British Politics

British Politics

FIFTH EDITION

Dennis Kavanagh

David Richards

Martin Smith

Andrew Geddes

OXFORD

UNIVERSITY PRESS

OXFORD

UNIVERSITY PRESS

Great Clarendon Street, Oxford OX2 6DP

Oxford University Press is a department of the University of Oxford.
It furthers the University's objective of excellence in research, scholarship,
and education by publishing worldwide in

Oxford New York

Auckland Cape Town Dar es Salaam Hong Kong Karachi
Kuala Lumpur Madrid Melbourne Mexico City Nairobi
New Delhi Shanghai Taipei Toronto

With offices in

Argentina Austria Brazil Chile Czech Republic France Greece
Guatemala Hungary Italy Japan Poland Portugal Singapore
South Korea Switzerland Thailand Turkey Ukraine Vietnam

Oxford is a registered trade mark of Oxford University Press
in the UK and in certain other countries

Published in the United States
by Oxford University Press Inc., New York

First published 1981
Fifth edition 2006

British Library Cataloguing in Publication Data

Data available

Library of Congress Cataloging in Publication Data

Data available

Typeset by Newgen Imaging Systems (P) Ltd., Chennai, India
Printed in Great Britain
on acid-free paper by
Ashford Colour Press Ltd, Gosport, Hampshire

ISBN 0–19–926979–3   978–0–19–926979–2

10 9 8 7 6 5 4 3 2 1

Dedicated to the Memory of John Richards (1933–2003)

SUMMARY CONTENTS

Summary contents

PART THREE Policy   521

DETAILED CONTENTS

Detailed contents

Detailed contents

PART TWO Institutions and processes   173

Detailed contents

Detailed contents

PART THREE Policy 521

Detailed contents

Dennis Kavanagh was appointed Professor of Politics in the School of Politics and Communication Studies, University of Liverpool in 1996. He graduated with a BA (Hons) in Politics and Modern History, University of Manchester in 1963 and with an MA (Econ) University of Manchester in 1967. His first academic appointment was as an Assistant Lecturer, Politics Department, University of Hull (1965–67). In 1967, he moved to the Government Department, University of Manchester where he was an Assistant Lecturer (1967–68), Lecturer (1968–74) and Senior Lecturer (1974–81). Between 1982–96, he was Professor at the University of Nottingham, and Head of Department (1995–96). He has held numerous visiting fellowships including: Visiting Professor, European University Institute, Florence. Spring 1977, Visiting Professor, University of California, San Diego, Winter and Spring Quarter 1979, Hoover Institution International Research Fellow, Stanford University, California, 1984–85, Visiting Professor, Department of Political Science, Stanford University, California, Winter Quarter 1985.

He has written and edited over 30 books, these include: *The British General Election of 2001* (Palgrave, 2002), with David Butler, *The Powers Behind the Prime Minister* (Harper Collins, 2001), with Anthony Seldon, *The Reordering of British Politics* (Oxford University Press, 1998), *Personalities and Politics* (Macmillan, 1992), *Thatcherism and British Politics: The End of Consensus?* (Oxford University Press, 1987) 2nd edn 1990, *British Politics: Continuities and Change* (Oxford University Press, 1987) 2nd edn 1990, *Political Science and Political Behaviour* (Allen and Unwin, 1983) and *Political Culture* (Macmillan, 1972). Has just completed the *British General Election of 2005* (with David Butler) and is presently writing on the development of the political science profession in Britain.

David Richards was appointed a Reader in the Department of Politics, University of Sheffield in 2004. He was awarded his PhD from the Department of Government, University of Strathclyde (1996). The thesis examined the politicisation of the Civil Service under the 1979–97 Conservative Government. He then became a post-doctoral research fellow at the Department of Political Science and International Studies, University of Birmingham (1995–98). In 1998, he joined the School of Politics and Communication Studies, University of Liverpool as a Lecturer, becoming a Senior Lecturer in 2001 and a Reader in 2004. In 2000, he was a Visiting Honorary Fellow at the Department of Government and International Relations, University of Sydney, Australia.

His main research interests are in British politics, Australian politics, public policy, governance, globalisation and state theory. He is currently researching the changing role of the British state, in particular, through a critique of the literatures on governance and the regulatory state. He is involved with Martin Smith and Andrew Geddes in an ESRC funded project on Policy Chains in the Home Office and he is writing a book on Whitehall and the Labour Government. In addition to a large number of journal articles, he has published *Governance and Public Policy in the UK* (with Martin Smith), *Changing Patterns of Governance in the United Kingdom* (with Martin Smith and David Marsh) and *The Civil Service under the Conservatives 1979–1997*.

Martin J. Smith was appointed to the Department of Politics at the University of Sheffield in 1990. He was promoted to Senior Lecturer in 1995 and Professor in 1998. Between 2001 and 2005 he was Head of Department. Before coming to Sheffield he worked at the Universities of Kent, York and Brunel. He did his PhD on agricultural policy at the University of Essex between 1984 and 1987. He has also been a visiting Professor at the University of Pompeu Fabra in Barcelona. In 2004 he was appointed Editor (with Matthew Festenstein) of the journal *Political Studies*.

His main research interests are in British Politics and Public Policy. In particular he is interested in the reform of the state, policy networks and policy making, the changing nature of central government and the Labour Party. He is currently directing a research project on delivery chains in the Home Office and writing a book on the changing nature of state power. He has published 11 books and numerous articles and book chapters. Recent books include: *Governance and Public Policy in the UK* (with David Richards) and *Governing as New Labour* (co-edited with Steve Ludlam).

Andrew Geddes has been a Professor of Politics at the University of Sheffield since September 2004. Before then he was Professor of European Politics and Jean Monnet Chairholder at the University of Liverpool. Andrew has published extensively on British, European and EU politics. His main interests centre on the ways in which international developments such as immigration, asylum and European integration affect our understandings of national politics in countries such as the UK.

His recent book publications include *Immigration and European Integration: Towards Fortress Europe?* (2000), *The Politics of Migration and Immigration in Europe* (2003), *The EU and British Politics* (2004) and *Britain Decides: The 2005 UK General Election* (2005, co-edited with Jonathan Tonge). He has also published in leading academic journals such as Political Quarterly, West European Politics, International Affairs, the Journal of Common Market Studies and the British Journal of Politics and International Relations.

ABOUT THE BOOK

The fifth edition of *British Politics* has dramatically increased in both size and scope since the fourth edition was published in 2001. The current book has two main sources. One is the existence of the well-established and widely read earlier editions by Dennis Kavanagh. A second is a frustration amongst the authors that many of the existing textbooks have failed to capture the vibrancy and rapid change of British politics. In addition, we wanted a book that introduced students to the facts of British politics but also demonstrated that the study of British politics is a social science which uses the concepts and ideas of social science to explain and understand how the British polity works. Whilst we want students to learn about British politics, we also want them to understand how to analyse politics. In this sense, we see a difference between what we do as academics and the ways journalists write about politics. Politics is not just about personalities and what is on the surface, but is often about context and the imprint of past institutions and ideas. For example, what the media often presents as a personality clash is often a clash of different institutional positions, party factions and ideas. We want students to move away from simplistic explanations of political phenomena and to realise that if we are to understand where power lies we need to investigate the organ-isation of society. So in this book we start by looking at ways of understanding politics, we then examine the historical and social context of British politics, before looking at its institutions and finally the way policy is made. So whilst the chapters in this book may be read individually and out of order, it is important to understand British politics in a holistic way.

No longer is it feasible for one author to undertake what has become an almost Herculean task of producing a wide-ranging and comprehensive textbook on British pol-itics. This fifth edition is the product of the combined efforts of a new four-person team. All the contributors are widely recognised as leading academics working in the field of British Politics. But at the same time, we each bring our own specialised subject-knowledge to produce what we hope is both a comprehensive and intellectually engaging textbook. That said, what has always marked out the past editions is the prominence of a fundamental narrative—that of continuity and change in British politics. We have felt it important to retain this core narrative, which we believe underpins many of the key strands explaining the nature of British politics. British politics and society has seen considerable rapid change in the last thirty years. Economic, social, technological and political changes have combined to make the Britain of the 21st century very different from the Britain of the 1970s. Yet, what we want to demonstrate is that these changes cannot be explained without understanding the traditions, institutions and ideas that have existed within the British polity for the last 100 years or more. For example, Britain's relationship with the European Union cannot be explained without understanding the existence and decline of the Empire.

Distinguishing features

We believe this completely revised and rewritten fifth edition contains a number of key distinguishing features that set it apart from comparable texts, namely the following:

- a significantly more comprehensive analysis of contemporary British politics than competing texts, that successfully combines a descriptive narrative with a range of conceptual analyses. An essential element of the book is that it demonstrates the ways in which theories help us understand and explain events in British politics;

- an international outlook that overcomes ethnocentrism and examines the global context in which British politics operates, paying special attention to the implications of Europeanisation, internationalism, governance and the marketisation of the state. We strongly believe that domestic politics cannot be understood without understanding the international context;

- it balances the traditional, descriptive, 'institutions-based' approach to politics with a lively, issue-led discussion of contemporary debates that considers topics of emerging importance, such as race and asylum-seeking; terrorism and the threat to individual liberty; Britain's destiny as a European partner and the future trajectory of British politics in the light of Labour's historic third-term electoral victory;

- it uses primary research from a large number of interviews conducted by the author team with key political actors, ensuring that the text is both theoretically informed and empirically grounded. All the authors of this book are actively engaged in research and we bring our research experience to bear on our understanding of British politics;

- it embraces a strong historical perspective to enable students to understand how the past has shaped present-day issues and the nature of British politics.

New to this edition

The fifth edition is considerably altered from previous editions of *British Politics* in three defining ways:

- the inclusion of work by three new authors of international repute who offer a fresh and more varied perspective on British politics, and who draw from an array of theoretical approaches to provide students with different 'pathways' for understanding political phenomena;

- a completely revised structure that incorporates an additional 16 chapters broadening the book's scope and allowing it to address more topical trends in greater detail, including immigration and ethic diversity;

- a dedicated section on policy that provides a detailed and accessible examination of economic, welfare, health, education, law and order, immigration and foreign and defence policies, and that draws from primary research findings obtained from interviews with policy-makers.

This text is enriched with a range of pedagogic tools to help you navigate the chapter material and reinforce your knowledge of British Politics. This Guided Tour shows you how to get the most out of your textbook package and help in your politics studies.

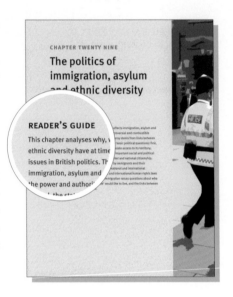

Reader's Guides

The key arguments and issues discussed in each chapter are outlined in the Reader's Guide that preludes each new chapter topics so that you are sensitised to the main themes that you are about to explore and have a framework for the material you are about to read.

'Politics in Focus' boxes

To promote your understanding of key areas of British political life, 'Politics in Focus' boxes throughout the text expand upon the chapter material and provide detailed illustrations of important political ideologies, events, institutions and policies in the social arena.

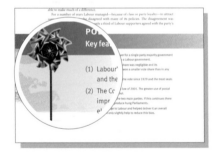

Key Points

It is important to put each chapter into context and reflect upon the issues that you need to think about throughout your reading of the text. Key Points help you to consolidate your learning by summarising the main arguments and issues raised in each chapter, and are ideal for use in revision.

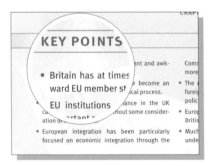

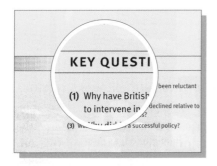

Key Questions

At the end of every chapter a suite of carefully devised Key Questions has been provided to help you assess your comprehension of core themes and readiness to move on to the next chapter topic. These may also be used as the basis of seminar discussion and coursework.

Important Websites

At the end of every chapter you will also find an annotated summary of useful websites that are central to the study of British Politics and that will aid your coursework and be instrumental in further research.

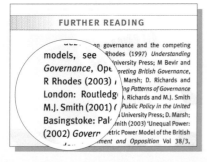

Further Reading

To take your learning further, reading lists have been provided as a guide to help you find out more about the issues raised within each chapter topic, and to help you locate the key academic literature in the field.

Online Resource Centre

Each chapter is supported by a range of online supplements to help you in your assessment and coursework. Follow the link to the Online Resource Centre at the end of each Further Reading section to access a comprehensive suite of learning resources.

www.oxfordtextbooks.co.uk/orc/kavanagh5e/

The Online Resource Centre that accompanies this book provides students and instructors with ready-to-use teaching and learning materials. These resources are free of charge and designed to maximise the learning experience.

For students

Multiple-choice questions

The best way to reinforce your understanding of British Politics is through frequent and cumulative revision. As such, a suite of self-marking multiple-choice questions has been provided for each chapter of the text, and includes instant feedback on your answers and cross-references back to the main textbook to assist with independent self-study.

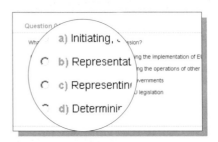

Political commentary

Each month a short essay written by a politics expert is added to the Online Resourse Centre to aid your awarness and understanding of British political life. All essays analyse a current and newsworthy political event in the UK from an academic standpoint, and are linked back to the chapter text.

Web links

A series of annotated web links organised by chapter has been provided to point you in the direction of important government new, elections, articles and other relevant sources of political information, to keep you informed of the latest developments in British Politics.

For instructors

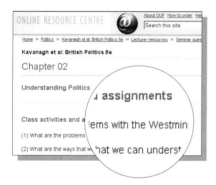

Class activities and assignments

A suite of challenging class activities and coursework assignments has been included to help students develop skills in research and presentation and apply their learning to new situations. Activities include debate topics, weekly research tasks and eassay questions arranged by chapter theme.

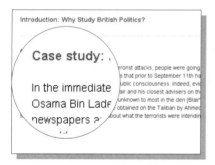

Case studies

Each chapter is supplemented with a short case study that is accompanied by critical thinking questions, designed to reinforce students' understanding of chapter themes and to encourage them to undertake more involved situational analyses of political scenarios.

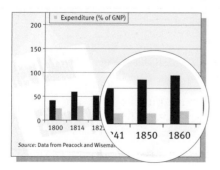

Figures and tables from the text

All figures and tables from the text have been provided in high resolution format for downloading into presentation software or for use in assignments and exam material.

ACKNOWLEDGEMENTS

The production of a book such as this inevitably depends on the help and assistance of many people. We have all learnt a lot about understanding and teaching British politics from the students that we have taught over many years in a number of institutions and we would like to thank them for their unconscious contribution to the book. The staff at OUP have been both professional and supportive, and contributed in a significant way to how the book has developed. Our biggest thanks go to Jane Clayton at Oxford University Press who proved to be a first-rate, sympathetic and astute Development Editor. We would like to acknowledge the effort she, our Commissioning Editor Ruth Anderson and the team at Oxford University Press have provided at all stages throughout the gestation of this book.

This book has also greatly benefited from being reviewed by a large number of reviewers who have been both professional and constructive in their approach, including Feargal Cochrane (Lancaster University); Richard Coggins (University of Oxford); Andrew Denham (University of Nottingham); David Denver (Lancaster University); Steve Kettell (University of Birmingham); Paul Lewis (University of Cambridge); Brian Tutt (London Metropolitan University); Simon Usherwood (University of Surrey, Guildford) and a number of anonymous reviewers. The reviewers have had a very important input into the development of this book and we are genuinely grateful for their time.

All the authors of this book have taught at either the *Department of Politics, University of Sheffield* or the *School of Politics and Communication Studies, University of Liverpool* and, in the case of two us, both institutions. We would like to thank both departments for the support and the stimulating environments they provide for teaching and researching politics. We would also like to thank Simon Lightfoot (University of Leeds) for his contribution to the writing of Chapter 8. Finally, we would like to thank Emma, Jean, Anna, Monica, Federica and Jacopo for being there.

David Richards
Dennis Kavanagh
Martin J. Smith
Andrew Geddes
December 2005

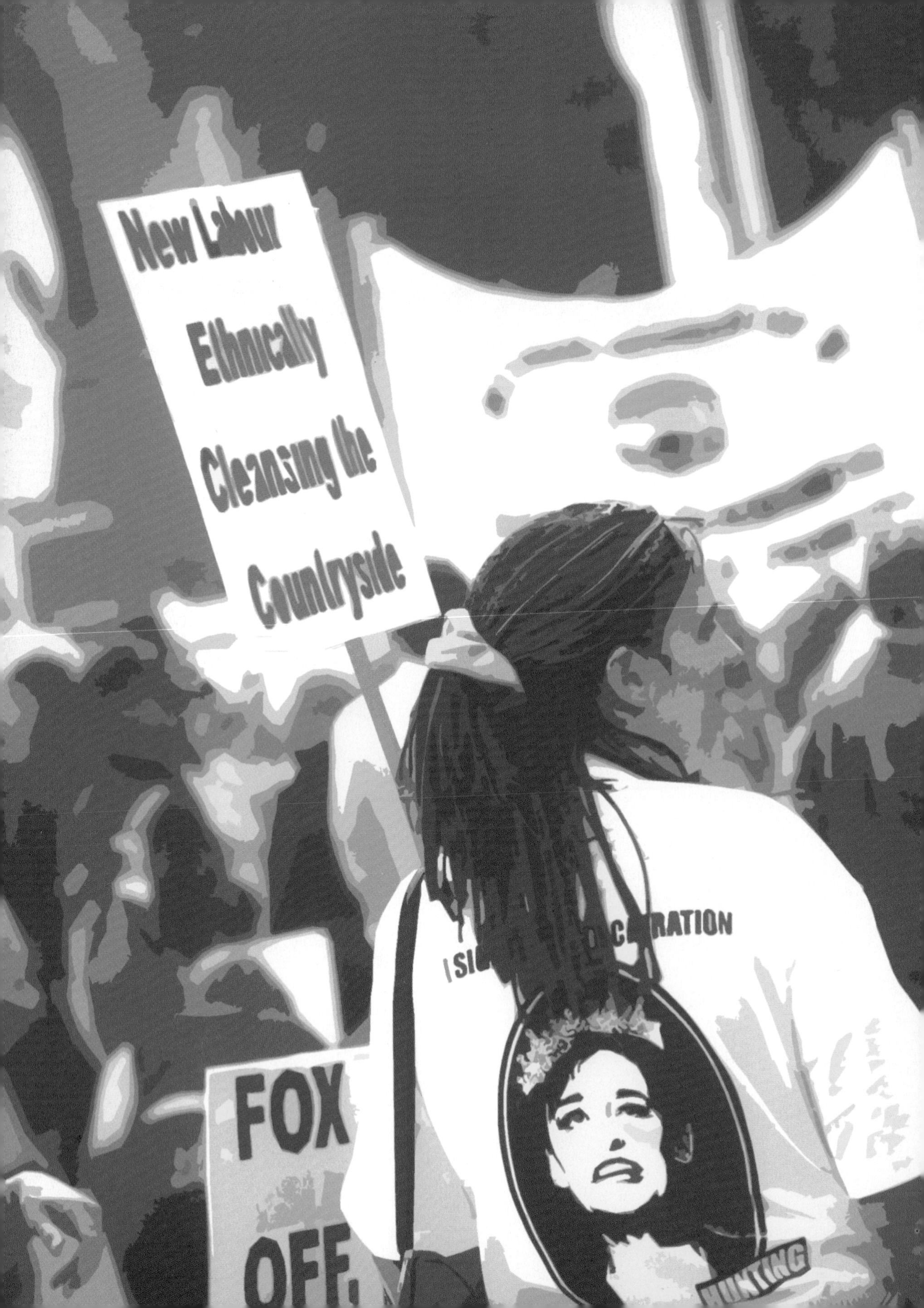
New Labour
Ethnically
Cleansing the
Countryside
FOX
OFF.

PART ONE

The context of British politics

CHAPTER ONE

Introduction: why study British politics?

READER'S GUIDE

In this chapter we first consider why the study of British politics matters. We look at different understandings of what is meant by politics. The chapter then focuses on the challenge facing British politics and those that study it, in what some have labelled an 'era of anti-politics'. This is reflected in a set of arguments associated with what is referred to as 'endism'—a set of contested ideas in mainstream political science today that aver that politics has now reached the end of history [ideology], the end of the nation-state, the end of authority and the end of the public domain. The chapter then reflects on the theme of 'continuity and change' in British politics—a central narrative to be found throughout the course of this book. It then concludes by considering what are the key questions and issues that should be addressed by anyone wishing to understand British politics today.

Introduction

Why does politics matter?

'A culture of detachment'—the 2001 and 2005 general elections

In the course of the last two general elections, we have witnessed a continuation of the steady decline in electoral turnout. On 5 May 2005, less than two-thirds of those eligible to vote did so, only 61.3%. This was a minimal increase of only 1.9% in turnout compared to 2001. In 2005, for the first time ever, the Labour Government won an historic consecutive third term in office. Yet, the party were far from being in a celebratory mode. They had been re-elected with only 36% share of the vote, 21.6% of the full electorate eligible to vote. The 9.56 million votes the Party received was the lowest for any governing party since 1923. For the Conservatives, who throughout the 20th century were one of the most electorally successful parties of any liberal democratic political system, their third consecutive defeat and the 33% of the vote they received, confirmed the party was now plumbing depths it had not experienced since the 1850s. Furthermore, the 2005 election was the first time since 1923 [an era of three-party politics] that the two main parties together polled less than 70% of the total vote.

Almost four years earlier on 8 June 2001, the Labour Government's second term victory, on one level, was crushing with the party returning 413 MPs to Parliament and holding an overall parliamentary majority of 165. Unlike 2005, there was a much greater sense of post-electoral euphoria, yet the real picture was much less rosy for the Government. The 2001 general election established a new record in the number of people who failed to turn out to vote. Voter participation fell to 59%, a reduction of over 12% from the 1997 election. Indeed, despite Labour's crushing victory, delivered on the back of a political system specifically designed to give an outright victory to one party, the problem facing the Government in its second term was that less than one in four people eligible to vote, supported the Labour Party in 2001. The low turnout generated a heated debate in Westminster, academic and media circles over whether a democratic deficit existed in which the Government no longer possessed a legitimate mandate to govern. This is a debate which, in the light of the poor turnout in 2005, has by no means gone away.

On 31 July 2001, a month after the 2001 election Brian Dowling was voted the winner of the Channel 4 *Big Brother* reality television series. As the final voting closed at 11pm, a total of 7,255,094 votes had been lodged by phone, text and interactive television. A notable feature was the number of people under the age of 35 who had participated in the vote. This contrasted with evidence from the *British Election Study* which showed that for the 2001 election, 41% of 18–24 year olds and 44% of 25–34 years olds had not voted. In February 2002, the creator of *Big Brother*, Peter Bazalgette appeared on BBC TV's *Westminster Live*, to argue that mainstream political parties had alienated most people under the age of 40. He suggested that most younger people had switched-off from politics, regarding it as an occupation pursued by middle-aged white men: '. . . arguing about things which have little to do with their lives'. Not surprisingly, during this period, many newspaper columnists drew a series of critical comparisons between the extent to which *Big Brother*, unlike the election, had captured the imagination of the general public.

A by-product of this debate was a call for an emergency 'health check' on British democracy to explain the perceived political disengagement by so many. Some commentators argued that politicians had become out of touch and so people were switching-off from politics. This is what the political columnist Peter Kellner (2004: 836) refers to as a 'culture of detachment'. An alternative argument was that we now live in a post-political age in which the perceived relevance of politics to the daily lives of people has diminished (see Mulgan 1994, 1999; Gibbins and Reimer 1999). Either way, the broader conclusion drawn by many, was that if interest in politics is gauged simply by the narrowest of benchmarks, that of voter turnout at a general election, then on this measure the figures for 2001 and 2005 indicated that the British parliamentary system was in much need of a comprehensive political health check.

'Life will never be the same again'—the 9/11 terrorist attack

In the aftermath of the 2001 general election, another highly significant political event took place—the terrorist attacks in the United States on Tuesday 11 September. On that day, millions across the world witnessed images of the destruction of the World Trade Center, one of the most prominent icons of international capitalism. Elsewhere, there was carnage at the Pentagon, Headquarters of the US Department of Defense, and a symbol of the dominance of US global military power in the post-Cold War era. During the first two days after the attack, CNN, a major US television network with broadcasting rights in many other countries, presented its coverage of the largest internal terrorist attack ever carried out on mainland USA under the back-drop banner of *'America Under Attack'*. The tone of the presentation was understandable. Many of the New Yorkers who witnessed first hand the events of September 11th testified that the whole episode had a surreal feel to it—a familiar refrain being that it was more like watching a *Spiderman* movie than a real event. By Thursday 13 September, CNN had changed the title of its news coverage to *'America at War'*. Numerous political pundits, many of whom had developed their careers in the Cold War era, called for immediate retribution and reprisal. Yet, unlike the Cold War era, where the Communist states of the Eastern Bloc and, in particular, the Soviet Union were portrayed as the enemy of the West, here the target was neither obvious, nor easy to pin down.

There was a stark contrast in the human response to the attacks carried out on September 11th. Many people in cities across North and South America, Europe and Australasia were outraged by what they had seen and openly mourned the deaths of those killed in this tragedy. Yet, in Pakistan, Iran, Egypt, Syria and Iraq, some people were singing, dancing and celebrating, responding to what they believed was a legitimate act of war carried out against a much hated enemy. What was striking was the subsequent often-heard comment on the television news by those who were both appalled by September 11th and those who had rejoiced in the events of that day—that from this moment: '. . . the world would never be the same again'. The collective view was that this was a turning point in history. Moreover, politics was once again at the forefront of people's thoughts.

The relevance of politics

These two contrasting events, the British general election of 8 June 2001 and the terrorist attack on 11 September 2001 provoked vastly contrasting responses. The first was the perception that the lethargic attitude shown by the British public to the democratic process was an indicator that politics was in terminal decline. The second was that one of the most extreme political acts, that of a terrorist attack, had had a dramatic impact on the views of people across the globe. In so doing, it had galvanised people's political views and, concomitantly, reinvigorated interest in politics (see Politics in Focus 1.1).

N FOCUS 1.1

In the immediate aftermath of the 9/11 terrorist attacks, people were going to their local bookstore to buy the first book they could find on al-Qaeda or Osama Bin Laden. These were two names that prior to September 11th had only fleetingly appeared in the overseas news sections of broadsheet newspapers and had barely penetrated public consciousness. Indeed, evidence of the depth of ignorance extended all the way to Number 10, as the account by Seldon (2004: 487) of a meeting by Blair and his closest advisers on the day of the attack demonstrated:

> The problem was that Bin Laden, al-Qaeda and the Taliban were all virtually unknown to most in the den [*Blair's inner-circle*]. Blair had heard of Bin Laden but knew little about him. [*Jonathan*] Powell asked for a book to be obtained on the Taliban by Ahmed Rashid which was later passed around Number 10 . . . Most left the meeting still feeling ignorant and bewildered about what the terrorists were intending and what was really going on. [*italics added*]

In retrospect, it might appear that, apart from those directly touched by the tragedy, claims that lives had irrevocably been changed by 9/11 were somewhat exaggerated. Nevertheless this event has had a profound political impact. Most obviously, it has altered the balance in the relationship between the state and the individual. The Labour Government reappraised its views on the relationship between domestic security and individual freedom. Such an issue is fundamental to politics and involves a trade-off between competing conceptions of, on the one hand, openness, individual liberty, freedom and human rights and, on the other, civic order, national security and the rule of law. Since 9/11, the pendulum has clearly swung more in the direction of the latter with, for example, the introduction of the Anti-terrorism, Crime and Security Act 2001 and attempts by the present Home Secretary, Charles Clarke to introduce new powers to impose house arrest on terrorist suspects, following a ruling by the House of Lords in January 2005 that the detention of 12 foreign terror suspects without trial breached human rights. This shift was compounded by the terrorist attacks in London in July 2005, in particular the '7/07' attacks when 56 people died, the first ever case of suicide bombers operating in the United Kingdom. The understandable response from the Government was relayed to Parliament two weeks later on the 20 July 2005, when Clarke announced a series of new measures to crack down on what he referred to as extremists who incite others to commit terrorist acts through preaching, running websites or writing inflammatory articles. He declared that the Government would draw up a list of 'unacceptable' activities intended to 'ferment or provoke' terrorism in the wake of the London bombings.

The reaction to '9/11' and more latterly '7/07' highlights how politics is an omnipresent force in human life, shaping the actions of people and conditioning their everyday existence. So, while at times, criticism might be directed at problems surrounding a political system, be it the apathy expressed at the British first-past-the-post electoral system of voting or, alternatively, anger and horror at atrocities undertaken by authoritarian regimes in, for example, Rhwanda, East Timor, Zimbabwe or Kosovo, politics is ever present. It is therefore important to recognise the extent to which politics and the state remain the key mediums conditioning the way humans interact with one another (see Politics in Focus 1.2).

POLITICS IN FOCUS 1.2

ief encounters—with the state the impact of politics on everyday life

A first year politics student wakes at a preordained hour in a national context that shares a common time. As she is summoned from her sleep by a radio-alarm clock to the dulcet tones of the state-funded Radio 1s *Breakfast Show*, she realises she is late for her lecture. In her condition of semi-slumber, she is bombarded with today's newsworthy events in the British nation-state and stories from 'elsewhere' which have significance for 'us', the national community of British people. She briefly tunes in to a pirate radio channel, and the likelihood is that as she dozes, state officials are monitoring the broadcast, tracking down the signals, or on their way to apprehend the culprits.

She reaches over to her bedside table and turns on her mobile phone to check for any text messages, for which Vodafone, Orange, O2, etc have paid the Government millions of pounds in order to secure a licence enabling them to sell her the product in the first place. Having then showered with privatised water regulated [she is led to believe] by Ofwat, she adorns herself in the 'costumes' considered appropriate within this national setting for attending university. Once dressed, she descends the stairs in a student house, built and subsequently sold-off by the state 20 years earlier. Whether or not the house was built by the state, one thing is almost for certain—it was constructed to state-regulated British building standards. She makes her way to the kitchen to prepare breakfast, grabbing a quick bowl of Coco-Pops. As she swills the chocolate-flavoured milk around the bowl, she glances at the cereal packet on which, state regulations require, must be printed both a list of ingredients and the nutritional value. At the same time, a new story comes on the radio informing her that the Government is about to embark on a campaign to improve the health of the nation, as part of a battle against the rise in obesity. She ponders this story, while drawing on her first cigarette of the day, taxed at 85%, the money going straight to the coffers of the Treasury.

Her morning routine complete, she leaves the house on the way to university—an institution that is both regulated and partly funded by the state and for which her fees are paid by a local education authority. She travels by car, relying on the assumption that at least within the British nation-state, everyone will drive on the left-hand side of the road, stop at red lights and negotiate roundabouts in a clockwise direction. When she steps into her car, she enters into an intensely state-regulated space. Not only must she abide by the 'highway code', she must also be in possession of a valid driving licence in a vehicle for which there is an insurance certificate, a tax disc and a current MOT.

She recognises that should she traverse the bounds of such legal stipulation then she is exposing herself to the legitimate sanctions of the state's judicial authority. As she drives at pace trying not to be too late for the lecture, she is constantly aware of the state's surveillance apparatuses and, sure enough, five minutes into the journey, she spots a speed camera and immediately reduces her speed by 15 mph. A few minutes later, she spots a police patrol car and instantly drops the mobile phone she is holding to her ear into her lap. Some of her friends are undertaking their journey on public transport, and here they are hardly escaping the institutional reach of the state. For even as they step on to a private double-decker on a deregulated bus route they enter, once again, into an arena thoroughly infiltrated and deeply structured by legal regulation. And all this before any of them have heard a word of their 'Introduction to political philosophy' lecture!

Adapted from Hay (1996: xii–xiii)

Broad v narrow definitions of 'the political'

A related issue is how we define and understand what is meant by 'the political'. If we return to the arguments contrasting the way in which *Big Brother*, unlike the 2001 and 2005 general elections, engaged the public, in particular its younger members, the conceptualisation of the political based on voting is especially narrow. At a broader level, non-participation could be interpreted as a highly political act by an individual. This has led some to argue that what we are witnessing is a conscious disengagement from formal or conventional politics (see Pirie and Worcester 1998; Park 1998). If we expand our understanding of what is meant by the political, then there is much contemporary research demonstrating that younger people in particular recognise the impact politics plays in their daily lives. For example, Henn, Weinstein and Wring (1999) argue that while the younger generation are disconnected from traditional political institutions, they are committed to the democratic process (see O'Toole et al 2003; Curtice and Seyd 2004; and Chapter 22).

If we recognise the extent to which politics plays such an important role in our daily lives and we embrace a broader and informal, rather than a narrow and formal conceptualisation of what is the political, then the task we now face is to define what remains a rather amorphous concept.

What is politics?

What makes politics fascinating is that one of its fundamental features is disagreement. Disagreement in many ways is the lifeblood of politics and without it politics would become a redundant feature in society. People disagree about how they should live together, over who should get what, how and why, how scarce resources should be distributed and who should have power. So, what is politics?

Politics: the art of the possible

A familiar quote, first attributed to Otto von Bismarck, the 19th century Prussian Prime Minister and subsequent Chancellor of Germany, but also used by the Conservative minister Lord Butler (1971) for the title of his autobiography, is that 'politics is the art of the possible'. This rather simple definition is useful as it presents a view of politics as a process of human participation in an exercise to find agreement amongst each other. A version of politics as the art of the possible can be identified in the work of Bernard Crick in his famous book, *In Defence of Politics*. Crick (1964: 141) argues that:

> Politics is not just a necessary evil; it is a realistic good.
> Political activity is a type of moral activity; it is a free
> activity, and it is inventive, flexible, enjoyable, and human.

Of course, this definition does not encompass what has gone on at a global level since 11 September 2001, and Britain in particular on 7 July 2005, where labels such as 'a free activity' and 'enjoyable' appear wholly inappropriate. Indeed, Crick regards terrorism as an amoral activity beyond politics. Nevertheless, in the real world politics, while often being a force for good, can clearly at times also be associated with extreme acts of terrorism resulting in murder and the destruction of a particular way of life. Crick's definition of politics should be understood as an ethical one—it is a view of politics based on compromise, co-operation and conciliation. The counter to this is that politics also involves conflict—based on disagreement between rival opinions, different wants, competing needs and opposed interests. Indeed, acts of terrorism can be regarded as one of the most extreme political acts perpetrated by humans. At the heart of an act of terrorism is the presence of conflict between opposing views. So, if we were to create a typology for understanding politics and at one pole, we were to place the ethically based view that politics is the 'art of the possible', then terrorism would be located at the opposing pole.

Politics at the extreme: terrorism

Terrorism can be understood as the use of violence and intimidation to achieve some goal. It might be conceptualised as legitimate versus the illegitimate use of coercion. We can define an act of coercion or control by the use of violence, fear or threats, coercive intimidation through the use of murder, injury and destruction, or threat to the same, to create a climate of terror, to publicise a cause and to coerce a wider target into submitting to its aims. From this, we might want to identify some characteristics of political terrorism as being: indiscriminate and arbitrary in nature, a willingness to engage in the indiscriminate murder of civilians; the creation of widespread fear, anyone and anywhere is perceived as a target; and, finally, ideologies of terrorism assume that the death and suffering of those who are innocent of any crime are means entirely justified by their political ends. Thus, from this perspective, terrorism is an explicitly amoral activity and directly opposes the ethical interpretation of politics provided above by Crick. Indeed, let us contrast Crick's view with that of Aron's (1968: 41) on terrorism:

```
An act of violence is labelled 'terrorist' when its psychological
effects are out of proportion to its purely physical result... The
lack of discrimination helps to spread fear, for if no one in
particular is a target, no one can be safe.
```

Clearly, we can recognise Aron's point if we imagine the reaction of those who work in Canary Wharf, the highest office block in London, when they had to go to work on 12 September 2001. An event that had taken place in another country, thousands of miles away and appeared to have no direct bearing on people's lives had created, in its immediate aftermath, a sense of fear which reached far beyond the borders of the United States. Likewise, in the aftermath of the London bombings in July 2005, the tourist industry was directly affected as some overseas visitors cancelled pre-booked holidays to the United Kingdom.[1]

There are two points we can make here: the first is that any act of terrorism, be it in Northern Ireland, Chechnya, the West Bank, or more specifically, the bombings in Bali (2002 and 2005), Madrid (2004), Baghdad (2003–05) and London (2005), is a political act, all be it one of the most extreme political acts that can be undertaken; second, politics is structured by identity. For example, the Bush Administration and much of the Western world had no hesitation in labelling the destruction of the World Trade Center as an act perpetrated by terrorists. Yet, as we have seen above, there were others who regarded this act as a justifiable response to US or Western imperialism carried out by heroic freedom fighters. What must be recognised is the important role that identity has in structuring political views. As Gamble (2000a: 7) observes:

```
Identity is the expressive dimension of the political, which asks
the question 'who are we?'. It is the space where choices have to be
made between values and principles, where people define who they are,
where they embrace or acknowledge an identity, and take on a
particular set of commitments, loyalties, duties and obligations.
Choosing or confirming an identity means seeing the world in
particular ways...Politics is here about understanding the world
in terms of us and them, of friends and enemies.
```

---

[1] The Tourism Industry Emergency Response Group, comprising officials from government and the tourist industry, estimated a £300 million reduction in spending by overseas visitors and a fall of 588,000 overseas visitors for the month of July in the wake of the 7/07 bombings.

But it is important to recognise that a person's identity shapes, *but does not necessarily determine*, their political outlook. Furthermore, identity is multi-dimensional—it can be both relatively unchanging and fluid, affected by for example age, gender, class, nationality, religion, occupation, ethnicity, etc. A significant force affecting identity is that of the state, because it shapes the nature of human social relations and creates the basis for other forms of politics. At the same time, human agency shapes the nature of the state—the relationship is dialectical. Throughout this book, we shall continually refer to the importance of the state in structuring political, social and economic relations and conversely, political, social and economic relations shaping the nature of the state. The key point here is that, in order to understand someone's politics or the nature of the state, we must explore the concept of identity.

Politics as conflict resolution

If we now return to our typology for understanding politics, then between our two existing poles of politics as the art of the possible and politics as terrorism, a third notion of politics can be located—politics as the search for conflict resolution. Note the emphasis here is on the search, as not all conflicts can be completely resolved. Instead, the best that may be achieved is that they are managed peacefully. Here, many of the international institutions created after 1945, such as the United Nations (UN), the Organisation for Economic Co-operation and Development (OECD) and the International Monetary Fund (IMF) were an attempt to create leviathan-like structures aimed at conflict resolution both within and between nation-states. Although it should also be pointed out that, since their inception, a number of commentators suggest that they have actually fuelled conflicts through exploitative economic arrangements, rather than acting as agencies of conflict resolution (see Archer 2001; Bayliss and Smith 2001).

So our understanding of politics can be linked to themes of both conflict and co-operation and the different ways in which politics is conducted by governments around the world can be located somewhere along the typology below. (See Figure 1.1.)

FIGURE 1.1
A typology of politics

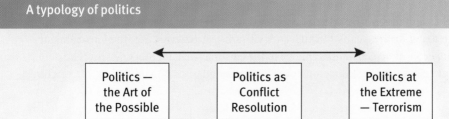

Studying British politics

Using the above typology, how do we best understand the nature of politics in Britain today? Clearly, examples of all three definitions can be recognised in the British context:

- Politics—the art of the possible: might be understood in terms of the establishment of the welfare state in the post-war era, in the light of the 1942 Beveridge Report (see Chapter 27), or the introduction of the London Congestion Charge in February 2003.
- Politics—as conflict resolution: might be understood in terms of the Downing Street Declaration of December 1993, that led to a para-military ceasefire in Northern Ireland, the signing of the Good Friday Agreement in April 1998 and the subsequent process of democratic, institution building in the form of the Northern Ireland Assembly (see Chapter 17).
- Politics at the extreme—terrorism: might be understood in terms of the London terrorist attacks of July 2005. Most notably, the events of the 7 July 2005, when the activities of four suicide bombers on the London underground and a double-decker bus led to the death of 56 people (see Chapter 30).

The point here is that there is no simple answer to conceptualising politics in Britain, it is a complex entity. Presently, there are many uncertainties surrounding both the future development of politics and how we as students of political science study such change. Indeed, one of the aims of this book is to equip the readers with both the theoretical and analytical resources in order to answer this question for themselves.

The future development of politics

If we focus on the first theme, politics in Britain today is undergoing a process of transition, most notably in the Labour Administrations' programme of constitutional reform and devolution. These reforms follow the neo-liberal reforms pursued under the guise of Thatcherism. The potential implications are profound; the topography of the British state has been, and is being re-drawn, and the nature of the political system recast. For some commentators, the Labour Government has opened up a Pandora's box, which may ultimately lead to the disintegration of the United Kingdom as a political entity. What must be remembered is that one of the factors prompting the Labour Government to initially embark on this course was the perceived need to revitalise a political system that it saw as creaking at the seams through lack of political renewal. Yet, the Government is attempting to graft on substantial change to the existing parliamentary system. The potential is that reform may produce outcomes unintended and, possibly, more far reaching than the Government intended (see Richards and Smith 2001 and Chapter 19).

Yet, one can argue that the flexibility of the British political system has previously enabled it to absorb and cope with internal and external shocks. Indeed, one of the themes emphasised throughout this book is the fluid and changing nature of the British state as highlighted through its territorial dimension—Wales was absorbed by Britain in 1536,

Scotland by the Act of Union 1707 and the Union of Ireland with Britain was achieved in 1801 (remaining until partition of Ireland on 6 December 1921 and the birth of the 26 counties of the Irish Free State—Eire and the six counties of Northern Ireland). The point here is that Labour's programme of reform, like that of the Thatcherite reforms that proceeded it, may be just another stage in the constant evolution of the British state (see Politics in Focus 1.3). The task for students of politics is to make sense of these changes by using a rich variety of theoretical and analytical models.

FOCUS 1.3

...olitics: continuity and change

A narrative that permeates our account of British politics is that of 'continuity and change'. The emphasis here is on the way that the British political system has over time been able to adapt and absorb new pressures that have developed in society, while maintaining the fundamental structure on which the modern British state is founded.

Some argue that Britain offers a model of stable government having transformed from a feudal kingdom into a modern representative nation-state. The British political system did not collapse, as Russia's had in 1917, Germany's in 1933, or France's in 1940 and again in 1958. Continuity and adaptation, rather than the creation of a completely new system at one point in time, are key elements of British political history. Some suggest that this is a reflection of the lack of a written constitution offering political flexibility to the ruling elite to adapt. Conversely others suggest it stems from the political adeptness of the ruling elite who have recognised critical junctures and pursued a course of reform to maintain the prevailing status quo. Elsewhere, others have argued that the 'load' or set of problems on a state is affected by the timing and intensity of conflicts, on such basic issues as securing its borders, forging a sense of national identity and establishing the authority of central government. If these challenges have to be faced more or less *simultaneously*, then fundamental questions of authority, legitimacy, and participation coincide and impose a heavy 'load' on the system. This has been the fate of many 'new' states which achieved independence after 1945. But the British state has been able to face many of these problems *sequentially*, thus allowing elites time to cope with or resolve one problem before confronting another. Britain provides a *model of low-cost political modernisation* in which the achievement of central authority and national identity preceded the democratisation of the political system.

Thus, a suitable label identifying the nature of British politics is 'continuity and change'. As we argue in Chapter 3, the British state never really modernised because the absence of a bourgeois revolution meant that many of the structures of pre-industrial society and the pre-modern state remained in place. Rather than Britain being a modern state, it is an *ancien regime* combining a pre-modern state, an anti-industrial commercial class and a remnant of a landed aristocracy (hence the continuing role of the House of Lords and the monarchy in the political process). The absence of revolution in Britain meant that much of the political development of the state in Britain has been a process of negotiated change punctuated by moments of crisis, for example, the Civil War and the Glorious Revolution in the 17th century, the Great Reform Act of 1832 and the present Labour Government's programme of devolution.

Studying the changing face of British politics

If we now turn our attention to the second theme, that of the state of political science today, then here again a brief survey of the discipline reveals a number of serious challenges. Indeed, they are brought about by the changing face of politics in recent times— clearly the two are not mutually exclusive. These challenges have been identified by Gamble (2000a: 1–2) as the rise of anti-politics as events over the last 50 years have:

> . . . spread scepticism about the ability of human beings any longer
> to control anything very much, least of all through politics.
> Alternative views of politics as an activity have become prevalent.
> The first scorns politics as irrelevant, conservative, riddled with
> corruption, waste, inefficiency and self-interest, a constant block
> to innovation and change and the least dynamic part of society. The
> other fears it as incipiently totalitarian, exacerbating conflict,
> fanning ideological commitment and encouraging a hubris about human
> abilities to shape their world that leads to vicious dictatorships.

This of course returns us to the issue addressed at the start of the chapter: why does British politics matter? A key theme is that of 'endism'—in particular, the recent growth of a body of literature diagnosing the end of history, the nation-state, authority and the public domain. Each of these endisms presents a serious challenge to political science, in that it forces us to question the core assumptions underpinning our very understanding of politics. Let us briefly look at each of these themes within a British context.

The end of history

Following the collapse of the old Soviet Union and the Eastern communist bloc in the late 1980s and early 1990s, the US political analyst Francis Fukuyama resurrected the Hegelian notion that the 'end of history' had been reached (see Fukuyama 1992). By this, he meant that the battle of ideas was finished, the communist experiment had failed, and the dominant ideology, that of liberalism had 'won'. At the heart of Fuyukama's argument was that the collapse of communism and the pursuit of democracy and capitalism in the old Second and Third Worlds (*sic*) had led to the conclusion that the ideological debate was now over. The history of ideas had ended. Western liberal democracy had triumphed or, to quote Fukuyama, liberal democracy is the 'final form of human government'. What Fukuyama really meant was not the end of history at all, but the end of socialism, the end of a particular ideological experiment, which in his view had been unwisely adopted by some countries during the 20th century. Fukuyama, in effect, was being highly political, championing the cause or triumph of Western liberal democracy and market economics.

Of course, with the events that have been going on around the world since 11 September 2001, Fukuyama's thesis appears both misconceived and outdated. Few would argue that

Western liberal democracy has triumphed over all else. Indeed, the views of Fukuyama have been most controversially challenged by Samuel Huntingdon's *The Clash of Civilisations and the Making of World Order* which averred that the world's major civilisations—Western, Chinese, Japanese, Hindu, Islamic, Buddhist, Latin American and Orthodox Christian—could react to globalisation in such a manner as to lead to a fundamental breakdown in world order.

Yet, the discourse of the 'end of history' (or ideology) has left an imprint on politics. As we will see in Chapter 4, in the British context, there exists a body of literature that argues that an ideological convergence has taken place, in which the old collective, Keynesian-welfare consensus predicated on a mixed economy and a welfare state has been rendered obsolete by a new, individualistic, neoliberal, laissez-faire consensus, established by Thatcherism and consolidated by the present Labour Government. The argument here is that the ideological debate in Britain is over, the ideas of Adam Smith, Hayek and Friedman have triumphed over those of Marx, Bernstein, Keynes and Beveridge.

The end of the nation-state

While globalisation is a contemporary and much-used buzzword, it is also a much misused, controversial and misunderstood term. In the context of the nation-state, the discourse of globalisation suggests that power is draining away from national governments, who no longer possess the capacity to control events within their own borders. National cultures, economies and, indeed nation-states themselves are being subsumed by an irresistible, new global order. In Britain, some argue that on one level, central government no longer has the capacity to determine its own economic destiny which assumes that there was once a golden era when Britain was resilient to external, economic shocks. At another level, the process of Europeanisation is rendering the British Parliament little more than a glorified parish council. As we explore in Chapter 6, the argument here is that what we are witnessing are the death throes of an old order—one in which Britain once had full control and command over its own political destiny, but that the forces of globalisation and Europeanisation have led to the terminal decline of the British nation-state. While these arguments are often much over-stated, they have induced considerable trepidation in some, witness for example the rise of the UK Independence Party.

The end of authority

The set of arguments here is associated with the notion that authority has either been seriously undermined or is near to collapse. The extent to which institutions, in this case governments, possess authority, why and how they wield that authority are contingent. As Gamble (2000a: 57) observes:

> We speak of actions and commands being authorised, which means that they are perceived as legitimate. The greater the perception of legitimacy, the more likely it is that commands will be obeyed voluntarily and coercion, even if it is available, will not be needed.

There are different elements to this particular set of arguments. Neo-conservatives argue that the traditional basis of society—the nuclear family, established customs, religious values, respect for institutions, etc—has been increasingly eroded (see Hitchens 1999). So also has respect for authority and the 'great institutions of the state', in particular Parliament, Whitehall, the Church of England, the judiciary, etc. The 'glue' holding society together and underpinned by a respect for the rule of law is rapidly vanishing (see Heffer 2000). A second, but not necessarily mutually exclusive, element is associated with those that wish to link the theme of globalisation to the collapse of authority. Here globalisation, rather than being a liberating force, has increased competition, insecurity and risk, and with it, devalued the authority of the rational-legal institutions of the British state, with people feeling increasingly insecure.

The end of the public domain

The public domain is one of the fundamental dimensions of the political world and its perceived decline or 'end' is one of the greatest threats to politics. Again, there are a number of strands to this particular theme. Within the British context, the most obvious form is that the neo-liberal reforms pursued after 1979 by the Conservative Government, coupled with 'globalisation' have led to the erosion of the public domain or, as some portray it—a 'hollowed out state' (see Rhodes 1997). The market is replacing government, while at the same time power has slipped away from its traditional sites—Westminster and Whitehall. Other strands to this theme include arguments that suggest that: as the dominance of the market increases, so the lines between the public and the private become increasingly blurred; as the emphasis on individualism intensifies so civic engagement evaporates; electoral participation diminishes with the decline of mass political parties; and lines of accountability are blurred in an increasingly fragmented polity. Ultimately, public interest in politics plummets.

The intellectual structure of the book

Throughout this book, we argue that many of the themes associated with 'endism' are often over-stated, but they do nevertheless offer important contemporary narratives of British politics that have to be taken seriously. We therefore consider to what extent the themes of endism present new challenges to political science. Our task is to explore the historical, ideological and institutional make-up of British politics, in order to present insights into the extent and impact of endism and whether or not we really do now live in an era of anti-politics. It is therefore important to recognise that when presenting this narrative, we are also providing our own interpretation of how we understand the nature of British politics today. With this in mind, one of the key themes conveyed throughout this book is that the British political system is best understood in the context of continuity and change.

Conclusion

In politics, there are no permanent solutions, and many of the once-praised features of British politics have been subject to criticism in recent years. There are always pressures to change or to adapt, from international forces, economic trends, interest groups and public opinion, to name but a few. When a country's political institutions and practices have been as moulded by the past as Britain's have been, this may act as a buffer against the forces for change. The long-established institutions and procedures may become too entrenched to adapt. Since the 1970s, attempts to promote social, political and economic change or modernisation have been a central part of the political agenda in Britain. Critics of the social class divisions, the education system, industry, the Civil Service and the political institutions claim that these are burdened by too much traditionalism. A growing body of opinion came to regard parts of the political system as a barrier to desirable social and economic development. Few member states of the European Union now look to Britain for democratic guidance. Indeed, the opposite is often the case, as supporters of electoral reform, a Bill of Rights, or a written constitution have looked to Europe for inspiration.

The Thatcherite 1980s did much to make Britain more of a market-dominated economy but did little to reform the political institutions. The Labour Government elected in 1997 was the first government in the 20th century to set out self-consciously on a programme of constitutional reform—'modernisation' is its preferred term. Yet, to what extent have recent governments successfully adapted to an increasingly globalised world, to a political arena that is seen as fragmented, and, more broadly, to the various 'endism' challenges identified above? These are important and wide-ranging questions—the answers to which are both complex, yet thought-provoking—but which we believe demonstrate why it is important to study British politics. The aim of this book is to address these questions by:

- providing an account of the continuity and change of British politics;
- furnishing the reader with an array of theoretical and analytical models for understanding British politics;
- providing a historical and institutional account of the evolution of the British political system; and
- presenting a state of the art survey of current and topical issues in British politics through a series of policy case-studies.

Visit the Online Resource Centre that accompanies this book
for links to more information on this chapter topic

CHAPTER TWO

Understanding politics

READER'S GUIDE

How we understand politics depends on the perspective we adopt. This chapter
reviews some of the many perspectives that can be used in analysing the political
process. Traditionally, British politics has been understood through the lens of
the Westminster model. This model reflected the institutional and constitutional
perspective adopted by many of the early writers on British politics. More
recently a range of approaches have been developed for understanding politics.
This chapter outlines these perspectives and examines their strengths and
weaknesses.

   'The first objective of a student of politics is to try and discover where power
lies in the system' (J.P. Mackintosh 1977: 36)

Introduction

In the last chapter we saw that politics matters to all of us and how, often unconsciously, we are concerned with political questions and even political activity. In this chapter we look at ways of understanding politics and how the way that we analyse politics affects what we see as important. The chapter will also illustrate how political science provides 'ways of seeing' that are distinct from the observations of journalists or voters. For instance, the media has paid considerable attention to the conflicts within the Labour Government. These are perceived as personal conflicts between Tony Blair and Gordon Brown. For example, Gordon Brown's speech at the 2003 Labour Party annual conference was seen as an explicit appeal for the Prime Minister's job. However, the role of the political scientist is to put these 'snap' judgements in a wider historical and political context. Understanding the relationship between Blair and Brown requires some understanding of Labour Party history and the role they played together in developing the New Labour project. It also requires an understanding of the role of the Prime Minister and the Treasury in British government and how a successful government depends on a strong relationship between the Prime Minister and the Chancellor. Whilst political scientists may look at politics differently to journalists, they also analyse politics in a range of ways. The perspectives used in political science have within them particular understandings of politics and power.

This chapter will look at how different understandings of politics have developed and what they say about how we understand the world. It will begin by examining the traditional approach to British politics. It will then examine the main theories which have been used to interpret and understand British politics including pluralism, elitism, rational choice and postmodernism. The chapter will also introduce a discussion of structure and agency, and it will examine the question of power. A key issue is how other ways of understanding politics offer an alternative to the Westminster model.

Textbooks and the Westminster model

Until the 1970s, the most common framework for analysing British politics was what was called the Westminster model. The Westminster model was in many ways a distillation of the key elements of the British constitution. The British constitution has been seen as vague, unwritten, uncodified and flexible (see Chapter 10). There is no single source that simply outlines the nature and rules of the British political system. Consequently, textbooks written in the 19th and 20th centuries were an interpretation and codifiers of the British constitution. Writers such as A.V. Dicey, Walter Bagehot and Ivor Jennings set out what they saw as the key principles of the British constitution and rather than being commentaries upon the British constitution, these texts became interpretations of the constitution. These interpretations were also normative, meaning that they saw the British system of government as the best form of government and believed that this was how political systems should be organised.

The system of government that was defined in these texts and through interpretations by ministers and civil servants has been known as the Westminster model. The key features of the Westminster model are:

- Parliamentary sovereignty—Parliament is the site of all political authority and there can be no higher power.

- Cabinet government—decisions are made through collective cabinet responsibility. Once a decision is made in Cabinet all ministers are bound by the decision.

- Individual ministerial accountability—ministers are responsible and accountable to Parliament—for the decisions and policies of their departments.

- The government is chosen by the electorate, in the sense that people vote for MPs and the party which has the support of the majority of MPs forms the government.

- There is a neutral and permanent Civil Service which is loyal to the government of the day.

The legitimacy of the Westminster model is based on the idea that ultimately governments and ministers are responsible to the people. Simultaneously the model establishes strong government because citizens do not become involved in day-to-day decision making. The system was representative, and because the Civil Service were neutral and professional, and politicians were accountable, they could be left alone to govern the country. Ultimately the probity of government was ensured because British government is bound by the rule of law which prevents excessive infringements on the rights of the individual. According to Sir Ivor Jennings an 'ordinary Englishman (*sic*)' is:

> not only a free man; he is truculently free. He is perhaps the most law-abiding citizen in the world, particularly when the law appears to him to be sensible; but no man is more ready to take offence when the law is broken. He does not obey orders because they are given by some person in authority: he obeys orders when they are lawful orders, issued by a person who has the legal authority to issue them (Jennings 1954: 10).

The Westminster model combines strong leadership with accountability, and limits on the executive. Decisions are made in the executive but those decisions have to be accounted for to MPs and the electorate. Tony Blair has stated that he had to take the unpopular decision of fighting the war in Iraq and he then had to face the electorate for that decision. The point here is that he does not necessarily have to take account of public views in making decisions because he is held to account after the event. Moreover, governments cannot act outside the law and all laws have to be passed through Parliament.

What has developed in Britain has been a particular understanding of the nature of government and the distribution of power. It is a liberal elitist approach which has developed within a context of a Whig understanding of history whereby the British constitution is seen to gradually evolve within the boundaries of its traditions. From this perspective, power is located within an elite of government ministers and officials but this elite is constrained by Parliament, the courts and the electorate. In addition rulers are constrained by the elite's duty of public service and awareness of the limits of the state. Underpinning this governmental framework is the 'Englishman's' sense of his own liberty and 'the rule of law'; the notion that laws have to be properly enacted and applicable to everyone equally. Changes in the system developed in the context of a Whig notion of history; reform occurs gradually within the existing traditions and in a way that allows the constitution to adjust to the new situations. From this conception, power is concentrated in the executive but it is power that is controlled and constrained both by internal conceptions of roles but also by other institutions and systems of accountability.

This understanding of British politics developed from a perception of how the British political system worked in the 19th century. When the British government was small, and parties had less control over the House of Commons, collective responsibility and ministerial accountability had relevance. Ministers did take most of the decisions in their departments and the Cabinet could discuss and agree the main elements of policy. In the absence of party discipline, MPs could and would vote against the government. However, as the role and size of government grew, as parties became more disciplined, the franchise extended and pressure groups developed, and as Britain became integrated into the European Union (EU), the established and integrated system of accountability broke down. The principles of parliamentary sovereignty and collective and individual responsibility became increasingly difficult to sustain.

Whilst British government has changed, as we will see through the course of this book, there have also been important changes in the nature of political science. Many of the original analysts of British politics were constitutional lawyers, historians, journalists and practitioners. Political science did not really exist. Politics lacked the scientific argot of the academy. For many this was a good thing, but language affects our understanding. Those who wrote on British politics spoke in the language of the constitution and were often part of the elite that they were studying. This limited their ability or willingness to assess the British political system critically. The only critics were a number of isolated Marxist voices. Harvey and Hood (1958) provided an analysis of how British government favoured the interest of the capitalist class. Ralph Miliband (1969, 1972) also examined the limitations on the Labour Party ever introducing a radical government and the upper class nature of British government. Marxist accounts of the state offered a very different understanding of how politics and government worked. From this perspective, politics was about sustaining the political dominance of the economically dominant class—the bourgeoisie. The British political system was very effective at doing this because it gave the pretence of being a democracy but actually allowed ordinary people very little say in political decisions. From the Marxist perspectives, concessions made to the working class such as the welfare state were merely tactical decisions made to ensure that the ruling elite remained in power and capitalism operated in an effective way.

The political and economic crises that affected the British state from the 1960s onwards saw a growing questioning of the Westminster model and attempts to analyse British politics in different ways. These new ways of seeing both reflect and explain changes that have occurred in the real world.

Approaches to politics

In this section we look at alternative ways of understanding politics. Each of these approaches has different understandings of power and the way that politics work. They also focus on different aspects of the political process. This means that it is possible to use a number of these perspectives together. We begin by examining pluralism which was a direct challenge to the Westminster model by seeing important elements of politics occurring outside of the Westminster arena.

Pluralism

For many commentators, particularly those in the United States, politics in democratic systems is not played out solely through the formal institutions of government but also outside of the state in formal and informal associations. Consequently, pluralism which was concerned with the development and interaction of groups, became an increasingly influential theory of government. For pluralists like Robert Dahl and Charles Lindblom, power does not exist in institutions but in the interactions and conflicts between groups. The role of the government is to provide an arena for group interaction. For pluralists, power is widely dispersed in society because if people have grievances such as the need for a crossing on their road or increased expenditure on schools they can form a group and lobby their MPs or Parliament. Pressure groups can have an impact by winning a high level of public support. Unlike Marxist approaches, pluralists are careful to separate political and economic power. Economically powerful groups or actors do not necessarily have political power. So although there may be groups without economic power, it does not mean that they do not have political power. Groups lacking in economic resources can use the media, or win widespread support and affect change. For pluralists, power is dispersed around the political system so that, like the traditional position outlined above, ministers, civil servants, Parliament and judges all act as constraints on each other. More importantly, groups act as a constraint on government and because different groups are successful in each policy area, no single organisation will come to dominate the political system. So, for example, it could be argued that the power of Rupert Murdoch has increased as he has concentrated control of a range of media outlets. Pluralists would point to the range of media outlets that now exist through the internet and multiple television and radio channels which make it more or less impossible for a single person or company to control all sources of information.

When pluralists examine the question of where power lies, they examine which interests or groups were involved in a particular decision, what demands they made and what was the final outcome. So for instance, if there is discussion about farming policy with the National Farmer's Union wanting increased support for farmers and the Friends of the Earth (FOE) wanting increased support for the environment and the outcome is increased environmental support, it appears for a pluralist that the FOE has power. The point that pluralists make is that no single group will dominate all policy arenas. At the same time governments are concerned with re-election so that they will not continually support the demands of a single group for fear of alienating another section of the electorate.

For Richardson and Jordan (1979) pressure groups effectively undermined the Westminster model. Rather than Parliament being central to the decision-making process, pressure groups have been routinely drawn into consultation, bypassing the parliamentary process. Richardson and Jordan see as one of the 'rules of the game' of British government that civil servants consult with pressure groups. Because groups have resources that are useful to government such as information, expertise and legitimacy then they can influence outcomes. However, for Richardson and Jordan the system remains pluralistic because in each policy area different groups are involved.

Whilst pluralism has been highly influential and appears to have resonance with the ways that politics is organised in Britain, there are a range of criticisms that have been made of the pluralist position:

- It pays too much attention to groups. Whilst pluralists may be right to focus on the role of groups, they perhaps over-emphasise their centrality to the political process. Particularly since 1979, governments have been less willing to consult with groups and Tony Blair has explicitly stated that he is concerned with the national, rather than group, interests. There is a whole raft of areas where governments have ignored popular pressure from the poll tax (1989), through to fuel tax (2001) and the war on Iraq (2003).

- Pluralists exaggerate ease of access. The rules of the game mean that many groups are excluded from government because they are not seen as having the authority, legitimacy or respectability for consultation.

- Pluralists concentrate on the observable behaviour of groups. They miss the ways in which ideologies, traditions, political institutions and economic constraints shape political outcomes. There are, as we will see in Chapter 5, a number of structural inequalities in Britain that make it easier for some groups to influence government more effectively than others (for instance, can the financial centre in the City of London and single parent families be seen as having equal influence? See Marsh 2002).

- Economic and professional groups have advantages over other groups (see Chapter 21). Economic and professional groups tend to be well resourced, well informed and to exist as easily defined groups—for example, doctors are a much more identifiable group than old people. Professional and economic groups often have resources that they can use in relation to government and in many cases the government relies on them for the implementation of policy, and this means that they are much more influential than consumer groups.

Elitism

Whilst pluralists generally see power as dispersed and citizens in a position to influence the government, elitists see the situation the other way round. For elitists, power is concentrated in the state and citizens have little or no impact on policy decisions. As Evans (1995: 228) suggests: 'At the core of elitist doctrine lies the belief that the history of politics is the history of elite domination'. There are indeed two types of elitists. Normative elitists such as Vilfredo Pareto and Robert Michels believe that only elites have the resources to rule and therefore democratic forms of government are unworkable. Analytical elitists believe that despite protestations by governments and pluralists that the political system is democratic, the empirical reality is that elites control the political process. We only need to see for instance how the middle class continue to dominate the House of Commons and the senior levels of the Civil Service (see Chapter 5). Both analytical and normative elitists believe that government is about a circulation of elites and whatever democratic institutions are in place, government is conducted by a small elite and not by democratic participation. Modern government is in effect about domination and democratic procedures are purely mechanisms for legitimising elite rule (see Evans 1995).

The Westminster model contains elements of both normative and analytical elitism. Analytically power is located at the summit of government within the Cabinet and the Prime Minister and democratic procedures exist largely to circulate elites (between Conservative and Labour elites) and not to allow citizen participation in the policy process. Normatively, it is argued that the Westminster model produces strong government, where politicians are able to make decisions in the national interests and not in response to sectoral or public pressure.

Rational choice theory

Rational choice theory is a perspective on politics that has developed out of economics. It is an attempt to apply an economic rationale to politics. It has also developed as a response to both institutional and pluralist approaches in politics (although it has combined with both). Rational choice theory suggests that politics will not operate in the way that either the Westminster model or pluralism suggests because people are rational actors. The basis of rational choice theory is that:

- Individuals are utility maximisers. In other word they will do what is in the best interest of themselves and their immediate families.
- People have clear preferences.
- People's preferences are transitive. In other words, if people prefer apples to pears and pears to bananas, they will choose apples over bananas if there are no pears.
- People have the information to make informed choices.

The consequence of rational self-interest is that people will not co-operate for the common good. The desire to achieve our own self interest means that we will not achieve what is good for society as a whole. We may desire a world without pollution and think it would be better if cars were used less. However, we want to use our own cars and a consequence of everyone making the same decision is pollution and congested roads. Building on assumptions of rational action, rational choice attempt to develop predictive models concerning the behaviour of actors and have used game theory as an analytical tool for understanding collective action problems (see Politics in Focus 2.1).

Rational choice attempts to develop simple predictive models using game theory. Two of the simplest games are the prisoners' dilemma and the chicken game. In the prisoners' dilemma, two people are arrested with the equipment to commit a burglary. The police suspect that they intended to burgle a house, but have no evidence. They therefore put the two, Janet and John, in separate cells. If they can get each to give evidence against the other they can get conviction for burglary and each will get 10 years in prison. If however, they both stay silent the police have no evidence and they will go free. If one speaks and the other stays silent then one will go to prison and the other will not. This produces the following matrix:

		Janet	
		Remain silent	Grass
John	Remain silent	0,0	0,10
	Grass	10,0	10,10

If both co-operate, they both remain silent and so neither goes to prison. But the question is can one trust the other when the police are trying to get Janet to give evidence against John. As they are both rational actors they will not trust their co-thief and will inform on the other. As a consequence of their both informing on the other, they end up with the worst outcome. The police have the evidence to send them both to jail.

The chicken game is based on the idea of who will back out first. Two farmers share a drainage ditch which is blocked. If they act quickly they can share the costs of mending the ditch and not have any further damage. However, being rational actors they wait for the other to act. As a consequence, the blockage causes flooding which costs the farmers much more (it is the chicken game in the example of the student bin see p 28 of this chapter). The matrix therefore is as follows.

		Farmer A	
		Mend ditch	Leave ditch
Farmer B	Mend ditch	50.50	0.50
	Leave ditch	50.0	200.200

You can try out these games at this website: www.gametheory.net/html/applets.html#PDi

Rational choice theorists see the workings of British government very differently to the Westminster model. Under the traditional approach, officials and ministers operate with a public service ethos, which results in their acting for the common good. For rational choice theorists, politicians and civil servants are self-interested actors. For politicians, this means that they see the electoral arena like a market and they have to attract the greatest possible number of voters. Rational choice theorists see voters spread along a left right axis. Voters tend not to have extreme ideological preferences and will align themselves near the centre. Consequently parties 'will normally try to align themselves with the median voter. To do anything else is to risk catastrophic defeat' (McLean 2001: 7).

The application of this theory to politics can be seen in the development of the Labour Party from 1979. After Labour's electoral defeat in 1979, the party moved to the left and subsequently performed badly in the polls, winning only 28% of the vote in the 1983 election. It was almost replaced by the Liberal SDP alliance as the main opposition party. Following the defeat, Labour started a gradual, concerted shift to the centre as it abandoned policies on nationalisation, increasing income tax, withdrawal from the European Community and a repeal of Conservative trade union reforms (Hay 1999). The Conservative Party, on the other hand, following its defeat in 1997 moved to the right, away from the median voter, and in 2001 and 2005 suffered significant defeats. Although with the election of David Cameron it seems to be confirming rational choice theory and moving the Conservatives to the centre.

Rational choice theory has also been applied to the way in which public servants work. In terms of bureaucracy and the Civil Service, rather than officials being loyal to ministers and concerned with the public interest, their motivation is their own interest. Consequently, this means, according to the original rational choice studies of bureaucracy, that civil servants are budget maximisers. Their concern is not the public good, but increasing budgets because this increases their power, status and job security. Dunleavy (1991) later adapted the rational choice theory of bureaucracy to say that bureaucrats were not budget maximisers, because they rarely received the benefits of increased budgets, but were bureau-shapers. What they want to do is shape their jobs so that they retain the most interesting and rewarding elements.

Rational choice theory seems useful at explaining certain situations. It can explain why students in a communal house only empty the rubbish bin when the bin is overflowing and the bag is split. Every student is a rational actor and therefore s/he believes that one more piece of rubbish can be squeezed into the bin leaving the next person to empty it. This of course, makes the situation worse. If the bin was emptied before bursting point it would be much easier and less would spill on the floor. Instead the job is a difficult one. This is an example of the chicken game (see Politics in Focus 2.1). Likewise, rational choice theory can show why it is difficult to obtain and sustain agreements on global warming or preserving fish stocks. Everyone wants to ensure that fish stocks are retained but they want someone else to bear the cost. Ideally, everyone else stops fishing and you can continue. What often happens is that an agreement is made but individuals break it because it is rational for them to do so and once one person breaks it then everyone does.

However, there are a number of major problems with rational choice theory. It assumes that rational self-interest is a universal motivation, whereas economists and psychologists have demonstrated that there are a whole range of motivations for people's behaviour. We can be motivated by greed, rage, altruism or the desire to avoid risk. Some of the most important decisions we make in life, such as who to marry or where to buy a house, are often driven by motives other than rationality. (For instance, Jane Austen's novels reflect the way in which, in the 19th century, love was taking over from economic interests in determining marriage partners. Before the 19th century, marriages were about economic relations and it is only relatively recently that marriage has been seen as a romantic relationship.) Often we are not rational in a conventional sense. It is more dangerous to drive down the M1 then to fly, but more people fear flying than going in the car. When we collect bottles to take to the bottle bank, we are not acting rationally in the rational choice sense. The rational response would be for us to throw the bottles in the bin and allow everyone else to improve the environment by taking the trouble to recycle. Often, much of what rational choice does explain is trivial. It is not particularly insightful to say that a Labour Party that has been in opposition for 18 years will move to a position where it attracts more votes. More interesting questions may be why did it take so long to change? Why did it change in the way it did? What is the impact of the change on party members? It is also clearly the case that we do not have complete information and often people are making choices out of prejudice or misinformation. Finally, rational choice theory is based on an individualist and agency-based approach to social explanation. It assumes that we are free to make choices (although contradictorily it sees people's actions as determined by self-interest) and that social phenomena are a consequence of the sum of individual decisions. However, increasingly social scientists are examining the way in which institutions shape our behaviour.

Institutional approaches

The underlying assumption of institutionalism is that organisations matter and that they are more than the sum of their parts. In other words, organisations are created by human activity, but they exist beyond the life of each of the individuals within it. Institutions can affect people through formal rules and the Westminster model is effectively an institutional approach that is concerned with the impact of formal rules on the operation of government. More importantly, for the so-called 'new' institutionalists, it is not formal rules that are important but the way informal rules—norms, values and culture—affect behaviour. For institutionalists, when we join an institution, whether it is a formal one like a university or an informal one like a group of friends, we inculcate the 'rules' of the institution and develop appropriate forms of behaviour. For example, at university there are no written rules on how a seminar should operate. There is nothing to say when students should or should not speak or how the tutor will run the seminar. However, we quickly develop certain understandings about how seminars in general operate and how particular seminar groups function. For instance, there may be strong expectations in some seminar groups that students should speak and whatever our rational self-interest in keeping quiet, the group expectation that we talk overrides immediate self-interest.

The other important element of institutional approaches is that certain patterns of behaviour become entrenched within institutions. One of the key concepts in institutional theory is the notion of 'path dependency'. Path dependency means that decisions made in the past, or particular patterns of behaviour, can be entrenched and these affect decisions that are made in the present. For instance, the licensing laws that were developed during the First World War in order to prevent munitions workers drinking too much set the pattern for licensing laws in Britain up to the present day. These laws have continued to shape the nature of licensing laws and have affected the whole attitude to drink in Britain. Any decision made about pub opening times is made within the context of rules about drinking that were made in very particular circumstances nearly 90 years ago. Even the recent decision to liberalise opening hours is made within the context of the rules established in the First World War and these rules shape how the new legislation is developed and implemented.

The impact of institutional norms and cultures can be seen in the operation of government departments. For instance, the Home Office has had a distinctive organisational and policy culture (see Chapter 31). In terms of organisation, it has been hierarchical and elitist with a strong conception that officials know best and ministers are there to serve the department. In terms of policy, the department's culture has reflected the need to find a balance between maintaining order and protecting individual liberty. Since the 1960s, the department has probably been more concerned with individual liberty and been quite progressive on issues such as gay rights and prison reform. This provided a problem for Conservative Administrations in the 1980s and 1990s which wanted a more socially conservative approach to these issues. The culture of the Home Office made it difficult for ministers to make the choices that they wished.

However, DiMaggio and Powell (1991: 30) ask: 'If institutions exert such a powerful influence over the ways in which people can formulate their desires and work to attention them, then how does change occur?' Institutionalism sees people as inculcating organisational norms and therefore it is difficult for it to explain why or how institutions change. Moreover, by extending the notion of institutions from formal bodies like Parliament or the Civil Service to informal organisations such as the rules of behaviour within a particular organisation, then it is very difficult to define any behaviour as being outside institutions. For many, institutional approaches go too far in examining the role of structures and pay too little attention to individuals.

Developing interpretive approaches

In the 1950s and 1960s, American sociologists developed an important approach to our understanding of the social world. Whereas before, social scientists had been concerned with the development of institutions and social structures and how they affected individuals or groups, interpretivist sociologists like Erving Goffman, Harold Garfinkle, Peter Berger and Thomas Luckman asked how the social world developed, and how did the social world look from the bottom up. How did individuals participate in the creation of the social world that they inhabited and how did they make sense of it? For these sociologists there were two important assumptions. First, society is socially created. In other words, the world we inhabit is not some organisation passed down from God, some natural way of being, but is created through the choices and actions of individuals. One example of the impact of social creation is English grammar. There is a lot of debate about English grammar and a suggestion that the standards of grammar have declined. The assumption is that grammar exists as something outside of people. There is a system of grammar to which people conform. Consequently, there is good grammar and a set of given rules about how we construct language. Yet, these rules of grammar are socially created, not given, and we could speak in completely different ways and at other times we have. In medieval times, the language of the educated class was Latin.

The second assumption of the social creationists is that there is not a single understanding of the world but a range of ways of interpreting it. Our interpretations of the world affect how and what we see. A seminar is not an independent institution but it exists because we, as individuals, reproduce certain forms behaviour—going into the room, presenting a paper, asking a question. Whether a seminar is a good or bad seminar depends on our interpretation. One student may see a seminar as good because she took lots of notes. For another, it may have been bad because no one spoke. There is no single interpretation of events that are correct and indeed different students may have different understandings of how one should behave in a seminar. For one student, the student who speaks throughout the seminar is clever and eloquent, for another, she is boorish and domineering. This is why we often cannot find a single view of events in political life.

These interpretativist approaches and assumptions about the social world have long been part of sociological perspectives on social life but have only recently been incorporated into political science. In international relations theory there has been the development of what is called constructivism (see Ruggie 1998). Constructivists emphasise the absence of an objective social reality that exists beyond human activity or understanding. From their perspective, the social world is inter-subjective, in other words, it depends on the interrelationship between humans and their interpretations and understandings (Hay 2002: 24). As a consequence, ideas play an important role in our understanding of the social world. So even in an event like the Iraq war which for social constructivists is a real event, how we understand it depends on ideas about the international system, the role of the United States, or the nature of the dictatorship in Iraq. Who is the sinner and the sinned against in the Iraq war will depend on our belief systems. For an Islamic fundamentalist, it is another example of US attempts to crush a way of life that is resistant to US liberal capitalist norms. To a Marxist it is about US attempts to secure its oil supply and to George Bush it is about destroying an evil dictator who is a threat to peace.

Interpretive approaches have also been developed by Mark Bevir and Rod Rhodes (2003) to examine the British political system. For Bevir and Rhodes, in order to understand the way in which officials and ministers behave within the British political system we have to understand how they interpret the world. Moreover, they argue that in developing understandings, individuals draw on particular traditions and it is these traditions that shape how they see the world. What people do and how they behave is related to their beliefs and understandings of the world. For instance, how we understand a political phenomenon such as Thatcherism will depend on the traditions upon which the analyst draws. For a socialist it may be an attempt to roll back the gains made by the working class in the post-war era. For a liberal conservative it may be about reasserting the sovereignty of Parliament in order to end Britain's economic and political decline.

The most extreme form of these types of interpretive approaches has been developed in what is known as postmodernism. For postmodernists, there is no real world that exists beyond our understanding. All truths are only such because they are sustained by sets of ideas or discourses. Our sense of the world is only what is conveyed through language and the meaning of language is never fixed because it is open to constant interpretation. There are no universal truths and it is impossible to develop an understanding of how the social world works. The world of politics and the state is fragmenting, and all the certainties of the post-war period are disappearing. Developments in new technology have changed how people relate to each other and the profusion of information sources mean that it is difficult to provide a single narrative concerning how the world operates. For writers such as Foucault, each society is characterised by an episteme and what are seen as truths within a particular episteme will not be true in another. Consequently, there is no fundamental truth. Truth is a function of power not knowledge.

Postmodernist relativism makes the notion of social science unsustainable. A social scientist cannot possible explain the social world but only proffer a different interpretation of the world. Postmodernism, although on the surface a radical philosphoy, is actually nihilistic and conservative because it does not believe that we can make society better (or indeed that there is such a thing as better). All notions of improvement are only an attempt to impose one episteme on another. Consequently, whilst appearing to offer an individualistic understanding of the social world, it actually denies individuals the ability to change the world. Nevertheless, postmodernism is a useful approach for making us think about how we take the modern world for granted and, in the West in particular, we tend to assume that through science we have the key to social progress, when it may indeed be the case that science creates new problems as it solves old one. Indeed, as Foucault and others have pointed out, it is difficult to separate power and knowledge.

Integrating the interpretive and the institutional: structure and agency

One of the key issues in social science is whether we as actors determine social outcomes or whether our actions are constrained or determined by social structures and institutions (what is often referred to as the agency/structure problem). This is the core of the argument between rational choice and institutional approaches. It is important because it helps us to understand how politics works. If we examine two approaches to the impact of Margaret Thatcher we can see that the focus of analysis is very different. Anthony King (1985) explains the success and impact of Thatcher in terms of her personality. Thatcher's dominant style was a reflection of her personality and it was with force of personality she was able to push through radical changes in policy. On the other hand Jessop et al (1988) see Thatcherism not as a derivative of an individual person, but the development of a political strategy that developed out of the consequences of the crisis of the post-war welfare state. Thatcherism was able to develop a coherent vision of an alternative to the post-war consensus that had dominated British politics. Her alternative attempted to resolve the crisis through re-asserting parliamentary sovereignty and privatising the economy. At the same time wealth was redistributed to the middle class through tax cuts. Thatcherism was not a consequence of an individual, but of the political and economic situation at the time. Indeed, Thatcherism could be seen as a particularly English phenomenon that developed from the organisational and ideological structures that have long been present within the British political system.

These two explanations offer alternative accounts of the nature of Thatcherism, one focused on individual action and the other on social structures. Now of course, it is relatively easy to see that any understanding of Thatcherism requires a sense of the social and political context and the decisions of individuals such as Margaret Thatcher. For instance, had Ted Heath (who was Prime Minister between 1970 and 1974) remained Conservative leader in 1975, it is unlikely that the political changes that unfolded in the 1980s would have done so in quite the same way. Consequently, individuals do make a difference. There have been a number of attempts to reconcile the relationship between structures and agents. Anthony Giddens (1985), for instance, examines how, through actions, individuals create social rules and these social rules provide the context in which individuals make decisions. Individuals are reflexive—they can think about the situation they are in and learn from experience. Therefore, they can make choices that are not necessarily determined by the social situation. Jessop (1990) develops this perspective further, suggesting that the structural contexts within which actors make decisions privileges certain outcomes. For neither Jessop or Giddens do individuals make completely free choices because their choices are shaped within a context, and if they act outside of expectations there is often a high price to play (for a discussion see Stones 1996 and Hay 2002). To return to the seminar example, a seminar follows a set of rules that are relatively clear even though they are not explicitly written down. Students know they will go into a room, sit down and wait for the seminar leader to speak and then when questioned or asked to speak they will speak. A student could decide that he is going to dominate the seminar. The costs of this may be high in terms of embarrassment or conflict with the tutor. But the student may have a belief that he has more interesting things to say than the tutor and so change the form that the seminar takes. This may be a one-off but if other students hear of it and think this is a good way to organise seminars they will eventually change the structure of seminars.

The approaches that we have outlined have a different conception of the relationship between structure and agency. Ironically, rational choice theory and postmodernism leave little room for individual choice because in these approaches the decisions we make are determined, in the case of rational choice theory, by the structure of preferences we face and for postmodernism, by the episteme in which we exist. On the other hand, social constructivists and institutionalists see the possibility for agents to change the structures that shape their lives. At the wider, macro-level the relationship between structure and agency can be seen as playing out in the discussions over the nature and meaning of globalisation.

Globalisation and the changing structural context

One of the key debates in political science in the past 10 years has been over the nature of globalisation. Many have used this to support structuralist arguments in relation to the nature of government in the modern era. It has been suggested that governments have been 'hollowed out' (Rhodes 1997 and see Chapter 3) and that there is a limit to what governments can now do. In other words with the development of globalisation, governments have had less freedom in terms of economic or social policy.

According to the governance literature, the cultural, political and economic processes of globalisation are permanently challenging the twin foundations of modern government: territoriality and sovereignty. A whole range of factors: technology, transportation, computerisation, the development of supranational organisations, the growth of transnational companies, etc have led to national borders being permeated and now nation-states have to react to, and operate within a global, rather than national, environment. It is argued there is a hollowing out of the state as transnational institutions and forces increasingly become the sites of key decisions.

Unfortunately, when analysing globalisation, there is a need for a degree of caution. This is because globalisation is not a neutral or meaningless label, but instead, is a value-laden and much-contested concept in both political and academic circles. When we are considering globalisation within the context of governance, the key questions are:

- What effect has globalisation had on governance?
- Has globalisation led to a more diverse and fragmented policy-making arena, which in turn, has led to greater pluralism?
- Alternatively, has the impact of economic globalisation (see below), led to a small number of very powerful, transnational companies controlling the domestic policy process?
- Is globalisation a recent phenomenon that has evolved in the last 30 years, neatly dovetailing with the governance era, or is it a process that has been occurring for more than 300 years?

The answers to these questions depend on what particular definition of globalisation one adopts (see below) and the extent to which one views globalisation as a recent, immutable process which renders national governments impotent or, alternatively, as a much over-stated and over-rated concept, with nation-states still remaining the key sites of political power. The point is that we cannot provide a definitive answer to the questions posed above because the nature of the subject is highly contested. Instead, we have set out to outline the different debates surrounding the concept of globalisation. We have to assess the British political elites' interpretation of globalisation, which is perhaps the most important consideration, given that our task is to evaluate the present day nature of the British policy process. For if Westminster and Whitehall consider globalisation, in whatever form, to be a reality, they will act in a different way than if they regarded globalisation as simply a debate discussed in university lecture theatres or late-night BBC2 political chatshows, but which has no bearing on the 'real' political world (for a discussion see Hay 2002).

Interpretations of globalisation

There is now a considerable literature on the nature of globalisation and its impact. But there is almost no agreement on what it is. Most people agree that something has changed, that the interconnectedness of the world—and the spread of that interconnectedness— has become greater. People also agree that capitalism has become an increasingly domi- nant global force and this is having an impact on how people live and the sorts of choices that they can make (for reviews of the debate see Scholte 2000; Held and McGrew 2000). Many disagree over the meaning of the processes. For some, globalisation implies a com- plete transformation of the pre-existing economic and political organisations and their replacement with a globally integrated state with transnational institutions of regulation (see Ohmae 1995). For others, they see globalisation as greatly exaggerated and therefore what we are apparently witnessing is nothing new (see Hirst and Thompson 1996). Consequently, as we see in Table 2.1, there are many interpretations of globalisation.

The question of power

Underlying all these different approaches to the study of politics is the question of power. Each of these approaches has a different assumption about where power lies and the nature of power.

The first issue of course is how we define power. The simplest definition is provided by Robert Dahl (1957). He sees power as existing when A gets B to do something that he would not otherwise have done. The Prime Minister has power if he can prevent the Chancellor raising income tax when the latter wished to do so. This is essentially a pluralist or rational choice definition of power. It sees power as something that attaches to agents and it is observable. We can see who has power because they can determine outcomes. Often from this perspective, power is attached to certain positions such as the Prime Minister or the chair of an important committee (Dunleavy 2003). Dunleavy, using a rational choice approach to examine the power of Cabinet committees, ascribes points to ministers and committees and uses the aggregation of points to determine who is the most influential minister. The problem with this approach is that it assumes that power is observable, that it is something that can be fixed to a person or a position and that it is possible to make some sort of abstract assessment of the influence of an individual or committee. Likewise, the Westminster model assumes that power is defined by the consti- tution and slowly the constitution will adapt to shifts of power within the Westminster system. Consequently, we can see power shift from Parliament to Cabinet to Prime Minister. The Westminster model defined much of the still on-going debate concerning whether power is now concentrated with the Cabinet or the Prime Minister. Power within this tradition is a zero-sum concept. There is a finite amount of power and if one person gains power another person will lose it.

Interpretation	Main argument	Main proponents
Globalisation as totalising process	The globalisation of the economy and culture is resulting in the disappearance of national boundaries and the declining importance of the nation state. Domestic states are being replaced by transnational states.	Ohmae (1995) Sklair (1995, 1998)
Globalisation as rhetoric	Globalisation is not really occurring (or it is nothing new) but is a useful rhetorical device for politicians either to hide policy errors or to promote the extension of neo-liberal economic policies.	Hay and Watson (1998) Hay (1999) Hirst and Thompson (1996)
Globalisation as imperialism	Globalisation is nothing new but is the continuation of imperialism by other means. Developing countries are no longer exploited through military conquest but through the exploitation of their resources and labour.	Hardt and Negri (2000)
Globalisation as restructuring of state power	There are significant changes occurring in the economy, culture and politics, but they do not mean the undermining of the nation state. It does mean, however, that the state is acting in different ways and making different choices. For some, it means policy being made increasingly in the interest of capital.	Mann (1997) Cerny (1990, 1995) Baker et al (1998)
Globalisation as Americanisation	Globalisation is not globalisation at all, but Americanisation: this is the successful export of US ideals, culture and economic methods to the rest of the world.	Fukyama (1992)
Globalisation as transformation	Globalisation is a continuation of patterns of global interaction that have occurred throughout history but they are now having more extensive and intensive impacts on the way people live and the nature of politics and economics. This process is still occurring, therefore there is no fixed notion of what globalisation means.	Higgott (1998) Held et al (1999)

Approach	Nature of power	Where power lies	Who exercises power
Westminster model	Constitutional	In key institutions	Prime Minister, Cabinet
Rational choice theory	Observable	Dispersed	Agents
Pluralist	Observable	Dispersed	Groups
Institutionalist	Structural	Within institutions	Institutionally embedded agents
Interpretivist	Ideational	In cultures and webs of meanings	Agents
Postmodernist	Ideational/discourse	Dispersed through discourse	Indeterminate

POLITICS IN FOCUS 2.2
Harold Wilson and the devaluation of sterling

When the Labour Government was elected in 1964, the Prime Minister was concerned with the vulnerability of the pound to international financial markets. There was significant pressure on sterling's position and one option was to voluntarily devalue the pound rather than let the markets force a devaluaton. Wilson's position was that Labour would maintain the existing value of the pound. A range of people within the Labour Party believed that Labour should devalue sterling in order to resolve a number of economic policies. Wilson's view was that any discussion of devaluation would lead to currency speculation and so he banned discussion of the devaluation option (although it was a perfectly legitimate policy option). The option of devaluation was removed from the agenda and called only 'the unmentionable'.

The notion of power as a zero-sum concept that can be observed has long been criticised. In the 1960s, the American writers Bachrach and Baratz (1962) argued that power was not always observable and that power was indicated more by what was not discussed rather than what was discussed. Those who had power were not those who could influence outcomes but those who could shape the political agenda and, therefore, exclude issues which threatened the interests of the powerful. This approach has been labelled the second face of power. The classic example of this type of agenda shaping was the Labour Prime Minister, Harold Wilson (1964–70 and 1974–76) and the devaluation of sterling in the period between 1964 and 1966 (see Politics in Focus 2.1).

This notion of shaping the agenda was taking even further by Steven Lukes (2004) in the so-called third face of power. He argued that power was exercised through more than the conscious exclusion of issues from the political agenda but through those in power engaging in the manipulation of wants, so that issues are prevented from even being developed. For example, with the development of the car a decision was made that the car would have primacy on the streets. There was no conception that perhaps people should have priority on the roads and that cars should drive at say, 5 miles an hour or even be eliminated from residential areas. The presumption, deeply embedded in our society is that the car comes first. Pedestrians have to watch out for cars whilst drivers need not give way to pedestrians. If a child runs out on to a road and is killed, it is the parent or the child that is at fault not the fact that a car driving at 30 mph will kill any child that it hits. An alternative conception of the relationship between cars and pedestrians has never been articulated because of the economic imperative of the motor car.

Lukes' third face of power is compatible with institutionalism. For institutionalists, organisations and cultures are ways of automatically keeping issues off the political agenda. Cultures for instance define what is acceptable behaviour. For example, Civil Service culture imposes on officials the need to be neutral and loyal to the government, and behaviour outside these rules is rarely conceived of by officials. Likewise organisations are concerned with delivering particular policy goals and do not consider alternative options. For instance, the Common Agricultural Policy has for 50 years provided farmers with subsidies and until the 1990s the government paid no attention to the impact of the policy on the environment, consumers or developing countries. Non-farm interests were automatically excluded from the policy process.

As Hay (2002) points out, the conception of power developed by Bachrach and Baratz is still linked to agents and a conscious sense of power. The exercise of power is something that powerful actors do (although this is less true in Lukes' third face of power). Interpretive and postmodern approaches see power as invoked less by individuals but existing in our conceptions and beliefs of the world. For interpretative approaches, power exists through cultures which determine our sense of what is the proper way to behave. Postmodernists take this further. For them power is everywhere. For example, the notion of a student involves a conception of power; the definition of student implies a set of power relationships. If you are a student you are placed in a relationship to your lecturer, your parents and to the government that is a power relationship. You are told that you should respect your lecturer's knowledge because you need it to pass the exam and you need your parents' assistance to pay the fee dictated by government. However, for postmodernists power is never set. It is not an object but a continually renegotiated relationship. The student-lecturer relationship can be subverted through attendance at lectures that are only of use to the student. Students know that because parents are imbued with a bourgeois notion of parental obligation they can be persuaded to lend a bit more money. The problem of postmodernism is that if power is everywhere can we ever hope to make life better or free ourselves from powerful relationships?

Power as dependency

Is there any way of making sense of all these different approaches to power? One of the problems of the power debate is there is no way of resolving the disagreements between different protagonist. Their views of the nature of power are so diverse that it is not possible for one perspective to accept that another may be right. Consequently, all we can do is try to develop a framework for helping us to understand the way power operates. One such framework is the notion of power dependency. This in some ways develops the more traditional notions of power that develop from pluralism with some of the ideas developed by institutionalist and postmodern traditions. From this perspective, all actors within a political system have resources. For example, the Prime Minister has the power to select the Cabinet whilst a member of the public has the right to vote. These resources are capabilities. In order to exercise power it is necessary to use the resources. However the use of resources is dependent on a range of other factors. The freedom of the Prime Minister to select a Cabinet may depend on his position in the party, the electoral strength of the government, the degree of public and party support. Power then is dependent on context and other actors. The Prime Minister, in order to exercise power, needs political support, and for people to accept his authority. Power then is not a zero-sum game but a relationship. It exists in the interactions between people and between people and institutions. Institutions provide the resources and people make the decision to use them. In this way power includes both agency and structure.

Conclusion

As we saw in the introduction, the role of political science is to try and understand and explain political events. Whilst the media concentrates on personalities and particular events, the role of political scientists is to understand events in a wider context. The various ways of understanding politics allow us to explain the motivations of actors and the context in which we operate. The theories outlined focus on different levels and on different forms of explanation. For example institutional approaches are concerned with the effects of institutions and structures. For instance one of the findings of the Macpherson report into the murder of Stephen Lawrence (see Chapter 5) was that there was institutional racism (Wight 2003). The report was highlighting how the attitudes and beliefs that were inherent within the police force led to an inadequate investigation of the crime. The explanation is structural. Rational choice theory and interpretivist approaches focus their analysis elsewhere. They examine the behaviour of individuals and their beliefs. By using alternative understandings we can look behind the superficial elements of politics and try to explain why certain events happened. Different understandings ask different questions and as a consequence come up with different answers.

What is important to understand is that the Westminster model was presented as a neutral picture of how the British political system operated. However, rather than being neutral it included a certain interpretation of how the political system should operate. At the same time, it legitimised the roles of ministers and civil servants and hence maintained an essentially elitist system. Other ways of understanding power help us open up the Westminster model to more critical appraisal and think about how power may be exercised within the British political system.

ICS IN FOCUS 2.3

nce and Britain and the Gulf War: two explanations

During the second Gulf War, France and Britain took very different positions. Britain was the closest ally to the United States. It supported the war without a second UN resolution and was prepared to provide a large number of troops to support the invasion. France on the other hand argued that the war was not justified because there was a lack of evidence of weapons of mass destruction and it was prepared to veto a UN resolution. How do we explain these different positions? The media and political science explanations focus on quite different factors when explaining the events.

The media

The media focused on the particular views and values of the British Prime Minister Tony Blair and the French President Jacque Chirac. Blair was seen as being close to George Bush, of wanting to maintain his approval and as being particularly pro-American. Britain's support for the war was seen as a personal decision of the Prime Minister. Chirac was seen as a proud and arrogant Frenchman who wanted to assert French independence.

The political science explanation

From the point of view of political science, these positions were completely predictable. As we will see in Chapter 6, Britain has long been caught in the middle between the EU and the US and it has been a central element of British foreign policy to retain a close relationship with the US despite closer integration into the EU. The continued alliance with the US is seen as a way of maintaining a world role for Britain despite a decline in its political power. In terms of power dependency, if Britain is to exercise any power on the world stage it is dependent on the support and assistance of the US.

France on the other hand has always attempted to develop a foreign policy that is independent of the US. It would not join NATO when it was established and it vetoed Britain's membership of the European Union (then the Common Market) because the then President, Charles De Gaulle, thought Britain was too close to the US. In addition, France has historical ties with Iraq and considerable overseas investments in the country.

Therefore the positions taken by France and Britain respectively in regard to the war was not the result of the whims of their leaders but reflect the relationships of the countries to the US and their particular views of the roles of the countries in the world. Britain thinks that it can have more impact through alliance with the US and France believes that it can have more influence through independence from the US.

KEY POINTS

- How we understand politics depends on the perspective that we use.

- British politics has generally been understood through the framework of the Westminster model which locates power within the Cabinet system.

- One of the crucial issues in understanding politics is the relationship between structures—the institutions that frame our actions—and agency—the ability to make choices.

- Different theories tend to focus on different factors. Rational choice theory focuses on the behaviour of self-interested actors, instuitional-ism on the ways that rules and institutions constrain and facilitate action, and interpretive approaches examine the ways in which people understand and interpret the political process.

KEY QUESTIONS

(1) What are the problems with the Westminster model?

(2) What are the ways that we can understand power?

(3) Are people rational actors?

(4) How may institutions influence political outcomes?

(5) What structures constrain the Prime Minister?

(6) Does globalisation limit what government can do?

FURTHER READING

An excellent introduction to a number of approaches used in political science can be found in D. Marsh and G. Stoker (2002) *Theory and Methods in Political Science*, London: Palgrave. If you want to follow up different approaches in more detail you should look at C. Hay (2002) *Political Analysis*. For a detailed account of pluralism see M. Smith (2005) 'Pluralism' in C. Hay, M. Lister and D. Marsh (eds) *State Theory*, London: Macmillan. Rational choice is applied in I. McClean, *Rational Choice and British Politics*. A good introduction to insitutionalism may be found in, V. Lowndes (2005) *Why Institutions Matter*, London: Palgrave.

 Visit the Online Resource Centre that accompanies this book for links to more information on this chapter topic

CHAPTER THREE

Models of the British state: from government to governance

READER'S GUIDE

This chapter argues that in the last three decades the traditional Westminster model, which presented an image of the British state and political system as unified, hierarchical, centralised and top-down, has been eroded. It provides a detailed analysis of what the Westminster model is by examining the evolution and nature of the modern British state in the 19th and 20th centuries. It then explores the evolution of the Keynesian welfare state in the post-war era before examining the extent to which different sets of pressures led to its breakdown. The chapter then focuses on the present nature of the British state, by using the governance approach and reflects on how change has affected the nature of politics and policy-making in Britain. In particular, it questions the extent to which the Westminster model has been undermined and examines two competing 'organising perspectives' of the British state—the differentiated polity model and the asymmetric power model.

Introduction

Observers of British politics, be they academics, journalists, politicians or other political activists, usually operate with an implicit, rather than an explicit, view of how British politics works. In part, this can be explained by the fact that only a small number of authors have developed an explicit model of the British political system. As Gamble (1990: 411) observes, for a long time: '. . . the majority of the political science profession were largely sympathetic' to the Westminster model. Yet, as we saw in Chapter 2, the Westminster model has always been used more as a shorthand, normative, organising perspective to portray a particular image of the British political system, rather than a theoretically developed and explicit model of how British politics works. As a consequence, there has been little effort to theorise the state, that is, to provide a more developed model of British politics. In particular, there has been, until recently, no real attempt to break from the view that British politics is an activity that predominantly takes places in and around Whitehall and instead look further afield to account for the impact of such features as governance, globalisation and Europeanisation.

Yet, there are now two exceptions to the paucity of explicit models of British politics. The first is provided by Rhodes (1997) who, in criticising the Westminster model, has developed the 'differentiated polity model'. This model aims to capture the changing nature of the British state in an era of governance. Rhodes argues that the Westminster model is too inflexible and monolithic to reflect the diverse nature and complex characteristics of the present-day British political system. In response, his differentiated polity model portrays a much more fragmented, pluralistic and segmented system.

An alternative perspective is provided by Marsh, Richards and Smith (2001, 2003) who argue that Rhodes overly stresses the pluralistic nature of the political system. Instead, they offer an alternative, the 'asymmetric power model'. This is an adaptation of Rhodes in which they focus on the structured inequalities that still exist in British politics. In this chapter we examine the much-maligned Westminster model and the alternative approaches offered by Rhodes and Marsh et al. This we will do by exploring the 'governance approach' (see also Chapter 14), which both sets of authors use to develop their competing organising perspectives of the British political system.

The Westminster model of government

As we saw in Chapter 2, the Westminster model has dominated studies of British government throughout the 20th century and is essentially an organising perspective which defines an area to be studied. Here, the British state is seen to be unitary in character—by which it is meant that all domestic sovereignty (power) is formally concentrated in the Westminster Parliament. This is underpinned by the principle of parliamentary sovereignty. Constitutionally, this principle allows for the overturning of any law by a majority in Parliament. So, from this perspective, power is clearly located at the centre.

However, as we will see below, this model presents an oversimplified version of the British system of government. In many ways, the British political system has been centralised, closed and secretive throughout the course of the 20th century. The justification for the development of this type of parliamentary system was based upon legitimacy through representation and public servants who were conditioned by a public service ethos and were therefore not self-interested actors. As such, the ruling elite, in particular, ministers and civil servants, could be trusted to act in the public good, rather than for their own narrow or self-serving needs (see Richards 1997; Richards and Smith 2000). Despite the Westminster model's normative prescription of power being centred on Parliament, the British state contained many 19th century features, its territory was contested and there were tensions between the local and the national levels, which weakened the model's utility.

Characteristics of the Westminster model

The Westminster model is built on the assumption that there is parliamentary sovereignty; all decisions are made within Parliament and there is no higher authority. Legitimacy and democracy are maintained because ministers are answerable to Parliament and the House of Commons is elected by the people. Decisions are taken by Cabinet and implemented by a neutral Civil Service. This view is derived from the Whig notion of the constitution being in self-correcting balance (see Judge 1993). The main characteristics of the model are identified in Table 3.1.

Westminster	Whitehall
Parliamentary sovereignty	Permanence
Governing party with a majority in the House of Commons	Anonymity
Cabinet ministers have collective responsibility	Neutrality
Party discipline maintained	Expertise/knowledge
Voters offered choice between disciplined parties	Informal 'village-like' networks
Accountability through free and fair elections	Accountability to political masters
Delivers strong Cabinet government [Executive dominance]	Ensures defence of the public interest

The importance of the Westminster model

As with all models, it is only intended to represent an 'ideal type'. For a long time this model has been criticised for not describing the reality of the British system of government. It undoubtedly reflects important features of the British system of government, but it is also a legitimising mythology. By this we mean that it justifies the maintenance of a closed and elitist system of government. The most important feature of this model is that because it is a legitimising mythology, it does reflect how most politicians and officials perceive the system. Within this model, both groups are portrayed as representatives and servants of the people and answerable to them. But they have to act in the public interest rather than directly responding to their own interests or other special interests. Hence, it continues to inform and condition the way in which both sets of actors operate. The Westminster model has been used as both an organising perspective on how the British political system works and as a model of power identifying the nature of sovereignty (see Table 3.1). It is also important to recognise that the Westminster model reflects a particular epoch in British politics, that of the modern British state in the post-war period.

Identifying the modern British state

During the 19th century, British government and society was dominated by the notion of laissez-faire or liberalism. The role of the government was limited to: maintaining a market economy and property rights; ensuring and protecting the freedom of individuals; and protecting citizens from external threat (Greenleaf 1983, 1987; McEachern 1990). It was in the course of the 19th century and throughout the 20th century, that the modern British state developed, but the process was gradual and piecemeal. The growth of the state was a response to a complex set of interweaving factors such as industrialisation, concerns over public health, urbanisation and developing bureaucracy.

19th century state evolution

The key developments in the 19th century were:

- The introduction of a range of social, health and education legislation that expanded the role of the state within these sectors. The key point here is that even at the high point of Liberalism in the 19th century, the state was never solely a night-watchman. The introduction of factory, education and health legislation in the 1840s gave the state a special role.
- Growing public expenditure (see Figure 3.1).
- The growth of the bureaucratic machinery (see Figure 3.2).
- The development of collectivist ideas through the dissemination of the ideas of political thinkers such as Marx, Engels, Hobson, Hobhouse and Weber as a response to the increasing complexity of a society undergoing an industrial revolution (see Politics in Focus 3.1).

E 3.1

vernment expenditure 1800–1900

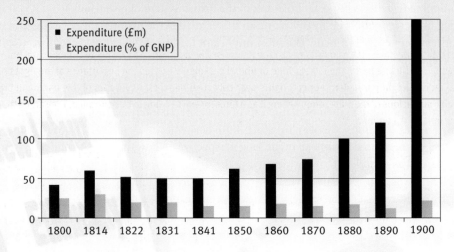

Source: Data from Peacock and Wiseman (1967: 37)

FIGURE 3.2
The growth of the Civil Service in the 19th century

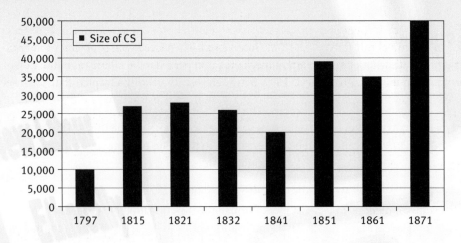

Source: Mueller (1984: 174)

Political philosophy was a major factor in shaping the role of the state in the 19th and 20th centuries. Put another way, ideas are very important in determining the type of state Britain has. At the heart of the philosophical debates in Britain over the nature of the state, we can identify two intellectual paradigms. On the one hand, the laissez-faire or liberal paradigm stresses the importance of the rights of the individual, in particular, property rights over collective benefits. Advocates of this paradigm are highly suspicious of the state, often seeing it as a force for evil needing to be controlled. They argue that any form of government intervention demands strong justification and the preferred solution to societal problems is to call upon charitable or private actors, not state agencies. The opposing paradigm is the collectivist model which argues for the importance of state action in order to promote the collective good. It advocates an active role for the state to alleviate poverty, social injustice and other pathologies it sees as symptoms of a market economy. Thus, the model places a higher priority on the use of state power, in order to promote collective good, than on the protection of individual liberty. 'This model ascribed no particular merit to the workings of the free market and saw governmental intervention as a rational force preferable to private philanthropy' (Peele 1999: 76; see also Greenleaf 1987).

During the late 19th century and throughout the 20th century, these two models have competed with one another for supremacy, as political parties, pressure groups and social movements contested what the role of the state should be. However, a key point is that, at no time throughout this period, did either position completely eclipse the other. So, for example, as we saw above, at the height of liberalism in the 1840s, the state was never relegated simply to a night-watchman role. If we look elsewhere, in peacetime Britain, the state reached both its greatest size and had the largest number of functions under its direct control in the late 1960s–70s. Yet, even here, the state employed only 30% of the workforce and the private and voluntary sectors still played a substantial role in social, political and economic life.

Yet, at the end of the 19th century, the British state was still relatively limited in what it did, how much it spent and how many people it employed. The predominant belief was still in a minimal role for the state; only intervening when faced with problems of internal or external disorder or when market mechanisms appeared to be failing (as in the case of providing public health). Before 1890, it was almost universally accepted that the level of government expenditure was kept at the minimum consistent with the provision of adequate protection against the Crown's enemies and the maintenance of order (Peacock and Wiseman 1967). Much of the social legislation was only implemented half-heartedly (MacDonagh 1958) and between 1841 and 1890 public expenditure declined from 11% of GNP to 9% (Peacock and Wiseman 1967).

20th century state evolution

It was only in the 20th century that the modern state really started to grow, when it acquired an increasing number of functions. As early as 1906, the state increased its role in the provision of welfare through health and unemployment insurance and old age pensions. Here, the Liberal governments between 1906 and 1915 advocated a more active role for the state in promoting social welfare. As important, the events of the First World War had a real impact in transforming the nature of the state and:

> ... with it the assumptions of the country's governing elite. An unprecedented degree of state intervention in the economy occurred between 1914 and 1918 and novel uses of discretionary powers were tolerated (Peele 1999: 76).

Throughout the inter-war years, the government became increasingly involved in the economy and the 'onward march of social policy' (Peden 1991: 105).

The post-war era: the evolution of the Keynesian welfare state

During and after the Second World War, the role of the state in both the economy and social policy substantially increased. The 1945 Labour Government continued the work started by the wartime coalition and established the welfare state which provided free education, health care and a comprehensive welfare benefits system. On the economic front, the Government committed itself to providing full employment, at least initially, planning the economy and, through nationalisation, it acquired control of large numbers of key industries. In addition, the Government committed itself to Keynesian demand management, so accepting responsibility for the aggregate level of demand within the economy (see Politics in Focus 3.2). Individuals were no longer solely responsible for their own welfare, nor was the economy left to the market. These economic and social responsibilities were more or less maintained by all governments until 1979.

This greater economic role increased the size of the state and raised levels of public expenditure. In absolute terms, the increase in state expenditure during the 20th century has been enormous. Even as a percentage of GNP, it has increased from 11% in 1910 to 52% in 1979 (see Figure 3.3). This increase in expenditure was accompanied by an increase in public employment. By 1976, 25% of the population worked for the public sector in one form or another.

One consequence of the evolution of the modern state in the post-war era and with it industrial society was the creation of powerful economic groups which need to be ameliorated to safeguard social order. In Britain, the form of the modern state after 1945 is described by Jessop (1990, 1994) as a Keynesian welfare state (KWS) (see Politics in Focus 3.2 and Chapter 27). This was a state in which different governments directly intervened in both economic and social policy. Yet, there were always limits placed on the development of the Keynesian welfare state, most notably in the shape of liberalism.

FIGURE 3.3

Government expenditure in the 20th century

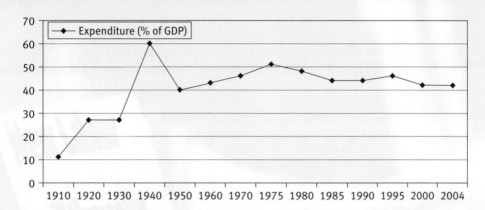

Source: Data adapted from Greenleaf (1983: 33) and Toynbee and Walker
(2001: 107), HM Treasury (2004)

...CS IN FOCUS 3.2

John Maynard Keynes was an English economist and Treasury advisor whose ideas had a major impact on economic and political thought in the post-war era. His most influential work, *General Theory of Employment, Interest and Money* (1936) was an attack on governments' response to the Great Depression of 1929 and the subsequent fall in global levels of economic production and the dramatic rise in the unemployed. His arguments centred on what he regarded as the fatal flaws inherent within capitalism and liberal market economic theory, asserting that economic systems would not automatically right themselves to attain 'the optimal level of production'. More specifically, he attacked existing macro-economic orthodoxy and its emphasis on the need for 'balanced budgets'. This he regarded as potentially harmful to the economy and a cause of unemployment. Instead, he suggested that governments should take an active role in the economy, in order to stimulate demand and so promote growth.

Keynes argued that the level of output and employment in the economy is determined by aggregate demand (the total demand for goods and services in the economy during a specific time period). Here, he was suggesting that demand creates its own supply up to the limit set by full employment. Growing employment and falling wages would reduce consumer demand and lead to a drop in aggregate demand for goods and services. This in turn would produce a reduction in consumer sales and a fall in revenue and profit levels for business. The cumulative effect would be to undermine business confidence, leading to a reduction in investment, and a collapse in business expectations. Furthermore, if wages and prices were falling, people would start to expect them to fall, making the economy spiral further downwards, as those who had money would simply wait as falling prices made it more valuable to save rather than to spend. This in turn would lead to further unemployment. In essence, the economy was a highly sensitive organ, receptive to the slightest change in perceptions of confidence. When Keynes published his *magnum opus* in 1936, his arguments appeared vindicated by the economic slumps of the inter-war years.

The solution for Keynes was to abandon the existing orthodoxy of balanced budgets. Investment was the key to economic success, and he argued that if business lacked the confidence to invest, then it was imperative that governments filled the void, in order to stimulate growth. Such a role was imperative in times of recession. Rather than cutting back on expenditure, governments should actively invest in the economy to promote new economic enterprises, which in turn would stimulate economic growth, increase consumption, stimulating further growth, reducing unemployment and so the cycle (or multiplier effect) would continue. In today's parlance, this would be described as governments' spending their way out of recession. Keynes' vision was the creation of a mixed economy, in which governments took on an active role in intervening in the economy in order to stimulate growth with the use of a range of economic levers to achieve full employment and planned economic growth. Underpinning this new economic vision was a series of social goals; Keynes believed that a mixed economy and an emphasis on full employment would alleviate the widespread hardship experienced by so many in the Great Depression, whilst also creating opportunities for social improvement.

It would not take long for a form of Keynesianism to be put into practice. In the course of the Second World War, the enormous expenditure by the National Government in almost all walks of life to successfully prosecute the war, effectively eradicated unemployment. This experience affected the economic views of leading politicians across the political spectrum. What followed in the post-war era was the establishment of a new economic orthodoxy—Keynesianism—embedded and pursued by both Labour and Conservative Governments for the next 30 years.

Analysing the British state

The continuing influence of liberalism

The British state developed in the context of liberal ideas from such thinkers as Jeremy Bentham, John Stuart Mill, Thomas Hill Green and Albert Venn Dicey (see Chapter 4). Consequently, Greenleaf (1983) identifies a continual tension between collectivist and libertarian thought. Whilst the state has become increasingly interventionist, there have been important ideological limits on how much the state should intervene. There is a strong tradition that the British state should be limited and consequently, there is no formally identified body of public law in Britain and governments have rarely relied on detailed state planning, unlike some continental European states (see Kavanagh and Seldon 1999). For instance, the comprehensive economic planning system created during the Second World

War was quickly abandoned and, subsequently, the Conservative Administration (1951–64) took a relatively hands-off approach to the economy.

A 'deformed' modern British state?

The problem of the British state—which in many respects persists today—is that the tasks and functions of a large and interventionist modern state were grafted on to a system that was essentially 19th century—hence, the evolution of the British system of government over the last 200 years is sometimes labelled a 'deformed modern state' (see Richards and Smith 2002: 60). By this what is meant is that notions concerning the role of the Civil Service, ministerial responsibility and Parliament were created in the 19th century and only adapted in a piecemeal and evolutionary way. Moreover, the process of adaptation was through negotiation between governing elites. Reform was therefore not about modernising government but about sustaining elite rule. It has only been at moments of crises of legitimisation that significant changes have even been hinted at. The consequence is that the modern British state takes a very particular form. To use Judge's (1993) term, it is a 'parliamentary state' which through party discipline and representative government allowed a considerable concentration of power within the hands of the executive. The executive's power is to some extent built on a system of departmental government that relies on the loyalty of officials who, as we will see, have considerable influence over policy. It also relies on local administration for the implementation of policy and thus considerable negotiation between the centre and the localities. It is through this framework that the modernist features of the Keynesian welfare state were established, but the deformed nature of this modernity created many difficulties for the government in achieving its goals (see below).

The state was (and is) undoubtedly large, centralised and bureaucratic. After 1945, it controlled a wide range of policies, it spent a vast amount of money and it had a significant impact on the lives of most people. This peaked in the 1960s. However, there were significant limits on what the state could achieve and control. As we will see in later chapters, the British state has always been constrained by external factors which are often portrayed as an explanation for not achieving domestic policy goals. It may even be the case that the maintenance of full employment was not a consequence of domestic control of the economy, but as a result of the post-war boom fuelled by US expansion. Nevertheless, the development of the modern state did affect both what British government did and the nature of the policy-making process (see Chapter 13).

Theorising the modern British state

An era of government

The modern state is characterised as hierarchical, centralised, territorially bound and omnipresent. Many of these features could be identified in the British state between 1945–79, but it was also, in many ways a deformed modernism. The state was hierarchical and centralised, but there were challenges from local and non-state forms of administration. Whilst the public sector was large, there was also an extensive private sector. Yet, it is also clear that the modern British state did take on many functions and, perhaps more importantly, policy-making was often closed, secretive and elitist.

So how should we interpret the modern state in Britain? Throughout the 19th and 20th centuries, this debate has oscillated between two contrasting models—collectivism and liberalism, each located at opposing ends of a philosophical spectrum. Yet, at different stages, the characteristics associated with one model dominated, but never eclipsed the other. A convincing argument can be made that the height of collectivism in Britain occurred in the late 1960s. It is important to recognise that while, at this stage, both the private and voluntary sectors still played an important role in social, political and economic life, the government was undoubtedly the most powerful and important actor in the policy process. It is from this perspective, that we can label the period from 1945–70s, an 'era of government' in which there was a high concentration of state powers. So, less than 40 years ago, it was widely accepted that government possessed the political power to control or provide direction to society where and when it so chose. This notion was reflected in the key normative, though rarely stated, element of the Westminster model: that the loci of political power in Britain centred on Westminster and Whitehall. Within this context, the British model of government implicitly espoused the view that 'government knows best'. This, in turn, reinforced the notion of Britain as a strong, unitary state in which the power invested in its governments remained largely unfettered.

An era of governance

In the last 30 years, the capacity of the state to control or direct society and the extent to which the institutions of central government retain a monopoly on political power have become a much more contested issue. The growth of globalisation, Europeanisation, internationalisation, devolution and market reforms of the state have changed the nature of the relationship between the state and society and have brought into question the extent to which Britain is, or ever was, a strong unitary state. In response, 'governance' has become an established concept within political science, used to portray the changing nature of the state in recent times. Pierre and Peters (2000: 1) argue that the popularity of the concept of governance stems from: '. . . its capacity—unlike that of the narrower term "government"—to cover the whole range of institutions and relationships involved in the process of governing' (see Politics in Focus 3.3).

Governance and the British state

A number of commentators have set about addressing the impact of governance (see Politics in Focus 3.4). In the British context, there have emerged two broad, competing analyses of the impact of governance on the British state—Rhodes' (1997) 'differentiated polity model' and Marsh, Richards and Smith's (2003) 'asymmetric power model'. Both of these accounts are critical of the Westminster model as being an outdated organising

POLITICS IN FOCUS 3.3
What is governance?

Governance is a concept which tries to make sense of the changing nature of the state in the last 30 years. The term stems from the notion that we now live in a more 'centreless society'. It is a reaction against those who continue to conceive of the state as being mono-centric or based on unitary government. As such, it is also a critique of the utility of the Westminster model. The main theme associated with the concept of governance is the recognition that there is not one, but many centres of power which link together a whole variety of state actors be they at the local, regional, national or supranational level. In the broadest terms, governance has been suggested as a way of conceptualising a new form of government. It is often portrayed as the combination of New Right reforms aimed at rolling back the state, globalisation, internationalisation, managerialism in the public sector and privatisation. It is argued that a product of these changes has been the loss of sovereignty for central government and a break-down in the nation-state. So, the term 'governance' refers to a change in understanding of what the process of governing is and refers to a new way in which society is now governed.

Unfortunately, one of the problems in trying to address these fundamental questions is that governance is a much contested concept which can often lead to a degree of incomprehension and misunderstanding. In order to make sense of this confusion, Richards and Smith (2002) argue that at a primary level, the term should be understood as a concept that reflects the shifting patterns of the state over the last three decades from an era of 'government' to an era of 'governance'. Government is seen to reflect a time when governing was basically regarded as one-way traffic from those governing to those governed. Yet, as the number of actors in the policy arena have multiplied, the boundaries between the public and the private sector have become more blurred and central government's command over a more complex policy process has receded a new era of governance has occurred. Here, governance should perhaps be best understood as:

> . . . a descriptive label that is used to highlight the changing nature of the policy process in recent decades. In particular, it sensitises us to the ever increasing variety of terrains and actors involved in the making of public policy. Thus, governance demands that we consider all the actors and locations beyond 'the core executive' involved in the policy making process (Richards and Smith 2002: 2).

perspective of the British political system. Yet they differ in their conclusions concerning the nature of power in Britain today.

The differentiated polity model

Rhodes (1997, 2000: 55) argues that the concept of governance sensitises us to: '. . . a new process of governing; or a changed condition of ordered rule; or the new method by which society is governed' which covers a whole range of institutions and relationships involved in the process of governing. What is being alluded to is the complexity involved in the many new forms of government, as a result of the fragmentation of traditional, centralised state apparatus in recent years. Governing is no longer seen as being confined to the nation-state, but instead involves a range of institutions, both public and private, from the

R.A.W. Rhodes (1997): One of the leading authors in this field, Rhodes argues that governance refers to a 'new process of governing'. He then notes that the multiplicity of meanings attached to governance is problematic, before suggesting that in the British case: 'Governance refers to self-organising, interorganisational networks characterised by interdependence, resource exchange, rules of the game and significant autonomy from the state' (p 15). Rhodes then identifies six separate uses of governance: the minimal state; corporate governance; new public management; 'good governance'; a socio-cybernetic system; and a self-organising network.

World Bank (1992) see also Davis and Keating (2000: 3): The World Bank adopts a simply expressed definition of governance, suggesting it refers to: 'the exercise of political power to manage a nation's affairs'. It then suggests that good governance is based on: an efficient public service, an independent judicial system..., the accountable administration of public funds; an independent public auditor, responsible to a representative legislature; respect for law and human rights...; a pluralistic institutional structure; and a free press.'

J. Pierre (2000: 3): Another leading author on governance, the Swedish political scientist, Jon Pierre argues that the concept has a dual meaning: 'On the one hand it refers to the empirical manifestations of the state's adaptation to its external environment as it emerges in the late twentieth century. On the other hand, governance also denotes a conceptual or theoretical representation of co-ordination of social systems and, for the most part, the role of the state in that process.'

J. Pierre and B.G. Peters (2000): Elsewhere, Pierre has collaborated with the US political scientist, Guy Peters. In their work on governance, they suggest that historically, four common governance arrangements have existed: hierarchies, markets, networks and communities. They then suggest governance concerns the process of steering and co-ordination, but make a distinction between the use of the term in Europe, in which it refers to 'new governance' ideas of the involvement of society in the process of governing, while in the USA, the term refers much more to the concept of steering.

J. Rosenau (2000: 171): Another US political scientist, Rossenau's area of specialism is International Relations. He therefore focuses on what he refers to as global governance and he adopts a perspective that: '. . . allows for governance occurring apart from what governments do, here governance is conceived as systems of rules, as the purposive activities of any collectivity that sustain mechanisms designed to insure its safety, prosperity, coherence, stability, and continuance.'

A. Gamble (2000a, 2000b: 111): The British political scientist Andrew Gamble has predominantly concentrated on the relationship between governance and the economy. One of Gamble's key arguments is that many of the governance mechanisms on which global markets rely are organised and sustained by nation-states. Thus, Gamble urges caution in an age in which many are rushing to embrace ideas associated with globalisation. More particularly, he defines governance as denoting: '... the steering capacities of a political system, the ways in which governing is carried out, without making any assumption as to which institutions or agents do the steering.'

J. Kooiman (2000): This Dutch political scientist is well known within the field of public administration, and his work concentrates on the relationship between government and society. He suggests that the governance of modern societies is a blend of all kinds of governing levels, modes

and orders. Kooiman argues that social-political governance implies: 'arrangements in which public as well as private actors aim at solving problems or create societal opportunities, and aim at the care for the societal institutions within which these governing activities take place' (p 139).

L. Hooghe and G. Marks (2001): One of the most oft-repeated terms from the governance lexicon is that of 'multi-level governance' (MLG). Hooghe and Marks suggest that governance is a multi-level activity. In other words, governing is an increasingly complicated process of decision-making operating at and between different levels (eg supranational, national or local). These levels interact to produce new forms of policy-making. The key premise of multi-level governance is that authority has dispersed away from centralised nation-states and that different decisions are made at different levels of government. Hooghe and Marks (2001: 7) argue: 'governance must operate at multiple scales in order to capture variation in the territorial reach of policy externalities'. Different actors have seen the opportunity to utilise new levels of decision-making, in order to influence the policy process. The assumption underlying MLG is pluralism. Essentially, authority is dispersed and decision-making occurs within a range of bodies through a process of negotiation. Policy-making is consequently about networks.

B. Jessop (2004): Jessop builds on the theme of MLG to suggest that states adopt a strategic-relational approach to the impact of governance. Here, he argues that the forces of governance have changed the strategic options available to government whilst also exacerbating complex social relations with other actors in the policy-making arena. Nevertheless governments engage in a process of shaping what he refers to as meta-governance, in order to exert control and influence over the policy networks within the policy process. For Jessop, policy networks do not function in isolation from their structured environment, but instead they are embedded 'in the shadow of hierarchy' (p 65). Here, of course, what Jessop is alluding to is the shadow cast by governments in setting the rules and regulatory order in which networks operate.

supranational to the national to the local level. Here, the suggestion is that governance is no longer about command, a key characteristic of the modern state, but instead, it is concerned with control (see Politics in Focus 3.5).

The concept of governance assists us, as students of political science, to understand changes in British government in the last quarter of the 20th century. In particular, it highlights the blurring or even the disconnection that has occurred between the state and civil society.

> The state becomes a collection of inter-organisational networks made up of governmental and societal actors with no sovereign actor being able to steer or regulate. . . A key challenge for government is to enable these networks and to see out new forms of co-operation (Rhodes 1996: 667).

POLITICS IN FOCUS 3.5
Steering not rowing the ship of state

'Steering not rowing' was an influential analogy produced by two New Right, US commentators—D. Osborne and T. Gaebler in their book, *Reinventing Government* (1992). They argued that the role of government should be to 'steer not row'. The central theme of their thesis is that, for too long, government has focused on extensive state control of all aspects of social life, leading to an ever-expanding state sector, bureaucratic growth, inertia and inefficiency. Osborne and Gaebler claim that the Weberian model of bureaucracy has become a bankrupt tool for governing. Instead, they argue (pp 19–20) that the old model should be replaced by 'Entrepreneurial Government' based on 10 principles:

> ... entrepreneurial governments promote competition [1] between service providers. They empower citizens [2] by pushing control out of the bureaucracy, into the community. They measure the performance of their agencies, focusing not on inputs but on outcomes [3]. They are driven by their goals—by their missions [4]—not by their rules and regulations. They redefine their clients as customers [5] and offer them choices ... They prevent problems [6] before they emerge, rather than simply offering services afterwards. They put their energies into earning money [7], not simply spending it. They decentralise authority [8], embracing participatory management. They prefer market mechanisms [9] to bureaucratic mechanisms. And they focus not simply on providing public services, but on catalysing all sectors [10]—public, private and voluntary—into action to solve their community's problems.

The essence of entrepreneurial government is that the state should radically withdraw from government (less rowing) and instead concentrate on good governance (more steering). By this, it is meant that government should take responsibility for controlling policy management, leaving service delivery ie how the policies are implemented or delivered to other actors, wherever possible, to the private sector. This, they argued, would allow governments to have a more efficient and effective role in 'steering not rowing' the economy, social policy, law and order, etc.

What Rhodes evokes is an analogy of government 'steering not rowing' and his comments are a plea that the government should act as a capable navigator in a state that has become fragmented. This has led to the advancement of a new role for the state that rejects the traditional model of state control to be replaced by the creation of an 'enabling state'.

So far, we have established that the concept of governance has a multiplicity of meanings attached to it. At its primary level, it sensitises us to the numerous actors, the variety of terrains and the different relationships involved in the process of governing. Moreover, it implies that the traditional role of central government has recently been curtailed to the extent that government is now only one actor among many in the policy-making process. Thus, central to Rhodes' understanding of governance is a tacit acceptance that the process of governing today involves a much more pluralistic conceptualisation of power. Put another way, power has been dispersed away from the traditional central-state actors to many different, often new arenas and a multiplicity of actors.

Within the British context, the concept of governance tends towards a position in which the Westminster model is no longer sustainable. In order to take account of the changing nature of the British state in the last 30 years and to recognise that the terrain in which politics is conducted has become much more diverse and complex, Rhodes (1997: 7) provides his own organising perspective of the British political system—the 'differentiated polity model':

> A 'differentiated polity' is characterised by functional and institutional specialisation and the fragmentation of polices and politics... This perspective is only one possible interpretation of British government, but it has three advantages. First, it identifies important weaknesses in the Westminster model. Second, it poses distinctive questions about British government. Third, it explains key problems confronting policy-making and implementation in the 1980s and 1990s.

The key characteristics of the differentiated polity consists of: governance; intergovernmental relations; a segmented executive; policy networks; power dependence; and a hollowed-out state. In the next section, we examine each of these characteristics (see Politics in Focus 3.6).

POLITICS IN FOCUS 3.6
The differentiated polity model

(1) Governance (see above)

For Rhodes, the key to conceptualising governance is to think in terms of 'governing without government'. It is a new state form which has shifted away from the corporatist model of mediating between labour and capital associated with the 1970s, towards one which attempts to reconcile the interests of consumers and producers at the sub-national, national and international levels.

(2) Inter-governmental relations

The notion of inter-governmental relations [IGRs] concerns the interaction between all the various state actors. It covers all public sector organisations including Westminster, Whitehall, the European Union, local government, quangos, agencies, regulatory authorities (Offwat, Offgas), etc: '. . . the term not only draws attention to the range of governmental organisations involved in service delivery but also to the increasing influence of the European Union [EU] on UK policy-making' (Rhodes (1997: 7)).

(3) A segmented executive

Highlights the departmental structure of Whitehall which creates 'policy chimneys' where policy is developed within a department without proper consideration being given to the fact that a policy initiative in one area may have unforeseen or unintended consequences elsewhere. In effect, the departmental structure conditions policy-makers to think vertically within the confines of their own specific policy area, rather than horizontally, on the impact of an issue across other policy areas in Whitehall. This is one of the besetting sins of the British system of government which has intensified in an era of governance.

JS 3.6

(4) Policy networks approach (see Chapter 21)

In an era in which the policy arena is portrayed as being increasingly complex and diverse, policy networks is an approach analysing the way government interacts with civil society, especially interest groups which are constantly voicing their own, sectional demands. The policy network approach is based on examining a particular policy area, for example, a policy of banning fox-hunting and identifying the range of actors involved in policy-making. Around each policy—be it health, defence, welfare policy for lone parents, asylum-seekers, etc—a network exists with a different range of actors involved. The approach recognises that much policy-making in central government is not through formal institutions but through contacts of informal networks.

(5) Power-dependence (see Chapter 21)

The notion of power-dependence argues that organisations depend on each other for resources and, therefore, enter exchange relationships. Politics is about resource exchange between different actors—departments, agencies, pressure groups, etc in order to achieve their policy goals or objectives. Hence, it is also implicitly about compromise. Thus, power is understood as an exchange relationship between different actors in the policy-making arena.

(6) The hollowing-out of the state

The hollowing-out of the state is perhaps the most radical aspect of the differentiated polity model. It summarises many of the changes which have and are taking place in British government in the last three decades arguing that central government's authority, autonomy and power have been reduced, by being dispersed:

- upwards to the supranational level that is Europe, IMF, G7 (8), etc;
- outwards through privatisation and market-testing;
- downwards, through the creation of quangos and agencies, etc (see Figure 3.4).

The importance of the 'differentiated polity' model lies in the fact that it is one of the most sophisticated attempts to reflect the changing nature of the British state over the last few decades. Unlike the Westminster model, it attempts to take account of the issues presented by the concept of governance. However, it is not without its critics. In particular, Marsh, Richards and Smith (2003), though sympathetic to many of the features identified by Rhodes, question the extent to which the differentiated polity model is underpinned by an implicitly pluralistic understanding of the British political system.

The asymmetric power model

Marsh, Richards and Smith (2001, 2003) observe that under the Westminster model, the locus of power was relatively clear; it was the executive whether defined as the Prime Minister,

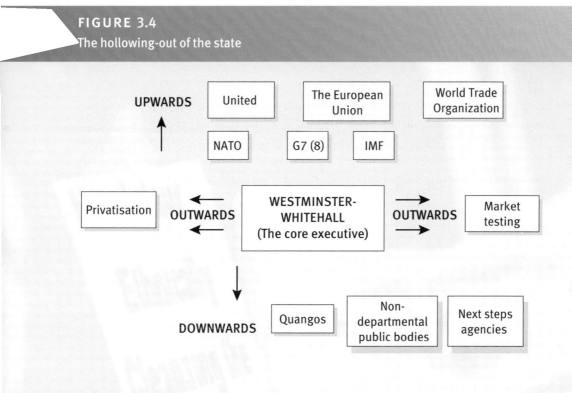

FIGURE 3.4
The hollowing-out of the state

Cabinet or departmental government. They also concur with Rhodes that with the internal and external changes that have occurred since the 1980s, the distribution of power appears to have become more fragmented. Yet, they are critical of the view of power presented by the differentiated polity model, instead suggesting that whilst there have clearly been changes in the policy process, the state remains the most dominant political actor within the British political system. The state has the most resources in terms of income (taxation), personnel, information and force. Whilst there are more actors involved in the policy process and the relationships between them and the core executive has changed, the relationship is asymmetrical, in that the central state continues to dominate when it chooses. So, although recognising that the state has undergone substantial change, they suggest that a high concentration of power remains at the centre. Thus, Marsh, Richards and Smith (2003) propose the 'asymmetric power model' (see Politics in Focus 3.7). The key characteristics of this model are:

- a society which is marked by continuing patterns of structured inequality;
- a British political tradition that emphasises the view that 'Government knows best';
- asymmetries of power;
- exchange relationships between actors in the system of governance;
- a strong, if segmented, executive;
- limited external constraints on executive power.

(1) Structured inequality

Actors have unequal access to the political process and political power. The poor, ethnic minorities and women are systematically discriminated against, in terms of access to power and the economy. Therefore, whilst the political system may be fragmented, there are still many groups that are excluded from the policy process.

(2) The British political tradition

The institutions and processes of British politics are underpinned by a view of democracy that continues to stress a limited, liberal notion of representation. Here the emphasis is on the holding of periodic, relatively free and fair elections; and a conservative notion of responsibility based on the need for strong and decisive rather than responsive, government. It is a model that expounds elite rule. The code that underpins the British political system is still one that emphasises that Whitehall, ie, the core executive, 'knows best'.

(3) Asymmetric power

There are crucial asymmetries of power in the British political system. The model recognises resources have, to an extent, shifted away from the core executive to other actors and that the process of governing has become more complex in recent years. Increasingly, the delivery of public goods involves the creation of networks including government, regulators and private and third sector actors. However, whilst the government is often dependent on these organisations for the delivery of the service, they in turn continue to depend on the government which has a unique set of resources: force; legitimacy; state bureaucracy; tax-raising powers; and legislation, which are unavailable to other actors. Thus, the relationship between the government and most other interests remains asymmetrical.

(4) A pattern of exchange relationships

Power is not zero-sum but involves exchange relationships that are based on patterns of dependence. Private companies, transnational organisations, voluntary organisations, quangos and agencies are involved in a process of exchange with different levels or sections of government. However, the continued strength of the executive and its control of significant resources mean that, whilst the government sometimes fails to get its way, it still continues to win policy battles much, indeed most, of the time.

(5) A strong, if segmented, executive

Despite recent constitutional reforms, Britain retains a strong executive. The core executive is clearly not a unified whole but has a segmented character. However, power continues to be concentrated within the core executive and the majority of policy decisions are made at departmental level.

(6) A limited pattern of external constraints

The pattern of external constraints on government is changing. However, it is important not to be too carried away by such arguments for a number of reasons. First, governments have always been

POLITICS IN FOCUS 3.7
(Continued)

constrained. Second, governments can be strategic, whilst markets cannot. Third, markets are dependent on government. Fourth, citizens are still subject to considerable state power. Thus, the relationship between global and national forces is contingent and interactive, not determined, and the British government still has considerable options. For example, Castells (1998: 330) argues that the EU is successful precisely because: '(it) does not supplant the existing nation-states but, on the contrary, is a fundamental instrument for their survival on the condition of conceding shares of sovereignty in exchange for a greater say in world, and domestic affairs . . .'. Like power, state-global relations cannot be conceived in zero-sum terms. So, for example, in relation to both globalisation and the EU, 'constraints' also provide opportunities for strategically calculating governments.

Conclusion

One of the key themes that will be addressed throughout this book is the extent to which phenomena such as globalisation, Europeanisation and internal reforms of the state have directly impacted on the nature of political power in the British political system. In particular, we explore the extent to which these forces have undermined the Westminster model. Here, we have suggested that the trends identified in the governance approach have rendered the Westminster model an inappropriate organising perspective which fails to reflect the reality of the contemporary British state. Put another way, the hermetically sealed nature of the Westminster model does not properly account for these phenomena and the challenge they present to the notion of parliamentary sovereignty.

In this chapter we have explored two alternative approaches to the Westminster model—the differentiated polity model and the asymmetric power model. First, it is important to recognise that both of these alternative models present a contrasting interpretation of the nature of power in the British state. Both offer, what their authors suggest, are more effective organising perspectives of the British state (see Table 3.2). When, in the subsequent chapters we examine key features of the British political system, it is important to keep in mind these two alternative models. This will allow you to determine which approach you think more appropriately reflects the contemporary British polity. Nevertheless, whilst we suggest here that the Westminster model no longer offers an appropriate organising perspective of the British system of government, this in itself does not render it an irrelevance. It is important to recognise that the Westminster model still leaves a vital imprint on British politics. Not only does it offer a defining image of the British political system, to which ministers and civil servants still pay lip service, but it is also the framework which has conditioned much that has been written about British politics and therefore cannot be ignored.

	Westminster model	Differentiated polity model	Asymmetric power model
Representation	Limited	Diverse	Limited with reforms
Organisation	Hierarchical	Diverse	Hierarchical but fragmenting
Distribution of power	Deformed pluralism/elitist	Pluralist	Elitist
Core executive	Unified	Segmented	Segmented
Role of executive	Dominant	Weak	Dominant
Sovereignty	Absolute within state	Sovereignty undermined	Sovereignty reconstituted
Form of governance	State centred	Governance without government	State-centred with new forms of power

KEY POINTS

- The state is a fluid and complex entity with changing boundaries and networks of relationships.

- Traditionally, the Westminster model was regarded as providing the 'ideal-type' model of the British state and how it operated.

- In the last 30 years, a series of external and internal forces, including globalisation, Europeanisation and internal state reforms have undermined the Westminster model and, in particular the concept of parliamentary sovereignty.

- As an alternative, the governance approach is a way of understanding the way in which the British system of governing operates and reflects the the complex nature of the policy-making process.

- There are a number of competing views concerning what governance means, but essentially it refers to a shift from a one-way hierarchical system of governance to an environment in which the actors in the public arena have multiplied, the boundaries between public and private have become blurred and government's central control has receded.

- The governance approach has led to two alternative models being present that challenge the Westminster model.

- First, Rhodes offers the differentiated polity which is underpinned by a more pluralistic conception of the nature of power than offered by the Westminster model.

- Elsewhere, Marsh et al while sympathetic to much of the Rhodes critique of the Westminster model, argue that he over-emphasises pluralism. Instead, they offer their own asymmetric power model, which argues that the core executive remains the dominant actor in the policy-making arena.

KEY QUESTIONS

(1). What are the key features of the modern British state?

(2) What is the relationship between the Westminster model and the modern state?

(3) Is Britain a deformed modern state?

(4) How have pre-modern elements affected the nature of the British state?

(5) What are the different interpretations of governance?

(6) Does the differentiated polity model or the asymmetric power model provide a more convincing organising perspective of the British state than the Westminster model?

IMPORTANT WEBSITES

On British government and changes in organisation see www.ukonline.gov.uk/, and more specifically, www.cabinetoffice.gov.uk/ and www.10downingstreet.gov.uk/. On global governance see www.worldbank.org/wbi/governance/, www.governance.qub.ac.uk/ and www.nottingham.ac.uk/politics/european-governance/. On regional and urban governance see www.unesco.org/most/most2.htm, www.saltireguide.co.uk/register. html and www.cf.ac.uk/euros/welsh-. For new forms of digital governance see www.digitalgovernance. org/governance/index.html. For a discussion of the modern state and its problems there is information at the sites of a number of think-tanks including: www.iea. org.uk/, www.demos.co.uk/pms2nded. htm, www.adamsmith.org.uk/, www.cer.org.uk/, www.npi.org.uk/, www.ucl.ac.uk/constitution-unit/, www. fabian-society. org.uk/int.asp, and for a libertarian view www.digiweb.com/igeldard/LA/. There is also useful general information on British politics at www.ukpolitics. org.uk/.

FURTHER READING

The debate on governance and the competing models, see R. Rhodes (1997) *Understanding Governance*, Open University Press; M. Bevir and R. Rhodes (2003) *Interpreting British Governance*, London: Routledge; D. Marsh, D. Richards and M.J. Smith (2001) *Changing Patterns of Governance* Basingstoke: Palgrave; D. Richards and M.J. Smith (2002) *Governance and Public Policy in the United Kingdom* Oxford: Oxford University Press; D. Marsh, D. Richards and M.J. Smith (2003) 'Unequal Power: Towards An Asymmetric Power Model of the British Polity', *Government and Opposition* Vol 38/3, Summer 2003, pp. 306–22; D. Richards and M.J. Smith (2004) 'The Hybrid State: Labour's Response to the Challenge of Governance' in S. Ludlam and M.J. Smith (eds) (2004) *Governing as New Labour: Policy and Politics under Blair*, Basingstoke: Palgrave, pp. 106–125; J. Pierre (2000) *Debating Governance*, Oxford: Oxford University Press and Pierre and Peters (2000) *Governance, Politics and the State*, Basingstoke: Macmillan; Fox and Miller (1995) *Postmodern Public Administration: Towards Public Administration*, London: Sage.

 Visit the Online Resource Centre that accompanies this book for links to more information on this chapter topic

CHAPTER FOUR

Ideas and ideologies in British politics

READER'S GUIDE

The chapter analyses some of the problems raised by the term ideology both generally and in the British context. For the most part British politicians do not like to be thought of as ideological, though they are more willing to talk of their values, beliefs or even 'vision'. But there do exist in British politics bodies of ideas which are akin to ideologies. The chapter analyses a number of them, including liberalism, conservatism, Thatcherism (and the new right), socialism and the third way, and notes how these have shaped policies when a party is in government. It also examines environmentalism and feminism and concludes by addressing the question: have we reached the end of political ideology?

Introduction

Britain is not noted for having a theoretical or ideological style of politics, rather the opposite. But ideas do play a part in politics—it would be difficult to conceive of political parties without them—although British politicians are shy of describing themselves as ideological; they think it smacks too much of dogma and intolerance and is potentially divisive. Most Conservatives, for example, have explicitly repudiated an ideological approach, contrasting it unfavourably to tradition and common sense and preferring these as a guide rather than abstract doctrines. Labour leaders (famously thought to owe more to Methodism than to Marxism) have spoken of values of fellowship and social justice, rather than overthrowing capitalism. In government, Labour's socialism has been muted by pragmatism, ambiguity and disagreements about what socialism entails for practical politics. Neither the Conservative nor the Labour Party has ever been dominated by the forces of right-wing reaction or Marxism respectively.

The lack of ideology in British politics is often, incorrectly, interchanged with claims about the rarity of political violence or political extremism, and consensus about the political procedures and institutions. One says *incorrectly* because they are all analytically separate concepts. Interestingly, a former British Prime Minister, Balfour, wrote in 1927, the year after the failure of the General Strike:

> Our whole political machinery presupposes a people so fundamentally at one that they can safely afford to bicker; and so sure of their own moderation that they are not dangerously disturbed by the never-ending din of political conflict (1927: xxiv).

Yet claims about the weakness of political ideology in Britain are relative; they are persuasive when set against the modern histories of, for example, Germany, Italy, France or Spain. In the latter states, ideologies of fascism, communism, monarchism, racism, republicanism and nationalism have all flourished at one time but attracted little following in Britain. This is not to say that the British system has not been immune to political ideas; a number have flourished in Britain and become associated with the British approach to politics. They include Cabinet government, collective responsibility, parliamentary sovereignty, the rule of law, the public corporation and constitutional monarchy.

Ideology

A problem with the term ideology is that it is often used in different contexts. At times it is used as a value-laden term. A politician may be attacked for being ideological, in the sense of not considering an issue or an idea on its merits and being closed-minded. But s/he may also be criticised for lacking an ideology, in the sense of not having a firm set of principles. Karl Marx dismissed ideology as unscientific thinking, a form of 'false consciousness' as opposed to a realistic perception of a situation; for example, when workers, consoled by religion or misled by the media, acquiesce in their poverty and exploitation, rather than realising it is the consequence of an unjust capitalist system. Michael Oakeshott argued that an ideological approach leads to a perverse style of politics because it fails to take account of the complexity and unpredictability of affairs and, above all, of circumstances. He likened the ideological approach to learning to cook from a cookery book, rather than learning by practice. He famously compared political activity to seamanship—a craft not a science:

> In political activity, then, men sail a boundless and bottomless sea; there is neither harbour for shelter nor floor for anchorage, neither starting-place nor appointed destination. The enterprise is to keep afloat on an even keel (1951: 22).

In politics, we take ideology to refer to a set of ideas which are coherent, used to interpret the world, and are action-oriented, that is, they have consequences for political behaviour. A familiar classification of ideology is the left–right dimension. This dates from the French Revolution in 1789 when the nobility, the King's allies, sat on his right in the Estates-General and the commoners, his opponents, sat on his left. At the time, the positions were identified, respectively, with support for or opposition to the monarchy, Catholic Church, aristocracy, and the values of hierarchy and inequality. But the continuum is not a simple one. There are gradations on the left between communism, socialism and social democracy, and on the right between fascism, conservatism and Christian democracy. A psychologist (Eysenck 1957) claimed that left and right should be further subdivided on the dimensions, authoritarianism and tenderness, for example, dogmatic versus open-minded and dictatorial versus tolerant.

Politicians like to claim their actions are rooted in values and principles. Tony Blair, on winning the 1997 general election, declared: 'We won as New Labour and we will govern as New Labour'. In January 2004, not long after he became Conservative leader Michael Howard took out a full-page advertisement in *The Times* stating his principles under the headline 'I Believe'. Although Mrs Thatcher had a reputation as an ideologue, she showed herself to be a pragmatic politician, taking account of the strengths and weaknesses of her position, until she miscalculated in 1990. Politicians, particularly in democracies, find it difficult to implement paper schemes in the real world. Often, the theories may be after-the-event rationalisations of what was done. For example, one leading Labour Cabinet minister in the 1945–51 Government said that socialism is what a Labour Government does. Or the theories may be revised to bring them into line with what happened. In the USSR, politicians and 'theoreticians' endlessly quoted texts from Marx and Lenin and claimed to be following the Marxist-Leninist line even when they changed course or manifestly were not, for example, the 'withering away of the state'.

Although the Conservative and Labour Parties may uphold, respectively, right and left outlooks on politics, the parties are not monoliths. Indeed, at times the differences within them have been as marked as those between them. This has been the case on foreign policy, Europe, state controls over incomes and prices in the 1970s, and House of Lords reform. But (see Chapter 18) there have been persisting differences between them, starker in the 1970s and 1980s than in the 1960s or over the past decade, on the broad themes of:

- state management of the economy versus the free market;
- collective provision of services versus more individual choice;
- promoting greater equality of outcome versus encouraging meritocracy;
- preferring low rates of income tax over boosting public spending.

Surveys suggest that only a small minority of the public think in tightly structured ways about politics. Knowing a person's position on one issue is not very useful for correctly predicting their views on other issues. A person who is right wing on capital punishment, that is, in favour, will not necessarily take a right wing view on defence, that is, in favour of more spending on it. Perhaps this should not be a surprise, given that less than a fifth of voters claim to be very interested in politics.

 ## The British political tradition

Until recently, most accounts of Britain's political development have regarded it as a success story. This view has not been confined to British historians and political scientists; foreign commentators, particularly from the United States, have made the case. Most accounts stress the successful adaptation of political institutions, the gradual spread of political liberties and rights to the adult population, the rule of law, and the way in which the executive was made accountable to Parliament. The consent of Parliament was required for raising taxes and making laws. Ancient (and pre-democratic) institutions such as the monarchy and the House of Lords survived because they adapted, however unwillingly, to democratic pressures.

After the end of the 1914–18 war many recognisable features of modern British politics were firmly established. These include adult suffrage, the emergence of a Labour–Conservative duopoly in the party system, new borders following the withdrawal of the 26 Irish counties which in turn greatly simplified Britain in terms of nationality, class and religion. Moreover, in the 1920s and 1930s Britain's social and political stability and the legitimacy of its political institutions contrast with the record of neighbouring France, Germany, Italy and Spain. These states were marked with bitter ideological rivalries between left and right, resort to political violence, extremism, instability and internal challenges to their legitimacy.

The experience of the political parties serving together in the coalition government between 1940 and 1945 is often regarded as a key step in shaping what some political scientists regard as a post-war consensus for the following 25 years or so (Addison 1994; Kavanagh 1987). The term consensus has been challenged (Pimlott 1988; Marsh et al 1999) on the ground that it does not do justice to the degree of party conflict which surrounded the introduction of many of the post-war Labour Government's policies, and thereafter. But what stands out, apart from the political rhetoric, votes in the division lobbies and manifestos—which emphasise differences—is the broad continuity of policy. Abroad, the 1945 Government began the retreat from Empire and established Britain as a member of NATO and a nuclear military power, and successor governments continued with the policies. On the domestic front the Labour Government was committed to an active state, which provided a universal system of welfare, managed the economy to deliver full employment, accepted that the main utilities would be publicly owned, and consulted on a wide range of issues with the trade unions. The state provision of social welfare required in turn relatively high levels of taxation and public spending and a large bureaucracy to service it. The Labour Government introduced a social democratic settlement after 1945 and the Conservatives in government for 13 years from 1951 did little to reverse it. As Samuel Beer (1965) and W.H. Greenleaf (1983) noted, the policy direction of modern British politics was towards collectivism, whether Conservatives or Labour were in power.

British conservatism has contained a traditional 'Tory' strand, which is prepared to welcome the constructive interventions of the state (Greenleaf 1983). It advocated a paternalist and pragmatic role for government in correcting instances of market failure, and providing welfare and other public services not provided by the market. Following the party's heavy defeat in the 1945 general election, many Conservatives felt forced to accept a positive role for the state in promoting full employment and welfare, not least because they calculated that this was essential to win elections in a largely working-class electorate. By 1951, the party was back in office and prepared to accept a good deal of the previous Labour Government's work—particularly public ownership, the National Health Service, and maintaining the welfare state and full employment. Before the 1979 Conservative Administration, all post-war Conservatives shared this outlook and regarded it as the key to good government and winning elections.

Following Mrs Thatcher's election as Conservative leader in 1975, the party gradually began to break with the above tradition. That approach was under attack after the failures of the Heath Government (1970–74) and the party's loss of two general elections in 1974. The Heath Government's introduction of statutory controls on incomes and bargaining with business and the trade unions over many aspects of economic policy (called neo-corporatism) undermined claims that the party was a credible defender of free markets and limited government. The party in government had also compromised the authority of government in its dealings with the unions.

Mrs Thatcher and her supporters claimed that by the 1970s collectivism had gone too far and that the so-called 'socialist' policies of post-war governments (Conservative as well as Labour) had damaged the qualities of individual self-help, self-reliance and thrift, and led to the country's economic decline. Not surprisingly, some colleagues (eg Gilmour 1992) regarded her as profoundly unConservative, because of her wish to limit the role of the state in welfare and economic policy and her hostility to so many institutions which the party had long regarded as bulwarks of a liberal democratic system. These included local government, the Civil Service, the professions, the BBC and the universities. Some defended them as examples of Edmund Burke's 'little platoons' and as a check on an all-powerful state. She, on the other hand, thought they had become vested interests. Even an admirer, like the economist Milton Friedman, saw her as a 19th century liberal.

During the late 1970s there was certainly a return of ideological politics, Labour was moving to the left, the Conservatives to the right. The evidence of the country's relative economic decline discredited the party elites and, for the ideologues, consensus politics. Rising inflation appeared to be the greater menace than unemployment and there was a growing concern about what was regarded as the problem of government being 'over-loaded' with commitments (not least in state spending on services and benefits) to voters. At a time of low economic growth, combined with double-digit inflation and statutory commitments to pay benefits, state spending grew steadily as a proportion of GDP, prompting the publication of a scholarly book, *Can Government Go Bankrupt?*

Classic liberal ideas gained a new hearing, under the label of neoliberalism, and became more influential on the right of the Conservative Party. Friedrich Hayek and Milton Friedman, both Nobel Prize winners in economics, attacked Keynesian (cf pp 48–9) views, claimed that inflation was primarily a monetary phenomenon and that controlling the supply of money, rather than the state trying to control rises in prices and incomes, was the key to restoring 'sound money'. They also called for less public spending, lower levels of taxes, and more limited government, apart from the traditional duties of maintaining law and order, defence and the value of the currency. They were generally suspicious of government attempts to replace the market in providing services in, for example, health, education and the utilities, because the service was then likely to be more responsive to vote-seeking politicians and be 'captured' by powerful producer interest groups, not consumers. Hayek also argued that society was too complex to be planned by govern-ments. There is, he claimed, a spontaneous natural order which is the outcome not of a plan or design, but of human action.

During the 13 years it was out of government, Labour struggled to decide whether it should consolidate the 1945 settlement or regard it as the first instalment towards the creation of a socialist Britain. In the 1950s the so-called revisionists on the party's right wing argued that Marxist analysis was outdated because of fundamental changes in capitalism and in British society. Anthony Crosland, in his *The Future of Socialism* (1956) argued that ownership of large enterprises was no longer synonymous with control; the latter was often dispersed among financial institutions and decisions were made largely by the managers. The rise of the welfare state and more progressive taxation was steadily improving the living standards of the working class. Keynesian techniques of economic management meant that public ownership, or the state control of the means of produc-tion, and economic planning were no longer necessary to achieve greater economic growth. Revisionists held the major posts in the Labour governments of 1964–70 and 1974–79 and these were widely judged to be failures. In turn, the left succeeded in reform-ing the party's institutions to give more power to the trade unions and party activists and the party manifesto for the general election of 1983 pledged to reverse many of the Thatcher Government's policies and introduce radical socialist policies. Labour suffered its heaviest defeat in modern times.

As the party suffered a series of election defeats so it began to move its policies to a middle ground that had been largely occupied by the Conservatives (Hay 1999). By the last decade of the 20th century the political left in Britain, as elsewhere, had been affected by the worldwide decline of communism and diminished confidence in the efficacy of state ownership and central economic planning. Under Tony Blair, the leadership openly accepted many neoliberal ideas about the positive role of incentives and markets can play, as well as an economic policy emphasising stability, modest marginal rates of income tax, a low (2.5%) inflation target; and a welfare system that should encourage people to leave benefit and return to work. But, like its West European counterparts, Labour also supported constitutional reform, environmental protection, minority rights, the EU's Social Chapter and public-private sector partnerships. To emphasise the break with his party predecessors, Tony Blair claimed that he led a New Labour Party, one designed to cope with the changed social and economic circumstances (not least from the effects of globalisation) and forge a 'progressive consensus'.

Party ideologies

Liberalism

Liberal ideas and values have been and remain important across the mainstream political parties. This was so even during the decline of the Liberal Party in the first half of the 20th century. From the late 17th century the English political theorist John Locke (*Two Treatises on Government*, 1690) provided a vindication of the English constitutional settlement of 1688–89. He defended the ideas of limited and constitutional government resting on a system of checks and balances, the need for government to have the consent of the people—the latter obeyed in return for the benefits of life, liberty and the protection of property. This is the basis of the idea that people have the right to overthrow their government if their rights are not being protected. The first half of the 19th century is generally regarded as the era of classic liberalism, particularly in economic affairs, when the ideas and practice of free trade, laissez-faire economics, and the minimal state were widely accepted.

But by the last third of the 19th century, a reliance on the outcomes of the marketplace came under attack, not least because of the social and economic problems emerging. The social or *new* liberals recognised that individuals are socially interdependent and advanced a positive role for the state, for example, to regulate the market, protect the relatively weak, prevent abuses of monopoly power, and provide public goods and services which the market neglected. The challenge was less of defending the individual's freedom from the state, than enabling the state to secure and extend people's freedoms and capabilities, particularly those of the less well-off. Political writers like T.H. Green and J.A. Hobson, and prominent Liberal politicians before 1914 propounded such views and these were reflected in some of the policies on welfare, trade unions and more progressive taxation of the 1906 Liberal Government.

The mass unemployment of the 1920s and 1930s severely undermined ideas that the economy was guided by an omniscient 'hidden hand' and that it maximised welfare. The economist, J.M. Keynes argued that unemployment was a case of market failure and that the state had an active role to play in managing demand. Where demand was deficient, the state could use the policy levers at its command, such as interest rates, public spending and public works, and taxation, to boost the level of economic activity and employment. After 1945 Keynesian ideas were accepted across the political spectrum (see Chapters 3 and 26).

Liberal ideas have certainly been influential on British public policy in the 20th century, notwithstanding the decline and formal demise of the party (until its recreation as the Liberal Democrats). Indeed, Keynes on economic policy and Beveridge on welfare were key shapers of Labour's post-war domestic policy settlement. Before 1997 Tony Blair invoked these two and even the pre-1914 'new' Liberals as influences in his own thinking about New Labour. He suggested that the Liberal Democrats and Labour shared so many policy goals that they could co-operate to forge a 'progressive consensus' in the 21st century. What is striking in the 21st century is the degree to which the idea of 'back to the market' gained more of an audience among the Conservative Party under Mrs Thatcher and her successors, and even some New Labour thinkers, than among the Liberal Democrats.

Conservatism

The great philosopher of British Conservatism is the Whig statesman and writer Edmund Burke, and he expounded his views at length in *Reflections on the Revolution in France* (1790). He extolled tradition and the wisdom inherent in many existing institutions and practices. He attacked the idea of designing a set of institutions according to universal and abstract principles. It follows that one should change the status quo only when not to do so will assuredly produce something worse.

There certainly are enduring Conservative principles such as respect for tradition, established institutions, hierarchy and private property; beliefs in the frailty of human nature and therefore the needs for curbs; an organic view of society compared to one divided into rival social classes; and the nation-state. But it is difficult to discern a clear Conservative ideology or coherent set of principles (Norton and Aughey 1981). Indeed, the party's attachment to winning or retaining office has required some flexibility over policy and a degree of political opportunism. The need to appeal to a mass electorate has dissuaded the party leaders from speaking for a narrow section of society, or being a party of reaction. Disraeli's claim that the Tory Party was 'a national party or it is nothing' has been echoed by many of his successors, and during the 20th century its electoral success rested on its ability to extend its support from the middle class to a large minority of the working class. The party has accepted many outcomes which it once stoutly opposed, such as the weakening of the House of Lords, self-government (or Home Rule) for Ireland, votes for women, state ownership of industries, relatively high levels of public expenditure and taxation, loss of empire, and so on. For such an electorally successful Party it has championed many lost causes. Some Conservatives have celebrated this adaptability but others (usually on the right) have criticised it as showing a lack of principle.

There have been two important strands in 20th century Conservatism. The 'neoliberal' element advocates a limited role for government, confined to certain 'essential' services (see p 70). In the 20th century Margaret Thatcher was the most politically influential advocate of these ideas. In John Major's Cabinet, right-wing ministers like Peter Lilley and John Redwood and various free-market think-tanks like the Adam Smith Institute and the Centre for Policy Studies advocated big cuts in income tax and state spending, and the extension of privatisation or market principles to the public services. But there has also been a 'Tory' or one nation element which accepts a positive role for the state and is sceptical of the benefits of markets in public services.

Impact of Thatcherism

In the 1980s the Conservative Party became more clearly associated with certain policies and values. The decade marked the rise of what was often described as *the new right*, including the *libertarians*, who advocate a free economic market and greater personal liberty in lifestyles, and the *authoritarians*, who believe in a strong role for social authorities and the state; Thatcherism was a blend of both. The policies included the following.

- *Monetarism*, or the claim that an increase in the supply of money above the rate of production would produce inflation—a case of too much money chasing too few goods.
- *The free market*, on the grounds that it was inherently more efficient than state planning, and that it was morally superior because it gave people the opportunity to make their own choices. Hence the Thatcher Government's policies of privatisation, reduction in subsidies to industry, sale of council houses, changes in industrial relations, including the abolition of the 'closed shop' (the requirement that one had to be a member of a trade union to work in a particular firm) and ending government controls on incomes, prices and dividends.
- *Curbing the economic role of the state*, particularly as a spender, taxer, employer and provider of services. Thatcherite commentators claimed that the more the state does, the less scope there is for individual choice and enterprise and that a shortcoming of politicians making decisions was that producer groups, lobbies, bureaucrats and other special interests could easily manipulate the political process.
- *Reducing marginal rates of income tax*, shifting the balance from direct to indirect taxes, partly to improve incentives to work, as well as promote freedom.
- *Rejecting egalitarianism* as an explicit goal of social policy, on the grounds that it could hold back talent and discourage hard work. Freedom meant the freedom to be different, the freedom to be unequal.
- *Reversing Britain's relative economic decline* (see Chapter 7).

Socialism

The Labour Party has always contained socialists but others as well. And, as a coalition of different interests and values, it has been ambiguous about the meaning of socialism. If, in the early days, some in the party looked forward to the replacement of capitalism and private property by the state ownership of the means of production, exchange and distribution, few hold such views today.

It is difficult to identify a Conservative ideology or a coherent set of principles. **Winning elections** seems to have been a guiding principle, together with an acceptance that this requires **opportunism and flexibility**.

Conservatism is traditionally associated with:

- pragmatism rather than doctrine;
- gradual reform rather than radical change;
- paternalism and an organic view of society.

Nevertheless, two strands co-exist in the Conservative Party which, although sharing some core values, can be distinguished by attitudes towards economic and social policy. The policies pursued and advocated by the party will depend upon which strand is dominant at the time.

Neoliberals emphasise the importance of limited government, free enterprise, low taxes and individual responsibility. They tend also to be Eurosceptic. But there can be a division between neoliberals who are libertarians (eg tolerating soft drugs and same sex relationships) and those who are more authoritarian.

One Nation Conservatives welcome state intervention to regulate the market, recognise links between social conditions and crime, emphasise the place of community and have usually been pro-EU.

It may be useful to distinguish four strands since 1918:

(1) The sectional interest of the *trade unions*. The unions have been prepared to accept economic planning and controls over the economy, but exclude wage bargaining. Although the unions have often paid lip-service to the idea of redistribution some have been lukewarm in practice about achieving greater equality of incomes; powerful unions have clung jealously to craft distinctions and wage differentials. The unions, as members of the party, have worked for the election of a Labour government because they thought they could influence its general economic policy and improve their bargaining position *vis-à-vis* employers.

(2) The *Fabian* belief in public ownership and the efficacy of gradual change. The founders of the Fabian Society in the late 19th century were intensely practical people; in so far as Sidney and Beatrice Webb, George Bernard Shaw, and others were socialists it was largely because they thought that state management and control of economic activities would be more efficient than unregulated capitalism. They saw the state as neutral, not exploitative, rejected Marxist notions of the inevitability of class conflict and revolution, and believed that if Labour gained a majority in Parliament then it could use the resources of the state and the political system to achieve its aims.

(3) The *socialist* strand, represented originally by the Independent Labour Party, and now by the left wing, has looked to the gradual transformation of capitalism into a more classless and egalitarian society.

(4) *Marxism*, with its class analysis, emphasis on economic structure as the determinant of political behaviour, and hostility to capitalism (Miliband 1972; Coates 1975). But its rejection of parliamentary methods for achieving the dictatorship of a class has had little following among Labour leaders. In the 1930s, reacting against mass unemployment, the collapse of the Labour Government in 1931, and the rise of fascism on the continent, some MPs cast doubts on the parliamentary route. In the 1980s some members of left wing groups, particularly those associated with the Trotskyite Militant Tendency, supported 'direct action' and rejected exclusive reliance on parliamentary methods to achieve reforms.

It is now difficult to apply a traditional left label to Labour or, as the modernisers have called it, New Labour. The leadership says it is in favour of what works, and that includes some of the policies of Thatcher and Major. Blair's contributions have been to: rewrite Clause IV of the party's constitution, the new version of which recognises the crucial role of business, enterprise and markets; acknowledge that Britain is now a largely middle-class society and Labour must appeal to all social classes; accept that the public wants value in the public services for the taxes it pays, and expects prudent management of the economy, low inflation and economic stability. Much of this package has been driven by the calculation that Labour had to demonstrate economic competence and gain the confidence of business and the middle class if it was to win a general election.

There has been something of a cyclical pattern of dominance in the Labour Party: in office the right/centre-right of the party is dominant. Loss of office has usually seen the left in ascendance until a prolonged period in opposition or being in government allows the right to recapture control over policy-making.

our Party

The Labour Party has traditionally been regarded as more doctrinaire than the Conservative Party. It was born from co-operation between trade unions, socialist societies, Fabians, and the Co-operative movement. All four strands have influenced the content of Labour Party ideology, which has championed:

- collectivism and co-operation;
- equality, although ambiguous whether it is of opportunity or outcome;
- the working class and the underprivileged;
- state provision of public services; and
- state ownership of key industries and utilities.

the Labour Party

Left Wing	Right Wing
Public ownership as the litmus test of socialism	Ambivalent or negative about public ownership, for mixed economy
Equality of opportunity	Equality of outcome
Against nuclear weapons	Retain nuclear weapons
Cool to NATO and USA	Pro- NATO and USA
Universalist public services, free for users	Diverse provision of services, some payment by user
Key role for trade unions in state and appeal to 'core' voters in working class and trade unions	No special position in state or party and appeal beyond 'core', be a catch-all party
Rely on traditional campaign methods and Party activists	Use marketing, opinion polls and public relations
Traditionalist—Old Labour	Modernising—New Labour

The third way

The term refers to the set of ideas developed by the British sociologist, Anthony Giddens (1998, 2000). Indeed, in his efforts to revise social democracy, he became so associated with Tony Blair's New Labour project that he was often called 'Blair's guru'. Support for the ideas was also found in Clinton's Democratic Party and, for a time, among German and Dutch socialists.

The third way starts from the assumption that the changes in society and culture and in the economic structure in Britain and beyond—partly because of globalisation—have made traditional ideas of the political left and right outdated. The changes mount a challenge to working-class parties but are not confined to them. Both the statist approach to economic management and to welfare, associated with old Labour, and the individualist approach, associated with neoliberalism, have severe shortcomings. The third way argues that traditional ideas of economic planning, Keynesianism and universal welfare benefits do not take account of globalisation, developments in technology, the knowledge economy and consumerism, as well as changes in the family structure and voters' resistance to high levels of income tax. It adds that the new right emphasis on the individual ('There is no such thing as society') and on markets fails to acknowledge that people are also social beings and that the welfare state is needed to help the losers from a competitive economy.

The third way claims to combine the best features of the old approaches in a new synthesis, and draws on various ideas; economic liberalism, or the role of markets; communitarianism, or the mutual obligations which tie individuals and groups; citizenship, or the social purpose of politics in creating opportunity for all and stakeholding, or the need for institutions and policies to take account of their effects on groups apart from producers and users. Governments have to achieve low inflation and higher productivity and levy rates of tax which do not dampen incentives. The ideal role of the modern state is well expressed in Labour's new Clause IV, with its praise for the dynamism of the market and its superiority to the state in generating economic growth (see p 74). The state can encourage the effective and fair working of the market by regulating sensitively, improving the infrastructure and educating and training the workforce. But it also needs to combat social exclusion, promote social justice and a sense of community and shared citizenship. Welfare should be reformed to balance obligations of the state (to develop self-reliance, initiative and curb the growth of welfare spending) and the individual's entitlement to rights and benefits. The third way rejects sole reliance on the first way (statism) and the second (markets) and tries to synthesise them in a third. Thus, it advocates community over either collectivism or individualism, and partnership between the private and public sectors.

Critics have complained that the third way is clearer about what it is against than what it is for, that there are ambiguities in the third way and that it is often all things to all people— perhaps exemplified in Blair' s claim that he 'is in favour of what works'. Is it primarily an updating of social democracy or a replacement for it? Is it a reinvention of social democracy or new Liberalism? Is it Thatcherism updated (see White 2001; Marquand, 2004)?

By 2005 politicians' mention of the third way had declined and it had few open supporters on the continent; Gordon Brown rarely mentions the term (nor New Labour, for that matter). It is also not clear how enduring some aspects will be. For example, in the 2001–05 Parliament many Labour MPs showed in votes in the House of Commons in 2003 and 2004 that they had no time for creating markets in higher education or the health service.

End of ideology

Commentators regularly proclaim a rise or a decline in political ideology. In the 1980s the rise of Thatcherism in the Conservative Party and of the left in Labour polarised the parties and lent an ideological tone to political debate. Since Mrs Thatcher's resignation in 1990, ideology is less evident, not least because Blair accepted a good deal of her programme.

The theme of the decline of ideology was much discussed in the late 1950s and 1960s among political scientists and sociologists. The collapse of fascism and the less radical stance of Communists parties in France and Italy led some to claim that the old battles between political left and right had declined in range and intensity, as had the divisions between social classes. What emerged, according to the American sociologists Daniel Bell and S.M. Lipset, were moderate policies of 'conservative socialism' or 'managed capitalism'. Parties competed on their ability to deliver economic growth and improve living standards rather than on alternative comprehensive and almost mutually exclusive ideologies. The commentators did not claim that there was an end to differences (which would mean the end of politics) but that the divisions were less intense.

The analysis seemed to fit much of the political debate in the United States and Western Europe at the time. But in the 1970s the slowdown of economic growth and the revival of neoliberal and radical left ideas heralded an upsurge in ideology. In Britain and the United States, the elections of Mrs Thatcher and President Reagan installed the two most right wing leaders for over a generation. Both introduced a sharper ideological edge to domestic politics and foreign affairs.

By the end of the 1980s, with the decline and then collapse of the Soviet Union, the victory of the West in the Cold War, and the right's dominance of the political agenda in Britain, it seemed that ideological division had declined again. Francis Fukuyama (1992) proclaimed an end to history on the grounds that capitalism had clearly triumphed over state planning of the economy and liberal democracy had triumphed over the one-party model. The end of history is a thesis about the end of the clash of rival ideologies and the triumph of political liberalism and free market economics (see Chapter 1).

But if the parties have become more pragmatic ideology flourishes elsewhere. The green or ecology movement campaigns against the costs of the pursuit of economic growth and materialism which dominate modern politics. Politics, it argues, should attend more to dangers of climate change, pollution and the depletion of natural resources, and promote sustainability and the value of sufficiency in material goods. Some of these ideas are partly accepted by the parties but are not endorsed by powerful interest groups which fear a loss of jobs or of profits. In some West European states, particularly Germany, the Green Party has attracted significant electoral support and the movement is well represented, thanks to proportional representation, in the European Parliament. In Britain, however, it has so far failed to gain more than 1% of the vote at any general election.

Feminists have long complained about the patriarchal bias or male domination of the British state and of the political system in particular. It is more than a lobby for women's rights. Having relatively recently achieved legal and political rights, they have increasingly criticised the male domination of key positions in public life, the professions and commerce, and how this bias is reflected in public policies and in females earning less than their male counterparts in equivalent positions. Some of this agenda has been taken on board by the parties, particularly Labour, both in all-women shortlists for selecting candidates for safe Labour seats and in policies, for example, child-care.

 ## Ideas and consequences

But do political ideas matter? The economist, J.M. Keynes (see Politics in Focus 4.4) clearly thought so and although Karl Marx dismissed them as subordinate to economic structures his own writings are a powerful refutation of his claim. Bulpitt (1986) in his analysis of Thatcherism argues that new right ideas were of secondary importance in understanding

IN FOCUS 4.4

actice

The ideas of economists and philosophers, both when they are right and when they are wrong, are more powerful than is commonly understood. Indeed, the world is ruled by little else. Practical men, who believe themselves to be quite exempt from any intellectual influence, are usually the slaves of some defunct economist. Madmen in authority, who hear voices in the air, are distilling their frenzy from some academic scribbler of a few years back.

J.M. Keynes (1936)

the Conservative Party's policies in the 1980s. What was decisive was what he calls 'party statecraft', to do with winning elections and being able to govern effectively, particularly in matters of 'high politics'. In running the economy free of the pressures from the trade unions, for example, monetarism was as crucial in giving ministers a degree of autonomy as in winning the battle against inflation. For ideas to have an impact they have to interact with other favourable conditions. These include the willingness of leading actors, for example, party leaders or senior civil servants and advisers, to be attracted by the ideas and push them, and circumstances, or dissatisfaction with the status quo and the sense that the existing set of policies are not working, that alternatives should be tried. One can point to the rise and fall of Keynesianism, or of comprehensive schooling, or of economic planning as examples. At a more personal level, politicians and parties need ideas to inspire active followers and are aware that political commentators look for 'coherence' or overarching themes in their policies. Most politicians like to be thought to 'stand for something' and, to use current buzzwords, to have core values.

Conclusion

Since the success of the Conservative Party in the 1980s in shifting the political agenda, clashes of ideology between the parties have waned, in line with the end of ideology thesis. Labour moved to the new middle ground on the economy and the role of the state largely defined by the Conservative's four successive general election victories between 1979 and 1992; since then the Conservatives have largely accepted Labour's constitutional changes and increased funding of key public services following that party's three successive general election victories between 1997 and 2005. There has been a convergence on many policies although it is still possible to place the Conservative and Labour Parties at different ends of a continuum on issues of equality-inequality, individualism-collectivism and level of taxation.

Indeed, in the 2001 and 2005 general elections many voters (and commentators) complained that there were only marginal differences between the main parties. The so-called 'big' issues like public ownership, powers of the trade unions, membership of the European Union, and nuclear weapons seem to have been settled. The rhetoric of party leaders is now about opportunity, value for money, greater consumer choice in public services, value for money, safe borders and helping 'hard-working families'. The parties' increasing reliance on political marketing at election time and concentration on appealing to target voters, who are not strongly attached to any political party, has probably encouraged the convergence.

KEY POINTS

- Ideologies are mental maps about such features as the purpose of politics, the nature of society, the nature of human beings, the role of the state, and relations between government and society.

- Claims that the first two decades of post-war politics were a time of relative consensus are contested.

- Conservatives are attached to the political status quo but, as with the new right, can offer radical reforms if it is unacceptable.

- Liberalism moved from a classic phase of limited government and individualism to accepting a more positive role for the state.

- The socialist strand in the Labour Party has declined due to a mix of calculations about electoral success and how to adapt to changes in the international economy and social and economic changes in modern Britain.

- There is now an end of political ideology between the left and right as the terms have been traditionally understood.

KEY QUESTIONS

(1) Does a political party need an ideology?

(2) What has been the lasting impact of Thatcherism on Conservatism?

(3) Why did the third way appeal to many Labour figures in the late 1990s?

(4) 'Liberalism has been more triumphant as a set of ideas than in helping a party to win votes'. Discuss.

IMPORTANT WEBSITES

For information on the ideas of the main UK political parties, see www.keele.ac.uk/depts/por/ptbase.htm; www.ukconservativesm.freeuk.com; www.labour.org.uk; www.consevative-party.org.uk; www.libdems.org.uk.

FURTHER READING

Good accounts of political ideologies and ideas are found in A. Birch (1964) *Representative and Responsible Government*, London: Allen & Unwin; W. Greenleaf (1983, 1987) *The British Political Tradition*, 3 vols, London: Methuen; R. Leach (2002) *British Political Ideologies*, Oxford: Philip Allan; K. Harrison and T. Boyd (2003) *Political Ideas and Movements*, Manchester: Manchester University Press; and A. Heywood (2003) *Key Concepts in Politics*, Basingstoke: Palgrave. On Conservative ideas see P. Norton and A. Aughey (1981) *Conservatives and Conservatism*, London: Temple Smith; N. O'Sullivan (1975) *Modern Ideologies: Conservatism*, London: Dent; and on the new right see N. Barry (1987) *The New Right*, London: Croom Helm. On liberalism a good guide is J. Gray (1995) *Liberalism*, Milton Keynes: Open University Press.

On an end of ideology see F. Fukuyama (1992) *The End of History and the Last Man Standing*, London: Hamish Hamilton. On socialism see T. Wright (1987) *Socialism: Theories and Practices*, Oxford: Oxford University Press is authoritative and succinct, but also see T. Fitzpatrick (2004) *After the New Social Democracy*, Manchester: Manchester University Press; on the left see R. Miliband (1972) *Parliamentary Socialism*, London: Merlin and on the third way see A. Giddens (1998) *The Third Way*, Oxford: Polity and (2000) *The Third Way and Its Critics*, Oxford: Polity; S. White (ed) (2001) *New Labour: The Progressive Future*, Basingstoke: Palgrave; D. Marquand (2004) *Decline of the Public*, Oxford: Polity; and R. Plant (2001) 'Blair and Ideology' in A. Seldon (ed), The *Blair Impact*, London: Little Brown, Chapter 25.

Visit the Online Resource Centre that accompanies this book for links to more information on this chapter topic

CHAPTER FIVE

The structure and evolution of British society

READER'S GUIDE

Britain has traditionally been characterised as a class divided society. However, some commentators have suggested that class is no longer important in British society or politics. This chapter looks at the social changes that have occurred in Britain over the past 30 years. It examines how inequalities continue to be important in understanding British politics. In particular it evaluates how class, ethnicity and gender continue to shape our understandings of politics.

Introduction

It is hard to understand British politics without some understanding of the structure of British society. The way society is organised and the divisions within it reflect past political decisions and are the source of many political pressures and conflicts. Many commentators argue that the social structure of Britain has changed rapidly in the last 25 years. The size of the manual working class has declined, class is less important in politics, most women now go out to work and Britain, it is said, has become a multicultural society. Yet for Marsh (2002), when analysing the nature of British society, it continues to be the happy hour for men with money, knowledge and power. What he means by this is that those with resources seem to be the ones who are continually blessed with even greater opportunities and wealth. This chapter will examine the nature of the British social structure and examine the cleavages in terms of class, ethnicity and gender. What accounts for inequality, how great is inequality and what are its implications for politics?

Much of the existing evidence supports the claim above by Marsh. In British society, white, middle class men are the ones who do best in terms of education, health care and life chances. There are three possible explanations for their success. First, they could be lucky. However, luck is a weak explanation for such a systematic and constant level of success. What could explain white, middle class men having more luck than anyone else. Second, they could be more able than others. They may be more intelligent, have more drive or be more competitive (see Politics in Focus 5.1). But it seems strange that all the attributes of intelligence, drive or competition reside in white, middle class men but it could be true that our notion of what is drive or intelligence is one defined by middle class men. Third, the way society is organised—the social structure—may privilege certain groups. In other words, society is organised in such a way that middle class men are more likely to succeed. The second explanation is based on the idea of agency and explanations of inequality are phrased in terms of choices and actions. From this perspective, women and ethnic minorities will start to reduce levels of inequality once they have equal education opportunities and then choose to compete with men. The third explanation is a structural explanation. In other words, inequality is a result of the ways in which institutions are organised. They can protect or promote certain interests or groups. Consequently, the end of inequality will depend on significant organisational change. The next section will examine the differing inequalities and examine the degree to which they are based on agency or on structure (see Chapter 2).

The end of class? Class, occupation and income

In 1940 the English writer and socialist, George Orwell, wrote: 'England is the most class-ridden country under the sun. It is a land of snobbery and privilege, ruled largely by the old and the silly' (1970: 87). However, by the 1950s politicians were talking about Britain being a classless society and in 1959, after Labour lost three elections in a row, the question

IN FOCUS 5.1
...equality

In her book, *Hard Work*, Polly Toynbee (2003: 207) asks a chief executive of a care home company, earning at least £250,000 a year, how he justified the low wages he paid to his care staff. His answer provides a perfect example of an agency based explanation of inequality:

> I believe this is a free country. I believe that in this modern age that everyone has their opportunity. Everyone who really wants to reach their goal is free to do it. If making money is your thing, you can go for it and make it. If its education you want, you can get education.

However, Toynbee (2003: 204) sees the situation very differently:

> At the heart of the low-pay problem lies the continuation of the low valuation of what are regarded as women's skills—caring, cleaning, cooking, teaching and nursing. Things your mother did for you she did freely out of love, and there is an unspoken expectation that all women at work should be society's mothers, virtually for free. The low value put on their labour springs from a deeply ingrained belief that they do these jobs because they love them.

was raised of whether Labour could ever win again because of the decline in the size of the working class. By the 1980s, Robertson was arguing that class was no longer important in British politics (Heath et al 1991). Likewise, the sociologist Peter Saunders (1996) argues that Britain is an open society where it is possible for people from working class backgrounds to move up into middle class occupations relatively easily. Failures in mobility are the consequence of ability rather than class structures. The British Election Survey concluded that class was no longer a significant determinant of the vote (Sanders et al 2004). It is clear that by 2001 the majority of people worked in white collar or what some people would see as middle class occupations.

As Table 5.1 demonstrates, in modern Britain just over 50% of the population are now in non-manual occupations compared with only 25% in the 1950s and only 20% in the early 20th century. Even the last 20 years has seen in a rise in the professional class from 22% to 32% and a decline in the working class from 34% to 29% (Park and Surridge 2003: 148). Mines have been replaced by call centres and steel factories have turned into leisure facilities. Sheffield, the steel city of Britain's industrial dominance, now produces as much steel as at its height of production but with a fraction of the workforce. The key employers in Sheffield are universities, hospitals and government offices. People have shifted from manual to non-manual occupations. With these changes in occupations it seems that some of the other markers of class have declined. The significant differences in dress, accent and education that existed between the middle class and the working class in the 1950s and 1960s seemed to have disappeared. By watching a film from the 1950s or listening to a BBC presenter even up to the 1960s and 1970s, it is apparent how class distinctions in accents have softened. Even things like travel have changed dramatically. In the 1960s and 1970s foreign and air travel was unavailable to the majority of people. Now nearly everyone has been on a plane.

Class	Number
AB Higher and intermediate, Professional	8,934,482
C1 Supervisory, clerical, junior managerial, administrative, professional	12,065,333
C2 Skilled manual	6,149,928
D Unskilled	6,976,630
E On state benefit	6,540,000

Source: British Social Attitudes (2005, London: Sage)

Does this mean that class has disappeared? Before writing off class as a significant factor in politics, it is worth considering a number of factors:

(1) The shift from manual to non-manual work does not mean that the working class has become middle class. Whilst people may now be working in call centres rather than mines, it does not mean that they have changed class. The work in call centres is highly routinised, the workplace highly structured with limited autonomy for workers, and pay rates and promotion opportunities are low. The non-manual category hides class distinctions based on occupation, autonomy at work, work conditions, pay and life chances.

(2) Whilst some of the markers of class may have lessened, others are crucially important. For instance, health and life expectancy are very closely related to class in Britain. Those on lower incomes are more like to be overweight, unhealthy and to die earlier (see Politics in Focus 5.2). Indeed the inequalities between the poor and rich have become greater in terms of health. As the Acheson report (1998: Part 2) on health inequalities said: 'Since 1980, although health and expectations of life have generally improved, the social gradients of many indicators of health have deteriorated or at best remained unchanged' (see Figure 5.1). In other words people are living longer but the difference between the life expectancy of the poorest and the richest has become greater. This reflects the general change in the nature of economic inequality. Between 1979 and 1995 incomes increased by 40% but for the richest 10% of the population they increased by 60–68% and for the poorest 10% they increased by only 10% (Acheson 1998: Part 2). If we look carefully in Britain, there are still important class markers in terms of what people eat, the cars they drive and where they go for their holiday (see Politics in Focus 5.3). In many ways the distinctions that exist in Britain between the lifestyles of different groups of people are much greater than in other European countries. Try spotting the difference between a middle class and working class Belgian for instance or see how different

Glasgow is a city where economic growth has led to much greater prosperity. However, this prosperity is not evenly distributed. Whilst some parts of Glasgow are becoming much wealthier others are becoming poorer. Life expectancy in the working class district of Shettelston is 63 which is 14 years less than the average and nearly 20 years less than in the wealthiest and healthiest parts of Britain. In the poorest parts of Glasgow life expectancy is becoming lower. 75% of Glasgow's unemployed are on sickness benefit and one family in 10 could not find £20 in an emergency.

Source: The *Guardian* (10 March 2004)

FIGURE 5.1
The income distribution in 2002/03

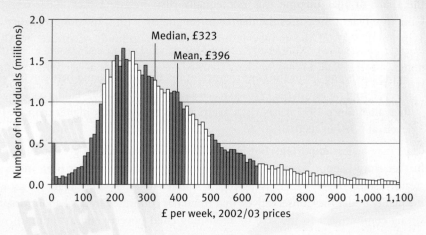

Source: M. Brewer et al *Poverty and Inequality in Britain 2004*, IFS, Commentary 96

the diet is of a middle class and working class Spaniard. As Jonathan Meades has said:

If you take a labourer in Marseilles and a Chief Executive, they will eat approximately the same food. In this country (the UK) there is no link between what a guy who is working in a building site in Southampton eats and the guy who runs that site—they eat completely different things (*The Guardian*, 12 March 2004).

5.3

Even shopping in supermarkets is highly structured by class in Britain. 'Verdict research has found that Waitrose has the highest proportion from the professional social classes A and B (47%) followed by Sainsbury's (34%), Marks & Spencer (22%) and Safeway (17%). At the bottom of the market, 72% of Nettos' shoppers are blue-collar Ds and Es, with Kwik Save (66%), Lidl (54%) and Somerfield (50%) close behind'. Even within chains the goods on sale in particular shops reflect the class composition of their clientele.

Source: The *Guardian* (12 March 2004)

(3) Whilst the size of the working class appears to have declined in Britain (certainly on some definitions) levels of inequality seem to have become greater. For instance between 1997 and 2001 Britain increased its wealth in real terms by 13%. However the share of that income was not equally distributed (Usher 2003: 63). The Gini co-efficient measures the degree of inequality with 0 meaning equality and 1 meaning that all the money is only in one household. According to Usher (2003: 63):

> In the 1960s and 1970s the Gini coefficient fluctuated in a band between 0.25 and 0.275. It rose rapidly in the 1970s to reach a peak of 0.37 in 1992, falling back slightly thereafter. Since 1997 it has risen again and is now slightly higher than its 1992 levels, at 0.384 in 2000–01.

Class may be less important, but income inequality has become greater and grown further since Labour were elected in 1997, and this inequality has been increasing steadily since the 1970s. It is politically interesting that after years of growing inequality under the Conservatives, that trend has continued under Labour despite a strong commitment to the goal of abolishing child poverty and a commitment to social justice.

(4) The rise of the underclass. There has been a long debate in British politics about whether Britain now has an underclass; a group of people locked into a cycle of deprivation who lack the means, ability or will to escape from deprivation. The consequence is a distinct cluster of people with low educational achievements who face long-term unemployment and poverty. The consequence in these areas is high levels of crime, high rates of teenage pregnancy and family breakdown. The economic restructuring of the 1980s, combined with neglect from the state, led to certain communities losing large numbers of jobs. These communities were not favoured by new social and economic development and consequently unemployment was passed through generations leading to deprivation in all aspects of life. From the perspective of those who support the notion of the underclass, younger

people learn from their parents that education and work are of little value and so the cycles of deprivation are socialised through daily life. Consequently, government has to encourage people to break with their dependence on the welfare state and crime. With policies such as Sure Start, Welfare to Work and initiatives on teenage pregnancies, the Labour Government is attempting to engender new forms of behaviour which encourage individuals to change their dependent behaviour. The concept of the underclass is a moral and agency based notion of deprivation. It sees people as responsible for their own poverty. Rather than moving for jobs, they depend on benefits or resort to crime. This perspective also sees family breakdown as a result of poor education and a lack of moral fibre rather than the social pressures under which they live.

What does class mean?

The crucial question is whether class makes a difference. Does it affect how we understand the world or how power and wealth is distributed? The simple answer is that class structures the life of everyone in Britain. Where we live, where we shop, how well we do in education and the jobs that we get can all be related to class. Indeed, it has a significant impact on when we are likely to die. Britain is a less rigid society than it was in the days when Orwell wrote, but class does still matter. Marshall et al (1997) demonstrate that even though differences in social mobility have declined, the chance of a working class person getting a top professional job compared to someone from a professional background are much less; even when they have the same level of education. In other words, 'a person's class of origin substantially influences his or her class of destination' (Marshall et al 1997: 134). More importantly, there has been little change in the extent of social mobility over the last 20 years. For example, whilst there has been a significant expansion of higher education in recent years, it appears that the extra places are not going to the working class but to middle class women.

The other sense in which class is important is in the way it shapes politics. In Chapter 20 we look at the relationship between class and voting but there is also the question of how government is shaped by class. We can see the way that class structures life chances but how does it structure politics? For Marxists, the capitalist state inherently favours the business class and in general disfavours the working class. For instance, one example would be the way in which the Labour Government has proclaimed a belief in social justice but has significantly reduced corporate taxation. At the same time, inequality has increased while they have been in office. Government rhetoric focuses on the need to develop a healthy, enterprise economy in order to achieve social justice, and to compete in an increasingly global market. This leads to policies that favour business—such as reducing taxation and regulation.

The other influential element of class is that those who work in the higher levels of the state are likely to come from middle class backgounds. Ralph Miliband's (1984) analysis demonstrated how all the key political, economic and military elites in Britain were from similar backgrounds and went to similar public schools and the universities of Oxford and Cambridge. Whilst there has been a significant change in the aristocratic nature of the

British state, there is little doubt that the key political and Civil Service positions in Britain are undoubtedly held by members of the middle class (see Tables 5.2 to 5.5).

There has been a shift in the class nature of the British state. Traditionally within the Conservative Party in particular, there was a significant aristocratic presence with a large proportion of the rest of the Cabinet being dominated by the upper middle class. Likewise, the senior Civil Service came largely from public schools and Oxbridge. However, the Conservative Party has become much more a middle class party and indeed the last three Conservative Party Prime Ministers have come from lower middle class or working class backgrounds. Likewise the Civil Service whilst still predominantly middle class, is not so completely dominated by Oxbridge and public schools. It is with the election of Labour in 1997 that we see an important change in the make up of the governing class. Labour Cabinet members (and Labour MPs) are more middle class than their predecessors but the range of educational backgrounds is much wider. What is apparent is that whilst much debate in the popular media has been about the decline of class, the British state has become more middle class. The Conservative Party is less aristocratic and the Labour Party is less working class. As Table 5.5 demonstrates it is increasingly the case that MPs are middle class and university educated, yet they are less likely to come from the traditional breeding grounds of the governing class, public schools and Oxbridge (see Kavanagh and Richards 2000). However, it is important to point out that public schools and Oxbridge universities still produce a disproportionate number of MPs, ministers and civil servants. At the same time senior officials are coming from a slightly wider range of backgrounds.

The class structure of Britain has changed but class still matters in terms of life chances, occupations, health and political behaviour. Moreover, whilst class is perhaps less significant in terms of people's perceptions and politics, inequality between the rich and poor is greater now than in the 1960s and 1970s. Whilst class may be less of a cleavage than 30 years ago, one form of division that is becoming of increasing importance is ethnicity.

Date	No	Etonian (%)	Public school (%)	Oxbridge (%)	All universities (%)	Women (%)
1923	258	25	79	40	50	1
1974	277	17	75	56	69	3
1997	165	9	66	50	81	8

Source: Kavanagh and Richards (2002)

…servative MPs, 1916–97 (%)

| | 1916–55 | | 1955–84 | | 1985–92 | | 1997– |
	Cons	Labour	Cons	Labour	Cons	Labour	Labour
All public school	76.5	26.1	87.1	32.1	85	61.9	30
Eton or Harrow	45.9	7.6	36.6	3.5	2.4	14.3	–
Elementary or secondary	4.0	50.7	36.6	3.5	2.4	14.3	–
Oxbridge	63.2	27.6	72.8	42.8	7.4	61.9	14
All universities	71.4	44.6	81.6	62.5	92.5	95.3	90.5
Aristocratic	31.6	6.1	18.1	1.8	11	28.6	–
Middle class	65.3	38.4	74.0	44.6	81	43	67
Working class	3.0	55.3	2.6	41	7.0	9.5	33
Women	–	–	3	2	11	4.7	24
Non-whites	–	–	–	–	–	–	–

Source: Kavanagh and Richards (2002)

…tish Cabinets, 1970–97 (%)

| | Class | | | Education | | | |
	Aristocratic	Middle	Working	Public school	Eton	University	Oxbridge
Heath 1970–74	22	78	0	83	22	83	83
Wilson/Callaghan 1974–79	1	67	26	33	0	77	49
Thatcher 1979–90	14	86	0	91	27	82	77
Major 1990–97	14	77	9	64	9	91	77
Blair 1997–	0	68	32	36	0	95	14

Source: Marsh (2002)

	1974–79	1979–97
All public schools	84	73.5
Eton/Harrow	11	3
Secondary school	11	7.5
Oxford or Cambridge	75	63
All universities	88	93
Middle class	95	94
Working class	5	6
Women	2	3
Non-whites	0	0

Source: Marsh (2002)

Ethnicity, race and racism in the British state

Until the 1950s Britain was perceived as an almost completely white society. Whilst there had long been a non-white community in Britain, the number as a percentage of the population was low. There were, nevertheless, significant non-white communities in port cities such as Bristol, Liverpool, Glasgow and London, but the majority of British people rarely saw a non-white face. It was only in the 1950s with the first wave of Commonwealth immigration (see Chapter 29) that the issue of race became important or that race developed as a significant social cleavage. Since then, there have been significant developments concerning the role of race in politics, the impact of discrimination and the nature of a multicultural society. The initial reaction to immigrants and non-whites was mixed. In some ways the reaction was benign, but it was always one where overt racism was accepted and the incomers were seen as different and not part of the British society. Well into the 1970s it was possible to have openly racist programmes such as *Love thy Neighbour* and the *Black and White Minstrel Show* on mainstream television. Initially the political position of blacks and Asians was weak. They were dependent on Britain for jobs and lacked the community or organisational links to develop any political response to their situation. However race riots in 1958 and growing levels of immigration combined with economic problems in the 1960s meant that the issue of race became increasingly controversial.

The issues concerning migration and immigration policy are discussed in Chapter 29. The focus of this chapter is how race structures British society. It is undoubtedly the case that Britain has become a more racially mixed society than at any time in its history. According to the British Social Attitudes Survey, 'Britain's minority ethnic population grew by 53 per cent from 3 million in 1991 to 4.6 million in 2001 and now represents 7.9 per cent of the UK population' (Rothon and Heath 2003: 190) (see Table 5.6). This population is concentrated in certain parts of the country. So, for example, in the London borough of Brent 45% of the population are non-white (CRE 1999), raising the question of whether the term 'ethnic minority' is still applicable.

But how does race shape lives and experiences? According to the British Social Attitudes Survey, the number of people who think of themselves as racist declined between 1983 and 2002 from 35% to 31% (Rothon and Heath 2003). Whilst only a minority of people think of themselves as racist, evidence of discrimination in Britain seems high. Ethnic minorities do worse in terms of education, income, occupations and housing. For instance, African-Caribbean children who start school at five at the average ability level have, by the age of 10, fallen behind the average. By 16 the number of Afro-Caribbeans achieving five grades A-C in GCSEs is less than half the national average. Pakistanis and Bangladeshis also perform worse than the national average, but Indian children slightly better (Parekh 2000). In terms of employment, Afro-Caribbeans and Bangladeshis are half as likely to have professional jobs as whites and whilst the employment rate for whites is 75%, for blacks and Asians it is only 57%. It seems that there is overt discrimination in terms of employment with blacks earning less than whites and

Ethnic origin	Total population	%	Ethnic minority %
White	54143898	92.1	
Mixed	677177	1.2	14.6
Indian	1053411	1.8	22.7
Pakistani	747285	1.3	16.1
Bangladeshi	283063	0.5	6.1
Other Asian	247664	0.4	5.3
Black Caribbean	565876	1.0	12.2
Black African	485277	0.8	10.5
Black other	97585	0.2	2.1
Chinese	247403	0.4	5.0
Other	230615	0.4	5.0
Total ethnic population	4635296	7.9	100

Source: Rothon and Heath (2003)

black and Asian school leavers having much less success gaining employment than whites (Parek 2000). On average ethnic minority workers earn £18,044 compared to £19,552 for whites but the average salary among Bangladeshis is £12,220 a year (*The Observer*, 21 November 2004).

In politics, the exclusion of ethnic minorities is even more apparent. It was only in 1987 that four ethnic minority candidates were elected to Parliament and by 1997 nine were elected (1.4% of the House of Commons). In the Labour Cabinet in 2005 there was only one black member of the Cabinet (Baroness Amos). Only 3% of councillors come from ethnic groups (see Table 5.7).

Legislation

Since the 1970s British government has attempted to legislate against racial discrimination in Britain. In 1976 the government introduced the Race Relations Act which was concerned with outlawing direct discrimination in employment and housing. This was followed by conscious attempts in education and welfare to make practitioners aware of issues of race and not to discriminate between different ethnic groups. In 2003, a new race relations law was introduced with the intention of strengthening equal treatment. Interestingly, this new legislation was a direct result of two new EU race directives which set minimum standards of protection for all people irrespective of race. The new legislation goes much further than the existing law because it outlaws indirect discrimination and racial harassment. It also abolishes a number of exceptions that existed in the original Act relating to small dwellings, employment in private households, charities and partnerships of less than six.

Ethnic group	Male		Female	
	Number	Percentage of group	Number	Percentage
White	15020	72	5741	28
Black Caribbean	66	68	31	32
Black African	13	76	4	24
Indian	149	94	10	6
Bangladeshi	30	94	2	6
Chinese	1	0	0	0
Mixed	54	67	27	33
Other	98	72	39	28

Source: Commission for Racial Equality

Institutional racism

Discrimination is clearly outlawed in Britain and overt racism in most public settings is taboo. For instance, in 2004, when a Conservative MP, Ann Winterton, made a joke about Chinese workers who had been drowned in Morecambe Bay, the Conservative Party whip was withdrawn. In the same year, when Ron Atkinson made a racist statement about a football player he lost his job as a television commentator and a columnist for *The Guardian*. Despite legislation, Britain appears to be rife with racism. In some cases this is overt with a large number of racial attacks. For the year 1999 to 2000 there were over 21,000 racially motivated attacks reported. Between 1994 and 1998 there were 13 racially motivated murders. Between 1998 and 2003 this figure increased to 35. However, probably more prevalent is the hidden discrimination of daily life in terms of the way ethnic minorities are treated in terms of jobs, housing and education and income as we saw above.

The explanations for continued discrimination can be related back to arguments concerning structure and agency set out in Chapter 2. An argument based on agency would see discrimination as partly a consequence of individual bad behaviour. There are people in the world who are racist and who may undertake racial attacks or discriminate on the ground of race in employment or housing. An agency-centred argument would suggest that legislation is a way to combat racism and the fact that it has not worked is a consequence of time. As ethnic minorities become increasingly integrated into British society, the degree of discrimination will decline and the unequal position of ethnic minorities will decline. We now have an Asian permanent secretary in Whitehall and an Afro-Caribbean member of the Cabinet. Over time their presence will grow.

The structural argument is based on the notion of institutional racism as identified by the Macpherson report into the murder of the black teenager Stephen Lawrence:

> Institutional racism consists of the collective failure of an organisation to provide an appropriate and professional service to people because of their colour, culture or ethnic origin. It can be seen or detected in processes, attitudes and behaviours which amount to discrimination through unwitting prejudice, ignorance, thoughtlessness, and racist stereotyping which disadvantage minority ethnic people (Macpherson 1999: para 6.34).

From this perspective racism is not about individual acts of discrimination, but how ethnic minorities are thought about in our society and how we all react to ethnic minorities. The conclusion of the Lawrence inquiry was not that the police were openly racist but that they acted in certain ways, and saw the death of Stephen Lawrence in a particular way, because he was black. The death of a white teenager would have been treated in a very different way. It is difficult to overcome institutional racism. To challenge it depends on people recognising biases that they may be unaware of, and changing amorphous things such as practice and culture (see Politics in Focus 5.4).

POLITICS IN FOCUS 5.4

Institutional racism: why does the black boy always play one of the three kings?

In predominantly white infant schools with black children, it is almost inevitably the case that a black boy will play one of the three kings in the Nativity play. In one sense this is not racist and may even be the result of teachers thinking they are not racist. The three kings come from the Orient and represent the nations of the world. It is not unreasonable that one of them is black and indeed it results in a black child having a key role in the play. However, that child is seen as being black and it is an easy decision. Why it is not the case that the black child is given the role of Joseph? In a way all of us have 'prejudices' in the sense of how we think of people and how they fit into the world. *Coronation Street* introduces an Asian character to reflect the more multicultural nature of our industrial cities but he runs the corner shop thus conforming to the traditional white assumptions.

This represents the way we all carry certain mental pictures and this influences our expectations of roles. There is now a lot of evidence concerning the way in which educational expectations affect performance. It is expected that Afro-Caribbean boys will perform badly at school and Asian girls well and of course, this expectation is then met in practice. Institutional racism is how we inculcate particular mental images that then affect our reactions to certain people.

Multiculturalism and citizenship

The changing ethnic basis of British politics has had an important impact on political debate, not just in terms of migration policy which is discussed in Chapter 29 but in terms of issues of citizenship, discrimination and multiculturalism. The key issue is, once people come into Britain, or indeed, are second or third generation children, on what terms are they deemed to be citizens of Britain? There are in effect three main positions around which these issues are debated. The liberal position sees everyone as equal in the eyes of the law and therefore skin colour is irrelevant and laws should be applied to everyone equally. On that basis there should be no discrimination. However, this can work two ways. People should not be disadvantaged in terms of jobs but likewise exceptions should not be made because of particular customs or practices. The law on crash helmets should be applied equally to Sikhs (who have to wear turbans) and non-Sikhs. In France, the Government has outlawed the wearing of headdresses by Muslims on the grounds that schools are secular and there should be no religious identifiers worn by students. This is not a racist position, but a liberal one. The law applies to everyone equally. Likewise the liberal position would not favour separate schools for different ethnic or religious groups.

The conservative position is that if people want to come to Britain they must actively integrate and accept local customs and practices. This is in a sense what is called the 'Cricket Team Test' after Lord Tebbit, the former Conservative Cabinet Minister, who argued that what mattered for second generation Pakistanis was which cricket team they supported; England or Pakistan. This is a flippant illustration of a particular notion which sees integration as about making immigrants English. In a similar view, the Labour

Government has introduced a citizenship test and a ceremony as a way of ensuring that immigrants are aware of the fundamentals of British life (see Chapter 29). Racial conflict will disappear if racial groups are integrated into British society.

The third position is the multiculturalist argument which believes we can ensure a harmonious society by allowing immigrants to integrate on their own terms by maintaining their cultures. The argument of multiculturalists is that immigration has changed British culture in positive ways, and society has become more diverse and pluralistic. Therefore, integration in the conservative sense of immigrants becoming 'English' is both impossible and negative. What we need to do is to develop a pluralistic society that learns to value the different ways of life of various groups. In this way, people can live together without imposing a single culture. For conservatives, however, by bringing in different cultures the core of Britishness has disappeared and this is leading to social disharmony. The practice of race relations policy by the Labour Government has been a combination of all three positions. Laws are applied to all equally, however at the same time the Government has actively encouraged multiculturalism in education and the police, for instance, whilst also introducing the new citizenship tests.

Gender and inequality

In the period since the end of the Second World War the position of women in Britain has changed dramatically. From 1945 to 1970 relatively few women worked. Often they were excluded from the vast array of both manual and professional occupations. What has happened since the 1970s is that women have taken on a much larger role in the labour market. In recent times, women have benefited from the development of a more flexible labour market which is based around part-time, and outside core time, work in the service sector. About 70% of women work (45% work part-time). The British workforce is now almost 50% male and female and in the over-50 age group women are

	Head count	Gender		Ethnic minority		Disability	
	All staff	Total women	% women	Total ethnic minority	% ethnic minority	Total disabled	% disabled
April 95	4,200	480	11.4	60	1.4	40	1.0
April 99	3,600	620	17.2	55	1.7	58	1.6
April 00	3,730	730	19.5	70	2.1	60	1.7

in the majority. However, this change in the position of women in work does not mean that inequality has disappeared. It is still the case that women earn on average only 73.7% of the average male wage, which is lower than other European countries like France, Germany, Spain and Sweden. Moreover, when women do enter the labour force they tend to do particular jobs such as clerical positions, nursing and teaching, and they tend to be relatively absent from senior positions. For example, whilst the vast majority of primary school teachers are women, the majority of head teachers are men. As Table 5.8 demonstrates, women only make up 11.4% of senior civil servants and very few permanent secretaries are women. As Figure 5.8 illustrates there may be more women in the labour market but gender segregation continues and this leads to continued inequality.

Gender and politics

Despite the fact that women make up more than half the population, they have been seriously underrepresented in politics at all level. However, the number of women MPs has

FIGURE 5.2

Occupational segregation, causes and consequences

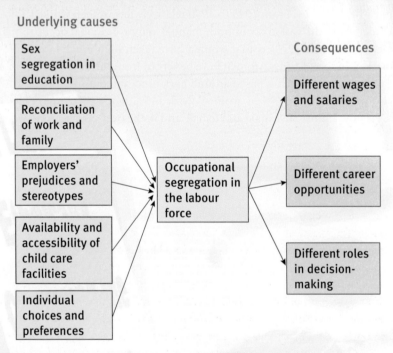

Source: Background Paper for 25th CEIES Seminar 'Gender Statistics', Stockholm, 21–22 June 2004

increased from 1 in 1918 to 128 following the 2005 election. Indeed, as Norris points out, the 1997 election marked a sea change in women's representation with the number of female MPs increasing from 19 in 1979 to a peak of 120 in 1997. In addition there is a high level of female representation in the new Scottish and Welsh Parliaments with 37% of Members of the Scottish Parliament being women and 40% of the Welsh assembly. Norris (2002) identifies a number of factors that account for the apparent sudden rise of women in Parliament and other political arenas:

- The growth of identity politics and a sense that women should have representation in politics
- Pressure for reform by women's groups such as the Fawcett Society
- Crucially, the decision by the Labour Party to adopt quotas for the selection of women and the development of all-women shortlists. Ironically, these were ruled illegal under sex discrimination legislation, but not until after Labour had got a considerable number of women in post
- The conscious attempt by the Labour leadership to attract more women voters
- The decision of constituency Labour Parties to adopt women for winnable seats.

However, in many ways the crucial issue is whether the selection and election of more women actually makes any difference. The first Blair Cabinet contained five women and so seemed to indicate that women were being placed in significant positions in politics. However, by 2005, the number remained at five and it continues to be the case that apart from Margaret Thatcher as Prime Minister, no women has held one of the senior Cabinet jobs of Home Secretary, Foreign Secretary or Chancellor of the Exchequer. There have also been some changes in the organisation of the hours of the Commons, with sittings ending at 7 pm in principle making being a MP more compatible with family. Yet at the same time, the new intake of female Labour MPs elected in 1997 were described in a derogatory and sexist way as 'Blair's Babes' and this has been followed-up with continual accusations in the press that they are less likely to rebel against the leader. There is evidence from Childs and Withey (2004) that women vote differently from men on Early Day Motions indicating that they do behave differently politically.

Is politics patriarchal?

To return to arguments concerning structure and agency, we can see different ways of accounting for the impact of women on politics. If we take a liberal, agency-based perspective, the argument would be that changes in legislation, like the Sex Discrimination Act of 1975 have formalised women's equality. Such measures combined with social change and positive measures like Labour's women-only shortlists, ensure a gradual but inexorable rise in the role of women in politics. If we believe that women act differently and are prepared to use their positions to change politics and policy, this will affect both the role of women in politics and in society. We have after all seen considerable changes in the position of women in the last 30 years. Over 50% of university graduates are now women, and women are now in many of the top professions. The numbers may be low but it is changing.

However, from a structuralist perspective work and politics are still structured in ways that favour men, and so whilst women are clearly developing a more important role, it is still secondary to men. For many feminists the way that politics, policy and government are constructed protects the interests of men. The state is, in other words, patriarchal. More women may be elected to Parliament but this does not mean that the patriarchal nature of the state has changed. How does this patriarchy reveal itself?

- First, in the definition of what is political. The argument of feminists is that politics is defined as the public and deals with issues in the public sphere such as economics and wages whilst issues that affect women like housework and domestic violence are seen as the private sphere and so they are not discussed. However, one important change in politics in recent years is the way in which the personal has become political. Increasingly, government is becoming involved in the regulation of family life, for instance, over issues such as physical punishment and parenting.

- Notions of citizenship and welfare have been built around the idea of a male head of household and male breadwinner. The Beveridge welfare state model was based on the notion of full *male* employment. It is argued that even recent policies such as the establishment of the Child Support Agency reinforce traditional conceptions of the family.

- Politics is defined as a masculine activity. It is often about working long hours, the ability to come across as strong and even arrogant, working in a conflictual environment and having to travel frequently. These, it is argued, are characteristics of politics which are different to women's views of how the world should operate.

- Policies reinforce traditional roles and conceptions of masculinity and femininity. It is interesting that for years women underperformed in education and this was taken as a fact with little political consequence. However, in recent years when women have consistently been doing better than men, the underperformance of men has become a political issue.

The position of women in society and politics has undoubtedly changed. Women are much more likely to work and to be in top positions than in the past. It is also the case that many more women are involved in politics and in senior political roles. Nevertheless, there continues to be an inequality between men and women in terms of roles, incomes and opportunities. For liberals this is because women choose family over careers. For structuralists this is because gender is constructed so that women rather than men will be expected to be carers. Moreover, success in a career is based on a traditional career structure that leaves little time for domestic responsibilities.

There are some that believe that women's equality has gone too far and there is a growing backlash against what is seen as the success of the women's movement with the rise of the men's movement who argue that it is now men who are discriminated against (see Extract 5.1). In 2005 Michael Burke made a television programme outlining ways in which women have come to dominate the labour market and Bob Geldolf made a programme arguing that fathers had no rights of access to their children following divorce. Geldolf's argument was that the law and the courts were systematically biased against men. It has also been pointed out that men do not have the same rights of paternity leave as women and whilst tremendous resources have been put into making

Extract 5.1: from the website of the Men's Movement

Why do we need a men's rights movement?

During the last 30 years or so we have experienced something not previously known. This is the general denigration of men, the limiting of the role of men, the reduction in employment prospects for men, state support for lone motherhood, and the elimination of many men's rights, especially within the family.

The reasons for this are not entirely clear. What we know however is that:

- there has been a massive increase in the representation of women's issues, due to the vast number of women's groups and organisations, while few exist for men;

- women have about 5.6% more votes than men, and this may not be lost on the political parties;

- the media reflect this situation in dealing with women's issues, together with denigration of men in articles and advertisements;

- feminists have obtained positions of great influence within the Government and with law makers;

- Parliament has passed measures which are unjust to men;

- corruption to the written law, especially in the matrimonial area, including serious malpractices by solicitors, barristers and court welfare officers, has resulted in the removal of all rights men once held in marriage, over children, home, life savings and future income;

- significant changes, of an anti-male nature, to laws have been introduced, often implemented through case law decisions by unaccountable judges rather than by Parliament in a democratic process;

- the democratic process has broken down, as we have not been able to obtain remedies through our MPs, etc. The majority of the population have not been involved in these changes, and in many cases are unaware that they have taken place. So the radical feminists have obtained influence beyond that which their numbers would suggest they should have, and they have been immensely successful at obtaining their unjust and unreasonable objectives.

It has been as a response to this that various men's and fathers' groups have been established. It is not only in the UK but across all of the Western World that these groups have arisen.

Source: www.ukmm.org.uk/

women aware of, and treating, breast cancer, much less attention has been paid to prostrate cancer, which is a bigger killer. Men's rights groups have been taking increasingly extreme actions such as climbing on to Buckingham Palace in order to publicise their arguments.

Do women organise differently in politics?

Much of the discussion about women and politics has been about the formal political arena. However, it may be the case that women approach politics differently and their influence is not through parties and Parliament but wider political movements. It is certainly the case that the period since the 1960s has seen the development of what is called the women's movement. This started out as part of and, reaction against, the civil rights and anti-Vietnam war movements of the late 1960s which were seen as radical but unsympathetic to the particular interests of women. Inspired by the writings of what were called the second wave feminists such as Betty Frieden and Germane Greer, the women's movement used demonstrations and consciousness raising as a way of highlighting issues like abortion, pay, rape and domestic violence onto the political agenda. This movement connected with women in the traditional trade union movement and it was important in the development of the Equal Pay and the Sex Discrimination Acts in the 1970s.

The argument of a number of radical feminists is that the traditional political sphere is inherently organised around the interests of men. Consequently, women who go into politics just become a female version of men in politics. To succeed in politics, it is argued, women have to be like men and Margaret Thatcher is the archetypical example of a woman politician who had no concern for the interests of women and replicated male behaviour. Therefore, it is argued that women should either organise separately from men or control the spaces in their own sphere like the family. Of course, whilst these positions are radical in one sense, they are deeply conservative in another because they suggest that the world cannot be changed.

Again, as with class, there is little doubt that there have been major changes in the position of women in the last 30 years and especially since the Second World War. Women are better educated, have a greater range of jobs and are more likely to have senior positions than ever before. However, it is still the case that women are underrepresented in most areas of public life and continue to earn less than men.

Globalisation, materialism and postmaterialism

In many ways, we have seen fundamental changes in the nature of the social structure in Britain in the last 30 or 40 years. As we said in the Introduction, British society was seen in 1950 as homogenous and hierarchical. It was a class bound, white society where the spheres of men and women were clearly delineated. Only exceptional women played a role in the world of decision-making either in the public or private sector. In many ways this social structure has changed fundamentally. Manual work as a percentage of work has declined massively. There has been social and geographical mobility and rapid economic change. Many parts of Britain have shifted from being white to being multicultural. Our sense of community and what possibilities and options we have in our lives has changed completely. Technology and travel have meant that a closed and bounded social community has disappeared and a sense of common values, or what it means to be British, may have gone as well.

Some people have also argued that class has become transnational as a consequence of globalisation. Maybe the key social relations in terms of wealth and power are between the rich West and the poor in the developing world who through their cheap labour enable us all to have a degree of material wealth that was unavailable even to our own parents and especially our grandparents. There is also, in the eyes of some, the development of a transnational ruling class which unlike the ruling class of the past has little attachment to that national state.

Perhaps what is crucial is the way that the role of class has changed in politics and how we think of ourselves. In 1967 Pulzer wrote, 'Class is the basis of British politics. All else is embellishment and detail'. Now whilst it is true that inequality still exists, it is not so certain that people think of their identities primarily in terms of class. In recent years politics has become about a whole range of other identities that are perceived as more important than class such as race, gender, sexuality or religion. One of the impacts of material wealth and the growth of a more diverse media is that production issues are much less important and politics is increasingly revolving around issues of identity and

	Sixties	Today
Population	52,807,000	59,432,000
Miles of rail routes	17,481	9,983
Litres of wine consumed per person annually	0.46	2.98
Numbers of hours of television available daily	24	3,000
Prison population	30,000	75,065
Number of first degrees awarded annually	25,000	250,000
Percentage of population smoking	56.5	27
Number of Britons holidaying abroad each year	3 million	39.9 million
Number of cars registered	5,776,000	24,543,000

Source: The Observer, 28 March 2004

what Inglehart calls post-material values such as the environment, peace and identity. Castells (1996) points to the rapid changes we have seen in the occupational structure. Britain like other countries is becoming post-industrial. Less people are working in manufacturing and the size of the managerial and professional classes is growing. Education is becoming an important resource that shapes the life chances of individuals and this is producing more mobility. These changes in occupational structure have had an impact on the traditional role of the family and the position of women and it cannot be doubted that the opportunities available to women are much greater than 50 or even 20 years ago.

Conclusion

Traditionally understandings of the British political system have focused on the existence and operations of institutions. If the country had free and fair elections it was suggested that people had political equality. However, it is impossible to understand the operation of the political system without understanding the social context. How can there be real political equality if there is discrimination against people on grounds of class, sex or race? It may be that everyone has the right to vote but not everyone has the same influence on political outcomes. It is also clear that some groups of people benefit more from the political system than others.

It is important to remember that politics is never a level playing field. It is about the distribution of resources and those resources are not equally distributed. It still seems that occupation, gender and race have a major impact on our life chances. Certain individuals may do well but if you are black, a women and working class you are likely to have less pay, worse housing and to live a shorter, less healthy life. As Polly Toynbee demonstrates, whilst the well-off are better off, the low paid have become worse off. Britain is shifting, as sociologists have pointed out, from a triangle shape structure to a diamond shape with most people somewhere in the middle but a significant number at the bottom on very low pay. The working class has become divided between those who are comfortable and those who are poor. Moreover, the cleavages of gender and race continue to have considerable impact on the life chances and political influences of particular groups. Class may be less important but inequality on a range of dimensions continues to persist. Moreover, as society becomes more fragmented and more diverse it could be that these divisions have a greater impact on politics and that issues of identity politics become much more important than class politics (see Chapter 22).

KEY POINTS

- Class has traditionally been a defining feature of British society. Class appears to be less important in terms of politics but inequality is greater now than it was 20 years ago.
- Other cleavages in British society seem to have become more important such as ethnicity and gender.
- There are clear indications of inequality between races with blacks and Asians significantly under-performing in terms of education and income.
- Explanations for inequality are structural and agency-based. A liberal perspective sees inequalities being overcome through legislation whilst structuralists see a much slower changing of values and ways of understanding the world.

- Women have become increasingly integrated into the workforce and are now in more senior positions. Nevertheless, women's incomes continue to be less than men's and women have a limited number of senior roles in politics.
- Some argue that the balance towards the interests of women has gone too far and there is a need for men to reclaim their rights.

KEY QUESTIONS

(1) How great is inequality in British society?

(2) What is the impact of inequality on politics?

(3) Has class become a less important cleavage in British society than race or gender?

(4) What best explains inequality—structure or agency?

(5) To what extent have social changes affected the traditional conceptions of politics?

(6) Is political equality possible without social equality?

IMPORTANT WEBSITES

The level of inequality in Britain is highlighted by the work of the Institute of Fiscal Studies, www.ifs.org.uk. The work of the Equal Opportunities Commission provides valuable information on the position of women in British society, www.eoc.org.uk. There is a lot of information of race and ethnicity at www.cre.gov.uk.

FURTHER READING

For a good sense of the continuing levels of inequality in Britain, Polly Toynbee's account of low pay in Britain, P. Toynbee (2003) *Hard Work*, London: Bloomsbury, is excellent and highly readable. A useful account of the changing social structure in Britain is given in the British Social Attitudes Survey. For a detailed examination of the impact and degree of social mobility see G. Marshall, A. Swift and S. Roberts (1997) *Against the Odds? Social Class and Social Justice in Industrial*

Societies, Oxford: Oxford University Press. For a counter argument see P. Saunders (1996) *Unequal but Fair? A Study of Class Barriers in Britain*, London: IEA. For an overview of class in British society see D. Canadine (1998) *Class in Britain*, New Haven, Conn: Yale University Press. The impact of class, gender and race on political recruitment is discussed in J. Lovenduski and P. Norris (1995) *Political Recruitment: gender, race and class in the British Parliament*, Cambridge: Cambridge University Press. A very useful review of the literature on gender and politics is provided by F. Mackay (2004) 'Gender and Political Representation in the UK: The State of the "Discipline" ', *British Journal of Politics and International Relations*, 6(1): 101–2. For a sense of the impact and nature of second wave feminism it is worth reading Germaine Greer (1999, 2nd ed), *The Female Eunuch*, London: Flamingo. For a good and comprehensive account of the role of ethnicity in British life see B. Parek (2000) *The Future of Multi-ethnic Britain: Report of the Commission on the Future of Multi-Ethnic Britain*, London: Profile Books. For an insight into the world of the early immigrants to Britain, read the novel by Andrea Levy (2004) *Notes from a Small Island*, London: Review.

Visit the Online Resource Centre that accompanies this book
for links to more information on this chapter topic

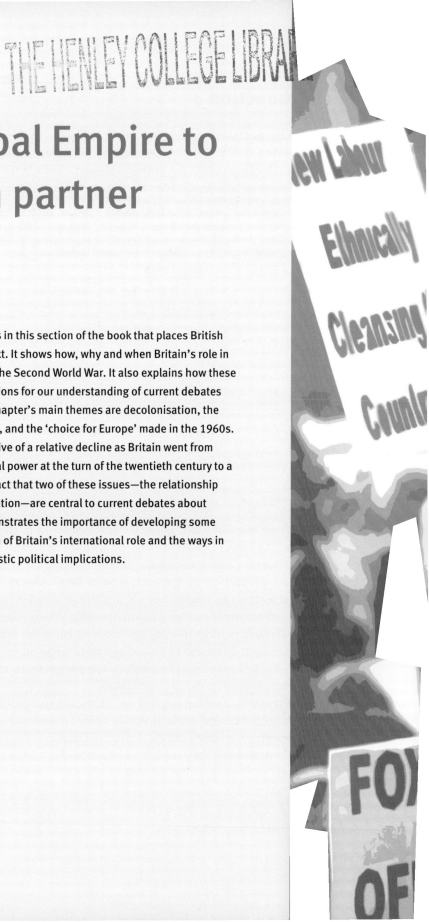

CHAPTER SIX

From global Empire to European partner

READER'S GUIDE

This chapter is the first of a series in this section of the book that places British politics in an international context. It shows how, why and when Britain's role in the world began to change after the Second World War. It also explains how these changes have important implications for our understanding of current debates about Britain in the world. This chapter's main themes are decolonisation, the 'special relationship' with the US, and the 'choice for Europe' made in the 1960s. Taken together, these are indicative of a relative decline as Britain went from being the world's leading imperial power at the turn of the twentieth century to a regional role within the EU. The fact that two of these issues—the relationship with the US and European integration—are central to current debates about Britain's place in the world demonstrates the importance of developing some historical depth to the discussion of Britain's international role and the ways in which it has had important domestic political implications.

Introduction

One of the most famous speeches about Britain's place in the world after the Second World War was made in 1962 by US Secretary of State, Dean Acheson. Acheson identified the strategic dilemmas facing the British in the early 1960s. It is worth quoting this speech at some length because it identifies the three core areas of perceived British interest at the time and addresses the basic question of Britain's role in Europe:

> **Extract 6.1: from speech by Dean Acheson, West Point military Academy, 6 December 1962**
>
> Great Britain has lost an Empire and has not yet found a role. The attempt to play a separate power role—that is, a role apart from Europe, a role based on a 'special relationship' with the United States, a role based on being the head of a 'Commonwealth' which has no political structure, or strength and enjoys a fragile and precarious economic relationship by means of the sterling area and preferences in the British market—this role is about to be played out. . . . Her Majesty's government is now attempting, wisely in my opinion, to re-enter Europe, from which it was banished at the time of the Plantagenets, and the battle seems about as hard fought as those of an earlier day.

We also get a sense of this quandary as it developed in the 1940s and 1950s when we consider the views of Winston Churchill who saw Britain's international interests in relation to three concentric circles: the Commonwealth, the special relationship with the US and Europe (Camps 1964: 4; see also Gamble 2003). After the Second World War Britain's political leaders asked themselves whether Britain's route to international influence could be through the newly emerging Commonwealth, through the special relationship with the US or through participation in supranational European integration. This question was pertinent in the 1940s and 1950s and aspects of it remain so today. They are key elements of the international context in which British politics needs to be located and which have important domestic political ramifications.

This chapter's main aim is to link the relative decline identified by Acheson to the reluctant 'choice for Europe' made by Britain's political leaders in the 1950s, 1960s and 1970s. The focus is on relative political decline articulated through a retreat from Empire, the 'special relationship' with the US and membership of the EC.[1] EC membership, when

---

[1] One potentially baffling element of EU politics is the number of terms used to describe it: EU, EC, EEC, Common Market, for example. In this text, we tend to refer to the EC in the period prior to the Maastricht Treaty which, in 1993, created the European Union (EU).

eventually attained in 1973, was not a positive, wholehearted or idealistic choice. Rather, it was based on calculations about the growing presence of the EC and the perceived absence of alternatives. One longer-term ramification of this half-hearted choice for Europe has been that Britain has been seen as an awkward, reluctant and semi-detached EU member state (George 1992, 1998; Gowland and Turner 1999). Also, in order to understand current debates about British relations with the US and the EU, it is necessary to locate them in their historical context and to understand the ways in which debates have evolved over time and how past decisions still influence current debates. For example, tensions between the 'special relationship' with the US and the EU were evident at the time of the second Gulf War which began in 2003. The next section explores Britain's post-war relations with the three circles of Commonwealth, the US and Europe. The chapter then examines the reasons why Britain opted for EC membership in the 1960s and the consequences of this choice.

 # The US, Empire and Europe

Britain's role in world politics during the 19th and 20th centuries was defined to a significant degree by Empire and by the retreat from Empire. The end of Empire and the search for an alternative role are core issues in Britain's international identity and, perhaps too, ones that are still not resolved when we consider the debate about Europe. There have also been domestic political ramifications of imperialism. It is impossible to understand immigration to Britain after the Second World War without knowing that many of those who came could claim *civis Brittanicus sum* (I am a British citizen) because they came from countries that had been or were British colonies.

After the end of the Second World War there were other dilemmas for Britain too. This period was dominated by the onset of the Cold War and the descent, as Churchill put it in his famous speech in the American town of Fulton, Missouri in March 1946 of an 'iron curtain' across the continent of Europe. The Cold War saw a military, political and ideological stand-off between the Warsaw Pact countries led by the Soviet Union and members of the North Atlantic Treaty Organisation (NATO) led by the US. Britain's economic, political and security interests and the choices made during the 1950s and 1960s were defined by this Cold War setting. Yet, when compared to other European countries, Britain did not see European unification as a necessary route to maintain prestige and secure peace and prosperity. There was to be a fundamental divide between Britain and the six other European countries (Belgium, France, Germany, Italy, Luxembourg and the Netherlands) that were to coalesce in 1951 within the European Coal and Steel Community (ECSC). The notion of a community founded on coal and steel may sound mundane nowadays, but its importance should not be downplayed: these were raw materials vital to economic reconstruction after the war while the location of their production in the Saarland and Ruhr Valley had been central to conflicts between France and Germany. The ECSC was the forerunner of what we now know as the EU.

The lesson learnt by the ECSC6 from previous conflicts was that economic and political integration within a supranational community with sovereignty 'pooled' was the way forward. The UK did not share this view about the desirability of supranational integration during the 1950s and came to accept it reluctantly only during the 1960s. By then, however, they encountered the opposition of French President De Gaulle who opposed British membership.

A key reason that the British were not prepared to accept supranational political and economic integration within the ECSC was that the experience of the Second World War produced entirely the opposite effect in the UK to that in West Germany and France and the other ECSC member states. For Britain, the Second World War vindicated national sovereignty with a powerful idea that Britain had 'stood alone' against Nazism and had ultimately been victorious. By this logic, Britain could continue to shape its own future and did not need to cast in its lot with European countries in the ECSC. As one of the founders of the EC, Jean Monnet put it: 'Britain had not been conquered or invaded; she felt no need to excoriate history' (cited in Fay and Meehan 2000: 211). The result of this attitude was, as Churchill put it, that Britain was *with them* in the sense of being a sponsor of European integration, but not *of them*, in the sense of being a participant in supranational European integration. Britain was determined not to be just a European power. Its aspirations were grander than this, but by 1961 we will see that the Conservative Government of Harold Macmillan sought EC membership. The remainder of this section explores reasons for this. It shows that by the 1960s the idea of the Commonwealth as a route to world power was dented, that the special relationship with the US was not as special as some had first imagined, and that the economic and political implications of European integration on Britain's doorstep could not be ignored.

Retreat from Empire

The immediate post-war period saw a retreat from an Empire that had reached its territorial height in 1921 and encompassed territories that stretched across Africa, Asia and the Pacific, as well as parts of Europe such as Cyprus. The British Empire built on trade, settlement and conquest encompassed between 400 and 500 million people and covered nearly 230 million square kilometres, around 40% of the world's land mass.

By the end of the Second World War British pre-occupations were much closer to home and centred on economic reconstruction. Moreover, in the colonies themselves British power was challenged by the rise of anti-colonialist movements seeking national independence (Darwin 1988; White 1999). Boyce (1999) has argued that the retreat from Empire was understood not as a loss but as the transformation of Empire to Commonwealth. The idea was that an association of states organised within the Commonwealth could be a road to international influence for Britain, although this would depend on the coherence of the Commonwealth. Britain could also look at the decolonising experiences of other European colonial powers, such as French experiences of decolonisation in Algeria where direct rule and the treatment of Algeria (treated as part of France until 1962) led to much blood being spilt during the war of independence.

Despite the impression that British national sovereignty had been successfully defended during the Second World War and that Britain had emerged victorious, it seems more plausible to contend that the war further undermined Britain's commercial and financial position and became increasingly reliant on the US for material support (Barnett 1986, 1990). During the Second World War it also became clear that countries such as Australia were not prepared to subordinate their interests to those of Britain. In 1952, Australia and New Zealand gave an indication of their desire to pursue their own interests in the Pacific region when they formed the ANZUS alliance with the US.

A particular blow to British imperial prestige and a stark illustration of Britain's place in the international order occurred in 1956. The nationalisation of the Suez Canal by Egyptian leader Colonel Abdul Nasser in July 1956 was seen to strike at key British and French commercial and strategic interests. Prime Minister Eden took an aggressive stance and with French backing used military force to reassume control of the Canal. The US was, however, unwilling to support what it saw as crude imperial manoeuvrings and brought intense economic pressure to bear on the UK (Dumbrell 2001: 46–9). In November 1956 the British agreed to a ceasefire and to the withdrawal of troops. In December 1956 a Bank of England official C.F. Cobbold reported that:

> The fundamental problem is that the economy and the public purse have been over-extended for many years, partly as a result of the war and partly because of the many commitments, social, military and political, which we have undertaken since (most of them doubtless justifiable on their own merits but adding up to a total bigger than we could afford) (cited in Dumbrell 2001: 47).

The costs of maintaining an Empire were beyond the reduced powers of a British state weakened by war, diminished in status alongside the United States and Soviet Union, and also economically and financially stretched in new ways, such as through the creation of the modern welfare state (see Chapter 28). As an interesting comparison, the French drew different lessons from the Suez crisis, which they saw as requiring the development of European strength, rather than reliance on the US. For the British, the emphasis was firmly placed on the rebuilding of the alliance with the US. This post-Suez division between France and Britain reflected different views on European integration and motivated General de Gaulle's rejection in 1963 of Britain's application for EC membership because he saw the British as too close to the Americans.

Britain then was not so much seeking a reason to leave its colonies as searching for reasons to stay (Heinlein 2002). Indeed, the argument for staying became less and less compelling because of domestic priorities. The case for withdrawal was strongly articulated by the Foreign Office after 1956 with the transition in India to its status as an independent republic in 1949 within the Commonwealth seen as the path to follow. The pace of decolonisation was rapid after the 1956 Suez crisis. Britain sought to divest itself of colonial possessions in light of its perception of changed strategic interests and the costs of maintaining an international role in the face of increased opposition to British rule in the colonies. In a speech in South Africa in 1960 Harold Macmillan referred to the 'winds of change sweeping through this continent and whether we like it or not, this growth of political consciousness is a fact'.

There were those who saw Britain's imperial past as offering a route to international influence through the Commonwealth based on co-operation between countries that shared strong historical links and, potentially, some common interests. By the 1960s this Commonwealth ideal had been dented. India and Pakistan were in conflict over the disputed state of Kashmir. In Kenya, the Mau Mau uprising against white minority rule was a vicious and bloody conflict while the racist apartheid system in South Africa was a deep source of bitterness and division within the Commonwealth until its end in 1994. Rhodesia was also a major problem. Northern Rhodesia gained independence as Zambia in 1964, but the white minority in Southern Rhodesia issued a unilateral declaration of independence in November 1965 and instigated a system of white minority rule with the support of South Africa until the resultant civil war was brought to an end in 1979 with the establishment of Zimbabwe (Kandiah 2002). Other former colonies such as Australia and New Zealand were charting a course for themselves in the Pacific region and were no longer so reliant on the 'mother country'. While ties of language, culture and history could be strong, British strategic and economic interests were no longer so closely attached to the Commonwealth.

It is also worth noting that the Empire and Commonwealth were to have other very tangible effects on British politics in the 1950s, 1960s and 1970s because they were the basis for immigration to Britain. The 1948 British Nationality Act extended British citizenship to all subjects of the Crown throughout the Empire. This gave around 800 million people the right to move freely within the Empire and, technically, settle in the UK. As people moved from former colonies to the UK they experienced some racist hostility based on these notions of racial superiority and the 'white man's burden' as Rudyard Kipling put it, that had been used to justify colonisation (see Chapters 5 and 29 for further discussion).

Between Europe and America

The other two influences, or circles of interest, as Churchill put it, were Europe and the US. It is worth analysing these two together if we are to develop an understanding of British economic and strategic interests in the 1950s and 1960s. The US saw vital economic and strategic interests in Europe and was concerned about the threat posed to these interests by the Soviet Union and its satellite states, as well as by strong Communist parties in countries such as France, Greece and Italy. The US saw a key role for Britain as a leading European power, but the UK did not see itself as an exclusively European power and had reservations about the role of supranational economic and political integration proposed by the French Foreign Minister, Robert Schuman on 9 May 1950. The US position towards Britain was made clear in a State Department paper of 1950 (cited in Bayliss 1997: 59, 61):

> The British attach great importance to the continuation of an
> especially close relationship with the US. This coincides with our
> own policy. The British, however, are inclined to make this
> relationship more overt than we feel desirable. . . . It should be our
> line with the British to assure them that we recognise the special
> relationship between our two countries and that we recognise their
> special position with regard to the Commonwealth. We should insist,
> however, that these relationships are not incompatible with close
> association in a European framework. . . . We should reassure the
> British that we do not advocate their political merger with the
> continent, but that we are convinced that closer economic and
> political, as well as military, ties between them and the continent
> are essential.

From the 1950s the only route in the pursuit of closer ties with the most important West European countries was for Britain to participate in a supranational community, which while not a political merger, did have important implications for national sovereignty. The question of supranational integration was difficult for Labour and Conservative governments. For Labour governments, supranational integration could inhibit the pursuit of socialist policies because the EC could constrain the ability of members to pursue national economic policies that conflicted with EC priorities and laws. For Conservatives, European integration was a distraction from Empire, which was, as R.A. Butler put it, 'the main religion of the Tory Party' during the 1950s. In more general terms, British ideas about national sovereignty and the centrality of Parliament to this vision had been emboldened not delegitimated by the Second World War. For example, why should the 1945–51 Labour Government cede sovereign authority in areas such as coal and steel production when these were vital raw materials and also had just been nationalised.

The British preference was for intergovernmental co-operation that would enshrine the nation-state as the basic legitimate unit of international politics. The six countries that were to form the ECSC favoured supranational economic and political integration. We need to understand the basic meaning of these two terms if we are to understand the split that emerged in Western Europe during the 1950s. Moreover, this preference for intergovernmentalism has been a long-standing feature of the British stance on European integration which we still can see when issues such as the proposed EU Constitutional Treaty are discussed.

Labour and Conservative governments during the 1940s and 1950s were prepared to support forms of European co-operation that established intergovernmental structures within which states would co-operate with each other, but they were not prepared to support new, supranational institutions with powers over national governments. This is a key

...national visions of Europe

Intergovernmentalism	Supranationalism
• The nation state as the basic unit of international politics	• The nation-state delegitimated by war and conflict
• Emphasis on co-operation between sovereign states	• Emphasis on the creation of common institutions able to pass laws that bind participating states
• Unanimity as the basis for decision-making	• Adoption of forms of majority voting
• European co-operation shaped by the interests of member states who control its scope and direction	• European integration capable of acquiring its own momentum as a result of transferred competencies
Further reading: Hoffmann 1966; Moravscik 1998	Further reading: Haas 1964; Sandholtz and Stone Sweet 1998

element of the distinction outlined in Table 6.1 above, which shows the basic differences between intergovernmental and supranational visions of Europe. British governments were firmly in the intergovernmental camp. Britain was prepared to participate in the Council of Europe created in 1949 because it accorded with this intergovernmental vision, but when it came to more ambitious plans for supranational integration then the sovereignty defended between 1939 and 1945 would not be sovereignty ceded. Ernest Bevin put it rather pithily in a famous mixed metaphor: 'If you open that Pandora's box, you never know what Trojan horses will jump out'. For the Foreign Office in the early 1950s a concern with international prestige meant that 'Great Britain must be viewed as a world power of the second rank and not merely as a unit in a federated Europe' (cited in Ellison 2000: 16).

Britain appeared to view the European circle as third in the order of pre-eminence behind the 'special relationship' and the Empire/Commonwealth. Britain did not see itself as an exclusively European country. These views about the relative ordering of interests had to be re-evaluated with an application for membership lodged in 1961, but this view of European integration's relative lack of prominence was an important influence at a time when early steps towards economic and political integration in Europe were being taken. With the gift of hindsight we now know that these first steps were to have very dramatic long-term effects on European politics and give rise to what we now know as the EU with 25 member states. In the early 1950s, this success could not have been anticipated. Indeed such a bold venture could have seemed more likely to fail. Moreover, within the British government there was not a widely held perception that participation in these continental European adventures accorded with British political and economic interests, or as Wolfram Kaiser (1996: xvi) puts it, those who criticise decisions made in the 1950s do so 'based on the normative assumption that the path taken by the six was not only successful but natural, and also morally preferable to the British preference for trade liberalisation within intergovernmental structures'.

The nature of the dilemma becomes apparent if we look at the declaration of French Foreign Minister, Robert Schuman made on 9 May 1950. He made it clear that the plan for a coal and steel community was not the endpoint of the ambitions of the founder six member states.

> **Extract 6.2: from the Schuman Declaration, 9 May 1950**
>
> Europe will not be made all at once, or according to a single plan. It will be built through concrete achievements which first create a de facto solidarity. The coming together of the nations of Europe requires the elimination of the age-old opposition of France and Germany. Any action taken must in the first place concern these two countries. With this aim in view the French Government proposes that action be taken immediately on one limited but decisive point.

Britain supported this vision to the extent of seeing it as appropriate for other European countries, but not to the extent of wanting to sign up to the ECSC. It could hardly be seen to oppose the creation of an organisation designed to foster peaceful relations between France and Germany. The United States had hoped that the UK would participate and could play a leading role in Western Europe to ensure that US interests were well represented. Britain was also firmly opposed to a 1952 plan (the Pleven Plan) for a European Defence Community with talk of a common European army and common defence policies. The French Parliament refused to ratify the Treaty so the plan never came to fruition. Instead, the West European Union fitted with British preferences for a strong link between Western Europe and the US in the context of NATO, an Atlantic alliance.

The lesson learnt by the ECSC6 was that ambitious plans for integration in areas of 'high politics' that impinged more directly on state sovereignty were less likely to succeed than more measured proposals for integration in areas of 'low politics' where interdependencies between participating states were most evident. This was taken forward when the ECSC foreign ministers met in the Sicilian city of Messina to discuss further economic and political integration. The discussions were to lead to plans for the creation of a Common Market (see Chapter 8 for more discussion). The British government indicated how seriously they took this event by sending a mere Board of Trade official. When the outcome of the meeting was published in November 1955 as the Spaak Report (after the Belgian foreign minister) it was asked that no reference to the British position be made. Britain effectively withdrew from the discussions that were to lead to the Treaty of Rome in 1957 that established the European Economic Community.

The 1950s are without doubt a key period in British contemporary history with important implications for today's debates about Britain's place in the world. Some historians argue that the 1950s were a decade of missed opportunities and that the leadership of

- NATO was founded by the Washington Treaty of 4 April 1949.
- There were 12 founder members: Belgium, Canada, Denmark, France, Iceland, Italy, Luxembourg, the Netherlands, Norway, Portugal, UK, US.
- Greece (1952), Turkey (1952), Germany (1955) and Spain (1982) joined during the Cold War.
- Czech Republic (1999), Poland (1999), Hungary (1999), Bulgaria (2004), Estonia (2004), Latvia (2004), Lithuania (2004), Romania (2004), Slovenia (2004) and Slovakia (2004) have joined since the end of the Cold War.
- The core provision is Article 5 which states that an armed attack against one or more of them in Europe or North America shall be considered an attack against them all. Consequently they agree that, if such an armed attack occurs, each of them, in exercise of the right of individual or collective self-defence recognised by Article 51 of the Charter of the United Nations, will assist the party or parties so attacked by taking forthwith, individually and in concert with the other parties, such action as it deems necessary, including the use of armed force, to restore and maintain the security of the North Atlantic area. This was first enacted after the 9/11 attacks on New York and the Pentagon.

Europe was Britain's for the taking if only it had possessed the resolve to take a leading role. Conservative politician, Anthony Nutting argued that 'Britain could have had the leadership of Europe on any term she cared to name' (cited in Young 1993: 52). However, there is a basic problem with this argument because as John Young (1993: 52) notes:

> Britain could not have had the leadership of Europe *on its own terms* because Britain saw no need to abandon its sovereignty to common institutions, whereas the Six saw this as vital. Britain could only have played a key role in European integration, paradoxically, *if* it had accepted the continentals' terms and embraced supranationalism, but very few people advocated this before 1957.

What kind of choice for Europe?

When the choice for Europe was made with Britain's first application to join the EEC in 1961 what kind of choice was it? Did Britain wholeheartedly embrace the supranational vision of a united Europe? This seems unlikely given the prevailing views in the 1950s. Or was the choice borne by the growing presence of the EEC as a major economic bloc with political implications on Britain's doorstep with which Britain had little option but to engage? We will see that this latter explanation is not only more useful, but also helps explain the ways in which European integration was subsequently viewed from Britain.

Britains initially attempted to sponsor an alternative organisation to the EEC with the creation of the European Free Trade Area in 1959 as a result of the Treaty of Stockholm. In numerical terms at least, the seven EFTA members (Austria, Britain, Denmark, Norway, Sweden, Portugal, Norway and Iceland), outnumbered the six EC member states (France, Germany, Italy, Belgium, the Netherlands and Luxembourg), but it was the EC countries that were the fast growing core of the European economy. This was made clear in a memorandum sent by Prime Minister Harold Macmillan to his Foreign Secretary, Selwyn Lloyd, in 1959:

> For the first time since the Napoleonic era the major continental powers are united in a positive economic grouping with considerable political aspects, which, although not specifically directed against the United Kingdom, may have the effect of excluding us both from European markets and from consultation in European policy (cited in Geddes 2004: 69).

These economic and political implications motivated the first application for membership lodged by the UK in 1961. The application however met the opposition of French President De Gaulle. In many ways, De Gaulle's vision of Europe accorded with what in later years would be seen as a distinctly Thatcherite position. De Gaulle adopted a distinctly nationalist position, distrusted EC institutions such as the Commission, and wanted to see the member states holding the upper hand. However, where he differed from Thatcherite views on Europe was that De Gaulle wanted to maintain the Franco–German axis as the key relationship within the EC with France as the dominant partner. De Gaulle also saw Europe as a third force between the US and the Soviet Union, with France at the helm. His opposition to UK membership was based on the fear that the UK would be a Trojan horse for US influence and would lead to the creation of an Atlantic Community dependent on America. Despite other member states favouring UK membership, De Gaulle imposed a unilateral veto in January 1963 based on his concern about US influence and his anger at a US–UK deal on nuclear weapons made at Nassau in July 1962 under which the US agreed to supply Polaris missiles to the UK.

The UK decision to seek EC membership was based on a re-evaluation of strategic interests rather than a positive acceptance of supranational economic and political integration. Ironically, as soon as membership had been decided upon as the appropriate course of action, there was implacable opposition from De Gaulle who saw the UK as a potential usurper of French influence wielded through the EC. Moreover, as we see in Chapter 9 the framework put in place by the Treaty of Rome, particularly the Common Agricultural Policy (CAP) and, after 1970, the budget system, were not in Britain's interests. Harold Wilson's Labour Government, elected in 1964, also pursued EC membership. Wilson sought to modernise the UK economy and to adapt to the 'white heat' of the technological revolution. However, the application lodged by Wilson's Government was again rebuffed by De Gaulle who expressed himself unsure of Britain's European vocation.

The political complexion of Europe changed in 1969 when de Gaulle was replaced by George Pompidou. Although a Gaullist, Pompidou was prepared to agree to British accession. The new Social Democrat West German Chancellor, Willy Brandt, also supported British membership. This combined with the election in Britain in 1970 of Edward Heath's Conservative Government. Heath was a committed European who had made his maiden speech in the House of Commons in favour of ECSC membership. Negotiations began in June 1970 and a 1971 White Paper outlined the implications of membership, which would include hefty budget contributions and an increased cost of living amounting to 3% over six years, mainly linked to a 15% increase in food prices because of the CAP.

The British negotiating team led by Geoffrey Rippon was not in a strong position. Some concessions were wrought on Commonwealth trade, but essentially, the British were forced to sign up to the 13,000 pages of EC law as it then stood (it has since risen to around 80,000 pages). Parliamentary approval was secured in October 1971 by 356 votes to 244, but only because 69 Labour MPs (including Roy Jenkins and future party leader John Smith) defied a three-line Whip to support membership. The Treaty of Accession was signed in Brussels on 22 January 1972 with Britain becoming a member of the EC on 1 January 1973.

The issue resolved?

The issue of Britain's EC membership was far from resolved. In February and October 1974 Labour governments led by Harold Wilson were elected. Labour had sought EC membership in 1967, but in opposition had moved to a contrary stance because of opposition from within the party and the labour movement to the 'capitalist club', as many saw the EC. Wilson's tactical device was to oppose the terms of membership, seek to renegotiate them and then put the result of this renegotiation to a referenda. This even led the former Conservative Cabinet minister Enoch Powell to call for a Labour vote in 1974.

The renegotiations were led by Foreign Secretary James Callaghan, who was far from being a committed European. Indeed, when he entered the Foreign Office he was presented by his new officials with a brief on relations with the EC that argued that there could be some room for concessions on the CAP and the budget. Callaghan referred them to the Labour Party manifesto and pointed out that the aim was a fundamental re-negotiation of the Treaty of Accession. The basic problem with this position was that there was no reason why the other member states should tear up the agreement that they had only just reached with the UK and enter into another process of tortuous negotiations. The end result of the 're-negotiations' were twofold: some minor trade concessions to the British and the irritation of other member states.

Despite their limits, the re-negotiated terms were placed before the British people in a June 1975 referenda. A powerful centrist coalition of politicians including all three main party leaders (Callaghan, new Conservative leader Margaret Thatcher and Liberal leader Jeremy Thorpe) advocated a 'yes' vote. The 'no' campaign was a disparate grouping of right and left-wing politicians such as Enoch Powell and Tony Benn. The 'yes' campaign also had the advantage of support from Fleet Street and financial backing that was 10 times greater than that of their opponents (Butler and Kitzinger 1976; King 1977).

> **Extract 6.3: from Yes Campaign Pamphlet**
>
> We do not pretend, and never have pretended, that we got everything we wanted in these negotiations. But we did get big and significant improvements on the previous terms. We confidently believe that these terms give Britain a New Deal in Europe. A Deal that will help us, help the Commonwealth, and help our partners in Europe.

Prior to the referenda campaign the opinion polls suggested a vote for withdrawal, but the powerful coalition of support that the 'yes' campaign gathered led to 67.5% of votes cast (on a 64% turnout) in support of continued membership.

Perhaps this would signify a new era based on full acceptance of Britain's EC membership. The Home Secretary and ardent pro-European Roy Jenkins hoped so and remarked that: 'it puts the uncertainty behind us. It commits Britain to Europe; it commits us to playing an active constructive and enthusiastic role'. 'No' campaigner and Secretary of State for Industry Tony Benn seemed to follow this line when remarking that: 'When the British people have spoken everyone including members of Parliament, should tremble before their decision and that's the spirit with which I accept the result of the referenda'. However, Britain's relations with the EC were to remain troubled in the years that followed, with further disputes about the level of budget contributions and a particular deterioration from the late 1980s as a right-wing Euroscepticism with its origins in Thatcherite opposition to the direction of the EC surfaced following her 1988 Bruges speech (see Chapter 9).

Conclusion

This chapter has explored the international context within which British politics was located after the Second World War. British political leaders identified three circles of influence: the Empire/Commonwealth, the 'special relationship' and Europe. The ways in which these international relations have been resolved is central to an understanding of contemporary debates about, for example, European integration (see Chapters 8 and 9) and to an understanding of migration to Britain in the 1950s and 1960s (see Chapter 30). Britain stood aside from early moves towards European integration because it opposed supranationalism and saw economic and political integration as not conforming with British interests, which were seen as not being entirely focused on Europe. As Churchill put it, Britain was *with* but not *of* Europe in the sense of being a sponsor and supporter of integration, but not a participant. This choice was re-evaluated by the late 1950s, but Britain's route was not as straightforward as imagined because of French opposition to British EC membership. France opposed British membership because it claimed that Britain did not possess a European vocation, while it was also the case that Britain could challenge France's leadership role and bring US influence to the heart of the European project. The 'choice for Europe' when it was made by British governments in the 1960s was not necessarily based on commitment to Europe, but the absence of alternatives and calculations about Britain's diminished role in world affairs. This was not to be the basis for full-hearted commitment to Europe and can be seen as a root cause of problems that still linger for Britain between Europe and America at the turn of the 21st century.

KEY POINTS

- Britain saw a decline in its relative power after the Second World War.

- The idea of three circles of influence comprising the special relationship with the US, the Commonwealth and Europe was quite powerful during the 1950s.

- The choice for Europe when it was made in the 1960s was not positive, wholehearted or idealistic.

- Neither the 'special relationship' with the US nor the Commonwealth provided a route to great power status.

- The US wanted Britain to take the lead in Europe.

- Britain was opposed to supranational integration between European countries and preferred intergovernmental co-operation.

- Joining the EEC was a recognition of Britain's diminished status in the world.

- A 1975 referenda agreed to Britain's continued membership but failed to decisively resolve the European issue in British politics.

KEY QUESTIONS

(1) What were Britain's foreign policy priorities after the end of the Second World War?

(2) What are the key differences between intergovernmental co-operation and supranational integration?

(3) Why did British governments prefer intergovernmentalism to supranationalism?

(4) Why did Britain decide to apply to join the EEC in 1961?

(5) How 'special' was the 'special relationship' with the US in the 1950s and 1960s?

IMPORTANT WEBSITES

The EU homepage can be found at www.europa. eu.int while the UK government position can be found at the Foreign and Commonwealth Office site www.fco.gov.uk. Two of the main campaign organisations are, on the pro-side Britain in Europe www.britainineurope.org.uk and, on the anti-side, the Bruges Group www.brugesgroup.com.

FURTHER READING

On the dilemmas of British policy towards the EU see H. Young (1998) *This Blessed Plot: Britain and Europe from Churchill to Blair*, London: Papermac. On the special relationship see J. Dumbrell (2001) *A Special Relationship: Anglo-American Relations in the Cold War and after*, London: Palgrave. On the end of Empire and decolonisation see F. Heinlein (2002) *British Government Policy and Decolonisation, 1945–1963: Scrutinising the Official Mind*, London: Frank Cass. On the debate about British decline see R. English and M. Kenny (eds) (2000) *Rethinking British Decline*, Basingstoke: Macmillan.

CHRONOLOGY

Empire, the special relationship and Europe in the 1950s and 1960s

1945	Clement Attlee becomes Prime Minister and Harry Truman US President, world's first atomic bomb detonated in New Mexico
1946	Churchill's 'iron curtain' speech
1947	Independence for India
1948	Marshall Plan aid from US to Europe established, independence for Burma and Ceylon
1949	Council of Europe and NATO established
1950	US–British mutual defence agreement, Schuman Plan outlines scheme for creation of ECSC
1951	Winston Churchill becomes British Prime Minister, Treaty of Paris creates ECSC
1953	Eisenhower becomes US President
1954	Plan for creation of European Defence Community fails
1955	Anthony Eden replaces Churchill as Prime Minister, Messina meeting on the future of Europe shows UK divided from ECSC6
1956	Suez crisis
1957	Harold Macmillan becomes Prime Minister, Treaty of Rome creates EEC, independence for Ghana
1959	Creation of European Free Trade Area
1960	Independence for Nigeria and Malaya
1961	British application to join the EC, independence for Sierra Leone and Tanganyika, John F. Kennedy becomes US President
1962	UK acquires Polaris missiles from US, independence for Uganda, Jamaica and Trinidad & Tobago
1963	De Gaulle says no to Britain's EC application, independence for Kenya and Zanzibar, Alec Douglas Home becomes Prime Minister, President Kennedy assassinated, Lyndon Johnson becomes US President
1964	Harold Wilson becomes Prime Minister, independence for Malawi and Zambia
1965	Independence for Gambia and Botswana
1966	Independence for Barbados and Lesotho
1967	Second British EC application rebuffed by De Gaulle
1968	Independence for Swaziland
1969	Richard Nixon elected US President, Georges Pompidou replaces General De Gaulle as French President

Visit the Online Resource Centre that accompanies this book
for links to more information on this chapter topic

CHAPTER SEVEN

Understanding decline

READER'S GUIDE

The ideas of relative British economic and political decline had powerful political effects on British politics throughout the 20th century. While Britain's international role changed after the Second World War, there was also a sense that Britain was falling behind economically compared to countries such as France, Germany, Japan and the US. As is discussed in this chapter and Chapter 27 on economic policy, the problems seemed to worsen in the 1970s as industrial relations deteriorated while unemployment and inflation were simultaneously high. This chapter centres on three issues in its analysis of economic decline. First, what exactly was it that declined? Second, what were the causes of decline? Third, has decline now been arrested? This chapter shows no single, shared understanding of decline and that the debate about economic decline was actually about relative decline.

Introduction

'We have ceased to be a nation in retreat', argued Margaret Thatcher to a meeting of the Conservative faithful in Cheltenham on 3 July 1982. 'We have instead a newfound confidence—born in the economic battles at home and tested and found true more than 8000 miles away' (in the Falkland Islands). The sub-text to this speech was that Thatcher was arresting British decline by tackling the enemies within (trade unions) and without (the Argentinean military junta). This contrasted sharply with the perception in the 1970s that Britain was locked into an inexorable political and economic decline from its imperial past and great power status to an uncertain future as a mid-ranking regional power within the European Community (English and Kenny 2000). The 'management of decline'—and those seen to espouse it, such as Foreign Office civil servants—were also Margaret Thatcher's enemies.

Ideas about decline were not a new component of British political debate. In 1903 Joseph Chamberlain began his campaign for domestic renewal, imperial co-operation and tariff reform in the face of what he saw as British decline (Marsh 1994). The Conservative and Unionist Party divided on this issue in similar ways to the divisions over Europe since the 1990s within the post-Thatcher Conservative Party (Baker, Gamble and Ludlam 1993).

Explanations for relative economic decline are closely linked to those about relative political decline because diminished international status after the Second World War seemed to go hand in hand with relatively poor economic performance in the 1950s, 1960s and 1970s. Thatcher's forceful remedies to her perception of the causes of relative economic and political decline contrasted with what Robert Cooper (1998) called 'post-imperial irony' as a potential component of Britain's self-identity as it seeks a new role for itself within the EU. Cooper argued that 'irony is at the centre of modern foreign policy-making' because 'what else is there left for a post-heroic, post-imperial, post-modern society? Provided it is tinged with humanity, irony is not such a bad thing. It suggests a certain modesty about oneself, one's values and one's aspirations. At least irony is unlikely to be used to justify programmes of conquest or extermination.' One, perhaps apocryphal, example of this was provided by Britain's ambassador in Washington DC between 1948 and 1952, Sir Oliver Franks. Along with colleagues from other leading countries, Sir Oliver was asked what he wished for in the coming year. His Russian colleague expressed the desire that colonial peoples would be liberated while the French ambassador yearned for a new era of peace and co-operation. Franks responded that a small box of crystallised fruit would be nice. Irony and modesty were, however, not obviously Thatcherite traits. According to *The Economist* (6 December 1999) Tony Blair too was: 'a stranger to irony. His eagerness to set the world's wrongs to rights and to turn Britain into a model country for the next century could not be more Victorian—or Thatcherite.'

This introductory discussion indicates that the politics of relative economic and political decline—or the political construction of decline as English and Kenny (2001) put it because the reasons and remedies for this decline have been seen in very different

POLITICS IN FOCUS 7.1
Explaining decline

Absolute decline—a permanent fall below a previously attained level.
Relative decline—a comparison with similar entities such as other European countries (Crafts 1995).
'Relative decline and absolute growth can and do co-exist' (Supple 1997: 10).

ways—have been staple components of political debates in the UK. The previous chapter explored the political and foreign policy dimensions of relative decline as Britain sought a new role for itself. Our focus in this chapter will be on the ways in which perceptions of, and ideas about, relative economic decline played a key role in shaping modern British politics.

Decline and the study of politics

By addressing this issue of decline we are also able to cast light on two other important issues for students of British politics. The first of these is the ways in which the contextual and conceptual vocabulary of political studies has changed. The debate about decline is actually a debate about the British state, its territory and its people. Thirty years ago an undergraduate student of politics would have pondered the question of nationalisation and state planning whereby the state assumed responsibility for the management of certain key industries such as coal mining, the railways, public utilities such as electricity, gas and water and (intermittently) steel. In turn this would imply certain assumptions about the role of the state and its capacity to provide the kinds of political, economic and social outcomes that political leaders and citizens sought. Nowadays it is almost unimaginable that students of British politics would encounter nationalisation as an issue integral to their studies. They would be more likely to analyse privatisation, the role of the market, European integration and those contemporary buzzwords 'globalisation' and 'multi-level governance'. These shifts do not imply that the state is now irrelevant, but that the ways in which it is analysed and understood have changed and that these alter the conceptual and analytical vocabulary that we employ when studying politics. The role of the state has changed, the organisation of state territory has changed too as a result of devolution, while Britain is now a diverse and multicultural society (see Chapters 5, 14 and 17).

The second issue is the relationship between the study of history and of politics. Students of politics obviously require a sound grasp of the history of the societies that they study and wish to understand. Yet, what becomes clear as we study the politics of relative economic decline (and other important political questions too, of course) is the existence of competing historical narratives from which analysts sometimes cherrypick those most convenient to their own preferred explanation. Remedies to supposed British decline often focus on certain aspects of British history—an ineffectual and anti-industrial upper class, the public schools, overly powerful trade unions, the dominance of commerce and finance over manufacturing or rural nostalgia—as explanations for decline. Because accounts of British decline often focus on different aspects of British history they can come to very different conclusions. They also show that history is not some neutral databank of facts to be deployed by students of politics. We need to explore differing narrative accounts of British history and of relative decline and seek to evaluate their usefulness. We can also consider the impact of history in other ways. Does the accumulated weight of past experience make change more difficult? Perhaps there are ways in which the ordering of political, economic and social life in times past can still affect current politics and, by doing so, the scope for political leaders to break from previously established paths, re-write the rules of the game and affect political change.

 ## Analysing relative decline

This chapter's analysis of the politics of decline in post-war Britain is focused on the economy and thus complements the analysis in Chapter 6 that focused primarily on foreign policy. In order to understand the relationship between the economy and the political system, Peter Hall (1989) wrote that we need to explore:

* the organisation of labour
* the organisation of capital
* the organisation of the political system
* the position of Britain within the international economy.

Each of these will be central to this chapter's analysis of the politics of decline and declinism in Britain.

We also need to be more precise about the meaning of decline. In some ways the idea of decline can appear rather ridiculous because at the time in the 1960s and 1970s when decline was apparently most evident, overall British people were wealthier than at any other point in British history. The point is that there was a sense of *relative decline* compared to competitor countries such as France, Germany, Italy, Japan and the US. These countries seemed to be more prosperous than Britain while their economies were growing more rapidly. In the mid-1970s, for example, the size of the Italian economy exceeded that of the British economy. *Il sorpasso* (the overtaking) as the Italians called it, was a source of great pride in Italy, but a further blow to national self-esteem in Britain. Table 7.1 shows GNP per capita in Britain compared to other EU member states.

Table 7.1 shows that at this national level British people experienced a relative decline in income per capita, but that this began to change in the 1990s. From being ranked 11th by this criterion in 1990, Britain rose to 4th in 2002. However, these national figures may not paint the whole picture. Within the EU the largest regional differences are in the United

02

	1960	1970	1980	1990	2000	2002
Austria	85.0	84.8	104.3	109.3	112.2	111.2
Belgium	114.9	112.8	122.5	104.1	107.7	107.3
Denmark	123.2	140.3	132.4	135.6	144.7	145.2
Finland	108.1	102.4	108.7	143.3	112.6	111.5
France	124.0	120.2	122.6	109.2	102.9	102.2
Germany	120.5	129.2	130.4	124.0	109.5	106.8
Greece	41.4	54.3	49.8	43.2	51.7	53.2
Ireland	63.2	61.2	61.3	70.5	121.4	134.7
Italy	73.4	85.0	78.8	101.5	89.6	90.8
Luxembourg	178.5	150.0	143.2	151.1	207.0	211.4
Netherlands	99.0	114.5	124.6	102.9	111.9	115.5
Portugal	31.5	35.9	30.3	37.7	51.2	53.3
Spain	36.5	49.4	58.3	68.6	67.7	70.5
Sweden	179.1	182.5	153.5	145.4	124.4	115.0
UK	127.3	94.4	94.2	90.0	115.3	116.4
	(3rd)	(9th)	(10th)	(11th)	(4th)	(4th)

Source: Adapted from *European Economy*, 2002

Kingdom, where there is a factor of 4.4 between the region with the highest per capita income (Inner London) with an income per capita 288% of the EU average and the region with the lowest (Cornwall and the Isles of Scilly) with a per capita income 65% of the EU average (*Eurostat, Regions: Statistical Yearbook 2004*). If we look at the distribution of income compared to other EU member states then income inequality was relatively high in 1997 in the southern member states, Belgium and the United Kingdom while relatively low in the Scandinavian countries and Austria. This is shown in Table 7.2 where the Gini co-efficient is used as a measure of inequality ranging from zero for complete equality (when everybody has the same income) to 100 for complete inequality (when only one person has all income) (see Chapter 5).

To these regional and distributive breakdowns could be added information on the comparative performance of economic sectors which would show decline of manufacturing industries (often concentrated in the Midlands and North) and a relatively strong performance by the service sector, particularly financial services.

ent

1997	GINI co-efficient
Austria	25
Belgium	34
Denmark	21
Finland	23
Germany	29
Greece	35
France	30
Ireland	33
Italy	32
Netherlands	28
Portugal	38
Sweden	23
Spain	35
UK	34

Source: Adapted from European Commission Directorate General Employment and Social Affairs

The contested meaning of decline

The basic questions that underpin an analysis of relative decline are what does decline mean and what exactly was it that declined? As is often the case in political studies, there are no quick and easy answers to these questions. As Gamble (2000: 1) put it: 'Decline has no single meaning. It has always been dependent upon seeing the world and Britain's place within it in a particular way.' It is also far from clear what declined. Was it the economy? All economic sectors or some sectors? All parts of the country or some parts? Some analysts of relative economic decline have focused on culture (Wiener and Barnett 1984; Sampson 1983), others on the role of finance and the City of London (Pollard 1982; Hutton 1995), some have pinpointed institutional weaknesses (King 1975; Marquand 1988), while others have identified the effects of empire (Hobsbawn 1968; Kennedy 1988; Callaghan 1997). We will look at each of these in turn in the chapter's next section.

While explanations of decline may differ, there are some common points of reference because debates about relative decline have been shaped by:

(1) Ideas about the national economy and national competitiveness. The notion of relative decline is usually understood in relation to other countries, but the idea that countries rather than firms or economic sectors can be competitive has been dismissed (Krugman 1994; Brittan 2000). As we have already seen, factors such as regional breakdown, income distribution and the relative performance of economic sectors question the notion of national competitiveness. Even though there are good reasons to doubt that it makes much sense, the idea of national competitiveness has long been to the fore in political debate. Chancellor Gordon Brown is prone to wax lyrical about the strength of the UK economy under his stewardship. The former European Commissioner Chris Patten was moved to suggest that so desperate did conditions seem to have become on the continent of Europe that perhaps food parcels would need to be sent. Lying beneath Patten's ironic observation was recognition that notions of success or failure can often depend on the criteria selected. So, for example, the UK economy has grown more rapidly than some comparable EU economies, but in some areas, such as productivity the UK still lags behind Germany while some parts of the UK such as Merseyside and Northern Ireland are in receipt of what is known as 'Objective One' special assistance from the EU as deprived areas. It may be that certain sectors of the British economy and certain parts of the country are doing quite well while others may not be doing quite so well. The same applies in France, Germany, Italy and other comparable economies. In fact, the language of national competitiveness can appear a bit ludicrous because, as Samuel Brittan (2000) has pointed out, we cannot all be more competitive while adopting the language of national success and failure renders trade and economic relations between states comparable to warfare.

(2) The extent to which governments can and/or should intervene in order to shape outcomes. Citizens may believe and hope that governments can and should intervene effectively, but the contextual and conceptual vocabulary of politics has been shifted in ways that reflect the development of multi-level governance as some powers move 'up' to Europe, 'down' to a sub-national level, and 'out' to the market and quasi-state organisations such as agencies. This may provide an escape route for governments who can say that these forces provide constraints on their ability to act and intervene (see Chapter 3; also Bache and Flinders 2003). While the role of the state has changed, some of the rhetoric about 'rolling back the frontiers of the state' should be taken with a pinch of salt. Gamble

ICS IN FOCUS 7.1
Objective One funding

Objective One funding is an EU scheme that aims to reduce deprivation in the European Union's poorest areas. A scheme funded by the EU and by national governments, Objective One targets the highest priority areas in the union—defined as those where per capita gross domestic product is less than 75% of the EU average. Cornwall, much of Wales, South Yorkshire and Merseyside are included in the scheme's current round.

(1983) identified the paradox of the free economy and the strong state whereby there was a tension within Thatcherism between economic liberalism and social conservatism. It has also been argued that supposed state retreat under the Conservatives and New Labour has actually been accompanied by new forms of state 'colonisation' to observe, monitor, target and manage (Moran 2003).

(3) The extent to which the decline identified in the 1960s and 1970s has been reversed. The quote from Margaret Thatcher that began this chapter emphasised national recovery. If we look at an indicator such as GNP per capita then we see that Britain is doing better in comparison with other EU member states. However, if we then break down these figures and look at different economic sectors or regional breakdowns then we see that this national story has some variance within it. From the centre-left, writers such as Will Hutton (1995) were keen to identify persistent weaknesses in the UK that still required radical overhaul if Britain was to be a modern, successful and socially cohesive society. Indeed, Hutton's critique and his vision of a 'stakeholder society' gave some intellectual ballast to New Labour.

Explaining relative economic decline

We can now move on to explore explanations for relative economic decline. One thing to note as a prelude to this discussion is that debates about decline have not been monopolised by academics because scholars have sometimes found political sponsors eager to use explanations for decline as the basis for their own particular remedies. For example, Martin Wiener's arguments about culture and anti-industrial attitudes influenced Sir Keith Joseph, who in turn was an intellectual force behind Margaret Thatcher (Denham and Garnett 2001). For a time in the 1990s there were many in New Labour entranced by Will Hutton's (1995) critique of Conservative Britain in his book *The State We're In*.

Table 7.3 seeks to identify some of the arguments that have been advanced to explain decline. These are then explored more fully in the rest of this section.

The cultural argument

This could be called the 'chinless wonder' approach to British economic decline. At heart the argument links culture and economic performance and argues that an elitist education system focused on public schools was not providing sufficient numbers of people with an aptitude for business.

Martin Wiener (1981), Corelli Barnett (1986) and Anthony Sampson (1983) all highlighted the weaknesses of an anti-industrial and anti-enterprise culture coupled with the effects of an education system that did little to encourage the 'useful' attributes seen in other countries. The key assumption was that 'cultural beliefs and values play the major role in determining economic behaviour' (Gamble 2000: 11).

Wiener argues that a cultural 'cordon sanitaire' was opposed to changes that would have brought about the modernisation of the British economy and society. Instead of challenging

Types of argument	Causes of decline	Advocates	Remedies
Culture	Anti-enterprise culture and elitist education system not attuned to the needs of modern economies	Martin Wiener, Corelli Barnett, Anthony Sampson	Attitudinal change and social modernisation to induce an enterprise culture
Empire	Empire a cushion against change inducing imperial overstretch and a national identity crisis	Eric Hobsbawn, Andrew Shonfield, Paul Kennedy, Stuart Hall	Recognition of and adaptation to changed status in the world
Industry	Poor management and overly powerful trade unions	Samuel Brittan, Martin Wiener	New management techniques, enterprise culture, reduced power for trade unions
Finance	City of London and short-termism	Will Hutton	Longer-term investment within a developmental state
Institutions	Overload	Mancur Olson, Anthony King, David Marquand	State as problem or state as solution?

the idle aristocracy, the middle classes opted for gentrification rather then industry. For Corelli Barnett the victory in the Second World War merely masked the endemic social and economic weaknesses that were beginning to become apparent before the war. The crucial period for him was between the 1870s and the 1940s when a: 'high minded but essentially hopeless' elite was produced in public schools (Barnett 1984: 37).

The post-war period became one of missed opportunities as Britain declined when it could have been putting in place the infrastructural and industrial changes necessary to compete with other countries in Europe and beyond. Perhaps too the impact of war can be considered in other ways. We must not forget that during the First World War 30% of British men aged between 20 and 24 in 1914 were killed. In *Our Age* Noel Annan wrote that: 'The shock of the losses stunned the British; and the lesion of trench warfare and its toll never healed'.

There are, however, some weaknesses with this cultural explanation. If the educated elite were quite so hopeless then why did Britain become the workshop of the world in the 19th century and the world's leading imperial power too? Presumably the elite at this time shared much in common in terms of their educational and social background with those that so messed things up after the war. Why was the British elite so singularly useless? In Germany the Prussian aristocracy were a driving force behind industrialisation (Moore 1966).

Even though we may doubt some elements of the cultural critique, there are reasons to take it seriously. In historical terms the work of Wiener possessed the merit of exploring questions of culture that were often neglected. Wiener became something of an academic celebrity with his book on British economic decline with Sir Keith Joseph and other like-minded Conservatives in the early 1980s keen to develop Weiner's ideas about anti-industrial attitudes and the role of the state. The cultural explanation for British decline was thus an influence on the intellectual progenitors of Thatcherism.

Empire

Did Empire provide a cushion against change? Did imperial grandeur prevent the kinds of changes that were necessary if Britain was to adapt to the challenges of the 20th century. Paul Kennedy (1988) in his book on the rise and fall of great powers refers to this syndrome as 'imperial overstretch'. Eric Hobsbawn (1968) argued that Empire was indeed a cushion that meant that the need for innovation and modernisation were neglected. Andrew Shonfield (1958) linked decline to Empire, the role of sterling and the cost of trying to maintain a world role.

That said, while there was evidence of decline in sectors of the economy such as manufacturing, some economic sectors such as finance and commerce continued to thrive as Britain entered a period of post-imperial decline. Rubinstein (1993) attributes a lot of the agonising to a 'post-Suez malaise' which, as we saw in the previous chapter, brought home the reality of Britain's diminished status in world affairs. Although Rubinstein contends that Thatcherism was successful because it marked a return to traditional strengths in financial services.

Arguments about the effects of Empire have been developed in other ways by sociologists such as Stuart Hall (1988) who focused on an embattled post-imperial national identity. The question of national identity, or to be more accurate national identities within a multinational and multicultural state has also been to the fore in discussion of decline and renewal in Britain (Favell 2002).

Industry

The focus here was on poor management and bad industrial relations. The so-called 'British disease' of workplace unrest and class struggle was powerfully satirised in the classic Boulting Brothers film, *I'm Alright Jack* (1959). Poor management is represented by the character of Stanley Windrush played by Ian Carmichael, newly graduated from Oxford, and to the horror of his upper class family, seeking a career in industry. Despite displaying no aptitude at all and experiencing a series of interview disasters, Windrush eventually finds employment in his uncle's armaments factory, but has to start on the shopfloor and work his way up within a structure that resembles the rigid, hierarchical and class-based structure of the British army. The workers are represented as bone-idle and strongly resistant to any measures that might improve efficiency. Union leader Fred Kite, played by Peter Sellers, is engaged in a permanent class struggle while fiercely resisting changes to the status quo. Industrial relations break down when Stanley is ostracised by fellow workers for 'an accidental display of efficiency'.

In more restrained fashion, academic analyses of decline compared British management and production techniques unfavourably with those in Germany and Japan (Elbaum and Lazonick 1986; Dintonfass 1992). A particular target for the Thatcher governments was the trade unions whose powers were dramatically reduced by industrial relations measures introduced in the 1980s and 1990s.

Finance and the dominance of the City of London

The influence of finance and the City of London has long been a bone of contention. Rubinstein's (1993) argument that British strengths had always lain with finance meant that the Thatcherite emphasis on finance and the City of London was a return to traditional strengths. For Will Hutton, on the other hand: 'The story of British capitalism is at heart the peculiar history of the destructive relationship between finance and industry' (Hutton 1996: 112). For Hutton this dominance bred endemic weaknesses because of a fixation on short-term returns rather than longer-term investment. Hutton's *The State We're In* and *The State to Come* (1995, 1997) were attacks on Thatcherite remedies to decline which, according to Hutton, exacerbated problems of social exclusion and highlighted the endemic weaknesses of key British political institutions. Historical reasons for this were traced to the 19th century by Tom Nairn (1979: 53) who described the late 19th century: 'defeat of industrialism by an older more powerful and more political bourgeoisie. This was, of course, the southern, London-based elite, first mercantile and then financial in its interests' this: 'strong hegemonic bloc then colonised and took over the growing state power of the Edwardian decade and afterwards'. This view has been criticised by Jonathan Clark (2000) for its overly stark portrayal of the City which, to his mind, conjured images of City types in top hats and smoking big cigars.

Institutional weaknesses and decline

The role of institutions is of course central to the analysis of politics. The relationship of important social and political institutions to the debate about British relative economic decline centres on the issue of whether institutions were part of the solution or whether they were part of the problem. Or put another way, whether the state needed to become better at attaining its objectives, or whether the state should be rolled back to allow market forces to flourish.

One common point amongst analysts of decline has been that weaknesses of industry, management, trade unions and/or the City of London highlighted institutional problems. For some, such as Hutton, the problem was that the state had abrogated responsibility and needed to be more active in countering the effects of market forces. For others, such as

Samuel Brittan, the state was not the solution, it was part of the problem; the state needed to be rolled back in order to un-harness enterprise and innovation.

A more general question here is the impact of institutions and the emphasis that has been placed upon it in both historical and contemporary terms by writers such as Nairn (1977a, 1977b), Anderson (1974) and Hutton (1995). Martin Smith (2000: 196) has, however, been sceptical about general claims about the British state and its institutions. Instead, he argues for contingency whereby, rather than painting a picture that is irredeemably bleak, it may well be the case that contingency has played a key role in the development of the state which: 'has grown in various ways, at different times, for a range of reasons'. Some aspects of this activity might have worked out quite well, others less well. In time, those areas that have been going badly may improve, while areas that are now doing quite well may worsen. Also, a lesson that could be derived from the history of state intervention in Britain over the last 50 years or so may be that the state has not been too successful in achieving its objectives through intervention. That said, those who advocate a dramatic reduction in the influence of the state may neglect important achievements such as the creation of the welfare state, which the majority of British citizens value highly. Caution in the face of 'generalised jeremiads', as Clark (2000) puts it, may be necessary.

The targets of the institutional critique were often parliamentary sovereignty, adversarial politics, the Civil Service, indirect rule and club government (for example, King 1975; Marquand 1988). Some of these targets were satirised brilliantly in the late 1970s and early 1980s by the TV series, *Yes Minister* and *Yes Prime Minister*. Academics' arguments have tended to be divided over whether a state that performed its tasks more effectively was necessary, or whether the real problem was the state itself with an urgent need for reduction in its powers. Central to both these views is, of course, the centrality of the national state. Indeed, arguments that Britain needed a 'developmental state' that would play a key role in the development of long-term infrastructure and the prioritising of growth rather than redistribution may require forms of intervention that would be illegal under EU law, although this may reflect some problems with EU priorities (Marquand 1988; Hutton 1995). The idea of the developmental state can also be located in relation to the work on the British political tradition by W.H. Greenleaf. Greenleaf emphasised the influences of collectivism and intervention rather than laissez-faire within the British political system. Smith (2000) argues that the mistake made by advocates of a developmental state is to confuse the failure of intervention with an unwillingness to intervene. A history of British industrial policy in the 1950s and 1960s would be full of references to intervention through, for example, the National Economic Development Council or the Department of Economic Affairs. All reflected attempts to plan and manage the economy, usually based on consultation with what are known nowadays as 'the social partners' (employers, trade unions and government).

For those interested in rolling back the state, the 'overload thesis' explained the ways in which the state had become overly burdened with tasks that it was not well-equipped to fulfil. This thesis was developed in the work of Anthony King (1975). Overload focused on the ways in which special interests could capture the state and potentially induce some kind of governing crisis. This overload thesis was taken up by those who wished to tackle corporatist structures (or the 'beer and sandwiches' culture of consensus building, as it was also known) and rein in the trade unions (Brittan 1973, 1978). The answer was to roll back the frontiers of the state, as Thatcher put it, through privatisation and liberalisation. There was thus a link between the overload thesis and the new right, which targeted corporatism and the 'beer and sandwiches' culture.

Conclusion

Notions of decline and remedies to it have been powerful mobilising forces in British politics from Joseph Chamberlain at the beginning of the 20th century to Margaret Thatcher and Tony Blair at its end. We began this chapter by raising three questions. First, what exactly was it that declined? We saw that the debate about decline is actually a debate about relative decline because in absolute terms British people were richer during the period of so-called decline than at any other point in history. Second, if decline did occur then what were its causes? We saw that in the absence of a single agreed meaning of decline then different interpretations of decline have been advanced that focus on culture, industry, empire, finance and institutions. Each may make some contribution to our understanding of relative decline, but also to our understanding of the ways in which decline was politically constructed by, for instance, the new right, as part of a set of arguments about the need to change the role of the state and reduce the power of trade unions. Finally we asked whether or not decline has now been arrested? This is a difficult question to pin down when it is not clear what declined. However, perhaps there is another dimension to this question that makes us think about the 'national' base of the debate about decline. Debates about relative decline may now been superseded by new debates about globalisation and multi-level governance. The debate about decline was a debate about *national* decline defined by the state, its territory and its people. In the 21st century the role of the state, the organisation of the state as a result of devolution and British national identity because of the development of a multicultural society have all changed.

KEY POINTS

- The idea of relative decline has had powerful effects on British politics.
- Different authors have had different ideas about what declined and why.
- It is widely agreed that the focus of the debate needs to be on relative decline.

- A key element of Thatcherism was that it provided a particular remedy to the problem of decline based on a particular perceptions of its causes.
- The origins of Thatcherism and New Labour can be related to a discussion of the causes of relative decline.

KEY QUESTIONS

(1) Explain what is meant by the term relative decline.

(2) Which explanation for Britain's relative decline do you find most useful?

(3) In what ways did interpretations of the causes of British decline influence Thatcherism?

(4) Are debates about British decline still relevant in the 21st century?

IMPORTANT WEBSITES

Useful sources for research and ideas about British relative decline can be found on the websites of the Institute for Historical Research www.history.ac.uk/ and the Centre for Contemporary British History http://icbh.ac.uk/.

FURTHER READING

There are a number of classic sources on the politics of decline. Most of these have particular takes on the issues and advance particular remedies based on this understanding. See, for example, A. Sampson (1962) *The Anatomy of Britain*, London: Hodder and Stoughton and (1965) *The Anatomy of Britain Today*, London: Hodder and Stoughton; W.D. Rubinstein (1993) *Capital, Culture and Decline in Britain 1750–1990*, London: Routledge. For an overview of debates see R. English and M. Kenny (2000) *Rethinking British Decline* Basingstoke: Macmillan.

 Visit the Online Resource Centre that accompanies this book for links to more information on this chapter topic

CHAPTER EIGHT

European Union institutions

READER'S GUIDE

This chapter analyses a specific aspect of the international context within which British politics is located through an analysis of key ideas underpinning European integration and a look at the EU's own institutional structure. We analyse these ideas and institutions because they have become integral components of the British political system. They are representative of a 'multi-levelling' of British politics whereby powers have moved 'up' to Brussels, 'down' to devolved government and 'out' to agencies and private companies and change the ways we think about the traditional loci of power within the British political system— Whitehall and Westminster. While discussing the more technical aspects of their role, the chapter also highlights why these roles have generated controversy in the UK. These themes are then taken forward in the following chapter which examines EU policy responsibilities and their relationship to policies pursued in Britain.

Introduction

We saw in Chapter 6 that during the 1950s, 1960s and 1970s Britain's political leaders made a reluctant choice for Europe. This chapter takes this historical discussion further by looking at EU institutions. We will analyse the main EU institutions (the Council, the European Parliament, the Commission and the European Council), their roles, how these have evolved and how they have been affected by important recent developments such as EU enlargement. We will also analyse what implications European integration has for some of the core ideas that underpin any discussion of Britain and European integration, such as that of 'national sovereignty'. We explore institutions and ideas because taken together they are now part of the British political process and we need to know how they work and have some understanding of the terms of debate about their role and development. By doing so, we avoid the perils of pretending that European integration is some kind of technical exercise when it is clear that it contributes in quite fundamental ways to how we understand British politics. So, while we learn about these institutions and what they do, we also think more broadly about Britain's role in the EU. At its heart, the debate about Britain and Europe is deeply and intensely political. But if we focus on just the formal aspects of the roles of EU institutions, then these political issues are lost in technical discussion. If we are to understand what many now refer to as the 'Europeanisation' of British politics (which is the topic we analyse in Chapter 9) it is necessary to also understand the development of European integration, the ideas that underpin it and then be able to relate these to the British political context (Geddes 2004).

Key ideas

What is at stake when a country joins the European Union? For some opponents of the EU, membership fatally compromises the history, institutions and traditions of member states and ends self-government. For supporters, Europe offers a forum for sustained interaction between participating states to create peaceful relations in a once war-troubled and divided continent while addressing the common problems that these countries face (Holmes 1996; Leonard and Leonard 2002).

The gap between opponents and supporters of European integration is wide, but they would probably agree on one thing: European integration has been of great significance in British politics for more than 30 years. Yet, what both opponents and supporters alike might also find rather troubling—particularly given the intensity of their own opinions on European integration—is that 'Europe' has rarely been a salient concern for the electorate as a whole. If anything, European economic and political integration has seemed a rather technical issue concerned with matters of 'low politics' such as the creation of a single European market. This is no longer the case because EU politics is now also 'high politics' with questions such as economic and monetary policy, foreign affairs, defence, immigration and asylum at the top of the EU agenda (Hoffmann 1965). This move from low to high politics helps explain why the debate about European integration has acquired such intensity, particularly since the negotiation of the Maastricht Treaty in 1991 and the subsequent 'uncorking' of popular opposition to Maastricht (Franklin, Marsh and McLaren 1994). That said, it is also worth bearing in mind that opinion poll evidence suggests day-to-day issues such as education, health care, employment and law and order are still the basis of British electoral politics (Geddes 2002). In fact, despite the EU's growing role, a lack of information about and knowledge of the EU is one of the most interesting features of British public attitudes towards the EU, as we will see in the next chapter. The remainder of this section will provide a guide to the key ideas and concepts that shape Britain's relations with the EU and give some analytical purchase to the question of what is at stake when the EU and British politics are discussed.

European integration can be understood as a process by which treaties between states agreed in international law are turned into laws that bind those states (Stone Sweet and Sandholtz 1997). The result is that within the scope of these treaties participating states cease to be wholly sovereign. EU institutions are central to this process by which treaties are turned into European law. Since 1951 the number of participating states has increased from six to 25 in 2004, with countries such as Bulgaria, Romania and Turkey waiting in the wings. The membership and Treaty basis of the EU are summarised in Tables 8.1 and 8.2 below.

The choice for Europe made by Edward Heath's Government in 1972 and confirmed by a referendum in 1975 has consequences because EU member states participate in a unique

1951 (6)	1973 (9)	1981 (10)	1986 (12)	1995 (15)	2004 (25)
Belgium	Denmark	Greece	Portugal	Austria	Cyprus
France	Ireland		Spain	Finland	Czech
Italy	UK			Sweden	Estonia
Luxembourg					Hungary
Netherlands					Latvia
West Germany					Lithuania
					Malta
					Poland
					Slovakia
					Slovenia

form of supranational governance:

- *Unique* because it is the only international organisation that possesses the capacity to make laws that bind member states and their citizens.

- *Supranational* because it has its own institutions located 'above' the nation-state and located mainly in Brussels, Strasbourg and Luxembourg.

- *Governance* because European integration contributes to a multi-levelling of British politics with power and authority exercised at points beyond Whitehall and Westminster, the traditional foci of British political analysis.

When Britain joined what was then known as the European Community back in 1973 it joined a Community with aspirations. Even though the scope of the treaties at that time was quite limited and mainly focused on the Common Market and Common Agricultural Policy, the founder members had much grander aspirations and saw the EC as a mechanism that would gradually build stronger economic and political union across the continent of Europe.

Year	Treaty	Intention
1951	Treaty of Paris	The creation of a common market for coal and steel.
1957	Treaty of Rome	Two treaties of Rome agreed to (i) the creation of a European Economic Community based on a customs union (Common Market) and a Common Agricultural Policy (CAP) and (ii) a European Atomic Energy Authority (Euratom).
1965	Merger Treaty	Bringing together ECSC, Euratom and EEC institutions to create a single EC institutional structure.
1986	Single European Act	Creation of a single European market defined as an area without internal frontiers within which the free movement of people, services, goods and capital would be assured.
1992	(Maastricht) Treaty on European Union	Creation of a European Union to replace the EC with the intention of economic and monetary union, as well as increased EU action in foreign and security policy and justice and home affairs.
1997	Amsterdam	Commitment to build the EU as an area of freedom, security and justice with enhanced powers in the areas of immigration and asylum.
2001	Nice	Aim to reform decision-making procedures prior to further EU enlargement in 2004.
2004	Second Rome Treaty	Puts in place a new EU constitution that seeks to state the EU's basic constitutional principles.

The capacity to make laws is a key defining feature of European integration and central to our understanding of the EU as a supranational system of economic and political integration that has implications for the national sovereignty of participating states. The relationship between European integration and national sovereignty has been central to debates about Britain's relationship with European integration. The trouble is that sovereignty is a slippery concept that means different things to different countries, at different points in time and to different people. It is, therefore, more important to know how the term is used rather than seek a definitive understanding of the term. At its heart, sovereignty is about power, or as Max Weber put it, the monopoly of the legitimate use of violence. By this he meant that a sovereign authority possesses the means to make and enforce laws. We tend to associate the idea of sovereignty with the nation-state. This means that we link law-making and law-enforcement to a particular piece of territory called the state and a people living within it. This leads to a relationship between a state, its territory and its people. This relationship is not constant. For one thing, nation-states are relatively recent creations that only became consolidated as the basic unit of international politics in the 19th century. For another, the nation and the state may not be the same thing. States and their borders can change and within these borders may live people who do not identify with what ostensibly is 'their state'. Britain is, of course, a multinational state. There are within some EU member states 'sub-state nations'. In Spain, Catalan and Basque identities show that national identity is not co-terminus with the borders of the state in the same way as British need not necessarily constitute an expression of national identity for the English, Scots, Welsh and Irish in the UK. The state and its sovereign authority can thus be challenged from below by separatist movements while they can be challenged from above by developments such as European integration. The key point to bear in mind about the understanding of national sovereignty in the UK is that it is closely linked to British history, culture and institutions. There are competing narratives about British history, culture and institutions with those who are either pro or anti the EU having very different understandings of Britain, its history and its place in the world.

The particular challenge to the nation-state that arises from European integration is linked to the fact, already mentioned, that a unique distinguishing feature of the EU is that it possesses the power within the scope of the treaties to make and enforce laws. This does not mean that the EU has replaced the nation-state. What it does mean is that the sovereign authority of states (understood as their power to make and enforce laws) has been compromised by the EU's emergence.

It is at this point that controversy arises. The argument could be seen to be between those who advance zero-sum understanding of national sovereignty compared to those who argue for a more positive, non-zero-sum understanding. Yet, if we explore the difference between zero-sum and non-zero-sum understandings of national sovereignty then we begin to see some of the issues at stake when sovereignty is discussed and the fallacy of zero-sum sovereignty. We also begin to see that the debate about sovereignty might actually disguise a more fundamental debate about state power, interdependence and the future of democratic government.

Zero-sum sovereignty is something that a state either possesses or does not possess. There is no middle ground. Sovereignty cannot be shared or pooled because to do so is to break the link between the territory, the state and its people that constitutes the basic and most legitimate unit in international politics. From this zero-sum perspective it is difficult to imagine legitimate forms of government that could exist above the nation-state.

Positive sum sovereignty is not a precious jewel to be guarded. Rather, in some areas, states can better attain their objectives if they work together with other countries to take on the common problems that they face. In other areas states might find their sovereign authority eroded by the operation of the international economy or the impact of international legal standards, such as international human rights laws. Sovereignty can thus be pooled or shared. From a non-zero-sum perspective it is feasible that post-national forms of democratic government can develop. Edward Heath, who as Prime Minister took Britain into the EC in 1973, made clear this idea of 'pooled sovereignty' when he argued in his memoirs that: 'When we surrender some sovereignty, we shall have a share in the sovereignty of the Community as a whole, and of other members in it. It is not just, as is sometimes thought, an abandonment of sovereignty to other countries; it is a sharing of other people's sovereignty as well as a pooling of our own' (Heath 1998: 357).

The essential point is that absolute sovereign authority is unattainable because sovereign states 'have rarely led free and easy lives' as though they could neatly demarcate the domain of their own sovereign authority and seal off external influences (Waltz 1979). Interdependence is a fact of life for modern states that led one analyst to refer to sovereignty as 'organised hypocrisy' in the sense that while it is proclaimed by some as a central political value, it is breached on a daily basis by a multitude of legal, social, economic and cultural processes (Krasner 1999). European integration is one of the ways in which the organised hypocrisy of sovereignty is breached, but so too are the operation of the international economy, privatisation of state activities and the creation of devolved government.

There are also contrasting views of the EU's impact on state power. For some, the creation of supranational institutions can set in train a gradual process of integration that slowly and steadily erodes the power of the nation-state. For others, European integration can actually make the state stronger by allowing it to more effectively attain its policy objectives by working together with other states. From this intergovernmental point of view, European integration makes member states stronger because they can achieve more acting together than they could acting alone (Moravcsik 1994).

While, for obvious reasons, the non-zero-sum conceptualisation of national sovereignty has tended to prevail in British debates about European integration, within this non-zero-sum outlook are very large differences regarding the legitimate scope for EU action and the role of the member states. It can be useful to distinguish between 'formal' and 'informal' sovereignty where the formal attribution of sovereignty to a state may actually not conform with the day-to-day challenges to this sovereign authority that emanate from the 'outside' such as the impact of globalisation (Wallace 1986). One example of this distinction between formal and informal sovereignty is the relaxation of capital controls by the first Thatcher Government, which reduced the power over economic life of the national government and made the UK economy significantly more open to the international economy. This decision deliberately reduced the ability of the British government to control capital movements and thus has implications for state power and the interests of key groups in British society such as business and the trade unions.

If we move on from the debate about sovereignty and begin to consider views about how the EU should proceed and how it should be organised, the essential difference tends to be between those who favour an *intergovernmental* European Union and those that argue for a more *supranational* or *federal* approach (see Chapter 6). It is here that we see other basic tensions about the EU's future role, scope and direction.

- Intergovernmentalists would be prepared to cede power and responsibility to the EU in certain areas but prefer to see a decision-making system that enshrines the supremacy of the member states through a reliance on unanimous agreement as the basis for decision-making. For intergovernmentalists, the ability to use a veto if national interests are threatened is very important. European integration should reflect the interests of member states and it is these states that should hold the upper hand. British governments have tended to prefer this intergovernmental vision of Europe's future.

- Federalists would prefer to see much more ambitious steps towards some kind of United States of Europe with a stronger institutionalisation of supranational authority. The essential features would be a constitution that defines the allocation of powers and money between supranational, national and sub-national governments, a bicameral assembly and a constitutional court. European integration can lead to the development of institutions independent of the member states and with substantial powers in their own right that seriously constrain the powers of the member states. British governments have not been enthusiastic about grand designs for a federal Europe.

The EU is, in fact, best understood as being a hybrid institution in that it contains both intergovernmental and supranational elements. In terms of its institutions, as we will see below, the Council and European Council reflect intergovernmentalism within the EU, while the Commission, Parliament and Court of Justice have a more decidedly supranational foundation. While British governments have tended to support more intergovernmental visions of Europe's future, this preference has not always tied in with the views of other member states that have preferred more ambitious federalising initiatives. Indeed, this has often been a cause of tension between more *minimalist* British governments and some more *maximalist* member states, such as the founder six. At its heart is a tension between the interests of states and the interests of an emerging European order centred on the EU as a supranational system. The EU has developed into a powerful and important set of institutions, but underlying it there still remain important debates about the relationship between states and this European order. Put simply, who holds the upper hand? Eurosceptics in Britain fear that too much power has shifted to the EU while Europhiles argue for further development of the EU's role.

As Table 8.2 above shows, over time the role of the EU has expanded. At some points the UK has been a supporter of European integration. For example, in the mid-1980s the Conservative government of Margaret Thatcher was an advocate of single market integration. Since 1997, Labour governments have been enthusiastic advocates of European economic reform, by which is meant market liberalisation. The Conservatives were less enthusiastic about the measures in the area of social, regional, economic and monetary policy that came in the aftermath of the Single European Act. As we will see in the next chapter, Labour's shift to pro-Europeanism since the end of the 1980s was linked to this developing social and regional policy dimension of European integration, but in power Labour's stance on these issues has been ambiguous. Of particular significance since the 1990s has been the shift into areas of 'high politics' that impinge far more directly on state sovereignty. This was best illustrated by the Maastricht Treaty that proposed EMU, more co-operation on foreign and security policy, and co-operation on justice and home affairs (which includes immigration, asylum and policing).

Over time, therefore, there has been the gradual development of competencies at EU level. If we think about what this means then it becomes apparent that the EU is not a foreign policy issue because its responsibilities in areas such as commercial, agricultural, environmental and social policy mean that the effects of European integration can be seen in the domestic political arena too. It is at this point that the term Europeanisation enters the analysis. The increased interest in Europeanisation reflects a shift from interest in European integration understood as the development of common institutions and policies towards an interest in the ways in which European integration then feeds back into the domestic political arena. Europeanisation is thus concerned with the impact on laws, institutions, policies and collective identities of European integration (Radaelli 2000).

To sum up, over the course of more than 30 years, Britain has become much more closely (albeit not always enthusiastically) involved with European economic and political integration. This has led to participation in a unique form of supranational governance with important implications for national sovereignty. British governments have tended to prefer a more intergovernmental vision of the scope and direction of European integration, although this has not chimed with the preferences of other member states, particularly France and Germany that have long been the EU's key players. We now move on to explore the EU's institutional structure, to look at the roles of important institutions and to explore the attitudes of British governments to these institutions.

EU institutions

The EU is a supranational system with independent institutions operating 'above' the member states with the capacity to make laws that bind those states. EU institutions are integral to the process by which treaties between states are turned into laws that bind those states. There are four main EU institutions:

- The European Commission
- The Council (of Ministers)
- The European Parliament
- The European Court of Justice (ECJ)

As we observe below, the EU's institutional structure is hybrid because it contains both intergovernmental and supranational elements. For example, the Council is composed of the member states and brings the interests of those states to the heart of the decision-making process while the European Commission has been seen as a potential engine of European integration because of its powers to propose and implement laws (Hayes-Renshaw and Wallace 1997; Cini 1997; Nugent 2000). For much of the EU's history the Council and Commission shared legislative and executive power, but since the 1990s the European Parliament has become a far more significant institution even though that has not necessarily been reflected in turnout for its elections or public knowledge of its activities.

Where does power lie within the EU?

Analysis of EU institutions could logically proceed from the identification of legislative, executive and judicial roles. The problem is that these are not as straightforward as might first seem because they are blurred.

- The Council performs both executive and legislative roles (shared with the European Parliament in a growing number of areas) as it is a forum for intergovernmental negotiations and law-making.
- The Commission has an executive role linked to policy implementation, but shares these powers with the Council in a 'dual executive'.
- The European Parliament has legislative powers but shares them with the Council.
- The ECJ performs a judicial role. A frequent mistake is to confuse the ECJ based in Luxembourg and linked to the EU with the European Court of Human Rights (ECHR) based in Strasbourg and linked to the Council of Europe. These are different courts, in different cities, in different international organisations. The ECJ operates within the supranational EU system and is mainly focused on economic matters while the ECHR is within the intergovernmental Council of Europe and has a much stronger focus on human rights questions.

The European Commission

The European Commission is a unique, multinational and multi-lingual international institution employing around 20,000 people, mainly in Brussels. Before we become too enthralled with the overblown language of a Brussels superstate it is worth bearing in mind that with around 20,000 staff, the European Commission employs fewer people than the City of Birmingham, but must administer an EU with around 450 million citizens. Many of the European Commission's problems stem from its small size which hinders its ability to perform key tasks.

What does it do?

The most common mistake made about the European Commission is that 'faceless Brussels bureaucrats' make laws. The Commission's roles are to propose and dispose, which means to make policy proposals and to implement measures agreed by the Council and the European Parliament. The Commission has the sole right of initiative except in the areas of common foreign and security policy and co-operation on judicial and police matters where the member states share the power of initiative with the Commission. Coupled with the power to make policy proposals is the responsibility to implement legislation. The Commission is regularly criticised for implementation failings, but it is important to bear in mind that it is reliant on co-operation from implementing agencies in member states. Because there is a strong 'national' dimension to implementation, its management is shared with the Council within a 'dual executive'.

In addition to proposing and disposing, the Commission manages the EU's finances (which amount to about 1.005% of the combined national income of the member states). The Commission also acts as an external representative of the member states in international negotiations such as world trade talks where the EU speaks with one voice. Finally, the Commission can act as the conscience of the EU and an honest broker because it is meant to transcend national interests and represent the European, common interest (Nugent 2001).

There is no single model of European public administration from which the Commission can draw. Rather, if we were to seek a parallel it would probably be with the French Civil Service that plays a more political role compared to the studied neutrality of the British Civil Service.

Who are they?

The institutional changes that accompanied the May 2004 enlargement saw the number of Commissioners increase from 17 to 25. The main change was instead of the 'big five' member states (France, Germany, Italy, Spain and the UK) having two Commissioners each, there would instead be one Commissioner from each member state. Between 1999 and 2004, the British Commissioners were former Labour Party leader, Neil Kinnock who was charged with the difficult task of reforming Commission management structures, and former Conservative Party chair and Governor of Hong Kong, Chris Patten, who was responsible for external relations. To call them the 'British Commissioners' might be slightly misleading because Commissioners swear an oath of loyalty to the European Union and are not supposed to be national representatives within the Commission. That said, it is no bad thing if Commissioners are in touch with national politics because this can offer a more acute sense of the European art of the possible. The British Commissioner between 2004–09 is ex-Trade and Northern Ireland secretary, Peter Mandelson. Mandelson was given the heavyweight task of external trade relations, by incoming Commission President Eduardo Barroso. This is a big and important job because the EU speaks with one voice represented by the Commission in world trade talks.

How is it organised?

The 25 Commissioners meet each week in the College of Commissioners chaired by the Commission President. Each Commissioner has his own personal cabinet. The day-to-day work of the Commission is conducted within Directorate Generals that have responsibility for key EU policies such as competition, agriculture, external relations, social policy, regional policy, and so on. The absence of a European model of public administration from which the Commission can draw because of the diverse traditions within the member states has proved a problem in the face of allegations of mismanagement and fraud because of suspicion that reform could be a vehicle for an 'Anglo Saxon' management culture alien to administrative traditions in some member states (Stevens and Stevens 2000).

The Commission aroused the ire of British Eurosceptics because it was seen as an engine of integration by stealth concocting plans for integration behind the backs of the member states. In fact, the growing distrust of the EC, and the Commission in particular, is evident in Margaret Thatcher's memoirs as she writes that by 1988 she 'had by now heard about as much of the European ideal as I could take' (Thatcher 1993: 473).

The Commission, particularly during the leadership of Jacques Delors between 1985 and 1994, played a prominent role in debates about the future of Europe. Indeed, Delors became a leading figure in British politics. This manifested itself in a number of ways. In 1988 he gave an impassioned plea at the British Trades Union Congress calling for the British labour movement to engage with European integration. This angered Margaret Thatcher who resented the idea of the Commission President speaking to an organisation she saw as 'the enemy within'. Delors became a bogeyman for right-wing Eurosceptics and even made the front page of *The Sun* newspaper who declared 'Up Yours Delors' on their front page and at one point in a subtle commentary on EU politics advised 'hop off you frog'.

The challenges for the Commission became rather different during the 1990s. Rather than advancing the cause of European integration, the Commission had to deal with serious internal management and administrative problem, as well as the weak leadership of Commission Presidents Jacques Santer (1995–99) and Romano Prodi (1999–2004). In fact, the entire Commission resigned in March 1999 in the face of embarrassing disclosures about mismanagement and, in the case of one Commissioner, nepotism.

With these difficulties and in light of the institutional changes introduced by the Maastricht and Amsterdam treaties, the traditional focus on the Commission and Council as the key EU institutions must be supplemented by consideration of the relationship between the Council and the European Parliament, institutions to which we now turn.

The Council

The Council plays a key role within the EU's hybrid institutional structure because it acts as a forum for member states. In these terms it could be seen as a manifestation of inter-governmental power at the heart of the EU. On the basis of Commission proposals, the Council acts as a forum for collective decision-making. Since the Single European Act of 1986 there has been a growth in issues determined by qualified majority vote (QMV), which means that for some issues, the national veto has gone while for others, such as taxation and social security, it remains. In this section we look at the Council's organisation, its decision-making procedures and the implications of more use of QMV.

Although we speak of the Council there are in fact a series of Councils organised along sectoral lines. So, if the issue is agriculture (as it often is) then agricultural ministers will go to Brussels. Similarly if economic and financial matters are to be discussed then it is finance ministers who make the trip. Some configurations of the Council meet more often than others because they deal with issues that are at the core of EU action. For example, the General Affairs Council composed of foreign ministers meets monthly while finance ministers and agriculture ministers also have the opportunity to get to know each other well. Some issues such as health care and education remain primarily national and the Council meets far less often in these configurations. Since the 1990s EU activity has spilled over into areas that were the domain of the Foreign Office or the Home Office. This means that in areas of high politics covered by these ministries there is now sustained and frequent interaction with colleagues in other member states. The significance of this inter-action should not be under-estimated. The former Head of the European Secretariat within the Cabinet Office, Sir Stephen Wall (2002: 16), identified the impact of European integration on Whitehall thinking:

> When I was dealing with European issues in the early 1980s, you had two or three departments that really knew about Europe: the Foreign Office . . . . The Ministry of Agriculture . . . and the DTI. Now when we have discussions in Whitehall, clearly we have British positions, but we also (and majority voting has been a factor) have learnt that you can't just say 'well this is the British position'. You have to say 'who are our allies?' 'How do we make alliances?' 'What is the endgame going to look like?'

It has become commonplace even in areas of high politics such as foreign policy, immigration and asylum to see these issues in European perspective. This does not mean that the scope for national action has gone, but that these issues are now understood as having an EU dimension.

What does the Council do?

It can be hard to know what the Council does. Even though it performs a legislative role, it makes its decisions in secret. This secrecy is because the Council is both a legislature and a forum for inter-state negotiations. Member states prefer to keep their bargaining secret. TV cameras are admitted for the preliminary sessions where the politicians meet and greet each other. There has also been more effort to make documents available from the Council website.

Council meetings could seem rather chaotic with 25 different national delegations around a table with ministers and officials from the member states supplemented by officials from the Commission and the Council's own secretariat. There could be around 150 people in the room. As the meeting progresses people may leave or enter, depending, for example, on the issue that is being discussed or something more mundane such as when their flight is leaving. There is also a small army of translators ensuring the proceedings are comprehensible to all participants. Indeed, language has been a tricky and controversial issue because of the number of official languages and because English has become a de facto working language—much to the chagrin of the French. English tends to be the second language in the accession states, which has confirmed its dominance. From within this scene the Council plays a key role as a forum for negotiation, a legislator and, with the Commission, as a branch of the dual executive. The procedures by which decisions are made are central to understanding the Council's role.

How are decisions made?

While the EU may attract a lot of criticism in the UK, it is worth reflecting for a moment on the remarkable change in international relations that it embodies. Would it have been thought possible 40 or 50 years ago that 25 European countries could have ceded aspects of their sovereign authority to participate in a unique form of supranational governance? This does not get to the nitty gritty of how decisions are made, but it could be seen as quite remarkable that we do now discuss this nitty gritty.

There are two key developments in EU decision-making. One has been the increased use of QMV while the other has been the increased role of the European Parliament, which we consider in the next section. As its name suggests, QMV is not a simple majority system. Rather it is a weighted voting system that gives more votes to larger member states. The QMV system was re-weighted prior to the 2004 enlargement to reflect the concerns of larger member states such as France, Germany and the UK that too much voting power resided in the hands of small states and that a minority of the EU population could outvote a majority.

British governments have tended to prefer intergovernmental decision-making but have also realised that if goals such as single market integration and economic reform are to be attained then this can require QMV otherwise issues could be blocked in the Council for ever. Many key single market objectives are subject to QMV, but sensitive issues such as taxation and social security remain subject to unanimity.

The distribution of votes within the Council is shown in Table 8.3 below.

3 votes	Malta
4 votes	Cyprus, Estonia, Latvia, Luxembourg, Slovenia
7 votes	Denmark, Finland, Ireland, Lithuania, Slovakia
10 votes	Austria, Sweden
12 votes	Belgium, Czech Republic, Greece, Hungary, Portugal
13 votes	Netherlands
27 votes	Poland, Spain
29 votes	France, Germany, Italy, UK

For a qualified majority vote to be successful it requires:

- 71.3% of votes cast
- At least half the member states
- At least 62% of the total population

This 'triple lock' introduced by the Nice Treaty in 2001 ensures that the hurdles to be cleared are high before legislation can be enacted within the Council.

While the Council clearly has a key role in EU decision-making it is also relevant to note that the European Parliament's powers have increased in recent years. This could be seen as signalling the emergence of a bicameral legislative system with the Council as an upper chamber representing the states and the Parliament as a lower chamber representing the peoples of Europe.

The European Council

Since 1974 the work of the Council has been supplemented by the European Council. The European Council brings together the heads of government and/or state from all the member states. They meet at least twice a year in the member state that holds the Council presidency (the Council presidency rotates on a six-monthly basis. The UK held it in 1998 and again in 2005). The European Council's role is to provide the EU with political leadership at the highest level. This means that some of the biggest decisions in EU history, such as the negotiation of the Maastricht Treaty were finalised at European Council. Indeed, the Maastricht Treaty has that name because it was negotiated in the European Council meeting held in the eponymous Dutch city. The focus of the European Council is not on detail, but on trying to conclude those history-making agreements that set the course of European integration. This also requires vision and leadership from EU leaders, which is a quality that is not necessarily always apparent.

The European Parliament

The June 2004 elections to the European Parliament were probably most notable in the UK for the success of the UK Independence Party. Indeed, one of their 10 MEPs, the ex-daytime TV host, Robert Kilroy-Silk, pledged to wreck the European Parliament (although he resigned the UKIP whip only four months after the election and formed his own party, Veritas, which he then left shortly after its dismal 2005 general election performance). This particular expression of political ambition was probably not what Europe's leaders had in mind when direct elections to the European Parliament were instigated. Indeed, pro-Europeans hoped that direct elections would give more democratic input to decision-making and boost the EC/EU profile in the member states.

Prior to the introduction of direct elections in 1979, members of the Common Assembly as it was first known, were usually national parliamentarians sent to Brussels, Strasbourg and Luxembourg (confusingly the Parliament has three locations, hence 'the multi-site problem'). The growth in European Parliament powers can be linked to a concern about the EU's so-called 'democratic deficit' which can be taken to mean that the transfer of powers from national to supranational level has not been accompanied by transfers of scrutiny and accountability. At a more theoretical level, the role of the European Parliament can also be linked to the possibility of democratic government above the nation-state and the means by which this could be achieved. While views differ on the practicality and desirability of such an endeavour, it is—to return to an earlier point— remarkable that we should be having this discussion at all in a previously war-torn and divided continent.

The basic evolution of the European Parliament's powers can be described in eight words: from *consultation* to *co-operation* and then to *co-decision*. The *consultation* process was the procedure that determined (and limited) the Parliament's role until the Single European Act. The European Parliament had to be consulted and its opinion sought on each Commission proposal, but the Council made decisions and could ignore the Parliament's view.

The Single European Act introduced the *co-operation* procedure which gave the Parliament the power to suggest amendments to Commission proposals in certain areas mainly linked to the creation of the European single market. The Council did not have to accept these (although it was easier to accept them than to reject them) but the Parliament was given heightened status within the decision-making system.

The *co-decision* procedure was introduced by the Maastricht Treaty and, as the name suggests, in certain areas, gives the Parliament the status of co-decision-maker alongside the Council. The process is lengthy (the description of the procedure on the Parliament's own website runs to 30 pages) but for an increasing number of policy issues it does give the Parliament a central role in EU decision-making. Thirty-two Treaty articles ranging from prohibition of discrimination on grounds of nationality (Article 12) to the independent supervisory body for the protection of personal data (Article 286) are covered by co-decision. Items such as immigration, asylum, taxation and social security remain within the consultation process.

Aside from its role in decision-making the most important issue for the European Parliament is turnout in its elections. The dilemma is that European Parliament elections are 'second order' elections, which means that, as with local government elections, they do not change national governments (Reif and Schmitt 1980). This also means that they can be a vehicle for protest votes both against the EU and national governments. The protest vote can have a magnified effect if turnout is low. This was the case in the 2004 elections in the UK when the UK Independence Party secured 16.7% of the vote cast and returned 10 MEPs to the European Parliament. Turnout in the UK for the June 2004 European elections was 38.8%, which is low but was an improvement on the 24% that voted in 1999. Experiments with all postal votes were seen as boosting turnout, although were also controversial with allegations of fraud. Table 8.4 maps turnout across the EU.

The role of the European Parliament increased through the development of the co-decision procedure to the extent that it does make sense to speak of an emergent bicameral system with the Council and Parliament as the two legislative chambers in

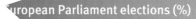

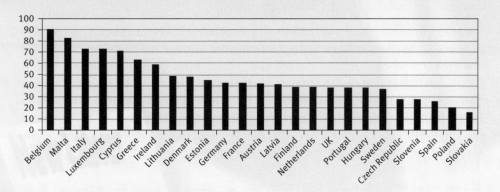

uropean Parliament elections (%)

Source: European Parliament, www.elections2004.en.int/ep-election/sites/en/index.html

those areas covered by co-decision. Increased powers for the Parliament can often be advocated as a quick and easy solution to the 'democratic deficit', but if turnout and levels of interest in its activities are low then a path that trades off power against legitimacy could be a risky strategy. The underlying issue is whether a strong sense of identification can develop across the EU with 'post-national' democratic processes (see Warleigh 2003).

The European Court of Justice

The ECJ plays a vital role in European integration. For Eurosceptic opponents in the UK, the ECJ has been a federalising and political court pursuing an agenda of European integration. For pro-Europeans, the ECJ is a vital institution ensuring that the laws agreed by the member states are implemented properly and that European law is respected. From a more scholarly perspective, the ECJ has been identified as creating the parameters of European economic and political integration through landmark decisions that have played a particularly important role in creating and sustaining the single European market (Burley and Mattli 1993; see also Dehousse 1998).

As noted earlier the Luxembourg-based ECJ must be distinguished from the European Court of Human Rights located in the French city of Strasbourg. The basic difference is that the ECJ has played a particularly important role in shaping the parameters of economic integration. This is hardly surprising when it is borne in mind that the principal impetus behind the EU has been economic in the sense of building the Common and later Single Markets. The ECJ interprets the treaties, seeks to identify breaches of Community law, and can decide whether European legislation is valid or not. The ECJ's powers rest upon two principles:

- community law overrides national law
- national law must be changed if there is a conflict.

The principle of *supremacy* was confirmed in English law in 1974 in the case of *Aero Zipp Fasteners v YKK Fasteners* when Mr Justice Graham stated that: 'relevant Common Market Law should be applied in this country and should, when there is a conflict, override English law'. The *Factortame* case (1990) saw a Spanish fishing company successfully argue that it was being unlawfully denied access to UK fishing waters because of restrictions on foreign companies using ships registered in Britain. The 1990 decision of the European Court of Justice in favour of the Spanish company meant that the 1988 Merchant Shipping Act was struck down because it contravened Community law.

Conclusion

Over 30 years European institutions such as the Council, the European Council, the Commission, the Court of Justice and the Parliament have become part of the British political process. They are not simply the home of things that happen 'over there' in Brussels, Luxembourg or Strasbourg because their decisions hit home and have reshaped British politics, as well as the ways that they are analysed. This could be seen to indicate a certain 'multi-levelling' of British politics as powers move 'up', 'down' and 'out'. It could be seen as indicative too of the shift from government as formal structure to new patterns of governance that go beyond the formal boundaries of the state (Marsh, Richards and Smith 2001). While it is important to understand the roles of the various EU institutions—and we have outlined the responsibilities of the leading five—we also need to know how they relate to the issue of national sovereignty, which is often seen as the key issue when European integration is discussed. We explored the meaning of this term quite closely, but also saw that behind discussion of sovereignty lie the questions of power, interdependence and democracy, which are touchstone issues in British politics. This also reveals that, while we need to know some of the more mundane technicalities, we also need to understand why, when and how European economic and political integration can be controversial. This chapter has shown that this is because the EU is a unique form of supranational governance that challenges national sovereignty as traditionally understood in British politics and by doing so exposes basic tensions concerning the power of the state, its level of interdependence and the future of democratic government. We now take these themes forward as we explore EU policy responsibilities and focus on debates about Europe in Britain with a particular focus on events since the late 1980s, when Euroscepticism emerged as a significant force in British politics.

KEY POINTS

- Britain has at times been a reluctant and awkward EU member state.

- EU institutions and policies have become an important part of the British political process.

- Changing patterns of governance in the UK cannot be accounted for without some consideration of the EU's role.

- European integration has been particularly focused on economic integration through the Common Market, then the Single Market and, more recently, EMU.

- The move into areas of high politics such as foreign, defence, immigration and asylum policies has generated a lot of controversy.

- Europe became one of the key defining issues in British politics in the 1990s.

- Much of the debate about Europe centres on understandings of sovereignty.

KEY QUESTIONS

(1) How relevant to the analysis of British politics is the concept of national sovereignty?

(2) Is it accurate to describe Britain as an 'awkward partner'?

(3) What factors influence public attitudes to European integration in Britain?

(4) Can Britain ever be at the heart of Europe?

(5) Why did Euroscepticism become such a powerful force in British politics during the 1990s?

(6) Outline and explain the roles of the European Commission, the European Parliament, the European Court of Justice and the Council of Ministers.

(7) How have treaty changes since the 1990s affected the roles of EU institutions?

IMPORTANT WEBSITES

The EU homepage can be found at www.europa.eu.int. The British government's EU policy can be found at www.fco.gov.uk. An excellent source of news and information about the EU is www.euractiv.com. A UK gateway to EU resources can be found at www.sosig.ac.uk/eurostudies. Research on current issues in European integration is available from the European Integration On-line Papers www.eiop.or.at. The BBC's 'Inside Europe' is also a good source of information at http://news.bbc.co.uk/1/hi/in_depth/europe/2003/inside_europe/default.stm.

FURTHER READING

There are many books EU politics and policy-making. Four of the best are N. Nugent (2003, 5th edn) *The Government and Politics of the European Union*, London: Palgrave Macmillan; S. Hix (2005) *The Political System of the European Union*, London: Palgrave Macmillan; S. George and I. Bache (2001) *Politics in the European Union*, Oxford: Oxford University Press; H. Wallace, W. Wallace and M. Pollack (eds) (2005, 5th edn) *Policy-Making in the European Union*, Oxford: Oxford University Press. On Britain and Europe see, A. Geddes (2004) *The European Union and British Politics*, London: Palgrave Macmillan.

CHRONOLOGY

Milestones in the history of the EU

1948	Congress of Europe
1949	Council of Europe created
1949	Washington Treaty establishes North Atlantic Treaty Organisation
1951	Treaty of Paris establishes European Coal and Steel Community
1957	Treaties of Rome establish European Economic Community and European Atomic Energy Community
1961	Harold Macmillan's Conservative government applies to join the EC
1963	French President de Gaulle rejects British application
1965	Merger Treaty creates common EC institutional structure
1967	Harold Wilson's government applies to join EU, rejected by de Gaulle
1973	Accession of Britain, Denmark and Ireland
1975	'Yes' vote in referendum on Britain's EC membership
1981	Accession of Greece
1984	British budget rebate secured at Fontainebleau summit
1986	Single European Act
1986	Accession of Portugal and Spain
1991	Maastricht Treaty
1995	Accession of Austria, Finland and Sweden
1997	Treaty of Amsterdam
2000	Treaty of Nice
2004	Accession of Cyprus, Czech Republic, Estonia, Hungary, Latvia, Lithuania, Malta, Poland, Slovakia, Slovenia

Visit the Online Resource Centre that accompanies this book for links to more information on this chapter topic

CHAPTER NINE

The Europeanisation of British politics?

READER'S GUIDE

This chapter provides a framework that looks at the policy role of the EU as an important international linkage and as a component of changing patterns of governance in Britain. The focus is on Europe as one source of policy change in British politics and thus on what is commonly referred to as 'Europeanisation'. The aim is not to provide detailed information on EU policies. Rather, the intention is to discuss some key ideas and then to relate these to some continuities in Britain's policy relationships with the EU. Essentially, the argument is that we need to understand current dilemmas as not simply the product of debate at particular points in time (contingent factors such as the Tony Blair–Gordon Brown relationship) but, rather, as having their roots in a series of earlier dilemmas that have had important effects on Britain's relations with the EU (structural factors). The chapter focuses, therefore, on policy implications of European integration and the identification of how, why and when European integration 'hits home', or put another way, the extent to which British politics has become 'Europeanised'.

Introduction

This chapter complements the analysis in Chapter 8 of EU institutions by analysing the policy dimensions of British relations with the EU and, thus, providing further insight into the EU framework within which British politics is now located. This intention to explore some policy implications of European integration which implies a shift in analytical focus from the ways in which Britain has participated in the EC/EU (Britain in Europe) to the effects of European integration on key British policies (Europe in Britain). It is shown that Britain's engagement with core EU policies can be understood as *conditional* in the sense that a full hearted choice for Europe has not been made and *differential* in the sense that European integration affects some policy areas more than others (Geddes 2004). The chapter does not outline and analyse the full range of EU policies in detail. This would be a task for a whole book rather than an individual chapter (see Bache and George 2002). Rather, the aims are fourfold. First, to identify key themes in the development of EU policy responsibilities and then relate these to the policy preferences and interests of successive British governments. Second, to examine core British governmental preferences and address the question of what outcomes British governments have sought to achieve from this venture. Third, to chart the shift from 'low' to 'high' politics in EU policies that occurred since the 1990s and see how this affected British relations with the EU. Finally, to outline scope for tension between policy priorities pursued by British governments and EC/EU priorities.

Rather than analysing the EU as some kind of external constraint, it is more useful to understand the ways in which Britain's choice for Europe has concrete and real manifestations in current policy dilemmas. EU policy has, therefore, become part of the British policy-making and policy implementation process. We need to understand why and how this has been the case and also to understand some of the implications. The argument presented in this chapter is that we need to take domestic politics seriously if we are to understand the ways in which EU policies have affected Britain and then explore the full implications of 'Europe in Britain'.

There is a useful framework in existence that has developed from the work of those interested in the study of Europeanisation. In terms of understanding policy linkages, it has been argued that EU member states such as Britain will seek to 'upload' their policy preferences to the EU level. If they are successful, then the task of 'downloading' EU policies can become easier because there is likely to be a higher degree of fit with the EU framework and the costs of adaptation are lower. If not successful then there can be tensions and misfit (Green Cowles, Caporaso and Risse 2000). The extent to which British governments have been successful players at European level and uploaded national policy preferences can then have a strong influence on the scope for tension between the domestic policy framework and the EU policy framework. We will see that the UK has not always been a successful player of the EU game. There are historical reasons for this and some areas where the UK does not seem to 'fit' too well with broader EU priorities. So, while in some areas such as single market integration, the UK has often been to the fore in pressing for integration, in others, such as the creation of a single currency, the UK stands aside.

Disagreements get far greater media attention than the steadier process of policy co-operation across a broad range of issues that occurs without major problem, or much public debate either. That said, it would be foolish to deny that there have been tensions. After all, there are good reasons why many books on Britain and the EU have words such as 'awkward', 'semi-detached' or 'reluctant' in their title (George 1992, 1998; Gowland and Turner 2000).

Analysing Europe in Britain

Before moving on to explore policy developments at EU level and think about their implications for the UK, we need to lay some analytical foundations. If the aim is to identify and specify the impacts of Europeanisation, then four factors need to be borne in mind. Each relates to the ways in which Britain's relations with the EU are analysed and understood:

(1) Since the 1990s there has been a shift in analytical focus from the creation of EU-level responsibilities to consideration of the ways in which Europe hits home and domestic politics becomes Europeanised. This involves complementing analysis of 'Britain in Europe' with the linked issue of 'Europe in Britain' (Bache and Jordan 2006).

(2) The history of British relations with the EU and the importance of domestic politics need to be factored into the analysis. When Britain joined the club in 1973 key priorities in areas such as the budget and agricultural policy had already been established that were not in Britain's best interests. Britain spent the first 10 years of its membership arguing about the conditions by which it had joined the club. The history of Britain's relations with the EU could be understood as the politics of perpetual catch-up: the UK agonises as new EU priorities are established, by the time the UK signs up—as it usually does in the end—the dogs have barked, the caravans have moved on, and new EU dilemmas confront British governments before previous choices have been properly digested.

(3) The dilemmas of the politics of perpetual catch-up have become more acute since the 1990s as there has been both an intensification of EU activity and a shift from EU activity in areas of 'low politics' such as the creation of the common market that are not seen to directly impinge on national sovereignty to matters of 'high politics' such as foreign policy, economic policy, the single currency, immigration and asylum that are clearly core sovereign concerns for the state. This has then been joined by discussion of a new EU constitutional treaty, although this was put on the backburner following the rejections of the proposed constitution by referenda held in France and the Netherlands in June 2005.

(4) Finally, if history and domestic politics are important then we need to ask a basic question: what have British governments sought from European integration? What has been the perceived British interest in participating in this unique venture in international politics? Perhaps a lack of alternatives rather than a positive choice for

Europe explains the initial applications in the 1960s. Since 1979 the pursuit of market liberalisation on a pan-EU scale has been a British key objective. But this domestic preference does not always rest easily with the policies pursued by other member states. The views of British governments about the respective roles of the state and market can differ from the view held in other member states. Hix (2000) notes that when compared to other member states: 'Britain has lower levels of welfare spending, lower levels of social protection, generally lower wages, more liberal markets … is more open to the global economy and is stronger in certain sectors such as financial services'.

The remainder of this chapter analyses the Europeanisation of UK public policy while accounting for the historical context of British membership, the shift from low to high politics, and a consistent British governmental preference for market liberalisation that has to a significant extent united Conservative and Labour governments. If we take these preferences seriously and relate them to the domestic political setting then we could suppose that apparent major shifts such as the election of the Labour Government in 1997 might not lead to such a dramatic reconfiguration of relations with the EU.

What is Europeanisation?

Conceptual clarity is necessary if we are to understand the ways in which European integration affects British politics. A slight difficulty is that the concept of Europeanisation is broad, applies to many different aspects of political life and can be hard to pin down. That said, to assess *Europeanisation* understood as the impact of European integration on domestic politics we need to think about three questions.

(1) How do we factor domestic politics into analysis of British relations with the EU?

(2) Where would we look for the impacts of European integration?

(3) How can we distinguish the effects of European integration from other sources of political change?

Bringing domestic politics into the analysis

European integration is not a foreign policy issue because its activities relate strongly to domestic politics. Each EU member state can be said to see European integration through a domestic political lens (Bulmer 1983). This means that the history, traditions and institutional structures of member states shape participation and refract the EU's influence.

Where would we look for Europeanisation?

The ways and places in which politics are done and occur could change as a result of European integration. The term 'multi-level governance' has become a useful way of describing the ways in which state-centred versions of political analysis have lost some of their analytical force (Bache and Flinders 2003). Whether we speak of multi-level or multi-locational politics, there are clearly important effects of European integration on law and policy-making in Britain. That said, some areas of law and policy are more affected than others because the EU's remit does not stretch across all policies. The EU's profile is particularly evident in those areas linked to economic integration and related areas such as regional social and environmental policy. When analysing Europeanisation we therefore need to bear in mind that the effects are likely to be *differential* depending on the extent of EU competence in particular policy areas (Geddes 2004). Over time, we could also suppose that the range of issues affected by European integration would increase. In the 1970s, only a small number of UK ministries had much to do with the EU: the Foreign Office because it dealt with day-to-day issues, the Ministry of Agriculture because of the CAP and the DTI because of the Common Market. This has changed. For example, environmental policy is now extensively Europeanised (Jordan 2002). Even an area that appears quintessentially domestic such as the Home Office now has a significant EU dimension because the EU is also active in areas such as immigration, asylum, policing and judicial co-operation.

How do we know when and where Europe makes a difference?

There is a real analytical problem when analysing Europeanisation because there are many possible sources of political change. Only the most determined conspiracy theorist could imagine that all political change in the UK can be linked to the EU. So, while we could ascribe all kinds of changes to the EU and assume that its effects on the British political system are direct and causal, this is likely to be too simplistic. The problem is that we have to distinguish between the EU as a source of domestic political change and other sources of change. To take one example, the EU has developed a stronger regional policy dimension since the 1980s. Since the Labour Government came to power in 1997 the UK too has seen the strengthening of devolved government. But are the two linked? Can we say that the moves by the EU to establish a stronger regional policy dimension have driven change in the UK? There was a strong domestic impulse to the creation of devolved government in both Scotland and Wales that was driven by a sense of national identity and neglect by a London-dominated political system rather than by European Commission ideas about a 'Europe of the regions'. Yet, European integration did give political parties such as the SNP and Plaid Cymru a way to re-imagine a future for Scotland and Wales as small, independent countries in the EU and, more substantively, funds to support regional economic development. European integration can thus be understood as *a* factor but not necessarily *the* factor in explaining domestic political change. If we put this point more broadly, those who analyse British politics tend to do so in the context of 'changing patterns of governance'. European integration is one among many components of these changing patterns of governance.

POLITICS IN FOCUS 9.1

...tures of the Common Market

- Tariffs and quotas were abolished between the (initially) six participating states.
- Within the common market goods, services, capital and workers could move freely.
- An external tariff was imposed on goods and services entering the customs union.

POLITICS IN FOCUS 9.2

...features of the Common Agricultural Policy

- Free movement of agricultural products.
- Community preference meaning that agricultural produce from within the EC would be given preference.
- Financial solidarity meaning a common pricing system and the creation of EC agricultural subsidies.

Core EU policies

This section of the chapter looks at those EU policies which developed in the 1960s. This gives us some historical perspective, which is important because a key argument of this chapter is that the disadvantageous conditions under which Britain joined the club in the first place have had a strong influence on Britain's 'awkwardness' since. The aim is to demonstrate that there have long been sources of tension that pre-occupied Conservative and Labour governments in the 1970s and 1980s.

What kind of club did Britain join in 1973? The three core features were the Common Market, the Common Agricultural Policy and, the budget.

In the 1950s more than 20% of the population of the six member states worked in agriculture. By 2001 this number had fallen to 7.1%, yet the CAP continued to consume

POLITICS IN FOCUS 9.3

...features of the budget

- Levies on goods entering the Common Market.
- Levies on agricultural goods entering the Common Market.
- A proportion of member states' sales tax (or VAT as it is known in the UK).
- A proportion of the national income of the member states.

nearly half the EU budget. This major shift in occupational profiles is one reason why the CAP has become a controversial policy area. Others are that it raises European food prices, has favoured large-scale producers and harmed producers in developing countries. When established, the CAP could be seen as a counterpoint to the creation of the Common Market.

While the Common Market provisions may have offered some advantages to the UK, the CAP had far more negative effects. These become clear when the third component of the EC's identity is considered: the budget. In a snappily entitled Treaty Amending Certain Budgetary Provisions of the Treaties (1970) the founder six member states put in place an EU budget process or 'system of own resources' as it is formally known that disadvantaged the UK.

The UK was disadvantaged because its trade was more globally oriented through strong trade links with the US and the Commonwealth rather than the EC6. Goods entering the UK from outside the EC paid a tariff that was re-directed to become part of the EU's own resources. Also, agricultural levies would raise the prices of agricultural goods entering the EC to those agreed within the CAP. The results were that the UK faced the prospects of being the largest contributor to the EC budget (paying 8.64% of the budget on accession rising to 18.72% in 1977, Geddes 2004: 69) and seeing increased food prices because of the CAP (the estimate was a 15% increase in the six years following accession, HMG 1971). The point is that these priorities were agreed in the UK's absence. For instance, it is hardly a surprise that the CAP reflected the interests of French governments. The costs in this instance of the politics of perpetual catch-up were summarised by Sir Con O'Neill, the official who led UK negotiations during the Conservative Government of Edward Heath, when he noted that the only option for the UK was to 'swallow the lot and swallow it now' (cited in Young 1999: 227).

While the EC clearly had a strong economic profile when the UK joined in 1973, it is important to dispel the myth that the UK joined a Common Market and that all subsequent movement towards political integration has been aberrant from this initial, more limited vision. The ambitions were always intensely political and quite grand. Indeed, a dislike of grand, supranational ventures was of course a key reason why Britain did not join in the 1950s. The 1970–74 Government of Edward Heath played down these implications and spoke of no loss of 'essential' national sovereignty. The obvious point here is the extent of the domain of 'essential' national sovereignty and those points at which it becomes 'non-essential'.

We can now return to our initial discussion of Europeanisation and explore the extent to which the EC measures that the UK had to 'download' as a consequence of accession matched with domestic policy preferences. As an outsider, the UK had no influence on the scope and direction of the EEC set up in 1957 and as it was elaborated during the 1960s. The most obvious sources of tension were the CAP and budget framework. The Labour Government elected in 1974 held a referendum on UK membership of the EC, although the 'renegotiated' terms on which this referendum was held made very little difference to either British budget contributions or the direction of the CAP. The Labour governments of Wilson and Callaghan (1974–79) made it clear that they had little truck with ambitious plans for European integration. Margaret Thatcher saw the business case for membership, but was by no stretch of the imagination a European idealist. She also brought a forthright negotiating style coupled with a determination to deal with the unresolved issue of Britain's budget contributions, or 'get our money back' as she put it. Until this matter was dealt with, the other member states would find it hard to think ahead because Thatcher was determined to ensure that no further agreements on anything substantive could be reached unless the British budget question was resolved.

The relaunch of European integration in the 1980s

The relaunch of European integration in the 1980s provides a good opportunity to explore the limits and possibilities of the Europeanisation of British politics. Moreover it was done at a time prior to the birth of modern Euroscepticism, which as a mainstream force in British politics can be linked to Margaret Thatcher's 1988 Bruges speech. For a time in the mid-1980s the British government was quite enthusiastic about a core component of the EC's agenda, namely the Single European Market.

We can now examine the extent to which Britain during the 1980s was able to 'upload' a domestic policy preference for market liberalisation to the EC level. When it comes to subsequent downloading we see real tension between the vision of Europe expounded by British governments and the views held by many other member states. Put simply, for the UK the single market was an end in itself. For other member states the single market was a means to an end; that end being much deeper economic and political integration that would involve social, regional and economic policies.

Prior to any discussion of future plans for economic and political integration the tricky issue of British budget contributions needed to be resolved. Labour governments had pursued this too, but Margaret Thatcher brought a new intensity and determination to the quest for a British budget rebate. Agreement was finally reached at the Fontainebleau meeting of the European Council held in June 1984. This meeting agreed to a British budget rebate, which still survives. The rebate was 66% of the difference between Britain's VAT contributions to the budget and its receipts. The UK remained a net contributor to the budget, second only to Germany in its level of contributions (HM Treasury, 2002).

The broader significance of the rebate was that it cleared the path to a far ranging review of future plans for economic and political integration. The context for this discussion was some doubt in the late 1970s about whether European integration actually had a future because, in the face of economic recession, the member states had appeared incapable of acing together. But what could be done? Into what areas should European integration move? The UK government at the time of its presidency of the Council of Ministers in 1984 had circulated a paper entitled 'Europe: The Future' that called for single market integration (HMG 1984). Such plans if proposed by one member state alone were unlikely to succeed, but the advantage for plans for the creation of a single market were that:

(1) The West German and French governments were prepared to back the plan. As the two leading players in the EC their backing was crucial.

(2) Influential business interests supported the idea of single market integration because Europe seemed to be falling behind its competitors, particularly in high technology sectors.

(3) Jacques Delors took office as Commission president in 1985 and was keen to pursue plans for further European integration.

There was thus a confluence of interests at national and supranational level that favoured single market integration (Moravcsik 1991). The plan for the single market was contained within the Single European Act of 1986. The two main features are outlined below.

The single market then can be understood as a progressive development from a customs union. Whereas a customs union seeks to allow people, goods, services and capital to move across borders, a single market seeks to remove these borders and create an area without internal frontiers.

There are clearly important implications for national sovereignty of these kinds of developments. Indeed, the SEA could be seen as a dramatic transfer of sovereign authority. Long-standing Conservative Eurosceptics such as Teddy Taylor MP made precisely this case. However, the Conservative Government of the day used their large majority and the 'guillotine' to move the ratification bill swiftly through Parliament.

The Conservative governments of the 1980s had a limited vision of Europe linked to economic integration. The SEA could be accommodated because it tied in with a domestic

ITICS IN FOCUS 9.4
eatures of the EU single market

- Article 8A of the Single European Act defined the single market as an area without internal frontiers which means that physical (e.g. border controls), fiscal (e.g. tax barriers) and technical (e.g. product standards) barriers to movement need to be dismantled
- Goods, services, capital and people would be able to move freely within the single market
  - Free movement of goods meant the abolition of customs duties and charges
  - Free movement of services meant the creation of a right of establishment so that Community nationals and/or Community businesses get equal treatment in other member states
  - Free movement of capital meant that restrictions on capital movements and payments would be removed
  - Free movement for people meant that border controls would be removed.

preference to 'roll back the frontiers of the state'. It was hoped—mistakenly as it turned out—that Thatcherism could be applied across Europe. The reason why this was a mistaken view was that, while the British government saw single market integration as an end in itself, other member states saw it as a means to an end; that end being further economic and political integration. While the UK had been able to upload its preference for single market integration, it also had to deal with plans for further integration in areas such as social, regional and economic policy that were linked to single market integration but were deeply problematic for British governments in the future. The SEA was a dramatic shift in the rules of the game: it expanded the EC's competencies and beefed up its decision-making powers. It was an important shift too in the sovereign authority of the British state. It laid the foundations for many of the tensions and perceptions of misfit between the UK and EC/EU that were to follow and for the rise of Euroscepticism in the Conservative Party.

Policy tensions, misfit and the rise of Euroscepticism

Euroscepticism as a force in British politics can be linked to the events that occurred in the aftermath of the SEA. We see a tension between Thatcherite Conservatism and plans for the development of EU competencies in areas such as social policy.

The EU's social dimension

The Treaty of Rome in 1957 had contained some social policy provisions that, for example, provided for gender equality in the workplace and the creation of a European Social Fund. Following the SEA there was concern that the freedoms given to business by market integration needed to be matched by the efforts to offer protection of workers' rights. This concern was shared by the Commission and by member states with Christian Democrat and Social Democrat governments that adhered to notions of social solidarity rather than Thatcherite ideas about 'rolling back the frontiers of the state'. In the late 1980s, dialogue with the 'social partners' (trade unions and employers) and the plans for beefed-up EU social policy competencies through the non-binding Social Charter of 1989 prompted the development of Euroscepticism as a potent force on the right of British politics. While Conservatives such as Margaret Thatcher had been able to accept European integration because it was seen as good for business, the proposed expansion of competencies in areas such as social policy was seen to threaten domestic policy changes made since 1979. In a seminal speech delivered in the Belgian city of Bruges in September 1988 Margaret Thatcher stated clearly her growing hostility to the direction of European integration.

> **Extract 9.1: from Margaret Thatcher's speech at the College of Europe, Bruges, 20 September 1988**
>
> But working more closely does not require power to be centralised in Brussels or decisions to be taken by an appointed bureaucracy. We have not successfully rolled back the frontiers of the state in Britain, only to see them reimposed at a European level, with a European superstate exercising a new dominance from Brussels.

The Bruges speech was to have dramatic effects on British politics:

(1) It brought Euroscepticism into the mainstream of Conservative thinking from the margins where it had languished.

(2) It provided ideological sustenance for an alliance of leading newspapers and Conservative politicians to pursue the Eurosceptic agenda outlined by Thatcher. European integration was seen as a threat to the British nation-state, or, more particularly, the Thatcherite version of the free economy and the strong state (Gamble 1988).

(3) The ideological critique centred on the EC's state-like aspirations and the idea that it would provide a back door for the re-imposition of legislation governing the work place and trade unions.

(4) It helped impel pro-Europeanism in the Labour Party both because the 'social dimension' was seen to offer something to the Labour Party and the labour movement and because Thatcher's opposition to European integration was seen to create some space on the centre ground of British politics. In 1988 Jacques Delors spoke at the TUC conference and called for the British labour movement to seize the new opportunities offered by European integration.

(5) Ultimately the speech unleashed internal divisions on the issue of Europe that were to contribute to Thatcher's own downfall in 1990 and the Conservative Party's landslide defeats in 1997 and 2001.

Thatcher refused to sign the non-binding Social Charter of 1989 which she saw as inspired by Marxist ideas of class struggle. The non-binding Social Charter was then to form the basis for the proposals brought forward in the Maastricht Treaty for a Social Chapter. Developments were not confined to the social dimension. The pursuit of social and economic cohesion led to an increase in the proportion of the budget spent on regional development policies to grow from 12.5% to 25% of the total between 1988 to 1992 and then to nearer 40% today. Areas such as Merseyside, Northern Ireland, the Scottish Highlands and South Yorkshire were to benefit from increased EC regional development spending, as will be discussed later. Here too there were some tensions with Conservative governments that held dear to the unitary state and had little enthusiasm for devolved government or

Commission-sponsored ideas about a 'Europe of the regions'. Single market integration also rekindled discussion of EMU. In 1988 a committee of European central bankers led by Commission President Jacques Delors produced a report that planned for EMU. This plan was the basis of the Maastricht Treaty EMU provisions.

Maastricht and the shift into 'high politics'

The Maastricht Treaty was a landmark event because it crystallised Conservative opposition to European integration. It also moved European integration into areas of high politics that directly impinged on national sovereignty (Hoffmann 1966). Following Thatcher's political demise in 1990, the new Conservative Prime Minister John Major faced the problem of reconciling strongly divergent strands of thinking within the Conservative Party on the European issue within his own party with the clear intention of leading member states such as the French and the Germans to make a further step in the direction of European unity. The Treaty on European Union agreed at Maastricht in December 1991 was to have dramatic effects on British politics, but as Major left the negotiating chamber at Maastricht his spokesman felt able to proclaim 'game, set and match' for Britain on the basis of:

- an opt-out from the third stage when the single currency would be established of Maastricht's plan for creation of an EMU;
- a refusal to agree to the proposed Social Chapter. The Chapter had to be added to the Treaty as a protocol covering the other 11 member states; and
- the creation of separate 'pillars' covering a Common Foreign and Security Policy (CFSP) and Justice and Home Affairs (JHA).

Amongst its other provisions, Maastricht created a co-decision procedure that would give the European Parliament a bigger say in decision-making alongside the Council and formalised EU environmental policy competencies.

With hindsight, claims of 'game, set and match' appear absurd, but the political fix offered by Maastricht held for the 1992 general election at which the EU barely registered as a topic of debate and at which Major secured a fourth Conservative victory. But a series of events in the summer of 1992 knocked the plan for Treaty ratification off course. First, the Danish people rejected the Treaty in a referendum. Then, in a September 1992 referendum, the French delivered only a '*petit oui*' by a narrow margin of 1% to the Treaty. The killer blow was dealt later that month when on 'black Wednesday' (16 September) the UK was forced out the Exchange Rate Mechanism (ERM), a device designed to link the values of EU member state currencies one to the other as part of the convergence towards creation of a single currency and EMU. The Conservative reputation for economic competence was shattered by the humiliating ejection from the ERM (see Chapter 27; also Stephens 1996). The ERM debacle also impelled Eurosceptic organisation within the Conservative Party. The Maastricht Treaty then limped through a long, agonising and

POLITICS IN FOCUS 9.5
The Maastricht Treaty created a three pillar structure

- The 'Community pillar' was all those activities that had previously been included within the Treaty framework since the Treaty of Rome.
- The second pillar dealt with Common Foreign and Security Policy (CFSP).
- The third pillar dealt with Justice and Home Affairs.
- The idea was that the first pillar would have a strong supranational element with a role for the Commission, European Parliament and European Court of Justice. The second pillar (CFSP) and the third pillar (JHA) would be intergovernmental with a central role played by member states and very limited roles for supranational institutions. Decisions made in the second and third pillars would not have the power of Community law. Other 'softer' mechanisms were created.
- After the Maastricht negotiations, the British claimed that this pillared structure was 'game, set and match' for Britain.
- Other member states disagreed and there has been some erosion of the pillars.
- The Amsterdam Treaty took migration and asylum from the third (JHA) to the first ('Community' pillar), for example.

tortuous ratification process that was only brought to a head in July 1993 when Major 'went nuclear' and turned the issue into one of confidence in his Government.

How can the dramatic effects of the Maastricht Treaty on the Conservative Party be explained and how can this help us understand the limits and possibilities of Europeanisation? The answer to the first part of this question centres on the divergence between British governmental views about the scope, direction and future of European integration and those of other member states and the Commission after the SEA. There was, of course, a longer history of British opposition to the Common Market, but in the wake of the SEA we see the emergence of Euroscepticism with a strong right-wing critique of the implications of European integration for the British state, nation and democracy therein (Forster 2002). Margaret Thatcher's Bruges speech was both a catalyst for this Euroscepticism and a source of validation from the very top of the party for views that had previously resided at the margins.

The second part of the question is equally important because it helps us to explore the impact of European integration on British policies. If we take the domestic political context seriously and, on this basis, consider the ways in which the longer-term patterning of British political life affects relations with Europe then this would incline us towards a view that there are likely to be long-term consistencies in British relations with the EU and that these impose limits on Europeanisation, or put another way, tensions between British policies and EU policies. We can now take this forward and analyse the relations between the Labour governments elected in 1997 and 2001 and EU policies.

New Labour and Europe

Europe was not a prominent theme in Labour's 1997 general election campaign. The determination not to be outflanked by Conservative Eurosceptics made Labour keen to close down discussion of Europe through the pursuit of an 'us too' approach. If the Conservatives were to have a referendum on the single currency then us too, responded Labour (Geddes 1997). That said, Labour had rethought its position on European integration. This rethink led to an ostensibly more positive approach to European integration that had three main sources:

• the EU's social dimension meant that the EU seemed no longer merely a 'capitalist club';

• the Conservative drift to a more Eurosceptic stance created political space in the centre ground of British politics that a 'modernised' Labour Party was keen to fill;

• economically competitive, prosperous and socially cohesive countries such as the Federal Republic of Germany with more consensual models of capitalism influenced New Labour thinking for a time (Hutton 1995).

When elected there appeared scope for a more positive approach to European integration. Blair professed the desire to play a positive, constructive and leading role within the EU. The Labour Government signed up to the Social Chapter and put their signature to the Amsterdam Treaty.

But within this Treaty the UK secured an opt-out from provisions on immigration and asylum, continued to press for CAP reform, made it clear that no concessions would be made on the UK budget rebate, and emphasised the centrality of NATO to European defence policy, albeit following the inadequacy of the EU response to the Kosovo crisis in 1999 with a strengthened EU military capability.

A key reason for this is the misfit between the policies pursued by New Labour in the UK and those pursued in other member states and have been most clearly evident in debates about the Euro (see Chapter 26). The Euro came into circulation in 2002 and by 2004 12 EU member states were members. The UK did not join. Figure 9.1 shows the reasons for this.

The Social Chapter of the 1992 Maastricht Treaty related to aspects of social policy.

John Major's Conservative Government opted out of the Social Chapter.

The Labour Government opted back into the Social Chapter when they came to power in 1997.

Rights included were free movement throughout the EC; 'equitable' remuneration; a maximum number of hours per working week; free association in trade unions and collective bargaining; professional training; sex equality; minimum health and security provision; employer–employee consultation and participation; a minimum working age of 16; minimum pension rights; and protection for disabled workers.

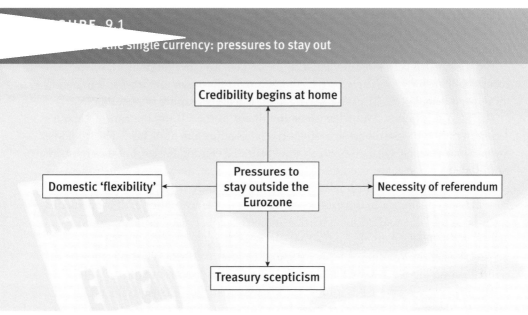

FIGURE 9.1

... the single currency: pressures to stay out

Figure 9.1 highlights reasons for a lack of fit between the UK policy framework and that being pursued by other EU member states. They provide the sub-text for evaluation of the Chancellor of the Exchequer's 'five tests' on whether Britain should join the Euro (see Chapter 27 for further discussion of British economic policy).

Credibility begins at home was the lesson learnt from the 1992 ERM debacle with an emphasis on domestic anti-inflationary policy rather than external mechanisms such as the ERM.

Domestic flexibility refers to the UK emphasis on market liberalisation and a suspicion that, despite EU wide initiatives within the 'Lisbon process', the level of commitment in other member states to market liberalisation and flexibility does not match that in the UK.

- Are business cycles and economic structures compatible so that we and others could live comfortably with euro interest rates on a permanent basis?
- If problems emerge is there sufficient flexibility to deal with them?
- Would joining EMU create better conditions for firms making long-term decisions to invest in Britain?
- What impact would entry into EMU have on the competitive position of the UK's financial services industry, particularly the City's wholesale markets?
- In summary, will joining EMU promote higher growth, stability and a lasting increase in jobs?

The necessity for a referendum means that Blair's large House of Commons majorities become less relevant because the appeal must be made to the court of public opinion and is thus beyond the control of the party whips.

The Treasury has been more influenced by the US than it has by European ideas about how economies function best. There is little enthusiasm for European economic integration in the upper echelons of the Treasury, right up to the Chancellor's office (Dyson 2000).

The Euro is a litmus test of British commitment to the EU. By the end of Labour's second term there was still no sign of when a referendum might be held. This could be linked to the personal tensions between Tony Blair and Gordon Brown, but the argument of this chapter is that we need to dig deeper and look at the ways in which there are longer-term patterns in British relations with the EU that have important influences on current policy dilemmas. In this case, we can see some evidence of the politics of perpetual catch-up as the UK agonised about participation while other member states moved ahead and established the parameters of the EMU. If we see it in these terms, then the politics of perpetual catch-up is a longer-term structural feature of British relations with the EU rather than simply a manifestation of tensions at particular points in time.

The EU barely registered as a topic for discussion at the 2005 general election. The reason for this was that the Conservative Party stopped talking about the EU and started to focus on other issues such as crime, tax and immigration (Geddes and Tonge 2005). By the end of Labour's second term the war in Iraq and disputes about British contributions to the EU budget had led to a deterioration in relations with the French and German governments. The budget question loomed over Britain's EU presidency in the final six months of 2005, but the bigger question was the future of Europe following the rejection of the proposed EU constitution in referenda in France and the Netherlands.

 ## Conclusion

This chapter has sought to outline the developing policy of the EU as an important element of the international context of British politics and as a component of changing patterns of governance. The focus has been on policy change and the relationships between policies pursued in the UK and those practised at EU level. The chapter complements those that have preceded it that attempt to place British politics in an international context. Many of the themes will be revisited when particular aspects of British politics and policy-making that bear close relation to EU competencies are the subject of analysis. The importance of the EU points to the growing 'Europeanisation' of British politics. This chapter sought to clarify the meaning of this term and highlight the necessity of seeing European integration as but one element of changing patterns of governance in the UK. The particular argument advanced in relation to policy integration is that it is important to understand the basic, underlying preferences of British governments. How did they see the EU? What did they seek to get out of it? How effective were they at playing the EU game? Or, put another way, to what extent have British governments been able to upload domestic preferences with the result that subsequent processes of downloading as EU legislation is adapted to become smoother and easier? From accession in the 1970s, we see tensions between the priorities of British governments and those of other EU member states. This has led to the UK being tagged an awkward partner. This awkwardness is not apparent in all policy issues because, for example, the UK has been keen to pursue market liberalisation. Also, the UK has been a good implementer of agreed measures because it has an efficient domestic administrative and bureaucratic apparatus. However, as we have seen, there were post-accession tensions in the 1970s, anxieties about the scope and direction of European integration in the 1990s, and a continued reluctance to embrace the EU's core project, the single currency, with Labour in power since 1997. This points to significant continuities in British relations with the EU and demonstrates some limitations on the Europeanisation of British politics in the sense that European influences have to be refracted through the lens of domestic politics.

KEY POINTS

- British politics has been Europeanised.
- We can understand Europeanisation as the impact of EU governance on domestic politics in Britain.
- Europeanisation is but one source of change in British politics.
- British policies towards the EU have been fairly consistent over time.
- Thee have been long standing preferences for the central role of the nation-state, a suspicion of extended powers to supranational institutions, and a fairly consistent set of policy preferences on key issues such as the budget and the Common Agricultural Policy.

- The EU's impact on Britain is conditional in the sense that Britain is not fully engaged with all aspects of EU activity and differential in the sense that some policy areas are affected more than others.

KEY QUESTIONS

(1) To what extent has British politics been Europeanised?

(2) Why have the budget arrangements and Common Agricultural Policy been a problem for British governments?

(3) Why did the movement into areas of high politics that occurred after the Maastricht Treaty cause problems for British governments?

(4) Why did Britain not replace sterling with the Euro?

IMPORTANT WEBSITES

On British EU policy see the Foreign Office website at www.fco.gov.uk. For news on the EU see www.europa.eu.int or www.euractiv.com. For the main pro-EU organisation in Britain see www.britain-ineurope.org.uk. The EU homepage can be found at www.europa.eu.int. The British government's EU policy can be found at www.fco.gov.uk. An excellent source of news and information about the EU is www.euractiv.com. A UK gateway to EU resources can be found at www.sosig.ac.uk/eurostudies. Research on current issues in European integration is available from the European Integration On-line Papers www.eiop.or.at. The BBC's 'Inside Europe' is also a good source of information at http://news.bbc.co.uk/1/hi/in_depth/europe/2003/inside_europe/default.stm.

FURTHER READING

On the Europeanisation of British politics see A. Geddes (2004) *The European Union and British Politics*, London: Palgrave Macmillan and I. Bache and A. Jordan (eds) (2006) *The Europeanization of British Politics*, London: Palgrave. On Euroscepticism see A. Forster (2002) *Euroscepticism in Contemporary British Politics*, London: Routledge.

CHRONOLOGY

The Europeanisation of British Politics

1970	Treaty establishes EU budget
1973	UK accession
1975	Referendum on UK membership
1984	UK budget rebate
1985	Jacques Delors appointed Commission President
1986	Single European Act
1988	Margaret Thatcher's Bruges speech
1989	Social Charter
1991	Maastricht Treaty
1992	Sterling ejected from ERM on 15 September, 'Black Wednesday'
2002	Single Currency in circulation

Visit the Online Resource Centre that accompanies this book for links to more information on this chapter topic

PART TWO

Institutions and processes

CHAPTER TEN

The constitutional framework

READER'S GUIDE

This chapter examines the nature and sources of the British constitution, paying particular attention to the key conventions of Cabinet government, the role of the monarch, the fundamental principle of parliamentary sovereignty, and the Labour Government's ambitious programme of constitutional reform since 1997. It also explores the reasons for the growing dissatisfaction with constitutional arrangements and why the Labour Party in its long period in opposition ((1979–97) took up the cause of reform. For most of the 20th century the constitution had suited the main parties; gradually Labour calculated that the arrangements were more helpful to the 'normal' party of government, the Conservatives. In conclusion, it discusses the question of whether Britain should have a codified (written) constitution and places contemporary debates about the constitution within their political context. After nearly a century in which the subject was neglected the constitution has become a matter of controversy.

Introduction

There is a learned debate about whether Britain actually has a constitution. It clearly lacks one in a widely used sense of the term: there is no single comprehensive written code, or document, which sets out the rules affecting the relations between government institutions and between these institutions and citizens. On the other hand, it does have one in the sense that there are established procedures and expectations affecting the conduct of government and politics, and these are largely adhered to.

Britain has often been regarded as an illustration of the claim that it is not necessary to have a codified constitution to be a constitutional democracy. After all, it has been a stable democracy for over a century and has scored relatively highly as a protector of civil liberties. Some commentators identify the term 'constitutional' with a *system of formal checks and balances between institutions* and a separation of powers between government and other bodies. They therefore dispute that Britain is constitutional because of the concentration of formal political power in Parliament, and the principle of that body's absolute and unlimited sovereignty (excluding the European Union, of course).

At times, dissatisfaction with the workings of the political system has broadened into a general concern about the health of British democracy and sometimes fuelled demands for the adoption of a written constitution. In the past, the existence of a competitive two-party system, with its implicit checks and balances, independent groups and a broad political consensus may have made constitutional safeguards seem unnecessary; the above provided some protection against the abuse of power. But critics complained that these safeguards could no longer be taken for granted. In opposition, both Conservatives in the late 1970s and Labour in the 1980s and 1990s pointed to the worrying potential for an elective dictatorship to exploit the absolute sovereignty of Parliament and a 'winner takes all' system. A legacy (probably unintended) of the long period of Conservative rule (1979–97) and the radical policy agenda of Thatcherism was a quickening of interest in creating a set of formal checks and balances, particularly in the Labour Party.

There is a *historical explanation* why the British constitution is not codified. Established ways of conducting politics in Britain existed well before written constitutions become the norm. It is only in the last 200 years or so, starting with the United States, that written constitutions have spread. Most constitutions were originally adopted by states when they became independent or suffered a rupture in their evolution through internal collapse or invasion. France has had many different constitutions since 1789 and the present Fifth Republic dates from 1958. The former USSR rewrote its constitution a number of times, and on its break-up in 1990 the former member states had to draw up new constitutions. In Britain, neither the system of government nor a formal set or rules has been adopted at one point in time. Instead there is a political system, or set of arrangements, and a style of politics that have evolved over centuries, rather than a constitution.

A liberal democratic constitution

Britain's constitution has not been the product of agreement. After all, in the 17th century a monarch was executed and another forced to flee, as the idea of parliamentary government triumphed over monarchical government. The political nation has often been bitterly divided over such constitutional issues as Catholic emancipation in the 1820s, the 1832 Reform Act, the powers of the hereditary House of Lords, Irish Home Rule and votes for women. But it is fair to claim that, since the flight of James II in 1688, the basic principles of a sovereign Parliament and a limited constitutional monarchy have been securely established. The absence of an upheaval since then and the long period of constitutional stability—always excepting Ireland, of course—provides a sharp contrast to the political evolution of so many other states.

The main constitutional and political steps towards *representative democracy* took place in the 19th century. The suffrage was gradually extended and the relative powers of the monarchy, Lords, and Commons were altered in favour of the latter. Successive extensions of the right to vote produced universal adult suffrage by 1928 and made the House of Commons representative of the nation. The principle of Cabinet responsibility to the House of Commons was established by the 1830s and the supremacy of the elected Commons over the Lords was formally recognised in the Parliament Act of 1911.

Two other reforms—referenda and proportional representation for election to the House of Commons—were often proposed between 1867 and 1918 but not introduced. The first was supported as a means of giving people a say on the issues of the day, the latter as a means of defending minorities against an overbearing party majority in the Commons. The two reforms were envisaged as devices to cope with the rise of organised political parties in the late 19th century (Bogdanor 1981: 7).

Constitutional change was therefore a live issue before 1918, indeed, until the partition of Ireland in 1922. Thereafter, constitutional issues virtually disappeared from the agenda. The two main parties had a vested interest in preserving the winner-take-all system of a sovereign Parliament, first past the post elections, and strong government. The Conservatives regarded government as hierarchical and defended its autonomy and authority. Labour also supported the idea of strong government, because it was the instrument whereby a working class party could use a majority in Parliament to reform the capitalist system. They also calculated, probably correctly, that the electorate was more interested in bread and butter issues than the rules of the political game.

As new democracies collapsed across much of Europe during the inter-war years, so British politicians and commentators became even more convinced of the merits of the British system. The satisfaction was increased by British success in the 1939–45 war. Defenders of the status quo and the lack of a written constitution were guided by various beliefs, some explicit and some not, including:

(1) a merit of the unwritten constitution was that it could be changed easily by statute, just like any other act;

oncepts

Constitution. A body of fundamental principles and rules according to which a state, or other organisation, is governed. A constitution usually specifies the composition and powers of governing institutions, the relationship between them, and the relationship between the state and the citizen.

Flexible constitutions. No special procedure is required for constitutional change. In Britain there is no difference in the process of passing an Act of Parliament affecting, for example, top up fees in higher education and one abolishing the House of Lords. This can be contrasted with the US, where constitutional laws are entrenched and a special procedure is required for amending the constitution.

Liberal-democratic constitutions. Constitutional arrangements which permit both a high degree of popular participation in politics and the opportunity for institutionalised opposition.

Sovereignty. Concept of the ultimate source of power within the state.

Sovereign. That person or institution which has the final power of decision.

Parliamentary sovereignty. This means (1) Parliament can make or unmake any law; (2) No judicial review is needed to determine the constitutionality of Acts of Parliament. But political reality places many constraints on this legal doctrine. Examples: public opinion; pressure groups; EU; NATO; international finance.

Unitary state. Subordinate authorities exercise power bestowed by Parliament and Parliament can remove those powers. Example: an Act of Parliament established metropolitan counties in 1972; in 1986 Parliament abolished them. This can be contrasted with federal states, where powers of subordinate units are set out in a constitution, eg Germany or the USA.

Civil liberties/rights. Rights to freedom of speech, freedom of person, etc. In Britain, until 2000, civil liberties were protected neither by a separation of powers nor by a Bill of Rights. Rights in Britain were said to be residual—a citizen can do anything not expressly prohibited by law. In reality civil liberties were extremely fragile, requiring government willingness to impose self-restraint. The Human Rights Act 2000 provides greater protection (see pp 490–1).

(2) the instability of many states which had liberal democratic constitutions showed the relative unimportance of such documents, compared to a country's traditions and culture; and

(3) the British system had proved its worth by surviving for so long; it was the product of experience rather abstract theories.

What emerged from the late 19th century was what is sometimes called the Westminster model (see Chapter 2) of the constitution, an amalgam of procedures, values and institutions, covering parliamentary sovereignty, one-party government, unitary state, first-past-the-post electoral system, collective Cabinet responsibility and executive dominance of Parliament. On one reading, often called a 'liberal' view of the constitution, parliamentary sovereignty enables the will of the electorate to be expressed as the executive depends on the support of Parliament and the House of Commons is elected by the people. In reality, however, the constitution was also a set of institutions and procedures tailor-made for elite rule. There were checks on the executive but they were often in the form of self-restraint and broad agreement across elites on the rules of the game (see Chapter 3).

 # Sources

Strictly speaking, the British constitution is not unwritten, for large parts are documented. An outstanding feature is that its principles are not codified but dispersed—across statute law, common law, judges' interpretations of the laws, and conventions—though texts and commentaries on the constitution do provide some integration.

There are several sources of the constitution, including:

(1) *Statute law*, or law made by Parliament, which overrides common law and provides a substantial part of the constitution. It includes such measures as the Bill of Rights 1689, the Act of Union with Scotland 1707, successive Representation of the People Acts, and the Government of Ireland Act 1920. These laws are made and may be unmade by Act of Parliament, like any other. During the First and Second World Wars Parliament simply extended its life rather that hold elections during war.

(2) *Case law*, or judges' interpretations of statutes. Judges do not rule on the validity of a law, duly passed by Parliament, but they do have the right to decide whether it has been properly applied. By their interpretations the judges have an opportunity to shape the application of the law. (See Chapter 24.)

(3) *EU law*, expressed in the European Communities Act to which Britain was a co-signatory in 1972, and subsequently amended by the Single European Act 1986 and later treaties, including the European Communities (Amendment) Act 1993, which gave effect to the Maastricht Treaty. British authorities are required to accept the rules and regulations of the treaties, commitments flowing from them, and future decisions taken by Community institutions. Crucially, the assent of the Westminster Parliament is not required and EU law takes precedence over UK law.

(4) *Common law*, for example, the traditional rights and liberties of subjects handed down by custom and precedent and upheld by the courts, such as freedoms of speech and assembly. But the common law can be overruled or limited by statute law. It also covers the royal prerogative (see below, pp 184–5).

(5) *Conventions*, or rules which have been adhered to for so long that, although lacking the force of law, they are regarded as having a special authority. The conventions differ in their firmness. Firm ones include the expectation that the monarch will give her assent to legislation which has duly passed through the appropriate stages in

the two Houses of Parliament, and that the Prime Minister and government will resign or seek to dissolve Parliament following defeat on a confidence vote in the Commons.

Conventions

Much of the British constitution is shaped by conventions. These derive from precedent and usage and their force depends on their being observed; continued breaches of a convention weaken its authority. Changes in conventions enable a constitution to adapt and evolve. In the 19th century, for example, Prime Ministers sat in either the House of Lords or the House of Commons. Even as late as 1902 the then Prime Minister, Lord Salisbury, sat in the Lords. Since at least the 1920s it has been accepted that the Prime Minister must be a member of the directly elected House of Commons. In 1963, when Lord Home was invited by the Queen to form a government following the retirement of Harold Macmillan, he was required to disclaim his peerage and seek a seat in the Commons on becoming Prime Minister.

At a time of political change or intense political disagreement there may be uncertainty about what is 'conventional'. The Labour Prime Minister of the day suspended the convention of Cabinet collective responsibility in 1975 to hold a referendum to decide Britain's continued membership of the EC and again in 1977 on the choice of electoral system for direct elections to the European Parliament—in both cases because the party was divided. Mr. Callaghan's rather cavalier response in 1977 to questions about the status of the convention in the latter case was that it still applied 'except in cases I announce that it does not!' His remarks captured the meaning of a convention—its force depends on politicians adhering to it. Taken literally, however, such an approach makes nonsense of the idea of constitutionalism, which is hardly compatible with the idea of the government deciding for itself what is or is not 'constitutional'. The politically impartial Cabinet Secretary in theory is a custodian of the constitution in the sense of what is and is not permissible may advise or warn the Prime Minister accordingly.

Responsible government

The term 'responsible government' has different usages; for example, that the government is responsive to public opinion, is prudent in the exercise of its duties, or is answerable to Parliament (Birch 1964). This last is the most important practical constitutional feature. The idea of responsible government is linked to two important constitutional conventions: (1) *the individual responsibility of ministers* to Parliament for the conduct of their departments, and (2) *the collective responsibility of the Cabinet* for the conduct of policies. If the Cabinet loses the support of the Commons, expressed in a vote on an important measure or on a motion of confidence, it is expected either to resign or to dissolve the Parliament.

Ministerial responsibility

According to the doctrine of ministerial responsibility each minister is responsible to Parliament for his own personal conduct, the general conduct of his department, and the acts or omissions of his civil servants. The last notable resignation on grounds of policy failure was that of the Foreign Secretary, Lord Carrington, and two other ministers in his department in the wake of the Argentine invasion of the Falklands in 1982. However, the list of ministers who might have been expected to resign because of policy failures, but did not, is a very long one. For example, nobody resigned over the expensive and abandoned poll tax under Mrs Thatcher, or Britain's humiliating exit from the ERM in 1992, or over the Dome project, or the misleading intelligence about Iraq's weapons under Tony Blair. Indeed, where resignations are forced it is usually not to do with admission of policy failures. The resignations in the 1992 Parliament of ministers like David Mellor, Tim Yeo, Michael Mates and Neil Hamilton were all over private scandals rather than policy matters, as were the resignations from Tony Blair's Cabinet of Peter Mandelson (his first) and David Blunkett's (his second). But in these cases the media coverage was damaging the authority of the minister and, ultimately, of the Government. More rare (because voluntary) are resignations because of disagreements with Cabinet policy as in the cases of Robin Cook and Clare Short.

Of more political significance is the idea that a minister is answerable to the House of Commons for the conduct of departmental policy. At one level, responsibility simply means answering questions on policy and departmental matters from MPs. A stronger interpretation is that Parliament can force the resignation of a minister in a case of demonstrated negligence. Demonstrating negligence, however, is difficult. Departments contain many civil servants, some of whom exercise a necessary degree of initiative and discretion, and it hardly seems practical politics to visit the personal responsibility for their mistakes on the minister. A hundred years ago, a conscientious minister might have been acquainted with most of the work done by his department. Today, however, so much is delegated that it is difficult for the minister to keep abreast of all the actions taken by civil servants (see Chapter 12). The delegation of work to agencies also weakens the principle of the minister's responsibility. Moreover, the turnover of ministers in office is so rapid (a little over two years on average) that by the time negligence or a mistaken policy has been uncovered, the minister will probably have moved on. Yet the convention remains (Politics in Focus 10.2).

The meaning of the convention has altered following the rise of disciplined political parties. Only exceptionally does a minister resign or suffer dismissal because of a policy mistake; in a classic study S.E. Finer (1956) noted that if a minister goes, it is probably because he is unpopular and/or because the Prime Minister regards him as dispensable. Here we have to take account of two important political barriers to the ability of the Commons to force the dismissal of a minister. One is *party loyalty*, as the majority of party backbenchers rally behind 'their' hard-pressed minister. The other is *collective responsibility*. Ultimately, the Cabinet is also responsible for policy, and a minister's resignation, however personally honourable, or even appropriate, often reflects badly on the government as a whole and is a source of encouragement to the opposition. The distinction between a minister's responsibility for policy and a chief executive's responsibility for operation matters is in practice not clear-cut (see Chapter 13).

10.2

esponsible government

Ministerial responsibility

Constitutional theory. Ministers are *answerable* to Parliament for the general conduct of their department and they are *accountable* in the sense that they are expected to resign if serious personal or departmental faults are disclosed. Example: Lord Carrington, Foreign Secretary, 1982, over Foreign Office misjudgement regarding Argentine intentions to invade the Falklands.

Political practice. In respect of ministerial responsibility for the conduct of departmental civil servants and departmental policy, this convention has weakened in recent years owing to the:

— increased workload of departments

— rapid turnover of ministers

— blurred lines of responsibility resulting from the creation of quangos (see Chapter 16) and executive agencies

— closing of ranks of disciplined political Parties

In 1996 William Waldegrave and Sir Nicholas Lyell refused to resign, in spite of heavy public and opposition pressure, following the Scott Report's claims that they misled the Commons over the guns for Iraq affair.

In 2004 attempts to impeach Tony Blair for presenting faulty intelligence to Parliament to make the case for the war with Iraq failed.

Resignation is probably a sign that a minister is unpopular in his party and/or dispensable to the Prime Minister.

Collective responsibility

Constitutional theory. Ministers are required publicly to defend government decisions or resign. Originally collective responsibility was limited to the Cabinet, but now is extended as a tool of party management to include approximately 100 or so members of the governing party. Examples: Sir Geoffrey Howe, Lord President of the Council and Leader of the House of Commons, resigned in November 1990 because he could no longer accept the Prime Minister's conduct of policy on Europe. In 2003, Robin Cook, Leader of the House, resigned from Tony Blair's Cabinet on the grounds that he could not support war on Iraq.

Political practice. Sometimes Prime Ministers may find it politically expedient to suspend this doctrine. In 1975 Harold Wilson allowed members of his Cabinet publicly to differ during the EC referendum campaign. He justified it as an exception to prove the rule, limited to the period of the referendum and to the specific topic of continued EC membership.

The convention still has some important consequences, however. It gives MPs and the opposition an opportunity to ask questions of ministers. Questions keep the civil servants in the department on their toes: their jobs may be virtually safe but their reputations and their career prospects are not. If an official has made a mistake—for example, if he has provided a poor briefing, failed to anticipate reasonable questions or criticisms from the opposition, has not carried out instructions, or has given an incorrect version of the minister's viewpoint—it is soon known in a department and circulated on the Whitehall grapevine. Finally, the convention helps to personalise politics in that the public tends to praise ministers for apparent successes and blame them for apparent failures.

Collective responsibility

This convention has two features. The first is that the Cabinet resigns if the government is defeated on a major measure in the House of Commons; this was clearly established in 1830 when the Government resigned after losing an important vote and faced almost certain defeat on the issue of parliamentary reform. After the Reform Act of 1832 the principle was established that a Cabinet depended on the support of the Commons. The second is that all ministers must, unless the principle is relaxed, accept and support in public Cabinet decisions or keep their dissent private; if they choose to express disagreement they should resign or expect dismissal.

The House of Commons may force a government's resignation by carrying a censure motion against it or by defeating it on a vote on an issue of confidence. An *issue of confidence* is one the Prime Minister declares to be so, the implication being that rejection of a government-sponsored measure entails the resignation of the government. Defeat on the Budget, on the second or third readings of government bills, or on the address in reply to the Queen's Speech have usually been regarded as votes of no confidence, because they are central to a government's programme. Such a defeat in the House of Commons has twice overturned governments in the 20th century, in 1924 and 1979. In 1940, although Neville Chamberlain won a vote of censure on his handling of the Norwegian campaign, his normal party majority was so reduced that he felt he had to resign.

The convention, however, has become an instrument of Cabinet dominance of Parliament and is now caught up in the politics of party management and stable government. For much of the period since 1945 it has been usual for one party to have a reliable majority in the Commons and not to lose important votes in Parliament. Even if a government faces a rebellion in its own ranks, it often pressures the potential rebels into line by making the issue one of confidence. In July 1993 rebels on his own side caused John Major's Government to lose a key vote on the Maastricht Treaty but the next day the decision was reversed on a confidence motion. The extension of the convention to include even parliamentary private secretaries (PPSs), or personal assistants to ministers, means that nearly a third of the governing party's MPs are on the 'payroll' (although PPSs are unpaid) and expected to support the government. Collective responsibility implies cohesion, and obviously fits more easily with a Cabinet whose members are drawn from one party, have been elected on a programme, and share a common philosophy. It also implies secrecy, so that the differences over a Cabinet decision are not made public. Presenting a united front to the Opposition in Parliament and to the public springs at least as much from considerations of political management as from constitutional propriety.

Yet there are signs that the convention, as applied to Cabinet unity, is declining. In the 20th century there were three notable agreements to differ; each occurred in circumstances when insistence on a common line would have split the Cabinet of the day. They concerned (1) the adoption of tariffs by the coalition National Government in 1932, when dissenters, notably the Liberal ministers, were allowed to support free trade; (2) the referendum on membership of the EC in 1975; and (3) the vote on the European Assembly Elections Bill in 1977. A constitutional consequence of the Cabinet waiving collective responsibility on such questions is that it is difficult for the House of Commons to hold it accountable for the result of a parliamentary vote. The myth of Cabinet unity has also been weakened as accounts of Cabinet proceedings and disagreements have been 'leaked' to the media more extensively in recent years.

The monarchy

Apart from a brief period (1649–60), England has had a monarchy since the 10th century. The monarchy has proved to be a durable institution, largely because it has acquiesced in pressures to change its role. Only a handful of monarchies remain in the world today. In the 20th century they have usually collapsed as a result of (1) events associated with military defeat (eg Germany, 1918); (2) the break-up of multinational empires, again usually after defeats in war (eg Austria–Hungary and the Ottoman Empire after 1914–18); or (3) failure to come to terms with the growth of democracy. The key to the monarchy's survival in Britain had been its willingness over the last three centuries to concede power in good time to head off demands for its abolition.

When we say that Britain is a constitutional monarchy we mean that the monarch plays a largely ceremonial role—for example, representing Britain on overseas tours, attending public functions, and so on—and on political matters acts on the advice of ministers. When Parliament is sitting, the monarch receives daily reports on parliamentary proceedings, government papers, and reports of Cabinet meetings, and meets the Prime Minister weekly for a confidential discussion of government policy. The traditional language of the constitution—dating from a time when the monarchy exercised power—remains. It is the Queen's government; ministers are ministers of the Crown; and courts and judges are Her Majesty's courts and judges.

The royal prerogative was described in the 19th century by the constitutional lawyer Dicey as 'the residue of a discretionary or arbitrary authority legally left in the hands of the crown'. This means that some powers may be exercised by the Crown without parliamentary authority; these include summoning, dissolving and proroguing Parliament, making treaties, declaring war, command of the armed forces, appointment of judges, conferment of honours, creation of peers, appointment of ministers, initiation of criminal proceedings, granting of pardons, and so forth. These actions, performed in the name of the

Crown and usually exercised by an order in council, are independent of the courts or Parliament, and underpin the power of the executive.

Today, however, the Prime Minister and Cabinet have assumed these powers, and in this regard the monarchy still has political significance. It was, for example, the Prime Minister who announced that the country was at war with Germany in 1939 and with Argentina in 1982. Tony Blair's decision to seek and win the approval of the Commons for war with Iraq in 2003 has probably set a precedent for Parliament to decide such a course in the future.

The monarch's right to appoint peers was of more significance before 1911, when the House of Lords was able to veto legislation, and was last exercised independently by a monarch in 1712. The monarch's threat to create extra peers to overcome the opposition of the Lords to the Reform Bill in 1832 and the Parliament Bill in 1911 was not carried out, because on each occasion enough members of the Lords eventually gave way to the governments of the day. The monarch's choice of a Prime Minister is normally uncontroversial, being the elected leader of the party able to command a majority in the House of Commons, and appointment of Cabinet ministers is made on the recommendation of the Prime Minister. Until 1963, whenever a Conservative Prime Minister resigned his office, the monarch's choice of successor was based on advice from senior party figures. The fact that the major parties now elect their own leaders has virtually removed any element of the choice of Prime Minister from the monarch (Politics in Focus 10.3).

Two areas are potentially more problematical. The first concerns the dissolution of Parliament. It is widely agreed that the monarch must generally agree to a request from the Prime Minister to dissolve Parliament. With one party or a group of parties having a clear parliamentary majority in all but one of the general elections since 1931, this has so far presented little difficulty. But what happens if a Prime Minister, who lacks a majority in the Commons, seeks a dissolution when another politician in the same party might be able to command a majority? Should the monarch agree to the request or invite somebody else? A second area of potential controversy may arise if no one party has a clear majority of seats or if the parties to a coalition do not agree on a leader; the monarch might then become involved, however unwillingly, in delicate negotiations to invite a politician to try and form a government. Such circumstances may draw the monarchy and its advisers into controversy, by expanding its political role. Conduct for which there are no clear precedents is liable to offend somebody and perhaps prompt allegations of political bias. The monarch of the day was criticised in 1931 over the formation of the National Government and in 1957 and 1963 over the appointments of Mr Macmillan and Lord Home respectively as Prime Minister. One way of avoiding controversy would be to transfer some of these decisions to the Speaker of the House of Commons or some other impartial figure.

Walter Bagehot succinctly laid down the monarch's role in 1865: the right to be informed, to encourage, and to warn, that is, the monarch reigns but does not rule. It requires the monarch to practice political impartiality: the monarch must act, and be seen to act, in a non-partisan manner and be willing to co-operate with any properly elected government. To play the role of constitutional referee requires the monarch to be even-handed between the parties, to avoid politically controversial statements or conduct, and to adhere to accepted rules. Problems are likely to arise, therefore, when the 'rules' are not clear or are in dispute. A crucial principle is that the monarch can do no wrong as long as he or she acts on the advice of a responsible government with a majority in the Commons. In this way the government assumes political responsibilities, and the monarch is kept 'above' party politics and protected from criticism. The advocates of abolition of the monarchy are few but the institution has attracted criticism. Much of this has been stimulated by negative media reporting of the behaviour of the younger royals and their failure to set a moral example to the nation, the size of the Civil List or revelations that the Queen did not, until recently, pay income tax. Other critics complain that the pre-modern and undemocratic values associated with hereditary monarchy are ill-suited to the 21st century.

Parliamentary sovereignty

The principle of parliamentary sovereignty has been perhaps the outstanding feature of the British constitution. For a strict theorist, absolute sovereignty is hardly compatible with the idea of a system being constitutional. Sovereignty, or the power to make law, is exercised by the Queen, Lords and Commons assembled. An Act of Parliament has not been constrained by any higher laws and no other authority may rule on its constitutionality. This meant that the courts could not set aside, but could only interpret, statute law. Before the mid-18th century, however, courts were prepared to void a statute if it was deemed to clash with common law. It was only in the 19th century that the idea of the absolute supremacy of Parliament developed.

One uses the past tense about the absolute supremacy of Parliament because membership of the European Union means that European law is now supreme where the European Court of Justice declares that it overrides national law. The *Factortame* case in 1990 was an important reminder of the impact of Europe on the British Parliament. As a result of a ruling from the European Court of Justice (ECJ) the House of Lords suspended the operation of a British law affecting the registration of fishing vessels for EC fishing quota purposes until the ECJ made a definitive ruling. The ruling starkly illustrated the subordination of British to European law. The ECJ, like the US Supreme Court, rules on whether the actions of the national government or legislature are in accordance with EU law. (See Chapter 8.)

The fact that (except for laws made by the EU) there are no formal checks on the sovereignty of the Westminster Parliament does not mean that in practice there are no limits. There have always been *political* checks on the government in the form of its sense of self-restraint, its need to bargain with powerful pressure groups and appease its own backbenchers, its duty to respect the right of opposition parties in the Commons, and, of course, fear that the voters may turn it out at the next general election.

The reform agenda

By the 1990s there were several signs of a loss of support for Britain's constitutional arrangements (Foley 1999, and for a defence of the status quo see Norton 1997). Some pressures were clearly *political*. These included opposition party complaints about the 'illiberal' actions of the Thatcher governments, the rise of a large centre party vote in the 1980s, which added weight to traditional Liberal demands for reform of the electoral system, and the rise of nationalism in Scotland. Other pressures were more narrowly *constitutional* (Mount 1992; Wright 1994). They related, particularly, to the apparent weakening of such conventions as collective and ministerial responsibility, the lack of settled rules regarding the conduct of referenda, the frequent rulings of the European Court of Human Rights against Britain on civil liberties cases, and the effects of membership of the European Union, notably the limits on the British Parliament and the supremacy of EU law. Groups like Charter 88 and Democratic Audit, based at the University of Essex, were influential campaigners for reform. There emerged from these various concerns a reform agenda comprising a Human Rights Act to protect citizens' rights, electoral reform, devolution, reform of the House of Lords and more open government.

The changed constitution

During its first term Tony Blair's Government implemented an ambitious programme of constitutional reform. In the past, Labour's left regarded proposals for limits on the executive as part of a campaign against a socialist government which would want to use its parliamentary majority to make radical social and economic reforms. In its early years Labour supported devolution as well as electoral reform. However once it became a potential party of government it accepted the supremacy of Parliament, the electoral system, and the dominance of the executive and hoped to use them for its own purposes. Its programme of an expanded welfare state, public ownership, national economic planning and redistribution required an active state and a strong centre. By the 1990s, however, its lengthy period of opposition converted some Labour leaders to the ideas of greater checks and balances, like a Human Rights Act and even electoral reform. What was the point of supporting such a pro-government system if Labour was usually in opposition (for two thirds of the 20th century)?

When Blair became leader in 1994 constitutional reform was a way of showing that his party was 'new' and could be identified with modernisation. He inherited some commitments, notably devolution for Scotland and Wales, from his predecessors. Constitutional reform was also a way of attracting support from liberal-minded people and the Liberal Democrats, and be a clear dividing line from the Conservatives. The measures include:

• A Human Rights Act (1998) which came into effect on 2 October 2000, although it began operation in 1999 in Scotland, Wales and Northern Ireland. The Act is based substantially on the European Convention on Human Rights. All bills before the Parliaments and

Assembly now allow judges to rule that ministers' decisions or legislation are incompatible with the Human Rights Act but not to strike down an Act (see Chapter 24). Ministers may use a fast-track procedure to amend legislation if they wish.

- A Freedom of Information Act came into effect in 2005. It creates a right of access to information held by public authorities. The measure, however, has disappointed reformers because ministers retain the right to exempt from release large areas, including discussion of many policy matters, and the proposed Information Commissioner only has a right to recommend, but not to compel, the release of information.

- Devolution was achieved in 1998, with the establishment of a Scottish Parliament, with tax-varying and primary legislative powers. There was also devolution for Wales in the form of an Assembly, but lacking the Scottish powers. In Northern Ireland, as ever, the arrangements were different. There was provision for a directly elected Assembly but with a requirement that the executive be drawn from members of both the Unionist and Nationalist communities, and seats allocated in proportion to the party strengths (see Chapter 17).

- For London a directly elected mayor and assembly were established in 2000, although the turnout in the 1998 referendum was only 34%. The mayor has modest powers, largely to devise strategies, for example, in transport.

- Proportional electoral voting was greatly extended, with the additional member system introduced in Scotland, Wales, London and the European elections. In Northern Ireland the highly proportional single transferable vote is used. In London the supplementary vote is used to elect the mayor, but for the assembly it is first past the post and a top up by the additional member system. The simplicity and uniformity of the British elections is no more (see Chapter 20).

- In 1999 the preponderant role of hereditary peers in the Lords was finally removed. It was agreed that 10% (92) of hereditary peers could remain in a transitional second chamber; most of these were elected on a party basis by the party groupings of peers. A Royal Commission headed by Lord Wakeham reported in January 2000 and recommended a second chamber of about 550 members, most of whom would be appointed by an Appointments Commission, with the remainder—between 65 and 195—elected to represent the regions (see Chapter 19). Although the Lords remains a largely nominated body—not much of an advance in democracy—in its 2005 election manifesto Labour promised to end the membership of the remaining 92 hereditary peers and consult on methods of choosing members.

- The use of referenda was greatly extended, being used for all the devolution measures. As of 2006, there have been 34 referenda during the lifetime of the Blair Government, some covering votes for introduction of elected local mayors. What in the 1970s was a controversial step (see Politics in Focus 10.3) is now firmly established as a part of the constitution—although politicians may dispute what counts as 'constitutional'. As critics and opponents of the 1975 initiative respectively feared and hoped, referenda have spread and are now regarded as the supreme (and binding) test of popular consent to constitutional change. All major parties were agreed at the 2005 general election that a referendum would be held in the event of a government recommendation that Britain should enter the European single currency and over the proposed EU Constitution (see Chapter 23).

US 10.3
...erenda

Theory

The electorate is asked to vote yes or no to a specific question. Example: June 1975, 'Do you think Britain should stay in the European Community?' The referendum until recently has been regarded as an alien device in British politics since it is problematic in relation to the constitutional doctrine of the sovereignty of Parliament. On the occasions it has been used, potential conflict has been avoided by making the referendum 'advisory'.

To date referenda have been used on (other than in local examples such as pub-opening times in some parts of Wales) constitutional issues. Before 1997 they were used in 1973 in Northern Ireland on the border question; in 1975 throughout the UK on continued European Community membership, and in 1979 in Scotland and Wales on devolution.

Referenda provide an additional opportunity for popular participation, the government consulting the governed on important constitutional questions. It is now almost a convention of the constitution that any radical constitutional change needs endorsement by the people as well as Parliament. Interestingly, the Local Government Act 2000 requires local authorities to hold a referendum if they wish to adopt a directly elected mayor system, and gives for the first time the power to 5% of the registered local electorate to require a local authority to hold a referendum on such a reform.

Practice

In practice the referendum has had as much to do with political expediency as constitutional principle or democracy. In 1975 the Labour Cabinet and party was split over the issue of continued EC membership and Harold Wilson resorted to a referendum and 'agreement to differ' to enable the government to survive in office. On a turnout of 64.5%, 64.5% voted in favour of remaining in Europe. In 1979 James Callaghan's minority Labour government depended for its survival on the Lib–Lab pact. Devolution for Scotland and Wales was introduced in return for continued Liberal and Nationalist support, but was unpopular with many Labour MPs. Devolution was, therefore, made dependent upon 40% of the electorate in each country voting in favour. In Scotland, 51.6% (but only 33% of the electorate) voted for devolution, and in Wales 20.3% (or only 12% of the electorate) voted for it. Devolution was abandoned and the government lost a censure motion in May 1979 and resigned.

In 1997 devolution referenda were a key part of Labour's ambitious constitutional reform agenda. They have been held because of long-standing promises (eg on devolution) or because a proposal raises fundamental questions (eg entry to the single European currency or acceptance of a European constitution) or clearly changes the conditions of popular participation (eg, the voting system). In referenda in 1997 in Scotland and Wales and in 1998 in Northern Ireland, the popular majority has supported the government's initiative. In Scotland, on a 60.2% turnout 74.3% voted for the establishment of a Scottish Parliament, in Wales on a 50.1% turnout 50.3% voted for a Welsh Assembly, and in Northern Ireland the Good Friday Agreement was approved by 71% of voters on a turnout of 80%.

• The potential conflict of interests stemming from the Lord Chancellor being both a senior politician and a judge as well as head of the judicial branch has been resolved by the Constitutional Reform Act and its creation of a Supreme Court and a Judicial Appointments Committee (see Chapter 24).

Critics have argued that Labour's reforms—more than a score of statutes were passed during the first term—have lacked an overall theme. In large part, this is because the measures have been responses to a variety of pressures. Devolution was unfinished business from previous Labour leaders. Electoral reform was in part a sweetener for the Liberal Democrats and a barrier to the Nationalists gaining and using a majority of seats in the Scottish Parliament to table a bill for independence. A merit of the various measures is that they have tried to respond to specific needs and political demands. Hence there is devolution in Scotland and Wales but not so far for the English regions where, on the evidence of the 2003 referendum in the North East, there appears to be little popular demand.

Political debate at the end of the 20th century returned to constitutional issues and at times divided the two major parties. Many of the issues discussed above arose piecemeal, in response to changing political circumstances and/or calculations about party gain. Reformers claimed, variously, that the changes would lead to a 'better' political system, would produce a more representative House of Commons, protect citizens against arbitrary government, or bring the United Kingdom into line with other West European democracies; and improve the policy-making process. For example, more open government might encourage more informed debate about policy, or proportional representation might weaken a class-based two-party system and promote more continuity and consensus in policy; or finally, an authoritative statement would preclude the rules of the game from being at the mercy of a temporary parliamentary majority.

Calculation of party advantage is rarely absent in discussion of the rules of the game. In the period 1974–79 when they were in opposition, a number of Conservatives supported the introduction of constitutional checks on what they condemned as the Labour government's elective dictatorship (Hailsham 1976). Once restored to government in 1979, however, such voices fell silent. Mrs Thatcher and her followers, who wanted to reverse the collectivist drift of much post-war policy, had little interest in constitutional reform. She was a radical on all matters except the constitution. In 1989 Mrs Thatcher reply to Charter 88's appeal for support was: 'The government considers that our present constitutional arrangements continue to serve us well' (Wright 1994: 29). But her long tenure as Prime Minister and some of her policies made the constitution a political issue. By 1989, according to Bogdanor:

> It is a paradox that a government so determined to resist constitutional change has made the constitution itself a political issue. . . It is a striking consequence of Mrs Thatcher's decade that all of the opposition parties, without exception, now favour constitutional change (1989: 139).

Opposition MPs may make demands for checks and balances as part of the party battle. Questioning the legitimacy or constitutional propriety of an action by the executive is a useful device for the opposition. It is remarkable how often politicians in opposition have advocated curbs on the executive until they are in office. The more distant a party's prospects of office the more advantageous proposals to limit the powers of government appear. It is interesting to observe how Labour's interest in proportional representation for Westminster has cooled since its election to power in 1997. There is nothing exceptional in this. Politicians calculate the advantages and disadvantages about changes in the rules of the political game, as they do about other issues.

It may even affect the judgement of commentators. Ridley (*Whatever Happened to the Constitution under Mrs Thatcher?* 1992) claimed that the flexible constitution proved to be too fragile a shield against the Thatcher government's abuses of power. He referred to its:

- use of the honours system to reward contributors to Conservative Party funds;
- manipulation of the time of publishing official statistics for party advantage;
- pressuring of officials to provide politically convenient advice;
- use of public funds to publicise government programmes and initiative, which also carried an implicit party political message.

Ridley clearly perceived a Thatcher effect at work and chose all his examples from her years in office. Yet all of the complaints equally apply to the Blair period. In his first four years as Prime Minister, Tony Blair created more peers than Mrs Thatcher did in her 11 years as Prime Minister, and some them had contributed to party funds; doubled the number of special advisers, often to promote party policy, and increased their influence *vis-à-vis* civil servants; and substantially increased spending on the Government's information campaigns.

A written constitution?

There has also been a growing body of support for a comprehensive restatement of the rules and even a written constitution. Charter 88, an all-party movement but dominated by Labour and Liberal Democrat supporters, has called for a written constitution, including many of the above, as well as fixed-term Parliaments and elected regional authorities. The centre-left think-tank, Institute for Public Policy Research (IPPR), drafted a written constitution in 1991, which included most of the 'reform' agenda. The programme closely resembled the manifestos of the two parties in the 1997 general election. And from the centre-right, Ferdinand Mount (1992) also expressed interest.

But drawing up a new constitution—let alone implementing it—is no easy matter. In Britain, the main practical difficulty involved in having a written constitution or an authoritative formal statement of the rules of the game is presented by the doctrine of the sovereignty of Parliament. This argument was often used to oppose virtually all the post-1997 reforms. Tony Wright (1994: 3) complains that 'It is the doctrine to be summoned up to explain why things cannot be done . . . It is the no-doctrine of British politics.'

As noted, the British have no experience of a system of government or set of rules being constituted at one point in time. In the United States, by contrast, one thinks back for a starting point to 1787, in France to 1958 and in West Germany to 1949. Similarly, the British have no concept of fundamental, or entrenched (ie difficult to change) rules but have taken pride in the flexibility provided by their unwritten constitution. Strict adherence to the doctrine of parliamentary sovereignty is essentially incompatible with genuine constitutional principles. Both features are of course part of 'the politics of power' or highly convenient for the government of the day. A written constitution is likely to increase the political role of the courts and the possibility of their coming into conflict with Parliament, as they would have to decide whether statutes infringed the constitution.

The main difficulty, however, in finding a set of rules acceptable to different viewpoints is likely to be *political*. A large measure of agreement is essential if a constitution is to be legitimate, that is, voluntarily accepted and widely regarded as 'above party politics'. A first step would presumably be to establish a body, say a Constitutional Commission, which in turn would formulate and then submit proposals to Parliament. These, when approved, might be subject to a referendum and, if approved, then entrenched. Yet many of the possible topics for inclusion, for example, whether Britain should accept an EU Constitution—the prospect of which has receded in 2005 following the rejection of the Constitution in France and the Netherlands—are highly political issues.

An additional difficulty is that governments are unlikely to be willing to sacrifice the necessary parliamentary time for a new constitutional settlement, when there are so many other pressing economic and social issues competing for attention. By tradition constitutions bills are referred to a Committee of the Whole House of Commons, and all MPs may participate. Legislation affecting membership of the EC and devolution for Scotland and Wales, both of which were also subjects of referenda, dominated debate and the legislative timetable in Parliament in the 1970s, and the Major Government spent the best part of two years in battling to pass the Maastricht Bill through Parliament. Governments also have little incentive to introduce any reforms which might constrain their own powers or undermine their authority in office. Political self-interest (particularly among the government of the day), therefore, is the major barrier to constitutional reform.

The adoption of a written constitution might well challenge many traditional assumptions about the conduct of British politics. The political elite has managed to operate without a formal constitution, in large part because the informal 'rules' were widely understood, and governments practised self-restraint and respected the rights of other groups, including the opposition in Parliament. In other words, there was a 'constitutional' political style or culture, without being based on law. In many West European states which have a Roman law background and authoritative written constitutions, the political culture is more legalistic and based on formal rules. Some of the legislative changes affecting constitutional issues in Britain have been controversial and politically divisive—extensions of the suffrage in the 19th century, reform of the Lords in 1911, partition of Ireland in 1922, and entry to the EC. Constitutional change has often come about less by general agreement than by power politics, by a party using its parliamentary majority to push through a change which is then accepted by opponents. In Britain the tradition has been more one of laws following behaviour than vice versa. Ultimately, however, constitutions, if they are to work as intended, need to rest on popular support and be acceptable to the major sources of political and economic power in society.

A French or American student writing about their country's constitution will inevitably concentrate on the formal constitutional document and legal decisions relating to it. Accounts of the British constitution, on the other hand, usually describe the way the system works, a situation that has allowed different writers to use evidence selectively in support of differing interpretations of the constitution. A politician's perceptions of the rules of the game may depend not only on whether or not his preferred party is in government or opposition, but also to which wing of the Conservative or Labour Party he belongs (Tivey 1988).

In 1867 Bagehot's *The English Constitution* distinguished between the 'real' and 'dignified' parts of the constitution, between the 'paper description' and 'living reality'. The 'outward show' provided by the monarchy did not, as many people believed, betoken effective power. Although the monarchy could 'excite and preserve the reverence of the population', it was the sober-suited Cabinet ministers who ruled. Some observers (usually critics) have invoked his famous distinction between the 'real' and the 'formal' constitution, when writing of unelected power-holders like officials, financiers and the European Commission.

Conclusion

Interest in constitutional and electoral reform has traditionally been 'the poetry of the politically impotent' (Mount 1992: 2) but a combination of pressures (from the EU) and dissatisfaction (largely from the political centre left under the 18 years of Conservative rule from 1979) altered the situation. Labour, assisted by the Liberal Democrats, took over the agenda and has achieved a remarkable programme of constitutional reform. Its long exclusion from power educated it to the merits of political checks and balances and a more pluralistic order. The constitutional changes enacted since 1997 are undoubtedly significant—indeed as of 2005 they are likely to be Tony Blair's most signal achievement as Prime Minister—and are almost entirely due to the change of government in May 1997.

But perhaps politicians, particularly in government, have been slow to adapt to the changes. Critics observing Blair's management of the party and Alastair Campbell's approach to the media (see pp 509ff) accused the government of 'control freakery'. Fearing that Ken Livingstone would be chosen Blair intervened to impose his own candidate in the selection of the party candidate for the first election of the London mayor and the choice of the First Minister for Wales, following the resignation of Ron Davies in 1998. There has also a distinct lack of pluralism in ministers' attitudes to local government or reactions to inconvenient decisions of the courts (notably when David Blunkett was Home Secretary). Yet the constitutional changes have produced a different political system, reflected in the expanded role of judges, the different electoral arrangements across the United Kingdom, and the devolved Parliament in Scotland.

There remains unfinished business for the reformers. They wait to see whether there will be a significant elected element in the House of Lords, whether the Freedom of Information Act will be effective, whether devolution will be extended to the English regions, and whether there will be reform of the voting system for Westminster elections. Supporters of the Human Rights Act complain that it lacks a supporting Human Rights Commission, which would promote a rights culture. And still unresolved is the so-called West Lothian question, in which Scottish MPs can vote on controversial matters affecting England but have no votes on matters affecting Scotland. Already since 1997 the British constitution has embraced more written and statutory elements, is more pluralistic, converges more with the European Union, and grants the judiciary a greater role. The reforms represent a significant step to the creation of a new political system. A constitution is a living thing and the British one may evolve perhaps in directions neither envisaged or desired by reformers or feared by opponents.

KEY POINTS

- The British constitution is partly written but uncodified.

- It has evolved in response to economic, social, and political change.

- It has five main sources: statute law, European Union law, common law, works of authority, conventions. The first two have grown in recent years.

- A constitutional monarch has a symbolic role.

- Britain is a parliamentary democracy: the executive is drawn from and accountable to Parliament.

- Parliamentary sovereignty is no longer the fundamental principle of the constitution. Britain is a unitary state in that subordinate authorities are empowered by Parliament and can likewise be disempowered. But the granting of powers to the Scottish Parliament has introduced an element of quasi-federalism and it is difficult to imagine the powers being taken away. Further, the extension of judicial review and membership of the EU are limits on a sovereign Parliament.

- A long period of Conservative Party dominance, a weakening of the observance of key conventions, and membership of the European Union placed constitutional reform on the agenda in the 1990s.

- The flexible nature of the constitution has facilitated piecemeal adjustments but constitutions are not above politics, and this partly explains the failure to introduce fundamental reform. Those out of power want change but cannot deliver it. Those in power can introduce change but do not need it.

KEY QUESTIONS

(1) Discuss the view that 'Procedure is all the constitution the poor Briton has' (Pickthorn).

(2) Do Labour's reforms since 1997 amount to a fundamental reshaping of the constitution or mere tinkering?

(3) Can the British system of government be described as constitutional?

(4) Discuss the view that 'Our so-called constitution allows a politician who doesn't want to play according to the rules, who isn't an "officer and a gentleman", almost unlimited power' (F.F. Ridley).

IMPORTANT WEBSITES

For up-to-date analysis of constitutional issues, see Constitutional Unit, www.ucl.ac.uk/constitution-unit. For the reformist agenda, see Charter 88, www.charter 88.org.uk. See also www.democratic audit.com.

FURTHER READING

For an introduction see M. Foley (1999) *The Politics of the British Constitution,* Manchester: Manchester University Press: N. Johnson, 'The Constitution' in I. Holliday et al (eds) (1999) *Fundamentals in British Politics,* Basingstoke: Palgrave; and Bogdanor V (1997) *Power and the People,* London: Gollancz. On the post-1997 developments see R. Hazell (ed) (1999) *Constitutional Futures,* Oxford: Oxford University Press; R. Hazell et al (2002), 'The Constitution Coming in From the Cold', *Parliamentary Affairs,* 55(2): 219–34; R. Blackburn and R. Plant (eds) (1999) *Constitutional Reform: The Labour Government's Constitutional Reform* *Agenda,* London: Longmans; A. King (2001) *Does the United Kingdom Still Have a Constitution?,* London: Sweet & Maxwell; S. Ludlam and M. Smith (eds) (2001) *New Labour in Government,* Basingstoke: Palgrave; and V. Bogdanor (1999) *Devolution in the United Kingdom,* Oxford: Oxford University Press. For a stimulating polemic see F. Ridley (1988) 'There is no British Constitution: A Dangerous Case of the Emperor's Clothes', *Parliamentary Affairs,* 41: 339–60 and (1992) 'What Happened to the Constitution under Mrs Thatcher?' in B. Jones and L. Robins (eds) *Two Decades in British Politics,* Manchester: Manchester University Press.

 Visit the Online Resource Centre that accompanies this book for links to more information on chapter topic

CHAPTER ELEVEN

The core executive I: Prime Ministers and power dependency

READER'S GUIDE

The core executive is the 'engine-room' of the policy-making process. This chapter examines what actors/organisations make up the core executive and to what extent the core executive has had to adapt to an era of governance. It then explores the nature of power in the core executive, in particular focusing on the role of the Prime Minister. Here, we review the traditional debate between prime ministerial v Cabinet power, before arguing that despite a more diverse and complex policy-making arena, political power in Britain is still best understood as a process of dependency between the key actors within the core executive.

Introduction

There is a tendency amongst even the more serious newspaper broadsheets and political television programmes to present a simple parody of the nature of power within the British political system. Discussions are couched in a formulaic manner, centred on a binary argument concerning the extent to which prime ministerial government and more recently presidentialism has replaced Cabinet government. For example, when in autumn 2001, the Labour Government was establishing its position in relation to possible military engagement in Afghanistan against the Taliban regime, a leader article in the *Guardian* entitled 'President Blair', spelt out in no uncertain terms the presidential thesis:

> Look at the contrast between America, with its presidential system in which the cabinet normally plays a negligible policymaking role, and Britain where, according to the textbooks, the cabinet is supreme, and the premier traditionally 'first among equals'. Today, the roles are reversed. President George Bush sits firmly in Washington, where he holds regular cabinet meetings, and sends his Defence Secretary through the Middle East and central Asia twisting arms and building alliances for the American position. In Britain, meanwhile, the Cabinet rarely meets and plays no meaningful role, while Mr Blair takes the decisions in private with advisers and conducts his own diplomacy across three continents... Presidentialism on this scale is neither smart nor right. (The *Guardian*, 6 October 2001).

This chapter outlines the broad parameters of the arguments between prime ministerial and Cabinet government, suggesting that it is a futile debate which is both irresolvable and, more importantly, ignores the way in which the core executive operates. The chapter suggests that in order to understand the core executive and how its key actors—the Prime Minister, the Cabinet and the Civil Service—operate, it is important to recognise that:

• each possesses an array of resources, and

• they are dependent upon each other.

As such, the key theme in this chapter is that the operation of the core executive is not about competition between rival sets of actors, but instead it concerns the structures of dependency, which both enable and constrain the core executive. The chapter outlines the traditional debate and its problems, then describes the core executive model of dependency as an alternative, more sophisticated approach to explaining power relations at the heart of British government and analyses the implications this model has for understanding the role of the Prime Minister.

Prime ministerial v Cabinet government

There is no constitutional definition of a Prime Minister's role, nor any statutory statement of his/her duties. Indeed, the first statutory reference to the office of the Prime Minister was only made in 1937. The checks and balances that operate on a Prime Minister are predominantly informal and political, not legal. Personality alone does not explain Tony Blair's dominance in his first term in office (1997–2001), especially when we contrast it with the travails he experienced at times in his second term (2001–05) stemming from the Labour Government's formal decision to go to war in Iraq in March 2003, or, the rhetoric surrounding Blair at the outset of his third term of being a 'lame-duck' Prime Minister, following his announcement in the lead up to the 2005 general election that this was the last election in which he would be standing as Prime Minister.

The growth of the prime ministerial thesis

We often classify Prime Ministers as 'strong' or weak, as a success or a failure. It is interesting that strong leaders so often fall spectacularly. When the Conservative Party withdrew from Lloyd George's coalition in 1922, he immediately resigned and was never a serious force again. In 1990, Margaret Thatcher was humbled when nearly 40% of Conservative MPs refused to vote for her in the party's leadership contest. In each case, it was the failure to gain the support of MPs, rather than of the electorate, that proved decisive. The election defeats of 'lesser' Prime Ministers like Callaghan, Heath and Major, or the retirements of Wilson and Eden are less dramatic. The British system, with the high place it has accorded to the Cabinet and the party in Parliament, has not been kind to strong Prime Ministers, even though it is the latter that leave their mark on history. Interestingly, the latter half of the last century has seen the relatively rapid accrual of new institutional resources to the Prime Ministers (see Table 11.1). This post-war growth in the Prime Minister's institutional support, combined with a declining role of the full Cabinet in policy-making led to a long and ultimately sterile debate over whether prime ministerial government had replaced Cabinet government. Unfortunately, personality was often placed at the centre of these discussions, leading to distorted commentaries on the real nature of prime ministerial power. Table 11.1 traces the genealogy of the institutional change in the role of the Prime Minister and Cabinet and the accompanying debate concerning the impact on power.

As Table 11.1 demonstrates, since the 1960s, academics, commentators and politicians have been arguing that prime ministerial government is replacing Cabinet government. For example, on 15 March 1968, George Brown, the then Foreign Secretary, left the Wilson Labour Government, stating that he had:

> . . . resigned as a matter of fundamental principle, because it seemed to me that the Prime Minister. . . was introducing a 'presidential' system in to the running of the government that is wholly alien to the British constitutional system (Brown 1972: 161).

Institutional change	Academic debate
Wilson 1964–70: establishes the Political Office at Number 10 and enlarges the press office.	Mackintosh (1963) initiates debate with history of the Cabinet. The decline of Cabinet government further supported by Crossman (1963, 1972).
Heath 1970–74: establishes the Central Policy Review Staff.	Brown (1968) and Jones (1975) argue that Cabinet government continues and point to constraints on Prime Minster.
Wilson 1974–76: formally creates the Policy Unit at Number 10.	
Thatcher 1979–90: denudes the role of the Cabinet; intervenes increasingly in departmental policy decisions and chooses to work through ad hoc groups, special advisors and bilateral meetings with Cabinet ministers.	A large body of literature highlights the style and dominance of Thatcher and questions the degree of prime ministerial government (see King 1985; Burch 1988; Kavanagh 1990; Hennessy 1986; Foster 1997).
Major 1990–97: attempts to increase the role of Cabinet in policy-making but the Policy Unit retains central role.	Literature by those involved in government under Thatcher and Major suggests Cabinet still important (see Lawson 1994; Wakeham 1994; Hogg and Hill 1995).
Blair 1997–to-date: Blair increases the size and centrality of the Policy Unit, creates the role of Cabinet enforcer and uses 'joined-up' government in an attempt to impose prime ministerial will on departments and improve policy delivery.	Literature on presidentialism (Foley 1992, 2000; Pryce 1997) developed with some analysis of Blair suggesting a shift to Bonapartism and increased one person control (Hennessy 2000; Kavanagh and Seldon 1999; Heffernan 2005).

Elsewhere, the prominent Labour politician, Richard Crossman, in his introduction to Bagehot's *The English Constitution* claimed that: 'if we mean by presidential government, government by an elective first magistrate then we in England have a president as truly as the Americans' (Crossman 1963: 22–3). Yet, by the 1970s, these arguments had already become somewhat stagnant—for example, Heclo and Wildavsky (1974: 341–3) described the debate about prime ministerial power as one of the 'chestnuts of the constitution'. As Rhodes (2005), observes they probably did not expect to see it thriving 35 years later as the presidentialisation thesis. A key theme was the perception of the declining role of Cabinet. This was seen as the culmination of a long-term process of centralisation of power in the hands of the Prime Minister and the increased development of

Prime Minister	Party	Dates	Hennessy Label
Clement Attlee	Labour	1945–51	'Weather Maker'
Winston Churchill	Conservative	1951–55	'Seasoned Coper'
Anthony Eden	Conservative	1955–57	'Catastrophe'
Harold Macmillan	Conservative	1957–63	'Promise Unfulfilled'
Alex Douglas-Home	Conservative	1963–64	'Punctuation Mark'
Harold Wilson	Labour	1964–70	'Promise Unfulfilled'
Edward Heath	Conservative	1970–74	'System-shifter'
Harold Wilson	Labour	1974–76	'Promise Unfulfilled'
James Callaghan	Labour	1976–79	'Seasoned Coper'
Margaret Thatcher	Conservative	1979–90	'Weather Maker'
John Major	Conservative	1990–97	'Overwhlemed'
Tony Blair	Labour	1997–to date	'System-Shifter'

resources inside Number 10. Until recently, academics have consistently drawn from within the parameters of this discourse when characterising the nature of different Prime Ministerships. For example, Hennessy (2001) attaches the following set of labels to individual post-war Prime Ministers.

Hennessy argues that of these 12 post-war Prime Ministers, only three have attracted the epithet 'presidential'—Harold Wilson, Margaret Thatcher and Tony Blair. In the case of Wilson, it was the testimonies of his own Cabinet ministers that provoked charges of presidentialisim. Denis Healey, who served as Secretary of State for Defence and Chancellor of the Exchequer in the Wilson governments, suggested that: 'no Prime Minister ever interfered so much in the work of his colleagues' (Healey 1990: 332); Tony Benn, Secretary of State for Industry 1974–75, and Energy Secretary 1975–79, but regarded by his Cabinet colleagues as an 'outsider' in the 1974–79 Labour Administration, argued that by the end of that particular term: 'the centralisation of power into the hands of one man . . . amounts to a system of personal rule' (Benn 1985: 222). Similar sentiments were expressed by some of Margaret Thatcher's ministers. Kenneth Baker (1993: 270), Secretary of State for Education, observed how Thatcher revelled in the soubriquet, 'The Iron Lady'. Three of her senior colleagues resigned predominantly because of the way she ran her Cabinets—Michael Heseltine (Secretary of State for Defence) in 1985, Nigel Lawson (Chancellor of the Exchequer) in 1989 and Geoffrey Howe (Foreign Secretary and then Deputy Prime Minister) in 1990. Of all Thatcher's ministers,

Francis Pym, Foreign Secretary (1982–83), was particularly damming of her style: 'I object to a system that deliberately pits Downing Street against individual Departments, breeds resentment amongst ministers and Civil Servants and turns the Prime Minister into a President' (Pym 1984: 17).

The growth of the presidential thesis

Under the Blair Administration, the presidential thesis has come to the fore. Popular wisdom deems that power within British central government is now increasingly concentrated in the office of the Prime Minister (see Foley 1992, 2000; Pryce 1997; Hennessy 2001; and Rose 2001). Peter Riddell sees the office in Number 10 Downing Street as a 'Prime Minister's Department' in all but name. Peter Hennessy talks of the 'Command Prime Ministership'. Michael Foley argues that the system has become presidential with the Prime Minister now standing above party, Parliament and even Whitehall. One Labour MP, Graham Allen (2002), has suggested that we forgo the pretence of Cabinet government and accept the inevitable: that we now have a presidential system which if acknowledged, and with proper constitutional checks and balances, would provide a more effective method of governing Britain.

These commentaries draw evidence from both 'insider accounts' by the circle of apparatchiks surrounding the New Labour camp, but more importantly, the institutional changes wrought by Blair since 1997. For example, weekly Cabinet meetings rarely last an hour and usually do not involve substantive policy discussions (Holliday 2002). Throughout the course of Labour's second term, there has been a reorganisation of Number 10 Downing Street with the Prime Minister developing much greater policy capabilities and means for intervening in a wide range of policy areas. The Prime Minister's Office is increasingly perceived as the source of policy, whilst it is argued that the role of Whitehall is to administer Number 10's agenda. As Tony Blair has admitted: 'I make no apology for having a strong centre. I think you need a strong centre . . .' (Liaison Committee 2002: para 5). This could be seen as a definitive break with the traditional constitutional position that sees the Cabinet as the ultimate political authority and government departments as the sources of policy. Further fuel is added to the fire by those who argue that the Blair Government relies much less on officials and increasingly uses special advisers and outside sources for advice. According to *The Times* (10 January 2002): 'Downing Street's battalions of political advisers and consultants have wrested power from the traditional Civil Service' (see Chapter 12). Again, this is changing the balance of power inside Number 10 and across government. Yet, defenders of the status quo still insist there have not been major changes in the organisation of government (see Politics in Focus 11.1).

A critique of the prime ministerial v Cabinet government debate

In order to understand the changing role of the Prime Minister, it is important not to oversimplify the argument. To see the current core executive as dominated by an over-powerful

11.1

...view of prime ministerial power

In 2001, Richard Wilson, a former Head of the Civil Service, appeared in front of the Public Administration Select Committee, and provided what can be regarded as the *de facto* constitutional view of the nature of prime ministerial power:

> I do not think that it is a Prime Minister's Department in all but name . . . we do not have a Presidential role for the Prime Minister in this country. We have a system where legal powers and financial resources are vested in the Secretaries of State. The Prime Minister has few executive powers other than the administration of the Civil Service . . . His or her power varies from time to time according to the extent his Cabinet colleagues permit him to have that power, depending on whether the Cabinet is split, depending also on the strength of the Government majority particularly in the House of Commons and also popular opinion in the electorate and attitudes in the Party. The structure that we have is one that meets the needs of the Prime Minister but it does not imply that the role of the Prime Minister has fundamentally changed. I think the term 'Prime Minister's Department' implies a different role for the Prime Minister and a major constitutional change that I would tell you has not taken place (Public Administration Committee, 2001).

Prime Minister is to misunderstand the complex network of relationships that are essential to the running of a modern state (see Politics in Focus 11.2). The prime ministerial versus Cabinet government debate is both irresolvable and unhelpful in discussions of British central government. A number of authors (see Bruce-Gardyne and Lawson 1976; Burch and Holliday 1996; Holliday 2002; Rhodes and Dunleavy 1995; Smith 1999; Richards and Smith

The term 'executive' is used here to refer to the centres of political authority which take policy decisions. In other words, the executive institutions are not limited to the prime minister and the cabinet but also include ministers in their departments. The term 'core executive' refers to all those organisations and procedures which coordinate central government policies, and act as final arbiters of conflict between different parts of the government machine. In brief, the core executive is the heart of the machine, covering the complex web of instuitions, networks and practices surrounding the prime minister, cabinet, cabinet committees and their official counterparts, less formalised ministerial 'clubs' or meetings, bilateral negotiations and interdepartmental committees. It also includes coordinating departments, chiefly the Cabinet Office, the Treasury, the Foreign Office, the law officers and the security and intelligence services.

Rhodes (1995: 12)

2002; Heffernan 2005) have been critical of this approach. They argue that it focuses too much on the personality of an individual; it sees power as an object rather than something that is fluid and relational; it ignores the constraints on actors and it simplifies the way decisions are made in central government. For example, as we will see in Chapter 12, it ignores the fact that departments in Britain have considerable autonomy and therefore, there are important resource, institutional and time constraints on what the Prime Minister can do. Furthermore, the debate is commonly couched in very insular terms, ignoring the broader constraints beyond SW1 that all political leaders have to confront. This theme is aptly caught in the title of Rose's (2001) *The Prime Minister in a Shrinking World*, in which he observes that whilst prime ministerial power has increased over the Westminster/Whitehall domain, this is no longer the sole nor key site of decision-making. In the areas where crucial decisions are made, such as the EU or G7[8], the Prime Minister has less power because s/he is one among many. Indeed, the present Labour Administration has recognised this change and advocates the need for mutual, inter-dependence at the European and supranational level, unlike the rhetoric of the previous Conservative Administration in defending the nation-state (see Chapter 9).

Essentially, neither the prime ministerial nor the Cabinet thesis can help us properly understand central government because both misconceive the nature of power and the institutional make-up of the core executive. There is a more analytically compelling alternative—the power dependency model—which highlights the complexity and inter-dependency of central government and can be used to analyse the fluctuating nature of relationships and power within government.

Understanding the core executive: the power dependency model

The 'power dependency model' avers that the Prime Minister is only one actor, albeit a significant actor, within the institutions and relationships that make up the core executive. This model is underpinned by the view that in order to appreciate the complexities of the policy making process within the core executive, it is necessary to recognise the following.

- All actors within the core executive have resources (see Table 11.3).
- In order to achieve goals resources have to be exchanged.
- Notions of prime ministerial government, Cabinet government or presidentialism are irrelevant because power within the core executive is based on dependency not command.
- In order to understand the operation of the core executive we need to trace the structures of dependency.
- These structures of dependency are often based on overlapping networks. Frequently, these networks do not follow formal organisational structures and this can lead to fragmentation and conflict over responsibility and territory.

- Even resource-rich actors, such as the Prime Minister, are dependent on other actors to achieve their goals. Therefore, government works through building alliances rather than command.

- Actors operate within a structured arena. Traditional approaches to central government have placed too much emphasis on personality. Prime Ministers, officials and ministers are bound by external organisation, the rules of the game, the structures of institutions, other actors and the context. Therefore, the nature and form of the core executive does not change with personality.

- Because of the distribution of resources, the strength of departments and overlapping networks, the core executive is fragmented and central co-ordination is difficult.

- The degree of dependency that actors have on each other varies according to the context. As the political and economic situation changes, actors may become more or less dependent. For example, a buoyant economy may provide a Chancellor of the Exchequer with more freedom, as witnessed during Gordon Brown's first term in office. A successful military campaign, such as that achieved by Margaret Thatcher in recapturing the Falklands Islands from the Argentineans in 1982, may provide the Prime Minister with greater room for manoeuvre. Economic failure such as that experienced by Norman Lamont in September 1992 with Britain's withdrawal from the Exchange Rate Mechanism may mean the Chancellor needs more support from his colleagues, especially the Prime Minister. Political failure such as the introduction of the Community Charge (Poll Tax) by the Thatcher Government in 1990, means the Prime Minister becomes increasingly reliant on his/her Cabinet for support.

Beyond personality—theorising prime ministerial power

The relationships between ministers, between ministers and officials and between ministers and the Prime Minister do not primarily depend on personality. They are structured relationships that are shaped by the rules of the Whitehall game, the institutions of government, past policy choices and by the external political and economic context. Asking whether there is prime ministerial government does not take us far in understanding the operation of central government. Different actors and institutions need each other. Cabinet ministers and Prime Ministers have resources, but to achieve goals they need to exchange resources. The process of exchange—the forging of alliances—depends on the particular context. If a Prime Minister has just won an election, he is less dependent than a Prime Minister who is very unpopular in the polls. It also depends on the tactics and strategies that ministers and Prime Ministers use. As John Major discovered in the latter stages of his term in office, if ministers do not recognise the authority of the Prime Minister, then s/he is rendered increasingly powerless. Continual overriding of the wishes of the Cabinet by the Prime Minister will undermine authority. Even dominant Prime Ministers need to exchange resources (see Figure 11.1).

Clearly, the Prime Minister has resources that are unavailable to other ministers, among them the traditionally cited formal resources of patronage, control of the Cabinet agenda, appointment of Cabinet Committees and the use of the Prime Minister's Office.

 officials

Prime Minister	Ministers	Officials
Patronage—the Prime Minister appoints MPs to government jobs.	*Political support*—ministers can often have considerable support within their party.	*Permanence*—officials are permanent and ministers temporary. Consequently, much of the minister's task is learning the job.
Authority—within the British system, the post of PM is recognised as carrying tremendous authority. Ministers immediately react differently to a colleague who becomes PM.	*Authority*—the minister within a department has a high level of authority. The British constitution means the minister's word is final.	*Knowledge*—officials have detailed information on policy areas and of course control the flow of information to the minister.
Political support/party—the Prime Minister usually has the support of the party.	*Department*—through the control of a department, a minister has access to tremendous bureaucratic resources.	*Time*—as a body, officials have considerable time.
Political support/electorate—The Prime Minister's resources are greatly increased if s/he has popular support.	*Knowledge*—departments have considerable informational resources concerning particular policy areas which are often absent to the Prime Minister.	*Whitehall network/information control*—officials have contacts throughout Whitehall which provide a good source of information. They can also regulate the information which ministers are exposed to.
Prime Minister's Office—The Prime Minister has institutional support through the office.	*Policy networks*—ministers become enmeshed within policy networks that control the making and delivery of policy.	*Keepers of the constitution*—senior officials see themselves as upholding the constitution. Consequently, they can define what behaviour is acceptable for ministers and officials.
Bilateral policy-making—The PM can have a major impact through intervening in departmental policy through policy-making with ministers.	*Policy success*—if a minister is seen to be successful, s/he is in a very strong position.	

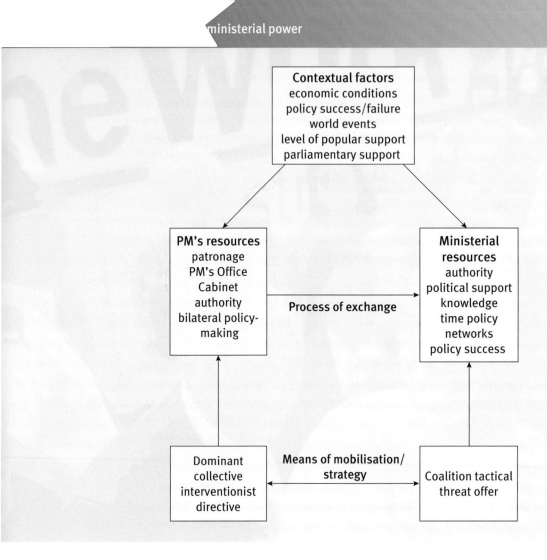

The Prime Minister also has less tangible resources including, particularly the ability to intervene in any policy area; only the Prime Minister really has any collective oversight; and most ministers lack the interest, time, ability or institutional support to be involved in other areas of policy. This oversight enables Prime Ministers to involve themselves in any area of policy-making they choose.

The Prime Minister does have a degree of authority that is greater than any other minister. A crucial convention within Whitehall is that ministers and civil servants accept the authority of the Prime Minister. Nevertheless, unlike other resources, which are fairly objective, prime ministerial authority is largely relational or contingent, dependent on the standing of the Prime Minister (see Politics in Focus 11.3). From this perspective,

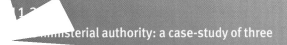

1 ...

...sterial authority: a case-study of three

Edward Heath (1970–74)

A Prime Minister has greatest authority after an electoral victory, particularly if it is an unexpected one such as that of Edward Heath in 1970 (Campbell 1993: 289). For two years, the new Prime Minister was at the vanguard of his government, but a mid-term economic recession mainly caused by an overseas oil crisis, followed by a series of perceived u-turns from Heath's own brand of neo-liberal Conservatism, coupled to the perception that he and his government could not control an all-powerful, trade-union lobby, increasing eroded Heath's political authority during the last two years of his term in office.

Margaret Thatcher (1979–90)

Margaret Thatcher provides a very good example of the contingent nature of prime ministerial authority. In 1981, Britain was in the middle of an economic recession, her Government was conceding wage demands to various trade unions and Thatcher was in a minority within her own Cabinet, in terms of her own brand of Conservatism. Within two years, she had overseen a successful military conflict to claim back the sovereignty of the Falklands Islands, banished what she regarded as 'non-believers' [or Wets] from her Cabinet and in the 1983 election returned her party to office with the largest post-war majority by a government. At this point her authority was regarded as almost unassailable. Seven years later, the picture was very different. The Conservative party had become increasingly divided over Europe, in particular, membership of the European Exchange Rate Mechanism (this had in part led to resignations by key Cabinet ministers such as Geoffrey Howe and Nigel Lawson), Britain had plunged back into recession and Margaret Thatcher's style of leadership was severely criticised for being aloof and isolated from her own Cabinet colleagues. She had chosen to surround herself by a cabal of advisers such as Charles Powell and Professor Alan Walters and finally, the Government's pursuit of a new taxation system for local government, the Community Charge, had led to widespread civil disobedience. Within months, Thatcher was forced to resign following a party vote of no confidence, the only incumbent Prime Minister to be ejected from office by her own party in the 20th century.

Tony Blair (1997–to date)

The authority of Tony Blair is an interesting study for popular accounts of his power always posit that it is subject to the ebb and flow in relations with his Chancellor, Gordon Brown (see Rawnsley 2001; Naughtie 2001). Again, these accounts misunderstand the nature of dependency within the core executive. The on-going Blair story is intriguing, founded on the back-drop of an enormous electoral victory secured by New Labour in May 1997, a Conservative Party in disarray, and an economy which on the whole has proved remarkably stable since both Blair and his Government were subsequently placed under immense strain in the autumn of 2000 in the shape of the fuel crisis and months later with the onset of the foot-and-mouth crisis. Yet, by the summer of 2001, Tony Blair's authority was again on the ascendancy as he became the first Labour Prime Minister to win two successive landslide Commons majorities. But his administration was heading for stormy waters, most notably, over the decision to engage in military conflict in Iraq. The Government was dogged by the continued failure of the intelligence community to find evidence of weapons of mass destruction which had been the justification for military engagement with Iraq in spring 2003, the suicide of the former UN weapons inspector Dr David Kelly on 17 July 2003, the subsequent imbroglio between the Government and the BBC over the reporter Andrew Gilligan's claim that the Government had placed undue pressure on the Joint Intelligence Committees in its compiling of the second dossier on Iraq's military capabilities and finally, the narrowest of margins on which the Government secured a majority of only five on the second reading of the Higher Education Bill following the dispute concerning university top-up-fees in January 2004. The latter was the largest parliamentary rebellion on the second reading of a bill for 60 years. Again, the contingent nature of the Prime Minister's authority was altering course, this time on a downward trajectory, as his standing in relation to both his Cabinet colleagues and the Labour Party diminished. This was compounded in May 2005 when, despite being the first ever Labour Prime Minister to deliver a third consecutive historic term in office, Blair's announcement that he would stand down as Prime Minister before the next election appeared to sound the death knoll on his premiership. Yet, by July 2005, talk of Brown replacing Blair had receded in the light of Blair's successful marshalling of the G8 summit in Scotland, his role in London's successful bid for the 2012 Olympics and his handling of and response to the terrorist attacks in London.

the key point about the Labour Administration is not that Tony Blair has become all-powerful, but that the resources of the Prime Minister have clearly increased and new patterns of dependency have developed (see Chapter 12).

The core executive and resource exchange

To understand prime ministerial power, it is necessary to examine the process of resource exchange between actors in the core executive that results from dependency. Even with an array of institutional resources and the authority of the Office, a Prime Minister can achieve nothing on his/her own. In order to translate capabilities into power, s/he is dependent on others for advice, information, support and assistance in making policy. Ministers and civil servants clearly have their own resources, as we will see in the next chapter. Perhaps most importantly, ministers have their own sources of authority. Many senior ministers have such high authority that it is almost impossible for a Prime Minister to dismiss them. For example, it would have been almost unthinkable for Tony Blair to have dismissed Gordon Brown as Chancellor of the Exchequer during Labour's first two terms. Similarly, in the period around 1987–88 another former Chancellor of the Exchequer, Nigel Lawson was in an exceptionally strong position. Then, he controlled significant institutional resources, not least the Treasury, which effectively gave him control of economic policy. Moreover, he was seen as the architect of Britain's economic revival in the mid-1980s and, subsequently, he had substantial authority within the Conservative Party. As he had little ambition to be Prime Minister he could take political risks. Lawson's stock rose further with his radical tax-cutting 1988 budget, which delivered a balanced budget. Consequently, despite major disagreements with Thatcher, Lawson was, in the Prime Minister's terms unassailable. Thatcher admitted to another of her ministers, Kenneth Baker that she could not have sacked Lawson because: 'I might well have had to go as well' (Thatcher quoted in Baker 1993: 315). Within a different context, at present, John Prescott has an independent power base in the Labour Party and it seems highly unlikely that Blair could remove him from Cabinet.

Not only is a Prime Minister confronted by ministerial resources, he is also highly dependent on the Cabinet for authority. The limits of authority are starkly illustrated in the case of Thatcher's resignation in November 1990. Then, a Cabinet she had appointed effectively removed the Prime Minister's authority. At the time of the leadership challenge, Thatcher would have gone on to a second ballot had she not realised that Cabinet support was slipping away. She admits in her memoirs that once she was convinced that she had lost Cabinet support, she decided not to stand in the second round:

> A prime minister who knows that his or her cabinet has withheld its support is fatally weakened. I knew—and I am sure that they knew—that I would not willingly remain an hour in 10 Downing Street without the real authority to govern (Thatcher 1993: 851).

The core executive and the importance of context

This process of exchange is also affected by the particular context. If the external context is favourable to the Prime Minister, in terms of economic policy or electorally, then the Prime Minister has less dependence on the Cabinet. If the external context is less favourable the Prime Minister requires more support.

Success in achieving policy goals for both ministers and the Prime Minister will depend on tactics. How resources are deployed is an important aspect in power and it means that in certain situations ministers with relatively low resources can defeat the Prime Minister or more highly resourced ministers. The three most recent Prime Ministers have had very different strategies and tactics. Thatcher's strategy was generally interventionist, Major was more collectivist and Blair appears directive (see Table 11.4).

Thatcher

Thatcher wanted to intervene in the work of departments. Many of her ministers recognised the effect she had on departments, especially when compared to Edward

	THATCHER	MAJOR	BLAIR
STRATEGY	Interventionist	Collectivist	Directive
TACTICS	Using small groups of ministers to build support for her goals. Bilateral meetings with ministers.	Working with Cabinet to build consensus. Delaying decisions until support.	Using PM's Office, Cabinet Office, Delivery Unit etc, to develop strategic direction. Use of 'Cabinet enforcer' to ensure ministers follow direction.

Heath. But she was often highly tactical in her approach—creating the right Cabinet committees, building the necessary alliances or working bilaterally with ministers to by pass Cabinet opposition. Even a dominant Prime Minister like Thatcher is dependent on colleagues, if she wants to intervene. In the initial years of her administration, Thatcher was successful at building alliances in order to achieve her goals. She was also effective at using relatively 'independent' figures like Lord Whitelaw and John Wakeham as conduits between her and Cabinet, so that compromises could be worked out without direct confrontation or capitulation.

Later, she found increasing opposition in Cabinet. Thatcher's tactic was to operate, to some degree, outside the Cabinet system. She depended on her political advisors for support and influenced policy by operating bilaterally with ministers who were not in a position to resist her demands. Consequently, even a Prime Minister with a dominant style who wants to intervene needs to understand the lines of dependence and work out tactics accordingly. For the first half of her period in office, Thatcher's tactics worked relatively well and she was effective at achieving her goals. Near the end of her administration, Thatcher failed to recognised the dependent nature of her position, she had cut lines of support with too many key actors in her own government and become overly reliant on her own politically appointed cortege and not her ministers and parliamentary colleagues. It was this, more than any other single factor that explains her subsequent ejection from the primary seat of power in British politics.

Major

On inheriting the premiership from Thatcher in November 1990, Major was clearly in a different structural position to Thatcher. He lacked his own electoral mandate and Britain was in the midst of an economic recession. Consequently, he adopted a different strategy. Thatcher was seen to have been removed from office because she would not listen and ignored her lines of dependency. Therefore as a new Prime

Minister, Major was expected to be more collegiate and he obliged. In Seldon's (1997: 738) assessment:

> Major by temperament and choice was a conciliator. Before he became prime minister, he had found Mrs Thatcher's style of 'macho leadership' personally distasteful. His chairmanship of cabinet and cabinet committees, in contrast, allowed ministers to express their views, and guided them to a conclusion in line with his intentions. Rather than have dissent in the cabinet he preferred to delay decisions until he could reconcile differences.

These changed tactics were not solely determined by personality, but were what the circumstances required. As Seldon (1997: 742) suggests: 'Major's leadership could be argued to have been exactly what was required for the times'. With the removal of Thatcher, the party and the Cabinet had different visions of Conservatism, and Major had to try to keep the Cabinet together. Yet leading the Conservative Party had become an almost impossible task. Fault lines in the party over Europe, which had been papered over in the late 1980s came much more to the fore, and a disastrous 'Back-to-Basics' campaign in which an array of misdemeanours by Tory MPs were revealed to the nation on an almost weekly basis, left the party in a state of almost ungovernability. Maybe here, the irony was that Major was able to keep his Government in power for almost seven years.

Blair

Clearly, Blair is still a work in progress, but he has already entered the history books having delivered Labour an historic third successive term in office (see Seldon 2004, Riddell 2004, Stephens 2004, Geddes and Tonge 2005 and Seldon and Kavanagh 2005). His strategy has been one of setting an overall policy direction with the Cabinet and then ensuring that the departments follow the broad policy outline. In some areas, he has been willing to become closely attached to certain policies. Here we might include education, Northern Ireland, Kosovo and even the issue of the 'millennium bug'.

However, it also appears that Blair is aware of his dependencies. Two ministers, Gordon Brown (Chancellor of the Exchequer) and John Prescott (Deputy Prime Minister) are in strong positions. Brown has agreed not to openly challenge Blair for the leadership of the party and so Blair owes his position, to some extent, to Brown who probably is the one Cabinet minister who could challenge Blair. As a result of Brown's support for Blair, which was most obviously witnessed in the 2005 election campaign when the two became almost inseparable on the campaign trail, he has assumed tacit control of the Government's economic strategy and the welfare-to-work programme. Labour's position on membership of European Monetary Union (EMU) is also a result of policy worked out between Blair and Brown.

Prescott also has a position of key influence because he was elected by the party as deputy leader and is seen as the 'voice' of the compassionate heart of 'old' Labour. He also provides a useful function for Blair in that he can often convince the party membership that key policy changes such as trade union reform and welfare-to-work are not at odds with Labour's principles. Prescott has too much party support and is too important in that position for Blair to be able to remove him.

It is also the case that ministers can win battles or at least concessions with the Prime Minister. This might be because the issue is unpopular with certain sections of the Labour Party, for example, the war in Iraq or university top-up-fees. Alternatively, it may be through the use of clever tactics. During the last Conservative Administration, Virginia Bottomley saved a threat to the Department of Heritage budget by releasing a letter from the Chancellor saying lottery money would be available in addition to, not as a replacement for, existing expenditure.

Prime Ministers undoubtedly have more resources than other ministers. However, as we see in the next chapter, ministers are in a strong position because they are the heads of departments and it is only departments that have the capability both to make and implement detailed policy. Therefore departments are crucial sites of power within the central state. This means that the relationship between Prime Minister and Cabinet is a fluctuating mediation between a Prime Minster who has authority and an overseeing capacity and departmental ministers who have their own varying levels of authority and a departmental machine as support. If a Prime Minister wants to make an impact, s/he is more often than not dependent on the departmental machine and the support of the minister. Clearly, then, we have argued throughout this chapter that in order to understand the core executive, an effective medium for analysis is the power dependency model. Our focus has been predominantly on the Prime Minister, as we look in more detail at the role of ministers and civil servants in the next chapter. Yet, despite the emphasis on dependency and a recognition that actors within the core executive operate within a structured context, we also need finally to recognise that the Prime Minister is an exceptional individual within the core executive.

The Prime Minister: *primus inter pares*?

The Prime Minister has more authority than any other actor in the core executive possessing the ability to change government structures and of course the make-up of the Cabinet. Two examples illustrate the particular position of the Prime Minister. The first is the way in which the Prime Minister can redraw the boundaries of government without consultation. In 1974, the then Labour Prime Minister Harold Wilson decided to split the Department of Trade and Industry into two departments in order to prevent one of his more difficult ministers, Tony Benn, having a significant economic power base. This change was made without consultation either in Cabinet or with senior officials. The Prime Minister can make changes in the machinery of government almost at whim and all Prime Ministers have done so. Tony Blair has made significant changes at the centre of his Government through the creation of the 'Cabinet enforcer', the strengthening of the Performance and Innovation Unit and bodies such as the Social Exclusion Unit and Delivery Unit which have an important impact in the way that the Prime Minister interacts with the rest of the core executive (see Chapter 13). But what it has also done is create much greater complexity at the centre (see Figure 11.2). One effect has been to leave those in the

entre

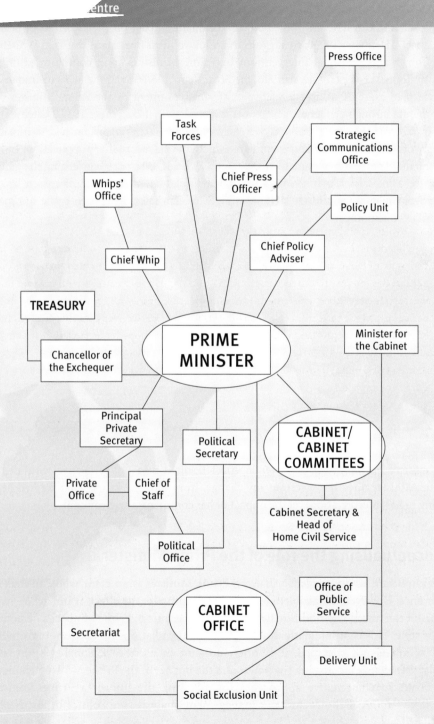

- Press Office
- Task Forces
- Strategic Communications Office
- Whips' Office
- Chief Press Officer
- Policy Unit
- Chief Whip
- Chief Policy Adviser
- TREASURY
- Minister for the Cabinet
- Chancellor of the Exchequer
- **PRIME MINISTER**
- Principal Private Secretary
- Political Secretary
- **CABINET/ CABINET COMMITTEES**
- Private Office
- Chief of Staff
- Cabinet Secretary & Head of Home Civil Service
- Political Office
- Office of Public Service
- Secretariat
- **CABINET OFFICE**
- Delivery Unit
- Social Exclusion Unit

Source: adapted from Barberis, 2000: 32

traditional government departments, unsure over which power centre to engage with, in order to secure their own departmental goals.

The second example is the way in which prime ministerial signals are read within Whitehall and can have an immediate and dramatic impact on the direction of policy. Since 1997, Hennessy (2000: 6) suggests that the two most important words in Whitehall are 'Tony wants'. Personal interventions by Prime Ministers are a common feature of British politics. For example, in 1996, the Scott Report looking at the arms to Iraq affair provides an example of how a relatively informal comment by the Prime Minister can reverberate through Whitehall. The report reveals that on 4 December 1984 Thatcher met Tariq Aziz, the then Iraqi Foreign Secretary. She told Aziz that Britain had terminated supply of weapons to Iran and even items which may have a military application. In her comments, Thatcher had gone further than the existing DTI rules concerning the guidelines for arms sales (Scott 1996: 215). Thatcher's statement was then discussed by the Interdepartmental Committee (IDC) dealing with arm sales. Scott reports the summary record as concluding:

> There was some discussion as to how this [ie the Prime Minister's statement to Tariq Aziz] might affect the Ministerial Guidelines. It was concluded that the guidelines were the prime source of policy on defence sales to Iran and Iraq and that the prime minister's comments as reported in the Private Secretary's letter, were compatible with these Guidelines. However, the IDC took the view that the prime minister's comments meant that the IDC should err on the side of strictness when deciding on cases where the evidence was inconclusive (quoted in Scott 1996: 215–16).

A comment by the Prime Minister in effect resulted in a policy change without the Prime Minister directly suggesting any change. Ironically, the Prime Minister had been wrong in her interpretation, yet the impact of her comments was profound.

Conceptualising the role of the Prime Minister

It is important to acknowledge that the Prime Minister is an actor who can make a difference. However, the problem is how to conceptualise the effect or impact a Prime Minister can make. The traditional approach focuses on the Prime Minister's personality or style. This is problematic not least because the relationship between personality and action is not specified, it is often difficult to ascribe personality traits and whilst personality is constant, the power and the impact of the Prime Minister changes. There are two alternative approaches for assessing the impact a Prime Minister can have—rational choice and risk management analysis (see Politics in Focus 11.4 and 11.5).

This approach sees actors as utility maximisers who act in their own self-interest. Whilst there are clearly examples of Prime Ministers acting as rational self-interested actors, the constraints on, and the visibility of, their actions can make this difficult. A concept developed within rational choice theory is the notion of political entrepreneurs who can use their power and selective incentives to overcome collective action problems (see Dunleavy 1991). Essentially the Prime Minister is surrounded by ministers who are concerned with protecting their own self-interests or more precisely the departmental interest (see Castle 1980; Ponting 1986). The pursuit of self-interest can undermine the broader collective goods/goals of government. So the role of the Prime Minister is to act as an entrepreneur who provides the leadership and benefits to ministers to persuade them to act for the common, rather than personal, good. The Prime Minister can use his/her control of patronage, his authority and control over resources like time and money to persuade ministers to act in certain ways. Moreover, the Prime Minister is an entrepreneur who not only creates incentives for certain choices but can use leadership and authority to shape preferences so that Cabinet members choose collective goods (Dunleavy 1991: 143).

The notion of the Prime Minister as a political entrepreneur is a useful way of understanding Prime Ministers. Thatcher and Blair have both attempted to set collective policy goals which they expect Cabinet ministers to follow and have emphasised the need to break down self-interested departmental interests. For example, one element of the Blair Government's modernising programme is to provide incentives for official and ministers to deal with cross cutting problems in a co-ordinated way rather than stick to departmental silos (see Chapter 13). Yet, while the notion of the Prime Minister as a political entrepreneur may be useful, it is not without its critics, most notably those who disagree with the assumption that the role of actors is underpinned by a view that they are self-interested, utility maximisers (see Ward 1995; Marsh, Richards and Smith 2000).

Traditionally, textbooks on British politics have clung to the rather pithy label that the Prime Minister is by convention—*primus inter pares* (Latin for 'first among equals'). Yet, in many ways this form of branding misrepresents the complexity involved in analysing the role and actions of the Prime Minister. Above, we have argued that the Prime Minister is locked into a co-dependent relationship of resource-exchange with other actors in the core executive. Yet, this model is complicated by the fact that the personalism of the British political system means that the Prime Minister does have a unique impact as an individual. There is therefore a need to conceptualise the Prime Minister beyond simply personality. We have suggested that one way to do this is to see the Prime Minister as a rational actor, a political entrepreneur, using the control of resources as a mechanism for ensuring collective action. This approach however is not without its problems. An alternative notion is to see the Prime Minister as a risk manager attempting to assess ways of managing risks to themselves and the government as a whole. As Winston Churchill once observed, a good politician: '. . . should have the ability to foretell what is going to happen next week, next month and next year. And afterwards to explain why it didn't happen.'

⊃CUS 11.5

¬nent approach

An alternative way of conceiving the impact a Prime Minister can have is that of the risk manager approach (Smith 2004). Here, it is argued that individual actors have the compulsion both to achieve security but also to take risks as a means of progress. The Prime Minister, in effect must attempt to juggle between these two competing needs. Much of the role of the Prime Minister can be seen as an attempt to manage risk to themselves and the government. An example of risk management is apparent in the present Labour Government's strategy toward economic policy. Blair and Brown's fundamental concern was to remove the risk that previous Labour governments faced of sterling crises (1967, 1976) that have thrown Labour Administrations off course and undermined their governing competence. Consequently, since 1997, Labour pursued a strategy of essentially continuing the previous Conservative policy of fiscal prudence as a mechanism for reassuring the markets. The potential next step in this strategy would be to join the Euro locking Britain into a potentially strong currency area less prone to currency speculation with the added benefits that economic decision would be made in the EU removing the dangers of the government's economic competence being undermined. However, membership of the Euro depends on a referendum which creates the risk for the government that it may lose. Consequently, the Prime Minister is in the difficult position of having to balance the economic risks of Euro membership with the political risks of a lost referendum. This analysis helps to explain some of the conflicts and ambiguities in Labour's approach to monetary union. It also provides a motivation for prime ministerial actions and helps to explain why s/he may shift from collective to individualist forms of government.

Conclusion

The traditional arguments concerning prime ministerial and Cabinet government provide a particularly narrow understanding of the key relationships within the core executive. If we are to understand how the Prime Minister and Cabinet interact, it is important to we move beyond the rather limited, often futile narratives that place the personality of politicians at the centre of explanations of political phenomenon. A much broader and theoretically developed approach to conceptualising the core executive is offered by the power dependency model. This model conceives of the relationships within the core executive as functioning in an interdependent manner. Both the Prime Minister and the Cabinet have resources and in order to achieve policy and political goals they need to exchange these resources. However, the degree of resource exchange and the nature of dependency varies according to circumstances. The freedom that the Prime Minister has depends on his political situation, the wider economic conditions and the authority and resources of the colleague that s/he is dealing with. This means that we must recognise that power within the core executive is fluid and cannot be simply ascribed to a particular actor—be it the Prime Minister or the Cabinet.

Nevertheless, the Prime Minister is not the same as any other Cabinet minister. S/he is an agent who can affect what goes on in government. This means that we need a theory of agency which is based on more than the style or personality of the premier. The Prime Minister can be seen as a political entrepreneur who attempts to induce his/her colleagues to act in certain ways and at the same time having to assess and manage risk to themselves and the government. Personality may affect risk management strategies and the tactics that Prime Minister uses, but it is not the main determinant of the operation of the core executive.

KEY POINTS

- The traditional textbook approach to understanding the power of the Prime Minister v the Cabinet, as well as the more recent 'presidentialism' model are misconstrued.

- A more analytically persuasive account requires that power should not be seen as an object, but rather something that is fluid and relational.

- The power dependency model which emphasises the complexity and interdependency of central government can be used to analyse the fluctuating nature of relationships and power within government.

- All actors within the core executive possess a range of resources which they need to exchange in order to achieve their goals. This creates a series of structures of dependency.

- The degree of dependency that actors have on each other varies according to the context.

- Within a structure of dependency, the Prime Minister has resources that are unavailable to other actors, yet context remains crucial.

- To understand prime ministerial power, it is necessary to examine the process of resource exchange between actors in the core executive that results from dependency.

- When conceptualising the impact of a Prime Minister, traditional approaches focusing on personality and style are inadequate. Two alternative approaches are rational choice and risk management analysis.

KEY QUESTIONS

(1) Does the growth of prime ministerial resources mean we now have a presidential Prime Minister?

(2) Why is the traditional debate between prime ministerial and Cabinet government a particularly limited approach to understanding power in British politics?

(3) How do conceptions of power influence our understanding of the relationship between the Prime Minister and the Cabinet?

(4) How useful is it to see the Prime Minister as a political entrepreneur or risk manager?

(5) What resources are only available to a Prime Minister that sets him/her apart from other members of the Cabinet?

IMPORTANT WEBSITES

The website for the Prime Minister's Office and Number 10 Downing Street is: www.number-10. gov. uk/output/Page1.asp and for the Cabinet Office: www.cabinetoffice.gov.uk/about_the_cabinet_ office/. For websites of the House of Commons, see www.parliament.uk, the websites on the main political parties are: for Labour www.labour.org.uk, for the Conservatives www.conservative-party.org. uk, for the Liberal Democrats www.libdems.org.uk, then SNP www. snp.org.uk and Plaid Cymru www. plaid-cymru. wales.com. For details on the work of both ministers and civil servants, a good starting point is www. open.gov.uk or, more specifically www.cabinet-office.gov.uk. For debates on the role of ministers and civil servants, an interesting site is the Democratic Audit www.fhit.org/ demoicratic_audit/ index.html.

FURTHER READING

J. Mackintosh (1962), *The British Cabinet*, London: Stevens and R. Crossman (1972), *Inside View*, London: Jonathan Cape together an excellent account of the history and functioning of Cabinet and they are still worth reading. The prime ministerial government argument is clearly outlined by R. Crossman (1963), 'Introduction' to W. Bagehot, *The English Constitution*, London: Fontana and again in R. Crossman (1972), *Inside View*, London: Jonathan Cape but dismissed by G. Jones (1975), 'Development of the Cabinet' in W. Thornhill (ed), *The Modernisation of British Government*, London: Pitman. Presidentialism is advocated by M. Foley (1992), *The Rise of the British Presidency*, Manchester: Manchester University Press. The debate is summarised by G. Thomas (1998), *Prime Minister and Cabinet Today*, Manchester: University Press and A. King (ed) (1985) *The British Prime Minister*, Basingstoke: Macmillan.

The history of the Prime Minister's Office is recounted in J. Lee, G. Jones, and J. Burnham (1998), *At the Centre of Whitehall*, London: Macmillan and D. Kavanagh, and A. Seldon (1999), *The Powers Behind the Prime Minister*, London: Harper Collins. The first sophisticated analysis of the core executive is in R.A.W. Rhodes and P. Dunleavy (1995), *Prime Minister, Cabinet and Core Executive*, London: Macmillan M. Burch and I. Holliday (1996), *The British Cabinet System*, Hemel Hempstead: Prentice Hall and M.J. Smith (1998), *The Core Executive in Britain*, London: Macmillan apply the term. Details on the importance of departments are provided in T. Daintith, and A. Page (1999) *The Executive in the Constitution*, Oxford: Oxford University Press and D. Marsh, D. Richards and M.J. Smith (2001), *Changing Patterns of Governance*, Basingstoke: Palgrave.

 Visit the Online Resource Centre that accompanies this book for links to more information on chapter topic

CHAPTER TWELVE

The core executive II: ministers, civil servants and power dependency

READER'S GUIDE

Departments are the key institutions in the policy-making process and they command a broad range of resources. Yet, despite being at the heart of the core executive, their roles are often marginalised in traditional accounts of policy-making in Britain. This chapter argues that within a dependency model of power, departments and the key actors located within them—ministers and civil servants—are absolutely central to how policy is made. It identifies the strengths of the resources that departments have available and how this can in some cases lead to problems of departmentalism. The chapter then uses a policy networks approach to chart how the role of ministers and civil servants have had to adapt to an era of governance.

Introduction

As we saw in Chapter 3, the image presented of the nature of governing Britain in the 1950s is one in which Westminster and Whitehall are portrayed as the central site of political authority and ministers and civil servants are perceived as the key actors who determine policy outcomes. In terms of policy, the British core executive was regarded as the most powerful actor in the policy arena, and policy was made and implemented in a top-down manner. During this period, even the institution conferred with formal powers to restrain the executive, Parliament, was seen as ineffective at carrying out this constitutional role. For example, Hill and Whichelow addressed this theme in 'What's Wrong with Parliament' (1964: 20–1). They observed the:

> . . . ease with which a determined government can achieve their ends, whether or not the House approves of them. . . The *raison d'être* of Parliament is called in doubt. In the public eye, the first thing that is wrong with Parliament is that it no longer controls the Government's handling of the people's money.

The thrust of Hill and Whichelow's observations are not dissimilar to those of Lord Halisham, Lord Chancellor in the first Thatcher Government who viewed Britain as an 'elective dictatorship' in which there was a misuse of power by the executive.

The importance of these arguments, within the context of this chapter is that commentators regarded the core executive (in particular ministers and civil servants) in the period after 1945, as omnipotent actors who dominated the policy process and operated with few constraints on their power. Then, policy-making was seen as taking place in a predominantly closed, secretive and elitist world, it was top-down and the core executive was the central, most powerful actor.

Yet, in the course of the last 30 years, the policy arena has become much more diverse and crowded. Policy-making is regarded as a process of interaction between many different actors, taking place across a variety of terrains. Now, ministers and civil servants are regarded as being only some of many actors involved in the making and implementation of policy. This shift from an era of government in the 1950s to the present era of governance has significantly affected both the role and power of ministers and civil servants in the policy process. As Pierre and Stoker (2000: 29) observe:

> Twenty years ago political institutions and political leaders were much more self-reliant and it was assumed—for good reasons—that the state governed Britain. Today, the role of the *government* in the process of *governance* is much more contingent. Local, regional and national political elites alike seek to forge coalitions with private businesses, voluntary associations and other societal actors to mobilise resources across the public-private border in order to enhance their chances of guiding society towards politically defined goals.

The impact of the changing nature of the state in recent decades, has led a number of authors to suggest that the process of governing Britain has now become a matter of multi-level governance in which politics is played out over many different terrains involving a wide array of disparate actors (see Marks, Hooghe and Blank 1996; Jessop 2004). A key theme of multi-level governance is that both the power and role Westminster (ministers) and Whitehall (civil servants) traditionally enjoyed in the policy-making arena have become much more circumscribed. In this chapter, we examine the changing role of ministers and civil servants in the context of changing modes of governance and, in particular, the changing nature of their relationships.

Ministers and civil servants: a dependent relationship

The Westminster model is based on a number of assumptions that create a particular set of relationships between ministers and civil servants (see Chapter 3). These assumptions are:

- Parliament is sovereign;
- ministers are accountable to Parliament;
- civil servants are neutral and loyal to ministers;
- that decision-making power is located in the executive;
- government is legitimised by a public service ethos;
- the system of decision-making is secret.

Thus, the constitutional position is that ministers decide, whilst officials advise and ministers then answer to Parliament (see Chapter 10). The underlying assumption is that officials are apolitical and that they do not have their own personal, political or policy preferences to pursue. However, the secrecy of the British government hides some of the key elements of the roles and relationships of ministers and civil servants.

The Westminster model and power: a legitimising mythology

Unlike the image portrayed in either constitutional textbooks, where ministers are meant to be dominant, or the 'yes minister model' where officials collude to undermine and override their minister, the daily reality of the situation is that ministers and officials are dependent on each other. As we saw with the Prime Minister in the previous chapter, ministers and officials have different resources and in order to achieve their goals, they have to exchange resources (see Table 11.3). Consequently, they are not competing with each other, but they are operating on different terrains. Ministers are concerned with particular policy decisions and officials are concerned with making decisions within a constitutionally informed framework. As long as they have ministerial (and therefore constitutional) cover, officials have considerable autonomy. They do not oppose ministers, but, through their reproduction of the Whitehall game and by providing 'facts' for the minister, they determine the terrain on which ministers operate. In so doing, they are then empowered to undertake decisions within an accepted (ie constitutionally proper) framework, reflecting the general goals of the ministers.

The basis of the post-war expansion of the modern state was the close inter-relationships between officials and ministers who were in effect working together to develop the welfare state. This fits in with the British conception of democracy and representation which assumes that decisions are made by those with knowledge and that the majority of people are excluded, only exercising their democratic function every five years. The central presumption is that 'Whitehall knows best' and decisions can be made in secret through the complex interactions of officials and ministers. Commentators, such as Marquand (1988) have referred to this as 'club government'. The issue here is that this system was convenient for both officials and ministers because the constitutional convention was that minister decide but officials advise. This convention was useful to both sides, as it allowed ministers to appear decisive and officials neutral and apolitical. Moreover, the much more complex reality of policy-making was hidden by the culture of secrecy. From this perspective, the Westminster model can be understood as providing a very useful legitimising mythology of core executive power which both ministers and civil servants appeal to when justifying their behaviour (see Richards and Smith 2004a).

Haldane and interdependence

This interdependent relationship of ministers and civil servants was actually established by the rules set out in the Haldane Report of 1918. The aim of Haldane was to fuse together both sets of actors to form: 'an ever-present, indissoluble symbiosis between ministers and civil servants so that they were almost one person' (Foster 2001: 726). In one sense then, ministers and officials operate as a single actor and it is the aim of a good civil servant to know the minister's mind (Richards 1997). As one former official said in an interview with the authors:

> Things actually work best when ministers and their staff have got a mutual understanding which was the kind of Civil Service I joined back in the '50s... it never struck me then that there would be any serious conflict between my minister and my bosses up in the office. They would all be in cahoots.

Another former official gave a good indication of how the Haldane model worked:

> Perhaps 10 or 12 people would spend the morning discussing, for example, majority verdicts (for Juries), which is what we brought in, which was a very important change. It is very difficult to say that the policy was decided by the Permanent Secretary or the Department or by the minister, it really developed from an interchange of views. *I thought this was perhaps the Whitehall machine at its best.* (Emphasis added.)

From this interdependent relationship, officials and ministers gave and received different things. Officials brought expertise, in terms of both policy-making and the bureaucratic process, they brought loyalty and the ability to protect ministers. Ministers brought the political authority for officials to act. Officials, who are regarded as neutral, therefore cannot act without ministerial cover. Ministers are the actors who have to authorise the decisions of a department. Without this ministerial support the officials can do little. This is why officials do not like indecisive or politically weak ministers.

Ministerial dependence on officials

In order to illustrate the dynamics involved in the relationship between a minister and his department, let us consider what either a department or a minister is capable of achieving without each other. For example, a department can draft policy, but it cannot ensure it will become law; it needs a strong minister to gain approval for its initiatives. Equally a minister who cannot win a battle in Cabinet or with the Treasury is a liability to his/her department. Moreover, it is usually only ministers rather than officials who can gain the support of the Prime Minister. Whilst the Prime Minister does not dictate policy, s/he can either veto a policy or, in alliance with a minister, get a policy through Cabinet and Cabinet committees (see Politics in Focus 12.1). A minister without the support of his/her department, or a department that lacks an effective minister is effectively rendered impotent. As

Much of the significant work of government is now conducted in Cabinet committees with only major strategic issues going to Cabinet. A matter will be referred to Cabinet if there is a major change in policy, or if there is significant conflict between departments, or if there is a particular crisis such as the fuel crisis (2000) or foot and mouth (2001). Cabinet committees are the institutional mechanisms for combining departmental autonomy with collective government. If ministers and departments are to succeed, they need to ensure that their proposals are supported in these committees. Without agreement in the committee, they will get no further. So, despite the decline in formal Cabinet, Cabinet government through committee is still important. However, an increasing number of commentators believe that committees are often being by passed, as Prime Ministers increasingly work directly with ministers or through ad hoc committees of ministers and close advisors. This particular allegation is one that is often associated with Tony Blair's style of governing. Indeed, Lord Bulter, the former Head of the Civil Service, made a number of caustic observations concerning Blair's informal style of decision-making and his reliance on a small coterie of advisers in his 2004 Report on the War in Iraq. Similarly, Seldon (2004) observes that decisions are often taken on the sofa in Blair's Number 10 office—known as 'the den'—rather than in formal, minuted committee meetings, much to the consternation of Whitehall officials. This approach was also criticised by Lord Hutton in the inquiry into the death of David Kelly (HC 247: 2004). Nevertheless, it is significant that Blair set up a War Cabinet to deal with the conflict in Afghanistan indicating the continuing legitimising role of Cabinet mechanisms.

a recent example, the DTI welcomed Peter Mandelson as their Secretary of State, if only briefly (1999–2000), as the department recognised the impact such a 'political heavyweight' could bring with him. A number of civil servants referred to him as their first 'heavy hitter' in Cabinet since David Young (1987–89) and Michael Heseltine (1992–95) (see Marsh, Richards and Smith 2001).

The political role of civil servants

Despite the constitutional mythology maintained by the Westminster model, officials have highly political roles. Whilst they are not political in a party sense, they are political in two senses. First, they frequently make decisions of highly political importance. Most decisions are not made by ministers, but by civil servants. These can be relatively small decisions, but for the person involved, highly significant, such as whether someone receives a benefit, or is given refugee status, or relatively large scale decisions, such as whether to grant an export licence to an arms company. Moreover, often when ministers make decisions, it is based on the advice of officials.

Second, officials play an important political role for ministers in terms of the political game in Whitehall and Westminster. Officials provide 'cover' for ministers by furnishing them with the answers they need for questions in Parliament and for select committees. Officials can provide the form of words that can enable a minister to respond to a question, but not necessarily to answer the question or even evade the question. For example, in the BSE crisis of the mid-1990s, it was civil servants who would have composed the phrase 'there is no evidence of a link between BSE and CJD'. They could say that because there was no evidence, but this did not mean that that there was no link between BSE and CJD.

The other important political role of civil servants is in the battles that exist within Whitehall. Despite the myths of collective responsibility, central government is not a unified organisation with ministers working together for the common good. Rather, it is the site of intense departmental conflicts. According to Ponting (1986: 102):

> Much of the work of Whitehall is institutionalised conflict between competing interests of different departments. Each department will defend its own position and resist a line that while it might be beneficial to the government as a whole or in the wider public interest, would work against the interest of the department.

Consequently, officials are often attempting to defend 'departmental turf' or work out alliances with other departments, in order to get departmental policy through. For example, the Scott Report into the sales of arms to Iraq indicated the extent of conflicts between the DTI, the Ministry of Defence and the Foreign Office over arms sales (see Smith 1999).

This symbiotic relationship also means that officials were highly influential in terms of policy-making. Below, a contemporary official provides a useful indication of how things have changed in recent years:

> My clear impression is that civil servants had much more weight in 1947. The then Permanent Secretaries were powerful, such as Donald Ferguson who obviously had a major influence on the promulgation of policy and there was one minister and one Parliamentary Secretary. It was very clearly established that in the minister's absence, the permanent secretary was in charge of the Department and I think that they had very great weight in the promulgation of policy. That probably continued through to the '70s, but perhaps it was linked to the rather sharper, or much sharper, division between political parties from the '70s onwards. The influence of civil servants did become less and there were more junior ministers around and they were given areas of responsibility and wanted to be consulted on those areas of responsibility and take decisions in them. (Interview with the authors.)

There was a sense that whoever the minister was, the department would generally continue on its own terms.

The effect of dependency on the policy process

This relationship had important implications for the policy process. As we see in the next chapter, despite attempts to standardise policy-making and to ensure rational processes of policy-making from Fulton (Cm 3638: 1968) to Blair, the nature of the policy process changes frequently across time, policy area, department, officials and ministers. There is no single or standardised form of policy-making in government departments. The most common methods of developing policy are:

(1) *To identify a problem and for an official, usually a Grade 7 (but there was variation from department to department) to review the evidence, consult interests and develop proposals which will then go to a Grade 3 or Grade 2 before being presented to a minister.*

Here, an example would be the development of the 1986 Public Order Act (see Hay and Richards 2000). The genesis of that review was a specific event, the murder of Blair Peach on 23 April 1979 while he was attending an anti-Nazi demonstration in Southall, West London. For over five years, the review slowly progressed until an official was asked to draft proposals for a White Paper. The official was then charged with reviewing the existing legislation and consulting relevant bodies. He established a consultative group, which met intensively over the first three months, reported back to the Home Office and led to the drafting of the 1986 Act.

(2) *To identify a problem and establish a committee to review and consult before reporting to a Grade 2 or 3 or maybe the minister.*

In health and social security policy, it has been relatively common when developing a major policy initiative to establish a formal committee involving ministers, officials and outside experts to review policy and develop policy proposals. The 1986 Fowler Review set up 'review teams' which took evidence of various elements of social security policy. Some of these teams were chaired by the Secretary of State and involved outside experts. More recently, in February 2004, following intense media and public pressure concerning the failure to find any evidence of weapons of mass destruction (WMD) in Iraq, the Blair Government established a five-member committee chaired by the former Cabinet Secretary, Lord Butler to examine the nature of intelligence gathering by Britain's various security agencies.

(3) *To respond to a problem identified by an agency at operational level.*

An example would be the case of (non)-payment of the Job Seekers Allowance. Agencies play a crucial role in identifying problems with implementation, anomalies in policy outcomes and contradictions in policy goals. Often, if they identify these problems in a non-political manner, they can be fairly successful at persuading the parent department to review the policy.

(4) *A response to a crisis.*

Two examples here would be the Football Spectators Act 1989 or the Dangerous Dogs Act 1991. There are enormous expectations on ministers to respond when things appear to go wrong. This is particularly true in the Home Office, where the media pays a great deal of attention to issues of law and order, following events such as the shooting in a school in Dunblane (1996) or the Lawrence Inquiry into the murder of Stephen Lawrence (see Cm 4262-I, 1999). The consequence is that the ministers are often required to act quickly and legislation is to some extent made in an ad hoc manner or, to coin a Whitehall phrase, 'policy-making on the hoof'. Thatcher responded directly to incidences of football hooliganism by pushing through the Football Spectators Act (1989) with the aim of creating a membership scheme. The difficulties of the scheme were revealed in the more considered review of the Taylor Committee following the Hillsborough disaster and the proposals were dropped. Elsewhere, the then Home Secretary Kenneth Baker was responsible for the 1991 Dangerous Dogs Act after a spate of vicious attacks by dogs alleged to be American pit bull terriers. The cases, which galvanised media and public opinion were six-year-old Rukshana Khan from Bradford and Frank Tempest from Lincoln, both of whom sustained horrific injuries by domestic dogs in the spring of 1991. Retrospectively, the Act has come in for much criticism for the speed it was pushed through Parliament and its overly repressive and unworkable nature.

(5) *A policy developed within the department and pressed on the minister.*

An example of such policy-making is the abolition of retail price maintenance which the Department of Trade kept pushing on ministers until it was finally accepted by the Home Conservative Government (1963–64) (Lawson and Bruce Gardyne 1976). Elsewhere, there was the decision to build pressurised water reactors that the Department of Energy first pushed on Tony Benn in 1975. He resisted, but it was later accepted by David Howell (Secretary of State for Energy 1979–81). In the 1980s and 1990s, the DTI developed policy on information that it presented to ministers.

(6) *Policies developed by a minister through either ideology or as a response to a particular problem.*

Such an example would include Peter Lilley's approach when he was Secretary of State in the DSS (1992–97). Lilley was clear that he wished to reform social security because he thought that there should be less reliance on state provision. Consequently, he was the main force behind reforms that occurred in social security policy in the 1990s. More recently in 1999, the Labour Government introduced anti-social behaviour orders, in order to combat the perceived growth in the problem of young offenders. The then Home Secretary, Jack Straw observed that:

```
. . . loutish and aggressive public behaviour, running on an
undercurrent of drugs, alcohol or violence, can, if left unchecked,
blight whole neighbourhoods. I hope and expect [these orders] will
help those communities run ragged by the anti-social behaviour of a
minority. (www.bbc.co.uk/worldservice/index.shtml)
```

It is also important to note that there is a great deal of variation in the manner in which policy is made in each department. Despite notions of a standardised Civil Service, departments have a great deal of autonomy in how they organise themselves. Nevertheless, it is the case that at the senior level, decision-taking often occurs in a seminar-type forum where officials and ministers discuss various ideas and come to an agreement about what is the best way forward. This, of course, assumes a seamless web between officials and ministers and no real tension in underlying beliefs and values.

Policy networks in Whitehall

Networks are important because much policy-making and intra-organisational contact in central government is not through formal institutions, but through contacts of informal networks. The variable nature of policy-making emphasises the difficulty of applying a policy networks analysis to Whitehall (see Chapters 3 and 21). Although there are clearly recognisable policy networks, rarely are they stable over a long period of time. Whilst there are a limited number of established and well-institutionalised networks—for example, the relationship between the Association of Chief Police Officers (ACPO) and the Home Office, the majority of networks are temporary and flexible. The fluid nature of the networks within Whitehall is possible (whilst retaining an identity of networks) because the rules of the game are well-established and when an official joins a network, s/he knows how to act and is aware of the sets of beliefs which underpin the system.

Characteristics of a network

Networks within the core executive, as opposed to those that are between Whitehall and outside groups, have a number of specific features:

- The absolute boundary of who is included is relatively limited, but within Whitehall, the networks tend to be messy and ill-defined and thus closer to issue networks than policy communities (see Chapter 21).

- Members of networks will often be institutionally defined. People with specific roles will have tasks that include them in particular networks. However, at the same time, some networks may be interpersonal and break down or change greatly with the removal of a particular individual.

- Many networks are informal and exist in order to overcome the rigidities of formal hierarchies.

- At different times and within different networks, both ministers and civil servants act as gatekeepers, determining who is part of and who is excluded from participation (see Hay and Richards 2000).

- If networks are more often informal, then the institutionalisation of power will occur more through cultures and values, rather than through institutional forms. Thus, as Heclo and Wildavsky (1981) suggest, it is important to understand the actor's perceptions of the organisational forms which face them. It is also important to understand the way in which actors recreate those organisational forms (Giddens 1986).

Networks are important because they affect policy outcomes. They provide the structure for organisational power and reflect past conflicts. By examining networks, we are looking at how power relations are institutionalised (Marsh and Smith 2000; Richards and Hay 2000). However, changes in the mechanisms of governance have had an impact on the way certain networks operate.

The impact of governance on networks

The increased complexity and interconnectedness of the policy-making arena in an era of governance has led to departments interacting with one another more now than in the past. This issue has come into focus since 1997 with the Labour Government's strictures upon the need for joined-up government (see Chapter 13), but it is also a response to a significant, long-term problem.

Obviously, Cabinet ministers and their departments interact with one another in a number of ways (and as we have seen above, there is often conflict). We have already briefly dealt with the Cabinet as a forum within which issues that cross-cut departmental interests can be discussed and resolved. However, in most cases, both Cabinet ministers and their departments have a vested interest in resolving issues earlier in the policy-making process. Clearly, Cabinet ministers are constantly involved in informal interactions with their Cabinet colleagues. Yet, departments also have a range of informal contacts with most other departments. Often, these may just be based on a series of telephone conversations between civil servants in departments who are most involved in some issue which cross-cuts departmental responsibilities. At other times, the issue will be of sufficient and most likely recurring, importance to warrant the creation of a committee which draws upon ministers and officials from all the departments involved. It is in this context that many, if not most, issues are resolved, because many of these issues involve the detail of policy.

Since 1997, the Labour Government has emphasised the problems that occur from the absence of adequate institutional machinery to deal with issues which cross-cut departmental responsibilities. The argument which underpins this view is that departments operate as 'chimneys'; that informal processes of the type sketched out above are insufficient to overcome such departmentalism and, thus, produce more effective policy-making (see Politics in Focus 12.2). Labour's response has been to pursue a strategy towards policy-making, labelled joined-up government, which has had a number of consequences that have affected both Cabinet ministers and their departments (see Chapter 13).

However, here it is important to note that ministerial and departmental discussion and co-operation, both within and between each other, is not new. There are some key points to observe:

- The nature of the British system of government means that there has always been the need for inter-departmental consultation and negotiation.
- In an era of governance, governing has become increasingly complex, making inter-departmental consultation and negotiation even more important than in the past.
- Recent changes, not all to do with the change in government in 1997, have accentuated the process.

The broadest meaning of departmentalism is the way in which a minister will pursue the narrow interests of his own department at the expense of wider government policy. In his book on ministers, Gerald Kaufman (1997: 15), a Labour Cabinet Minister in the 1970s, refers to this occurrence as departmentalitis: 'It stems from a preoccupation with the department to which the minister is assigned, to the exclusion of all the other considerations including the fortunes of the government as a whole.'

The manner in which the policy-making process has been organised around Whitehall departments has provided the structured context that has shaped the way agents, ministers and civil servants act. One consequence of the establishment of departmental government has been the problem of departmentalism. The term departmentalism covers a mix of political, policy and governmental pathologies. Essentially, critics argue that the departmental perspective can impact adversely on the wider system and the broader objectives of the government. In a major speech in 1999 Tony Blair complained of having 'scars on my back' from his attempts to get Whitehall departments to improve public services; they were slow to provide initiatives or respond to ministerial prompting. Civil servants, he implied, were concentrating on protecting their turf and their own interests rather than advancing government programmes.

Departmentalism flourishes for many reasons. Politics in Whitehall—as elsewhere—is about spoils, about who gets what. This can cover resources, media attention and political capital—for the minister and his department. Barbara Castle, as Employment Minister, reflected on a meeting with other ministers: 'I wasn't in a political caucus at all. I was faced by departmental enemies' (*Sunday Times*, 10 June 1973). She was complaining that ministers were protecting their departmental interests as ends in themselves rather than an overall programme. When Richard Crossman was Minister of Housing and Local Government in 1964 he surrendered responsibility for physical planning to another department and was immediately assailed by his formidable Permanent Secretary, Evelyn Sharpe, on the grounds that he had significantly weakened the capacity and standing of the department.

In policy terms, departments have accumulated 'wisdom', derived from experience about which approaches work best, which lobbies should be consulted and how to negotiate effectively with the Treasury and other departments. Civil servants educate the new minister to 'ongoing reality'. Ministers frequently bear the imprint of their departments, singing a different tune when moving from one department to another in the same government. A minister's concern with protecting turf, within as well as between departments, means that co-ordination tends to be done at the lowest common level which can weaken cross-departmental initiatives. Departmentalism should therefore be understood as a pathology that prompts ministers to think of the micro-political interests of their department, at the expense of the macro-political goals of their own government.

The breakdown of dependency

Policy-making is based on interdependent networks that involve officials and ministers. However, there have been a number of occasions when relations between ministers and official have broken down and this has created problems. The breakdown in relationships often occurs when trust fails to develop between ministers and officials. The symbiotic relationship between ministers and official depends on each playing particular roles. Civil servants are happy to obey their ministers but that is if they have involved officials in the discussion of policy. They are less happy when ministers attempt to impose a policy which undermines the departmental approach or occurs against the advice of civil servants. Consequently, ministers who have not operated in the way that officials want, often encounter problems, frustrations and delays. Usually, a breakdown occurs when ministers have had distinct policy proposals that run counter to the departmental agenda. Here the officials are mistrustful of what the minister plans to do and the minister believes that officials will try to undermine his/her goals. When Michael Howard was Home Secretary (1993–97), he had a clear idea that the best way to counter crime was through harsher prison sentences. This view ran counter to the departmental line that prison did not work as a deterrent. So in the Howard era, conflict occurred in the Home Office.

The changing role of ministers

Traditionally, government at the centre has depended on a close and symbiotic relationship between officials and ministers and it is within this relationship that the key decisions are made. However, an argument of the governance literature is that this relationship has changed or, to an extent, broken down (Campbell and Wilson 1995; Foster and Plowden 1996; Scott 2004; Foster 2005). The particular problems associated with Tony Benn in the 1970s and Michael Howard in the 1990s have become more widespread since 1997. An example here would be the clash between Stephen Byers and his officials in the Department of Transport which subsequently led to Byers' resignation in May 2002 (see Woodhouse 2004). Furthermore, there are also the numerous accounts of the perceived dysfunctional relationship between the Prime Minister Tony Blair and his Chancellor Gordon Brown (see Naughtie 2001; Rawnsley 2001; Scott 2004; Seldon 2004; Short 2004; Stephens 2004; Hyman 2005). Although it should be pointed out that both individuals went to extraordinary lengths to put on a 'united' front in the 2005 general election. At times it appeared the pair were almost inseparable. The point here is that both recognised the dependent nature of their relationship. Brown recognises his dependence on Blair, in order to secure a harmonious and smooth transition to leader of the party. At the same time, the vocal support Brown offered Blair, particular when the Prime Minister was receiving a barrage of criticism over the war in Iraq, was crucial (see Richards 2005).

POLICY ROLE	POLITICAL ROLE	EXECUTIVE OR MANAGERIAL ROLE	PUBLIC RELATIONS ROLE
Agenda setting	Advocacy of department's position in Cabinet	Departmental management	Overseeing department's relations with: (1) interest groups (2) public (3) media
Policy initiation	Parliament	Executive decision maker	
Policy selection	European Union		
Policy legitimation	Party		

Source: Marsh, Richards and Smith (2001: 133)

In order to evaluate the changing role of ministers, we can first turn to Marsh, Richards and Smith (2001) who have constructed a typology of what they regard as the present-day role of ministers (see Table 12.1).

Table 12.1 identifies four generic roles that ministers presently perform; a policy role, a political role, a managerial or executive role and a public relations role. These roles are not necessarily mutually exclusive. Indeed, often they complement one another. For example, if a minister is to be pro-active in his/her policy-making role, s/he will need to perform managerial or executive functions; these could include deciding on the extent of intradepartmental and inter-departmental discussions and interest groups consultation. Subsequently, the minister needs to steer the policy through Cabinet and Parliament, while perhaps, at the same time, playing a public relations role, convincing the electorate of the benefits of a particular policy.

In the next section, we will examine the different roles of ministers, focusing in particular on the extent to which these roles have change in the last few decades.

The policy role

The Marsh et al typology argues that it is useful to sub-divide the policy initiator role because, while many ministers attempt to initiate in narrow policy areas, there are some, although very few, who try to change a department's broader policy agenda; the latter they term an agenda setter (see also Marsh et al 2000, 2001). Let us look at each of these categories in turn.

(1) Agenda setters

Definition: *These are ministers who act as 'agents of strategic change'. They attempt to instigate a permanent change in a department's institutionalised policy preferences and culture which privileges certain policy outcomes.*

In the last 30 years, a number of Cabinet ministers, both Labour and Conservative, have set out to change the broad agenda or policy line in their department—they can be referred to as 'agents of strategic change' or *agenda setters*. Below is an example of an agenda setter.

Gordon Brown—Chancellor of the Exchequer (1997–to date)

Gordon Brown is an interesting case-study, as the economic policies he has pursued since becoming Chancellor in 1997 have centred on creating a new legacy for a Labour government, in terms of its ability to successfully manage the economy. His policies have not therefore entailed an explicit break from the preceding Conservative Administration. To explain this, it is important to recognise the historical context, in the light of the devaluations that occurred under previous Labour Administrations—1947, 1967 and 1976—that left the Labour Party with the tag of being incompetent managers of the economy. On coming to power in 1997, one of the main elements in Labour's economic policy has been the need to reassure the City and the markets that it could run the economy. As a consequence, the prime aim of Brown's strategy has been a commitment to macro-economic stability based on low inflation and promoting sound public finances, not raising income tax, nor returning to public ownership (see Chapter 26). This contrasts with the Keynesian-influenced, demand-side approach of previous Labour Chancellors.

Yet, since 1997, the policies of Brown can allow us to label him as an agent of strategic change. Most notably, in what at the time was seen as a radical and bold move, Brown gave independence to the Bank of England, established a new 'independent' Monetary Policy Committee to determine interest rates in his first month in office and set up a new Financial Service Agency to regulate the activities of the City. At the time, the opposition parties and some members within Brown's own party were highly critical, although most have since done a u-turn and accepted these changes. Senior civil servants from the Treasury were also up in arms, but that was primarily because Brown had sprung such major changes on them with no consultation (see Seldon 2004: 280–1). Brown has also embedded a commitment to what he refers to as the 'golden rule'—expenditure and income have to balance out over the economic cycle whilst borrowing can only be for investment, not for current expenditure. He did however, receive some criticism in July 2005 for altering the framework under which the 'golden rule' was applied. Nevertheless, the impact of Brown can allow us to conclude that whether or not the next Chancellor of the Exchequer comes from the ranks of the Labour Party, his legacy will be that of a set of now institutionalised policy preferences in the Treasury.

(2) Policy initiators

Definition: *This is a minister who, though lacking the goals or vision of an agenda setter, is nevertheless prepared to 'take-on' his/her department, in order to initiate a specific policy that may be counter to the department's strategic preferences.*

Some ministers do not aim to change the overall direction of their department, but are willing to attempt particular policy initiatives that may rub against the grain of the department's own culture. Here, an example might include:

David Blunkett: Home Secretary (2001–04)

David Blunkett provides an interesting case-study of a policy initiator, for in many ways, one could argue that if he had been a Labour Home Secretary in an earlier era, the policies he pursued would have placed him in the category of an agenda-setting minister. But, in Blunkett's case, when he became Home Secretary in 2001, his pursuit of a variety of measures to tackle anti-social behaviour, street crime, immigration, asylum control, organised crime and the introduction of identity cards in the aftermath of the 9/11 attack in America, led liberals to label Blunkett, a 'Michael Howard in Labour clothes'.[1] The point here is that Blunkett did not need to take on the mantle of being an 'agent of strategic change' in the Home Office, Howard had already carried out that task a decade earlier. The culture of the Home Office had shifted in Howard's time from a socially-liberal to a more socially conservative disposition. Much of the Blunkett rhetoric was not dissimilar to that of the former Conservative Home Secretary, particularly when, in an infamous comment in November 2001, he declared: 'We could live in a world which is airy fairy, libertarian, where everybody does precisely what they like and we believe the best of everybody and then they destroy us.' Yet, as we see in Chapter 30, Blunkett's more socially conservative approach to policy-making was underpinned by an ideological value-set that saw the working class as the main victims of crime. He therefore concluded that greater action by the state was required to protect such communities. An obvious example of Blunkett's desire to pursue this agenda can be seen in the introduction of Dispersal Orders.

Dispersal Orders were part of a broad package that Blunkett introduced in the Anti-Social Behaviour Act 2003 to protect the public from what it claimed was behaviour that was likely to cause harassment, alarm or distress—for example, noisy neighbours, abandoned cars, vandalism, graffiti, litter and youth nuisance. Dispersal Orders provide the police with the power to require any group of two or more young persons in a specified location to leave if the police believe members of the public have been intimidated, harassed, alarmed or distressed, or if anti-social behaviour is a significant and persistent problem in the relevant locality. If the individuals refuse to leave, or returns within 24 hours, they can be arrested. If they are under 16, they can be taken home or to a 'place of safety'. Dispersal Orders can be extended for anything up to six months. The Home Office's official figures indicate that between January 2004 and September 2004, 418 Dispersal Orders were issued nationally 'to tackle the problem of intimidating groups'. Yet, initially, the Home Office was against the inclusion of Dispersal Orders in the 2003 Act, fearing for their implications on civil liberty grounds.[2] Yet, despite Home Office resistance,

---

[1] Michael Howard was a former Home Secretary 1992–97 (see Chapter 30 for details).

[2] These fears were realised in July 2005, when the use of Dispersal Orders was successfully challenged in the High Court by a 15-year-old boy.

Blunkett continued to pursue their introduction. As he observed in an interview with the authors:

> The Dispersal Orders... were entirely driven through by me for good or ill because the Department [*The Home Office*] were frightened about them... and the Association of Chief Police Officers were frightened that we were going back to the Sus laws.[3] (Italics added.)

Thus, Dispersal Orders offer an example of a minister pursuing a particular policy, despite the institutional resistance from both a Whitehall department, in this case, the Home Office and other key agents including the Association of Chief Police Officers.

(3) Policy selectors

Definition: *This is a much less ambitious type of minister, who, rather than being pro-active in making policy, is instead prepared to choose a particular policy initiative from a range of options presented by the department. These ministers are content to play the role of policy selectors: choosing from the alternatives set out by officials.*

Helen Liddell: Secretary of State for Scotland (2001–03)

Helen Liddell, the MP for the Scottish constituency of Monklands East provides an interesting example of a minister who can be identified as a policy selector, although structural rather than agency-based reasons explain why. Following the programme of devolution pursued by the Labour Government and in the light of the creation of the Scottish Parliament in 1998, much of the portfolio of Secretary of State for Scotland has been transferred to the Scottish Parliament. As we see in Chapter 17, the Scottish Parliament possesses legislative powers with responsibility for a variety of policy areas including health, education, housing, economic development and transport. When the Scotland Bill was passed in November 1998, the Act led to the abolition of the old Scottish Office. In Whitehall, the Scotland Office came into being to assist the Secretary of State in representing Scottish interests at Westminster and acting as the 'guardian of the constitutional settlement'. Due to the constitutional complexities involved in the embedding of the new institutional arrangements, the Scottish Secretary of State became increasingly reliant on the advice of civil servants, in order to navigate a path through both the legal and institutional maize created by devolution. This was a role that was performed by Helen Liddell between 2001–03. It can be argued in this case, that the changing nature of the job, rather than the personality of the individual minister, can allow us to label her as a policy selector.

---

[3] Sus Laws were introduced as part of the Vagrancy Act of 1824, authorising the arrest and punishment of suspected persons frequenting or loitering in public places with criminal intent. They became highly politicised in the 1960s and 1970s, when accusations were made against the police authorities that the Sus Laws were being used to target young males, particularly from ethnic minorities.

(4) Policy legitimator/minimalists

Definition: *This is a minister whose role and impact within a department is relatively marginal and whose main function is to legitimise or rubber stamp departmental policy.*

During the Conservative Government led by Heath [1970–74], Lord Carrington and Patrick Jenkin admitted that when they were put into the newly created Department of Energy, they were so overwhelmed by an energy crisis (1973–74) that there was little, if anything, they could do (see Carrington 1988: p 262–63). The last Conservative Administration also provides examples of a number of ministers who made almost no impact when in office and who we can label 'policy minimalists'. In most cases, this was because they were in office only briefly or they became overwhelmed by events. For example, Peter Lilley's short tenure at the DTI (1990–92) left no discernible legacy. Elsewhere, John Moore, Social Security Secretary (1987–89), despite using rhetoric promising 'big ideas' on the reform of welfare policy, became overwhelmed by the task and was quickly removed. Most notably, David Waddington, as Home Secretary (1989–90) argued that he was constrained by both the lack of time and the impact of the riots at Strangeways Prison. Consequently, he accepted he made little impact on the direction of the Home Office:

> I wasn't really there long enough to bring about major change and, particularly, with all the problems we had in prisons and the Strangeways' affair, one did tend to be absolutely overwhelmed by events as they unfolded. There wasn't really a lot of chance to bring about radical change even if one had wanted to do so. But then again, we did just begin... it was when I was at the Home Office that we were shaping up to big decisions about introducing the private sector in to the running of prisons but the actual decisions were not being made.

Since 1997, there have been a number of Labour ministers who can also be placed in this category, but for a variety of different reasons. Most obviously, Peter Mandelson's period as Trade and Industry Secretary in 1998 was so short lived, after he was forced to resign over an undeclared loan, that he made little or no impact. In July 1998, Harriet Harman, after just over a year in office was sacked by Blair from her job as Secretary of State for Social Security in July 1998, having failed to deliver on Labour's welfare agenda and following a series of public spats with Frank Field, one of her junior ministers. Similarly, in September 2004 after two years in office, Andrew Smith resigned as Secretary of State for Work and Pensions, following constant media criticism of his performance and in the wake of suggestions that Blair was about to sack him. For very different reasons, Estelle Morris, the former Education Secretary found that she could not meet the demands placed on her and so voluntarily resigned in October 2002 (see Woodhouse 2004). She reflected afterwards that she had felt more comfortable in her previous role as Schools Minister, rather than as a Secretary of State having to undertake major strategic decisions and run a huge department. In an interview she observed that:

> If I'm really honest with myself I have not enjoyed it as much and I just do not think I'm as good at it as I was at my other job. I'm not having second best in a job as important as this.
> (news.bbc.co.uk/1/hi/education/2359695.stm)

Analysing the role of ministers today

The Marsh et al study raises some importance issues concerning the role of ministers:

- The role of ministers should not be compartmentalised. They each undertake a variety of roles, all of which are component parts of a minister's remit and all are mutually reinforcing.
- All ministers have a policy role and this policy role has cumulatively increased in the last three decades. Partly because of ideology, partly because of external advice and partly because of increased public scrutiny of government activity, ministers now have more concern with formulating effective policy and making a difference.
- The impact of ministers depends on four main factors: the nature of the minister; the nature of the department; the relationship between the minister and the Prime Minister; and the wider political and economic context. Thus, the impact of a minister is not solely dependent on his/her perception of the ministerial role, but it develops within a particular context and a certain set of structural relations.

Ministers cannot be ascribed a particular role. Rather it is more useful to conceive of what they do as being on a continuum which reflects the degree of activity involved in the four different policy roles of ministers (see Figure 12.1). At one end of the continuum, we can identify agenda setters, as those ministers who were pro-active while in office. At the other end of the continuum, we can identify policy legitimators based on the minimal role they adopted as ministers. We can label this end of the spectrum, the inactive pole.

Despite the complexity and variability of ministerial roles, there are a number of points we can make about the position of ministers today:

- It would appear ministers have assumed a more proactive role in the last 30 years and, to this extent, there is more, rather than less, power concentrated in the core executive. One explanation of this greater emphasis on proactivity by ministers might be that, in an increasingly complex and fragmented policy-making arena, ministers have to take greater action and more direct involvement in the policy process, in order to simply maintain some semblance of control.
- The balance of power between civil servants and ministers has shifted, with ministers becoming increasingly dominant. A number of authors (Campbell and Wilson 1995;

FIGURE 12.1
A continuum of policy roles

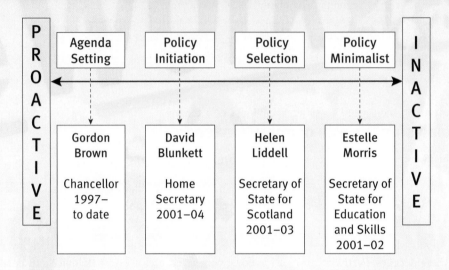

Foster and Plowden 1996; Foster 2005) claim that the Whitehall paradigm, by which they mean the dominant position of the Civil Service within the policy making arena, has been destroyed by the changes wrought during the era of governance.

- Ministers are increasingly looking to outside sources for policy advice. The number of special advisers (political appointments paid for by the taxpayer) has fluctuated over time, but there is no doubt that it has increased in the last two decades, most significantly since the election of the Labour Government in 1997. For example, during the Major Government, there were on average 32 special advisers. This figure has risen to an average of 74 during the course of the first term of the Blair Labour Government (see Table 12.2). The cost of this increase in special advisers rose from £1.9 million a year under Major to over £4 million a year under Blair. Yet, as Toynbee and Walker (2001: 216–17) observe:

> Many more special advisers were brought in to strengthen the influence of ministers over their departments, and to act as political brains bridging the divide between departments and politics. For all the venom poured on them by the Opposition, and resentment at usurpation from within Whitehall, the best of them were good brains collating bright ideas from outside the narrow Whitehall loop. They were able to explain policy better than civil servants, they made government more open.

Generally, special advisers have tended to be of two types, policy advisers or public relations experts (or to use the current jargon 'policy-wonks' and 'spin-doctors'). Both types of advisers can cause tension within departments; but the pattern is not uniform.

So, one Treasury civil servant argued after the 1997 general election:

> There is quite a lot of resistance [to special advisers]. Certainly
> for the first 6—9 months [of the Labour Government] officials were
> heard to say: 'this will soon settle down and go back to normal'.
> But of course it never has. I think officials have increasingly
> understood that this is how it is going to be.

In contrast, a current DSS Grade 5 civil servant claimed:

> I've never seen the current special adviser, which is some indication.
> I think the current adviser is a detail man, more than a spin-doctor.
> The first lot of ministers had two advisers who were both into spinning
> rather than anything else. We had a fair degree of contact with
> them, which was fine. However, I think one of the advisers stirred up
> a lot of mistrust with the minister.

Of course, not all ministers have, or like, special advisers. So, one Labour DTI minister asserted:

> I'm not all that keen on special advisers if I'm honest. I'm all for
> peer review but I don't think we make enough of our officials. They
> are very bright people and they certainly want to help and be part
> of transforming public administration. . . but in a sense they are
> being sidelined. . . they are now really there to [assess] radical
> suggestions coming from outside the department.

Finally, a current special adviser in the DTI offers a more critical view from the 'other side':

> I remember when I was a civil servant, I hated special advisers. . .
> I think that the officials don't like advisers attending meetings
> with ministers and contributing, but what they hate most is advisers
> getting involved in the Department lower down. That is exactly what
> we have done to try to shape the way that policies are coming up by
> talking to more junior officials in order to see who is working on
> areas in which the minister is interested.

The pattern is complex and evolving, but clearly a minister with a special adviser has to ensure that the relationship between the adviser and the department is co-operative, rather than competitive. This issue was brought into focus in July 2005, when the Committee on Standards in Public Life, chaired by Sir Alistair Graham, criticised the Government for changing the rules governing special advisers without informing Parliament. The Committee's concern focused on moves by the Government to change the wording in an Order of Council to allow special advisers powers to order civil servants to do their 'ministers' bidding', a shift from advising ministers to assisting them which would potentially allow a special adviser to override a civil servant. Graham commented: 'I am very disappointed that the Government has chosen to make changes to the legislation governing the role of special advisers using prerogative powers without any proper parliamentary and public debate'.

There are of course, other sources of external advice. For example, the last Conservative Administration bought in an increasing amount of advice from consultancy firms. The use of consultants was a practice that continued throughout much of the 1980s, but in the Major years, their use came under scrutiny and was subsequently reduced on grounds of cost-efficiency. As one contemporary official observed:

> Consultancy was the thing in the 1980s, but it was then rather criticised by Ken Clarke [Chancellor of the Exchequer 1993–97] in the 1990s due to the amount of money which was being spent on consultants. In particular, because he recognised he could get similar advice, at much cheaper cost to the tax-payers, from his own civil servants.

Thus, at the start of the Thatcher Administration, the use of consultants became an additional component of the policy-making process and one that altered the balance of resources within the core executive. Their use was cut back during the 1990s, but they still remain a key alternative resource which ministers can use.

The present Labour Government has also being willing to make substantial use of consultancy firms, which, they argue is a practical manifestation of third-way thinking in relation to policy-making (see Chapter 4). Thus, KPMG, Arthur Andersen, Price Waterhouse Coopers, Siemens and McKinsey & Co to name but a few, have all benefited from lucrative contracts from the Labour Government for a wide variety of consultancy projects ranging from advice on how to impose the windfall tax on privatised utilities (Andersen) to how to deliver a computer software system for the processing of asylum applications (Seimens) (see Cohen 2003).

The changing role of civil servants

As we have seen above, from the 1950s to the 1960s, officials were integral to the policy process and intimately involved in the making and taking of decisions. However, from the late 1970s onwards ministers, driven by both ideology and the apparent failure of the Civil Service to solve Britain's recurrent social and economic problems, developed a

Year	Total	No 10	Departments
1979/80	7	n/a	n/a
1989/90	35	n/a	n/a
1994/95	34	6	28
1995/96	38	8	30
1996/97	38	8	30
1997/98	70	18	52
1998/99	74	25	49
1999/00	78	26	52
2000/01	79	25	54
2001/02	81	26	55
2002/03	81	27	54

Source: Adapted from the Committee on Standards in Public Life (2003), Toynbee and Walker (2005) and Richards (2005)

greater policy role. In addition, there was, as we saw in Chapter 4, a broader new right critique of the efficiency of the state and public sector organisations.

The changing role of ministers and the managerial reforms to Whitehall had a significant impact on the role of officials. To some extent, they had a monopoly of policy advice and almost a total monopoly of political advice (political, in the sense of how to play politics in the arenas of Whitehall and Westminster). A number of commentators argue that the reforms of the Thatcher years destroyed the traditional role of officials. For example, according to Campbell and Wilson (1995: 60), the Whitehall model has been undermined with:

```
. . . civil servants increasingly defining their role as policy
implementors rather than policy analysts, people who gave ministers
what they said they wanted, rather than functioning as what they
disparagingly call 'quasi-academics' who tried to show politicians
the full consequences, adverse as well as positive, of their policy
proposals.
```

In some ways, this is an accurate representation of changes that have occurred. After 1979, there was an attempt to assert a managerial culture across Whitehall and this has affected the nature of the relationship between ministers and officials. According to Foster

(2001: 9), during the 1980s ministers continued to listen to officials: 'but often seemed less responsive'. He also suggests that many officials were indifferent to statistics and this of course produced poor legislation, such as the Community Charge and the Child Support Agency. Of course, one of the traditional rules of the Whitehall system is that officials are the arbitrators of 'facts'. Ministers are expected to trust the official presentation of facts, when of course, they can be interpreted in different ways. In a sense, the official version of the facts was used as the basis of policy but with more ideological ministers in the 1980s, they had a different value-set to draw on. This then created a conflict between the official framework of facts and the ministerial ideological framework.

It is increasingly the case that ministers rely much less on officials for policy advice. For example, recently one of the main conflicts that has occurred within the Treasury is over how the Chancellor, Gordon Brown, is using his own advisers rather than Treasury officials in developing policy (see Naughtie 2001; Rawnsley 2001; Scott 2004; Foster 2005). However, it is the case that many officials rejected the notion that relationships had broken down in the 1980s and 1990s. According to one, commentating towards the end of the Major Administration: 'I think certainly the senior Treasury officials all get on very well with the Chancellor and the Chief Secretary'.

It is also the case that, as in other areas, the personalism of the system and the degree of ministerial autonomy means that the nature of the relationship depends on the department and the minister. As one official pointed out:

> Your experience around Whitehall depends very much on who your minister is and what his/her attitude is. Some ministers think they are there to run the Department and others think that the Permanent Secretary is there to do that and they are only there to give broad instructions. I think that will continue to vary depending on the personality and predilection of ministers...

Nevertheless, there have been some important changes in the day-to-day work of the senior Civil Service and, in some ways, contradictory changes in the way their work is organised and what they do. There have been three important changes: an increased managerial role, a delayering of the senior Civil Service and a greater role for Next Steps agencies (see Chapter 13).

The changing role of the Treasury

For most of the post-war period, the role of the Treasury was essentially negative; it attempted to stop departments spending. Often, it was not very successful in this goal because many of the welfare policies were demand-led, in other words, the amount spent on health depended not on Treasury targets but on how many people needed to be treated. In the 1990s, both Conservative and Labour governments attempted to make the Treasury more proactive. With the Fundamental Expenditure Review (1994) under the Conservatives and the Comprehensive Spending Review (1998) under Labour, departments had to justify their spending and keep within targets set by the Treasury. The Treasury, in particular under Gordon Brown, has become much more active in dictating policy developments within departments especially in areas such as social security policy (see Smith 2005). According to Rawnsley (2001: 147), the Comprehensive Spending Review was: 'an opportunity to delve deep into every department which he further exploited by binding ministers to his will with "public service agreements" with the Treasury'.

The Treasury now has spending teams, headed by a Grade 5 official, responsible for each expenditure area. In each department, the key contact is still the Principal Finance Officer. Of course, the main responsibility of these teams is for expenditure. However, inevitably, their brief involves policy, given the focus that the Treasury has upon improving economic performance. Once again, the Department for Social Security, now rebranded the Department for Work and Pensions, offers an excellent example of how this works. As Deakin and Parry (2000) argue: 'After the 1997 election, the Treasury and the DSS formed something of an axis within government because of a shared ministerial agenda of targeting and means-testing.'

The Treasury's involvement in this policy area stemmed from at least two factors. First, Gordon Brown and a close colleague Harriet Harman, the first Secretary of State for Social Security (1997–98), were both committed to a policy change which was at the core of the Labour Government's pledge to reform the welfare state. In the Treasury's view, the New Deal, which was the flagship policy in this area, would contribute to a more skilled and flexible workforce and, thus, improve economic efficiency. Second, this policy was funded from the public utilities windfall tax which also gave the Treasury a key concern in this policy area.

There is little doubt then, that the Treasury is now crucially involved in labour market policy, most specifically in the welfare to work programme (see Chapter 26). Indeed, it has established a 'Work Incentives and Policy Analysis Unit' and there are regular meeting between the teams responsible for this policy area in the Treasury, the Department for Work and Pensions and the Department for Education and Skills. Of course, this in part reflects the Labour Government's emphasis on joined-up government, but it also shows that the Treasury is now much more pro-active in policy terms, when a policy area impacts upon its concerns. So, despite arguments concerning governance decentralising control, recent years have seen much greater Treasury dominance.

Analysing the changing role of ministers and officials

It is undoubtedly the case that a range of internal and external factors have changed both the roles of ministers and officials and the dynamics of the relationship between them. The main sets of arguments that have been identified in this chapter are:

Ministers

- Ministers often have clearer policy ideas than officials and will not always work to the departmental agenda.

- Ministers will use a range of sources for advice such as think tanks, pressure groups, task forces and special advisors in developing policy. Indeed, officials may sometimes be excluded from policy discussions.
- Ministers are less trustful of officials than 30 years ago.

Civil servants

- Officials are taking on a role that is increasingly managerial.
- Officials are less policy experts and more experts on policy implementation.
- Detailed policy work has shifted down the departmental hierarchy.
- Prime Ministers have become more policy active but departments continue as the sites of the majority of policy making.
- The Treasury is now a stronger force on the activities of departments.

However, despite these changes, it is important to remember that the relationship between officials and ministers is highly variable. It depends on personalities, circumstances and departments and many officials and ministers have maintained relatively traditional relationships. The relationship between ministers and civil servants is and remains an exchange relationship. The nature of Britain's political system ensures that departments still want strong ministers, capable of defending their interests within Whitehall and beyond. On the other hand, ministers need good civil servants capable of giving sophisticated advice, drafting good policy documents and legislation and implementing policy effectively. The terms of the exchange are not equal or constant. Ministers are agents with significant resources. Only they have the authority to make policy. A department with a weak minister can achieve little or nothing. In addition, civil servants are trained to, and most wish to carry out government policy. This view of their role is still strongly held by civil servants. As such, they expect ministers to make policy; indeed they admire strong ministers with a policy agenda which they can get through Cabinet. Of course, not all ministers want to adopt, or are capable of adopting, such a pro-active role.

Conclusion

The relationships involved in the core executive are based on an understanding of the nature of dependence between the various actors. The exact nature of dependence is determined by the skills, values and interpretations of those occupying each ministerial post. The personality of some ministers may push them towards a relatively inactive ministerial role. Others may feel too constrained by a departmental culture to innovate. However, ministers, and to a lesser extent civil servants, clearly do make a difference. The nature of the exchange is also affected by the broader context. So, if for example the Thatcher Government is informed by a view that civil servants are too powerful, or the Blair Government believes that officials have been less than effective at policy delivery, then this view is likely to affect how ministers conceptualise the nature of the exchange between themselves and civil servants.

In the last Conservative Administration, most ministers had a different view of what the relationship should be between ministers and officials, than that enshrined in the traditional, Westminster model. The Westminster model regarded officials and ministers as partners; civil servants could be trusted to exercise considerable discretion. In contrast, the Thatcher Governments were more critical of civil servants whom they viewed as a cause of, rather than a solution to, what they saw as the core of the governance problem; weak, ineffective government pursuing consensual policies because it was in thrall to particular interests. To break out of this stultifying embrace, they claimed government and ministers needed to exercise executive autonomy. As such, for the Conservatives, the chief role of the Civil Service was not to advise on policy but to assist ministers in carrying out government policy. At the same time, the Conservatives were more willing to use special advisers (see above), although not to consult interest groups (see Chapter 21), as alternative sources of information. All this meant that Conservative ministers were encouraged to lead their department, to change departmental thinking and, in Bulpitt's (1986) term, project an image of governing competence. Under the present Labour Government, the emphasis has been much more on achieving greater joined-upness in government and, in particular, improving on policy delivery (see Chapter 13). Foster (2001, 2005) avers that under New Labour, the old 'Haldane-style' of relationships have not been re-established, so that ministers still rely much more on outside advice and special advisers.

KEY POINTS

- Contrary to the normative assumptions of the Westminster model, a more appropriate reflection of the relationship between ministers and civil servants is one of co-dependency based on resource exchange.

- Power between ministers and civil servants is, more often, better understood as a positive-sum, rather than a zero-sum game.

- The context, resources and structure of the different actors within the core executive changes over both time and policy area. This affects the nature of the dependency relationship.

- Since the mid-1970s, ministers have become more pro-active and, in particular, the policy role of ministers has increased.

- Ministers have been increasingly willing to use sources of advice outwith Whitehall.

- Senior civil servants have increasingly taken on a managerial role with policy advice being pushed further down the Whitehall hierarchy.

- In the last two decades, the balance of power between ministers and civil servants has shifted, with ministers becoming more dominant, but they both remain locked into a co-dependent relationship.

KEY QUESTIONS

(1) From your understanding of the contemporary role of ministers and civil servants, provide a critique of the Westminster model.

(2) How and why has the relationship between ministers and civil servants changed in the last two decades?

(3) What are the different sets of explanations that account for ministers and civil servants embracing an elitist model of the policy-making process?

(4) Why is it that in order to achieve their goals, different actors within the core executive have to engage in a process of resource exchange with other actors?

(5) What impact have the forces associated with governance had on the roles of ministers and civil servants in the last 30 years?

IMPORTANT WEBSITES

For websites of the House of Commons, see www.parliament.uk, the websites on the main political parties are: for Labour www.labour.org.uk, for the Conservatives www.conservative-party.org.uk, for the Liberal Democrats www.libdems.org.uk, then SNP www.snp.org.uk and Plaid Cymru www.plaid-cymru.wales.com. For details on the work of both ministers and civil servants, a good starting point is www.open.gov.uk or, more specifically www.cabinet-office.gov.uk. For debates on the role of ministers and civil servants, an interesting site is the Democratic Audit www.fhit.org/demoicratic_audit/index.html.

FURTHER READING

The original and most enduring account of the relationship between ministers and civil servants, written over 25 years is that of B. Headey (1974) *British Cabinet Ministers,* London: George, Allen and Unwin. The most contemporary and comprehensive analysis of their present role is: D. Marsh, D. Richards, and M.J. Smith (2001), *Changing Patterns of Governance: Reinventing Whitehall,* Basingstoke: Palgrave, but see also: P. Norton, (2000) 'Barons in a Shrinking Kingdom: Senior Ministers in British Government' in Rhodes, RAW (ed) *Transforming British Government,* vol 2, Basingstoke: Macmillan. For a critical account of the effect of change on Whitehall see: C. Campbell, and G. Wilson (1995) *The End of Whitehall: Death of a Paradigm,* Oxford: Basil Blackwell, C. Foster, and F. Plowden (1996), *The State under Stress,* Buckingham: Open University Press and C. Foster (2005) *British Government in Crisis,* London: Hart. An account of the power-dependent relationship between ministers and civil servants can be found in: M.J. Smith (1999), *The Core Executive in Britain,* Basingstoke: Macmillan and Rhodes, RAW (1997) *Understanding Governance: Policy Networks, Governance, Reflexivity and Accountability,* Buckingham: Open University Press.

 Visit the Online Resource Centre that accompanies this book for links to more information on chapter topic

CHAPTER THIRTEEN

Policy-making and the managerial framework

READER'S GUIDE

Traditionally senior civil servants have been the main policy advisors to ministers. Their control over information and departments has meant they have been in a symbiotic relationship with ministers which has given them considerable influence over policy. The last 25 years have seen civil servants face almost a permanent revolution with a continual stream of reforms from both Conservative and Labour governments. This chapter examines the reform process, and the impact that it has had on the role and power of the Civil Service. It examines whether the balance of power between ministers and officials has changed and the extent to which civil servants have lost their monopoly of policy advice.

Introduction

We have seen in an earlier chapter how important the Civil Service has been in both shaping the nature of British government and making policy. The Westminster model placed the senior Civil Service at the centre of government as an essential element of the policy-making process. Their relationship with ministers was symbiotic. However, since 1979 we have seen radical changes to the nature of the Civil Service and the development of a new framework for policy-making. This chapter is concerned with examining how the role and nature of the Civil Service has changed and how new patterns of policy-making have developed. It will look at how the role of civil servants has changed and the extent to which they have lost their monopoly of policy advice. Do officials continue to have an intimate relationship with ministers?

The British Civil Service has often been portrayed as a 'Rolls Royce machine' and most politicians will say in public how excellent the civil servants they have worked with have been. Despite this public discourse concerning the nature of the Civil Service, politicians have, at least since the mid-1970s, been attempting to reform the Civil Service. From 1979, in particular there has been almost a permanent revolution with a continual stream of reform programmes aimed at improving the efficiency and effectiveness of the Civil Service. Politicians have a continual frustration that the goals they wish to achieve do not seem to have been delivered on the ground and hence they see the Civil Service as being ineffective. Officials, on the other hand, see ministers as having unreasonable expectations and in reforming the Civil Service they are damaging what are the unique abilities of Whitehall. However, whatever the arguments, there can be little doubt that the Civil Service has changed considerably in the last 25 years and that the traditional relationship between ministers and civil servants has changed considerably.

The chapter will begin by outlining the traditional model of policy-making. It will then look at the reforms that were undertaken by the Conservative governments between 1979 and 1997. The chapter will then examine New Labour and policy-making looking at public sector reform and delivery before finally outlining the impact of the EU and devolution on the policy process. There are two key questions. How has the role of the Civil Service changed? Have we seen a decline in their power?

The traditional pattern of policy-making

Traditionally, and probably up to 1979, policy-making was largely left to the Civil Service. The role of the Civil Service was to advise ministers on policy. Officials were neutral and permanent, and at the top of the Civil Service they were experts in making policy. Policy-making had two key elements. The first was making sure that ministers had the right advice. So, for instance, if a minister wanted to examine the prospect of building a new road the civil servants could provide the information on the cost of the road, its impact on traffic flows, the environmental impact and how many houses may need to be demolished. Often officials would assess

POLITICS IN FOCUS 13.1

Traditional models of policy-making

There was never a single process of policy-making in central government. The way policy was made would vary from department to department and according to policy area. Two of the typical processes were the seminar approach and the hierarchical approach. These can be described as being at either end of a continuum on policy-making.

The seminar approach

In the seminar approach a minister would call in his key Civil Service advisors which may include the Permanent Secretary, his number 2s and perhaps his principal Private Secretary and they would sit in his office and discuss the problem and the range of solutions. The discussion would be open and the views of everyone there treated with respect. At the end of the discussion the minister would make a decision.

The hierarchical approach

This was more often the approach adopted in a more long-term development of policy. An official at Grade 7 or HEO would do the background work on policy and then pass it up to the Grade 5 who would examine the brief and then pass it to the Grade 3 or 2 who may go directly to the minister or through the Permanent Secretary. A quote from a retired civil servant gives a good sense of this process:

> What would happen was that the principal would write two or three pages, closely argued, and put it up to his Assistant Secretary. That night he would add another two pages and would then pass it up to his Undersecretary who would add his own page and, if it was terribly important, it would then go through the Deputy Secretary and the Permanent Secretary and it would land on the minister's desk in a great think thing which had contributions all the way from the top down.

the strengths and weaknesses of a particular proposal and lay out alternatives. Officials were not experts in all areas of knowledge. The top civil servants were generalists—their expertise was in gathering information from a range of sources and presenting it to ministers. They were gatekeepers who would summarise all the evidence and arguments about a particular policy and present it in an easily digestible form for the minister (see Politics in Focus 13.1). This process gave officials tremendous influence. They could, as the second face of power would suggest, shape the policy agenda (see Politics in Focus 13.2). Civil servants had a monopoly of policy advice and this meant that they were central to the policy process.

The second aspect of the civil servants' role was, and continues to be, to advise ministers on presentation. Although civil servants are politically neutral, in the sense that they have no attachment to a party, their role is often highly political. They live in a political world where much of their work is concerned with ensuring the ministers, departments and governments appear effective. Much of their time is spent advising ministers on how to avoid public criticism. Officials will provide briefs for ministers when they are facing questions in Parliament or in front of a Parliamentary Select Committee. (See Politics in Focus 13.3.) One of the skills of a top civil servant is felicity

.2

Civil Service

Tony Benn's special advisor said that she felt that the Civil Service was sabotaging his industrial policy and Benn agreed. In his diary he recorded that the Permanent Secretary was 'making no progress, they just turf back things . . . Professor Peacock is utterly wedded to laissez-faire, and it is extremely difficult to operate with that sort of advice coming to you. I just have to think of ways of outflanking them. One way is by public speeches that commit them to a public policy that they then have to defend.'

Tony Benn, *Against the Tide: Diaries* 1973–76, (London: Arrow, 1990)

IN FOCUS 13.3

try of Defence

When the media was first aware that an official within the MoD had talked to the journalist, Andrew Gilligan about weapons of mass destruction, they tried to identify the official. Officials within the MoD prepared a 'defensive briefing' to deal with questions.

Q&A

Who is the official?
> The official works in MoD.

What is his name and current post?
> We wouldn't normally volunteer a name.
> If the correct name is given, we can confirm it and say that he is senior advisor to the
> Proliferation and Arms Control Secretariat.

How long has he been in MoD?
> He has been in his current position for 3 to 4 years. Before that he was a member of UNSCOM.

Did the official play any part in drawing up the dossier?
> He was involved in providing historical details of UNSCOM's activities prior to 1998.

Is he a senior figure?
> He is not a member of the SCS—he is a middle-ranking official.

Is he still working for MoD?
> Yes.

Is he in Iraq?
> No, though he visited Iraq recently for a week.

Is he a member of the ISG?
> No.

Do you believe he is the single source?
> It is not for us to say—only the BBC can confirm that.

with language which allows officials to present material in the best possible light (see Politics in Focus 13.4). A famous example of this was during a court case in Australia when a former British spy, Peter Wright, was fighting for the right to publish his memoirs. The then Cabinet Secretary, Sir Robert Armstrong, was called to give evidence. When asked if he had lied, he said not. He had merely been 'economical with the truth'.

This traditional role of the official has been challenged since the 1960s. In 1968 the Fulton Report criticised the generalist nature of the Civil Service, saying that they did not have the necessary specialised knowledge to make policy in the modern age. In addition, politicians and academics were becoming increasingly sceptical in relation to the Civil Service's supposed abilities. A number of diaries by former politicians like Richard Crossman, Barbara Castle and Tony Benn implied that officials had too much influence and were not responding to the demands of ministers. Simultaneously, the New Right were developing public choice criticisms of bureaucracy (see Chapter 2), and suggesting that officials were responsible for ever-increasing public expenditure. The Conservative Government of Edward Heath 1970–74 was concerned with engendering a greater degree of managerialism in government, and introduced a number of measures designed to improve the processes of policy-making. The Labour Government of James Callaghan 1976–79 was presented with an economic crisis and demands by the International Monetary Fund to cut the number of civil servants. The period from 1977 saw the first fall in the number of civil servants in the post-war era (see Table 13.2). These events provided a backdrop to what was to become a permanent revolution in terms of the Civil Service and central government.

Civil servants and power

In examining the role of the Civil Service we have to be clear that we are not just looking at a simple administrative process but sets of power relations. These power relations are conceptualised in different ways:

The constitutional view sees civil servants as intimate advisers to ministers who are there to present ministers with the facts (and so constrain the wilder ideological ambitions of politicians). Nevertheless it is for the minister to make decisions and it is he who is

ICS IN FOCUS 13.4
rvants and the art of presentation

Throughout the case of BSE there were many examples where officials developed ways of fully informing the public concerning the development and likely impact of BSE. For a long time the Government sustained the position that there was 'no evidence of a link' between BSE and the human variant of the disease, CJD. However, what eventually became apparent was that what was meant by 'no evidence' was not that that there was no link between BSE and CJD but that the Government did not have the evidence. The research had not been done to demonstrate a link between BSE and CJD. Once the research was done there was clear evidence of a link between the two diseases and the Government changed its position.

accountable to Parliament (see Chapters 10–12). Within the constitutional view, the Civil Service sees itself as being constrained by its commitment to the public service ethos; the notion that it is serving the public good and so can be trusted to act with propriety. One political scientist, J.P. Nettl, saw the Civil Service as a benign elite, able to mould and maintain a consensus in British society. This is the conceptualisation of the role of officials that derives from the Westminster model.

The conspiracy view is the position developed by people like the former Labour ministers Tony Benn and Richard Crossman and a number of Conservative politicians. It sees the civil servants as dominating departments and using their control of information to subvert the wishes of ministers. Tony Benn suggests that for the civil servants government is like a hotel that they run but ministers are the guests who come and go and therefore are not able to take over the running of the government. Officials have the long-term view and therefore their views should predominate (Marsh, Richards and Smith 2001).

The Marxist view developed in particular through the work of Ralph Miliband sees senior civil servants as coming from the same social background as leading figures in the military and business. Therefore their interests and the policies they support generally reinforce the interests of the ruling class.

Power dependency—the notion of power dependency is discussed in Chapters 2, 11 and 12. From this perspective we can see officials and ministers as dependent on each other. Officials have knowledge, and expertise and the ability to implement policies. Ministers have political authority and can win the political authority for developing and funding policies. Ministers and officials need each other.

Reforming policy-making

Thatcherism and new public management

The Conservative Government, elected in 1979, initiated a process of reform that continues today. The accumulation of these reforms has resulted in a significant shift from the precepts of the Westminster model. Yet the Thatcher Government, in starting a programme of reform, was trying to reassert the key principle of the traditional model: the sovereignty of Parliament. For Margaret Thatcher, civil servants were obstacles to the wishes of ministers and therefore they had to submit to the sovereignty of Parliament, or more accurately, the executive. What the Thatcher Government wanted was a more responsive Civil Service that was at the same time small and efficient. Thatcher and some of her ministers did not see the relationship between officials and ministers as symbiotic but one where ministers made decisions and officials implemented them. Thatcher believed that civil servants were wedded to the idea of big government and the post-war consensus. She wanted an invigoration of the Civil Service with the introduction of free market criteria into public service. These reforms led to what some people called New Public Management (NPM).

The main features of new public management are:

- a belief in the private market and a concern with introducing market mechanisms into the public sectors;

- a view that organisations should be flexible and they have to be adapted to the task rather than a notion that one size fits all;

- where possible there should be decentralisation and delayering so that organisations are less hierarchical;

- the use of performance indicators and targets to allow audits of performance and to act as incentives;

- a focus on efficiency and costs savings; or

- the belief that managers have to be free to manage.

NPM measures were introduced by the Thatcher Government through a number of programmes:

- Deprivileging the Civil Service—the Thatcher Government was concerned with reducing the number of civil servants (see Table 13.2) and removing some of their employment rights. The early 1980s saw a bitter strike over pay and privileges.

- The Rayner Scrutinies—the Thatcher Government appointed Sir Derek Rayner to head an efficiency unit which looked at the functions carried out by departments and examined whether they were carried out efficiently or if another supplier could provide the same service for less (see Chapter 16).

- The Financial Management Initiative (FMI)—this programme was concerned with developing a clear management system for the running of departments with the aim of improving financial management.

- Marketisation—a crucial element of the Thatcherite programme was to import market mechanisms into the public service. This was done through a number of policies such as contracting-out, which forced public sector organisations to see whether services could be provided more cheaply by private sector companies. For instance, in local and central government many services, ranging from cleaners in hospitals to refuse collection and secretarial services, are now provided by private companies. Marketisation was developed further through the creation of competition between services such as health care and education. The government tried to create a market in health care by splitting the purchasers of health care, which were the local health authorities from the providers, which was the hospital.

The Major Government from 1990 to 1997 continued the reform process initiated by the Thatcher Administration, and oversaw some significant changes in the role of the Civil Service. Whilst the Thatcher Government established Next Steps Agencies, it was the Major years that saw a significant and rapid shift of civil servants from departments to the new agencies (see Chapter 16). The Major Government also created the Competing for Quality Initiative which was intended to identify the core task of the Civil Service, to increase competition and improve delivery. The period from 1990 saw four significant changes developing from this initiative:

- The Citizens' Charter—the Citizens' Charter was an attempt for the first time to set out the rights of the consumers of public services. Government departments had to establish charters with targets for the levels of public service and clearly state the means of redress available for the public when the delivery of services was poor.

- Market testing—all services provided by the public sector were to be 'market tested' to see if they could be provided more efficiently by the private sector.

- Senior management review—as a consequence of the development of agencies and the reduced role of departments, there was a review of the role of central government departments. This review removed a layer of senior civil servants and pushed detailed policy work down the hierarchy of the Civil Service. The aim according to the 1994 White Paper, *Continuity and Change in the Civil Service* was to create 'leaner, flatter management structures'. The process led to the development of what was called the Senior Civil Service (SCS). The intention was that the new SCS was to become much more flexible than the old system based on grades and that decisions were delegated to the most suitable level.

- Fundamental expenditure review—the senior management review was reinforced by the fundamental expenditure review which was a systematic attempt to evaluate the performance and expenditure of departments and to examine whether there could be improvements in efficiency and reductions in departmental expenditure.

Reform under New Labour

Whilst the process of reform was initiated by the Conservatives, and to an extent influenced by New Right thinking, it did not come to an end with the election of a Labour Government in 1997. The New Labour Government under Tony Blair has undertaken a permanent revolution in relation to the role of the Civil Service and the public sector. New Labour has developed an agenda based around the notion of modernising central government, public sector reform and improving delivery. Labour has built on, rather than rejected, the managerial framework of the Conservative government. However, the end point has been rather different. Whilst the Conservatives were distrustful of the state and saw reform as a mechanism for reducing the size of the state and imposing the private sector, for Labour the development of public sector reform is a mechanism for improving the effectiveness of the state and public services. Labour's reform programme has been based on the 'Modernising Government Agenda' which has been extended to reforming the public services programme.

The *Modernising Government* White Paper (1999) aimed at reforming (again) how government works. This included:

- Improving policy-making through the identification of best practice, the development of evidence-based policy-making and increased training for ministers and civil servants.

- Making public services more responsive to the public—developing, for instance, the one stop shops where benefits and state supports can be accessed as one site.

- Improving the quality of public services through targets, identifying the best suppliers and monitoring performance. A crucial element of the Government's policy has been the development of targets in all areas of public service activity from the top of government down to delivery in schools and hospitals. Public services are being set clear targets concerning what they should achieve. (See Politics in Focus 13.5.)

Tony Blair was frustrated by the lack of progress in terms of public sector reform in the first term. It was his belief that despite the extra resources the Government had put into the public sector, better delivery and quality of service was not being achieved. He spoke graphically of the scars on his back from trying to push through changes in the public sector. Consequently, following the election in 2001 a second White Paper, reforming public services was produced. This paper outlined the need for:

- National standards—with hospitals, schools, the police and local government being set tough targets.

- Devolution of decision-making to frontline staff. For instance, Local Primary Care Trusts are now responsible for 75% of NHS funding. The new foundation hospitals will have even more control over how they use funds and deliver services.

- Increased flexibility by allowing those who deliver services to make changes in organisations.

- Improving consumer choice.

ITICS IN FOCUS 13.5
c service agreements

PSAs have been developed by the Treasury and the Delivery Unit. Their aim is to create targets and incentives for improving public services. PSAs set a list of objectives and aims which are then linked to performance targets. Most of these are set for departments but some cross departments. These targets enable the Treasury and the Prime Minister's Office to shape the direction and policy goals of departments and to improve co-ordination (James 2003). PSAs are not only being used in central government but at all levels of public service delivery. There are targets in schools for abilities at different ages and targets for the level of truancy. There are targets in hospitals for the length of waiting lists and the time it takes for patients to be treated.

Many commentators suggest that targets distort the delivery of public goods. It is argued that public sector workers are spending their time filling in forms and chasing targets rather than serving the public. For instance, the leader of the British Medical Association, Dr Ian Bogle said that the NHS was more concerned with ticking boxes than the needs of patients and those targets were undermining the clinical autonomy of doctors. He also pointed to the game playing that is a consequence of audit as those under scrutiny attempt to meet the targets set by the auditors.

A cultural change?

One of the main aims of the process of reform has been to try to change the culture of the Civil Service. So one of the key questions is whether there has been a shift to what could be called a managerial framework. Many Conservatives saw the Civil Service as a closed and insular organisation more concerned with its own interests than the interests of the government or serving the public. For others, the Civil Service was dominated by what could be called 'the public service ethos'. This is the view proffered by the Westminster model which sees civil servants as loyal and neutral political actors who, often through self-sacrifice (they could be earning more in the private sector) have dedicated themselves to public service. Civil servants also had a particular style of speaking and presenting themselves. They were the typical Oxbridge graduate who spoke in a deliberate and mannered way (with a pronounced upper middle class accent) and dressed in the ubiquitous pinstriped suits.

There are indications that there have been significant changes in the nature and role of the Civil Service. First, an increasing number of senior civil servants are being drawn from the private sector and other public bodies outside Whitehall. Traditionally civil servants grew up in Whitehall and eventually some would make it to Permanent Secretary. Now nearly all senior appointments are openly advertised and a growing number of senior figures have come from outside. Of the 146 appointments made in 2002, 42 (29%) were filled by civil servants, 47 (32%) by candidates from other organisations in the public sector and 57 (39%) were from the private and voluntary sectors. This is quite a change in a short period of time. Twenty years ago almost no senior appointments would have come from outside, whereas now only a third of posts are filled by traditional civil servants. One of the worries of the Civil Service commissioners, who are responsible for overseeing senior appointments, is that many of the outsiders are unaware of the code of practice that governs the behaviour of officials. In certain instances outsiders have certainly been aware of a culture clash in terms of the values of the private sector and the Civil Service (see for a good example of the clashes between the former Home Secretary Michael Howard and Derek Lewis the former head of the Prison Service.

Second, whereas the role of the official in the Westminster model was very much concerned with advising ministers on policy and ensuring that ministers 'knew the facts', the role of officials now is much more related to the management of the policy process rather than the making of policy. What we have seen in recent years is the development of the 'can do' official. Their role is to deliver what ministers want. In other words, officials are expected to be effective managers and enablers rather than policy advisers (Richards 1997). Third, the structure within which officials operate has changed greatly. The types of organisations in which officials work have now become much more varied. There is no longer a single model of a government department (see Chapter 14). Officials can now find themselves working at the interface between the public and the private sector, and increasingly they are working outside London. It is probably not a coincidence that a previous Cabinet Secretary, Andrew Turnbull, said that civil servants no longer had to wear ties—indicating a change in dress code and culture.

The impact on Civil Service power

Christopher Foster and Frances Plowden have argued that the changes that have occurred since 1979 have had a fundamental impact on the relationship between ministers and officials and reduced the power and influence of the Civil Service (Foster and Plowden 1996; Foster 2001). They believe that ministers have become much less willing to listen to the advice of officials, that decisions are often now made in informal meetings between ministers without the presence of officials, and that ministers are concerned only with rapid decisions rather than undertaking a careful policy process. Foster (2001) outlines the key changes that he believes have occurred:

- Ministers and special advisors meet without officials and they are more concerned with media reaction than the quality of policy.
- There is greater reliance on alternative sources of advice outside the Civil Service. One of the major innovations of the Labour Administration has been the development of task forces. Literally hundreds of task forces have been developed to advise ministers on a whole range of policy areas. These task forces include people from business, the voluntary sector and trade unions.
- There is less consultation with pressure groups (see Chapter 21).
- Officials have lost control of ministerial diaries.
- There has been a decline in the number of senior officials, leading to a decline in the quality of the advice.

A number of commentators have complained about increased politicisation of civil servants, the extent to which political advisers are replacing civil servants and the decline in the quality of the advice that is going to ministers. Increased conflicts are developing between officials, ministers and civil servants over roles and relationships. Fundamental to the process has been the increase in the number of special advisers (see Chapter 12). Labour has substantially increased the number of special advisers. In some cases they have taken over the role of senior officials as the closest policy advisers to the minister. Both Tony Blair and Gordon Brown have relied very closely on special advisers. For much of the period of the Labour Government Alistair Campbell and Jonathon Powell have been Blair's most important advisers. Likewise in the Treasury, Gordon Brown, for much of the first two terms of the Labour Government, depended on his special advisers Ed Balls and Ed Miliband rather than Treasury civil servants. The Labour Government has also changed the pattern of relationship involving officials, ministers and special advisers. In 2003 the Government announced that special advisers could instruct officials on behalf of ministers. Special advisers are able to work in a relationship with ministers that places them between officials and ministers. Martin Stanley makes the point that now: 'special advisers now have more power than private secretaries in that they can commission work on their own account, and not just on behalf of ministers. Civil servants now therefore serve special advisors as well as ministers' (www.civilservant.org.uk/spads.shtm).

A number of commentators have highlighted the problems with the growth in the number of personal advisers. Two previous Cabinet Secretaries (Robin Butler and Richard Wilson)—the post which is the head of the Home Civil Service—have expressed concern about the role of special advisers and the dangers of politicisation that they bring. It is clear that special advisers are reducing the role of officials in the policy process especially in the Home Office and Number 10. However at the same time it has to be remembered that there are 4,500 senior civil servants and only 81 special advisers (see p 241). Most departments have no more than two advisers and so their impact on government may be more limited than the critics suggest. In other Westminster systems such as Australia, the Prime Minister has a much greater number of special advisers.

Policy failure

As we saw above, some of the critics of special advisers and the wider reforms to the Civil Service have suggested that these changes are leading to a growing number of policy failures. The poll tax, BSE and the foot and mouth crisis are all pointed to as failures resulting from the declining effectiveness of the Civil Service, the unwillingness of ministers to listen to advice and the increased perception that policy has to be introduced rapidly without proper consideration either inside Whitehall or by Parliament (see Table 13.1). The study by David Butler and his colleagues of the poll tax fiasco illustrates the problems that can arise when policy is not developed in a considered and informed manner (Butler, Adonis and Travis 1994). The Conservative Government introduced a tax to replace the rates based on the notion that every individual over the age of 18 should pay local tax. Such was the opposition to the tax that there was a huge campaign of non-payment, there was a large and violent anti-poll tax demonstration on 31 March 1990,

Date	Policy
1989–90	Poll Tax—Community Charge
1995–97	Privatisation of the railways
1991	Child Support Act
1991	Dangerous Dogs Act
1989	Football Supporters Act
1986–	BSE crisis
2001	Foot and mouth crisis

and it was a key factor in the removal of Margaret Thatcher as Prime Minister (see Chapter 22). The poll tax was a consequence in part of ideological dogma not being properly constrained by the Civil Service and partly a consequence of the officials not gathering sufficient information concerning the consequences of the tax.

However, it is important to point out that in all the policy failures mentioned, it is difficult to allow officials to abdicate all responsibility and blame poor policy on the breakdown of the Haldane relationship. In some ways these policies are not a consequence of changing relationships between ministers and officials—although that may have exacerbated the failings or created new problems—but a consequence of the nature of the Civil Service. In all the examples outlined above, officials were closely involved in the development of policy. Therefore policy failure has not been a result of officials being ignored, but with their involvement. Critics point to a number of continuing problems within the Civil Service:

- The Civil Service remains a closed and insular organisation. Despite greater exchanges with other sectors, and the increased employment of outsiders, the majority of officials are career civil servants.

- The civil servants in key positions remain generalists rather than specialists and lack expertise in policy issues. Their focus is much more on process—how policy is made— rather than outcomes—the actual delivery of policy (this is very much Tony Blair's criticism of the Civil Service).

- Much policy-making continues to be closed and secretive. The Freedom of Information Act (discussed in Chapter 10) still does not allow the publication of policy advice to ministers. This means that the advice to ministers cannot be tested in a public arena. Many of the problems to do with the handling of BSE were a consequence of secrecy.

- Despite attempts at joined-up government departmentalism remains endemic. Most policy-making occurs within departments without sufficient reference to what other departments are doing.

- The culture has not changed enough. Officials remain wedded to the old ways. Whilst they may have picked up the language of managerialism, they retain the practice of the traditional public service ethos.

Foster and Plowden suggest that ministers are much more hands on and much less willing to take the advice of civil servants. Their assumption is that the advice of the traditional Whitehall mandarin is good. The reality is that what officials have often been good at is offering advice on presentation and dissembling, rather than good policy. It also ignores the fact that people elect ministers to make decisions and implement policy. There is no constitutional or democratic reason why officials should be involved in making policy—this is just a remnant of the Westminster model which sees officials as the keepers of the system. What is clear, is that the policy process has changed from the top to the bottom. Officials have lost the monopoly of advice. Ministers are now looking to a wide range of sources for policy initiatives and they have become much more pro-active in terms of the policy process. Senior officials are increasingly confined to two jobs. The first is managing the policy process, in other words, co-ordinating the range of policy advice and then ensuring that decisions are implemented. The second is supporting the minister on a day-to-day basis through the private office. However, perhaps one of the most significant changes in the long term is the way that devolution is fragmenting the Civil Service.

The decentralisation of the Civil Service

One of the arguments that has been consistently put forward by civil servants and ministers is that despite the fact that there has been considerable change and fragmentation of government, there is still a unified Civil Service. Despite a quarter century of reform, it is maintained that a core Civil Service, governed by the unified rules and sharing similar values, remains. Whilst this may be the case legally, it is certainly true that devolution in addition to the reforms outlined above has had a major impact on the reality of a unified Civil Service. This problem arises particularly in relation to the issue of loyalty. Officials have to be loyal to their minister but they are also loyal to the Crown—in practice the government in London. This may not be a problem when Labour controls the government in London and in Scotland, but it could become a big problem if there is a Conservative government in Westminster, but a Labour Administration in Scotland. Could a civil servant who is obeying an order of his minister in Scotland be overruled by the government in Westminster? In order to try to resolve this problem a loyalty solution has been put forward: 'civil servants will have to delineate between "practical loyalty" to the minister they serve and "ultimate loyalty" to the Crown' (Rhodes et al 2003: 96). However, this compromise does not really address the question of what would happen should there be a real conflict between Crown and minister.

More generally this relates to a wider question of whether a genuinely unified Civil Service continues to exist. In Northern Ireland, there has long existed a separate Civil Service which to some extent has had a separate set of rules. It seems increasingly the case that the Scottish Civil Service will develop differently from that based in London. It will become less likely that officials working in Scotland will develop a career path that takes them into Whitehall-based departments and over time a different culture may develop. Likewise, even in England there has been a shift to the development of regional offices where the departments of Trade and Industry, Education, Work and Pensions and Environment, Local Government and Transport have shared offices in regional locations. The aim of these offices is to:

- to ensure better co-ordination of area based initiatives;
- to bring regional perspectives to bear on central initiatives;
- to act as representatives of government in the regions (Rhodes et al 2003: 132).

As a consequence, large numbers of civil servants are employed outside London (see Table 13.2). So whilst the government may wish to maintain a unified Civil Service, the

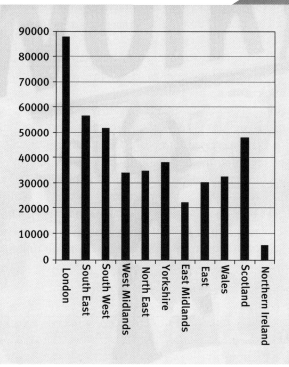

reality could be that this is increasingly difficult as different ways of working develop in the various parts of the United Kingdom. As Rhodes and his colleagues conclude:

> We have found a distinctive Civil Service with their own ways of working, servicing territorially specific policy networks. Most of the Civil Service lives and works anywhere except Whitehall. And location matters. The Civil Services of Scotland and Northern Ireland have distinctive histories...

For Rhodes et al devolution will result in even greater distinctions because the process encourages difference.

The Europeanisation of the Civil Service

A further important change in the roles and practice of the Civil Service is its greater integration into the European Union (see Chapter 8). Europe has affected officials in a number of ways. For some officials nearly all their work is tied to the EU. For instance, in areas of agriculture, trade and much of the environment policy is determined almost solely at the EU level. As a consequence officials are involved in developing policy within Europe and then implementing EU policy. It is also increasingly the case that officials are spending some time seconded to the EU and there is a suggestion that they may be bringing back elements of European working practices, and thus Europeanising the British Civil Service. With increased European Union activity, officials in devolved and regional institutions are often in consultation with officials directly without working through departments in Whitehall. However, Bulmer and Burch (1998) note that in many ways the EU has had remarkably little impact on the work of Whitehall and that in many ways the EU has been absorbed into the existing machinery. There has been little reassessment of ministerial responsibility, Cabinet responsibility or even parliamentary sovereignty in the light of Britain's membership of the European Union.

Conclusion

The last 25 years have seen a permanent revolution in Whitehall. Officials in government departments have been subject to a continual reform programme that started with the election of Margaret Thatcher in 1979 and continues today. This reform process has been about attempting to make government more efficient and effective, and improving the process by which policies are delivered. The consequence of the programme of reform is the role of civil servants has changed significantly. Civil servants have transformed from being at the centre of policy-making to a role where they are more concerned with management. Officials have lost their monopoly of policy advice and ministers are obtaining policy suggestions from a wide range of sources. This has resulted in a change in the nature of the power relations between ministers and civil servants.

However what we have seen is not the complete restructuring of British government but a battle between new public management and the Westminster model. As the NPM attempts to create greater managerial autonomy, the Westminster model attempts to re-impose control. On the one hand the government has attempted to introduce managerialism into the public service. It has tried to give officials more autonomy and managerial discretion. The argument is that this will improve delivery on the ground because officials can respond to local circumstances and make decisions quickly without having to refer up the hierarchy. However, this has contradicted the desire of ministers to control. So what has happened is that whilst on one side the government has increased autonomy, on the other hand it has attempted to restrain the autonomy through the use of targets. The government has in other words tried to re-impose the Westminster model.

Nevertheless, it is clear that the relationship between minister and civil servants has changed considerably since 1979. The role of officials in policy-making has declined. Increasingly their role is being seen as one of management. Moreover, ministers are using a wider range of advice than just their civil servants and so the symbiotic relationship that gave officials a crucial role in the determination of policy has been diluted. Officials are less important to ministers and as a consequence have less impact on policy. For some this is seen as an attack on the constitution, whilst for other it is reasserting the constitutional position that it is ministers that decide. Whichever is the case it cannot be denied that the balance of resources between ministers and officials has changed and officials have lost influence.

KEY POINTS

- The power of the Civil Service has changed considerably over the last 25 years.
- Governments have introduced a range of reforms to try to improve the efficiency and effectiveness of the Civil Service.
- Civil servants have lost their monopoly of policy advice and ministers now use a range of sources for policy.
- There has been further fragmentation of the Civil Service because of devolution.

KEY QUESTIONS

(1) Why have governments been so keen to reform the Civil Service?

(2) What are the main reforms?

(3) What impact has reform had on the relationship between ministers and civil servants?

(4) How has the role of civil servants changed?

(5) What has been the impact of devolution on the Civil Service?

(6) Has the power of civil servants declined?

IMPORTANT WEBSITES

Information on Civil Service reform can be found at the Cabinet Office website: www.cabinet-office. gov.uk/. There is a large amount of information on the Civil Service at: www.civilservice.gov.uk/. There is also a wealth of information and analysis at the site of the Public Administration Select Committee: www.parliament.uk/parliamentary_ committees/public_administration_select_ committee.cfm.

For international information see: www. worldbank.org/publicsector/civilservice/.

A great insight into the workings of the Civil Service and the core executive in general is to be found on the Hutton Inquiry website: www. the-hutton-inquiry.org.uk/index.htm. Here you can access many original government documents which would not normally be availed for thirty years. Likewise similarly sources are provided by the Phillips inquiry into BSE site: www. bseinquiry.gov.uk/report/.

FURTHER READING

The key changes in the Civil Service under the Conservatives are examined in C. Foster and F. Plowden (1996) *The State Under Stress*, Buckingham: Open University Press and D. Marsh, D. Richards, and M.J. Smith (2002) *Changing Patterns of Governance in the UK*, London, Palgrave. The reforms under Labour are explored in D. Richards and M.J. Smith (2004) 'The Hybrid State: Labour's Response to the Challenge of Governance' in S. Ludlam and M.J. Smith (eds) *Governing as New Labour*, Palgrave: London and D. Richards and M.J. Smith (2002) *Governance and Public Policy in the UK*, Oxford: Oxford University Press.

 Visit the Online Resource Centre that accompanies this book for links to more information on this chapter topic

CHAPTER FOURTEEN

The British state today: power, meta-governance and regulation

READER'S GUIDE

The state in Britain has been transformed over the last 30 years. Yet understanding the impact of state change is a complex task generating a diverse body of literature. In this chapter, we examine two contrasting narratives of the nature of state transformation—governance and the regulatory state. The chapter argues that while these two narratives are not necessarily mutually exclusive, it is important to understand the differing implications each presents in their interpretations of the impact of state change on the core executive and political power. Implicit within the governance narrative are arguments that suggest that state fragmentation and an increase in actors in the policy-making arena has led to an increasing plurality of political power. Alternatively, the regulatory state narrative suggests that the response by governments to the forces of governance has led to a rise in regulation, which has reinvigorated the power of the core executive.

Introduction

In the preceding chapters in Part Two, we have examined the impact of change on both the policy-making process and the machinery of government. We have addressed some of the most important forces shaping the nature of British politics today—globalisation, internationalisation, Europeanisation, neoliberal reform and devolution. Collectively, these forces have changed the way in which politics in Britain today operates. Yet, while the themes we have examined looking at the impact of change on the constitution, the core executive, government departments, agencies and the policy arena are all important when constructing a picture of how the British polity now functions, what is lacking is a holistic narrative describing the contemporary nature of the British state. What this chapter provides is a macro-analysis of the changing nature of the British state by examining the two most dominant, but not necessarily mutually exclusive, sets of literature on the state—that of 'governance' and 'the regulatory state'.

As we saw in Chapter 3, the literature associated with the governance narrative identifies both the nature of state transformation in the last 30 years and also the forces that have been responsible for this change. The governance narrative presents a set of images of the state as being diffuse, fragmented and differentiated. In particular, the role and power of government is seen as having altered to being only one of many actors now involved in the making of public policy. The implications are that the power of the core executive has diminished from being able to command (order) the policy process to being now, at best, able to impose some form of control over policy.

Yet, there is a second competing set of literature which, while recognising the very real impact governance has had on the power of the core executive, instead suggests that it is still an actor which commands a powerful set of resources enabling it to respond strategically to change, in order to retain its power over the policy process. This is most clearly manifested in the regulatory agenda pursued by recent governments in order to retain central control. Clearly, this second set of literature presents a contrasting understanding of the impact of governance on the British state. The aim of the chapter is to explore these two sets of literature, in order to highlight how changes in the nature of the state have led different commentators to competing conclusions as to the impact rendered on political power.

The governance narrative

In Chapter 3, we surveyed a number of the key themes related to the term governance. The focus was on the variety of ways governance has been used as an analytical tool for explaining state change within the discipline of political science. It seeks to understand and explain the impact of a variety of forces including, neoliberal reforms aimed at rolling back the state, globalisation, internationalisation, managerialism in the public sector and privatization that have affected the nature of politics since the mid-1970s. The substantive arguments associated with the majority of the literature on governance are that both the state and the policy-making arena in the last three decades have substantially changed. Traditional means of governing based on a top-down, hierarchical, centralised and elitist model—traits that are more often than not associated with a Keynesian-welfare state—have been eroded. Today, the policy-making arena has become a cluttered environment, involving numerous actors operating at different levels (supranational, national, devolved, regional and local). In this changing governing environment no one actor, be it a government or a supranational institution such as the EU or the G8, dominates. Policy-making has increasingly become a process of evolving policy networks in which a range of actors are dependent on each other in order to secure their goals. In this environment, the best that a national government can hope to achieve is some semblance of control over the policy network. The process of governing has become a mixture of markets, networks and hierarchies. Fundamental to this analysis is that the policy-making arena has become an increasingly pluralistic environment. Clearly, the governance narrative provides a direct challenge to the Westminster model examined in Chapter 3. In particular, it suggests that power is no longer centred in or round the core executive, but has been dispersed away from traditional central-state actors to many different, often new, arenas. One potential weakness of this approach is the broadly implicit assumption that the net impact of these changes has been a residual loss of control by the core executive, where political power has seeped elsewhere in an increasingly pluralised policy-making arena.

The regulatory state narrative

The governance literature is not the only body of work that has attempted to describe and analyse the changing nature of the state in the last 30 or so years. A second body of literature has also questioned the utility of the Westminster model in describing the nature of the contemporary state in Britain. As with the governance literature, the 'regulatory state' narrative also argues that many changes have taken place in the policy-making arena, but its conclusions on the impact of change are in marked contrast to that of the goverance school. Central to the regulatory state narrative is the notion that the response of governments to the rise of such forces as globalisation, internationalisation, marketisation and Europeanisation has been to increase state regulation in an attempt to maintain a semblance of control. Indeed, the conclusion of some of the key authors from the regulatory state school is that rather than seeing a rise in pluralism in the last 30 years, governments' pursuit of regulation as a means to assert control has further increased the centralisation of power at the core executive level.

The rise of the regulatory state

One of the most coherent accounts of the rise of the regulatory state in Britain is provided by Moran (2001, 2003). He observes that while regulation is by no means a modern invention and, within the British context, the 19th century was a notable period for the construction of a wide range of regulatory institutions—the Prison Inspectorate, the Raliway Board, Factory Inspectors, the Mining Inspectorate, etc—the period in which there has been the greatest transformation in regulation has been the last three decades. Moran (2003) refers to this period as an era of 'hyper-innovation' in state reform triggered by the crisis of the Keynesian welfare state in the 1970s. Previously, government would predominantly opt for a legisaltive approach in order to affect change or secure order in society. The complex challenges presented by governance forces, most notably the fragmentation of hierarchical control by the core executive, led to a new strategy emerging in which government created a range of inter-mediary bodies—regulatory agencies—to exert control over both the public and private spheres on its behalf. The impact of the regulatory approach pursued by both the last Conservative Administration and the present Labour Government has meant that:

> Vast new areas of social and economic life have been colonised by law and by regulatory agencies. The food we eat, the physical conditions we work under, the machines and equipment we use in our home, office and on the road—all are increasingly subject to legal controls, usually adminstered by a specialised agency (Moran 2001: 20).

What is striking about this observation is that the contemporary image of life in Britain is far removed from the intentions of the last Conservative Administration to create a more minimal state. The rhetoric of the 1979 Thatcher Government was that in response to what it regarded as a bloated, inefficient and over-expanded public sector, it had been elected on a popular mandate to 'roll back the frontiers of the state', remove red-tape from constraining the entrepeneurial zeal of Britain's private sector and free individuals from the pervasive shackles of the state. Conversely, the arguments associated with the regulatory state suggest that by the time the Conservatives fell from office in 1997, the reach of the state through various regulatory agencies was greater than ever. The rise of the regulatory state in Britain in recent decades should be understood through a:

> . . . series of concurrent transformations in the system of government: the retreat of some historically established forms of intervention, like public ownership; the advance of new forms of control, typified by the extension of regulation over a wide range of potential risks to health and safety; and the transformation of some institutions of public control, typified by the changes that have come over the bureaucracy of the central state in Britain (Moran 2001: 20–1).

In the next section, we examine the different elements that contribute to the British regulatory state today, before considering what has caused its growth and why its evolution is so far removed from the suggested neoliberal aspirations of the New Right 30 years ago.

Britain's regulatory state

First, it is important to recognise there is no single form of regulation in Britain; it has evolved in a complex way in recent decades as governments have tried to assert some form of control over political, social and economic forces that are in flux. The rise of the regulatory state is a multi-faceted phenonemon and, as such, Moran provides a useful schema to illustrate the different forms regulation can take: the regulation of privatisation; the transformation of self-regulation; the rise of self-regulation; and the regulation of government.

The regulation of privatisation

Fundamental to the New Right project in the late 1970s was the role of the market as a mechanism for delivering public goods in 'the most effective and efficient manner'. The aim was either to return elements of government to the private sector (through privatisation) or, where that was not possible, to introduce the market to aspects of the public sector (the creation of internal markets). For many ministers who were in office during the last Conservative Administration, privatisation was regarded as the most successful policy carried out during the 18 years of Conservative government (see Richards and Smith 2004a). The origins of this wave of privatisation can actually be traced back to the previous Labour Government when, as part of the IMF package in 1976, they were forced to sell shares in the then publicly owned British Petroleum (BP) as a mechanism for raising finance. The Conservative Administration of 1979 positively endorsed privatisation, nevertheless the policy developed in a piecemeal and gradual way. It began by selling more BP shares so that it became a minority shareholder, it then followed a similar strategy for British Aerospace and then Cable and Wireless. The first 100% sale of a publicly owned company was Amersham International and this was followed by the sale of the National Freight Corporation to its managers and workers. The first large-scale privatisation, aimed at the general public, was British Telecom in 1984 which subsequently became the largest UK privatisation. Following a comprehensive advertising campaign, 2.4 million people applied for shares. The next large-scale privatisation, British Gas, attracted 6 million applications for shares. By 1992, the Conservatives had sold off nearly all the major utilities and privatised companies. The only large companies left in public ownership were British Coal, British Railways and the Post Office. The first two were privatised by the Major Government (see Table 14.1).

One of the biggest impacts that privatisation had was in changing the mode of governance for a large part of the economy and for the provision of public goods. For nearly 40 years, responsibility for delivering different forms of energy, public transport, a range of public utilities and even the production of a variety of manufactured goods such as steel were with the government. With the privatisation programme, the Conservative Government was disengaging from the economy, effectively arguing that the market was

Company	Date
British Petroleum	1979
British Aerospace	1981
Cable and Wireless	1981
National Freight Corporation	1982
Britoil	1982
Amersham International	1982
Assn of British Ports	1983
Cable and Wireless	1983
British Telecom	1984
Enterprise Oil	1984
Jaguar	1984
British Gas	1986
Rolls Royce	1987
British Airways	1987
British Airports Authority	1987
British Petroleum (2nd tranche)	1987
British Steel	1988
Powergen	1995
National Power	1995
British Coal	1995
British Nuclear Power	1996
British Rail	1996

a more effective way of delivering services such as water, gas and electricity. However, the process of privatisation was not a shift from state control to a free market. In most cases, the government retained some mechanism of control over the newly privatised industries. For example, in some industries, the government retained, at least for a period, a golden share. This meant that the government could have a substantial influence if it so desired. More importantly, the privatisation process did not create competition in a range of areas, especially the utilities like water, gas, electricity and railways.

Therefore through privatisation, the government introduced a system of regulation. It set up regulatory bodies which effectively restricted the price increases that the new private monopolies could impose if they were left to the market—Ofwat, Oftel, etc. Some of these bodies have been relatively effective. For instance, the railway regulators can impose heavy fines for poor performance and in 1995 the electricity regulator reconsidered the prices previously agreed. In 1997, both the water and electricity regulators imposed price reductions. As Feigenbaum, Henig and Hamnett (1998: 80) point out: 'The regulators possess considerable power over the operation, service standards and pricing structure of the privatised utilities'. Moreover, as with the case of Railtrack, the government can impose direct government control if it believes that the standard of service falls below a certain level. Richards and Smith (2002) argue that privatisation has changed the nature of government control rather than ended state control. They point

ties in the UK

OFTEL—the regulator or 'watchdog' for the UK **telecoms** industry. It is also responsible for broadcast transmission. Its stated aim is 'for customers to get the best possible deal in terms of quality, choice and value for money'.

OFGEM—Office of the **gas and electricity** markets, it regulates the gas and electricity industries in Great Britain. Ofgem's stated aim is 'to bring choice and value to all gas and electricity customers by promoting competition and regulating monopolies'.

OFWAT—regulates the UK **water and sewage** industry overseeing quality, protecting customers' interests and proscribing the rate of return on capital invested by the industry companies.

ORR—the Office of the **Rail Regulator** is the independent UK government department responsible for the regulation of the railways in Great Britain.

Ombudsman—is given the power to **investigate grievances** with **government bodies**. An example is the UK Parliamentary and Health Service Ombudsman who will investigate complaints free of charge with the power to award compensation where there is justification.

Postcomm—is the Post Office Commissioner with power to regulate and encourage competition as the Post Office (now Consignia) becomes a plc.

Trading Standards—a one stop shop for **consumer protection** information in the UK. The site is supported and maintained by TSI, the Trading Standards Institute.

Competition Commission (formerly the Monopolies and Mergers Commission MMC)—government body which **investigates monopolies,** price fixing, etc.

European Competition Commission—investigates monopolies and anti-market practices across the whole of the EU; it can overrule the **UK Competition Commission**.

Financial Services Authority—this authority will eventually be the only overall **regulator** of the financial markets.

Source: Adapted from www.raynet.mcmail.com/official.htm#Government%20regulatory

to the numerous regulatory bodies created by government whose *modus operandi* is also set by government (see Politics in Focus 14.1).

Moran (2001: 22) observes that the nature of this type of regulation is intensely political:

> Issues that elsewhere in the private sector are usually thought to be properly settled by managers responding to the market—issues of executive pay, of pricing of products, of level and direction of investment—are in the case of the privatised industries subjects of intense political dispute.

This was demonstrated in the case of Railtrack, whose 50,000 shareholders took the government to the High Court in 2005, claiming the government deliberately forced the company into insolvency in October 2001 to avoid paying out compensation. During the case, the former Transport Minister Stephen Byers admitted he had not been wholly truthful to a Commons sub-committee about the events leading up to Railtrack's collapse.

Interestingly, Professor Stephen Littlechild, commissioned by the Department of Industry to write the original report for establishing the regulatory framework for the first major privatisation, that of British Telecom (Littlechild 1983), argued that regulation was: 'essentially a means of preventing the worst excesses of monopoly . . . until competition arrives'. He conceived of the need for regulation as only a temporary measure until normal market conditions had been established. With hindsight, we can see that the original expectations of Littlechild—that regulation was a short-term measure, 'holding the fort' as he infamously observed—were very much wide of the mark. The history of regulation indicates that it is a process that once started takes on a momentum of its own. This leads Richards and Smith (2002) to conclude that while the nature of the delivery of services in the form of utilities has dramatically changed, a clear shift from the public to the private sector, the power of the state to maintain control has been retained, but in a different form.

The transformation of self-regulation

The evolution of the 'chartered' professions in Britain—doctors, lawyers, accountants, engineers, etc—produced a system of self-regulation based on public trust, legitimised by each profession's standards of practice founded on professional qualification. For the professions themselves, this created a cosy state of affairs, not only ensuring that they acted as lord and master over their own realm, but at the same time creating a monopoly in which they were the only service supplier. Moreover, such an approach acted as a bulwark against state interference, providing the professions with an enormous degree of autonomy and secrecy in determining the parameters and practices of their own existence (see Vincent 1998). The origins of this form of regulation can be largely traced back to the 19th century. As Moran (2003: 51) observes: '. . . the idea of a profession as a college of gentlemen, preferably sanctified by grace of the Royal touch (a Royal Charter), raised the status of occupations that were being created, or reshaped, by industrialism' (see Politics in Focus 14.2). The system that evolved was, in the words of Marquand (1988) and Moran (2003), a system of club regulation and government, based on informal, gentlemanly

POLITICS IN FOCUS 14.2
Professional bodies and Royal Charters

Below is the official definition given by the Privy Council as to what constitutes a Royal Charter and how a professional body acquires one. Also listed are some of the key bodies that have the status of a Royal Charter.

Chartered bodies

There are 400 or so chartered bodies. A Royal Charter is a way of incorporating a body, that is turning it from a collection of individuals into a single legal entity. A body incorporated by Royal Charter has all the powers of a natural person, including the power to sue and be sued in its own right. Royal Charters were at one time the only means of incorporating a body, but there are now other means (becoming a registered company, for example), so the grant of new Charters is comparatively rare. New grants of Royal Charters are these days reserved for eminent professional bodies or charities which have a solid record of achievement and are financially sound. In the case of professional bodies they should represent a field of activity which is unique and not covered by other professional bodies. At least 75% of the corporate members should be qualified to first degree level standard. Finally, both in the case of charities and professional bodies, incorporation by Charter should be in the public interest. This last consideration is important, since once incorporated by Royal Charter a body surrenders significant aspects of the control of its internal affairs to the Privy Council. Amendments to Charters can be made only with the agreement of The Queen in Council, and amendments to the body's by-laws require the approval of the Council (though not normally of Her Majesty). This effectively means a significant degree of Government regulation of the affairs of the body, and the Privy Council will therefore wish to be satisfied that such regulation accords with public policy. (www.privy-council.org.uk/output/Page44.asp)

Examples of key professions with a Royal Charter:

Association of Chartered Certified Accountants
British Psychological Society
Chartered Institute of Bankers
Chartered Institute of Public Finance and Accountancy
Chartered Institute of Management Accountants
Chartered Management Institute
Institution of Engineers
Royal Astronomical Society
Royal College of Physicians of London
Royal Institute of British Architects
Royal Statistical Society
The Chartered Institute of Taxation
The Royal Meteorological Society

agreements and an unspoken, yet clearly recognisable, set of 'rules of the game'. This is a classic British trait of preferring to rely on trust and implicit understandings, rather than establish a formal set of codified rules. The end product was a system of self-regulation possessing predominantly oligarchic, secretive, elitist, informal and anachronistic characteristics. From its evolution in mid-Victorian Britain until the 1960s (and a then growing sense of the amateurism of the ruling elites and professions being, in part, responsible for Britain's relative decline), the system was largely allowed to evolve unchecked with few questioning its legitimacy. Indeed, club regulation in many ways replicated many of the characteristics of the Westminster model—closed, elitist, hierarchical and secretive. As Moran (2003: 4) observed:

> . . . the system survived as a deliberate anachronism, because in the twentieth century it protected elites from more modern forces: from the threats posed by the new world of formal democracy; and from an empowered and often frightening working class.

Yet, by the 1970s, a growing sense of crisis in the Keynesian welfare state concomitantly led to a crisis in the world of club regulation by the professions. The impact on the system of self-regulation of professional bodies triggered a creeping process of 'institutionalisation, codification and juridification'. This might for example take the form of including 'outsiders' on a regulatory board, such as in the case of the General Medical Council, or, elsewhere, the introduction of legislation to formalise or codify working practices, such as the Financial Services Act (2000). The aim of the professions has been to restore public trust in what they do. Yet a number of high profile scandals in recent years, such as the Harold Shipman case in the medical profession, the Nick Leeson/Barings Bank fraud in the banking profession and the Price Waterhouse scandal in the accounting profession have continued to raise numerous questions concerning the effectiveness of regulation in the professions.

The rise of social regulation

The rise of social regulation can be traced to a number of different features within Britain: the introduction of legislation to ensure equality of opportunity in different social, political or economic settings; the creation of new agencies or organisations to combat dis-crimination, such as the Equal Opportunities Commission and the Commission for Racial Equality; and finally, the growth of regulation to protect citizens against the potential exposure to hazardous environments. This last feature is associated with the notion of risk avoidance and is manifested in the creation of such bodies as the Health and Safety Executive to ensure safe practice in the workplace, or the Food Standards Agency created to monitor the quality of food in the light of various recent scares such as salmonella in eggs or BSE. The first two features are not mutually exclusive, so we will examine these together.

Much of the rise of social regulation in Britain stems from inequalities that were occurring in the workplace. This might take the form of discrimination over religion, disability, gender, age or ethnicity. From the late 1960s onwards, pressure groups such as

Equal Pay Act 1970

Under this Act, every employment contract is deemed to include an 'equality clause' which guarantees both sexes the same money for doing the same or broadly similar work, or work rated as equivalent by a job evaluation study. Such a clause operates unless an employer can prove that pay variation between the sexes is reasonable and genuinely due to a material difference between their cases.

Anti-Discrimination (Pay) Act 1974

An Act to ensure equal treatment, in relation to certain terms and conditions of employment, between men and women employed on like work.

Sex Discrimination Act 1975

An Act to render unlawful certain kinds of sex discrimination and discrimination on the ground of marriage, and establish a Commission with the function of working towards the elimination of such discrimination and promoting equality of opportunity between men and women generally; and for related purposes.

Race Relations Act 1976

An Act to make fresh provision with respect to discrimination on racial grounds and relations between people of different racial groups; and to make in the Sex Discrimination Act 1975 amendments for bringing provisions in that Act relating to its administration and enforcement into conformity with the corresponding provisions in this Act.

Employment Equality Act 1977

An Act to make unlawful in relation to employment certain kinds of discrimination on grounds of sex or marital status, to establish a body to be known as the employment equality agency, to amend the Anti-Discrimination (Pay) Act 1974.

Disability Discrimination Act 1995

This Act provides for disabled people to have the legal right to be treated equal to able-bodied persons. This means that all service providers have to ensure that their business is accessible to do business with people with disabilities.

Human Rights Act 1998

An Act to give further effect to rights and freedoms guaranteed under the European Convention on Human Rights; to make provision with respect to holders of certain judicial offices who become judges of the European Court of Human Rights; and for connected purposes.

the Anti-Nazi League (race) and the Fawcett Society (gender) spearheaded the growth of large-scale political protests over various forms of discrimination in British society. This led in the 1970s to a series of landmark pieces of social legislation (see Politics in Focus 14.3).

Intially, the legislation that was passed such as the Equal Pay Act 1970 or the Anti-Discrimination Act 1974 concerned itself with discirmination that was occuring in the workplace. Yet, with the passage of time, the scope of social legislation broadened to address society-wide discrimination culminating most recently in the 1998 Human Rights Act. Accompanying the legislation, a series of intermediary, state-funded agencies or regulatory systems were created to enforce and maintain the progress in these areas, including: the Equal Opportunities Commission (gender equality); the Government Women and Equality Unit; the Commission for Racial Equality; the Disability Rights Commission and the most recent proposal by the present Labour Government to establish an Identification, Referral and Tracking System (child protection) in response to the Victoria Climbié inquiry (see Munro 2004: 180, see also www.victoria-climbie-inquiry. org.uk for details of the case).

Another element to the growth of social regulation concerns increasing pressure on government to protect individuals from harm in society, most notably, in the workplace. This takes the form of regulations concerning health and safety practices. Here again, there are established intermediary state agencies to maintain standards and regulation, most notably Britain's Health and Safety Commission (HSC) and the Health and Safety Executive (HSE). These two organisations are responsible for the regulation of all the risks to health and safety arising from work activity in Britain. Their mission is to protect people's health and safety by ensuring risks in the workplace are properly controlled. The scope of the regulation is enormous, ranging from: the type of boots workers should wear on building sites; ensuring chemical industries avoid releasing hazardous emissions into the environment; and the regulation of food standards in the light of numerous public health scares in the last two decades concerning infected or poor quality food products.

Elsewhere, there has been the decline in certain practices in social life that were previously deemed acceptable, but that in an era of increasing litigation are now perceived to be too risky. We might think for example of the decrease in outward-bound school trips. This trend links in with a set of literature on the rise of what has been referred to as the 'risk society' and how government responds to this feature (see Smith 2004). Another key actor in this area is the European Union, which has been active in passing on a wide array of regulatory directives to its member states (see Majone 1996). For example, British government policy on BSE and foot and mouth was directly affected by EU regulation, with the EU paying much of the compensation for the loss of sheep and cattle during the 2001 foot and mouth epidemic. Likewise, food regulations at the EU level have resulted in major changes in issues of food hygiene and the operation of slaughterhouses in Britain.

The regulation of government

As we saw in the first part of this chapter, a key theme of British politics in the last 30 years has been the changing nature of the state. The highly centralised Keynesian welfare state has undergone a series of dramatic changes in the form of privatisation, agencification, the growth of quangos and non-departmental public bodies, and the marketisation of public services. These changes, detailed in the governance literature, reflect what might be referred to as the rise of 'entrepreneurial bureaucracy' (see Osborne and Gaebler 1992). The analogy being presented is that government should 'steer rather than row the economy' (see Chapter 3, Politics in Focus 3.5). The role of government should be to create the framework in which the private sector can flourish. The aim is to establish an 'enabling state' in which the private sector can flourish.

Yet, in the British context over the last 30 years, government has been prepared to abandon its role of service provider in many areas, but it has been much less willing to relinquish its controlling capacities. The topography of the British state has undoubtedly changed dramatically in recent decades (see Chapter 3, Figure 3.4). Yet, government's response has been to ensure it maintains control by establishing what Hood et al (1999, 2000) refer to as a new 'regulatory state inside the state'. This has involved:

- The creation of numerous regulatory agencies; by the mid 1990s. It is estimated that the number of national-level regulatory organisations ranged from between 135–200 with running costs ranging from between £750 million–£1 billion.

- The appointment of a set of regulatory or inspectorate officials; the figures were estimated in the mid-1990s to be between 14,000–20,000. There are numerous examples: the Chief Inspector of Prisons for England and Wales created in 1980 to look at the condition of prisons and the treatment of prisoners; or the GM Inspectorate created in 1990 to inspect release sites of genetically modified organisms (GMOs) to ensure that they comply with the terms of the consents granted for trial release or marketing of a GMO. Inspectorates cover almost all areas of social life including health, education, building, the fire service, police, wildlife, vehicles, etc.

- Most importantly, the establishment of a wide array of performance indicators and league tables for services. The most obvious institutional form in which target-setting has been pursued by the present Labour Government are Public Service Agreements (PSAs), set up after the 1998 comprehensive spending review. PSAs establish in one document the aims, objectives and performance targets for each of the main government departments. They include value for money targets and a statement of who is responsible for the delivery of these targets. PSAs are agreed on by the individual department following discussions with the Treasury and the Prime Minister's Delivery Unit. In 2005, the Treasury estimated it had 130 PSAs in place (see Cm 5571 2002, HM Treasury 2005a). An obvious example would be the Department of Health's PSA, which includes a variety of targets set for the National Health Service: no patient should have to wait longer than six months for an in-patient appointment; no patient should have to wait longer than 15 months for surgery; no patient should be waiting longer than three months for an outpatient appointment; patients should not have to wait more than four hours from arrival to admission, transfer or discharge in Accident & Emergency (see HM Treasury 2005b; and Chapter 13).

Where organisations fail to meet the prescribed targets laid down by government, they can incur an array of prescribed penalties ranging from a simple cut in government funding to the outright closure of an organisation, such as has occurred for example with a number of 'failed' secondary schools. The practice of target-setting has become a key tool of control now exerted by government, as a report by the Comptroller and Auditor General, focusing specifically on Next Steps Agencies testifies: '. . . performance measurement and reporting are intrinsic to the whole process of public management, including planning, monitoring, evaluation and public accountability' (HM Treasury 2000: 2).

The growth of a regulatory state within the state reflects an attempt by central government to ensure it maintains control over those agencies or actors delivering services to the public. It is argued that the regulation of public sector bodies has grown substantially in the last two decades coinciding with the perceived fragmentation of the state, reflected in the governance literature. Hood et al (1999) contend that individuals employed in 'oversight bodies for public organisations' rose by approximately 90% between 1976–95, whilst at the same time Civil Service numbers were cut by about 30% and local government service by 20%. Moreover, the institutionalisation of this process by central government is reflected elsewhere in such initiatives as the 'Citizens' Charter' introduced by the Major Government and then extended and re-branded by the Blair Government as 'Service First'. The rationale behind this approach was to shift power away from service providers to consumers. In effect, this has become an explicit process of auditing the public sector—by publishing performance lists for schools, hospitals, universities, etc. Accompanying this process has been the rise in magnitude of an array of regulatory units including: the Deregulation Unit, also created by the last Conservative Administration but again re-branded by Labour—first as the Better Regulation Unit and later, the Regulatory Impact Unit; the Better Regulation Task Force; the National Audit Office; the Audit Commission; and the Public Sector Benchmarking Service. It is important to recognise that the use of targets in public services has attracted some criticism. For example, during the course of the 2005 general election campaign, both main opposition parties believed political capital could be made from attacks on the Government over what they regarded as the excessive use of targets (see Richards 2005). The Conservatives argued that people's real needs and priorities under Labour had been overshadowed by centrally imposed targets, the growth in 'Whitehall inspection regimes' and a rapid rise in 'stealth taxes' (Conservative Party 2005: 22). Similar sentiments were expressed by the Liberal Democrats who averred that Labour ministers were trying to: 'pull the strings with pointless targets and endless bureaucracy' (Liberal Democrats 2005: 4).

Analysing the rise of the regulatory state

Moran (2001, 2003) suggests that there are five key explanations for the growth of regulation in the last 30 years:

- *the exhaustion of established modes of intervention*—refers to the collapse of the Keynesian welfare consensus of the post-war era;
- *the impact of the European Union*—argues that due to the lack of institutional capacity of the European Union (in terms of finance and bureaucracy), the EU acts as a regulatory agency, generating regulations that it then passes on to members states to implement;

- *the audit explosion*—involves the absorption and application of accounting/auditing mechanisms previously associated with the business/finance sector into other social areas of life such as health, education, local government, etc;

- *scandal*—refers to the various scandals in the field of health, finance, accounting, food, defence, etc (see above) which triggered a government response in the shape of new and/or more regulation. This has also been referred to as an 'audit explosion';

- *the risk society*—linked to the preceding two themes, in which developments in modern technologies, industry, etc have created new risks, sometimes unknown or unforeseen, and the growth of the perception of risk, from which individuals in society need protecting.

Moran's analysis is an attempt to further our understanding of the nature of the regulatory state. What is implicit in his narrative, but needs further elucidation, is the relationship between the changing nature of the state in the last 30 years, reflected in the governance literature, the growth of the regulatory state and the impact on political power. These three features are intrinsically linked.

The reconstituted power of the core executive

As British governments, both Conservative and Labour, have attempted to make sense of recent changes to the nature of the state, underpinning their response to forces such as globalisation, internationalisation, privatisation, Europeanisation, etc has been the need to maintain control. In this context, control is shorthand for more prosaic terms, used by the likes of Jessop (2004: 61), such as 'meta-governance' or 'meta-steering'. These expressions refer to: 'governance in the shadow of hierarchy'. What might appear to be a policy-making arena that is fragmented or made up of 'self-organising networks' is in fact shaped by various political authorities operating at different aggregate levels.

In the British case, there are those who argue that the key political authority shaping the policy-making arena remains the core executive (see Saward 1997; Holliday 2000; Marsh et al 2001, 2003; Richards and Smith 2002, 2004b; Jayasuriya 2004). They directly challenge much of the governance or 'hollowing-out' literature and its conclusion that power has seeped away from the central executive territory of the state. Instead, they portray the nature of the state as having undergone a process of reconstitution, in which the power and the size of the state remains, but in a more diffuse, decentralised form. In particular, Richards and Smith (2004b) argue that the last Conservative Administration created a hybrid state between the Keynesian welfare state and a neoliberal notion of the laissez-faire state. They argue that while Thatcherism disengaged from crucial elements of the economy through policies such as privatisation and cuts in state subsidies, it was unable to break many of the welfare policies of the post-war settlement. So, while the Conservatives viewed state intervention as problematic, they were unable to overcome the weight of past institutional practices. In particular, characteristics associated with the 'British political tradition'—elitism, hierarchy, strong government, etc (see Chapter 3) were vital in shaping the government's response to the changing nature of the state. The subsequent regulatory model that has evolved over the past three decades, in many ways, has allowed both the Conservative and Labour governments to sustain, even rejuvenate, the British political tradition. This is because the model portrays the core executive as retaining broad control and power over a fragmented policy-making arena through the use of regulation. It is a process based on the widespread introduction of managerial and regulatory mechanisms, imposed largely on the existing structures of welfare provision such as the NHS and the welfare state and in other areas, such as law and order, defence and education.

Richards and Smith (2002) therefore argue that the state has undergone extensive reconfiguration, not hollowing-out. This is because the core executive possesses greater capacity than many other actors in the policy-making process to respond to the changing environment and protect its own status and power; it acts strategically. So, whilst the government is often dependent on a variety of organisations for the delivery of a service, they in turn continue to depend on the government which has a unique set of resources: force, legitimacy, state bureaucracy, tax-raising powers and legislation.

Conclusion

Understanding the changing nature of the state is a complex task. To compound this problem, there is at present a broad dichotomy in the literature accounting for the impact of globalisation, governance, Europeanisation, etc on power within the British state. On the one hand, the governance literature broadly avers that in an era of state change, governments have increasingly become only one actor amongst many in an increasingly pluralised policy-making arena. Conversely, the regulatory state literature highlights the extent to which state change has led to new modes of governing based on control or 'meta-steering'. The suggestion here is that government has relinquished an array of tasks it previously found problematic (*it has stopped rowing*), for example, running large-scale industries such as the railways or coal. This has enabled it to concentrate on more effective modes of governing through increased control via regulation (*it has started steering*). The often implied conclusion of the regulatory state literature is that, in an era of governance, the power of the central state has in many ways been enhanced not diminished. Furthermore, the regulatory state literature also highlights the extent to which Britain does not replicate a neoliberal model of the state, as advocated by the New Right 30 years ago. The power of intermediary state agencies to intervene in political, economic and social life through regulation suggests government still very much retains an active role. Indeed, one of the intellectual challenges presently facing the New Right is the need to consider if, to use the language of Friedrich Hayek, the state today in Britain is now further down the road to serfdom than it was in 1976[1].

---

[1] Friedrich von Hayek (1899–1992) achieved fame with his critique of collectivism and planning in his most famous book *The Road to Serfdom* (1944). As an economic liberal, he believed centralised economic planning by government reduced individual and group liberty, upset the balance between political institutions by making the executive too strong and undermined the rule of law. This then led to pressure for yet more controls as the 'logic of intervention' fed on itself. He attracted controversy in Britain because he challenged the belief in the so-called 'middle way' which combined both freedom and planning, prevalent in both the moderate 'One-Nation' wing of the Conservative Party and among the Labour Party elite such as Attlee, Gaitskill and Wilson.

As Jordana and Levi-Faur (2004: 1) observe:

> ... the institutional advance of regulation in the context of
> privatisation and the neo-liberal hegemony presents a paradox. In an
> era in which regulation has become synonymous with red tape, and
> deregualtion has become a major electoral platform of the New Right,
> regulatory authorities have been created in unprecedented numbers.

Conversely, from a centre-left perspective, what the regulatory state literature highlights is that there is a wide array of regulatory tools or controlling mechansims available to government, in order to deliver a social-democratic based project for the creation of what Marquand (1988) would refer to as a truly developmental state.

It is important that students of political science recognise the dichotomy in the governance and regulatory state literatures—for in many ways it goes right to the heart of many of the key, contemporary debates in politics. Questions concerning the changing nature of the state, the effect of globalisation or Europeanisation, the impact that governments do or do not have when in power, etc are viewed through different conceptual lens depending on which set of literature is being sourced. Most importantly, both sets of literature implicitly, sometimes explicitly, embrace contrasting macro-models of state power. The present task for students of politics is to decide which set of literature provides the most convincing explanatory account of the British state today.

KEY POINTS

- It is important to recognise that there are a number of competing accounts analysing the nature of state change. Presently, two of the most dominant we can refer to are 'governance' and the 'regulatory state'.

- The governance literature broadly avers that the British state has been hollowed-out in the last three decades—transformed into a complex mix of markets, networks and hierarchies.

- Central to the conclusions of this narrative is that, in relation to power, there has been a shift to much greater pluralism.

- The 'regulatory state' narrative argues that there has undoubtedly been a fundamental shift in the mode of governing in recent decades, yet, the core executive has attempted to retain control over an increasingly diverse and crowded policy-making arena by pursing an array of regulatory mechansims.

- The suggestion here is that the Britsh state has undergone a process of reconstituting itself, through a 'hyper-innovative' regulatory programme. The core executive remains the most powerful actor in the policy-making arena having available a wide array of governing tools and mechanisms to deliver its political programme.

KEY QUESTIONS

(1) What are the key changes to the nature of the British state in the last 30 years?

(2) What are the key features that explain why change has occurred?

(3) What has been the impact on core executive power of state transformation?

(4) To what extent and why does the regulatory state literature present a contrasting view of the British state to that of the hollowing-out literature?

(5) With the rise of regulation, can we now argue Britain is 'further down the road to serfdom' than it was in the mid-1970s?

IMPORTANT WEBSITES

On regulation agencies see: www. raynet. mcmail. com/official.htm#Government%20regulatory. For information on Royal Charters see: www. privy-council.org.uk/output/page26.asp. For regulation by government see: www.cabinetoffice. gov.uk/improving_services/ and the Better Regulation Task Force: www.brtf.gov.uk/. On British government and changes in organisation see www. ukonline.gov.uk/, and to see some of the specific details look at www.10downingstreet. gov.uk/. On global governance see www. worldbank.org/ wbi/governance/, www. governance.qub.ac.uk/ and www.nottingham.ac.uk/politics/european-governance/. On regional and urban governance see www.unesco.org/most/most2.htm, and www.cf. ac.uk/euros/welsh-. For new forms of digital governance see www.digitalgovernance.org/ governance/index.html.

FURTHER READING

For key texts on the debate concerning governance see: G. Davis and M. Keating (eds) (2000) *The Future of Governance*, St Leonards, NSW: Allen & Unwin; L. Hooge and G. Marks (2001) *Multi-Level Governance and European Integration*, Maryland: Rowman and Littlefield; B. Jessop (2004) 'Multi-Level Governance and Multi-Level Metagovernance' in I. Bache and M. Flinders, *Multi-Level Governance*, Oxford: Oxford University Press; D. Osborne and T. Gaebler (1992) *Reinventing Government*, Reading Mass: Addison-Wesley; J. Pierre and B.G. Peters (2000) *Governance, Politics and the State*, Basingstoke: Macmillan; J. Pierre *Debating Governance* Oxford: Oxford University Press; R.A.W. Rhodes (1997) *Understanding Governance: Policy Networks, Governance, Reflexivity and Accountability*, Buckingham: Open University Press; J. Rosenau (2000) 'Change, Complexity and Governance in a Globalizing Space' in J. Pierre, *Debating Governance*, Oxford: Oxford University Press; P. Weller (2000) 'In Search of Governance' in G. Davis and M. Keating, *The Future of Governance*, St Leonards, NSW: Allen & Unwin; World Bank (1992) *Governance and Development*, Washington, DC: World Bank.

For the literature on the regulatory/reconstituted power see: J. Jordana and D. Levi-Faur (eds) (2004) *The Politics of Regulation: Institutions and Regulatory Reforms for the Age of Governance*, London: Edward Elgar; U. Beck (1992) *Risk Society: Towards a New Modernity*, London: Sage; I. Holliday (2000) Is the British State Hollowed-Out?' *Political Quarterly* Vol 71(2): 167–76; S. Littlechild (1983) *Regulation of British Telecommunications' Profitability: A Report by Stephen C Littlechild*, London: Department of Industry; M. Moran (2003) 'The British Regulatory State: High Modernism and Hyper-Innovation' in G. Majone (ed) *Regulating Europe*, Routledge: 1996; M. Marinetto (2003) 'Governing Beyond the Centre: A Critique of the Anglo-Governance School', *Political*

Studies Vol 51(3): 592; D. Richards and M.J. Smith (2002) *Governance and Public Policy in the United Kingdom*, Oxford: Oxford University Press; D. Marsh, D. Richards and M. Smith (2003) 'Unequal Power: Towards An Asymmetric Power Model of the British Polity', *Government and Opposition* Vol 38(3), (Summer 2003c: 306–22; C. Hood, O. James, C. Scott and T. Travers (1999) *Regulation Inside Government*, Oxford: Oxford University Press; D. Richards and M. Smith (2004) 'New Labour and the Reform of the State' in S. Ludlam and M.J. Smith (2004) (eds) *Governing as New Labour: Politics and Policy under Blair*, Basingstoke: Palgrave; M. Saward (1997) 'In Search of the Hollow Crown' in P. Weller, H. Bakvis and R.A.W. Rhodes, *The Hollow Crown*, London: Macmillan; D. Vincent (1998) *The Culture of Secrecy: Britain 1832–1998,* Oxford: Oxford University Press; K. Jayasuriya (2004) 'The New Regulatory State and Relational Capacity', *Policy and Politics*, 32(4): 487–501.

Visit the Online Resource Centre that accompanies this book
for links to more information on this chapter topic

CHAPTER FIFTEEN

Local government

READER'S GUIDE

Over the past three decades the role of local government in British political life has been transformed and, depending on interpretation, severely weakened or reinvented. This chapter reviews the arguments for and against local democracy and local government, describes local government's structure and organisation and analyses relations between councillors and officials and the changing state of central–local relations. Finally, it assesses the effects of the post-1997 changes—covering devolution, reforms of public services and pressures to improve their delivery, regionalism and the regime of inspection and audit—on the role of local government. What is its place in the system of governance and 'new localism'?

Introduction

Arguments for local government have often been advanced on the grounds of greater democracy and/or greater efficiency, two different but not mutually exclusive arguments. In recent years both have been strongly challenged. Supporters of democracy claim that local government provides opportunities for people to participate in politics, develop a sense of citizenship and political responsibility, and promote a sense of community. Supporters of efficiency claim that central government and Parliament are already over-loaded and that policies and services developed and delivered locally are more likely to be appropriate for and supported by the local population. Some political theorists see demo-cratic vitality emerging from the existence of various independent groups; pluralism allows many groups to have some influence and to check one another. According to this view genuinely local government may act as a buffer between citizens and central govern-ment, a check on the latter, and a source of experimentation in policy. For example, Leicestershire pioneered comprehensive schooling in the 1950s and the Greater London Authority introduced congestion charging.

There is, however, always a tension between local autonomy and inequality and the 'cent-ralists' argue that the national government is better able to handle issues of redistribution. They add that the likely variations in policies and quality of services may lead to undesir-able inequalities in services between areas, or that local units will be less efficient than cent-ral government. They also point to the evident lack of a sense of community in many larger conurbations and the typical turnout of less than 40% in local elections. Because distinctions between local and central government responsibilities are unclear it is often the more 'visible' national government which gets the blame if things go wrong and local elections are often decided on national not local grounds, largely due to the dominance of national political parties. The many changes made to local government structure and organisation have done little to clarify the distinctions between different tiers or increase democratic accountability.

Local government structure

The origins of local government in England can be traced back to the Middle Ages, when a number of boroughs gained Royal Charters from the monarchy and were allowed to run their own affairs. In the 19th century a new system of local government was established and it largely lasted until 1974. By then changes in patterns of employment and residence, development of new forms of transport, and demands for new types of services all com-bined to undermine the logic of the system drawn up in the late 19th century.

After much debate about structure and functions, the Local Government Act 1972 came into effect in 1974. This established a two-tier system of 39 counties and six metropolitan counties for the major conurbations outside London. Within the metropolitan counties was a lower tier of 36 metropolitan districts. At the time, reorganisation of Whitehall departments, of many public services and of local government reflected a belief that 'big is beautiful'. A large authority, it was argued, was able to provide a more specialised staff and service because of the greater scale of its operations. Demands for a more integrated approach to decision-taking also seemed to require the creation of larger local authorities. Interestingly, studies for the Royal Commission on Local Government in the 1960s did not find any clear-cut relationship between population size and quality of service provided by the local government. But nor did they support claims that a person's 'social attachment' and 'interest in local affairs' increased with the smaller types of authority (Newton 1982).

In the 1980s, local government, reflecting national party politics, became increasingly politicised and there were frequent battles between central and local government. In 1985 the Conservative Government abolished the Greater London Council (GLC) and metropolitan authorities—all Labour-controlled—and devolved their responsibilities to London boroughs and metropolitan districts respectively. The history of local government reform is one in which negotiations, government inquiries and commissions, and discussions have been coloured by the partisanship and the self-interest of different political parties and groups.

Variety and complexity have been the order of the day in the local government system which has emerged since 1997, as a consequence of the creation of the devolved legislatures in Scotland, Wales and London, models of city governance, and the possibility—remote since the rejection the rejection of the proposal in the North East in 2004—of elected regional assemblies in England. A system of quasi-federalism has been introduced and with little thought apparently given to its consequences for local government. Britain now has a multi-tier system of government—operating at local, regional, national, and European levels. England and Wales have a mix of single-tier authorities in metropolitan areas and two-tier district and county councils, all elected by the first past the post method. Scotland since devolution, however, has 29 single-tier authorities elected by proportional representation. Since 2005 the future role of local government is uncertain as Labour ministers are proposing plans to set up city-wide authorities, devolve powers to community and 'neighbourhood' groups and take away many powers from local education authorities.

Councillors and officers

To be eligible to serve as a councillor a person must live or work in the seat or have some connection with it. Holding a paid office with the local authority disqualifies one from election. Also ineligible are undischarged bankrupts, lunatics, and anyone who has been sentenced to more than three months' imprisonment over the previous five years, or convicted of illegal electoral practices. Many work long hours and may spend 20 hours or more a week on council duties. The reduction in the number of authorities and number of councillors (to about 26,000, or half of the earlier numbers) has led to an increase in their typical workload. The tradition of unpaid public services is still important in local

FOCUS 15.1

...plicated system?

(1) Local elections take place annually on the first Thursday in May.

(2) Not every council votes every year, however:
   — County councils are elected *en bloc* every four years.
   — Districts can opt for either *en bloc* four-year elections at the mid-term point of county elections or
   — 'by thirds', one-third of councillors standing for re-election each non-county election year.

(3) Eligibility to vote:
   — 18 years or over
   — citizen of Britain, Ireland or the Commonwealth
   — resident in the locality
   — registered.

(4) Eligibility to stand as a candidate:
   — 21 years or over
   — citizen of Britain, Ireland or the Commonwealth
   — on the local electoral register
   — resident or employed in local authority for at least 12 months prior to standing
   — support of 10 registered electors in the ward.

government and proposals for the payment of salaries have been largely resisted, although attendance and other allowances have been increased.

Average turnout at local elections is less than 40%. Since 2002 there have been pilot schemes of new ways of voting, for example, placing ballot boxes in shopping centres, extending voting over a number of days or over weekends, or postal voting to boost turnout. Only the last has made much difference.

Local elections are now portrayed by the media, and to some extent accepted by politicians, as a verdict on national government. Note that the Liberal Democrats in 2004 campaigned strongly on their opposition to the Iraq war—hardly a local government issue. Councillors, like MPs, are sociologically unrepresentative of the population, being dis-proportionately male, middle-aged and middle class. Unpaid council work is most easily combined with certain types of employment—particularly such self-employed professions as the law, estate agency and small businesses—and being trade union and political organisers, housewives and retired. People stand for council for a variety of motives. For some it is a step on the road to national politics—in recent Parliaments about 45% of Labour MPs and 25% of Conservative MPs had been councillors before election. For some council membership is an alternative to a humdrum job, or a means of enjoying enhanced social status and membership of 'a good club', or exercising influence in the local community. Many recruits are already community activists and typically belong to an average of seven or more local voluntary 'organisations'. Nomination by a political party is now a virtual precondition to pursuing a local political career.

As local government acquired more functions during the 19th century, so Parliament insisted that officers be appointed. The chief officer of a department, in contrast to the councillor, will usually possess professional training and qualifications. An officer is also expected to be politically impartial and debarred from standing for political office until a year after his retirement as an officer. The officer's task is to provide the best professional advice to the councillors and then carry out the policy decisions of the council, short of breaking the law.

In theory, the relationship between councillors and officers often resembles that between ministers and civil servants. But there are differences: a councillor, unlike an MP, is usually a member of the executive; there is closer contact between officials and councillors than between civil servants and MPs; each authority decides its own staff structure, compared with the uniform structure of Whitehall departments; most chief officers are appointed for their relevant professional expertise in a specialist area (engineering, accountancy, planning, and so on) while Whitehall administrators remain generalists, and whereas the officer is appointed by the council, senior civil servants are promoted by colleagues and the Prime Minister. In some cases an officer's personality and skills may enable him to 'lead' the councillors; in others, a strong committee chairman or a small group of councillors will provide the direction. The legal position is clear enough. Officers are employees and servants of the *council* and, in the last resort, take instructions from it.

The top-down model

Different models have been employed to describe the central–local relationships (Rhodes 1988 and 1999). The *agency* model emphasises the resources at the disposal of central government, notably its power to create or abolish the units and powers of local government; establish the national framework of a policy; financing of many programmes, and that local authorities in implementing policies have little scope for discretion or variation. In the *partnership* model the authorities do have some scope for local choice, their own political legitimacy from being elected by local voters, finance (from the council tax), resources and even legal powers.

The relationship between the two levels of government is based on a mix of controls, dependence and co-operation (see Politics in Focus 15.2). Local authorities have few legislative powers of their own; Parliament confers powers and can amend or withdraw them. If a local authority exceeds its powers then its actions will lack legal validity, and the courts may decide that it has acted *ultra vires*. In 1983 the London borough of Bromley challenged the GLC's 'Fares Fair' policy of cutting fares by 25%. The court ruled that the GLC was acting *ultra vires* and the policy was in breach of its fiduciary duty to ratepayers. Some responsibilities are mandatory, such as the compulsory sale of council houses to tenants, and some are permissive, such as whether or not local authorities introduce a congestion charge. Responsibilities may move between categories—for instance, the reorganisation of secondary education was made compulsory by a Labour government in 1965 and 1976, and then permissive by a Conservative government in 1970 and 1979, a good example of the ping-pong effect on policy of changes of government in Westminster.

There are also controls that stem from central government's involvement in many services. Local education authorities provide state primary and secondary education, although increasingly their role is being reduced. The scope of the national curriculum and training and the supply of teachers has long been largely in the hands of the Department of Education and the school-leaving age is decided by Parliament. But the Thatcher and Major Governments assumed greater power over the curriculum and introduced nationwide assessment of pupils, and the Blair Government has intervened further (see below pp 298–99).

Another source of central influence is the power to approve the appointment and dismissal of certain chief officers. The approval of the Home Secretary, for example, is required for the appointment of a local Chief Constable, and the approval of the appropriate minister is necessary for appointments of chief education officers or directors of social services. The power was dramatically illustrated in 2004 when the then Home Secretary David Blunkett insisted, against the wishes of the local police authority, that the Chief Constable of Hull be dismissed for poor performance.

External inspectors in education, police, fire and social services have for some time been employed by central government to report on the standards and efficiency of the services, but the inspection regime has been made more rigorous in recent years. The inspectorates include Ofstead (the Office for Standards in Education), the Food Standards Agency, HM Inspectors of Constabulary, the Social Services Inspectorate and various branches of the Audit Commission, to name but a few.

A local authority's building plans for schools and the making of by-laws, require the approval of the appropriate department. Central government circulars also contain advice and guidance to local authorities. In finance the government has the power to reduce a local authority's central grant if the latter is deemed to have 'overspent', and it has to approve local authority applications to raise a loan for new capital expenditure. The Audit Commission appoints auditors to inspect the local authority accounts each year to establish that all expenditure has been duly authorised. Individual councillors may be held responsible and surcharged for any unauthorised expenditure and even disqualified from membership of a local authority. In 1986 Labour councillors in Liverpool and Lambeth, for example, were surcharged and disqualified for refusing to set a legal rate.

Between 1945 and 1979 the local authorities lost jurisdiction over a number of functions (including hospitals, gas and electricity supplies, trunk roads and water) and were subject to more central controls and guidance on other services. In Northern Ireland the British government unilaterally suspended the Stormont Parliament 1972 and imposed direct rule from London. In the same year the Government took powers to set the level of rents for local authority housing (subsequently repealed). For all the support Westminster politicians (usually in opposition) have expressed about local democracy and the virtues of decentralisation, the record suggests that it is not deeply held. Westminster governments have felt it necessary to intervene to ensure that *their* national policies are delivered. Before 1979 Conservatives usually intervened on grounds of macroeconomic policy, particularly to control public expenditure, Labour on grounds of redistribution and equality. Both parties when in government have used central funding to reward their geographical areas of political support.

But Conservative ministers in the 1980s increasingly viewed local government as *just* another body delivering services to customers. But they also complained that it, like much of the public sector, was over-staffed, enjoyed too 'cosy' a relationship with trade unions, was protected from competition and, as long as it could raise money from household ratepayers, lacked financial discipline. The Conservative approach was to subject local government to competition in service provision and to external controls. The Audit Commission acquired an important position in measuring the performance of local authorities and encouraging greater economy, effectiveness and efficiency, and private-sector management techniques are used increasingly. Above all, a consistent theme of the central government interventions has been to curb the growth of spending by local authorities.

The loss of local powers and the increase in central control continued under the Thatcher governments. Grant penalties were introduced for local authorities spending more than the government thought appropriate. Local authorities were compelled to put out to competitive tender many of their services, including cleaning, refuse collection, road maintenance and house repairs. In 1980 the Government required authorities to make council houses available for sale to tenants at substantial discounts. Councils lost responsibility for further education and polytechnics, and schools were allowed to 'opt out' of local authority control and be funded directly by central government. The Government set a national

FOCUS 15.2

Central and local government

Central government

— Control over legislation and delegated powers

— Provides and controls the largest proportion of local authorities' current expenditure through the Revenue Support Grant

— Controls individual authorities' total expenditure and taxation levels by 'capping'

— Controls the largest proportion of local capital expenditure

— Sets standards for and inspects some services

— Has national electoral mandate

Local government

— Employs most personnel in local services, far outnumbering civil servants

— Has, through both councillors and officers, detailed local knowledge and expertise

— Controls the implementation of policy

— Has limited powers to raise own taxes and set own service charges

— Can decide own political priorities and most service standards, and how money should be distributed among services

— Has local electoral mandate

Source: Wilson and Game (2002)

curriculum for all state schools, backed up by regular assessment of pupils and published league tables of school performances on various criteria, including the assessment tests. The GLC (Greater London Council) and the metropolitan authorities were abolished and in 1990 the rating system was replaced with the poll tax and that was then replaced with the council tax. Such incursions on local choice and accountability would be unthinkable in a federal system where the local or regional units have their own powers.

Both parties, when in government, have found the 'top-down' or Westminster model of British administration convenient, notably the supremacy of Parliament as lawmaker, Whitehall control, party discipline and the absence of formal checks and balances. Conservatives, with a belief in 'strong' government, have understandably found the model congenial, as has Labour which, traditionally, has regarded centralised decision-making as the most effective way to promote equality. Entitlement to and levels of welfare benefits, or the school-leaving age, for example, are the same wherever one lives in the United Kingdom, though there are differences in the *quality* of service across regions.

The localist model

Advocates of localism argue that the British state evolved from the bottom up. Effectively, many services, including health care, education and the provision of utilities developed at local level and were only nationalised after 1945. For instance, the creation of the National Health Service in 1948 involved the consolidation of many local authority and charity hospitals under Ministry of Health control. A consequence of this bottom-up evolution of service provision was that the local level continued to have considerable impact on the policy process, not least in funding, delivering and regulating a range of welfare and other services. Professor Rod Rhodes in various works emphasises the degree of mutual dependency between the centre and locality. Ministers may lay down national policies on housing and education, for example, but they do not build houses or schools, or directly employ teachers and builders. Teachers are employed by a local education authority or school governors rather than by central government; they are not civil servants, as they are, for example, in France.

A major analysis of the evolution of sub-central government in the UK in modern times is Jim Bulpitt's *Territory and Power in the United Kingdom*. He argues that between 1926 and the early 1960s, the relationship between the centre (ie Westminster/Whitehall) and the periphery (local government) took the form of a 'dual polity', and central and local government coexisted relatively independently of one another:

> a state of affairs in which national and local polities were largely divorced from one another. Those contacts which existed [between them]...were bureaucratic and depoliticised. In this period, the Centre achieved what it had always desired—relative autonomy from peripheral forces to pursue its High Politics preoccupations (Bulpitt, 1983: 235–6).

Central government dealt with what Bulpitt called 'high politics', issues relating to the economy, law and order, social welfare, defence of the realm and foreign policy, whereas local government addressed 'low politics' issues concerning schools (but not higher education), social services, and keeping the streets clean and tidy, etc. As Rhodes (1997: 114) observes:

> In sharp contrast to the French system, Britain has neither a Napoleonic tradition of using central field agents to supervise local authorities, nor a system of *cumul des mandats* whereby politicians collect electoral offices, leading to the close interpenetration of national and local elites. The British territorial code stresses the autonomy of the centre in matters of high politics.

Yet, Bulpitt contends, the corporatist era of the 1970s witnessed the breakdown in the relationship between the centre and the periphery. The centre became increasingly embroiled in 'low politics' issues and this compromised central government's ability to be seen as 'governing competently'. During the 1980s, the Thatcher governments sought to reassert a degree of autonomy for the centre. One target was what they regarded as the increasing power and over-spending of local government, typified by the so-called 'hard left' councils.

The Bulpitt thesis sensitises us to the ebb and flow of power at the sub-national level. In spite of the centre's relentless pressures in the 1980s to limit their autonomy and resources, local authorities still account for about a fifth of total public spending and still deliver many local services. Although all central governments have used their substantial powers over finance (in the form of the government grants), structure and policies to influence local government, they depend on local governments to deliver many of their policies on schools or crime. The normal pattern is one of co-operation, consultation and even bargaining; Rhodes concludes that the balance between centre and locality fluctuates according context and that there is too much variation in local services to sustain the agency model, even though local authorities are clearly subordinate in the partnership.

Critiques

Local government came under increasing attack during the late 1970s. The first recognisable critics were the so called New Left of the Labour Party, who exploited party grass-roots disaffection with the Wilson and Callaghan Labour Governments, and then used local government as a base from which to oppose the Thatcher Governments. A younger generation of left-wing activists was determined to expand services and increase spending, in defiance of Labour ministers (1974–79). Labour councillors in such cities as Manchester and Liverpool and a number of London boroughs were dismissive of what they regarded as their right-wing parliamentary leaders, and were determined to use local government as a base from which to challenge Thatcherism (Gyford 1985). They pursued policies of local

S IN FOCUS 15.3

...ative changes affecting local government, 1979–2000

1980	Local Government Planning and Land Act: powers to cut government grants to 'overspending' local authorities
1982	Local Government Finance Act: abolition of supplementary rates
1984	Rates Act: rate-capping
1985	Local Government Act: GLC and six metropolitan councils abolished
1986	Local Government Act: statutory prohibition of local authority publicity of a party political nature
1987	Rate Support Grant Act: local authority grant fixed to expenditure
1988	Local Government Act: local councils to put public supply services out to tender
	Housing Act: allowed council tenants to choose their own landlords and created Housing Action Trusts to take over poor performing council estates
	Local Government Finance Act: rates abolished, replaced by community charge
	Education Act: allowed schools to opt out from local authority control and be funded directly from Whitehall. National curriculum for state schools
	Local Government Act: extended compulsory competitive tendering (CCT)
1991	Poll tax abolished, replaced by council tax, to begin April 1993. 'Capping' power retained by centre
1997	Referenda approve devolution for Scotland and Wales
1998	Referendum approves directly elected executive Mayor for London. White Paper, *Local Government: In Touch with the People*
	Ken Livingstone elected, as an independent, as Mayor for London
1999–2000	Local Government Acts: new forms of executive, eg elected mayors. Best Value replaces compulsory competitive tendering.

economic development, and equal opportunities, and defied government guidelines on spending and levels of local domestic and business rates. Their policies on education, housing, transport and employment led to a confrontation with the Thatcherite agenda. The conflict was one reason why an impatient Conservative Government in 1985 abolished the GLC and other metropolitan authorities.

The New Left attitude was countered by a New Right critique (fashioned largely in think-tanks) of local government and the public sector among some Conservatives. Traditionally, Conservatives have praised local government as a means of checking interventionist (probably Labour) central government, encouraging diversity and providing an opportunity for experimentation with different policies. This was one reason why, for example, the party opposed mandatory comprehensive secondary education, and insisted that it was for each local authority to choose its own system. Yet the New Right critique questioned the legitimacy of local government. Election turnouts were low, local elections were usually fought on national not local issues and small electorates could be dominated by a public sector workforce (for example, teachers, direct labour workers and transport employees), council house tenants, and many who did not pay rates. In other words, the claims by local government to possess a local mandate were bogus. Moreover, more than half of the money spent locally actually came from central government.

New right critics therefore urged the importation into local government of greater competition and a more business-like approach to management. Local government should be forced to compete with other groups in the delivery of such services as school education or refuse collection, and act as an 'enabler', administering and contracting out local services, with funding and standards of services determined by central government. Such reforms would make local services more efficient and more responsive to consumers and depoliticise local government. The Thatcher Government's introduction of compulsory competitive tendering (CCT) obliged local authorities to put such services as street cleaning, refuse collection, catering and cleaning of buildings out to tender to the private or voluntary sector and was then extended to include professional, technical and financial services.

Of the two critiques the new right won out and in some respects it has been implemented by the Blair Government.

Local party politics

Party politics in some form or other has long been a feature of local government. In the mid-19th century many councils were divided between rival factions and even parties. In the 1870s Joseph Chamberlain used the Liberal Party and a party programme in Birmingham to show what could be done to give political leadership to local government. The Liberals and Conservatives became dominant in local politics towards the end of the 19th century, especially in the North and the Midlands. The major expansion of the Labour Party in the 1920s in many parts of the country formalised and accentuated partisanship.

Following the 1974 reorganisation the national parties consolidated their hold over local government. The number of 'Independents', or non-party councillors, was drastically reduced and the proportion of uncontested seats fell from 40% to 16% (Game and Leach 1995). Parties, alone or in coalition, now control some 90% of councils in England and Wales. In the ruling party councillors usually take decisions in secret meetings and are expected to abide by the majority view.

The arguments for and against party politics in local government, particularly where it duplicates the national rivalry, are well known: partisanship may frighten off able people who would otherwise offer their services to the community; many local services require good administration rather than the application of party ideology, and the sense of community identity is weakened as national parties with national programmes move in. Against this, it may be argued that parties provide a focus and coherence for local political debate; they stimulate political interest and turnout in elections; and they are important in enabling voters to pin political responsibility at elections.

Yet, viewed in a wider perspective, particularly in comparison with the United States, France or West Germany, it is the disjunction between local and national politics in Britain that is so striking. In the countries cited, parliamentarians are expected to act as local spokesmen and the advancement of a political career depends on having a local base. In Britain, by contrast, many local councillors have indeed been 'localists', and may regard Westminster politics as remote. John Major and David Blunkett are among the few to have reached a top position in Westminster, having already served as local councillors. Apart from Northern Ireland, national political elites are usually securely based in London. National political elites are sharply separated from local politics, understood as the maintenance of local positions of political influence. As a result, interest and influence do not flow up continuously from the base to the top of British political life.

Finance: from rates to poll tax to council tax

Local government's spending is so significant in the national context that central government cannot turn a blind eye to it. If we aggregate expenditure (about 20% of total public spending) and employment (over two million employees) by local authorities, then we are talking about big government.

There are three main sources of local finance. The first is the grant from central government. The second is revenue from rents, fees and charges from housing, sites for markets, services in parks, leisure centres, for example. For long, the third source were the household and business rates, a tax levied on the owners of premises, including houses, offices and factories. Rates were a form of local property tax and were replaced by the short-lived poll tax in 1990, which in turn was superseded by the council tax in April 1993.

A local source of finance is essential if local independence and accountability are to be maintained. But Whitehall and the Treasury in particular, have steadfastly rejected schemes for a local income tax or a local sales tax. A result is that that Britain has one of the most centralised tax systems in Western Europe. The central government raises 96% of total taxation in Britain, local government only 4%, and that from the council tax (see Politics in Focus 15.4).

The largest source of finance for local authorities is the Revenue Support Grant from central government. As a proportion of local authority spending, the central grant steadily grew from 29% in 1938–39 to 65% in 1976–77 and has since fallen back to around 50%. The Treasury has consistently tried to reduce or hold steady public spending as a share of GDP and to restrain both local spending and the proportion financed by central government. The grant is fixed each year after negotiations have taken place between associations of the local authorities and the departments most concerned with local government.

Yet for all the battles and extra controls imposed by the centre, local government current spending continued to increase in real terms. In some frustration, the Thatcher Government finally decided to abolish the rates, replacing them with the community

POLITICS IN FOCUS 15.4

Local government finance: key terms

Rates A tax on rentable value of business and domestic property. It is paid by the owner or occupier. It is a regressive tax because it takes no account of income. Property values are periodically revised. The last revision in England was in 1973. The 1985 revision in Scotland brought rate rises of 50%, and fear of likely repercussions of a similar rise in England prompted the Government to seek an alternative. Many people were exempt from rates, and this weakened the link between voting for increased local spending and responsibility for footing the bill. Rates were abolished in Scotland in 1989 and in England and Wales in 1990.

Community charge A 'poll tax' introduced by the Local Government Finance Act in 1988. It was a flat-rate tax to be paid by every adult with a few exemptions. It had the advantage of simplicity and it revived the link between voter, charge, and service. But it was regressive, a very visible tax, and difficult and costly to collect. In the face of its extreme unpopularity, the Government abandoned this tax as of 1993.

Council tax A tax introduced in 1991 to replace the community charge, effective in 1993. It combines a personal and property element and is levied on households; it assumes two adults, and single occupants can claim 25% rebate. It reflects property values: each property is allocated to a valuation band set by the Inland Revenue and council sets the level.

Uniform business rate Replaced rates in 1990. It is based on business property values and therefore similar to the old rating system, but set and collected nationally and redistributed to councils through government grants.

Rate capping In 1982 the Local Government Finance Act removed the right of councils to levy a supplementary or extra rate in the middle of the financial year. The Rates Act 1984 gave the Government the power to cap the level of rates charged by a local authority. It still applies in the form of council tax capping.

Revenue support grant This is the main contribution of central government to the current income of local authorities. The Government determines the **total standard spending** for local government. It then decides what proportion will be met from national taxation. The remainder has to be met from locally determined sources.

charge, or poll tax, as it became known. The tax was a flat-rate charge for local services levied on all adults over the area, although the Government reserved the power to cap it in each authority. In addition, central government set a uniform charge for businesses.

An attack on the rating system was an important part of the New Right critique (see above, pp 293–94). As long as only a minority of the electorate paid rates voters had little incentive to protest at wasteful spending or the imposition of high rates by the council. Conservative ministers calculated that if all adult residents paid a fixed charge, then they would be more likely to vote in local elections and to vote against a 'high' spending and 'high' taxing local authority. In other words, the Government hoped that by restoring the link between taxation and voting, people would be mobilised to vote in local elections to punish 'wasteful' (presumably left wing Labour) councils. Government spokesmen also complained that local authorities were driving business away from cities through high business rates. By imposing a *uniform* business rate across the counties, local authorities would be able to increase local spending only by increasing the poll tax. External control would remain in the form of an enhanced role for the Audit Commission to scrutinise local spending and ensure value for money.

A detailed study of the poll tax, titled *Failure in British Government*, has described it as the single most disastrous democratic policy decision made by a post-war British government (Butler, Adonis and Travers 1995). The principle of charging virtually every adult a flat-rate charge was bitterly opposed. The new tax was difficult to collect because people had to register, was widely regarded as unfair because it was not progressive and proved expensive to administer because of the need to set up new machinery. It led to riots, a slump in Tory electoral support and widespread evasion, and was a factor in Mrs Thatcher's downfall in 1990. Many Tory MPs were convinced that the party would lose a general election badly unless the tax was repealed—and that appeared to be out of the question, as long as she was leader. When John Major replaced Mrs Thatcher as Prime Minister the search for a substitute tax began, although in the short term the Treasury had to make generous settlements to keep the poll tax down to acceptable levels.

A new council tax, based partly on property values and partly on a personal element, replaced the poll tax with effect from 1 April 1993. It is calculated according to the value of the property and is levied on the current owner of the property. Like the old rating system, and in contrast to the poll tax, it is notionally fair (the largest tax is paid by owners of the wealthiest properties) and is relatively easy to collect. The Government retained the power to cap the tax—so much for local choice—and the tax now raises around 20% of local spending. The fact that the Government ended up with a form of property tax, not dissimilar to the old rates, is a tribute to the complexity of the problem and the failure of a decade of reform.

But the long-running battle over local finance is set to continue. Local authorities continue to complain that the centre imposes duties on them without providing adequate funding. In turn ministers claim that some local authorities manage resources poorly, and central and local government blame each other for above average increases in council tax or cuts in services. In recent years the increases above the rate of inflation in the council tax have become a political issue, particularly among pensioners. Before the 2005 general election the Labour Chancellor of the Exchequer offered a one-year reduction of £100 in the tax for pensioners, the Conservatives offered a reduction of up to £500 per household for the over-65s and the Liberal Democrats promised to end the tax and replace it with a local income tax. The future of local government finance is again under review and the forthcoming report by Sir Michael Lyons will try to balance the competing needs for the Treasury to have some control over total levels of public spending, provide adequate funding for locally delivered services and allow some independence to local authorities in raising and spending money. The lack of transparency in the present system means that voters are unclear about whom to hold responsible for spending and taxing. Not surprisingly, the Labour Government decided to retain 'reserved' powers under which the central grant may be reduced if the Secretary of State decides that an authority's expenditure exceeds its 'target', that is, what it should spend.

The controversy concerning local government finance shows how difficult it is to separate questions of financial independence and political autonomy. As Labour and Conservative governments in the past three decades have tried to control the growth of central public expenditure by imposing cash limits on many programmes, so they have tried to 'export' similar controls to local government. Some three-quarters of local authority spending is effectively determined in the policies laid down by central government, particularly in transport, education, housing and social services. And global assessments about the 'correct' level of local authority finance may overlook the differences between frugal and high-spending authorities. Variations in levels of local expenditure on particular services are partly a consequence of the different levels of resources available to authorities, as well as of different local needs and demands for particular services. Inner-city areas, for example, with high levels of social and economic deprivation, face a greater demand on housing and family support services. But the different political values of Labour and Conservative matter also, and may be reflected in shifting the allocation of resources between different areas of the country (often favouring those in which they enjoy strong political support), or altering the support for different services.

New Labour

In his battle to reform the Labour Party, Tony Blair weakened the people, policies, and organisations he associated with what he and his supporters dismissed as old Labour. Not surprisingly, along with some trade unions, local government was also a target. Labour modernisers were aware that in some Labour-dominated councils' services were poor, often more responsive to the producers than the customers and were plagued by cronyism; they noted how Conservative governments and a sympathetic media had made great play with the excesses of 'loony left' local councils in government, particularly in parts of London and Liverpool.

In government many of Tony Blair's ambitions, not least in improving state education, housing and social services, depend on delivery by local government. Ministers have wanted to attract higher calibre people into local government, improve the quality of management, increase the level of responsiveness of local service providers to consumers and promote greater interest in local politics. It is part of the Government's programme of modernising public administration and improving the delivery of public services (see Chapter 13 on the Civil Service).

Despite some changes, what stands out since 1997 is the degree of continuity with the preceding Conservative governments' mix of 'sticks and carrots' to achieve greater value for money and ensure better delivery of high quality public services. This includes by passing local councils. The Labour Government has transferred the running of social housing to social landlords and its encouragement of city academies and specialist schools, the former with part private funding, and controlling more of their intake and curriculum, is steadily eroding the role of local education authorities. In its 2005 Education White Paper, the

Government proposed that all schools would become self-governing 'trust' schools—rather similar to the Conservative-created grant maintained schools the Government inherited in 1997. Indeed, following the dispute over school funding in 2003–04 when some schools claimed that they had received less than they had been led to expect, the Government has decided to ring fence money for schools in its allocations to local authorities.

It also includes vigorous audit and inspection. In 1999 Labour abandoned the compulsory element in competitive tendering (see above p 294) and replaced it with 'best value'. This requires local councils to draw up plans for the efficient delivery of services, including the freedom to decide whether the public or private sector should be the provider. Services have for long been subject to inspection but Labour has greatly extended the regime of audit, inspection and assessment of local government performance in all services measured against 'targets'. The aims of 'best value' are to promote value for money, good quality and greater customer-focus in the provision of services. In 2003 the Audit Commission assumed the task of compiling a Comprehensive Performance Assessment (CPA) for each authority based on ratings for the quality of its service provision, and these range from excellent to poor (leading to 'league tables'). The Audit Commission's ratings and verdicts on whether best value has been achieved provide an opportunity for external intervention: if it judges a council to be 'failing' then it may recommend that the minister steps in and invite a successful local authority to take over a 'failing' service. The best local authorities are subject to lighter inspections in future, have less of their central funding ring-fenced, and are given more freedom to borrow funds. This is sometimes called 'earned autonomy' but, crucially, it is the centre that decides.

In 2000 the Government also obliged councils to replace the committee system, dating back to the 19th century, with more streamlined procedures. Authorities were given the choice of three management models:

- directly elected executive mayors, with a cabinet drawn from the council; or
- a cabinet and leader elected by the council; or
- a directly elected mayor and a council manager.

To introduce the elected mayor there has to be approval in a referendum triggered by a petition signed by at least 5% of the council electorate. Ministers reserve the power to order a referendum if they are not satisfied with the reformist intentions of the council.

The Labour Government has supported the introduction of elected executive mayors or a cabinet system, because of its concern about the quality of local leadership. Compared with the American or French mayor or German *Bürgermeister*, British local government lacks 'visible' local political leaders. Indeed, the fact that, for example, local American and German leaders are directly elected gives them a function and standing separate from that of their parties. The point of the mayoral option is to separate the executive tasks from those of scrutiny. The mayor is expected to provide strategic direction and propose the budget, and the councillors not in the executive to scrutinise the work and propose amendments to policy and the budget. However, the experiment has had mixed results. Only a dozen authorities have gone down the elected mayor and cabinet route. When mayoral elections have been held voters have shunned the established parties—in Hartlepool they elected 'Angus the Monkey', a candidate dressed as a monkey and Ken Livingstone was first elected as London Mayor in 2000 as an independent. Moreover, there has been no boost to turnout. So far councils appear to be more sympathetic to the cabinet model and few have supported the executive mayor model. Surveys show a large majority of the public favour the introduction of elected mayors, but surveys report that less than 10% of councillors support the idea. No doubt the lack of support is connected with the fact that such a system would usually involve a substantial reduction in the number of councillors.

More successful has been the restoration of an elected city-wide government for London, the Greater London Authority (GLA) in 2000. The system combines an elected executive mayor and a 25-member elected assembly which to scrutinises the mayor's policies. The idea of the elected mayor is innovative but so also are the electoral arrangements. The mayor is elected by the supplementary vote, in which the voter ranks two candidates in order of preference and the assembly by the additional member method, in which the voter has two votes, one for a party list and one for a constituency member. The former vote is used to achieve a more proportional legislature. The effect has been to help the 'other' parties like the Liberal Democrats and Greens gain assembly representation. The mayor's powers relate largely to transport, strategic planning and promotion of London. Ken Livingstone, elected mayor in 2000 and re-elected in 2004, has made his mark with the congestion charge, introduced in 2003, and paid by vehicles entering the 'congestion' zone. So successful has Livingstone judged the charge that he plans to extend it (Travers 2004) and other authorities are studying it.

The Government, particularly the Deputy Prime Minister John Prescott, has also favoured the introduction of more regional government. In part, the interest reflects a lack of confidence in local government and in part is an 'English' response to devolution in Scotland and Wales. But a difficulty has been lack of much public demand for this or of strong regional identities, certainly when compared to Scotland. The Government established regional development agencies (RDAs), regional assemblies of non-elected notables and envisaged these as a stepping-stone to elected regional councils. The bodies, however, were criticised as 'talking shops' and for lacking powers. The project received a major setback in November 2004 when the first referendum on the idea was held in the North East, widely regarded as the most likely region to support a regional body. In a 48% turnout (on a postal vote ballot) voters, perhaps fearing more taxes and the creation of yet another tier of government and more politicians, rejected the proposal by 78% to 22%. No further referenda are planned and regionalism now seems to be off the agenda for the foreseeable future. What has never been resolved is what effect, if any, the creation of regional assemblies would have on local government.

Conclusion

The past two decades have seen much controversy and much change surrounding the structure, role and financial basis of local government. And, while waiting on the Lyons review of local finance (see p 297) this will continue. What remains true is that local government operates within an environment which is the product of each authority's social, historical, political and economic conditions. It also operates within a national environment—councillors belong to national parties, officers to national associations, policies are made in Whitehall and the state of the national economy is always important.

The steady reduction in local financial independence and responsibilities and the imposition of a regime of central inspection and assessment has led some observers to talk of a 'crisis' of local government. It has been squeezed between greater control from the centre, competition and 'takeover' from other agencies, and the role given to parents, school governors, tenants and other consumers of services. The Treasury's determination to control public expenditure and effectively monopolise taxation has reinforced this 'top down' model. Does local government, some ask, have any purpose beyond satisfying the convenience of Whitehall?

In contrast, a number of other countries operate federal systems, which guarantee independent powers to local units. An insight into the culture of Whitehall was how officials ignored European experience when devising the poll tax; the verdict of the authoritative study on the subject (Butler, Adonis and Travers 1995: 3) was: 'The neglect, bordering on contempt for wider European practice in local government . . . is a telling commentary on Britain's rapport with its continental neighbours.'

Ministers of both Conservative and Labour Parties have found traditional local government wanting. Both now appear to regard local government primarily as a service provider, one competing with other providers and needing to be subject to regular checks that its performance meets Whitehall standards of quality and value for money. Labour ministers have retained the power to cap the council tax and the authority to set business rates and are looking to new structures to provide for better leadership and attract more able people.

Yet the above developments have to be set against Labour's introduction of devolution for Scotland, in particular, and Wales and the London mayor, and the interest in electing city mayors. There is an inconsistency in Labour's attitude to decentralisation. Conservative and Liberal Democratic attacks on the plethora of Whitehall targets for services and central control have been coupled with calls for a revival of local government (a traditional call, it is true, of the opposition). Labour ministers in 2005 have talked of 'letting go' and decentralising more decisions to local managers and professionals. Such talk has not satisfied Simon Jenkins (2004) who urges a root and branch abandonment of the trends of the last two decades and favours councils raising more of their own funds, having more responsibilities, entering partnerships with the private and voluntary sectors and embracing the idea of elected mayors. As yet, the overriding problems remain: the difficulty of sustaining genuine local government when it raises only a fifth of its revenue and depends on central government for the rest; local government's dependence on the centre for its existence and powers; and, as a consequence of the first two, the failure to attract high quality people to local politics.

KEY POINTS

- Local democracy is defended on the grounds of participation and efficiency; but these arguments are undermined by low turnouts for local elections, low interest in, or awareness of, what local government does and unacceptable inequalities in standards of service provision.

- Local government is subject to central control: the powers of local authorities are conferred, and may be withdrawn, by Parliament. Various legislation on education, housing or social services, etc affect local government's powers and responsibilities and often specify particular central–local relationships. Both main political parties when in power favour a 'top down' model of central control.

- Councillors have local connections, are usually members of a party, sociologically unrepresentative and unpaid but receive expenses. Some regard local government as a stepping stone to national politics.

- Local government officers are full-time officials usually having expertise in particular fields of local government work, eg planning or education. The relationship between councillors and officials is similar to that between ministers and civil servants.

- Party politics now dominate local councils and the leader of the majority party usually becomes the council leader.

- Central–local relations vary to some extent from department to department. In some ways it is more like a partnership, in others local government is more like an agent of the centre. The relationship is based on a mix of controls, dependence and co-operation. Central government is closely involved in overseeing the provision of many services in an attempt to ensure minimum or equal standards.

- Increased central control has eroded local autonomy and the old partnership model has been superseded by a greater emphasis on the agency model.

- The New Right argues that local government's lack of legitimacy means that its defiance of Whitehall on grounds of a local mandate is bogus and local government needs greater exposure to the market.

- The New Left in the 1980s saw local government as a base from which to oppose Conservative policies.

- New Labour's local government reforms are part of its wider plans for modernisation of government. In particular it looks to local government to be a more efficient deliverer of services.

- Finance comes from three main sources: grants, council and business tax, and income from rents, fees and charges for local amenities. The poll tax was an unsuccessful attempt to link local spending to local accountability.

- Local government has been subjected to more stringent financial controls and bypassed in many policy fields, eg housing, urban development and education.

KEY QUESTIONS

(1) How legitimate is the local electoral mandate?

(2) Why is local government subject to central government control?

(3) British people attach little importance to local democracy. Discuss.

(4) In what respects have the role and powers of local government changed in recent years?

(5) Why was the community charge introduced and then subsequently abolished?

IMPORTANT WEBSITES

For comprehensive and up-to-date news, see the following: www.nlgn.org.uk (New Local Government Network); www.lga.gov.uk (Local Government Association); www.lgiu.gov.uk (Local Government Information Unit).

FURTHER READING

For an introduction see D. Wilson and C. Game (2002) *Local Government in the United Kingdom*, 3rd edn, Basingstoke: Macmillan. On the poll tax and Whitehall's attitude to local government see Butler, A. Adonis and T. Travers (1995) *Failure in British Government*, Oxford: Oxford University Press. More generally see G. Stoker (ed) (1999) *The New Politics of British Local Governance*, London: Macmillan; G. Stoker (2004) *Transforming Local Governance: From Thatcherism to New Labour*, Basingstoke: Palgrave; J. Bulpitt (1983) *Territory and Power in the United Kingdom*, Manchester: Manchester University Press; R. Rhodes (1988) *Beyond Westminster and Whitehall*, London: Unwin-Hyman; and R. Rhodes (1999) *Control and Power in Central—Relations*, 2nd edn, Aldershot: Ashgate. On Labour since 1997 see D. Wilson, (1999) 'Threats and Promises: New Labour and Local Government', *Politics Review*, Vol 8(4); T. Travers (2001) 'Local Government' in A. Seldon (ed) *The Blair Effect*, London: Little Brown; T. Travers (2005) 'Local and Central Government' in A. Seldon and D. Kavanagh (eds) *The Blair Effect 2001–5*, Cambridge: Cambridge University Press; S. Jenkins (2004) *Big Bang Localism. A Rescue Plan for British Democracy*, London: Policy Exchange; and T. Travers (2004) *The Politics of London: Governing an Ungovernable City*, Basingstoke: Palgrave.

CHRONOLOGY

Three decades of local government

1964	Maud Committee on Management of Local Government
1966	Redcliffe-Maud Commission on Local Government
1969	Wheatley Commission on Local Government in Scotland
1970	'Fair Rents' Act: rent on council houses to be based on ability to pay
1972	Local Government Act: rationalises the previous 1,400 local authorities into 420-plus parishes. Government sends commissioners to administer housing in Clay Cross; councillors refuse to implement the 'Fair Rent' Act
1974	The 1972 Local Government reorganisation comes into force
1975	Reorganisation of local government in Scotland
1976	Local Education Authorities are instructed to reorganise education on comprehensive lines
1980	Local Government and Planning Act: grants penalties for overspending authorities. Housing Act: mandatory sale of council houses
1982	Local Government Finance Act: abolishes supplementary rates
1984	Rates Act: introduces rate-capping

1985	Local Government Act: GLC and metropolitan counties abolished. Transport Act limits powers of local authorities to subsidise and regulate public transport
1986	Widdicombe Report into the Conduct of Local Authority Business
1986	Local Government Act prohibits local authority publicity of a party political nature
1987	Rate Support Grant: grants fixed to expenditure
1988	Local Government Act: introduces Compulsory Competitive Tending, Housing Act: tenants can form Housing Action Trusts, Local Government Finance Act: rates to be replaced by community charge and uniform business rate, Education Act: introduces opting-out, national curriculum, local management for schools
1989	Community charge (poll tax) introduced in Scotland
1990	Community charge replaces rates in England and Wales
1991	Council tax replaces poll tax as of 1993, Commission for Local Government to examine structure and make recommendations
1992	Education Act: every school subject to inspection at four-year intervals
1994	Local Government Acts for Scotland and Wales: new single-tier authorities to be introduced in 1996
1997	Referenda approve devolution in Scotland and Wales
1998	Referendum approves directly elected executive mayor of London, Regional Development Agencies Act
2000	Local Government Act: new models of management, including elected mayors
2004	Referendum in North East overwhelmingly rejects proposed elected regional assembly, idea appears to be off the political agenda.

Visit the Online Resource Centre that accompanies this book
for links to more information on this chapter topic

CHAPTER SIXTEEN

Quangos and agencies

READER'S GUIDE

This chapter examines the way in which the British state has been fragmented as a consequence of the growth of Quangos and agencies. It outlines the development of these bodies, what they do and how they operate. It analyses the impact that the creation of bodies at arm's length from government have on the question of accountability. The chapter will then review the growth of agencies at the European level.

Introduction

Over the past 30 years there has been a considerable growth in the number of Quasi Non-Governmental Organisations (Quangos) and agencies. Quangos have responsibility for the delivery of public goods at arm's distance from government. They include a wide range of bodies such as the Arts Council, the Higher Education Funding Council and the Food Standards Agency, and they have responsibility for both regulating a range of public and private activities and distributing public money. Agencies are organisations hived-off from central government departments that have responsibility for the implementation, regulation and delivery of public services.

Quangos and agencies are often seen as an obscure element of administrative politics with little interest either for the general public or for political scientists. However, this view misses the way in which the lives of all of us are increasingly touched by Quangos and agencies. As members of the public, our contact with government is often through agencies and Quangos rather than the core executive or government departments. As Rhodes (1997) highlights, someone with HIV may receive support from up to 20 agencies or Quangos, none of which are direct representatives of central government

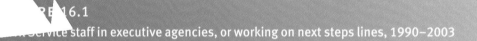

FIGURE 16.1

Service staff in executive agencies, or working on next steps lines, 1990–2003

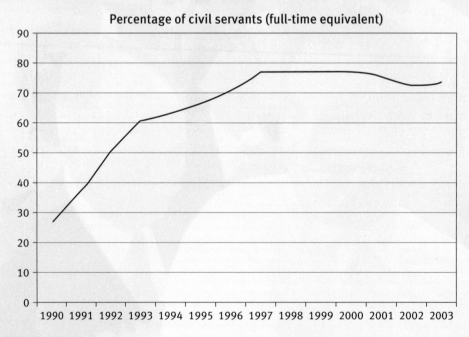

Percentage of civil servants (full-time equivalent)

Source: Civil Service Statistics

FIGURE 16.2

Total number of Agencies and percentage of civil servants

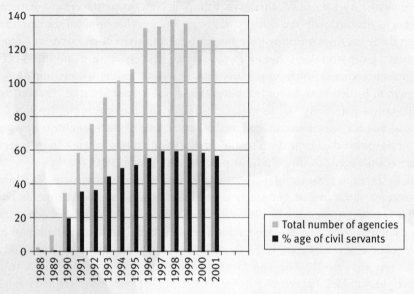

(*Source*: Civil Service Statistics)

departments. Quangos are nearly always spoken of in pejorative terms. They are seen as unelected and unaccountable bodies that spend vast amounts of public money. One of the themes that has always come from opposition parties during elections is the need for a cull of Quangos.

What these agencies and Quangos represent is a significant change in the nature of British government. No longer is policy delivered through standardised, hierarchal government departments but through a range of bodies that are developed to suit their particular task (see Chapters 3, 13 and 14). However, the consequence of these new organisations is a fragmentation of the state and a development of serious concerns about the nature of accountability. This chapter begins by looking at agencies and then goes on to examine the development of the growth of Quangos. It concludes by reviewing the growth of Quangos and agencies at the EU level.

Next Steps agencies

The development of Next Steps agencies can be linked directly with the Thatcher Administration's belief that traditional government bureaucracies were costly and inefficient. As a consequence, the Government developed a programme of reform that was outlined in Chapter 13. The Next Steps agencies developed from a report written in 1988 by Sir Robin Ibbs—a former director of Marks & Spencer. The Ibbs report, *The Next Steps*, was concerned with how to consolidate the reforms introduced by the Conservative Government during the 1980s (and discussed in Chapter 13). It proposed a division of departments between the policy advisers and the policy-makers at the core of a department, and those concerned with the delivery of policy whether this involved the provision of motor vehicle tax discs, printing government publications or social security payments. The parts of departments responsible for service delivery were to be hived-off into Management agencies, which would have much greater freedom to determine how services were to be delivered, to control budgets and to hire and fire staff. The aim was to separate out responsibility for the making of policy and the operation of policy. It was suggested that the reform would lead to the dismantling of the monolithic and unified Civil Service established in the 19th century and develop a model where a 'loose federation of many smaller agencies, units and core predominate' (Kemp 1993: 8).

Initially there was considerable resistance to the establishment of agencies. The Treasury had concerns about loss of budgetary control and a number of departments resisted attempts to establish agencies. In 1988 only three agencies were established and in 1989 a further seven were created. However, from 1990 onwards there was an explosion in the number of agencies (see Figure 16.2). By 2003 over 70% of civil servants were working in agencies (see Figure 16.1). There are two explanations for the rapid development of the core-periphery model of government. One is what is called the bureau-shaping model (see Dunleavy 1991). This approach argues that civil servants are self-interested actors and therefore act in ways that best protect their own interests. At a time when the government was trying to cut public expenditure and was critical of the way in which the Civil Service worked, the best way that senior civil servants could protect their interests was to hive-off the difficult work of managing large delivery units and restrict their role to the more interesting and rewarding policy work. They were therefore very keen to see the development of agencies which relieved them of responsibility for managing delivery and allowed them to concentrate on developing high-level policy and advising ministers (James 2003). The second explanation is political. It suggests that agencies did not develop because of the preferences of officials—indeed many opposed agencies—but because politicians pushed the agency agenda (Marsh, Richards and Smith 2001). It was Thatcher who set up the review under Ibbs and it was John Major who pushed through the agencification programme. He was strongly committed to the notion of public sector reform. For the Major Government, it was an opportunity to introduce a radical reform which was relatively low cost. Whatever the causes of this radical change, it is clear that it has an important impact on the structure and operation of government.

In principle, agencies released government departments and the delivery of public services from uniformity. They can organise not according to some standard practice but in ways that best suit the service they are delivering. Agencies can be divided into three main types: delivery services such as the Benefits Agency; regulatory bodies such as the Inspectorate of Education or trading concerns such as Her Majesty's Stationery Office (now privatised as the Stationery Office) (see Table 16.1 and see Chapter 14). By being semi-autonomous they have the freedom to decide how services can be best delivered.

Moreover, they differ in size and form greatly. The largest has over 72,000 and the smallest fewer than 50 staff. The goals and functions of agencies are set out in a framework agreement which is negotiated between the department and the agency. The framework agreement sets out:

- the agency's aims and objectives
- its relationship with Parliament, ministers and the department
- financial responsibilities
- personnel responsibilities
- control over pay, training and industrial relations.

Agencies were important institutional innovations because they changed both the roles and relationships of ministers and civil servants. For the first time ministers were identified as having responsibility for policy alone and not how it is delivered. It was for the Chief Executive of the agency to provide operational leadership. Gains (2004) shows that for a number of commentators, agencies were seen to have a positive impact on the delivery of policy, allowing Chief Executives much greater flexibility and the ability to concentrate on management and a more customer-orientated service. One of the questions which emerged

Department	Agency
Ministry of Defence	Defence Animal Centre
	Defence Dental Agency
	Joint Air Reconnaissance Intelligence
	Ministry of Defence Police
Department of Environment, Transport and Regions	Driver and Vehicle Licensing Agency
	Highway Agency
	Ordinance Survey
	The Rent Service
Home Office	UK Passports
	Fire Service College
Department for Education and Employment	Employment Agency
	Teachers' Pension Agency
Department for Work and Pensions	Benefits Agency
	Child Support Agency
	War Pensions Agency
Department of Health	Medical Devices
	National Health Service Estates

from this process was how much freedom agencies had in terms of their control over the implementation of policy. James (2003) points out that in a trading agency—that is, agencies that are selling a good, for example, HMSO which sold government publications— there is considerable autonomy, with agencies able to expand activities and control their internal management systems. However, in other areas Chief Executives have expressed concern at their lack of freedom. James (2003) highlights that ministers and other senior officials in the parent departments often did intervene in the day-to-day running of the agencies. One of the problems within British politics is that responsibility ultimately lies with ministers and as a consequence they have a tendency to intervene when they believe that the activities of agencies have political implications (however narrowly defined). Whenever a crisis becomes the focus of media attention, a minister is likely to intervene, whatever the nature of the framework agreement.

James (2003) points out that a number of benefits have developed as a consequence of the creation of agencies. There has been some reduction in running costs in providing services—overall a fall of 4.6% in running costs and ministers have been satisfied with the performance of most agencies. The majority of agencies have met their targets in terms of performance. As James points out, 'The semi-detached organisational structure of the Benefits Agency allowed a better focus on the delivery of the agency's objectives'. Nevertheless, the issues of agencies has raised a number of problems and issues.

Issues of accountability

The official position is that agencies improve accountability. According to ministers, agencies mean that there is transparency with ministers having responsibility for policy and the Chief Executive having responsibility for operations. Ministerial accountability still exists and the minister is responsible for the activities of his department. The Chief Executive is directly responsible for the delivery of services and has a clear set of targets. If these targets are not met, the contract of the Chief Executive can be terminated. A number of Chief Executives including Ros Hepplewhite, the former Chief Executive of the Child Support Agency, have resigned because of failures in their agencies. Chief Executives are dealing with issues of accountability directly in a way that has not been the case with civil servants in the past. The new agencies therefore end the fiction that ministers can be responsible for everything and therefore officials are not directly answerable. It is clear with agencies that officials are making very significant decisions which affect the lives of ordinary people in direct ways and therefore should be answerable for errors. The problem arises if ministers are avoiding responsibility by passing the blame to Chief Executives. Following a prison escape by IRA prisoners in 1994, there was some confusion over who was responsible. The report by John Woodcook on the incident stated: 'There exists some confusion as to the respective roles of the minister, the agency headquarters and individual prison governors'. Indeed, many people felt that the Home Secretary, Michael Howard, avoided responsibility for the escape by saying that it was an operational rather than a policy matter and it was the Chief Executive, Derek Lewis who had to resign. Brian Landers, who was the first Finance Director of the Prison Service agency, said Michael Howard 'wanted direct control but would not accept responsibility' (Landers 1999: 122).

What is policy?

The notion of an agency is built on the idea that there is a clear distinction between policy and operations. However, in reality it is often difficult to make a clear distinction. One of the arguments that arose between the Home Office and its agency, the prison service, was whether the issue of putting televisions in prisoners' cells was an operational or policy matter. For the Chief Executive it was an issue about making sure that prisons were well run and if prisoners were not bored then there were likely to be less problems. For the Home Secretary it was a policy matter concerning the conditions within prison cells. Sir John Woodcock, in his report on the IRA prison escape, said that the distinction between policy and operations was not clear and this made it difficult to assign responsibility. However, other agencies have made less of an issue over the relationship between policy and implementation. In the Department of Work and Pensions there is recognition that there is not a neat division between policy and operations. Therefore the Benefits Agency does have a policy role and it reflects back to the department issues of operations which need to be considered in policy (Gains 2004).

Clashes of cultures

The Government was keen to have a process of open recruitment when it established the agencies and therefore a number of Chief Executives came from the private sector (by 1998 31 out of 138 Chief Executives came from outside the Civil Service). One of the problems which arose was that those from the private sector had a different conception of the role of the Chief Executive than those within the departments. In the private sector the Chief Executive is at the top of the organisation and has considerable autonomy. However within the agencies the Chief Executive is ultimately responsible to the minister. For some Chief Executives this led to too much interference. Derek Lewis, the first Chief Executive in the Prison Service, believed that Michael Howard was continually interfering in operational matters and this made it very difficult for him to do his job (Gains 2004).

The Westminster model notion of ministerial power

The clash of cultures is in large part a consequence of the notion of ministerial power implicit within the Westminster model. Within the British political system, the minister is the apex of power. The minister heads a department and is responsible for all policy and actions. Consequently, ministers ultimately have responsibility concerning what happens on in an agency. This means that it is difficult for ministers not to become involved when issues appear politically salient, particularly when the minister may fear that the media may focus on issues which could create political difficulties. For instance, when Jeffrey Archer was in prison for perjury, he was allowed weekend release and a newspaper reported that he had broken the condition of the release by having lunch in the home of the MP Gillian Sheppard. This consequently became a major political issue and the Minister for Prisons commented on the case. It was undoubtedly an operational issue which should not have involved the minister. The British political system makes it almost impossible for ministers to stay out of issues, even if they are defined as operational.

An agency that has had a troubled existence is the Child Support Agency. This was a new agency created to deal with the issue of child maintenance payments following divorce. The aim was to take the issues of maintenance out of the courts and to have an agency that set payment levels and ensured the payment of maintenance. After a few months of operation there was considerable criticism of the agency. First, it was argued that the agency focused on those who received benefits payments and thus it was only a mechanism for reducing social security. Second, many men affected believed that the amounts they were being asked to pay were unrealistic. Third, many women reported difficulties in receiving payments because of the problems of the CSA. After only 18 months the Chief Executive of the CSA, Ros Hepplewhite, resigned. Since the early days of the Child Support Agency the problems have continued. Many women say that they are still not receiving sufficient support. On the other hand many fathers claim that they are being forced to make large payments without being guaranteed access to their children. In addition, they claim that the CSA takes no account of second families and it is throwing these families into poverty. Problems have been exacerbated by the introduction of a new computing system which has slowed down the payment process even further. It was later revealed that because of staff shortages staff were deliberately not dealing with cases by passing them on to colleagues who were away. In 2006 the government announced a fundamental review of the child support system.

Quangos

Quangos affect nearly every aspect of our lives. For example, as a student in a university, the circumstances in which you work are likely to be affected directly by Higher Education Funding Council for England (HEFCE), the Quality Assurance Agency (QAA), Office of Fair Access (OFFA), the Economic and Social Research Council (ESRC) and often indirectly by organisations such as the Health and Safety Executive. Despite their ubiquity, there is little agreement concerning what constitutes a Quango (see Politics in Focus 16.2). The most comprehensive definition includes any body that relies on public money to carry out a public task but with a degree of independence from government (see Flinders 1999). This definition involves literally thousands of bodies and could include BBC, Primary Care Trusts (PCTs) or universities. On the other hand, the definition preferred by government is those organisations defined as non-departmental public bodies, although the Labour Government has widened the definition to include public spending bodies at the regional and local level. The narrow definition of Quangos produces about 309 but the widest definition involves nearly 6,000 bodies. Whatever the definition it is clear that there is a range of bodies that provide public services but which are unelected and are not directly controlled by central government. As Table 16.2 indicates the Labour Government has created a considerable number of new bodies since 1997. It is also clear from the table that these bodies cover a wide range of functions.

Quangos are public bodies which operate at arm's length from government, but for which ministers are ultimately accountable. For this reason, ministers are usually responsible for appointments. The term, which is American in origin, stands for quasi-autonomous non-governmental organisations. These days, the preferred acronym is NDPB, for non-departmental public body. The full cast list includes major players such as London Transport, the Environment Agency, the BBC, the pay review bodies and the nationalised industries. But many are more obscure. Have you heard of the zoos forum, the advisory committee on historic wreck sites or the apple and pear research council?

Source: 'All you ever wanted to know about Quangos...but were afraid to ask', Andrew Cole, (The *Guardian*) 20 November 2000

One of the most important questions in relation to Quangos is why is it that parties in opposition are highly critical of Quangos but once in government they tend to create more. The usual pattern is for governments to come into office with a commitment to reduce Quangos. For a period there is a review and a Quango cull—usually as the result of amalgamation rather than abolition—and then the process of Quango-creation starts again. For instance, Flinders (2004a) indicates that the number of non-departmental public bodies declined from 1073 in 1998 to 849 in 2003. However, as he points out, this reduction in numbers is largely a result of responsibility being devolved to the regions, amalgamations and reclassifications. Perhaps more importantly, expenditure by public bodies has not declined, and is now about £25 billion a year (Flinders 2004a).

Why do governments seem so keen to establish Quangos?

- British government traditionally has not been closely involved in the implementation of policy. In most areas, policy is delivered closer to the ground whether it is through Local Education Authorities, Police Authorities or Health Authorities. Quangos are in many cases mechanisms for the delivery of policy.

- There is a belief that most of the areas Quangos are dealing with are relatively technical areas of policy such as health, education or the running of the national parks. These services require people with specialist knowledge to understand how policies should be delivered. For instance, what knowledge does a minister have to decide whether a grant should go to a particular artist or a researcher, and indeed, if ministers were deciding there would be accusations of patronage and political bias. Tasks such as the distribution of grants are much better carried out by the Arts Council or the Economic and Social Research Committee which are able to judge the quality of an artist or a researcher. Moreover, there is a practical issue. The government would not be able

Policy area	Quasi-Autonomous organisation
Local Government	Standards Board for England
Northern Ireland	Parades Commission (NI), Sentence Review Commissioners (NI), Commission for Racial Equality (NI), Human Rights Commission (NI)
Regulation	Postal Services Commission (POSTCOMM), Office of Communications (OFCOM), Gas and Electricity Markets Authority, Consumer Council for Postal Services, Gas and Electricity Consumer Council, Statistics Commission
Food Policy	Food Standards Agency
Constitutional Policy	House of Lords Appointments Commission, Electoral Commission, Commissioner for Judicial Appointments, Office of the Information Commissioner
Criminal/Legal Policy	Civil Justice Council, Sentencing Advisory Panel, Sentencing Guidelines Council, Legal Services Complaints Commissioner, Youth Justice Board, Criminal Records Bureau, Independent Police Complaints Commission, National Police Training and Development Authority (CENTREX), Assets Recovery Agency, Security Industry Authority
Industrial/Business Policy	Low Pay Commission, Better Regulation Task Force, Fair Trading Authority, Small Business Service, Ethnic Minority Business Forum, Nuclear Decommissioning Authority, Fuel Poverty Advisory Group
Lottery	National Lotteries Fund, National Lottery Commission
Transport	Strategic Railway Authority, Commission for Integrated Transport, Independent Railway Industry Safety Body
Rural/Agriculture	British Potato Council, Countryside Agency
Economic Policy	Competition Commission, Financial Services Authority, Monetary Policy Committee, Statistics Commission
Social Policy	New Deal Task Force, New Opportunities Fund, Race Relations Forum, Disability Rights Commission, Youth Justice Board, Pensions Compensation Board, Independent Pensions Commission, Community Forum, Children and Family Court Advisory and Support Service, Pensions Regulator
Education	Qualifications and Curriculum Authority, General Teaching Council for England, Learning and Skills Council, Medical Education Standards Board, Schools Funding Agency, University for Industry, Office of Fair Access, National College for School Leadership, Adult Learning Inspectorate, Office of the Independent Adjudicator

Policy Area	Quasi-Autonomous Organisation
Health	Commission for Health Improvement, National Institute of Clinical Excellence, Independent Reconfiguration Panel, National Care Standards Commission, Health Development Agency, Foundation Trusts, Primary Care Groups/Trusts, Commission for Health Care Audit and Inspection, Commission for Patient and Public Involvement in Health, General Social Care Council, Air Quality Expert Group, Patient Information Advisory Group, NHS Information Authority, National Patient Safety Agency, National Treatment Agency, Retained Organs Commission, National Clinical Assessment Authority, Council for the Regulation of Health Professionals, Council for the Quality of Health Care, NHS Information Standards Board, Medical Education Standards Board, Nursing and Midwifery Council, Health Professions Council, Social Care Institute of Excellence, National Shared Standards Initiative, NHS University, NHS Bank, Commission for Social Care Inspection, Health Protection Agency, NHS Independent Appointments Commission, Family Health Services Appeals Authority, Counter Fraud and Security Management Service, Office of the Independent Regulator for NHS Foundation Trusts
Security	Office of Surveillance Commissioners, Security Vetting Appeals Panel, Interception of Communications Commissioner, Intelligence Services Commissioner, Investigatory Powers Tribunal
Genetics	Human Genetics Commission, Agriculture and Environment Biotechnology Commission, Genetics and Insurance Committee, Committee on Novel Foods and Processes, Sustainable Development Commission, Distributed Generation Co-ordination Group
Misc.	Statistics Commission, National Archives, Independent Football Commission, Spoilation Advisory Panel, Committee for Monitoring Agreements on Tobacco Advertising and Sponsorship, Consumer Council for Postal Services, Brownfield Land Assembly Trust Co., Commission for Architecture and the Built Environment (CABE), National Endowment for Science, Technology and the Arts (NESTA), Land Registration Rule Committee, Office of the PPP Arbiter

Source: Flinders (2004a)

to cope with the large number of decisions that need to be made in relation to policy implementation.

- Since 1979, government, particularly under the Conservatives, has been suspicious of local government which they saw as highly political and not very effective (see Chapter 15). As a consequence a whole range of services shifted from local authority control to Quangos. One of the most prominent examples is in the provision of public housing. Until the 1980s, public housing was provided almost solely by local councils but under the Conservatives it was made the responsibility of a Quango, the Housing Corporation. This meant that for the Conservative Government services were not in the hands of Labour controlled local authorities but in the hands of Quangos whose members were appointed by government ministers.

- By shifting functions from central and local government to Quangos, governments concerned with reducing the size of the state could claim that the numbers employed by government had declined.

- Ironically, with the reforms that have occurred in government over the past 25 years, the pressures for the creation of Quangos are greater than ever. First, the response to marketisation and privatisation has been an explosion of regulation (see Chapter 14) and as a consequence a whole range of regulatory bodies—which are Quangos—have been set up. Second, the latest move in the process of reform is to move away from the notion that one size fits all in terms of policy delivery and therefore the government has used a range of different organisations in order to deliver policy. For instance, even in the rarefied area of monetary policy, we now have the Monetary Policy Committee within the Bank of England as the Quango responsible for setting interest rates (see Chapter 27).

- Often the issues that Quangos are dealing with are moral or controversial issues concerning the distribution of funding. By having an issue resolved through a Quango, the government is able to depoliticise it and avoid ministers having to take sides and alienate voters or being held responsible for outcomes. Flinders (2004a) makes the important point that Quangos fit into the strategy of New Labour for running the country. They give both independence and control, and they are mechanisms that allow for mixing both public and private mechanisms of delivering services.

Problems caused by the expansion of these bodies

Fragmentation

Flinders (2004a) indicates how with the growth of Quangos and agencies when developing new policies, there are a growing number of linkages between bodies that need to be made and as a consequence, there are an increasing number of veto points (arenas where decisions can be stopped or delayed). This can lead to situations where the responsibilities and relationships of the various bodies are unclear. For instance, whilst the British Board of Film Classification has the power to advise on the classification of films, it has statutory powers in relation to the classification of DVDs. The combination of internal management reform discussed in Chapters 12 and 13 and the establishment of agencies and Quangos have produced a significant change in the way decisions are made. Nearly all policy areas have become more fragmented. For instance, in areas like agriculture where policy was once controlled almost totally by the Ministry of Agriculture, it will now include the department (which is now called the Department for Environment, Food and Rural Affairs), a number of agencies such as the Intervention Board, the Meat Hygiene Service, the Rural Payments Agency and a new Quango, the Food Standards Agency. In all other areas, there has been a similar process of fragmentation. This means that policy is not made in a hierarchical line bureaucracy but through a network of departments, agencies and Quangos—and government is increasingly concerned with the management of these networks. This makes it increasingly difficult to join up policy and to achieve policy goals.

Accountability

The issue of fragmentation raises another problem: how does the system of accountability work when decision-making and policy delivery is fragmented across a range of institutions? The system of ministerial accountability in Britain means that ministers are responsible for their departments and Quangos have a parent department to which they are responsible. However, the problem is that they are supposed to be independent and the minister cannot be held responsible for their decisions. If the Monetary Policy Committee raises interest rates, the Chancellor will say that he is not responsible for that decision. Quangos can become mechanisms of blame-shifting for ministers—they pass the buck to the Quango (Flinders 2004a). Within the British political system, however, the mechanisms for holding Quangos directly responsible are limited. They are not elected and often they are remote from the people whose lives their decisions affect. As any university lecturer will know, the ESRC—the main Quango responsible for distributing research funding in the social sciences—does not enter into correspondence with those to whom it does not award grants, there is little transparency and there are no easily accessible mechanisms for changing the policies or managers of the ESRC. A corresponding problem is that the membership of Quangos is appointed by ministers. This led to accusations that under the last Conservative Administration Quangos were packed with Conservatives. Whether this accusation was true or not (only about 15% of members of Quangos say that they have a political affiliation), what was clear was that ministers were appointing up to 10,000 people each year (Wright 2001). Serious issues have been raised concerning the representativeness of members of Quangos and whether members of Quangos fully declare their interests. Such was the criticism of this level of patronage that the Major Government set up the Nolan Committee which led to the creation of a Public Appointments Commissioner to review appointments. However, the powers given to the new commissioner were very light, and had no statutory basis, and not all public appointments fall within the remit of the commissioner. The 2004 report highlighted that a number of departments were breaking the rules on appointments by showing lists of candidates to ministers, which implies they were influencing the appointment process. In addition, a number of Quangos which have an advisory role, do not even publish an annual report and often contain representatives from the sectors over which they are giving advice (Flinders 2004a).

It is also the case that Select Committees have a role in the scrutiny of Quangos. However, the number of Quangos means that the Select Committees do not have the resources to review the work of all of them. There have been proposals that Select Committees have a role in the appointment process but this has been rejected by the Government.

The Government's position is that Quangos have downward accountability to the public rather than upward accountability to ministers, and Quangos are expected to consult their users. However, as Flinders (2004a) points out, there are a number of problems with these recommendations:

- There are no legal requirements that Quangos consult users.
- Because much of what they do is legally and commercially sensitive, there is a limit on what can be discussed publicly.
- Only a small number of public bodies do hold open meetings—in 2000 it was only 17%.

Despite the problems and issues of democracy, it is clear that Quangos are here to stay and are an important element in the process of delivering public goods. Increasingly as government develops new policies, it establishes another body to either administer or regulate the policy. Public services are no longer being supplied by local or central government but from bodies that are developed specifically for the task. These bodies have advantages in that they can adapt to suit the task and they can be run by people with particular expertise. The drawback is that they do not fit easily into the British constitution as defined by the Westminster model and there is a need to give more thought to how these bodies can be held to account and operate democratically. So whilst Quangos may seem mundane and unimportant they are an important new element in the way that Britain is now being governed. Perhaps one of the most striking developments is how Quangos and agencies are now operating at the European level.

Quangos and the European Union

One of the features of the European Union is that it relies on nation-states for the implementation of policy (see Chapter 8). However, as Flinders (2004b) points out:

> . . . in certain areas the Treaties or specific EU Acts require tasks to be implemented centrally at the European level to ensure coherence, operational efficiency and confidence. Responsibility for these tasks lies with the Commission who may, in certain areas, decide to delegate or distribute defined tasks to quasi-autonomous Agencies. This is particularly common in relation to areas demanding a high level of technical expertise and where citizens must be confident that decisions have not been influenced by political or contingent factors. The creation of an independent agency is dependent on the adoption of a specific legislative instrument by the European Parliament (EP), based on the Commission's initiative.

Founding Basis	Agencies
EC Treaty	European Environment Agency
	European Agency for Reconstruction
	European Maritime Safety Agency
	European Food Safety Authority
	European Aviation Safety Agency
	Community Plant Variety Office
	Translation Centre for Bodies of the European Union
	European Agency for Safety and Health at Work
	Office for the Harmonisation in the Internal Market
	European Agency for the Evaluation of Medicinal Products
	European Monitoring Centre for Drugs and Drug Addiction
	European Training Foundation
	European Foundation for the Improvement of Working and Living Conditions
	European Monitoring Centre on Racism and Xenophobia
	European Centre for the Development of Vocational Training
Euratom Treaty	Euratom Supply Agency
Second and Third Pillars	European Union Institute for Security Studies
	European Police Office-Europol
	European Union Satellite Centre
	EuroJust
Autonomous Financial Institutions Proposed	European Central Bank
	European Investment Bank
	Management of Community Programmes Agency
	European Railway Agency

Source: Flinders (2004b)

As Table 16.3 demonstrates there are now a range of agencies which exist at the EU level. Some of these organisations such as the European Central Bank (ECB), which has responsibility for interest rates within Europe and the efficient operation of the single currency, have considerable influence over the lives of European citizens. Like Quangos in Britain, the ECB is not elected, and the lines of accountability are not particularly transparent, especially as the ECB was created specifically to be independent. What is of most significance concerning EU agencies is that their existence means that policy is being developed and implemented independently of nation-states and there is a European level of regulation developing that covers issues such as food, the environment, crime and transport. These bodies are significantly increasing the capacity of the European Union.

Conclusion

Under the Westminster model the delivery of policy was undertaken by government departments headed by a minister. It was the minister who was responsible for making policy and who was answerable when policy failed. The departments took a fairly standardised form and all those working within departments were civil servants who had the same conditions of work and similar prospects in terms of promotion and salaries. In the last 25 years there has been a major change in this structure. Whilst it is clear that agencies and non-departmental bodies have always existed in different forms in British government, there have been two significant changes. First, is the creation of agencies responsible for delivery that are separate from parent departments. This change has now become an established feature of British government. Central government departments are no longer responsible for policy delivery. Today the majority of civil servants work in agencies and each agency operates on different lines and with different conditions of work. Second, is the explosion of non-departmental public bodies or Quangos. All of our lives are in some way affected by these bodies which are involved in processes of regulation of both public and private services and the distribution of public money and services (see Chapter 14). The problem is that whilst these bodies are undoubtedly necessary, the British constitution has not kept pace with the degree of administrative change and the old concept of ministerial accountability does not allow the development of new forms of accountability to ensure that the new bodies are run on democratic lines. Moreover, with these bodies proliferating under a whole range of guises, it is not always clear who they should be responsible to and what mechanisms for maintaining legitimacy exist. In addition, they fragment the state even further.

KEY POINTS

- One of the most significant administrative reforms of the last 20 years has been the hiving-off of the delivery of policy into agencies.

- The majority of civil servants now work in agencies rather than government departments.

- Policy is increasingly being delivered and regulated by Quangos.

- Despite attempts by successive governments to cut the number of Quangos, the number has increased.

- The growth of Quangos and agencies has fragmented the policy-making process so that policy-making is in large part about the management of networks.

- The fragmentation of policy-making raises question about the accountability mechanisms that exist within British government.

- Quangos and agencies are now becoming important mechanisms for the delivery of policy at the European Union level.

KEY QUESTIONS

(1) Why has there been such a growth of Quangos and agencies in the last 20 years?

(2) What are the advantages and disadvantages of Quangos and agencies?

(3) Why do some agencies seem to work better than others?

(4) What are the implications of Quangos and agencies for ministerial responsibility?

(5) What are the implications of the growth of Quangos and agencies at the European Union level?

(6) What are the implications for Quangos for the process of governance?

IMPORTANT WEBSITES

The Government has two official websites concerned with Quangos: www.cabinetoffice.gov.uk/Agencies-publicbodies and www.public-appointments. gov.uk. A very useful and more crictical site is www.democraticaudit.com/issues/quangos.php which focuses directly on issues of accountablity, democracy and appointment processes. The webpage of the Public Commissioner on Appointments also has a large amount of informaton about those who are on Quangos and how they were appointed: www.ocpa.gov.uk/index2.htm. A useful site on agencies is www.dh.gov.uk/AboutUs/RelatedBodies/ExecutiveAgencies. Most Quangos and agencies now have their own websites which can easily be found on through Google.

FURTHER READING

There is not a vast amount of literature on Quangos and agencies. The development of agencies is covered in P. Greer (1994) *Transforming Central Government: the Next Steps Initiative*. Milton Keynes: Open University Press and in S. Zifcak, (1994) *Administrative Reform in Whitehall and Canberra*, Milton Keynes: Open Univerisity Press. A more recent and theoretically informed analysis is O. James (2003) *The Executive Agency Revolution in Whitehall*, London: Palgrave. Some of the theoretical issues surrounding agencies are covered in P. Dunleavy (1991) *Democracy, Bureaucracy and Public Choice*, Hemel Hempstead: Harvester Wheatsheaf and in D. Marsh, D. Richards and M.J. Smith (2000) 'Bureaucrats, Politicians and the Reform of Whitehall: Analysing the Bureau Shaping Model', *British Journal of Political Science*, 30: 461–82.

A useful article on some of the problems of agencies is F. Gains (2004) 'Hardware, Software or Network Connection? Theorizing Crisis in the UK Next Steps Agencies', *Public Administration*, 82: 547–66.

A good introduction to the issues surrounding Quangos is M. Flinders and M.J. Smith (1999) *Quangos Accountability and Reform*, London: Macmillan. The parliamentary view of Quangos is available in HC 367 *Mapping the Quango State,* Fifth Report of the Select Committee on Public Administration, Session 2000–01, (London: HMSO). A recent account of Quango development is M. Flinders (2004) 'Distributed Public Governance in Britain', *Public Administration*, 82 and at the European level in M. Flinders (2004) 'Distributed Governance in the European Union', *Journal of European Public Policy*, 11: 520–44.

 Visit the Online Resource Centre that accompanies this book for links to more information on this chapter topic

CHAPTER SEVENTEEN

A (dis)United Kingdom? Devolution and the policy process

READER'S GUIDE

Since 1997, one of the most radical aspects of the Labour Government has been its programme of devolution. Yet, its success in achieving devolution has been somewhat mixed. This chapter examines the evolution of relations between the centre and the territories and, in so doing, questions the extent to which Britain is a unitary state as portrayed by the Westminster model. It then considers why the relationship between the two came under increasing stress during the last Conservative Administration prompting the Labour Party to re-examine the institutional make-up of the UK. The chapter then explores the programme of devolution for Scotland, Wales and Northern Ireland which Labour embarked on in 1997, and considers how devolution has affected the policy-making process. The chapter concludes by considering whether devolution will strengthen the union of the United Kingdom, as Labour hopes, or in fact whether a chain of events have been set in motion which will lead to the potential break-up of the United Kingdom.

Introduction

As we saw in Chapter 3, the Westminster model has dominated studies of British government throughout the 20th century and it is essentially an organising perspective which defines an area to be studied. The British state is seen to be unitary in character—by which it is meant that all domestic sovereignty (power) is *formally* concentrated in the Westminster Parliament (see Politics in Focus 17.1). This is underpinned by the principle of parliamentary sovereignty. Constitutionally, this principle allows for the overturning of any law by a majority in Parliament. From this perspective, state power can be seen to be firmly located at the centre. What this leads to, at least in theory, is that, *the British state commands a high concentration of power at the centre*, in particular, the executive which dominates both Parliament and the judiciary. As Smith (1999: 9–10) observes, the Westminster model:

> . . . is built on the assumption that there is parliamentary
> sovereignty; all decisions are made within Parliament and there is
> no higher authority. Legitimacy and democracy are maintained because
> ministers are answerable to Parliament and the House of Commons is
> elected by the people. Decisions are taken by Cabinet and implemented
> by a neutral civil service. This view is derived from the Whig notion
> of the constitution being in self-correcting balance.

While both ministers and civil servants have continued to pay lip-service to the Westminster model, political science tends to view it in a more sceptical light, regarding it as an outdated and inaccurate portrayal of the British political system.

...G IN FOCUS 17.1

...unitary state?

Although the United Kingdom is composed of four nations it is a **unitary state**. Laws are passed by the Westminster Parliament and by the Scottish Parliament. The state is governed from London. Any power exercised by subordinate authorities is bestowed by, and can likewise be taken away by, Parliament.

For example, an Act of Parliament established a Parliament for Northern Ireland at Stormont Castle in Belfast, but in 1972 Parliament suspended Stormont and imposed direct rule from London. Similarly, the Assembly established in Northern Ireland in 1999 under the terms of the Belfast Agreement has up until 2005, been suspended four times, most recently in October 2002, each time reintroducing direct rule from Westminster.

This **unitary arrangement** in the UK can be contrasted with **federal states** such as the United States of America or Germany, where written constitutions define the legal rights and status of various levels of government. In the UK, it is Parliament that is legally and constitutionally supreme.

The supposed unitary nature of the British state has always been somewhat of a misleading feature of the Westminster model. As Bogdanor (1997: 15) argues: 'The United Kingdom is a unitary, though not necessarily uniform, state'. In principle, parliamentary sovereignty means that there is a single authority that governs the whole of the nation of the United Kingdom. But, Britain does not have a *uniform political or administrative structure*, there are a number of other dimensions to consider: the territorial dimension (see below); the sub-central government dimension (see Chapter 15) and the European dimension (see Chapter 9). In particular, we need to recognise how each of these dimensions, individually and collectively impacts on the original notion that formally, state power is highly concentrated at the centre in Britain. We then consider Labour's programme of devolution and assess to what extent reform has further affected the unitary character of the British state.

The British state—unitary but not uniform

As we saw earlier, the growth of the modern British state can be characterised as a process of peaceful evolution, rather than shaped by a series of revolutionary crises, as experienced by an array of contemporary, mainland European states. One element of this process of evolution is that at times of potential state crisis—the challenge from Oliver Cromwell and the New Model Army (1640s), the 'Glorious Revolution' (1689), the first Great Reform (1832) and the partition of Ireland (1920–22)—both the British state and its constitution have been adapted, in order to absorb and to an extent ameliorate the discontents within the political system. This can be clearly demonstrated if we examine the evolution of territorial relations in the United Kingdom.

The territorial dimension

The flexibility of the British constitution has allowed for the development of a unique set of institutional arrangements in each territory, such as distinctive legal and educational systems in Scotland and varying forms of government in Northern Ireland. As Mitchell (2002) points out, the United Kingdom developed without disrupting the existing institutional arrangements. Indeed, a clear example of the fluid and changing nature of the British state can be seen in the evolving nature of relations with the territories. Scotland, Wales and Northern Ireland have all been component parts of the British state for a long while—Wales was absorbed by Britain in 1536, Scotland by the Act of Union 1707 and the Union of Ireland with Britain was achieved in 1801 remaining, until partition of Ireland in 1920 and the creation of Ulster in 1921.

The pattern of Britain's evolving territorial relations has during the course of the 20th century been conditioned by a view, held by both the Conservative and Labour Parties, of the importance of political centralisation at Westminster. This development, from the 1920s onwards was not inevitable. Until then, Labour was also a party of Home

Rule for the different nations and of municipal socialism, while the Conservatives defended local government and with it the idea of limited national government. However, when Labour was faced with the prospect of political power in the early 1920s, it settled for power centralisation (for economic planning, public ownership of the main utilities and redistribution) over decentralisation (for participation and local choice). Help for the peripheral parts of the UK (and Labour strongholds) would come through central allocation of government spending, rather than through constitutional change. The importance of the centre in shaping territorial relations should not be understated and, as we saw when examining the sub-central level (see Chapter 15), one of the most compelling narratives for analysing centre-territorial relations throughout much of the last century is provided by Bulpitt (1983; see also Politics in Focus 17.2). Bulpitt (1983: 2) observes that his analysis of centre-territory relations is conditioned from a 'centre' perspective

e dual polity model

Jim Bulpitt's *Territory, and Power in the United Kingdom* examined the nature of territorial politics in Britain between the 1920s–80s. He argues that when analysing territorial politics it is best characterised as a structural dichotomy between the centre and periphery:

> ...to put the point in seventeenth-century and eighteenth century political terminology, the basic division has been between the court and country. To begin with, the centre meant the court. Later, it came to mean the Cabinet and then a 'political-administrative community' of senior ministers and top civil servants. Whatever the precise location, a court ethos has always dominated the Centre's activities. The periphery, or country, was usually, from the Centre's viewpoint, all other places... The Centre or court sought increasingly to operate a distinction between 'High Politics' and 'Low Politics'. The former involved matters which, at any one time, were regarded as primarily the responsibility of the Centre, the latter covered those residual matters which in normal circumstances could be left to governments and interests in the periphery... In pursuit of this High/Low politics distinction, what can be called the official mind at the Centre developed an operational code for territorial politics which emphasised the desirability of autonomy for the Centre in matters of 'High Politics' and indirect rule of the periphery by local elite collaborators. In practice, this system involved an operational separation of powers between the national institutions of government in London and a considerable amount of reciprocal autonomy for peripheral governments and interests. The apotheosis of the Centre's official mind was realised in the period roughly from 1926 to 1961. In those years a Dual Polity operated in territorial terms: both Centre and periphery achieved a relative autonomy from one another, the degree of interpretation between national and local politics was low... Much of what has happened in territorial politics since the early 1960s must be seen in terms of the emergence of various challenges to that Dual Polity. Up to the present (1980s), it is argued, the most serious challenges have come not from the periphery but the Centre itself'.

(Bulpitt 1983:3)

The concept of Bulpitt's dual polity and in particular, the extent to which the centre conditions relations with the periphery remains important today, when examining the process of devolution pursued by the Labour Government since 1997. In particular, the extent to which it is the centre, to use Bulpitt's terminology, that has dominated the way in which the reform process has evolved.

because: '...this perspective is to a large extent a forced one, since it is doubtful if any macro-study of territorial politics can be carried out without viewing the subject from the centre'.

Despite the concentration of power at Westminster, Scotland and Northern Ireland had for long possessed their own distinctive political institutions. Until 1972, Northern Ireland had its own Parliament based in Stormont, a classic case of devolution, long before the case of Scotland became an issue in the 1970s. Scotland, Wales and Northern Ireland had their own ministers in the Cabinet and a separate local government system existed in Scotland and Wales. Before the creation of its Parliament, Scottish legislation at Westminster was dealt with by a Scottish Grand Committee, and non-Scottish MPs were reluctant to intervene in its work. The Welsh and Scottish Offices negotiated with Whitehall departments for money to cover their national responsibilities.

British governments had no consistent view about the relations between the constituent nations of the Union. From 1972, local self-government in Northern Ireland had been suspended and direct rule imposed from London until 1999. Yet the 1974–79 Labour Government was prepared to devolve powers to directly elected assemblies in Scotland and Wales (see Nairn 1981). Today, the mainstream British parties have now accepted the right of Northern Ireland to leave the UK and join the Irish Republic at a future date, if a majority so wish. Yet separatism and federalism have been rejected for Scotland and Wales.

Scotland and England co-existed as two separate kingdoms under one monarch for a century before the union of *Scotland* with England and Wales in 1707. This involved the creation of a new Parliament of Great Britain within which Scottish MPs were a distinct minority. Scotland, however, retained its own legal system, the national Church of Scotland and many other national institutions which may be said to provide a 'Scottish political system' (Kellas 1989). Since 1885, there has been a Scottish Office, whose head has sat in Cabinet since 1895, except for the war years, and has its headquarters in Edinburgh. It was responsible for health, education, housing, economic development and agriculture, and Home Office matters. Although variations of national policy were permitted by the Westminster government when applied to Scotland, decisions remained with London. The Labour Government in 1978 passed bills to create an elected Scottish legislative assembly, to which a Scottish executive would be responsible, and would have dealt with matters then in the hands of the Scottish Office. Nationalists in Scotland called for independence and the Labour Government offered *devolution*; this would be a halfway house, creating a Scottish Assembly and allowing it some legislative power. The plan collapsed when an insufficient number of Scots supported it in a referendum in 1979.[1]

During the 1980s, devolution disappeared from the Westminster agenda. The Thatcher Administration was vehemently opposed to the idea, the Nationalists were eclipsed, and Labour, although still in favour of devolution, was in decline. Yet in these years, Scotland's sense of distance from England probably increased. Although the Conservatives had only

---

[1] The referendum was held on 1 March 1979. The result was a narrow majority in favour of devolution (51.6% in favour, 48.4% against). However, because of the low electoral turnout (63.8%), the percentage of the electorate that voted 'yes' was less than the required 40% needed for devolution.

minority support in Scotland, they enjoyed a commanding majority in Parliament, thanks to their electoral dominance in England. Increasingly, the Conservative Governments of 1979–97 were seen by Scots as simply English governments. A particular indignity was the decision to implement the unpopular community charge in 1989, a year before doing so in England and Wales. According to opinion polls in 1991, one-third of Scots favoured outright independence, 40% devolution and 20% the status quo.

Wales has been governed virtually as part of England since its absorption in 1536. A Welsh Office was established in 1964 with a Secretary of State for Wales in Cabinet. The areas of responsibility are broadly similar to those of her/his Scottish counterpart, although less significant in total. In the 20th century, the Welsh political differentiation from England has been expressed in strong support for the Liberal and the Labour Parties, rather than the Unionist Conservatives. Support for political nationalism is weak on the evidence of the pro-devolution vote in 1979 and the small vote (about 10%) for Plaid Cymru, the Welsh nationalist party. The appeal of Plaid Cymru is primarily cultural and linguistic, but only a fifth of the population is now Welsh-speaking compared with half in 1901.

Pressures for devolution

When Labour was elected to power in 1997, a number of serious stresses had developed in the unitary nature of the United Kingdom. After the partition of Ireland at the start of the 1920s until the 1960s, there was very little discussion about the nature of the United Kingdom. In a sense, for some this was part of the post-war consensus that Britain was and would remain unified. The regions were given autonomy over particular areas of policy, but in return, devolution was not discussed. However, from the 1960s onwards, there were growing nationalist feelings within Scotland and Wales and an increased desire for some form of devolved government. In the case of Northern Ireland, there was a growing demand for a united Ireland in the Catholic/Nationalist community (see Nairn 1981). Following a failed attempt at gaining greater independence in the 1970s, when a 1979 referendum did not secure the necessary majority for devolution, tension within the United Kingdom again grew in the 1980s, as people in Scotland and Wales increasingly felt that they were being governed by a government they did not elect. Whilst Conservative governments were being elected in the United Kingdom, support in Scotland and Wales practically disappeared. Moreover, the perception of England dominating Scotland was exacerbated by the last Conservative Administration's apparent modus operandi that the United Kingdom was just an extension of England. As McConnell (2000: 220) observes: '... the Thatcher Government came to power in 1979 with moves for devolution apparently at a dead-end ... In retrospect, it is clear that devolutionary sentiments were not dead. Supporters of devolution were merely reeling from the shock of the referendum result and were about to be galvanised by the activities of the Thatcher and Major Governments between 1979–97.'

Labour's programme of devolution

Labour's response to regional demands and concern over democracy was a commitment in its 1997 manifesto to devolve greater power to Scotland, Wales and Northern Ireland. Indeed, their commitment to this policy is arguably one of the most radical policies acted on in the course of their first two terms in office.

Labour's approach, in particular to Scotland and Wales, has been based on political pragmatism. Their programme of reform has been framed in the context of devolving greater power to the territories in order, paradoxically, to strength and reinvigorate the unitary character of the British state, not as a transitory stage on the path to complete separation or federalism. The key dynamic underpinning this stance has been Labour's reluctance to risk the strong, electoral position it secured in 1997, reaffirmed in 2001 and which it had spent 18 years striving to achieve. Again, it is worth recalling Bulpitt's analysis, in particular the extent to which it is the centre which plays the dominant role in shaping relations with the territories. This is clearly the case in the way in which devolution has been pursued since 1997.

In the following sections, we examine the variation for each territory in Labour's programme for devolution. Indeed, as with Labour's approach to constitutional reform (see Chapter 10), the process of devolution might be understood as a rather pragmatic, ad hoc and geographically variable responses to pressures that had built up within the Union. Our approach will consider three principal problems arising from devolution:

- devolution is a threat to parliamentary sovereignty;
- there is not one, but at least four forms of devolution proposed;
- a consequence of devolution may be greater fragmentation and conflict within the British state, exacerbating the problems associated with governance.

Scotland

In the late 1980s, a number of groups and the Labour and Liberal Democratic Parties formed a Scottish Constitutional Convention which prepared a scheme for a Scottish Parliament which would have taxing and spending power and would be elected by proportional representation (PR). Notable absentees from the Convention were the Scottish Nationalists and the Conservative Party, for whom devolution was an unacceptable middle way between their preferred options of, respectively, independence and the status quo. At the 1992 and 1997 general elections there were effectively three options represented by the political parties.

The first was for the constitutional status quo or marginal changes to it. The Conservative Party resisted devolution on the grounds that it would be a first step on a slippery slope or, in another metaphor, a Trojan horse, leading to independence, and the break-up of the United Kingdom. The party's stance only reinforced its image among many Scots as the English and alien party.

The second position was devolution for Scotland within the United Kingdom. Labour and the Liberal Democrats claimed that such a reform was necessary to acknowledge Scotland's distinctiveness and to keep the United Kingdom together. A commitment to devolution had been present in every Labour Party manifesto since October 1974 and it was approved in the Lib–Lab Commission on Constitutional Reform in the run-up to the 1997 general election.

A third option was that of the Scottish Nationalists, who called for outright independence and supported devolution in the short term as a bridge to achieving it. Nationalists claimed that once they gained a majority in Parliament they would call a referendum on the issue and if successful would open negotiations over separation with the Westminster Parliament.

The popular support for the three positions in the 1992 and 1997 general elections is shown in Table 17.1. By 1997 the status quo or Conservative position was effectively killed off, supported by less than one-fifth of the Scottish electorate, and the Conservative Party had no Scottish MPs. In all, a clear majority of voters supported devolution. It is worth noting, however, that surveys suggest that devolution was not the most important issue for Scottish voters, whose views on social and economic issues were broadly similar to those of voters in England.

For the 1997 general election, the details of Labour's devolution plans were affected by its acceptance of the Conservative Government's plans for future public spending and rates of income tax. A Labour-led executive in Scotland, according to Tony Blair, would not increase income tax for the lifetime of the first Parliament. Indeed, he offended Scots by comparing the spending powers of the proposed Scottish Parliament to those of an English parish council.

The Scottish Parliament

In government, Labour moved quickly to prepare a White Paper, *Scotland's Parliament*. This explicitly recognised that Scotland was a nation. In September 1997, a referendum was called to vote yes or no on two questions: (a) should a Scottish Parliament be created and (b) should it have tax-varying powers? From a near 50-50 split on the devolution proposals in 1979, the referendum in 1997 provided a three-to-one majority for the Parliament and a clear majority for giving it tax powers (see Politics in Focus 17.3). Since

	1992	1997
Status quo (Conservative position)	25.6	17.5
Devolution (Lib–Lab position)	52.0	52.6
Independence (SNP)	21.5	22.1

The Scotland Act and the Wales Act 1978 provided for the establishment of legislative assemblies in both countries respectively, but subject to approval by 40% of the electorate in national referenda. In the event, even in Scotland the 'yes' vote fell well short of the required 40% of the total electorate.

The 1979 result was:

Scotland (% who actually voted)	51.6% voted for devolution	48.4% voted against
Overall %	33% voted for devolution	31% voted against
Wales (% who actually voted)	20.3% voted for devolution	79.7% voted against
Overall %	12% voted for devolution	47% voted against

The 1978 Acts were repealed and in 1997 new legislation providing for a Scottish Parliament and a Welsh Assembly, subject to approval by referendum.

The 1997 result was (% of those who voted):

Scotland	74% voted for devolution	26% voted against
Tax-varying powers	63.5% voted in favour	36.5% voted against
Wales	50.3% voted for devolution	49.7% voted against

1979, public opinion had become more familiar with the idea of a Scottish Parliament and more disenchanted with Conservative rule from London. The Scottish Labour Party was now united in support, and Labour had a large majority at Westminster. Proportional representation was expected to have a number of effects, including rewarding parties which were willing to negotiate and/or form a coalition with other parties because it was unlikely that any one party would get an overall majority of seats—Labour and the Liberal Democrats had co-operated during and before the 1997 general election campaign, over the passage of the Scotland Bill through Parliament, and during the referendum—and making it more difficult for the Scottish Nationalists (the only pro-independence party) to achieve a majority in Parliament and open negotiations for independence.

In the light of the referendum result, Labour set about establishing a new Parliament in Edinburgh for Scotland and the formal transfer of power from Westminster occurred in July 1999. The new Scottish Parliament enjoyed powers covering education and training, environment, agriculture, fisheries and forestry, housing, law and order and policing crime, local government, health and most transport. It also had power to vary income tax by up to three pence in each pound, although not in the first session of the Parliament (Mitchell 1999). The Scottish Executive, headed by a First Minister, would be accountable to the Parliament. The Parliament would have 129 members, 73 of whom would be elected by first past the post in existing constituencies for Westminster elections and an additional 56 'top-up' members for regions and drawn from a party list which would be used to achieve a more proportional outcome (see Politics in Focus 17.4).

Membership and organisation:

129 Scottish Members of Parliament (SMPs). 73 SMPs are directly elected on a constituency basis, with the remaining 56 members elected by the Additional Member System drawn from a party list. The Cabinet is headed by a First Minister. The Secretary of State for Scotland retains a seat in the Cabinet in Westminster. Scottish ministers are entitled to participate in meetings of the EU Council of Ministers.

Duration:

A maximum four-year term, but with the possibility of early dissolution.

Powers:

The Scottish Parliament possesses legislative powers and is responsible for: health, education and training, local government, social work and housing, economic development and transport, the law and home affairs, the environment, agriculture, fisheries and forestry, sports and art, research and statistics in relation to devolved matters. It is also vested with tax varying powers + or −3p, in relation to the basic rate of tax established by the Westminster Parliament.

In conceding the above range of powers to a Scottish Parliament, the Labour Government made clear that the UK Parliament would remain sovereign. Westminster would retain powers over issues concerning: UK defence and national security; UK foreign policy including relations with Europe; the UK constitution; the stability of the UK's fiscal, economic and monetary system; common markets for UK goods and services; employment legislation; social security; and over most aspects of transport safety and regulation.

There have been two elections to the Scottish Parliament (May 1999 and May 2003) since its inception and in both, the Labour Party has been the largest party in Scotland (see Table 17.2). However, it has not enjoyed an outright majority (65 seats required for a majority) in Scotland in either election and has had to govern in an uneasy coalition with the Liberal Democrats on both occasions. Interestingly, the May 2003 election saw a rise in the share of the vote for the smaller minority parties—most notably the Scottish Socialists and the Greens and also a decline in the vote for the SNP. This suggests that, for the moment anyway, further moves towards outright separation have been dampened. It should also be noted that the turnout for the elections fell by over 10%, partly explained by the escalating costs of a new parliamentary building constructed in Holyrood.

Analysing Scottish devolution

When analysing the political impact of Scottish devolution, let us first highlight Labour's argument that devolution neither threatens parliamentary sovereignty, nor undermines the integrity of the United Kingdom. 'Sovereignty rests with Westminster because we are

	Seats won in 1999	Seats won in 2003
Conservatives	18	18
Greens	1	7
Labour	56	50
Liberal Democrats	17	17
Scottish Socialists	1	6
SNP	35	27
Other	1	4
Turnout (%)	60.2	49.2

proposing devolution—local services to be run here by the people of Scotland. It's not separation.' (Cf Riddell 2000: 105). However, as we have seen above, the central tenets of the reform package have been to establish a Scottish Parliament, based in Edinburgh, with powers to make law, provide limited scope for raising taxes and to represent Scotland in the European Union. In terms of public policy, there have been clear examples such as the provision by the Scottish Parliament for free personal care for the elderly, which are at variance with the policies pursued south of the border and are used to highlight the impact the new political arrangements have made. Likewise, certainly policies, such as the Scottish Executive's abolition of up-front, higher education tuition fees for all eligible full-time Scottish and European Union students in Scotland, while in July 2005 it announced plans to increase tuition fees for English students in a bid to discourage 'fee refugees' from overwhelming Scotland's universities from the introduction of top-up fees in England in 2006, have led to clashes between Edinburgh and London. There has also been a conscious attempt to reject the Westminster model. This can be seen in the way ideas embracing proportional representation, more sociable working hours and the use of electronic voting methods have been instituted.

However, despite Labour's reassertion that the sovereignty of the UK Parliament remains intact, a number of issues have arisen over the interpretation of the nature of sovereignty:

- It is questionable whether tax raising powers are compatible with notions of sovereignty.
- The fact that MPs are pressurising the Westminster government to prevent Scottish MPs from voting on English matters indicates that the unified sovereignty of Parliament is not guaranteed. This is often referred to as the West Lothian question, named after Tam Dalyell, one-time Labour MP for West Lothian, and then MP for Livingston until his retirement at the 2005 general election.

- The de facto sovereignty of Parliament could be further threatened if proportional voting increases nationalist representation and breaks the links of dependence that would be maintained through a Labour Scottish Assembly.

- The rejection of the Westminster model may produce a less executive centred, more open and responsive Assembly unbound by the Westminster traditions and consequently less elitist.

- The Assembly may have greater legitimacy than Westminster, thus effectively restraining central government from ever reducing the powers of the Scottish Parliament.

Wales

Labour's proposals for Welsh devolution set out in the July 1997 White Paper, *A Voice for Wales* were more modest than those for Scotland. Labour's aim was to revitalise Welsh participation in the political process and reinvigorate the principality's faith in the UK political system. As we saw in Politics in Focus 17.3, support for devolution in both 1979 and 1997 was not as strong in Wales as Scotland—in the referendum in September 1997 the package was narrowly approved by 50.3 to 49.7% of the vote. The White Paper offered only executive, not legislative, devolution of power to the principality. Unlike Scotland, the Welsh Assembly has not been conferred with either power to raise taxes or primary legislative powers. Instead, the Assembly only constitutes 'executive devolution' (see Politics in Focus 17.5).

The May 1999 elections could not be regarded as a ringing endorsement for devolution. The turnout was low with only 25% of the electorate bothering to vote. The party which

Membership and organisation:

The Assembly consists of 60 members elected by the Additional Member System. Forty members are elected on a constituency basis and the remaining 20 are taken from a party list. The Cabinet is headed by the First Secretary. The Secretary of State for Wales retains a seat in the Westminster Cabinet. Only the Secretary of State is entitled to participate in meetings of the EU Council of Ministers.

Duration:

A fixed four-year term, in which early dissolution is not permissible.

Power:

The Welsh Assembly does not have any legislative powers, nor does it possess any tax raising powers.

The Assembly possesses executive powers only and these cover the areas of health, education, industry and training, agriculture, environment, roads, planning, arts and heritage.

	Seats won in 1999	Seats won in 2003
Labour	28	30
Plaid Cymru	17	12
Conservatives	9	11
Liberal Democrats	6	6
Others	0	1
Turnout	45%	38.2%

enjoyed the most success in relative terms was Plaid Cymru on a platform advocating outright separation from London, while Labour's share of the vote compared to the 1997 general election was sharply reduced (see Table 17.3).

Unlike Scotland, the establishment of a Welsh Assembly has not created the same degree of tension surrounding issues of sovereignty, nor is it presently likely to provide a staging post on the path towards full separation. However, the danger Hazell and O'Leary (1999) identify is leap-frogging, whereby a Welsh Assembly sees a successful Scottish system and therefore starts to push for more powers. Indeed, as early as autumn 1999, the Welsh Assembly were calling for more powers to place the Welsh Assembly on a similar footing to that of the Scottish Parliament.[2] There is an argument that suggests devolution has increased tensions with Westminster and may lead to greater autonomy for Wales. Already there have been conflicts over BSE and foot and mouth, and the fact that Blair's chosen leader Alun Michael was forced out of office to be replaced by Rhodri Morgan in 2000, indicates that the Welsh Assembly perhaps has already more independence than was at first intended. However, Westminster has retained considerable powers over Welsh matters. Again the Bulpitt analysis of the centre shaping territorial relations remains pertinent. The relationship was further strained in June 2003, when Lord Falconer was made Secretary of State for Constitutional Affairs and inherited a number of residual responsibilities for the devolved countries as the Scottish and Welsh offices were abolished. The Secretaries of State for Scotland and Wales have been replaced by 'spokespeople' in the Cabinet. After the 2005 general election, Peter Hain acts as the Secretary of State for Northern Ireland and Wales, while Alistair Darling is Secretary of State for Transport and Secretary of State for Scotland.

---

[2] As it had promised before devolution, the Labour Government established an independent review committee— the Richard Commission—to consider the 'sufficiency' of the Assembly's current powers (for details see www.richardcommission.gov.uk/).

Northern Ireland

An historical overview

Northern Ireland has for long posed a major challenge to many of the assumptions about British politics, not least to that concerning the authority of government. The union of Ireland with the United Kingdom was achieved in 1801, but the present borders date only from 1921. Northern Ireland was created in 1922 under the threat of force. The 26 largely Catholic southern counties formed the new Irish state but the six largely Protestant northern counties were allowed to remain part of the United Kingdom. Since the partition, many Irish Catholics and almost all Protestants have continued to protest their exclusive loyalties to the Irish Republic and British Crown respectively, and constitute separate sub-cultures (see Politics in Focus 17.6). In Northern Ireland, Protestants outnumber Catholics two to one, but in a united Ireland, Catholics would be in a clear majority. Many of the Irish felt 'cheated' by the partition and looked to eventual union, while the Protestants in Northern Ireland continued to feel threatened by the claims made by the South.

Eire	Gaelic for Ireland, often used to refer to Southern Ireland
Irish Free State	Southern Ireland, 1922–49
Irish Republic	Southern Ireland since 1949
Ulster	Ancient province of Ireland—9 counties of the north-west often used to refer to Northern Ireland
Northern Ireland	6 counties of Ulster politically part of the UK
Dail	Southern Irish Parliament
Stormont	Northern Ireland's Parliament, 1922–72
IRA	Irish Republican Army, a paramilitary terrorist organisation formed in 1919. Evolved out of the Fenians
Sinn Fein	('Ourselves Alone')—political wing of IRA
Provos	Provisional wing of IRA and Sinn Fein active in Northern Ireland
Unionists	Supporters of union with Britain—usually Protestants living in Northern Ireland referred to as Loyalists, ie loyal to the English Crown
Nationalists	Supporters of united Ireland; today the term is used usually in association with Catholics in Northern Ireland
UDA	Ulster Defence Association—Protestant unionist paramilitaries
UVF	Ulster Volunteer Force—as above, but more extreme and violent
UUP	Official Ulster Unionist Party—moderate unionists
DUP	Democratic Unionist Party—populist, extremist
SDLP	Social Democratic Labour Party—moderate Catholic party in Northern Ireland
Alliance	Non-sectarian party of Northern Ireland with very limited support—unsuccessful in breaking the sectarian mould of Northern Ireland politics

Northern Ireland's physical separateness from the mainland and its distinctive problems make it seem 'non-British' in many respects. Certainly, many of the statements made about British politics for the last 50 years—on political consensus, the rule of law, tolerance, secularism, class voting—hardly apply to Northern Ireland. Since the late 1960s, however, the region has increasingly mattered and irritatingly to British politicians, both because of the violence, which has received international publicity, and because of the seemingly impossible task of finding 'a solution' which is acceptable to both Protestants and Catholics. At issue are such fundamental questions as the borders of Ireland and the United Kingdom, national identity and the legitimacy of British rule (Whyte 1990).

Bitterness has been increased because the national and religious rivalries between the two communities are so long-standing. Catholic Ireland had refused to conform to Henry VIII's Protestant Reformation. For the next two centuries, Ireland was a security threat to Britain, as a hostile France or Spain could exploit dissatisfaction there. During the 19th century, a party of Irish Home Rule (or greater autonomy) developed and by the end of the century the 80-plus Nationalist MPs threatened to paralyse Parliament unless their demands for self-government for Ireland were granted. The Liberals were prepared to grant it, but the Conservatives and Protestant Northern Ireland were bitterly opposed. A Home Rule Act was passed and was due to come into effect in 1914, despite threats of insurrection in the North.

After the First World War, the Government of Ireland Act 1920 partitioned Ireland and offered Home Rule to both North and South. The Northern Protestants, iron-ically, accepted Home Rule, but as a guarantee against separation from the United Kingdom, not a step towards it. In the rest of Ireland, however, Home Rule was rejected as insufficient, and a guerrilla war launched against British rule. Eventually a treaty was signed in 1921 by which the Irish Free State was created as a dominion within the Commonwealth. Gradually, however, Ireland moved towards a republic and left the Commonwealth in 1949. Northern Ireland was given a separate Parliament and control of virtually all administration that did not affect other parts of the UK. The province's public services were to be maintained at the same level as those in the rest of the UK.

Devolution to the Unionist-dominated Stormont Parliament gradually became discredited as the Unionists systematically discriminated against Catholics in housing and public employment (see also Politics in Focus 17.7). Many Unionists are members of the anti-Catholic Orange Order (see Politics in Focus 17.8). Successive British governments were prepared to let the Stormont government go its own way until 1969. In that year, the British government intervened to restore law and order, which had collapsed in the face of violent protests by many Catholics at civil and social discrim-ination and equally violent Protestant reactions. Various reforms were introduced, and the British government gradually came to play a greater role in the province. Eventually, in 1972, the Stormont Parliament and executive were suspended and direct rule from London was imposed. The presence of British troops did not halt the escalation of violence by the sectarian forces of both sides nor prevent the spread of terrorism to the mainland. Since 1969 over 5,000 people have died as a result of violence.

The British pride themselves on the consensual nature of their political culture and a squeaky clean record on human rights. The history of Anglo-Irish relations is incompatible with this self-image.

— **1919–21** The notorious Black and Tans were given an almost free hand to brutally suppress the IRA and Irish rebellion. 'Things are being done in the name of Britain which make her name stink in the nostrils of the whole world.' Report of the Labour Party Commission on Ireland, 1921.

— **1922–72** British governments ignored political and economic discrimination practised by the Protestant majority against the Catholic minority in Northern Ireland.

— **1971** The army was accused of torturing detainees. The government of the Irish Republic took Britain before the European Court of Human Rights. The finding (1978) was that the interrogation methods did not constitute torture but were inhuman and degrading treatment.

During the last 30 years Northern Ireland has been an exception to the rule in respect of civil liberties. Civil rights of the citizens of the province were significantly more restricted than those of citizens of Britain. The Northern Ireland Emergency Powers Act 1973 and the Prevention of Terrorism Act since 1974 permitted trial without jury and allowed the police to arrest and detain suspected terrorists for seven days without charge. In 1988 the accused's right to silence was removed in Northern Ireland.

— **1988–94** A ban was imposed on broadcasting interviews with terrorists or their spokesmen.

The Orange Order was founded in response to the Catholic uprising in 1798. Its activities declined during the 19th century until revived by the Home Rule crises. Officially the Order describes itself as a religious organisation. In practice its objectives blend religion with politics, defending the Protestant religion and supporting union with Britain. For many years the Order has had close links with the Unionist Party and it plays a significant part in uniting Unionists. Between 1922 and 1972 some two-thirds of adult male Protestants in Northern Ireland belonged to the Order. It played a key role in maintaining the public displays and ceremonies associated with Protestant Unionism and served as a link between different sections of Protestant society. Since direct rule from Westminster (1972) its influence on government in Northern Ireland has declined.

The legacy of history and the conflicts of religion and national identity have made politics in Northern Ireland distinctive in the United Kingdom, and it is an exception to all generalisations about the British political culture. Until the July 2005 bombings in London and the subsequent demonisation in some quarters of the Islamic community in Britain, religion has tended to be of limited political significance, but it dominates political life in Northern Ireland.[3] Until early 1995 riots, assassinations and terrorism were everyday occurrences in spite of a heavy military presence. Indeed, one commentator has claimed that the United Kingdom was only 'almost a state', or 'Except for Northern Ireland the United Kingdom is a state' (Rose 1982). The claim was reasonable enough, given that the British government lacked support from a substantial minority, its rules were openly defied, it did not have a monopoly of force and the frontier was not secure.

The options for Northern Ireland

Northern Ireland has been a great strain on British governments, making significant demands on the military and exchequer and damaging Britain's reputation as an upholder of democratic standards and the rule of law. Partition was a failure and direct rule was always seen as transitional. But transitional to what? Each suggested option was not without problems:

- *An independent Northern Ireland* has so far attracted little support; if violence broke out between Protestant and IRA paramilitary groups, it would probably spill over to Ireland and the rest of Great Britain.

- *Repartition*, or a redrawing of the boundary to create more homogeneous Catholic and Protestant communities, would require substantial and probably unacceptable shifts of population.

- The Protestant demand for a restoration of *majority rule* has been rejected by Britain until there are satisfactory safeguards for the minority; suggested safeguards have invariably been rejected by Unionist politicians (see Politics in Focus 17.9).

The Westminster system of government has not been regarded by British leaders as suitable for a society divided into two mutually antagonistic religious communities. Majority rule, a basic feature of British politics, is rejected for Northern Ireland because it means permanent Protestant rule. Successive British governments have therefore experimented with forms of *power-sharing*, which effectively allow the Catholic minority a veto. In many West European states (Switzerland and the Netherlands, for example) bitter social divisions have encouraged leaders to adopt power-sharing arrangements (for example, minority rights to veto, legislation and coalition government). British governments have already recognised Northern Ireland's 'difference' from the mainland by introducing proportional systems for local and Euro elections.

The peace process

In November 1985, the British and Irish governments drew up the *Anglo-Irish Agreement*. This pledged both governments to work towards a framework of rules which would

---

[3] It is interesting to draw parallels between the discourse used in the case of Northern Ireland, where there was a labelling of specific groups—IRA terrorists or UDLA terrorists, rather than Catholic terrorists or Protestant terrorists, compared to the more implicitly racist language used in some sections of the media, in their reporting of the 2005 London bombings in which the term Islamic terrorists or Islamic militants was constantly banded around.

Ireland question

Suggested solutions	Favoured by
United Ireland	Catholic Nationalists; Southern Ireland less enthusiastic
Independent Ulster	Some Protestants who suspect Britain will renege on border/nationality pledges
Total integration of Northern Ireland within Britain	Some Unionists (little support in Britain)
Repartition	Few supporters since recognised as only a partial solution—residual Catholic population
Devolution	Moderates on both sides who are willing to participate in power-sharing
Direct rule	Least worse option; everyone, except Britain, has someone to blame

recognise the different identities of the two communities. It also accepted that any scheme for a united Ireland would depend on the support of a majority of Northern Irish people. But to the fury of Protestants, it also set up an Intergovernmental Conference to allow the two governments to confer on political, security, economic and legal matters affecting Northern Ireland. Significantly, this was the first formal recognition by the British government of the legitimate interest of Dublin in the Northern Ireland question—hitherto an internal matter exclusive to London. The Dublin and London governments effectively decided that they should do something because the two communities were too entrenched to come up with a solution.

In December 1993, John Major and the Irish Prime Minister, Albert Reynolds, signed the so-called *Downing Street Declaration*. The British government offered to hold talks about Northern Ireland's constitution with groups which renounced violence—a clear signal to Sinn Fein—and accepted the right of the North and South to unite if the people so wished. In 1995 peace broke out and the Dublin and London governments moved closer. British ministers opened negotiations with representatives of Sinn Fein and accepted the right of the people in Northern Ireland to choose to join the Republic of Ireland. Government by consent—as in the rest of Britain—might require, in the case of Northern Ireland, a redrawing of the boundaries of the United Kingdom. The stance was a contrast to its defence of the union with Scotland, and was an acknowledgement by ministers that Northern Ireland was different (ie was less 'British' than Scotland). In February 1996, the IRA resumed its bombing campaign when it targeted Canary Wharf in London, and the problem of finding a solution appeared as intractable as ever.

The search for peace resumed under the new Labour Government in 1997 and culminated in the *Good Friday Agreement* signed on 10 April 1998. The former US Senator George Mitchell chaired the talks, and the main political parties signed up to the so-called Mitchell principles for democracy and peace. Crucially, all had to agree to 'democratic and exclusively peaceful means of resolving political issues', as well as the disarming of paramilitary organisations. Progress to the agreement was fraught with problems: some Unionist groups refused to participate in the talks, there were resignations and divisions in parties on both sides about the process, and sectarian killings continued.

The *Good Friday Agreement* was drawn up between the British and Irish governments. It accepted that Northern Ireland's constitutional status would be decided by the majority consent of its people, and that the current wish of the population was to support the union with Great Britain. This was a significant step by Sinn Fein. The parties agreed that if in the future a majority wished to see a united Ireland, both governments would support legislation to bring this about. The Irish Republic undertook to repeal Articles 2 and 3 of the 1937 constitution, which spoke of the eventual goal of a united Ireland. An international commission to review policing—and by implication reform the Royal Ulster Constabulary—was established, and provision made for the gradual release of prisoners from organisations which observed the ceasefire. The Blair Government wished to consolidate the peace by restoring democratic government in Northern Ireland, at the same time as it was creating devolved legislatures in Scotland and in Wales. But in Northern Ireland, it was always understood that there would have to be a power-sharing executive, with membership drawn from all the parties in a new Assembly. It would have executive and legislative authority over matters currently in the hands of the Northern Ireland departments. The Assembly would have 108 members, elected by single transferable vote, based on the existing Westminster constituencies in Northern Ireland (see Politics in Focus 17.10). The British and Irish governments also insisted that the road to devolution would move in tandem with the decommissioning of arms. Referenda on the Agreement received overwhelming support in the South and substantial support in the North.

The Northern Ireland Assembly

As a result of the implementation of the *Good Friday Agreement*, the Northern Ireland political system has been extensively revamped. A North–South Ministerial Council has been established to enable representatives of the Irish government and of the Assembly to consult on matters of shared interest. There is also a British–Irish Council, which contains representatives of the British and Irish governments and representatives from Scotland, Wales and Northern Ireland, as well as the Channel Islands and the Isle of Man. It meets twice a year to discuss shared concerns. A commission on policing was appointed under Chris Patten, which made proposals to make the Royal Ulster Constabulary (RUC) more representative of the community as a whole. This culminated in the abolition of the RUC to be replaced by the Police Service of Northern Ireland (PSNI) in November 2001. Finally, commissions for equality, human rights and reviewing the release of prisoners were also established.

...FOCUS 17.10

...land Assembly

Membership and organisation:

The Northern Ireland Assembly is made up of 108 members, elected by a single transfer vote based on the existing Westminster constituencies in Northern Ireland.

Duration:

A maximum four-year term, but with the possibility of early dissolution.

Organisation and powers:

- The Assembly operates where appropriate on a cross-community basis and is the prime source of authority in respect of all *devolved* responsibilities.

- The Assembly has authority to pass primary legislation for Northern Ireland subject to a number of checks including the European Court of Human Rights and the Westminster Parliament which continues to legislate on *non-devolved* issues.

- A North/South Ministerial Council has been established to bring those with executive responsibilities together in Northern Ireland and the Republic to develop consultation, co-operation and action on matters of mutual interest.

- A British–Irish Council has been established under a new British–Irish Agreement to promote the 'harmonious and mutually beneficial development of relationships between the North, South and the mainland'.

Important elements of the agreement of Ireland bring non-Westminster elements into the policy process and further question the notion of territorial sovereignty within the United Kingdom.

In June 1998, elections to the Assembly were finally held (see Table 17.4). An executive-designate was drawn in proportion from the parties in the Assembly.

The First Minister-designate was David Trimble from the Unionists and the Second Minister-designate Seamus Mallon from the SDLP. The barrier to establishing the executive was decommissioning of arms. The IRA never agreed to this and Sinn Fein only pledged to use its good offices to achieve it. After much agonising, the Ulster Unionist Party finally agreed in November 1999 to take part in the executive—on the understanding that decommissioning would begin in January 2000. Yet, the issue of decommissioning has proved a constant thorn in the early life of the Northern Ireland Assembly. There has been claim and counter-claim on both sides of the divide over the state of play concerning decommissioning and it has prompted the British government to suspend the Assembly on a number of occasions: first on 12 February 2000 the Assembly and the associated institutions were suspended, but were restored on 30 May 2000; they were again suspended for 24 hours on 11 August 2001, 22 September 2001 and once more from 14 October 2002. In the interim, another set of elections took place in November 2003, which the Labour

Party	Votes won	Percentage of vote	Nos of seats in assembly
SDLP	177,963	21.97	24
UUP	172,225	21.25	28
DUP	146,989	18.14	20
Sinn Féin	142,858	17.63	18
Alliance	52,636	6.50	6
UKUP	36,541	4.51	5
PUP	20,634	2.55	2
NIWC	13,019	1.61	2

Government in London hoped would change the balance of the Assembly and reinvigorate the process of devolution in Northern Ireland. Unfortunately for Labour, the hardline Protestant Democratic Unionist Party (DUP), which campaigned against the 1998 Good Friday peace accord, became the biggest party in the new Northern Ireland Assembly having won 30 seats in the election (see Table 17.5). This has raised the fear for Labour that it is now much less likely to achieve a breakthrough in the peace process which continues to remain deadlocked. In June 2005, Peter Hain, the Secretary of State for Northern Ireland requested that the political leaders in Northern Ireland should follow the example of Nelson Mandela in South Africa and go the 'final mile' for peace. Hain observed:

> Obviously, Northern Ireland is not a replica of that situation. But if you are going finally to crack the end of the process that culminated and then went beyond the *Good Friday Agreement*, these are the two parties that can most effectively deliver if they choose to do so. They are polarised. But talking to both sides privately and in public positions, I think there is a will to crack it (*The Times*, 27 June 2005).

On 26 September 2005, a report submitted by General John de Chastelain, head of the Independent International Commission on Decommissioning confirmed to the British and Irish governments that the decommissioning process by the IRA was now complete. The report however was met with a degree of scepticism by some elements with the Protestant community, most notably from the DUP. The key issue was the lack of actual

Party	Votes	Percentage of vote	% change since 1998	Seats won	Nos seats change
DUP	177470	25.6	+7.5	30	+10
SF	162758	23.5	+5.9	24	+6
UUP	156931	22.7	+1.4	27	−1
SDLP	117547	17.0	−5.0	18	−6
Alliance	25372	3.7	−2.8	6	±0
PUP	8032	1.2	−1.4	1	−1
Kieran Deeney (West Tyrone)	6158	0.9		1	+1
NIWC	5785	0.8	−0.8		−2
UKUP	4794	0.7	−3.8	1	−4

substantive evidence confiriming decommissioning. This provoked the leader of the DUP, Ian Paisely to claim:

```
This afternoon the people of Northern Ireland watched a programme
which illustrates more than ever the duplicity and dishonesty of the
two governments and the IRA. Instead of openness there was the cunning
tactics of a cover-up, the complete failure from General John de
Chastelain to deal with the vital numbers of decommissioning. . . . We
do not know how many guns, the amount of ammunition and explosives
that were decommissioned. Nor were we told how the decommissioning
was carried out. . . The so-called Independent International
Commission for Decommissioning could only say to the people of
Northern Ireland that the proof that all the guns and material of
the IRA were decommissioned was in an assurance given to them by the
IRA. Not one iota was given to verify that assurance.
```

As is often the case with the politics of Northern Ireland, attaining any form of a consensus often appears an almost insurmountable task. In the light of the contrasting responses to the formal completion of the IRA decommissioning process, it is worth referring back to the themes addressed in Chapter 1; the politics of Northern Ireland does not clearly fit the Crick definition of 'politics as the art of the possible', but instead, as the Labour Administration, now in its third term continues to discover, it still appears to reflect more an environment of conflict resolution.

Analysing Labour's programme of devolution

A comparison of the various institutions established in Scotland and Northern Ireland indicates that they each have different models of devolution. However, both Scotland and Northern Ireland (when operable) have been given considerable autonomy. In Wales, policy competence is much less. While Scotland has experienced a real and discernible transfer of power from Westminster to Edinburgh, the same cannot be said for Wales. Constitutionally and practically, it may not seem a problem that the constituent parts of the UK have different forms of devolution, but two issues arise:

• these developments undermine the notion that Britain is a unitary state because not all people are being governed in the same way; and

• if devolution is popular in Scotland and Northern Ireland, pressures may develop for similar forms of government in Wales. Such developments, and the pressures they may cause for greater independence, will further undermine the Westminster model as a value system for legitimising government.

The notion of a unitary state is difficult to maintain when a range of forms of governance are operating within various parts of the UK. This problem has been exacerbated by conflicts that have developed between Westminster and the regions in such policy areas as the funding for higher education and the provision of care for the elderly. A crucial point is that devolution is not an end point, but a process of continual negotiation and development. Relationships vary according to circumstance, political control and the tactics of the various parties.

In terms of the policy-making process, what devolution has produced is new structures of dependency within the British system of government. Whilst currently, the most important relationships within the core executive are between the Prime Minister and departments, the Treasury and departments and ministers and officials, devolution has established important new relationships between the centre and the regions. For certain policies, the Prime Minister and departments are dependent on devolved bodies for delivering policies and important processes of exchange occur over issues such as finance and legitimacy. This may create an important constraint on the activities of the centre, especially where devolved governments are controlled by nationalists or coalitions. These new structures of dependency are likely to make greater co-ordination and joined-up government difficult to achieve because London will not have direct control over the devolved bodies. The impact of these new dependency networks have been made apparent already in the area of agriculture, where the Welsh and Scottish bodies have levered extra assistance to all farmers and, in return, the Secretary of State for Agriculture has had to put pressure on his Welsh and Scottish counterparts to lift the ban on beef on the bone before he can do so.

 # Conclusion

It is important not to be too apocalyptic about the potential impact of devolution. Here, it is worth recalling that 30 years ago there was a high profile discourse consigning the union of the United Kingdom to the scrap heap. These views were most coherently expressed in Nairn's (1981, revised 2000) *The Break-up of Britain: Crisis and Neo-Nationalism*. Yet the predictions made then of the likely splitting of the various Celtic nations from England in the face of a rising tide of nationalist demands and the increasing perception that the British state was becoming ungovernable proved wide of the mark. Today, the identity of the United Kingdom remains intact and its breakdown does not appear imminent. This again may reflect the ability of the British state to reform and adapt in order to survive. Mitchell (1999: 608) for example argues that it is possible to classify Britain as a union, rather than a unitary state where: 'integration is less than perfect and that pre-union rights and institutional infrastructure preserving some degree of autonomy and serving as agencies of indigenous elite recruitment are preserved'. In other words, a strong degree of autonomy has always existed, especially in Scotland, and devolution is about changing the form of legitimation rather than governance. In addition, the choices that the Scottish Parliament makes remain constrained, particularly by financial imperatives. Elsewhere, the fact that all EU negotiations have to be conducted through UK representatives reinforces the position of national sovereignty. As far as the EU is concerned, the United Kingdom remains the nation-state that is recognised within Europe and the Scottish Parliament and Welsh Assembly can only lobby informally.

If we return to the analytical approach presented by Bulpitt (1983), it is clear that in an era of devolution, it is the centre that has continued to try and dominate the nature of the new relationships which are being developed with the territories. Yet, their efforts at control have often escalated tensions. For example, the attempts by the Labour Party to impose 'New Labour' candidates on the regional elections generated much local resentment: in Wales, the Blairite Alun Michael failed where the distinctly 'off-message' and 'old Labour' Rhodri Morgan succeeded as First Minister; while in Scotland, Labour successfully ensured that Dennis Cavanagh was not selected to stand as a Labour candidate for the Scottish parliamentary elections creating much friction and anger within the Scottish Labour Party. The usefulness of the Bulpitt analysis, more than 20 years on, is that it continues to explain the nature of Celtic political expression, as a response to the political machinations being emitted from London.

KEY POINTS

- The UK is a four-nation state in which England, as the centre of the unitary government and having 80% of the population, is the dominant nation.

- Scotland has distinctive political, legal, economic, religious and cultural institutions. It now has power to tax and legislate.

- Wales now has an Assembly to add to its Welsh Office. But nationalist sentiment has focused more on cultural recognition than on independence.

- Northern Ireland, though part of the UK, is distinctive. Since its inception, the power-sharing executive in Northern Ireland has been suspended four times, pending progress on decommissioning of arms.

- Violence has ensured that Northern Ireland has remained high on the political agenda in Britain in the last 30 years. The ideological nature of the conflict, coupled with its deep historical roots, makes it less amenable to the British liberal tradition of resolving conflicts by a process of bargaining, negotiation and compromise.

KEY QUESTIONS

(1) To what extent is Bulpitt's 'dual polity' model still a useful analytical approach in an era of devolution?

(2) To what extent has Labour's programme of devolution since 1997 undermined the Westminster model?

(3) Has the 'Irish problem' been solved?

(4) To what extent has Labour's reforms, in particular devolution, affected the nature of power in the policy-making arena?

IMPORTANT WEBSITES

For websites on the Labour Party see www.labour.org.uk, information on reform of the House of the Lords, see www.parliament.uk. For Labour's programme of state reform, the Constitution Unit's site is very useful: www.ucl.ac.uk/constitution-unit/. For issues concerning Labour's reform of the state, go to: the Democratic Audit www.fhit.org/demoicratic_audit/index.html or the site of Charter 88 at www.charter88.org.uk. There are many sites on devolution, including the Scottish Parliament's site: www.scottish.parliament.uk, the Welsh Assembly: www.wales.gov.uk/assembly.dbs and the Richard Commission: www. richardcommission.gov.uk/, and the Northern Ireland Assembly: www.ni-assembly. gov.uk/.

FURTHER READING

For traditional accounts of Labour's relationship with the state, see: R. McKibbin, (1974) *The Evolution of the Labour Party 1910–24*, Oxford: Oxford University Press and D. Kavanagh, (1985) (ed) *The Politics of the Labour Party*, London: George, Allen and Unwin. There are many academic texts on Labour's reform programme and devolution after 1997, these include: S. Ludlam, and M.J. Smith, (eds) (2003) *Governing as New Labour*, London: Palgrave, D. Coates, and P. Lawler, (eds) (2000) *New Labour in Power*, Manchester: Manchester University Press and S. Savage, and R. Atkinson, (eds) (2001) *Public Policy under Blair*, Basingstoke: V. Palgrave, Bogdanor (1999) *Devolution in the United Kingdom*, Oxford: Oxford University Press, A. Marr, (2000) *The Day Britain Dies*, London: Profile Books, C. Pilkington, (2002) *Devolution in Britain Today*, Manchester: Manchester University Press and J. Tonge, (2002) *Northern Ireland: Conflict and Change*, London: Longmann.

CHRONOLOGY

A United Kingdom?

1536	Wales absorbed into England
1707	Act of Union between Britain and Scotland
1801	Act of Union between Great Britain and Ireland to form the United Kingdom
1905	Aliens Act: the first modern immigration control
1920	Government of Ireland Act: partition, Northern Ireland remaining under British rule
1922	Six out of Ulster's nine counties became Northern Ireland
1948	Commonwealth Nationality Act, encouraging immigration from the West Indies
1949	Southern Ireland becomes a republic, but Irish citizens continue to enjoy rights as British citizens
1962	Commonwealth Immigration Act: end of 'open-door' policy
1964	Robbins Report: expansion of higher education creates greater opportunities for children of working-class families
1965	Race Relations Act outlaws discrimination in public places
1968	Race Relations Act establishes Race Relations Board Commonwealth Immigration Act, to reduce flow of Kenyan Asians 'Troubles' begin in Northern Ireland. Enoch Powell makes 'rivers of blood' speech in Birmingham
1969	British troops sent to Northern Ireland as peacekeepers
1971	Immigration Act introduces 'patrials' rule
1972	Direct rule in Northern Ireland; Stormont suspended
1973	Referendum in Northern Ireland on border question
1976	Race Relations Act establishes Commission for Racial Equality
1978	Devolution Bills in Scotland and Wales
1979	Referenda in Scotland and Wales on devolution
1981	British Nationality Act tightens immigration controls

1985	Anglo-Irish Agreement recognizes role for Republic of Ireland in Northern Irish question
1993	Downing Street Declaration
1994	Announcement of IRA and Protestant paramilitary ceasefire
1996	Breakdown of ceasefire
1997	Referenda held on devolution to Scotland, Wales and Northern Ireland
1998	Good Friday Agreement and elections to the Northern Ireland Assembly
1999	Start of Scottish Parliament and Welsh Assembly
1999–2005	Northern Ireland Assembly suspended four times (February 2001, August 2001, September 2001, October 2002)
2000	IRA decommissioning commences
2001	Abolition of the RUC and the creation of the Police Service of Northern Ireland
2003	Second election to the Scottish Parliament, Welsh Assembly and Northern Ireland Assembly
2003	Abolition of the Secretaries of State for Scotland and Wales
2005	Report by the Independent International Commission on Decommissioning that the process now complete

 Visit the Online Resource Centre that accompanies this book
for links to more information on this chapter topic

CHAPTER EIGHTEEN

Political parties

READER'S GUIDE

This chapter considers the important functions carried out by political parties and the different types of party system Britain has had over the past century. It then examines development of the Conservative, Labour, Liberal Democrat and minor parties. It also analyses the structures of the two main parties, tackles the question of where power resides in them, the forces making for cohesion and factionalism and assesses their impact on government policy. Finally, it explores some of the ways in which declining party support and membership is changing the nature of the parties and forcing them to seek alternative ways of performing some of their traditional functions. The ideological aspects of the parties are considered above in Chapter 4.

Introduction

The conduct of democratic politics today is almost inconceivable without organised political parties. By nominating candidates for election parties play the main role in political recruitment; they also mobilise many thousands of people into political activity, influence the political preferences and outlooks of many voters and, by aggregating policies into programmes, enable people to make choices at elections about how they will be governed. Britain is often said to have responsible party government, in the sense of being accountable to Parliament (see Chapter 10). The term 'responsible' refers to the ability of the electorate to elect a government and hold it accountable for its record in office at the next election. The fact that the British parties stand on programmes or manifestos and MPs are highly disciplined in the division lobbies also encourages this sense of electoral responsibility, and is an important part of the Westminster model discussed earlier.

A party's survival depends upon its ability to adapt to the changing political climate. Britain's first past the post electoral system favours a two-party system, but, over time, not necessarily the same two parties. In the early years of the 20th century the Conservative and Liberal Parties were dominant. After 1918, however, Labour was able to capitalise on the extension of the vote to the working class, the growth of the trade unions, a change in

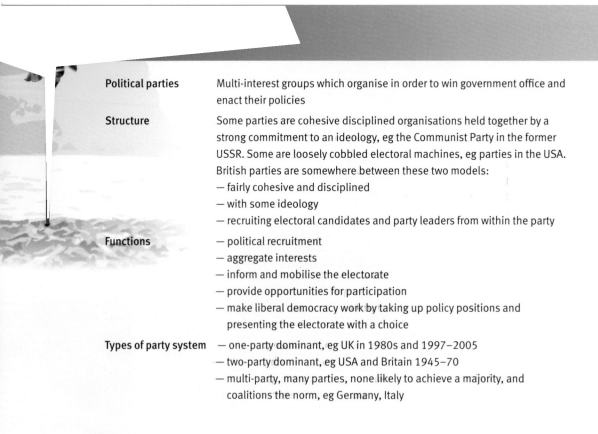

Political parties	Multi-interest groups which organise in order to win government office and enact their policies
Structure	Some parties are cohesive disciplined organisations held together by a strong commitment to an ideology, eg the Communist Party in the former USSR. Some are loosely cobbled electoral machines, eg parties in the USA. British parties are somewhere between these two models: — fairly cohesive and disciplined — with some ideology — recruiting electoral candidates and party leaders from within the party
Functions	— political recruitment — aggregate interests — inform and mobilise the electorate — provide opportunities for participation — make liberal democracy work by taking up policy positions and presenting the electorate with a choice
Types of party system	— one-party dominant, eg UK in 1980s and 1997–2005 — two-party dominant, eg USA and Britain 1945–70 — multi-party, many parties, none likely to achieve a majority, and coalitions the norm, eg Germany, Italy

attitudes towards the state, and divisions in the Liberal Party to replace the latter as a dominant party. After 1992 Labour responded to successive electoral defeats and broader social, economic and cultural change by radically changing its policies and structure. The electoral success of the Conservative Party throughout the 20th century was a testament to its adaptability. It responded flexibly to changes brought by the 1914–18 war, economic depression, universal adult suffrage and the rise of the welfare state until the end of the century. It has been unsuccessful in responding to the social and political changes since 1992.

The party system

Party systems are often defined according to the *number of significant political parties, measured in terms of votes or seats*. Whether Britain is regarded as having a two-party system depends on which criterion is applied. There is a two-party system in Parliament, since the Labour and Conservative Parties between 1945 and 2001 regularly gained over 90% of the seats. But support for the two parties among the electorate is much lower and has steadily declined since 1970. It is also worth noting that the perception of a two-party system being 'normal' in Britain is, strictly speaking, based on a short period of recent political history. Before 1914 the Liberal–Conservative dominance was challenged by the Labour and Irish Nationalist Parties. In the 1920s there was effectively a three-party system, as Labour gradually displaced the Liberals as the second party. Since 1970 the Labour–Conservative dominance has been challenged by the growth of political nationalism in Scotland and Wales, and of the Liberal Party and its successor the Liberal Democrats. Thus the term two-party system is more accurate for the 1945–70 period (see Chapter 20).

Similar qualifications apply to the 'norm' of majority one-party government. Between 1910 and 1915 the Liberal government depended on the support of other parties for a working majority in the Commons. There were also two periods of minority Labour government (10 months in 1924 and 1929–31) and some 13 years of coalition government between 1915 and 1945. Yet since 1945 the Cabinet has consisted of members of one party, and for all but a period of 38 months one party has had an overall majority in the House of Commons.

While no party system is immune to change, the British party system in the 20th century was more stable than those in most other West European countries. In every general election since 1918 the two largest parties in votes and seats have been Conservative and Labour. The 1918 general election witnessed Labour's replacement of the Liberals as the second largest party and the withdrawal from Parliament of the Irish Nationalists. It was the last realignment of the British party system. Since 1918 the effect of the first past the post electoral system (which penalises third parties, whose vote is dispersed) and the adaptability and opportunism of the two established parties have prevented the breakthrough of a viable third party, although the Liberal Democrats with nearly a quarter of the vote in 2005 poses a serious threat. The relative weakness in the 20th century of other social differences has also lessened the opportunity for significant third parties, based for example on language, race or religion, to emerge. But as we see below the dominance of the two parties is under threat and in different parts of the United Kingdom the top two parties differ.

Conservatives

The Conservative Party was the most electorally successful right-wing party anywhere in the 20th century; it was in office, alone or in coalition, for 67 years. It has managed to thrive without a large peasant or rural vote, or exploiting religion or nationalism, sources which have been important for right-wing parties elsewhere (for discussion of Conservative ideas, see Chapter 4). The party's electoral dominance began when the Liberals split over Irish Home Rule in 1886. The party has gained from coalition and from splits in the other parties. But it is also a tribute to its political skill and opportunism that it has managed to win so many elections.

During the post-war period the party has enjoyed two lengthy periods of office, between 1951 and 1964 and between 1979 and 1997. During the first period, it accepted many of the Labour Government's more popular policies, an expanded welfare state, full employment, the NHS, progressive taxation, retreat from Empire and public ownership of the main utilities. Not all Conservatives welcomed this convergence with what regarded as social democratic policies, but they remained a minority in the party, The roll-call of party leaders—Churchill, Eden, Macmillan and Heath—were all in the One Nation tradition (see p 72).

Margaret Thatcher, after she became Prime Minister in 1979, set the party in a different direction, making it more free market in orientation. Mrs Thatcher was no supporter of many aspects of the post-1945 settlement and inevitably, this involved a break with many of her Conservative predecessors' policies, but she was electorally successful and helped to change the political agenda.

Since her dramatic departure from the leadership in 1990 the Conservatives have struggled to assert a clear identity or sense of direction. On the EU, the sceptics have gradually become dominant, particularly in opposing the single currency and an EU constitution. Although the old divisions on economic policy between the drys and wets of the early 1980s have faded, the party lost its reputation for economic competence after the 1992 ERM failure. Surveys for over a decade have shown that voters believed (unfavourably) that the Conservatives place tax cuts above spending more money on public services, and do not trust the party on the core issues of health and education and suspect that the party wishes to privatise them. After a second successive election disaster, in 2001, the party leaders, first Iain Duncan Smith (2001–03) and his successor, Michael Howard (2003–05), declared that tax cuts are secondary to funding good health and education services. But it still failed to change the voters' image of the party (see Chapter 19); surveys show that voters' approval for policies falls when the policy in question is identified with the party. The party takes its traditional firm line on defence, law and order, asylum and immigration (what Andrew Gamble calls 'the strong state'), opposes further integration in the EU and calls for a smaller state, in the sense of less central direction of public services.

Labour

The first steps towards the creation of a Labour Party were taken in 1900 with the establishment of a Labour Representation Committee; the party's name was adopted in 1906. In 1918 it adopted a programme, *Labour and the New Social Order*. This called for the public ownership of the major industries, full employment, and a financial and economic policy to redistribute wealth to the working class; the programme enabled the party to distinguish itself from the Liberal Party. The Liberal Party had split in 1916 and Labour seized the opportunity to become both the second largest party in Parliament and the official opposition. Although the extension of voting rights to all adult males (in 1918) and then women (in 1918 and 1928) made the electorate predominantly working class, Labour enjoyed only two short spells of minority government (1924 and 1929–31) over the next 20 years. It entered the wartime coalition in 1940 and formed its first majority government in 1945. That government did much to shape social and economic agenda of British governments for the following 25 years (see Chapter 4). Its achievements in coping with challenges and in its far-reaching legislation also set the standard for succeeding Labour governments.

Labour then had to decide whether it would consolidate the policies of the 1945 government, notably in extending state ownership to other sectors of the economy and going further with redistribution, or in consolidating the policies. The choice divided the left, who wanted to go further, and the right who wanted to consolidate. There were other divisions between the two factions over foreign policy, membership of the European Community and defence, and the party was an unstable coalition for much of the second half of the 20th century. In 1981 nearly 30 Labour MPs, mainly on the centre right of the party, defected to set up the Social Democratic Party. Electorally, the party went into decline after 1951; between 1951 and 1997 it was in government for only 11 years. The reasons for the decline are explored below. Only once, in 1966, did Labour win an election with a clear parliamentary majority and it usually governed against a background of a weak economy and the pound under pressure, conditions which precluded Labour governments from making their promised advances in welfare provision. By the time James Callaghan's divided government fell in 1979 Labour was associated in many eyes with incompetent economic management and being closely attached with over powerful trade unions. All this was grist to the mill of Labour modernisers who branded the party before Blair as old Labour and unelectable.

Blair and New Labour

By the time Blair succeeded John Smith as party leader in July 1994 he was able to benefit from the actions of Neil Kinnock (Labour leader between 1983 and 1992) who had expelled the extreme left group *Militant* from the party, and abandoned a number of electorally damaging policies. Blair had also concluded that politics had to move beyond the old battles between left and right and that people were resistant to paying higher taxes, to public services which did not provide choice and had no particular identification with state-owned enterprises. These views were a challenge to traditional Labour values (see Chapter 4). A symbol of his break with old Labour was his reform of Clause IV of the party constitution, with its open-ended commitment to public ownership. The new clause states that the party accepts the market. Blair also declared that Labour now accepted virtually the entire Conservative package of trade union reforms and privatisation measures. And, to live down the damaging 'tax and spend' label, which the Conservatives had attached to the party, he and Gordon Brown pledged that there would no increase in income tax rates and for the first two years they would accept the very tight Conservative plans for public spending. Blair's transition to what he called New Labour in his first party Conference speech and a convergence with a number of the Conservative policies, was influenced by various factors, including:

- *Demographic change.* Labour's traditional core voters among manufacturing industry, the working class, council estates and trade unions were all declining. De-industrialisation and new patterns of work were shrinking the working class and trade union membership, creating problems for centre-left parties.

- *Changing public opinion.* Labour's survey research showed how during the 1980s the Conservative Party had captured the themes of choice, ownership, prosperity, and educational standards. Thatcher's income tax cuts, council house sales and trade union reforms were all popular with the voters. Labour modernisers were challenged by further research after the 1992 election defeat, which showed how former Labour voters and 'soft' Conservatives in the south-east felt that the party might be good for the poor, but that it also held back the ambitious and those wanting to get on, that is, people like themselves. The research shaped a largely conservative set of social and economic policies.

- *Circumstances.* The passage of time meant that it was impractical for Labour to maintain its 1983 pledges of reversing many Conservative measures. Britain was now too entwined in the EU to contemplate withdrawal. Returning privatised utilities to public or part-public ownership, and compensating shareholders in the process, would be a major drain on public finances and preclude spending on other more popular programmes.

- *Globalisation and the interdependence of states.* The experience of the Mitterrand government in France in the early 1980s showed that socialism—or even Keynesianism—in one country was no longer possible. Regimes in the West were converging around business-friendly policies of low taxes, low borrowing and flexible labour markets.

- *Shifts in the left.* The collapse of communism in Eastern Europe and break-up of the former Soviet Union in the late 1980s, and the decline of faith in the state as a solution to problems, affected centre-left political parties everywhere. Parties of the left in Australasia and much of Western Europe turned away from public ownership and government intervention in the economy, and squeezed entitlements to welfare benefits.

- *Constitutional reform.* Labour's acceptance in the mid-1990s of what had traditionally been a Liberal Party agenda was in large part a reaction to the long period of Conservative rule (see Chapter 12).

Liberal Democrats

Since the 1918 general election the Liberals, now Liberal Democrats, have been the major third party in the United Kingdom and qualified the accuracy of the label 'the British two-party system'. Until then it was one of the two parties of government and still in office in 1916. In that year it split between the supporters of Asquith, the Prime Minister, and Lloyd George, his successor, and thereafter the party steadily lost support. Since the late 1950s, however, the party had a number of spectacular by-election successes and has seen its general election vote rise to over a fifth of the total, although only since 1997 has it elected a substantial number of MPs. Ironically, the number (51 in 2001 and 62 in 2005) has mattered less because of Labour's large parliamentary majority.

The creation in 1981 of the Social Democratic Party posed the most formidable challenge yet to the two-party system. A number of right-wing Labour MPs became increasingly disillusioned with the left-wing drift of the party's policies and the constitutional changes (particularly those which gave the trade unions greater power in the election of the party leader), and formed the new party. The SDP broadly agreed with the Liberals on many policies, including British membership of the EC, proportional representation, industrial co-ownership, incomes policy, and constitutional reform. In the 1983 general election the Alliance of the two parties gained over 25% of the vote—coming close to overtaking Labour—but fell back slightly in the 1987 election. But on both occasions the operation of the electoral system ensured that it gained only a handful of seats. After the 1987 election leading figures in both parties pressed for outright merger. This was accomplished in 1988 and the new successor party eventually called itself the Liberal Democrats.

Traditionally, the Liberal Democrats (and their predecessor parties) were even-handed in their attitudes to Labour and Conservative. They were regularly embarrassed at general elections by questions about which of the two major parties they would support in the event of a deadlocked Parliament. But after the 1992 election the party abandoned the policy of equidistance between the major parties and agreed to work with others 'to assemble the ideas around which a non-socialist alternative to the Conservatives can be constructed'. As Tony Blair moved the Labour Party even more to the centre ground after 1994 and appropriated many of their policies, so the Liberal Democrats found it difficult to be distinctive. Before the 1997 election the two parties agreed a programme of constitutional reform which they would try and achieve in the new Parliament. Blair and Ashdown, the two leaders, even planned a coalition government with Liberal Democrats taking seats in a Labour Cabinet. Although Labour's landslide majority ruled this out, Blair invited the Liberals to sit on a Joint Cabinet Committee, which discussed constitutional matters and over time other policy questions and set up a Commission to examine electoral reform (see p 398).

In the 2001–05 Parliament Charles Kennedy (party leader 1999–2005) distanced the party from the Labour government. The party abandoned the Joint Cabinet Committee (made difficult anyway because of the lack of government action on the Jenkins Report on electoral reform) and opposed the Iraq war, top-up fees in higher education, and an appointed House of Lords, and advocated a higher tax rate for those earning over £100,000 and a local income tax—something rejected by Blair. Surveys in 2005 showed that Lib Dem supporters were as likely as Labour to regard themselves as left of centre on the political spectrum and the party is to the left of Labour on a number of policies. The election slogan in 2005 was 'The Real Alternative', presumably to Labour.

Other parties

The Scottish National Party emerged as a major electoral force in Scotland in the 1970s but in Westminster elections it has since stalled. Initially, its call for independence was helped by the unpopularity of the Conservative and Labour Parties, the weak UK economy and the discovery of North Sea oil. 'It's Scotland's oil', cried the Nationalists. In 2005 it gained 17.7% of the vote, its lowest share since 1987, and six of Scotland's 59 MPs. In Wales, Plaid Cymru, or nationalist party, gained 12.5% of the vote and returned three of the 40 Welsh MPs. The nationalist parties favour greater autonomy for their nations, leading to independence in the case of Scotland. In the elections for the devolved Scottish and Welsh legislatures the Nationalists do better than at Westminster and have emerged as the main opposition party in both.

In Northern Ireland, the once-dominant—and largely Protestant—Unionist Party has splintered into rival successor parties. Ian Paisley's Democratic Unionists takes a strong line against the IRA and Sinn Fein, regarding the latter as the political arm of the former; it refuses to work with Sinn Fein until it is convinced that the IRA has decommissioned all its weapons. By 2005 the DUP had replaced the Official Unionists as the main voice of Unionism. On the other, mainly Catholic side, Sinn Fein, the political arm of the IRA, has overtaken the Social and Democratic Labour Party (SDLP).

There are also other smaller parties which gain relatively tiny numbers of votes in general elections. Support for the environmentalist Green Party soared to 15% in the European election in 1989, with a good deal of its support coming from disillusioned Alliance voters and it does well in non-Westminster elections which have proportional representation (PR). Its highest share in a general election, however, was in 2005 when it gained 1%. More extreme parties like the BNP and newer ones like the United Kingdom Independence Party (UKIP)—which gained 16% of the vote in the 2004 European election with its simple 'No' cry—or Robert Kilroy-Silk's Veritas failed to reach 1%. But in 2005 George Galloway, having been expelled from the Labour Party, founded his Respect Party and, appealing to a large Muslim vote and hostility to the war with Iraq, captured a seat from Labour.

In the last nine general elections (1974–2005), the combined 'third party' vote (including Liberals) has varied between a fifth and a third of the total and averaged 43 MPs, or 8% of the seats. But in 2005 it reached a third of the vote and 93 seats, the highest figures since 1923. The number of third party MPs proved to be significant between 1974 and 1979 and after 1992, as John Major's Government, hit by rebellions, struggled to find a parliamentary majority. Indeed, in most post-war general elections the figure of 93 seats would have produced a 'hung' Parliament. The 'third force' covers a highly diverse and unstable set of parties and offers little prospect of changing the political landscape. The Scottish Nationalists in 1974 and the Alliance in 1983 seemed to be poised for a breakthrough, but on each occasion they failed. But with PR, as in the elections for the European and Scottish Welsh legislatures, the minor parties do better: the Greens and UKIP have gained seats at Brussels. In view of the different patterns of voting there has emerged a two-tier system of elections and voting.

Constituency parties

The tasks of local parties are to fight elections, nominate candidates, raise funds and propagate party policy. The most important power of the constituency party is the selection of parliamentary candidates, particularly in those seats which the party has a good chance of winning. In all the main parties candidates are selected according to national guidelines and subject to approval by the party headquarters. This is rarely refused, although Labour has assumed the power to impose candidates in by-elections. The Conservative and Labour Parties also have powers to suspend or dismiss a candidate or MP who is judged to have brought the party into disrepute. The Conservative leader Michael Howard dramatically exercised this power on the eve of the 2005 general election when he dismissed the MP Howard Flight because of remarks he made (at a private function) which contradicted official party policy.

The two main parties have had problems attracting and retaining members. Compared with the 1950s, the Labour and Conservative Parties now have considerably fewer members. A similar decline is occurring in many parties in other Western states also—leading some observers to wonder if the age of mass political parties is over—but contrasts with the increase in membership of many voluntary groups. Labour's individual membership in 2004 is just over 200,000, giving an average constituency figure of about 350, with an average of 80 or so 'activist' members in each constituency. The Conservative Party estimates its national membership to be about 300,000. Some strong local Liberal Democratic parties have substantial memberships and compare favourably with any party in the country, but most depend on a small group or an enterprising individual and may come to life only with the stimulus of a general or a by-election. The Liberal Democrat figure is about 90,000.

Parties need active members to raise funds, fight elections by canvassing and addressing and delivering leaflets and to represent the political party in the local community. It is also from such members that local party officers and candidates for local elections are drawn. Knocking on doors at election time is declining, but the modern technologies of telephone canvassing, direct mail and keeping computerised data up to date still require activists. The decline over the years in the number of political activists amounts to what Seyd and Whiteley call a 'de-energising' of grass-roots politics. So-called Conservative modernisers campaigned for the local membership to lose its power to elect the party leader on the grounds it is elderly (average age 62), retired and unrepresentative of the electorate. Interestingly, Labour members do not share Blair's views on income tax, trade unions and economic planning (Seyd 2002).

Organisation and authority

Power within the British political parties has effectively been centralised for many years. Model rules, drawn up by the party headquarters, govern the operation of the constituency parties, which can be disbanded by the centre. In this respect, the 'top down' formal structure of the parties resembles that of the British political system. By tradition, the main task of the parties outside Parliament is to support the party in Parliament. The most formidable challenge to this model was posed by Labour in the early 1980s. Demands by activists for more 'accountability' and 'participation' resulted in the party, between 1979 and 1981, introducing the mandatory reselection of MPs and the election of the party leader by an electoral college in which the votes of MPs were outnumbered by the trade unions and constituency parties. Within the Conservative Party the 'Charter' movement had campaigned for more party democracy, including direct election of the party chairman by members, fuller reporting of party accounts and a greater policy-making role for the annual Conference. William Hague's reforms gave the grassroots a greater say, not least in electing the party leader (see below).

Structure of the Labour Party

There are three major institutions in the Labour Party.

Party Conference meets annually and, according to the party's constitution, it is sovereign and directs the work of the party. Second, there is the *National Executive Committee* (NEC), the *supreme body between conferences*. It traditionally represented the different sections of the party, the unions, MPs, women (for historical reasons) and constituency parties. Reforms in 1997 resulted in the abolition of the women's section and replaced it with a 50% quota for women representatives among the trade union, constituency and MP sections. Representation was also increased for ordinary members, local government and back-benchers. The third major institution is the *Parliamentary Labour Party* (PLP), consisting of Labour MPs.

Under Blair, partly because of his reforms and partly because of the decline of the left, the NEC and the Conference have become more supportive of the parliamentary leadership, or at least provide less of a forum for opposition to the leadership. In 1998 NEC members were forbidden to leak details of its proceedings and were obliged to clear in advance any public comments on NEC business with the party's press office and MPs could be disciplined for 'bringing the party into disrepute'. Blair wished to avoid a repetition of the situation in the Conservative Party under John Major when dissenting MPs regularly broadcast their criticisms and undermined the leadership; the same had happened with Labour in the 1970s and 1980s. Conference still occasionally defeats the platform but ministers ignore it.

Labour differs from other British parties in that it has affiliated to it a major producer interest—trade unions. As an organisation the party has been weak in terms of finance and members, while the trade unions have long been strong in both. This strength helped them to have a major voice in the policy-making bodies of the party, the NEC and Conference.

Union influence was reinforced by new arrangements for electing the leader (1981) which gave the unions 40% of the electoral college vote, later reduced to one-third. Trade union power in Conference rested on the block vote, whereby the majority decides how the entire union vote is cast. In the 1970s the five largest unions or, more precisely, majorities in them could together decide the outcome of a Conference vote. The result was that if party leaders and big unions agreed, then they could 'manage' Conference. Not surprisingly, a key to successful leadership involved keeping the unions on side.

Yet for all this 'power' of the unions, it is an exaggeration to see them as manipulating the party. The unions are not of one mind on many issues and have traditionally left 'political' or non-industrial issues to the parliamentary leaders. The unions' effective power was usually concentrated on the few issues they regard as priorities. Hence the importance of events in the 1960s and 1970s when Labour governments transgressed the traditional separation of spheres by 'invading' trade union areas of wage bargaining and industrial relations (Minkin 1991). The outbreak of strikes in the 'winter of discontent' in 1979 dealt a fatal blow to an already weak Labour government and for several years the public perception of the close links between the party and the unions was an electoral handicap.

New Labour was keen to show its independence from the unions. As part of its drive to 'modernise' its policies and its image, it reformed its institutions and the role of the unions in the party. In spite of significant union opposition the then Labour leader John Smith persuaded the 1993 Conference to adopt 'one member one vote' (OMOV) for elections at all levels of the party, effectively ending the union block vote. In 1993 the party reduced the size of the union vote at Conference to 70%, with the intention of providing more incentive for constituency parties to recruit members, and reduced it further to 50% in 1995. Some of the unions, including the largest, the Transport and General Workers Union, which opposed Blair's revision of Clause IV in 1995, did not ballot members—a poor advertisement for union democracy. Unions are kept at arm's length in the modern Labour Party. But when it came to selecting a party candidate other than Ken Livingstone to contest the London mayoral election in 2000 the leadership was happy to mobilise the union block vote to get its way.

Structure of the Conservative Party

Until 1998 the Conservative structure was simpler, largely because the ultimate authority of the party leader was clear. The *parliamentary party* consisted of Conservative peers and MPs, and the latter until 2001 elected the party leader. In opposition the leader selects members of the Shadow Cabinet or so-called Consultative Committee. The party leader appointed the chairman and major officers of Central Office, which directed the *party organisation*, including the Research Department. Finally, there was the *National Union*, a federation of the constituency parties, which organised the party's annual Conference.

In 1998 William Hague sought to emulate Blair in modernising the party. His aims were to boost individual membership—and this could be done by allowing members a greater voice in forming policy and electing the leader—and give the centre more power to discipline wayward MPs (in the 1992 Parliament a dozen Conservative ministers were forced to resign from the Government because of personal misconduct). A ballot of members approved the proposals. They included the creation of a Board to be responsible for a single party outside Westminster, and control the organisation, including Central Office budgets, senior party appointments and finance. Conservative MPs, the constituency associations, and the party bureaucracy at Central Office are now united in a single organisation. The Board also oversees a new Ethics and Integrity Committee, which has the power to suspend or expel any member judged to have brought the party into disrepute. In 2000, this body expelled for five years the disgraced Lord Archer (who had been selected as the party's candidate for the London mayoral election) from the party. Hague also introduced a centralised national membership, partly to allow the party to conduct ballots. Most controversially, the members were given the right to elect the party leaders from a short list of two chosen by MPs.

The new arrangements in turn weakened the MPs because they no longer controlled the choice of leader, the leader surrendered some powers to the Board, and members clearly were the gainers from the reforms. When the new election procedure was put to the test for the first time in 2001 the members elected Iain Duncan Smith over Ken Clarke as leader. Only a third of MPs, however, had voted for Duncan Smith and a large number were bitterly opposed to him. The grassroots members elected a candidate who lacked the support of many of the MPs, hardly a formula for effective leadership. In November 2003 MPs carried a vote of no confidence in Duncan Smith and, to avoid a contest and the participation of the membership, they elected Michael Howard by acclamation. But Hague's hope that the reforms would boost membership was not fulfilled and, backed by most Conservative MPs, Michael Howard proposed after the May 2005 general election that the choice of the leader be reserved for the MPs. Although a majority of members voting supported this change to the constitution it fell short of the necessary two-thirds majority to make the change.

Conservative Conferences have differed from Labour's. The Conference resolutions are only 'advisory', expressions of opinion and the party leaders may or may not act on them. But Richard Kelly's studies of Conservative Conferences argue that the support shown by representatives at Conferences has less to do with deference than with the leadership correctly anticipating and responding to the concerns of members. When dissent breaks out it is usually because the leadership has been out of touch.

 ## Power in the parties

There has long been debate about the distribution of power in the parties, particularly in the Labour Party. Labour has caricatured the Conservatives as elitist, with the party leader and his colleagues being relatively immune to grassroots pressure and the extra-parliamentary organisations being supportive and deferential. Conservatives, by contrast, have praised the support and loyalty shown by the members and the opportunities this provides for the exercise of firm leadership. Labour's doctrine of intra-party democracy, according to which the party Conference makes party policy and the parliamentary leadership is accountable to the membership, has long been defended by party supporters and attacked by Conservatives. Robert McKenzie's classic book *British Political Parties* (1963) claimed (like many Conservatives) that Labour's intra-party democracy and the sovereignty of the party Conference are incompatible with the British constitution. He posed the question: to whom Labour MPs are ultimately responsible—the party Conference or parliamentary leadership—when the two bodies disagree?

But, according to McKenzie's reading of the party histories, the actual distribution of power in the parties, when in government, is similar. He showed that Labour leaders managed, by various stratagems, compromises, accidents, and through the willingness of the large trade unions to back the parliamentary leadership, to avoid the strict regime of Conference control. The impact of Conference resolutions which were contrary to the wishes of the parliamentary bodies was softened by other provisions in the party constitution which allowed the parliamentary party to decide 'the timing and application' of the policy in Parliament, and that only Conference resolutions carried by a two-thirds majority automatically become party policy. Labour Party leaders since 1935 have been reasonably secure in office—indeed, their average tenure has been longer than that of Conservative leaders and none has been pushed out. The Conservative Party outside Parliament has been more supportive of the leader, particularly when the party is in office. Loyalty to the leadership has been a more reliable rallying cry than loyalty to something as debatable as Conservative principles. Yet Conservative MPs have been willing to withdraw support and force out several leaders, including Austen and Neville Chamberlain, Sir Alec Douglas-Home, Edward Heath, Mrs Thatcher, Iain Duncan Smith, and severely hampered John Major after 1992.

Disappointment with the record of the Labour governments (1974–79) and their failure to implement a number of left-wing Conference resolutions encouraged the left to work for a change in the formal structure of the party. Between 1979 and 1981 the reformers wrested from the MPs their exclusive right to elect the party leader and deputy leader, made the reselection of MPs mandatory for all local parties, and won a series of Conference votes for left-wing policies. MPs were made more accountable to local activists, the PLP to extra-parliamentary pressures, and the leader's election was decided by a largely extra-parliamentary electorate. Many of the changes were made in the name of making the party more democratic. These developments appeared to refute McKenzie's thesis about the autonomy, in practice, of the PLP. There was no doubt that the extra-parliamentary party was in the driving seat at this time.

The victory was short-lived. Successive election defeats encouraged beliefs that the party (a) should be less responsive to the activists, assumed to be left-wing and unrepresentative of Labour voters (Smith 1994; Hughes and Wintour 1990; Shaw 1996) and (b) required a strong leader to compete with Mrs Thatcher, one who was clearly not beholden to the trade unions or Conference. Neil Kinnock, in spite of the constraints of the new rules, managed gradually to get his way on most policies and undo some of the effects of the constitutional changes. Labour leaders appear to be as strong as ever in relation to the extra-party structure.

After the 1992 election defeat Labour established a 180-member National Policy Forum (NPF), to oversee the work of eight policy commissions. It reports to a Joint Policy Committee, chaired by the party leader, and which decides the policy motions on which Conference votes. As a result Conference has become 'tamer' and more stage-managed, particularly since Tony Blair became leader in 1994. The weight of the unions has been reduced in the new structure; they have only 42 seats on the NPF and 12 of the 32 places on the NEC. Blair also bypassed the Conference by using ballots of members to force through his changes to Clause IV to the party constitution (see Politics in Focus 18.2) and again for the party's draft general election manifesto before 1997. Constitutional purists objected (correctly) that bypassing the activist-dominated party Conference was unconstitutional.

The power relationships in each party have varied over time with the issues, personalities, and events, and according to whether or not the party is in office. It is clear that the centre of power in the Conservative Party has always lain with the parliamentary party. The main challenge to the authority of the Conservative leader has come from parliamentary colleagues; to the Labour leader from the NEC, leaders of the major trade unions, and senior politicians who can count on the support of these groups. In recent years, the balance within the Conservative Party has shifted between the leader and the MPs, as the former is now is short listed and may be dismissed by the latter in an annual election, and leader and mass membership, as the latter choose the leader.

After 1987 Kinnock, Smit and Blair had their way on the important issues and, even in opposition, wielded as much power over the party as previous Labour premiers. They exploited the party's sense of frustration at being out of office for so long and a realisation that the spectacle of Conference defying the leader was not calculated to enhance the party's appeal to voters. The 'electoral politics' meant that the desire to support the leadership, provide an image of a united party, and adopt policies to please the electorate rather than Conference have mattered more in strengthening the leader's position.

Two conclusions may be offered about the party structures and how they operate. First, the parties outside Parliament should be seen as pressure groups on the parliamentary leadership. This is more apparent with Labour because of the position granted to the trade unions in bodies like the annual party Conference and the NEC. Second, the different histories and origins of the parties have been important. Labour, unlike the Conservatives, was created from outside Parliament, and during its first 20 years the trade unions were a more substantial and influential body than the small number of Labour MPs. The party and movement acquired a marked extra-parliamentary character early on, one that it has never entirely lost. But for most of the 20th century, the Conservative leader was also Prime Minister and his colleagues were Cabinet ministers, while Labour leaders have spent more time in opposition. Since 1922, all 13 Tory leaders except the last four Hague, Duncan-Smith, Howard and Cameron have been Prime Minister at some time: as of 2006 this has been so for only five of Labour's 12 leaders.

Party finance

British parties, locally and nationally, struggle to raise the money to run effective organisations. Both Labour and Conservative Parties depend on contributions from individual members, wealthy supporters and interest groups—in Labour's case from affiliated trade unions.

Until recently, the sources of Conservative finance have been (a) quotas from constituency associations, (b) contributions from business and, (c) other funds, routed through such bodies as Aims of Industry or British United Industrialists, or secret 'one-off' gifts. Yet in recent years the loss of members and widespread doubts that the party could win an election hit those sources. During the 1990s the party was substantially in debt and the secret and substantial donations from overseas were linked in the public mind with other evidence of sleaze in the party.

Labour has traditionally relied heavily on affiliated trade unions for its finance. In the 1980s, however, unions had their own problems, including a decline in membership and resources. Labour has succeeded in diversifying its sources of finance. But the party still draws two-thirds of its funds from the unions. The party has turned to wealthy individuals for donations and standing order payments from members to boost finances.

Labour's 1997 manifesto promised to 'clean up politics', particularly over party financing, and regulate the parties. The Registration of Political Parties Act 1998 required parties to register with the Registrar of Companies. The Government also largely accepted the Neill Committee's proposals on party finance for its Political Parties, Elections and Referendum Act 2000. The Act requires that donations over £5,000 nationally and £1,000 locally should be publicly declared, including payments in kind and 'blind trust' arrangements, or the provision of funds by donors, who are not known to the beneficiary. It refused to allow tax relief for small contributions and ruled out donations from people who are not eligible to be registered to vote in British elections. It also imposed a limit on the amount parties could spend on campaigns, locally and nationally. The Acts have introduced a substantial degree of regulation of the activity of parties and greater transparency in their finances.

'Cash for favours' had been strongly and damagingly associated with the Conservatives before 1997. And for many years researchers have reported that many large donors to the party's coffers received political honours. But Blair's Labour Party has not escaped controversy. The change in government policy on tobacco advertising in sport following the £1 million donation to the Labour Party from Bernie Eccleston, head of Formula One racing, seemed to be a clear case of cash for influence. It was followed by revelations of similar benefits for large contributors like Mittal and the Hinduja brothers and Blair has been as attentive as any Conservative Prime Minister in ensuring that party donors receive political honours.

Convergence and divergence

Study of the parties' election manifestos shows that there have been clear and persistent differences between Labour and Conservatives on such issues as public ownership (more or less), council house building (more or less) and the priority accorded to increases in public expenditure versus reductions in income tax. Labour Party rhetoric refers to 'equality', 'redistribution', 'investment' in public services and 'social justice'; Conservative Party rhetoric refers to 'personal responsibility', 'freedom', 'incentives', 'the burden of taxation' and 'enterprise'. The forces making for differentiation arise from party tradition and ideology, calculations about electoral support (particularly among existing and potential supporters), reactions to what the other party in government is doing, and the need to justify a party's established policy. In some other areas, such as foreign policy, defence (apart from Labour's support for unilateralism in the 1980s) and Northern Ireland the parties have not sought out distinctive and well-publicised policy lines. But much of the pressure for divergence or convergence depends on which policy group is dominant in the party. A Thatcher-led Conservative Party presented a sharper contrast to Labour than did the party of the 1950s and 1960s, and when the left is stronger in the Labour Party, as in the early 1980s, it promises to break with the policies of consensus and continuity.

The parties' images of themselves and their opponents and the media presentation of policies as the struggle of the government versus the opposition may suggest that the two parties are monoliths. This has rarely been the case and several issues in recent years have proved especially troublesome for the two parties. Entry to and attitudes to greater integration in the EU, defence, the poll tax, the Iraq war, health and welfare reform, anti-terrorist legislation and top-up fees in higher education have all triggered major divisions within one or both of the major parties.

The continuities in many policies between the two parties when in office, even when they have promised differently, and the U-turns which governments in the 1960s and 1970s made in mid-term, encouraged the suspicion that a good part of the difference between the parties is between the 'ins' and 'outs', that is, that a party's policies depend largely on whether or not it is in government. In the 1960s and 1970s the party in opposition usually criticised the government of the day, particularly for imposing controls on incomes, social and economic policies, and public expenditure priorities. Yet when that party was in office it usually pursued policies not dissimilar to those it criticised. Proximity to, or occupation of, office appears to be a powerful educator. Of course, a government may claim that circumstances are never exactly as similar as they appeared when it was in opposition. In office the pressures and influences are different, and the 'governmentalists' in the party have greater sway. It is also the case that a series of election defeats can force a party to move to new ground. After the severe defeat in 1983 and losses in subsequent general elections Labour steadily accepted a number of Conservative policies it had earlier opposed. After the 1997 and 2001 election defeats the Conservatives have had to come to terms with Labour's new agenda, particularly the constitutional changes and big increases in spending on health and education. In 2005 the Conservative manifesto pledged that it would match Labour's spending plans on health, education and pensions, although voters were not convinced.

In Britain the two largest parties have usually tried to be 'catch-all' parties, appealing to a wide range of groups in search of votes and playing down ideological or sectional appeals (Labour's left-wing platform in 1983 and the party's worst election result for over 50 years only confirmed the lesson, as did the Conservative defeat in 2001). Blair has deliberately sought to attract traditional non-Labour voters into his New Labour 'big tent' and been highly successful. In 2001 and 2005 the party attracted almost as large a share of the middle class vote as the Conservatives did. As explained in Chapter 20 the Conservatives are no longer the successful 'catch-all' party they once were. The existence of two large parties has also meant that the parties themselves have been embryonic coalitions, embracing their own left and right wings.

In many respects New Labour's agenda has grown out of acceptance of or built on the Thatcherite policies of the 1980s. This is particularly so in respect of the economic liberalism (eg privatisation), flexible labour markets (eg the trade unions reforms) and social conservatism (eg proposals for sacking incompetent teachers, increasing targets and measurements of performance across the public sector) and a tough stand on law and order. Richard Heffernan (2002) has pointed to the 'uncanny' resemblance between Labour's economic priorities in the 1997 manifesto and the 1979 Conservative manifesto: to control inflation as a first priority; curb public expenditure; reduce public borrowing; oppose punitive taxation; restore incentives to business and enterprise; and regulate trade unions. In other words, the 1997 general election was more about policy continuity than discontinuity, and convergence rather than divergence, because of Labour's acceptance of many of the policy changes of the 1980s. By 2005, as noted, the boot was on the other foot as Conservatives had accepted much of Labour's agenda.

Old Clause IV (1918)   'To secure for the workers by hand or by brain the full fruits of their industry and the most equitable distribution thereof that may be possible upon the basis of the common ownership of the means of production, distribution and exchange, and the best obtainable system of popular administration and control of each industry and service'.

New Clause IV (1995)   'The Labour party is a democratic socialist party. It believes that by the strength of our common endeavour, we achieve more than we achieve alone, so as to create for each of us the means to realise our true potential and for all of us a community in which power, wealth and opportunity are in the hands of the many not the few, where the rights we enjoy reflect the duties we owe, and where we live together, freely, in a spirit of solidarity, tolerance and respect'.

Party unity and discipline

British parties have long been noted for their remarkable unity when it comes to voting in divisions in the Commons. Party loyalty has been crucial to the executive's dominance of the House of Commons, to its secure tenure of office until the next election, and to the idea of responsible, programmatic, party government. The commitment of most MPs to a party programme and the likelihood that one party will have a majority in Parliament enables the British electorate to choose between two potential parties of government at general elections.

Discipline is one reason why party MPs vote together in the House of Commons. A party line is agreed after soundings and discussions between the Chief Whip and MPs, and the final decision is expected to be binding on all MPs. A member who defies a three-line whip (the strongest form of instruction to follow the line) runs the risk of having the party whip withdrawn; this is tantamount to expulsion from the party. The Conservative leader always appoints the Chief Whip, the Labour leader only when s/he is Prime Minister; in opposition Labour's Chief Whip is elected by the PLP. Significantly, Blair broke with the tradition and appointed his own Chief Whip in 1995. The tasks of the Chief Whip and his assistants are to try and ensure that enough members are present in the House of Commons or nearby to vote the appropriate way in divisions, and to act as intermediaries between the leaders and backbenchers. Whips try to gauge the mood of members, assess how they will express their unhappiness with party policies, and cajole, bully or conciliate the potential dissident. Expulsion is very rarely used if the number of likely dissidents is large, because it may then be counter-productive. In 1971, when nearly a third of Labour MPs defied the whip and voted for membership of the EC, there were so many rebels that the whips were powerless; safety for the rebels lay in numbers. This happened again in the 2001 Parliament when many Labour MPs broke ranks over top-up fees and the war on Iraq. In 1995 the Conservative whip was withdrawn from nine MPs who had persistently rebelled on European issues. But as most of the rebels gained the support of their local associations and the government's majority in the Commons was threatened, the whip was soon restored. Invoking disciplinary sanctions reflects the failure of the normal process of decision-making in the parliamentary party.

We therefore have to look for more positive reasons for party loyalty. Most MPs are aware that they are more widely known to constituents for their party label than for their personalities and political ideas; if they want to be re-elected by the voters then a party label is virtually a prerequisite. Moreover, they will have built up loyalty to the party and to the parliamentary colleagues and local supporters with whom they have been associated for many years. MPs also know that a divided and faction-ridden party is not likely to be well regarded by the electorate.

The increase in the number of government appointments in the hands of the Prime Minister has also helped the executive; around a hundred MPs receive some kind of appointment, from Cabinet ministers down to parliamentary private secretary. As all are bound by collective responsibility, a Prime Minister is virtually assured of the support of a third of his party in any vote—the so-called payroll vote. Office, or the hope of it, helps loyalty. But again, this is not a complete explanation, for many MPs have no hope or expectation of office. The threat of dissolution is hardly a sanction to wield against dissident MPs. The likely outcome is that a divided government would be defeated in the election, the Prime Minister lose office, and many MPs in marginal constituencies forfeit their seats.

Party government?

A British government, which has an assured majority in the House of Commons and some control of the parliamentary timetable is usually able to carry through its major legislation. Yet if the ability to pass measures through Parliament reflects the government's strength, then the failure of the government to realise its broader policy goals *vis-à-vis* society and the economy may correlatively be taken as a sign of its weakness. Advocates of responsible party government in Britain, and representative government in general, usually assert that parties should have an impact—an intended one. For parties to play a minimal role in government weakens the influence of elections and the electorate. Yet parties in office often disappoint their supporters.

There is no completely satisfactory way to test for the effects of a party in government (Rose 1984). One may compare the promises and statements of intent of governments with actual outcomes at the end of their terms. But one then has to speculate about what might have happened if a different party had been in control. Perhaps, given the circumstances, another party might have acted similarly. Governments may have other effects—on public opinion or patterns of public spending, for example—than those planned, or their policies may be modified in response to changing events or shifts in public opinion.

Academics and politicians have propounded two rival views about the effects of parties. One is that parties are too strong because in government they can wield the power of the elective dictatorship. This view is primarily a statement of the ability to pass legislation rather than to shape society—look at the failures to promote greater economic equality or less violent crime or better public transport. But it seemed appealing during the long period of Conservative rule under Thatcher between 1979 and 1990, although less persuasive under John Major after 1992.

A contrasting view is that parties are weak. Parties usually are poorly prepared in opposition, whereas civil servants are well entrenched and have many strategies for frustrating ministers who pursue policies which the civil servants regard as impracticable. Moreover, the same recurring problems and similar constraints, or the sense of 'ongoing reality', may steer parties, regardless of ideological leanings, into following a broadly similar set of policies (Rose 1984). A good part of 'reality' comes in the form of inheritance of public policy and government spending from previous governments. In 1990 almost three-quarters of public spending still went on policy commitments made by governments before 1939 (Rose and Davies 1995). Another limit on national government is the impact of events beyond its borders, for example the quadrupling of Arab oil prices in 1974, or of policy decisions taken elsewhere, for example from the European Union. If one tries to relate party incumbency to trends in economic conditions—rates of inflation, unemployment, growth and prosperity—it is striking how modest have been the differences associated with party control of government.

The Thatcher governments were an exception to the weakness thesis. They were committed to shift the balance from the state and collectivist values to market forces and individualism. Many nationalised assets were sold off to private investors, and many services and goods provided by local and central government were either contracted out or 'privatised'. It shifted the balance from direct to indirect taxation. Its industrial relations legislation, aided by changing patterns of work and high unemployment, severely weakened the trade unions. It would be difficult to argue, in the light of this experience,

Current trends and pressures for change include:

(1) The arrangements for electing the Conservative leader hardly command confidence. 61% of the membership voted for a change (to confine the vote to MPs) but the status quo remained because two-thirds did not vote for change. More seriously, the party needs to 'reinvent' itself if it to be a realistic challenger for office again.

(2) The parties are now subject to greater regulation by law in the form of the Political Parties Act 1998 and the Political Parties, Elections and Referenda Act 2000. Their operations are also affected by the deliberations of the Electoral Commission set up to oversee the legislation and conduct of elections and referenda.

(3) Labour might review its link with the trade unions, in part to shrug off its sectional image and perceptions that it is 'in hock' to the trade unions. A weakening of ties might pose a major question for party finances.

(4) Financial pressures affect the main parties. Even the Conservative Party, traditionally the wealthiest British party, has struggled with persistent deficits for at least a decade, and relied on loans from wealthy supporters. The two main parties are relieved that there is now a limit on election spending. The limit is less of a bother to the Liberal Democrats because they do not spend even near to the limit.

(5) A question on the agenda is whether Britain, like most other Western democracies, should provide state funding for political parties. There is a relatively small amount (approx. £3 million) of 'Short Money' available to the opposition parties for their parliamentary work, but at present all funding of election campaigns has to be raised by the parties themselves.

(6) The question of funding has been exacerbated by dwindling party membership. Between 1953 and 2004 Conservative Party membership fell from 2.75 million to some 300,000. Labour membership over the same period fell from 815,758 individual members to some 200,000.

Falling membership also brings associated problems of narrowing the field of political recruitment and reducing the campaigning and educational effectiveness of parties at local level.

that a determined government 'makes no difference'. Since 1997 Blair can point to the many constitutional changes, redistribution via the tax credits system to the working poor, child care, the minimum wage, Social Chapter and independence for the Bank of England, all of which are likely to outlast his Government and would probably not have been introduced under a Conservative government. But his 'big idea' is to transform the welfare state by introducing more diversity among providers (encouraging more private providers) and choice for consumers, particularly in health and education. He hopes that his third term will enable his Government to entrench was he calls a 'progressive consensus'. If he succeeds his Government will probably be ranked along with those of Attlee and Thatcher as agenda-setting (Seldon and Kavanagh 2005).

 # Conclusion

There have been claims that the decline of political parties suggests that the era of the mass political party may be drawing to a close (Politics in Focus 18.3). Declining levels of strong party identification and falling levels of party membership and activity indicate the marginal role of political parties in the lives of most people across much of Europe and the US. Surveys report that very few people are willing to carry out demanding political activities for the party they support. In 2004 about 800,000, or less than 3% of voters, are members of all parties.

The widespread agreement among voters on many values means that the Labour and Conservative Parties do not represent sharply contrasting values or issue preferences among their supporters. In some respects the parties have become less ideological, perhaps a response to the growth of a more middle class electorate and a decline in the so-called 'great' issues. Politics appears to be more technical and managerial. Parties may also be less deeply rooted in society compared to the time when social class identities and trade unions were stronger. Interest groups are reluctant to associate closely or openly with political parties and Labour's connections with the trade unions have been loosened. Party leaders also complain that they are unfairly treated by the mass media and this limits their ability to make their cases to the public. For example, no party has a direct connection with a national paper and parties cannot purchase broadcasting time (Kavanagh 1994; Mulgan 1994).

Parties are adapting to these broader changes by contracting out some of their functions. Before and during election campaigns they recruit technical experts to assist with publicity, media presentation, opinion polling; the latter is often more important than party Conferences in informing party leaders about the public mood. Parties have increasingly turned to independent or sympathetic think-tanks for ideas about policy, Labour to Demos and the Institute of Public Policy Research (IPPR), the Conservatives to the Social Market Foundation (SMF), Adam Smith Institute (ASI) and Centre for Policy Studies (CPS). Parties have also drawn on cross-party sources for policy advice. The IPPR Commission on Social Justice and the Welfare State included experts from outside the Labour Party. Blair has been keen to look outside established party figures (eg Lords Sainsbury, Falconer and Birt) in making appointments as ministers and advisers.

The immediate futures for all three main parties are shrouded in uncertainty. What direction will a post-Blair Labour Party take? How deeply rooted in the party is Blair's commitment to more market-oriented public services? In trying to 'reconnect' with the voters how will the Conservatives reconcile the division between advocates of a smaller state and less state provision and financing of services and advocates of well-funded public services? Is David Cameron's emphasis on changing the party's image more to do with presentation than substance (after all, he wrote the party's 2005 election manifesto)? Because the party is so broadly Eurosceptic it may be that the bitter divisions over Europe of a decade may have passed. And how do the Liberal Democrats position themselves against the other two parties; do they emphasise economic liberalism and a greater role for markets as some wish or do they cling to the collectivism (more taxes and state spending) and alliance with public service producers as in the 2005 manifesto?

The changed rules on party finance, new electoral arrangements for non-Westminster elections and emergence of coalition governments in Scotland and Wales, acceptance of a political marketing ethos and multi-tier levels of governance are providing a changed context for political parties. Yet British government, for good or ill, is still party government, and the health of one is inseparable from the health of the other.

KEY POINTS

- Parties perform essential functions of recruiting political leaders, mobilising voters and presenting voters with policy choices.

- Responsible party government depends on programmatic disciplined parties, which allow the electorate to reflect upon the governing party's record and choose between competing programmes for the future.

- In terms of voter preferences Britain has a multi-party system, but in terms of parliamentary seats and chances of forming a government, Britain has a two-party system.

- The Conservative Party's electoral success in the 20th century is a testament to its adaptability, the political skill of its past and present leaders, and a divided opposition. In the new century, however, it has not displayed these strengths.

- The Labour Party began life as a political wing of the trade union movement. The close association between the trade unions and the Labour Party has been a source of criticism and serves to undermine the Labour Party's claim to be a national non-sectional party. This relationship has been changed under Blair's leadership.

- With the notable exception of the nationalist votes concentrated in the Celtic fringes, third parties are disadvantaged by the electoral system. But the support for the Liberal Democrats is proof of the dissatisfaction with the two main parties, whose dominance in the House of Commons owes much to the electoral system.

- Party unity and discipline is partly explained by the whipping system and expectations of constituency parties, but ambition, linked with patronage and shared values also play a significant role.

- The weakening of partisanship among the electorate has had an impact throughout the party system, reducing numbers of activists and potential recruits, etc. This has forced parties to revamp their images and to contract out some traditional functions. The introduction of PR or the continued decline in support for the two main parties may lead to coalitions, and in that event may bring about other constitutional changes.

KEY QUESTIONS

(1) Why has the Labour Party been more prone to splits and factions than the Conservative Party? Is this still true?

(2) Why has the Conservative Party been so unsuccessful electorally since 1992?

(3) Can the Labour Party claim to be more internally democratic than the Conservative Party?

(4) Does Britain have party government?

IMPORTANT WEBSITES

For the main party sites see www.conservatives.com; www.labour.org.uk; http://libdems.org.uk.

FURTHER READING

A good introduction is R. Garner and R. Kelly (1998) *British Political Parties Today,* Manchester: Manchester University Press. On recent developments see P. Webb (2000) *The Modern British Party System,* London: Sage; L. Baston and S. Henig (2005) 'The Labour Party' in A. Seldon and D. Kavanagh (eds) *The Blair Effect 2001–5,* Cambridge: Cambridge University Press. On Labour ideas and practice see A. Giddens (2000) *The Third Way and Its Critics,* Oxford: Polity; A. Seldon and K. Hickson (eds) (2004) *New Labour Old Labour,* London: Routledge; C. Hay (1999), *The Political Economy of New Labour,* Manchester: Manchester University Press; S. Ludlam and M. Smith (eds) (2001) *New Labour in Government,* Basingstoke: Palgrave; and E. Shaw (1996) *The Labour Party Since 1945,* Oxford: Oxford University Press. On the Conservatives see M. Garnett and P. Lynch (eds) (2003) *The Conservative Party in Crisis,* Manchester: Manchester University Press; A. Seldon and S. Ball (eds) (1995) *The Conservative Century,* Oxford: Oxford University Press; S. Ball and A. Seldon (eds) (2005) *Recovering Power. The Conservative Party Since 1867,* Basingstoke: Palgrave; S. Ludlam and M. Smith (eds) (1996) *Contemporary British Conservatism,* Basingstoke: Palgrave; and the special issue on the Conservative Party, *Political Quarterly,* vol 75 (2004).

 Visit the Online Resource Centre that accompanies this book for links to more information on this chapter topic

CHAPTER NINETEEN

Parliament

READER'S GUIDE

The chapter reviews the development, organisation and functions of Parliament. It traces the emergence of the elected House of Commons from being relatively co-equal with the 'upper' House of Lords to being superior and then examines the factors that have weakened the Commons' independence (from the executive) and therefore its ability to hold the executive to account. It assesses the role of the political parties in the life of Parliament and the rise of dissent on the back benches. After analysing the stalled attempts by the Blair Government to reform the composition of the Lords it concludes by assessing Parliament's continuing importance in the British system of democracy.

Introduction

For at least a century commentators have mourned 'the decline of Parliament' and claim that it has become part of the 'dignified' constitution. Some looked back to a golden age when the Commons made and unmade governments and when many MPs were relatively independent of party whips. But this is to look back on a short period of the mid-19th century, and one that has little relevance to the very different political, administrative, and economic circumstances of today. That view of Parliament's role has been undermined by three developments in the 20th century:

(1) *The growth of disciplined party voting* in the Commons from the late-19th century, with the vast majority of MPs voting in the division lobbies as directed by the party whips. Effective pressure by backbenchers takes place less in debates on the floor of the House than in private party meetings. The development of the programmatic, disciplined political parties has led some observers to talk of 'party' rather than 'parliamentary' government.

(2) *The emergence of the dominant two-party system*, largely after 1945, and the control of government by one party with an assured parliamentary majority. This enabled the government to dominate the business of the House and get its way in the division lobbies.

(3) *The trend to more interventionist government* and membership of the EU have meant that Parliament has struggled to cope with an enormous amount of legislation and this has reduced its ability to deliberate and scrutinise. It may be countered that the transfer of responsibilities to Brussels and the three sub-national bodies because of devolution has eased the burden of work, but equally it can be argued that Parliament is being bypassed.

The three factors are interlinked. They help the government to carry out its legislative programme for which it claims a mandate (see Chapter 20). The task of the majority party in Parliament, as most of the MPs see it, is to support the government and give Parliament what a commentator has called an executive cast of mind.

In a brilliant study, David Judge claims that in our system of government by parliamentary democracy the emphasis is firmly on the former not the latter, and:

> By the end of the nineteenth century. . . the modern British state was inimitably structured in its present institutional form: parliament was sovereign in constitutional theory but the executive was 'sovereign' in practice. In terms of the central relationship between parliament and government the imbalance has never subsequently been redressed (1993: 26).

Judge (1993: 27) adds that governments of all parties have found the formula of parliamentary sovereignty convenient for the exercise of executive dominance, and that British government may be representative but this 'is not a synonym for "democracy"'.

Parliament today therefore does not make policy—that is a matter for the executive—but it may influence policy. It also plays a debating role, criticises and scrutinises the policies and legislation of the government, and is a channel of recruitment to the government. And it is not enough to say that power has gone to the executive (see Chapters 11 and 12). The executive is not a unitary body; the departments, Cabinet and senior Civil Service all have their own resources and preferences and depend on each other (Rhodes 1997; Richards and Smith 2002). Moreover, these actors have to take account of the decisions in external arenas like the EU, networks and the global economy.

Development

The development of Parliament occurred in two stages. First, it asserted, following a civil war, its independence *vis-à-vis* the Crown; second, the House of Commons became representative of the public at large through election by universal suffrage. During the 17th century the House of Commons established its supremacy over the Lords in financial matters; it became accepted that the House of Lords could not amend finance bills, although the principle was not formalised until the 1911 Parliament Act laid down that all money bills certified as such by the Speaker of the Commons should be presented for the Royal Assent, regardless of the views of the House of Lords.

The conventions of the accountability of the government to the Commons and its dependence on majority support there—rather than on the support of the monarchy—were established in the 19th century. The convention of collective responsibility also grew; it meant that defeat on a vote of confidence, or the inability of the government to command support in the House, entailed its resignation (see Chapter 10). But the rise of one-party majority government and the use of procedural devices have given the government a high degree of control over the Commons. And many elements of the monarch's prerogative power (or powers vested in the Crown)—such as dissolving Parliament, appointing ministers, declaring war and making treaties with other countries—have now passed to the Cabinet. Because civil servants and ministers are servants of the Crown, British government has a substantial degree of autonomy from Parliament. In this model, Parliament may debate and criticise, but any realistic analysis of how Britain is governed acknowledges that initiative on legislation and policy lies with the Cabinet.

Members

For all the differences in their personalities and views, the combination of their intense political interest, ambition and activity makes MPs distinctive (Searing 1994). Being elected as an MP immediately makes one unrepresentative. The pressures and satisfactions of living in the public gaze appeal to only a minority of people. Some backbenchers find life in Parliament frustrating, particularly if they have not been promoted, largely because they feel that their opportunities to influence the government are limited. Indeed, because of Labour's substantial overall majority between 1997 and 2005 the party whips encouraged MPs to stay home for so-called 'constituency weeks' and few MPs are still in the House after Thursday afternoon. Some MPs try to be all-rounders, seeking to speak on a wide variety of issues. Others specialise in a particular area, for example, defence, the disabled, even the procedure of Parliament. Some are content to be party loyalists; some calculate carefully how to mix loyalty to the whips with threats of disloyalty to ascend the ministerial hierarchy; others seem to be natural 'mavericks' and spurn the opportunities to please their leaders—for example, the Conservative Nicholas Winterton and Labour's Bob Marshall-Andrews and, until his retirement in 2005, Tam Dalyell. For most MPs, increasingly it is relations with the local party and local organisations, and handling the problems of constituents that are the most time-consuming (Norton 1994).

Because Prime Ministers are limited to selecting MPs and peers for government posts, Parliament, mainly the House of Commons, is the source of recruitment. A Prime Minister who is dissatisfied with the available talent can create new peers and give them ministerial posts, as Blair has done with David Sainsbury, Charles Falconer, Andrew Adonis, Gus McDonald, David Simon and Chris Haskins, all successful in other walks of life.

The idea that MPs should be paid a salary and, the implication perhaps, that they did a full-time job was slow to gain acceptance. Payment was introduced in 1911, largely at the behest of Labour MPs who lacked private incomes. It may be telling that the chamber of the House of Commons only contains seating for some two-thirds of members. The salary has been raised since on a number of occasions, and is now comparable with the pay of successful middle-aged people in the professions, or members of legislatures in other Western democracies. Salaries are reviewed each Parliament (or at four-year intervals) by the Review Body on Top Salaries and additional allowances are made for travel, secretarial and research expenses. Many MPs, particularly on the Conservative side, receive additional remuneration from outside 'interests' or draw salaries from other employment. Indeed, a Conservative Party leader in opposition may find some difficulty in appointing the party's brightest talents to the Shadow Cabinet as they prefer to earn money from company directorships. Defenders of these outside activities suggest that the House gains from this type of experience. However, the range of such activities is rather narrow, being largely confined to business directorships, the law, journalism or public relations related activity.

As Leader of the House of Commons between 2001 and 2003, the late Robin Cook brought in a number of reforms to make the work of the House more topical and effective. Working hours were changed so that they were timed to catch news programmes and to fit in with MPs' family commitments, more bills were published in draft form to allow pre-legislative scrutiny by members, and Government bills were allowed to 'carry over' from one session to the next instead of having to be re-introduced anew. And the development of the Select Committee system (see below, pp 379–80) provides an alternative potential career path for ambitious MPs who have either left the front bench or never made it and wish to specialise. Backbench MPs may complain of their lack of influence on the executive, of media intrusiveness in their private lives and of a decline in status, but few willingly leave it. MPs who lose their seat at an election compare the loss to bereavement and some eagerly seek membership of the House of Lords. Winston Churchill was not alone in having a deep emotional attachment to Parliament. During a fraught stage in the 1914–18 war he was leaving the House of Commons late one night with a fellow Liberal MP. Looking around the empty dark chamber he said:

'This little place is what makes the difference between us and Germany . . . This little room is the shrine of the world's liberties' (Hennessy 2004).

The legislative process

It is ironic that legislation in Britain is largely a matter for the executive and that the most significant stages in the genesis and shaping of a bill have often already occurred before Parliament is involved. Although there are private members' bills and MPs have opportunities to press amendments to bills, most legislation arises from government departments. Even before a new government enters office, civil servants have drafted proposals to try and give effect to the party's manifesto promises. Stimuli for legislation may come from pressure groups, press campaigns, energetic MPs, reports of Royal Commissions and recommendations from committees, working parties or other expert bodies. Outside pressures or events may help to give momentum to a framework for legislation. Providing the substance and detail of a bill, however, usually rests with the department. Parliament remains supreme in making statute law—except for EU law and some Scottish matters—and once a bill becomes law it is entered in the statute book. The operation of an Act, however, depends in part on the interpretation of those who carry it out, in part on the views of the courts if they are involved, and in part on the consent of those who are subject to it.

Although the government and opposition front benches dominate the parliamentary timetable and legislative process, there is some scope for members. Early in each session a ballot is held for private members' bills to be considered—usually on Fridays. Only those drawn in the top 10 or so have a reasonable chance of making progress to the statute book. Most private members' bills are 'talked out' before reaching a vote, and

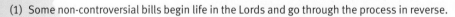

(1) Some non-controversial bills begin life in the Lords and go through the process in reverse.

(2) If the Lords propose amendments, Commons can accept, reject or propose further amendments and return the bill to the Lords and so on until Houses are agreed.

(3) If no agreement can be reached between the two Houses the Commons can insist (except in case of a bill extending the life of Parliament) and the bill can then be passed again through the Commons and then for Royal Assent under the terms of the 1949 Parliament Act.

on average only eight such bills have been passed per session in post-war Parliaments. Many successful bills, often prompted by interest groups or other MPs, are uncontroversial but some have been path-breaking, for example, ending capital punishment and decriminalising abortion and homosexuality, all in the 1960s. The last depended on a sympathetic government prepared to make time available. In 1997 Labour MPs strongly backed Michael Foster's private members' bill to ban fox-hunting. In the end the Government overcame opposition in the Lords by using the Parliament Act to force the measure through.

The Queen's Speech, which is delivered at the beginning of each session, promises various 'bills', 'legislation', 'measures', items for 'discussion', and 'proposals'. Some proposals eventually introduced by ministers may not have been mentioned in the speech, because they were not anticipated when it was written, were not considered important at the time, or are perennial items. To become law a government bill must navigate what has been called the Whitehall 'obstacle race'. Where a department has recognised an issue as suitable for legislation and decides to make out a case for a bill, it will then circulate a draft proposal to other departments likely to be affected, and to the Treasury. If the Cabinet agrees, the proposal goes to its Future Legislation Committee, then to Parliamentary Counsel, who will draft a bill. Finally, the proposal will be included in the Queen's Speech, along with statements of the government's other plans for the forthcoming session. Once the Cabinet has granted the time, the bill is then forwarded to its Legislation Committee, which is responsible for piloting the bill through Parliament. The Cabinet's decision (or its committee's) is therefore important at three stages: on the substance of legislation in the policy committees, the wording and form in the Legislation Committee and the parliamentary timing in the Future Legislation Committee.

Within the Commons, the *first reading* of the bill is formal, being a statement of the bill's purpose. On the *second reading* the bill's contents are subject to a fuller debate. If its general principles have been approved it goes to a standing committee for detailed consideration. The composition of the standing committees must, according to Standing Order No 65, 'have regard to . . . the composition of the House', that is, reflect the party balance of the Commons. The bill, with any amendments, then goes back to the whole House for a *report* stage and may be subject to further amendments. On the *third reading* there is a final debate and then a *vote* on the bill. Except in the case of money bills, the bill goes through a similar process in the House of Lords, but the Lords have no standing committees: all bills are considered in a committee of the Whole House. If the amendments are made by the Lords and insisted on, against the wishes of the Commons, then the bill falls. It may be reintroduced in the same form by the Commons and, if passed again, will become a law, notwithstanding the objection of the Lords. Finally, the bill goes to the monarch to receive the *Royal Assent* and becomes law.

A British government is well placed to get its legislation through the Commons. The rules of the House give it ample opportunity to get its business considered when and in the form it wants. Ministers are responsible for drafting the vast majority of bills and amendments. In a typical session about 150 bills are introduced, of which up to two-thirds receive the Royal Assent. Yet in terms of time it is perhaps surprising that government business accounts for only about half of the time of the Commons.

The pressures of time, the ease with which governments can pass legislation, and the growing constituency workload of many MPs have probably impaired the quality of legislation. In the last decade it has been usual for at least one and sometimes two Criminal Justice Acts to be passed per session. Various Hansard Society reports have fairly expressed concern about declining standards in drafting bills and the lack of scrutiny of delegated legislation.

Delegated legislation

The term, *delegated legislation* refers to Acts which contain enabling clauses allowing the minister to issue directives and regulations at a later stage. The growth in delegated legislation has accompanied the growing social and economic responsibilities of government. In a typical session over 100 bills might be passed but some 3,000 statutory orders and regulations will also be passed, with only about half of them laid before Parliament. Approval of broad purposes in legislation and delegating detail in theory frees Parliament to concentrate on the principles of laws and allows the legislation to be adapted to special circumstances. The Joint (of the Houses, the Commons and the Lords) Statutory Instruments Committee reviews such legislation. There is, however, a political aspect to delegated legislation; ministers may use it avoid detailed scrutiny of controversial measures (Blackburn and Kennon 2003).

Committees

Most of the work of the House of Commons is now done through committees. *Committees of the Whole House* are used for certain major bills, often on constitutional issues. *Standing committees* established in the 1880s, examine the details of a bill once it has passed its second reading and party whips appoint members in proportion to party strength in the Commons. These committees provide the opportunity to examine and tidy up each clause of the proposed legislation and take account of views expressed in groups outside the House. But the great majority of the amendments accepted are those from the minister who is piloting the bill through the House. And if a government is defeated on an important point in committee it can usually have it reversed on the floor of the House. The standing committees, largely because they deal with legislation (mostly government bills), are subject to close management by the party whips, and party solidarity is the norm. The committee stage of some legislation is taken in the Committee of the Whole House (all MPs minus the Speaker) rather than in a standing committee. These may occur with one-clause bills which can be passed quickly, some financial bills which involve an increase in public expenditure, and bills of a constitutional nature. If the government meets what it considers unreasonable delay or obstructions then it can try to impose a timetable to get a bill through.

There are different types of *Select Committees*, again set up by the House. Investigatory committees have long been used for in connection with public expenditure, legislation and ad hoc inquiries; in his diary Samuel Pepys records giving evidence to one in 1688. They may summon ministers and civil servants to give evidence, commission papers and issue reports, and are concerned more with the application than the formulation of policy. The membership of these committees also reflects party strength in the House of Commons. The Public Accounts Committee (PAC), set up in 1861, is perhaps the most notable. It is chaired by a member of the opposition, and is supported by a staff of auditors, under the Comptroller and Auditor-General, and an independent National Audit Office (NAO). As well as checking that a department's expenditure has been duly authorised, the NAO is able to mount 'value for money' investigations of many bodies which receive public funds. Although it is precluded from judging policy decisions, its investigations into, for example, housing benefits, NHS costs and defence procurement have all instigated debate and savings. A limit, however, is that the PAC only reports on the use of public spending *after* the event. Other investigative committees include those for Statutory Instruments, Standards & Privileges, and the European Scrutiny Committee. Compared with the standing committees, which reflect the government–opposition adversarial side of Commons life, MPs on the select committees are expected to adopt a 'non-partisan' approach.

Since January 1973, Britain's membership of the European Community has meant that all EU legislation is automatically enforceable in Britain, as in all member states. The relations of the House of Commons with the Council of Ministers and the European Commission are indirect, as is Parliament's scrutiny of European legislation. With few exceptions the House has no powers to withhold consent. The European Scrutiny Committee reviews directives and draft legislation from the Commission, but not when these are being prepared, and its role is limited. Moreover, in expressing views MPs compete with British members of the European Parliament, which has gained authority as a result of the Single European Act and the Maastricht Treaty and subsequent treaties.

A major reform of the committees followed a report of the House of Commons Select Committee on Procedure (1978). The report was approved and led to the setting up in 1979 of 14 departmental select committees (at present reorganised and extended to 19) to examine expenditure, administration and policy within a department or two or more related departments, as well as in the nationalised industries and other organisations operating within a department.

Because the committees are established by standing orders for the lifetime of a Parliament, rather than on an annual basis, a committee has a measure of independence. And selection of MPs (usually about 11) to serve on committees is not in the hands of whips but a Committee of Selection, although party managers still play a key role. But it is salutary to recall how MPs in the 19th century were able to extract information from the executive and when they regularly secured the release of government papers and sat on Royal Commissions. The ability to extract information is more limited today, although the select committee system has helped. It was notable that Lord Hutton's inquiry in 2003 into the circumstances leading to the death of Dr David Kelly and Lord Butler's inquiry into the intelligence prior to the war with Iraq were more successful than any select committee in summoning ministers (including Tony Blair in the case of Hutton) and officials, and gaining access to documents and e-mails.

The new system has the merit of coherence: the work of each committee is directed to a specific government department. It has attracted the support of many backbenchers, encouraged a degree of specialism among MPs and is a force for improving the quality of the debate. It also provides an opportunity for pressure groups to present their case in public. Some useful reports have been published, although pressure of time means that few are debated on the floor of the House. At times a department may anticipate a committee's criticism by changing policy or issuing a consultative document. The Prime Minister and his key aides have traditionally refused to appear before a select committee, a notable illustration was Mrs Thatcher's refusal to appear before the Defence Select Committee and answer questions over the Westland affair in 1986. But from 2002 Tony Blair has agreed to appear twice a year before the Liaison Committee (consisting of the chairs of the committees) and answer questions.

Other commentators are more critical, notably of the quality and irregular attendance of members and the way in which most reports are largely ignored. It remains the case that ambitious MPs would rather have a post on the front bench, preferably in government, than on a committee. If one discounts the 80 or so government appointments, members of the opposition front bench, and others who are either unsuitable or unwilling to play a part, perhaps only about one half of the House is available for membership of the committees. In the 1997–2001 Parliament there were cases of Labour members of committees passing drafts confidential reports and other information to government ministers. But in the 2001 Parliament select committee chairmen were paid a salary and the research capacity of the committees has been increased.

There are also party committees, which are unofficial because the House did not set them up. The Conservative *1922 Committee* consists of all backbench MPs when the party is in government and all, except the leader, when in opposition. It meets weekly, elects an executive of 18 MPs who regularly confer with the party leader and whips, and arranges ballots for the Party leadership election. The Conservative and Labour Parties have a wide range of regional and subject committees and a minister or shadow minister will want to be sure of the support of members of his subject group.

Control of the executive

As noted elsewhere, the executive-centred British system has affected the influence of Parliament. The phenomenon of one-party majority government has helped to make a government fairly secure for the lifetime of a Parliament and the passage of its legislation predictable. In the 20th century, governments have been dismissed by Parliament on only two occasions, in 1924 and 1979, and both were minority Labour governments. Walter Bagehot drew attention to the *fusion* of the executive and legislature in Britain compared to their separation in the United States. This produces a paradox. It is the fact that most members of the executive sits in the Commons that makes it important. But it is also the fact that the Commons is weakened because the majority party supports the executive; nearly a third of the majority party in the Commons is in the government and therefore part of the 'payroll vote'.

CS IN FOCUS 19.2

nd practice: Question Time

Theory

The Government is recruited from, but also accountable to, Parliament. Question Time is perhaps the best known of several procedures incorporated into the parliamentary timetable to provide opportunities for backbenchers to scrutinize the government's activities.

— Question Time takes place for approximately one hour on Monday to Thursday
— Ministers rotate
— Since 1997 PM answers government-wide questions for 30 minutes on Wednesdays
— 48 hours' notice is required of a question, but one unscripted supplementary question is allowed
— questions may be for written or oral answer

Political practice

— ministers are thoroughly briefed, and civil servants are adept at predicting supplementaries
— 'friendly' questions are planted from a minister's own side
— general rowdiness
— lengthy evasive replies of recitation of government's achievements
— the procedure can be subverted, serving to reduce the time available for answering and enabling ministers to avoid awkward questions lower down on the list

Question Time has become something of an elaborate parliamentary charade

— it may occasionally lead to the revelation of, and redress of, an injustice, but the dominance of the parties results in the opposition using QT as an opportunity to embarrass the government and boost morale in its own ranks, and the government defensively closing ranks to outwit the opposition
— reputations are occasionally on the line and inexperienced ministers do seem to be apprehensive about taking their turn at the Dispatch Box

Another factor has been the government's growing control of the proceedings of Parliament; in effect members acquiesce in the executive controlling its proceedings. This was largely achieved in the late 19th century as a result of agreement between the Liberal and Conservative front benches—a response to the obstructionist tactics of the 80-plus Irish Nationalist members who were paralysing the work of the House of Commons. The Government assumed the powers of 'closure', to limit the time for debate on a bill and force a vote, and 'guillotine', to decide how much time would be allowed to each stage of a bill. Other reforms, revealingly called 'Balfour's Railway Timetable' (after the then Leader of the House of Commons), were introduced to speed the passage of business. Henceforth, the Government had control of the time of the House, subject to the opposition party's rights of Supply Days and private members' time. The opposition acquiesced in the redistribution of power because it anticipated that it would soon have a turn in office.

But the House of Commons has become more of a front bench system, particularly of the government front bench.

Finally, Parliament has effectively lost control of supply, that is, the authorisation of expenditure. The annual estimates are presented to the House of Commons and show in detail how much is to be spent on each area of activity. But they are invariably passed and scrutiny takes place afterwards. The Comptroller and Auditor-General and his staff of over 500 audit the work of each department, ascertaining whether money has been spent as authorised and whether it has been spent with proper economy. The accounts and reforms of the Comptroller and Auditor-General form the starting-point of the work of the Public Accounts Committee. The committee has a good record of identifying extravagant items of expenditure by departments.

Commentators, writing from a 'liberal' perspective, often complain that the sovereignty of Parliament has been transformed into the sovereignty of a whipped party majority of MPs. And the lack of many effective checks and balances on the Commons means that we have a dictatorship, albeit elected, of the executive and, at times, of the Prime Minister in particular. Lord Hailsham made a particularly eloquent analysis and attack on recent developments in his lecture in 1976. He declared:

> The sovereignty of Parliament has increasingly become, in practice, the sovereignty of the Commons, and the sovereignty of the Government which, in addition to its influence in Parliament, controls the party whips, the party machine, and the Civil Service. This means that what has always been an elective dictatorship in theory, but one in which the component parts operated in practice to control one another, has become a machine in which one of these parts has come to exercise a predominant influence over the rest.
>
> ('Elective Dictatorship', BBC Dimbleby Lecture 1976, cit *Listener*, 21 October 1976)

The opposition

The idea of a legitimate political opposition in Parliament to the government of the day dates back to the 18th century and is reflected in the Speaker's statutory duty to designate the leader of the largest party not in government as the *Leader of Her Majesty's Opposition*. Since 1937 the Leader has also been paid a salary out of state funds, making Britain unique among the European states in having such a state-funded office. The work and character of the House of Commons, particularly debates and votes, are coloured by party. The existence of the opposition reminds the public that there is an alternative government with an alternative 'Shadow Cabinet' and policies.

In recent years the simple government versus opposition portrait of the House of Commons has had to be modified, because of the fragmentation of the party system and the rise of a larger, though diverse, third-party force in the Commons. For example, in the October 1974 Parliament, Labour started out with a lead of 42 seats over the official Conservative opposition. But five other parties had 39 between them, leaving Labour with a precarious overall majority of only three seats. This disappeared by 1977, and Labour depended on the support of the Liberals. The Government was able to survive as long as it did because it was not until March 1979 that it was simultaneously in the interests of virtually all non-Labour MPs to combine on an issue of no confidence.

At the start of the 1992 Parliament John Major's Conservative Government had a comfortable 65 majority over Labour but, because of the number of MPs from 'other' parties, only 21 overall. The loss of by-elections, rebellious Conservative backbenchers and the withdrawal of the whips from nine Conservative Eurosceptics played havoc with the Major Government's ability to pass its legislation, at one point turning it into a de facto minority government. Although the Labour Government, with its massive majority, did not lose a vote in the Commons in the 2001–05 Parliament (although it lost many in the Lords) it still struggled to pass its contentious bills on higher education finance, foundation hospitals and terrorism (Cowley 2004).

The opposition's conduct is shaped in part as a reaction to what the government does, in part by pressure in the party, and in part by events. A large proportion of the parliamentary timetable is taken up with predictable matters, such as six days of debate on the Queen's Speech and days allocated to the Finance Bill. Here the opposition can make both negative and constructive criticisms. On opposition days or no-confidence motions, it can choose its own line of attack. But like a Prime Minister, a Leader of the Opposition has to be concerned with the unity of the party and of the Shadow Cabinet. Just as in government a principle of collective responsibility operates, by which shadow ministers are expected loyally to defend Shadow Cabinet policies and take care not to express controversial views on the policy area of another colleague.

The parliamentary opposition has a number of resources at its disposal. It may choose the subject for debate on the 20 opposition days. It may also persuade the Speaker to grant an adjournment debate because an issue is considered to be an emergency. And, of course, it may at any time move a motion of censure on how a government or minister has conducted business. In March 1979 a Conservative motion of no confidence, carried by one vote, brought about the downfall of James Callaghan's Labour Government. The opposition parties are represented on the select and standing committees in proportion to their strength in the House of Commons. Finally, it is traditional for an opposition MP (in 2005 the Conservative MP Edward Leigh) to be chairman of the influential Public Accounts Committee. In comparison to the time and opportunities allowed in legislatures elsewhere, arrangements in the British House of Commons must be judged as relatively generous to Her Majesty's Opposition.

Opposition activity in Parliament is shaped by the need to agree with the government on procedure and allocation of time. For example, the programme of business for the following week is arranged by the parties' whips each Thursday, arrangements referred to as 'the usual channels'. Ministers who have to be absent from votes in the Commons because of government business are usually 'paired' with an opposition MP. Government business managers are aware that the opposition, by withdrawing goodwill and co-operation, can seriously disrupt their conduct of parliamentary business. This was the case, for example, in 1951 and 1993 when the government of the day had only a precarious majority.

The essence of the relationship is not accurately captured in such phases as 'the Cabinet versus Parliament' or 'the executive versus the legislature'. Because many members of the executive (about a third of the governing party) sit in Parliament we have to extract the government (around 100 MPs hold a government post) from Parliament to appreciate its role. Anthony King (1976) has pointed to four distinct groups of actors in the 'normal' two-party-dominated Parliament. These are the government frontbenchers, government backbenchers, opposition frontbenchers and opposition backbenchers. The variation in the role of Parliament may be analysed in three broad styles.

The first is the *opposition* style, in which the main actors are the government and the opposition. This is the view of Parliament conveyed by the mass media and the rhetoric of General Elections. It is the classic adversary system which overlaps with a two-party system, and the arguments and votes are often predictable. The opposition can achieve various limited objectives: it can deny the government time in Parliament; it may expose the administrative or political weakness in a government's case; or it may undermine public and parliamentary confidence in a minister or a government, and so promote its own chances of winning the next general election. Above all, the opposition is poised to take advantage of a government's mistakes; its activities remind voters that there is an alternative government.

A second mode is the *non-partisan* one, when MPs act in relative freedom from the party whips. The work of select committees sometimes shows MPs in a bipartisan mood; the desire to gain information, or expose policy failures by the executive, is found across the political spectrum of backbenchers. The other major opportunity for the relaxation of partisanship is on a free vote (when the whips do not operate and the issue is judged as a matter of individual conscience) in the Commons. The government is relatively safe from defeat in both of the models outlined so far. In the former, party loyalty will usually secure its majority; in the latter, its position is not, by definition, at stake.

What does matter for the government, however, is King's third or *intra-party* model. For the ministers the most important MPs are their backbenchers. The leaders listen to the backbenchers, partly because they are in the same party, partly because they may represent opinion outside Parliament or in the party in the country, and partly because the executive is not monolithic. Divisions among backbenchers may reflect divisions in the Cabinet. The government may take the opposition of other parties for granted but, as Tony Blair found when struggling to pass his top-up fees bill in 2004, its security depends on keeping its own party majority intact.

There are many examples of the government having to bow to pressures from its own supporters and either losing or modifying a bill. Mrs Thatcher's Government had to withdraw proposals to increase sharply the parental contribution to students in higher education (1984); lost the Shops Bill (1986); withdrew proposals to sell off parts of British Leyland to General Motors (1986); and withdrew proposals to introduce identity cards for football spectators (1990). John Major's Government made many concessions on the bill to ratify the Maastricht Treaty (1993). A core of Conservative Eurosceptics could combine with Labour to threaten the Government's majority. The motion to ratify the Treaty was carried in July 1993 only after the Government declared that it was a vote of confidence—and that defeat would lead to a general election. And in the 2001 Parliament the Blair Government had to make concessions on bills about top-up fees, foundation hospitals and gambling to get them passed. The pattern continued in 2005–06 over bills on schools and ID cards. It was not enthusiastic about the private members' bill to ban fox-hunting but, pressed by Labour MPs, it backed it.

Dissent

MPs in the two main parties have become more rebellious, even to the point of voting against their own party. The first student to document this was Philip Norton (1980). His study of the division lists in Parliaments since 1945 shows that in the Parliaments from 1970 the proportion of divisions in which cross-voting (or a member defying his whip) occurred increased. A consequence of this rebelliousness has been that governments have been defeated more frequently on the floor of the House of Commons and in standing committees. This feature flies in the face of claims that as MPs have become more ambitious for and dependent on ministerial advancement, so they would be more loyal to the party whips.

It was no surprise that the Labour Governments of October 1974 to 1979 were defeated on 42 occasions, for they were in a minority for much of the time and were divided on a number of issues. Similarly, John Major's losses were not unexpected given his slender majority and his party's divisions on Europe. The rebellions, however, continued under Mrs Thatcher, particularly with her greater majorities since 1983. The second reading of the Shops Bill was lost in 1986, when 72 Conservative MPs entered the opposition lobby; this was the first time in the 20th century that a government with an overall majority has lost such a vote. 139 Labour MPs refused to support Blair's decision to go to war with Iraq and the revolt against legislation to introduce top-up fees in higher education were the biggest revolts on the governing side for over a century. On the last issue, at least, the rebels could claim that were being loyal to the party's 2001 election manifesto pledge that there would no top-up fees in the Parliament.

There appear to be four possible causes of the changes in behaviour. One is that a number of issues—Iraq, top-up fees and foundation hospitals for Labour, and Europe for Conservatives under John Major—offended party instincts. A second is that dissenters rarely have the whip withdrawn; compared with the sanctions visited on left-wing Labour rebels or Conservative dissenters in the 1950s, the party leaders have become more tolerant. Thirdly, the Labour Governments between 1974 and 1979 and John Major's 1992 Government had to be more relaxed about the consequences of a defeat in the division lobbies; the Government lost votes on a number of important issues and then invited the rebels to support the Government on a vote of confidence. The ultimate attempt by government leaders to defuse the impact of a backbench rebellion on a crucial issue is the refusal to issue a three-line whip, because the party is too divided. Finally, it may be that the more 'professional' MPs have become, the more they are frustrated by the conditions of parliamentary life and with lack of promotion, and they decide to make a name for themselves as rebels. The long period of Conservative government resulted in a large number of disappointed and potentially troublesome MPs—what an exasperated John Major was overheard to call 'the dispossessed and the never-possessed'. Tony Blair could echo the remark as he surveys the number of ex-ministers, notably Clare Short, Glenda Jackson and Frank Dobson, who rebel and routinely call for his resignation.

House of Lords

For much of its history the House of Lords possessed co-equal powers with the Commons. In the 19th century the gradual extension of the suffrage for elections of the Commons emphasised that body's more democratic credentials. The government of the day was also clearly responsible to the Commons because a defeat on an issue of confidence entailed its resignation; such a consequence did not follow from its defeat in the Lords. But before 1909 a constitutional clash over the powers of the two Houses was avoided. Late 19th-century Cabinets still drew half of their members from the Upper House and Lord Salisbury sat as Prime Minister in the Lords until 1902. Indeed in 1940, following the resignation of Neville Chamberlain as Prime Minister, the King was faced with a decision to appoint Winston Churchill or Lord Halifax, the Foreign Secretary, to the position. Although he chose Churchill he did not consider Halifax's membership of the Lords as a barrier. The Peerage Act 1963 permitted hereditary peers to renounce their title and stand for election to the Commons. Using this procedure Lord Home gave up his title, won a by election and became Prime Minister in 1963. Until 1911, therefore, apart from the supremacy of the Commons on the matter of finance bills, the two Houses were more or less co-equal in their powers.

The sharper conflict between the Liberal and Conservative Parties—particularly over the former's willingness to grant Irish Home Rule—and the preponderance of Conservatives in the Lords led to the clash. In 1909 the House of Lords took the unprecedented step of rejecting Lloyd George's budget and paved the way for the Parliament Act 1911. Two provisions of the Act clearly established the subordinate position of the Lords. The first was that bills passed by the Commons and certified by the Speaker of the Commons as money bills were to receive the Royal Assent a month after being sent to the Lords, whether or not approved by the latter body. The second was that any other public bill (except one extending the life of a Parliament) passed by the Commons in three successive sessions and rejected by the Lords would receive the Royal Assent, provided that two years had passed between the bill's second reading in the first session and the third reading in the third session of the Commons. In 1949 the Lords' power to delay was further reduced to one year by the Labour Government.

Until 1999, the majority of peers were hereditaries. Nearly half of the peers took the Conservative whip and around 30% were cross-benchers. Creating peers involves considerable prime ministerial patronage and no Prime Minister has been as lavish as Tony Blair. In his first two terms as Prime Minister, he appointed over 250 peers and for the first time ever the number of Labour peers nearly equals those on the Conservative side. Just before Parliament was dissolved in April 2005 there were 233 Conservatives, 195 Labour, 61 Liberal Democrats and 181 crossbenchers. Blair, like other premiers, has found the patronage useful for rewarding supporters (including donors to party funds), recruiting people he wished to appoint to government and encouraging Labour MPs in safe seats to retire. But the Lords can still make life difficult for any government.

The present-day powers of the Lords are relatively minor. But its powers of delay may sometimes amount to obstruction if the government's term is nearly complete, its legislative timetable is already crowded, or it is unable to get the defeated measure through the Commons again. Since 1945, the Lords have generally felt free to reject or offer substantial amendments to a government bill which has not been mentioned in the government party's election manifesto (the 'Salisbury Convention'). It frustrated the minority Labour Government (1974–79), was an irritant to the Thatcher Government and blocked the Hunting Act 2004, to outlaw fox-hunting (until the Parliament Act was used), and forced concessions from the Blair Government on bills, notably the Anti- Terrorism, Crime and Security Bill.

Defenders of the second chamber claim that it has a number of uses. Governments may introduce relatively non-controversial legislation in the Lords. In revising and amending legislation it eases the legislative burden on the Commons and the great majority of amendments it passes are accepted by the government—indeed ministers increasingly introduce amendments in the Lords. In comparison with the Commons the Lords also has more time and, since the introduction nearly 50 years ago of life peers, more members with expertise in various walks of life, who can make informed contributions to debate. Indeed because prominent figures from business, finance, culture, the Civil Service and trade unions are members, the House has been called a meeting place for yesteryear's elites (Shell 1992). In view of the increasing professionalisation of MPs there is probably a greater wealth of all round expertise and experience available in the Lords. The House also has had a judicial function in that the Lord Chancellor and the Law Lords at present sit in the House and act as the highest court of the land—and will remain there until a building is found for the Supreme Court (see p 482). Because it can veto a proposal to prolong the life of the House of Commons it may act as a check (however fragile) against the potential elective dictatorship of a temporary majority of MPs in the Commons.

Critics of the Lords divide into two schools. One, found largely on the Labour left, would like to abolish it, and this was proposed in Labour's 1983 election manifesto. Some other liberal democratic countries, such as Sweden, Finland, Denmark and New Zealand, manage without a second chamber. It is worth noting, however, that these countries, except New Zealand, also have proportional representation, a Supreme Court and a Bill of Rights; the members of these single chambers operate in a system of formal constitutional checks and balances.

Other critics accept that a second House is necessary but argue that it should be a reformed chamber that carries out its functions. Proposals for changing the composition include: the direct election of members on a regional and/or proportional electoral basis, the appointment of members in proportion to party strength in the Commons, with voting rights restricted to them, or some other mixture of nominated and elected members. The reformers have usually wanted to introduce the elective principle, reduce or abolish the hereditary peers, and not replicate the party balance in the Commons. For example, the Webbs in 1920 and Winston Churchill in 1930 favoured the creation of a second chamber more directly representative of the major economic interests. The proposals for changing the powers have ranged from reducing the delaying power to six months to increasing it to two years. Disagreement among would-be reformers has prevented change of a fundamental nature.

Reform (or abolition) of the Lords and its consequences present several political and administrative difficulties, which is one reason why since 1911 the only 'fundamental' reform has been Blair's culling of the hereditary peers. Labour's commanding majority in 1997 enabled it at last to tackle the House of Lords. It has done so in two stages. In 1999, as a result of compromise between the ministers and Lord Cranborne, the Tory leader in the Lords, the Lords agreed to reduce the number of hereditary peers to 92 pending the implementation of the second stage of reform; these were elected by separate constituencies of Conservative, Labour, Liberal Democrat and cross-bench peers. The Government then appointed a Royal Commission under Lord Wakeham to consider what would follow, making clear that it did not want a wholly or even largely elected House which might enable it to rival the Commons. In January 2000, the Wakeham Commission reported and offered a number of options for electing some members (see Politics in Focus 19.3). The report received a mixed reception (many critics called for a larger elected element) and it seems to have died.

In February 2003 the two Houses voted on a range of options for reforming the composition of the Lords. There was no majority support for an appointed chamber or having different proportions elected (Politics in Focus 19.4). For all the dissatisfaction with the status quo, MPs seem to fear the alternative of the extension of the Prime Minister's patronage by having an appointed chamber or creating a rival to the Commons by conceding the principle of election to another chamber. 218 MPs voted to abolish the Lords. In 2004 the Government set up a new Statutory Appointments Commission to appoint all members of the Lords, although the political parties will make the majority of the nominations. Blair has set his face against any elected members. Meanwhile the interim House, shorn of most of its hereditaries and perhaps feeling more legitimate as a result, has been more assertive and willing to defeat the Labour Government during the 2001–05 Parliament (Cowley and Stuart 2005).

Lord Wakeham's commission reported in January 2000. Its main proposals were as follows:

- *Life peers*. Existing peers to remain but gradually disappear. They could also be offered 15-year terms renewable on the same basis as those newly appointed.
- *Elected members*. Between 65 and 195 could be elected for 15-year periods. One third of the total would come up for re-election at each five-year cycle. The committee felt that 15-year terms were long enough to enable such members to be independent. Because they could not be re-elected such members were therefore not beholden to the party

whips. An elected member, once his term has been completed, could be appointed by the new Appointments Commission. Wakeham favoured a limit on the number of elected members because of fear that political parties would dominate the process and recruit failed or retired professional politicians.

– *Appointed members* by the Appointments Commission. The Commission was enjoined to respect the need for recruiting people of practical experience, eg business, farming, trade unions, etc. Note that this second chamber would remove patronage from the Prime Minister, although party leaders could make nominations to the Commission. 20% of appointments should be cross benchers. When new appointments were made their numbers should reflect the balance of the voters cast at the previous general election.

– *Law Lords.* The 12 Law Lords to remain as the highest court of appeal in the land.

– *Powers.* To remain as at present and should continue to respect the Salisbury Convention, under which the House does not reject the bill from the Commons which has been mentioned in the governing party's manifesto.

CUS 19.3
House of Lords

Plans to reform the House of Lords are frequently mooted, especially by Labour and the Lib Dems, but they are rarely high on the agenda. It was a Liberal Government in 1911 that changed the Lords' veto into a two-year delaying power, and a Labour Government in 1949 that reduced the delaying power to one year.

Before Wakeham the last major attempt to reform the Lords was introduced in 1968. It proposed that:

— hereditary peers be phased out

— members be appointed

— voting rights be dependent upon attending 30% of sittings

— delay be reduced to six months

It was defeated by the combined efforts, for different reasons, of the Labour left and the Conservative right.

Pressure for reform
Source of proposed reforms

Liberal Democrats: Replace with a Senate elected by PR on a regional basis; two-year delaying power (except money bills)

Tony Benn: Commonwealth of Britain Bill 1991: members should be elected proportional to populations of component nations of Great Britain; one-year delaying power

Labour: In 1997 Labour proposed to end sitting and voting rights of hereditary peers; create a more equal balance between the major parties; leave powers as at present

FOCUS 19.4

...mong MPs on future of the Lords

Vote on range of options on 4 February 2003.
Amendment on abolition of Lords: for 172 against 390

(1) All appointed House: for 245 against 323

(2) All elected House: for 272 against 289

(3) 20% elected defeated without vote

(4) 80% elected: for 281 against 284

(5) 40% elected: defeated without vote

(6) 60% elected: for 253 against 316

(7) 50% elected: defeated without vote.

Conclusion

The House of Commons remains a focus of public interest on major occasions—a Budget Statement, a motion of censure on a minister or the government, or an emergency, such as the Falklands debates in April 1982, or the decision to go to war with Iraq in 2003, or the debates on tuition fees in 2004 and the London bombings in July 2005. 'Winning the argument' in the House is important in maintaining the morale of the party in Parliament and transmitting this mood to the party in the country. Political leaders are recruited and socialised in the Commons and politicians' reputations and career prospects are affected by how they perform in parliamentary debates. Former ministers in their memoirs frequently recall their sense of elation or despondency depending on how they had performed in a key parliamentary debate. A minister's rising stock in the Commons may be reflected in a positive working atmosphere among his senior officials, poor performance in a gloomy one. Paradoxically, if it is because so many ministers are members of the Commons that the latter has lost some of its influence and independence *vis-à-vis* the executive, by the same token this has made it a more important forum than might be the case with a strict separation of personnel, as in the US.

Yet Parliament plays little part in formulating policy, or changing legislation, and has struggled to come to terms with its loss of power to, for example, Brussels, the Scottish Parliament, Quangos or the bodies regulating the utilities. Given the longstanding cry of the 'decline of Parliament' it is not surprising have looked beyond the reform of Parliament itself as a means of seeking checks on the executive and promoting more accountable government. They have turned to proportional representation, more openness, incorporation of the European Convention on Human Rights, more free votes or devolution as levers of desired change. Some of the decline in the standing of Parliament has stemmed from the behaviour of MPs. The well-reported cases of sleaze (including MPs being paid cash to ask questions of ministers) in the 1992 Parliament and spin and deception since 1997, and former ministers' backbiting memoirs and diaries have damaged the reputation of politicians and Parliament. There has been an increase in self-regulation, for example, a Committee on Standards in Public Life, a Parliamentary Commissioner who monitors the registration of MPs' interests, stricter controls over MPs' paid consultancies and a ban on payment to MPs for advocacy of a cause in Parliament.

Far from restoring the vitality and independence of the House, however, insecure government gives power to small groups of potential dissenters, maintains the opportunity for 'backstairs' deals and gives scope for pressure groups, while making 'strong' government unlikely. It is not clear how such a government would necessarily be more representative of the public mood. The fragility of the Major Government in the Commons was as much a reflection of the party's divisions on Europe, resentment of frustrated or resentful Conservative MPs and the bargaining power of a small number of rebels because of the Government's narrow majority.

No doubt criticism of the workings of the Commons, of the damaging effects of the adversarial party battle, and of its lack of power *vis-à-vis* the executive or the European Union will continue. The institution, however, has a long, continuous history, well-established traditions and a strong sense of institutional identity. It commands a deep-seated loyalty among most MPs (few leave it willingly), and defenders of the 'right' of Parliament strike a sympathetic chord in most parts of the House.

KEY POINTS

- Parliament's functions and role have evolved over several centuries. Its present-day functions include representation, debating, converting proposed legislation into law and recruitment to and scrutiny of the executive.

- Democracy gave rise to the convention of House of Commons supremacy in most matters *vis à vis* the Lords. This was given formal statutory recognition by the 1911 and 1949 Parliament Acts.

- Disciplined parties, one party majority government, and the emergence of interventionist government have contributed to a 'decline' in Parliament in the sense of its being an institution independent of party control. Pressure groups, devolution and the EU have weakened Parliament's role as a consenting forum.

- The government is usually able to use its majority and legislative procedures to convert most of its desired legislation programme into law. An increasing tendency towards rebelliousness amongst backbenchers has produced some notable exceptions since the 1970s.

- There are three main types of committee in Parliament: standing committees which scrutinise and amend legislation; select committees which scrutinise spending and the policies of executive departments; and committees of the whole House which deal with short bills, and financial and constitutional bills. There are also various party committees.

- The party system, giving all but a few governments an assured majority in the chamber and in the committees, has weakened Parliament's control over the executive.

- There is formal recognition of the role of the opposition in Britain. The Leader of Her Majesty's Opposition and the Opposition Chief Whip receive an additional salary. Specific opportunities in the parliamentary timetable are allocated to the opposition.

- The House of Lords is in a transitional stage, regarding its composition. Insufficient support for any particular proposal has meant that any reform, apart from the reduction in the number of hereditary peers, has so far failed to materialise.

- Approximately 25% of legislation begins its life in the Lords—mainly of a non-controversial nature. The House has no power over money bills and only a one-year delay over other legislation.

KEY QUESTIONS

(1) How effective are the House of Commons select committees as a means of scrutinising the executive?

(2) 'Even if it is not effective in holding the executive to account the Commons still performs many valuable functions' Discuss.

(3) The sovereignty of Parliament is a meaningless concept and should be abandoned. Discuss.

(4) Why have attempts to reform the composition of the House of Lords proved so difficult?

(5) Does the record since 2001 confirm the view that political parties have transformed backbenchers into lobby fodder?

IMPORTANT WEBSITES

www.Parliament.uk—for Parliament; www.charter88.org.uk—for Charter 88; www.parliament.uk/commons/selcom/cmsel.htm—on select committees; www.revolts.co.uk—for dissent.

FURTHER READING

For an introduction see Riddell, P. (2000) *Parliament under Blair*, London: Politicos; P. Cowley and M. Stuart (2005) 'Parliament' in A. Seldon and D. Kavanagh (eds) *The Blair Effect 2001–5*, Cambridge: Cambridge University Press; Hansard Society (2001) *The Challenge for Parliament. Making Government Accountable*, London: Vacher Dod. On dissent see Cowley, P. (2002) *Revolts and Rebellions*, London: Politicos. On the House of Lords see *Political Quarterly*, 70 (1999, special issue): 368–416; the Wakeham Report, *Unfinished Business: Reforming the House of Lords*, Stationery Office, Cmnd 4534; and I. Richard and D. Welfare, (1999) *Unfinished Business: Reforming the House of Lords*, London: Vintage; and M. Russell (2000) *Reforming the Lords: Lessons From Abroad*, London: Macmillan.

CHRONOLOGY

Major events in the history of Parliament

1689   Bill of Rights: creates parliamentary monarchy

1832   Reform Act: golden age of Parliament; the House of Commons makes and unmakes governments

1861	Public Accounts Committee established
1867	Reform Act: party rule begins
1909	Lords defy convention and reject the budget
1911	Parliament Act: powers of Lords reduced to two-year delay; no power over money bills, maximum life of Parliament reduced from seven to five years, payment for MPs
1937	Ministers of the Crown Act: payment for Leader of the Opposition
1949	Parliament Act: delaying powers of Lords reduced to one year
1958	Life Peerage Act: life peers can be created and women peeresses can inherit a title and sit in Lords
1963	Peerage Act: permits hereditary peers to resign a title for their own lifetime
1972	European Communities Act: Parliament accepts supremacy of EC law in areas of EC competence
1978	Report of the Select Committee on Procedure leads to setting up of select committees to scrutinise the work of government departments
1979	Callaghan Government defeated on a vote of no confidence
1990	Lords reject the War Crimes Bill
1991	The War Crimes Bill becomes an Act of Parliament under the provisions of the 1949 Parliament Act
1994	Committee on Standards in Public Life
2000	Wakeham report on House of Lords
2003	Record number (139) of Labour MPs revolt over Iraq war

 Visit the Online Resource Centre that accompanies this book
for links to more information on this chapter topic

CHAPTER TWENTY

Elections and voting

READER'S GUIDE

This chapter analyses the role of elections in Britain and the different electoral systems under which they are held. It shows how the effects of the first past the post system in general elections have changed over the past 50 years and examines the arguments for electoral reform and how election campaigns have changed, as a result of new technology and changes in voting behaviour. It then analyses the shifts in voting, notably the decline of support for the two main parties, the fall in turnout and the diminishing significance of social class on voting. Finally, it discusses the continuing relevance of the idea of the mandate in British politics.

Introduction

General elections serve several political purposes in democracies. In Britain they reinforce the legitimacy of a regime in so far as people are disposed to accept a government and recognise its right to rule if it was chosen by known and accepted procedures. An Act of Parliament may be disliked and unwelcome but it is recognised as legitimate if it has been passed by a majority of representatives elected in the accepted manner. Elections are also mechanisms of choice and help to choose a government, though the nature of the party and electoral systems determines whether this is done directly by voters or indirectly by elected members of the legislature; where a coalition is formed, bargaining between the party leaders determines the government's policies and composition. Elections also offer cues for the direction of public policy, particularly where parties and candidates stand on programmes. Finally, they provide an institutionalised and non-violent method for resolving political disagreements and changing governments. Open, competitive elections are a peaceful means of achieving political and constitutional change.

...SS IN FOCUS 20.1
...he constitution

Britain's electoral system is the product of history and convenience. Most rules governing the franchise (voter eligibility) are contained in statutes and thus form a written part of the constitution.

Parliament The Parliament Act of 1911 reduced the maximum life of Parliament from seven to five years. Within those five years the Prime Minister, by convention, advises the monarch on the exercise of the Royal Prerogative to dissolve Parliament and sets a date for a general election. During both world wars the maximum life of Parliament was extended by statute, as allowed under the Parliament Act.

Voters The franchise was gradually democratised by a series of Electoral Reform and Representation of the People Acts (see the Chronology at the end of this chapter). Today there is universal adult suffrage: everyone aged 18 and over can vote, except convicted felons, certified lunatics and peers of the realm. In 2001 there were just short of 44.3 million people registered to vote.

Candidates Any British citizen or citizen of the Commonwealth or the Irish Republic who is
— resident in Britain
— 21 years or over
— eligible and registered to vote
— has the signatures of 10 electors
— has £500 deposit (forfeited if less than 5% of the vote in the constituency is received)

There are some exceptions, notably Anglican and Roman Catholic clergy, judges, members of the armed forces and some local government officers.

General elections are not of course the only means by which people may seek to influence public policy (see Chapters 22 and 23). Membership of interest groups is one arena open to people. In recent years referenda have been extensively used, although usually on constitutional issues. As well as elections for the European Parliament and local government the past decade has seen the introduction of elections for the Scottish Parliament, Assemblies in Wales and Northern Ireland and for the London Mayor. But only general elections provide the opportunity for citizens to choose the government of the country.

The electoral system

Only Britain and France (although it has a second ballot) in Western Europe do not use a form of proportional representation (PR) to elect MPs. In the British first past the post system, the candidate with the most votes, whether or not it is a majority, wins the constituency. Since 1997, various PR forms of voting have been introduced for European elections and for the new devolved legislatures in Scotland, Northern Ireland and Wales, but not for Westminster.

An electoral system includes procedures for translating individual votes into seats in the legislature. Systems may be considered on the criteria of representativeness (ie producing a proportional relationship of seats to votes) and majoritarianism (ie producing a government majority). At post-1945 general elections the system, coupled with the dominant two-party system, has always, except for February 1974, produced a majority of seats for one party and one-party government. It has been less successful in producing a House of Commons in which seats are distributed between parties in proportion to their electoral support. The disparity between votes and seats for parties has sometimes been marked. In 1983, for example, the Conservatives gained 63% of the seats for 42.4 per cent of the votes, and in 1997 Labour gained 65% of seats for 43.2 per cent of votes. There has usually been a marked bias (in seats) for the winning party and a smaller one for the opposition, although in 1992 it was the second party, Labour, which gained the most from the bias. The two exceptions, when the party with the most votes did not get the most seats, were in 1951 and February 1974 (Labour and Conservative respectively). Similar disproportionality is evident in the handful of other states—India, Canada and the United States—which use this 'British' first past the post method. The 2005 general election was notable for Labour winning 55% of the seats on 36% of the vote, the lowest share for a winning party in over a century.

Yet the price of these disproportional outcomes has widely been regarded as acceptable. Proportionalism was often unfavourably associated with a multiplicity of parties, coalitions and unstable governments. The fact that most other West European states had a form of PR did not recommend itself when one remembered the political instability of inter-war Germany, post-war Italy and pre-1958 France. Defenders of the British system often argued that if a choice had to be made between the goals of representativeness and majoritarianism, then the latter was more desirable—the claims of government, as it were, won out over those of representativeness. Majority government by one party could be held accountable for its record to Parliament and to the electorate. This was the key to the British idea of responsible party government, something not possible in the United States, because of its separation of powers, and in many West European countries, because of coalition governments. A system giving full power to the winning party and condemning the opposition party to virtual impotence was accepted by the latter because it hoped to gain the full fruits of office at a later election. The saving graces of the British system were that it produced strong stable government, provided voters with a choice between clear party alternatives and ensured that a government with a majority could be held accountable at the next election. One could say that this is a key feature in the British political tradition.

But the effects of the electoral system have altered over time. In general elections between 1951 and 1970 the aggregate shares of votes and seats for the two main parties did not diverge too sharply: the Conservative and Labour Parties between them gained an average of 92% of votes and 98% of seats. The small Liberal Party was penalised because its votes were not geographically concentrated. The system also exaggerated the amount of change: a swing of 1% in votes either way between Conservative and Labour could transfer approximately 20 seats from one party to the other, so adding a difference of forty to any gap in seats between them. In fact, there was little turnover of seats at general elections and the battleground was the 50 or so marginal seats which decided the outcome of a general election.

From the 1970s, however, the electoral system ceased to work in the regular ways defended by its supporters, largely because of the rise of the centre party. The changes included:

(1) It was less successful in producing parliamentary majorities. In the two 1974 general elections the outcomes failed to produce a government majority sufficient to last for a full Parliament, and in February 1974 there was a minority government for the first time since 1929.

(2) Declining support for the two main parties meant that one could form a government backed by less than 40% of the votes (as Labour did in October 1974), and even gain landslide majorities with just 42%—as Thatcher and Blair did.

(3) Finally, the system has operated with more disproportional results. The combined Labour–Conservative share of the votes in the nine general elections from February 1974 to 2001 slumped to an average of less than 75%, but their average combined share of the seats in the House of Commons was hardly affected, at 93%. In 2005 the decline was confirmed as the two parties gained a combined 69.4% of the vote for 85% of the seats. In 1983 and 1987 the Liberal SDP Alliance gained 23 and 22 seats respectively instead of the 160 plus which its votes would have gained in a completely proportional electoral system. Although changes in electoral behaviour and the fragmentation of the party system have reduced aggregate Labour–Conservative support among the electorate, the electoral system has protected the two parties' dominance in parliamentary seats.

Electoral reform

Discussion of electoral reform is not new. A Speaker's Conference (1916–17) recommended the adoption of a form of proportional representation in urban seats. Since 1945 arguments for PR have been based on 'fairness', and were voiced largely by the Liberal Party, which was disadvantaged by the system. In the 1990s, however, two new arguments supplemented the case for reform. They were:

(1) The European dimension. With first past the post, Britain was the odd nation out in elections for the European Parliament, which were held every five years. European leaders pressed for a common system, or at least adherence to a common principle, one of proportionality. A defence of first past the post, that it is more likely to deliver majority one party government, was hardly relevant, because the Euro-elections were for electing MEPs and not a government. Mrs Thatcher opposed the step because she feared that it might open the door to reform of the Westminster system.

(2) The change of mood in sections of the Labour Party, particularly after successive election defeats in 1987 and 1992. Parties have a keen interest in electoral systems because the translation of votes into seats affects their political fortunes. A number of Labour supporters became increasingly pessimistic about the chances of the party winning a majority of seats on its own and joined the Liberal Democrats in campaigning for electoral reform. Neil Kinnock in 1992 set up a commission to examine the case for reform. His successor, John Smith promised to hold a referendum on reform and Tony Blair acquiesced in that promise (although he has reneged on it).

Prior to the 1997 election the Liberal Democrat and Labour Parties agreed a package of constitutional reform, including the establishment of a Royal Commission to examine alternatives to the first past the post system. In government, Tony Blair quickly appointed an Independent Commission on Voting Systems, under Lord (Roy) Jenkins, the former Labour deputy leader and more recently leader of the Liberal Democrats in the House of Lords. In making a recommendation the Commission sought to balance the needs of:

• achieving stable government;

• preserving the link between constituency MPs and voters; and

• producing more proportionality in the relationship between votes and seats.

The Commission sat for a year and recommended a mixed system of AV plus (see Politics in Focus 20.2). Voters would have two votes. Some 85% of MPs would be elected under the AV system for single-member constituencies. To be elected a candidate would have to gain more than 50% of the vote. The voter would also have a second vote for a top-up list of some 15% of MPs who would be allocated to large regional seats. MPs elected on the top-up list would be allocated in a way to rectify some of the disproportionality arising from the first stage. The top-up candidates could be elected either individually or from a

TICS IN FOCUS 20.2

electoral system

First past the post (FPTP)   Voters have one vote for a candidate, usually in single-member districts. The candidate with the most votes wins, even if he does not secure an absolute majority. The system is used in Britain for Westminster and most local elections and in a number of other English-speaking countries.

Alternative vote (AV)   The voter indicates his preferences among candidates in single-member constituencies. A candidate requires an overall majority of votes cast to be elected. If no candidate secures an absolute majority of first preferences, the lowest-placed candidate is eliminated and his second preference votes are transferred among the remaining candidates. The process continues until one candidate has a clear majority. It is used for the Australian House of Representatives.

Regional list proportional system   Electors choose from a list of candidates in large regional constituencies. Seats are then allocated according to the proportion of votes gained by each party. The party list of candidates may be 'open', where voters can choose between individual candidates, or 'closed', where electors can only vote for the party list. The last obviously gives party managers greater control over the election of MPs because the higher one is listed the greater the chance of being elected. The system is used for the European elections in Britain and for the election of 'additional members' in the Scottish Parliament and Welsh Assembly.

Single transferable vote   This refers to the use of preferential voting in multi-member constituencies, as in the Irish Dail and the Australian Senate. Electors number the candidates in order of preference. A quota is calculated and a candidate has to reach this to be elected. Surplus votes for an elected candidate are reallocated according to his or her supporters' second preferences. Bottom candidates are successively eliminated and their preferences redistributed until all seats are filled.

Additional member system (AMS)   This is the system used in Germany, where the elector has two votes, one for a constituency representative, as in Britain, and one for a party list. Half the members are elected by first past the post voting in single-member constituencies. The other half are for party lists and allocated in such a way that the seats in the legislature are made proportional to the votes cast in the country. In Germany a party must gain at least 5% of the total votes to be eligible for additional members. A similar system operates for the London Assembly.

party list. The report's impact, if it had been implemented, would have been modest, because it did not recommend a fully proportional system; the top-up seats were too few in number. Under the proposals, 10 of the 17 post-war elections would still have given an overall majority for one party, in spite of that party not achieving 50% of the vote. This figure is not far short of the 14 achieved under the present system.

As of 2006, PR is effectively off the agenda and there is little prospect of a referendum in the near future. The two main parties still calculate that the established electoral arrangements, a key part of the traditional Westminster system and its underpinning of elitism, still operates in their interests. But is also the case that some in the parties are less confident about this than was the case perhaps a generation ago.

The Conservatives have long opposed electoral reform. Since 1997 they feared that it was a key part of Tony Blair's plan to forge a Lib–Lab centre-left progressive alliance and to minoritise them. Yet the Conservatives are seriously disadvantaged by the existing electoral system. In 2005 it finished over 150 seats behind Labour, although only 3% behind in vote share and 93 seats behind Labour in England even though it gained more votes. The party's fairly even (or inefficient) spread of votes across the country and a vote share of less than 40% means that the party will do badly. In 2005 it took some 27,000 votes to elect each Labour MP, compared to 45,000 for a Conservative MP and 96,000 for a Liberal Democrat. Electorates in Conservative-held seats were on average 6,000 larger than in Labour-held seats, turnout on average was 6.6% higher, and the Conservatives on average won by larger majorities. This means that reviews of boundaries to make seats more equal in size (see below, p 401) are no answer to such anti-Conservative and pro-Labour factors. Psephologists calculate that even with substantially fewer votes than the Conservatives in a 2009–10 general election Labour will still have a comfortable majority of seats over the Conservatives. In the event of the two parties being equal in vote shares the Conservatives would trail Labour by over 100 seats.

Few Labour ministers or MPs show much enthusiasm for electoral reform. A large number of Labour MPs stand to forfeit their seats in the event of a more proportional system being introduced. Both Scotland and Wales are Labour strongholds in Westminster elections but they are in a minority in the elections for the devolved legislatures elected under PR. The decline in interest in reform of voting for Westminster in the Labour Party is an illustration of the opportunism which invariably accompanies discussion of electoral reform. As of 2005, PR is effectively off the agenda and there is little prospect of a referendum in the near future. The two main parties still calculate that the established electoral arrangements, a key part of the traditional Westminster system and its underpinning of elitism, operates in their interests. But is also the case that some in the parties are less confident about this than was the case perhaps a generation ago. And away from Westminster, electoral reform has made great strides, being used for the Euro elections, the London mayoral elections and elections for the devolved assemblies (see Politics in Focus 20.2).

 ## Party regionalisation

The electoral system in Britain has also been a force for a sharper geographical division of political representation. North Britain has remained solidly Labour at most general elections since 1951 (even at times of national swings to the Conservatives) while until 1997 the South and Midlands were moving sharply to the Conservatives over that time. Urban and city centre seats have become more Labour, while suburban and rural seats have become more Conservative. By 1992 only a handful of Labour MPs represented rural seats and few Conservatives represented seats in heavy industrial areas, inner cities or the urban North. Labour's landslide in 1997 changed this and it remains to be seen whether Labour's redrawing of electoral geography is sustained. A likely effect of the adoption of a more proportional electoral system is that the parties' seats would be more evenly distributed across the country than at present and the parties might be encouraged to pay more attention to aggregating interests across regions.

To ensure that there is an approximate equality in the individual weight of votes across the country, impartial Boundary Commissions (a separate one for each of the four nations of the United Kingdom) periodically review and make recommendations (between every 10 to 15 years) about the size of constituencies, with a view to rendering their electorates more equal in size. The Commissions work out a quota for each nation by dividing the total electorate by the total number of seats although recommendations for particular seats may take account of sparsely populated constituencies and the sense of a community in an existing seat. They are also required to respect the boundaries of counties and London boroughs. The Commissions have a reputation for political impartiality in submitting recommendations, but political pressures from parties for the retention of politically 'safe' constituencies also play a part in affecting recommendations. Scotland and Wales were guaranteed a minimum number of seats by the 1944 Redistribution of Seats Act, and the result is that they have long been given more seats in the House of Commons than the size of their electorates justify. The delay of a decade or so before the Commissioners consider the census data and their recommendations take effect means that, for example, the boundaries for a general election in 2009–10 will be based on the 2001 census. The arrangements for Scotland and Wales have for many years provided a 'bonus' for Labour, which is the dominant party in those nations (although in 2005 Scotland's number of seats has reduced by 13). Moreover, the slowness of the process means that by the time constituency boundaries have been drawn new anomalies have occurred and the principle of the equality of constituencies weakened.

Changes in election campaigns

A paradox about British elections is that they are more national but also more differentiated. The growth in the 20th century of the mass media, nationwide industries and services, and organised, disciplined political parties has produced (except for Northern Ireland) a 'nationalisation' of the election campaign. The main political issues and events are more national in scope, and local influences and issues have declined in importance (although there have been interesting local variations in swing in recent general elections). In the 19th century parties had to rely on local candidates and supporters to carry the message in the constituencies. Today, however, mass media and modern transport enable the leaders to communicate these policies more directly to the voters across the country, and technology allows them to direct the campaign from party headquarters. Campaigning has become more professional, with the parties borrowing many techniques and ideas from the United States. They now invest heavily in spin doctors, opinion polling and computers to understand and court public opinion, direct messages at voters, manage the media and collect data so that they can rebut (rapid rebuttal) charges from opponents. Parties are now equipped to concentrate their efforts at target voters—those who are not firmly attached to any party but have declared they are likely to vote—and whose support will prove decisive in the marginal seats. The parties concentrate direct mail, telephone-canvassing and DVDs on them to win their support. A result is that for voters in relatively safe seats (the majority) or who are firmly attached to a party can feel that the campaign is bypassing them, as the parties respond to the concerns of the target voters. Not surprisingly, activists complain about this effect of political marketing (see Politics in Focus 20.3).

Yet, offsetting this nationalisation, there has also emerged in recent general elections more differentiation in the voters' choice in different parts of the country. The normal Labour–Conservative contest has been upset in Scotland and Wales by the intervention of the Nationalists, and in South England by the progress of the Liberal Democrats who are now often the main challengers to the Conservatives. There is now less of a national campaign and less of a national pattern to election results and general elections provide less of a national verdict.

British constituency elections are remarkably cheap by comparison with those in other Western states, largely because of the strict limits on local expenditure. The permitted maximum varies to take account of the electorate and geography of the constituency and works out at around £6,000 per candidate for the main parties. Until 2001, however, there was no limit on expenditure by the party headquarters. In the 1997 general election the two main parties spent a total of nearly £33 million (£20 million Conservative, £13 million Labour) in the 12 months prior to polling day. Labour spent some £7 million with its advertising agency, the Conservatives some £13 million. It was with some relief that the parties accepted the Neill Committee on Standards in Public Life proposals to end the arms race of election expenditure. These included a maximum spend for each party of £20 million (the limit for each party depends on the number of seats it is contesting) and required each party to submit accounts after the election. In the 12 months up to the May 2005 general election the Conservatives spent £17.8 million, Labour £17.9 million, and the Liberal Democrats £4.3 million.

Robin Cook was an advocate of electoral reform and in his *Point of Departure*, he wrote:

> It puzzles me that many of my colleagues who complain that Labour's core voters are ignored also stoutly defend the first past the post system which is the reason why core voters are ignored. The image, language and policies of the Labour leadership are angled to the right because they know that the only electoral battleground that matters is for the centre. A more pluralist electoral system that obliged them to fight for every vote would promptly produce a more diverse pitch (2003).

In contrast to the position in the United States, the British parties are provided with free time on radio and television and precluded from purchasing advertising time on these media. Another contrast to the United States is that advertising on regional broadcasting media and such other initiatives as the use of telephones for canvassing and conducting private local opinion polls are not legally possible unless the spending limits on local parties are lifted drastically.

There is some evidence that active local parties can boost voting support. In marginal seats a popular candidate and good organisation may be worth a few hundred votes, enough to affect the result in some seats. Research also suggests that an established MP, because of the media attention he may attract and the constituency services he may provide, is able to build up a personal vote, that is, support himself as an individual rather than as a representative of their party. Curtice and Steed (1997) have calculated that the effect of an established MP is to attract between 750 and 1,000 votes which would have otherwise gone to his opponent. But it is well to keep these figures in perspective; they would have made little difference in most recent general elections which have been won by landslides.

Declining turnout

Voting in general elections is still widely regarded as a minimal criterion of being a good citizen, is the most widespread form of political participation, and elections remain an important indicator of a government's legitimacy, or right to rule. But the sharp fall in turnout to 59% in the 2001 general election shocked the political establishment. It was not a 'one off' because the turnout at the previous general election in 1997 had been a post-war low and there were similar trends in elections for the EU Parliament and the devolved legislatures. There were other indicators of disengagement. A major study of voting in the 2001 general election claimed that many voters felt little incentive to vote when they did not feel close to the parties, perceived few differences between the major parties, and regarded the outcome (a clear Labour victory) as a foregone conclusion (Clarke et al 2004). These factors were still present in 2005. The importance of choice may be confirmed by the impact of UKIP, the only party to call in the 2004 European election for outright British withdrawal from the EU; turnout did increase substantially, from 24% in 1999 to 39%. Distrust in politicians and the parties also correlates with non-voting and these are both very low in Britain.

Immediately after the 2001 general election some Labour leaders claimed that the low turnout reflected the voters' satisfaction with the work of the Labour Government. Few were persuaded. Low turnout matters for two reasons. There is a socio-economic bias to participation; it increases with age and social status. Second, satisfaction with democracy in Britain appears to derive in part from engagement with politics and positive evaluations of the political system's performance (Clarke et al 2004). Because the same research found that young people are much less likely than older people to regard voting as a civic duty, turnout may be even more of a challenge in the future.

Politicians have shown an interest in the measures taken by other states to boost turnout. Experiments with voting on Sunday or having ballot boxes in shopping centres have made little difference and so far there has been little support for making the vote compulsory, as in Australia. Postal voting in the 2004 local and European elections certainly increased the number of voters, by at least some 10%, but even with some 15% of votes cast by post in the 2005 general election turnout increased only by 2% to 61.3%. The evidence of some abuse of postal votes by party activists led the Electoral Commission to warn about the lack of proper controls. There are good reasons for suspecting that changes in the mechanics of voting alone will not be sufficient to boost general election turnout to the levels of a generation ago. Surveys show that levels of interest in public affairs has not declined but interest in parties and voting has.

Electoral decline of the two-party system

Post-war support for the two main parties divides into two periods, with a sharp break occurring in 1974. The two parties' 'normal' votes for the three periods (1945–70, 1974–92 and 1997–2005) are shown in Table 20.1. Each party's 'normal' vote can be compiled from figures on Party identification and recent local and national election results. It is probably misleading to call this average a 'normal' or underlying level of support, in view of the weakening of strong party loyalties. In the first period, the two main parties gained an average of over 90% of the vote at general elections, and were evenly matched in shares of the vote (around 45%) and in the years spent in government. But in subsequent general elections the combined average has fallen to below 75%, with Labour the main casualty until 1992, and the Conservatives since. The Conservative vote (1974–92) averaged 40.7%, 6.3% higher than Labour's share, but in the elections of 1997, 2001 and 2005 it trails Labour by an average 8%. In general elections Britain has moved from a competitive two-party system to a dominant one-party system, first of the Conservatives and now of Labour.

	Cons	Lab	LibSDP/Lib Dem	Other
Mean, 1945–70	45.2	46.1	7.1	1.6
Mean, Feb 1974–92	40.7	34.4	19.5	5.5
Mean, 1997–2005	31.5	39.4	21	8.1

Source: Calculation of the author

The main 'third' party in the post-war period has been the Liberal Party, now Liberal Democrats. In general elections since 1970 it has gained an average of nearly a fifth of the vote, rising to a quarter in 1983 when it was part of the Alliance with the new Social Democratic Party. Its share of the vote by 2005 is still less than 1983 or 1987. But it has significantly increased its number of seats. It has been successful in concentrating resources on winnable seats, often having a strong local candidate or a well-established MP. The party gained 26 seats in 1997 and 2001 by such 'targeting'. In 2005 its opposition to top-fees and to the Iraq war won it support in seats with a concentration of Muslim voters and university students. The centre-party supporters have constituted a social microcosm of the electorate, being drawn fairly evenly from different classes, but by 2005, largely because the party took a position to the left of Labour on a number of issues, its supporters see it clearly as a party of the left.

The decline of Labour–Conservative dominance has been marked throughout Britain. In England this has been affected by the rise of the centre party, in Scotland and Wales by the rise of nationalism. In Scotland the high point for the Scottish Nationalist Party (SNP) was October 1974 when it gained a third of the vote, and it has not approached that share since. In Wales, the nationalist (Plaid Cymru) party scores around 10%. There has been little popular support for Welsh independence or devolution and the party's support is cultural, mainly confined to rural and Welsh-speaking areas.

In Northern Ireland, the main change has been not so much in voting behaviour between the two communities as in the relative electoral support for the parties speaking for them. Until 1972 the dominant Protestant party, the Ulster Unionists, supported the Conservatives at Westminster. In 1972, however, the Conservative Government forfeited that support when it suspended the Stormont Parliament, and the Unionist Party has since split. Ian Paisley's Democratic Unionist Party, which has opposed the Good Friday Agreement (see Chapter 17) has overtaken the Unionists as the voice of the Protestant community. In the 2005 general election the DUP gained nine seats, the Unionists a solitary one. Sinn Fein has become the dominant voice of the nationalist community.

What is clear is that the new proportional systems for European, Scottish Parliament, Welsh Assembly and London Assembly elections have enabled small parties to win seats they would not gain under first past the post. Some Labour voters used their second or top-up votes in Scotland tactically to help the election of Green and Militant Socialist candidates. In the European Parliament the Greens (three seats) and the United Kingdom Independence Party (two seats) have gained representation. Electoral reform has chipped away at the dominance of the two big parties, encouraged fragmentation of the party system and led to power sharing arrangements in Scotland and for a time in Wales.

The most striking features of the post-war period therefore are: (a) Labour's long-term decline after 1970, (b) the rise of a centre party since 1974 and fragmentation of the party system, and (c) the decline of the Conservative Party after 1992.

Electoral behaviour

Because the social structure and partisanship (or party identification) change only gradually they are forces for continuity in the short term although, as they change over time, they may provide the basis for an eventual shift in voting behaviour. Changes in the composition of the electorate due to deaths and comings of age of voters, and to emigration and immigration, mean that about a tenth of the electorate has changed over the lifetime of a five-year Parliament. Nearly a half of those on the electoral register in 2005 had not cast their first ballot before 1979. It is often said that voters have become more volatile, and the explanation for electoral changes lies more with such short-term factors as shifts in leadership, issue perceptions and assessments of competence, as well as the events preceding the election. It is true that attachments to party are more lightly held but it is interesting that out of some 600 opinion polls conducted between the beginning of 1993 and the beginning of 2005 the Conservatives have been ahead of Labour (and then only narrowly) in only five and have flat-lined in support at around 32–3%.

Many factors dispose a person to vote as he did at the previous election. Party loyalty or identification, the tendency of voters to think of themselves as a Labour, a Liberal or a Conservative, is one important force for stability. Some 70% of the British electorate identify with a party, though the proportion of electors identifying with the Conservative and Labour Parties has fallen from 1964, and the proportion of 'strong identifiers' with the two parties fell even more, from 44% to less than a fifth. The decline has been fairly even across all social groups but more marked among the young; each new cohort of voters has tended to be less partisan than its predecessors.

Compared with other voters, the strong party identifiers are more likely to agree with their party's policies, cast a vote, participate in politics and believe in the usefulness of the electoral process. They are 'reliable' supporters and likely to remain loyal, however badly the party is performing. Surveys have indicated that party allegiance tends to harden over time; a reason why many young or first-time voters are so changeable is that they have not 'learnt' party outlooks and are therefore less 'immune' to the influence of contemporary issues and events. Older voters, with a more settled allegiance, are more adept at screening new political issues and personalities, so that existing partisanship is maintained. Understandably, when many voters were firmly loyal to a party, the parties concentrated on mobilising traditional supporters.

Social class and voting

Social class has been important in studies of voting behaviour largely because of the weakness of other social factors. However, if we again divide post-war general elections into two halves, the decline in class voting is quite marked. In the 1945–70 period the Conservatives regularly gained four-fifths of the middle-class vote and Labour three-fifths of the working-class vote. But over the next two decades, these shares fell to less than three-fifths and one-half respectively. In the first period about two-thirds voted with their class-party, compared with less than half in the second period.

In their classic study Butler and Stokes (1974) show that the generation that came of age in the 1940s moved decisively to Labour. This generation had the highest level of class alignment and contained the highest proportion regarding politics as the expression of class conflict. The balance of class political loyalties was still moving in Labour's favour up to 1970. As the Conservative-inclined old died and left the electoral register and the Labour-inclined young entered it, so the net effects of deaths, comings of age and higher birth rates of the working class worked to Labour's advantage. Labour was the 'natural' majority party if it could mobilise its potential maximum vote. The Conservatives, to overturn the forces of electoral demography, had to rely on superior performance in office, more attractive leaders and policies, and Labour's shortcomings—and they usually did judging by their success in winning general elections. Social changes, particularly the decline in manual workers, council house tenants and trade unionists, and the more middle-class character of society, were eroding Labour's advantages and working in the Conservative Party's favour.

But demography turned out to be less important than politics. The 1997 election was remarkable for the record inroads Labour made on the middle class (see Table 20.2). Labour modernisers realised that Britain was becoming more middle class—it was not enough for the party to rely on the working class. New Labour adopted policies which brought it closer to the views of voters (Clarke et al 2004: 40), and Blair's appeal to the middle class in 1997 was remarkably successful and remained so in 2001 and 2005.

Some features remain clear. The Conservative Party has until recently been a cross-class party, drawing some 40% of its support from the working class and 60% from the middle class. Even while Labour was a relatively unsuccessful working class party it still drew two-thirds of its support from that class. Labour's electoral decline in the 1970s and 1980s was faster than changes in social structure or values. But the experience in other countries showed that such features as wider home ownership, affluence and the embourgeoisement of the working class are not necessarily electorally damaging for social democratic parties. A good deal of the electorate's disenchantment with the Labour Party at the time must be explained in political rather than sociological terms. The 1997 and later elections strongly reinforce the point. It was Labour's gain among the middle class that contributed

ad over Labour)

	Oct 74	1983	1992	1997	2001	2005
ABC1	+37	+39	+32	+5	+4	+3
C2	−23	+8	−1	−23	−20	−12 (this is for C2DE)
DE	−35	−8	−18	−38	−31	

Sources: MORI and You Gov for 2005

Notes: AB = professional and managerial workers, C1 = other white collar workers, DE = unskilled and casual workers. Columns do not total 100 because voting for other parties is not shown.

further to a weakening of the relationship between social class and vote. As well as party dealignment, or the falling support for the two main parties, there is also a class dealignment, that is, there is less relationship between a person's social class and his vote. In recent elections less than half the voters have been voting with their 'natural' class party.

Issues

Issues must satisfy a number of criteria if they are to shift voters from an established loyalty. These include:

- public opinion is unevenly divided on the issue
- a voter feels strongly about the issue
- a voter identifies the parties with different positions on the issue and believes that one of them can do something to improve matters.

These criteria greatly limit the scope for issues to shape voting. Ordinary voters may not be interested in many of the issues which deeply concern political activists or commentators. Unless voters think an issue is salient, they are not likely to hold considered and stable views on it. Often the typical voter's thinking is of the nature that higher taxes, unemployment, crime and strikes are 'a bad thing' and that 'something' should be done about them. A voter may agree with a party's policy on an issue but not believe that a party might be able to make much of a difference.

For a number of years Labour managed—because of class or party loyalty—to attract support among voters who disagreed with many of its policies. The disagreement was particularly sharp in 1983, when only a third of Labour supporters agreed with the party's

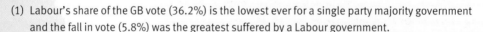

ITICS IN FOCUS 20.4

...res of the 2005 general election

(1) Labour's share of the GB vote (36.2%) is the lowest ever for a single party majority government and the fall in vote (5.8%) was the greatest suffered by a Labour government.

(2) The Conservatives gained 33 seats but its gain in vote share was negligible and its improvement was largely confined to the South East. It won a smaller vote share than in any election between 1857 and 1997.

(3) The Liberal Democrats won their third highest share of the vote since 1929 and the most seats since 1923.

(4) Turnout (61.2%) was only a little more than the record low of 2001. The greater use of postal voting does not appear to have helped to boost turnout.

(5) One in seven MPs is now not attached to either of the two main parties. If this continues there is a significant chance that British elections will produce hung Parliaments.

(6) The electoral system gives a massive advantage to Labour and helped deliver it an overall majority. New constituency boundaries will only slightly help to reduce this bias.

promises to extend public ownership, increase spending on the social services and protect existing trade union rights and immunities, and in 1987 when many disagreed with the party's defence policy. Labour's difficulty in the 1970s and early 1980s was that the psychological (party identification), social (class) and ideological (policy) sources of support had all been weakened.

More significant than particular issues as an influence on the vote is the party's image—perceptions of the strength of its leadership, competence and trustworthiness—and Labour until 1997 trailed here. Memories of Labour's record in office, particularly the winter of industrial disruption in 1979, impressions of Labour cultivated by opponents, critical newspapers, the party's divisions and perceptions that it was not 'sound' on such economic issues as tax and inflation, all fostered this sense of distrust, and were still present in the 1992 election. Since then Labour has moved into a commanding lead over the Conservatives on many questions about economic competence. Meanwhile, the negative perceptions of the Conservatives on handling key public services—something exacerbated by its talk about income tax cuts—was damaging in recent general elections. In 2001 the Conservative emphasis on such issues as 'saving' the pound, tax cuts and curbing asylum seekers seemed designed to please party members and loyalists rather than non-Conservative voters for whom these issues were not salient. This was frequently criticised as a 'core vote' strategy, designed to appeal to convinced Conservatives supporters when the party needed to reach out to non-Conservatives. In 2005, the party under Michael Howard attracted support for its hard line on asylum and immigration, on which his party led Labour in the polls, but this was not enough to offset the deficits on health, education and the economy. The emphasis did nothing to improve the image of the party; it was still seen as stuck in the past, sectional, divisive, extreme and not having its heart in the right place (see Table 20.3). Labour lost support in 2005 but this did not redound to the benefit of the Conservatives (see Politics in Focus 20.4).

Short-term factors

The events during and preceding an election campaign can also change votes. The industrial disputes and disruption in the winter of 1979, the recapture of the Falklands in 1982, the honeymoon period of John Major's first year as Prime Minister in 1991 and the Iraq war and its fallout in 2003 and 2004 were all given extended coverage by the mass media and influenced voters' perceptions of the parties.

Another short-term factor causing voters to shift allegiance is the state of the economy, or rather the combined effects of the voters' perceptions of how the economy has performed, changes in voters' economic circumstances, and their personal expectations for the future. Survey evidence shows that voters who feel that their economic circumstances have improved are likely to 'reward' the party in government by switching to it, and to defect if they feel that their conditions have worsened. Governments of both parties, aware of the voters' mood, have often tried to manufacture short-term economic 'booms' and a 'feel good' mood by tax cuts and increased spending on popular programmes during the run-up to a general election. The perception that the Conservative Party was the best party to guard the increased prosperity was significant in influencing voting behaviour

Irrespective of how you intend to vote (or have already voted by post), which of the following statements do you think apply more to the Conservative Party and which apply more to the Labour Party?

	Applies more to . . .			Don't know	Lab minus Con (%)
	Con (%)	Lab %	Both/ neither		
It seems to have succeeded in moving on and left its past behind it	17	42	24	17	25
Its leaders are prepared to take tough and unpopular decisions	19	42	28	11	23
Even if I don't always agree with it, at least its heart is in the right place	22	40	22	17	18
It is led by people of real ability	19	36	34	12	17
The kind of society it wants is broadly the kind of society I want	33	40	19	8	7
It seems to chop and change all the time: you can never be quite sure what it stands for	35	26	26	12	−9
It is too extreme	29	16	33	22	−13
It seems to want to divide people instead of bringing them together	41	20	25	14	−21
It seems rather old and tired	44	18	27	10	−26
It seems to appeal to one section of society rather than to the whole country	48	20	22	10	−28
It seems stuck in the past	45	11	27	17	−34
It has very little chance of winning this election	63	6	16	15	−57

Source: Populus. Fieldwork, 29 April–1 May

in the 1983 and 1987 elections. Voters who believed that they had prospered economically over the lifetime of the Parliament were particularly likely to vote Conservative (Sanders and Price 1994). In 1992, a crucial number of voters calculated that Labour would do a worse job than the Conservatives in improving their living standards. Such issues as health and education favoured Labour but 'pocketbook' voting favoured the Conservatives.

The relationship between (a) the state of the economy, (b) how it is perceived by voters (which may be shaped by media coverage), (c) changes in individual voters' living standards and how these are perceived, and (d) to which party voters attribute blame or credit for bad/good times, is a complex one. In 1997 the Conservative Government could point to lower inflation, unemployment, and interest rates. But this record made no difference to the voters; they felt disillusionment with the Conservative Party, as a result of tax increases, the ERM débâcle, sleaze and divisions over Europe. Moreover, Blair had done much to transform the Labour Party, which had now overtaken the Conservative Party on most survey questions about party competence and managing the economy. The result was that voters acknowledged the improvements to the economy but would not give the Conservative Party credit for it. The party's image was so negative that it presided over a 'voteless recovery' (see Finkelstein 1998; Sanders 1997). The economy, alone, does not decide voting behaviour.

How did Labour achieve one of the most remarkable turnarounds by any British party in the 20th century? After all, in the wake of the 1992 election defeat, many analysts could point to social trends and political factors which suggested that the Conservatives were the new majority. Some part of the explanation is to do with voters' disillusion with the Conservatives but some is also due to the modernisation of Labour (see pp 353–4). Modernisation in electoral terms involved not only the use of modern communication techniques but also broadening Labour's electoral base. For a number of elections Labour had been weak among the middle class, homeowners, women and the South East. Labour went out of its way to reassure these groups—often termed 'middle England'. Labour proclaimed that it was no longer a party of tax and spend, would not be 'soft' on the trade unions and crime, and that it was now safe to vote Labour. In 1997 the party made big gains, particularly among the middle class, first-time voters and women. Labour had become a successful catch-all party. Its image is greatly superior to the Conservative's; on questions of party unity, trustworthiness, leadership and competence in managing the economy Labour moved into and retained a decisive lead over the Conservatives. For the first time ever the bulk of the press swung behind the party, although some of this reflected dissatisfaction with the Conservatives, and has remained pro-Labour in later elections.

Opinion polls

Opinion polls are almost inseparable from the conduct of general elections in Western states. The mass media, which commission polls, are concerned to make a story about which party is in the lead and is likely to win an election. The political parties also conduct private polls to help them plan and monitor their campaigns. The major polling organisations such as ICM, NOP and MORI have been established for some years now and they supply most of their political polling to the mass media. By interviewing a sample of 1,000 or so voters, drawn randomly from the electorate, the polls claim to be correct within a margin of plus or minus 3% in 95% of cases. The polls have a good record in predicting election winners, though they have been spectacularly wrong on three occasions, 1970,

February 1974 and 1992. In 1992 the final forecasts of the five major pollsters averaged a 1.3% Labour lead in contrast to a 7.6% lead in votes for the Conservatives on polling day. In 1997 and 2001 some pollsters claimed credit for correctly predicting the outcome. But most of them substantially overstated Labour's actual lead on polling day. Had the election result been close there was a huge potential for another embarrassment. In 2005 the polls had a good record in their predictions.

It is frequently alleged that the polls, by making forecasts, influence the election result, for example, by creating a 'bandwagon' of support for the leading party. Since 1964 the number of opinion polls has increased and their findings have become more publicised. More voters are now aware of what the polls are saying and are potentially more open to influence. But there is no evidence that the polls do create a 'bandwagon'. In most general elections since 1964 the party ahead in the final survey did worse than predicted on polling day. In 1997, for example, Labour began the campaign with an average lead of 22% in the polls; on polling day this had fallen to 16%, and Labour led in votes only by 13%. The polls may also have a 'reverse bandwagon' effect. In 2005 Labour campaign managers feared that polls that showed the party was heading for a clear victory would encourage some supporters not to turn out on polling day and allow the Conservatives to sneak a victory or lead to a 'hung' Parliament.

There has been clear evidence in by-elections, however, that voters use the reported findings of constituency opinion polls to 'punish' one or other of the two main parties, and the Liberal candidates often benefit from this tactical voting. And there is no doubt that the findings of polls influence the morale of the politicians and how the media reports a campaign. They increasingly focus on what Americans call the 'horse race'—which party is ahead in the polls, which is gaining/losing, why this is so, and what its significance is. Opinion-poll-related stories are usually among the three most heavily covered features in the press in election campaigns.

In 1970 commentators and bookmakers wrote off the possibility of a Conservative election victory because Labour was so far ahead in the polls. In 1992 few anticipated a Conservative majority because all the polls pointed either to a Labour victory or to a hung Parliament with Labour as the largest party. Almost inevitably perhaps, commentators wrote of a brilliant Labour campaign and a poor Conservative one, until the result was known.

Manifesto and mandate

British political parties are programmatic. They fight general elections on manifestos and promise, if elected, to carry them out. Leaders present the promises of a manifesto as a 'contract' between the party and its voters, and on the whole parties in government do carry out a great many of the specific legislative promises. Manifestos are also designed to persuade the voters. In addition to making proposals for specific policy areas, the tone of a manifesto is important in colouring a party's image as, for example, 'national', 'sectional' or 'radical'. They are final statements of party policy and within the party may be regarded almost as a draft legislative programme for the new Parliament. When governments introduce policies which are sharply at variance with the promises, or which were not foreshadowed in the manifesto, the opposition is apt to cry, 'You have not got a mandate!' or 'You have broken your promises!'

Newly elected ministers invariably choose to regard an election victory as conferring a mandate on their policies. The idea of the electoral mandate has changed over the years and even today it has no agreed meaning. Essentially, it refers to the authority of a government to carry out its election promises—which may or may not be enshrined in a manifesto. In some general elections, a particular issue may have predominated and the main parties' positions may have been so clearly differentiated on it—and recognised as such by many voters—that the outcome of the election is widely regarded as having clear implications for the subsequent direction of policy. In 2001 Tony Blair declared that Labour's election victory was a mandate for him to press on with his reform of public services. Occasionally it has been argued that a government should not introduce a major policy, or one concerning constitutional matters, without putting the issue clearly before the voters. In 1992 the Conservative manifesto made great play of its record in cutting taxes, promised to cut them again, and warned that Labour would increase taxes. It lost much credit when, having won the election, it increased taxes in 1993 and 1994. Blair's breach of his 2001 manifesto pledge not to introduce top-up fees in higher education almost certainly cost the party a handful of seats in university towns in the 2005 election.

Another and a related meaning of the mandate is that the election enables the voters to indicate their preferences between broad party programmes rather than for a particular policy. Since 1945 the manifestos of the main parties have become longer and more detailed. As central government has extended the range of its activities and responsibilities, and more pressure groups have organised to press a policy on government, so the number of issues on which parties are expected to take a line has grown. Governments now claim to have a mandate for a battery of items in the manifesto, however picayune each may be. As pledges are fulfilled, so the government spokesman claims that he has kept faith with the electorate, regardless of the popularity of the measure. But voters for a party simply cannot be expected to be aware of all the proposals, let alone agree with them.

Surveys have dented the idea that voting decisions are largely determined by specific policy considerations. A voter's decision is based on many considerations, including traditional allegiance and perceptions of the parties' records, competence and leadership, as well as policy preferences. It is unrealistic to expect most voters to be aware of or, if aware, even agree with all of them. Parties present a broad package of policies and voters have no way of voting for or against particular items in a programme at general elections.

What then remains of the idea of the mandate? One can certainly make out a case that party leaders invoke it when they find it expedient to do so. Yet parties in office do carry out the great majority of their election promises when these can be cast in legislative form. A clear policy commitment strengthens the hand of a minister with his civil servants if he wants to initiate a new policy. A government is also likely to be at its strongest *vis-à-vis* public opinion, pressure groups and the opposition in the first year or so of office when the memory of its electoral success and 'mandate' is still fresh. Ministers who break promises are likely to get into trouble not only with the opposition but with their own supporters, both inside and outside Parliament. The mandate, in its modern form, means that most voters broadly approve (or prefer in comparison to anything else on offer) a party's general sense of policy direction rather than its specific policies, and agree with its right to carry out policies it laid before the country. But voters are more interested in manifesto aspirations (such as full employment, lower inflation, better public services, and safer neighbourhoods, etc) than specific policy promises.

 # Conclusion

Modern political representation assigns an important role to political parties and elections which provide the opportunities for popular choice. In another, less institutional, sense representation also has to do with a high degree of trust and identification between voters and politicians. The government's authority or right to claim obedience from citizens rests in large part on its representativeness (that is, it has emerged through a competitive election).

Many features of representation and the electoral system have become matters of political dispute in recent years. Some critics complain about the conduct of modern elections and/or question their significance. They suggest that the growing importance of modern public relations techniques—expensive advertising, use of opinion polls and focus groups, and the role of spin-doctors—promote presentation and packaging at the cost of substance. They allege that the use of sound bites and photo opportunities reduces the scope for meaningful political debate. But politicians and some commentators retort that the media as well as the parties are to blame for growing voter disillusionment (Norris 1998). It is certainly possible to argue that general elections now have less impact for public policy than used to be the case. British governments have lost decision-making initiatives to the EU, to a devolved Parliament in Scotland and Assemblies in Northern Ireland and Wales, and to referenda.

Electoral reform (ie the adoption of a system of PR) has been introduced for various elections, but not for Westminster. The system has been turning smaller minorities of votes into a majority of seats. In the first nine general elections between 1945 and 1970, the party in government was elected by an average of 47.5% of the votes. But in the next nine general elections, between 1974 and 2005, this average fell to 41%. With more than two major political parties the present electoral system works less predictably and it may produce even more disproportional results than before. In 1983 the Conservatives actually had a smaller share of the vote than in 1979, but they trebled their overall majority in seats to 144. Between 1979 and 1992, thanks in part to the electoral system, Britain had a dominant Conservative Party system. With just over 42% of the vote, it managed to win handsome parliamentary victories, as Labour and the Liberal Parties have divided the non-Conservative vote. Since 1997, it has been a dominant Labour system. The referendum has been introduced as a supplementary channel of electoral opinion, but with little debate about its constitutional implications (see Chapter 10). Finally, the 'mandate' concept has been attacked, as more interventionist governments have liberally interpreted their election as a blanket approval for their policies.

The fragmentation of political choice, partly because of the decline of aggregate support for the two main parties, partly because of the growth of minor parties, and partly because of the different line-ups of parties in various parts of the UK, means that British general elections now give less of a national verdict. But the trends also undermine a dichotomous view of British politics and society—a political dimension of left and right which correlates with two political parties and two social classes.

KEY POINTS

- Britain's first past the post electoral system has traditionally been defended on the grounds that it produces strong, stable and accountable governments; voters have a clear choice between party alternatives; and it is accepted and easily understood.

- Since the 1970s this view has been challenged. Pressure for electoral reform at Westminster is widespread but not strong. Labour is at best ambivalent and the Conservatives opposed; the electorate is not interested and, crucially, those in a position to introduce reform, the ministers of the day, have few incentives to do so.

- The media, the issues, and the strategies of the parties have all contributed to a growing nationalisation of election campaigns.

- Since the 1970s, partisanship has declined, relative sizes of social classes have changed and become more differentiated, and class party loyalty has weakened. These trends have helped to undermine a dichotomous view of British politics and society—a politics of left and right correlating with two political parties and two social classes. The emergence of the Liberal Democrats means that the two main parties now struggle to reach an aggregate 70% of the vote at general elections.

- Voting behaviour has become more volatile and less predictable.

KEY QUESTIONS

(1) Why has pressure for electoral reform increased during the last 20 years?

(2) If the case for electoral reform is self-evident, why has reform not been introduced?

(3) Examine the cases for and against publishing opinion poll findings during an election campaign.

(4) Why has turnout in elections declined?

IMPORTANT WEBSITES

The Electoral Reform Society—www.electoral—reform.org.uk/; the Electoral Commission—www.electoralcommission. org.uk; the Commission's reports—www.electoral commission.org.uk; UK general elections since 1832—www.psr.keele. ac. uk/area/uk/edates.htm; parliamentary by-elections since 1945—www.geocities.com/by_elections/; votes that determine elections—www.psr. keele. ac.uk/area/uk/makediff.htm; UK Elect—http://ourworld.compuserve.com/homepages/timb/.

FURTHER READING

On voting see P. Norris (1997), *Electoral Change Since 1945*, Oxford: Oxford University Press; D. Denver (2002) *Elections and Voting Behaviour in Britain*, Hemel Hempstead: Harvester Wheatsheaf; and H. Clarke et al (2004) *Political Choice in Britain*, Oxford: Oxford University Press. On campaigning, see D. Kavanagh (1995) *Election Campaigning*, Oxford: Blackwell; Wring D (2005) *The Politics of Marketing. The Labour Party*, Basingstoke: Palgrave and J. Lees-Marshment (2001) *Political Parties and Political Marketing*, Manchester: Manchester University Press. On electoral systems, see D. Farrell (2001) *Electoral Systems. A Comparative Introduction*, Basingstoke: Palgrave. On the 2005 general election see D. Kavanagh and D. Butler (2005) *The British General Election of 2005*, Basingstoke: Palgrave and P. Norris and C. Wlezien (eds), (2005) *Britain Votes 2005*, Oxford: Oxford University Press. For discussion of ideas of representation, see A. Birch (1964) *Representative and Responsible Government*, London Allen & Unwin.

CHRONOLOGY

The role of elections in Britain

1832	Reform Act: middle class gain vote, subject to property qualification
1867	Reform Act: urban skilled workers gain vote
1872	Secret ballot
1884	Reform Act: vote extended to rural labourers
1911	Parliament Act: maximum life of Parliament reduced from 7 to 5 years
1918	Representation of the People Act: votes for men 21 and over and for women 30 and over
1928	Representation of the People Act: votes for women reduced to age 21
1949	Representation of the People Act: abolition of plural voting (business, universities)
1975	Referendum on continued membership of Common Market
1998	Report of Independent (Jenkins) Commission on voting system. No action taken
1997	Referenda in Scotland and Wales on devolution
1998	Neill Committee proposal to limit party expenditure on general election campaigns to £20million accepted
2001	Electoral Commission established to oversee elections and referenda

Visit the Online Resource Centre that accompanies this book for links to more information on this chapter topic

CHAPTER TWENTY ONE

Pressure Groups and Policy Networks

READER'S GUIDE

This chapter analyses the relationship between the state and civil society. First, it examines the role of pressure groups within the British political system before presenting a set of typologies classifying different types of pressure groups. The policy networks approach is then explored as a meso-level tool of analysis linking macro-theories of the state to more specific micro-policy decisions. The chapter then analyses the changing relationship between government and pressure groups from 1979 to the present. The chapter concludes by arguing that network analysis on its own is inadequate and should be applied to broader macro-theories of the state, in order to provide a richer explanatory analysis of political phenomena in British politics.

Introduction

If people in Britain were free to influence the government only at general elections, then Rousseau's 18th-century gibe about the British being slaves between elections, might still have some validity. But during the last century, two major channels for representing popular opinion have evolved. The first is the party electoral one, in which a person votes for a party as a member of a territorial constituency, and the second is the interest group-functional one, in which a person joins a group consisting of people who have shared attitudes or occupations. Most individuals possess both a vote and belong to a group. But whereas a vote can only be used periodically, perhaps every four years or so in the case of general elections, pressure groups allow citizens a continuous opportunity to try and influence policy in particular areas. This underpins one of the basic principles of contemporary liberal democracy—the freedom to associate. Pressure groups are one of the fundamental components of the British political process providing a key medium through which civil society can engage in political discourse and engagement. In particular, while the basic role of political parties in a democracy is to seek to attain power, the aim of pressure groups is to influence power, or, more particularly, the making of public policy (see Politics in Focus 21.1).

In this chapter we explore the role of pressure groups as a fundamental component of civil society. Underpinning any analysis of pressure groups is the extent to which they can influence both the political decision-making process and, in turn, affect the making of public policy. In order to understand this crucial interaction between core policy-makers (be it at the local, national or supranational level) and executive and pressure groups, we examine different typologies used in political science to characterise the role and impact of pressure groups. Here, we suggest that the 'insider/outsider' framework offers the most analytical sophisticated approach for addressing the key issue of pressure group influence on centres of political power. We then look more specifically at the policy-network approach which can be understood as a 'meso-level' tool for exploring the various degrees of influence different types of pressure groups exert across different policy areas. Finally, we consider the crucial relationship between the policy-network approach and macro-state theory. As we see below, different types of networks have implications for our understanding of the broader nature of political power in the British political system. Here, it is crucial to recognise that Marxist and elitist models of the British state embrace a different understanding of the nature of policy networks than that which pluralist accounts would offer.

Interest groups and democracy

The role of interest groups in a liberal democracy can appear somewhat contradictory. On the one hand, between general elections, they can offer a vital channel of political expression between government and society. Yet, alternatively, they can be associated with

Pressure group A generic term for any kind of group seeking to influence the government to adopt or change particular policies.

Types of group
— **promotional**: advocating a cause, eg Child Poverty Action or Campaign for Nuclear Disarmament
— **interest**: representing those engaged in a particular sector, eg trade unions, Automobile Association, British Medical Association
— **peak**: representing a set of interests, eg TUC
— **episodic**: these spring up to pursue a particular project, eg a proposed site for nuclear waste or the Countryside Alliance.

'Insider group' A group with direct access to the corridors of power, eg National Farmers' Union and the Department of Environment, Food and Rural Affairs.

'Outsider Group' A group which does not have access to the key policy-makers in the core executive. This is because such a group explicitly chooses not to attain such status, or because the core executive chooses not to engage in any form of dialogue, eg Black Flag, Reclaim the Streets.

Polyarchy A term coined by Robert Dahl (an American political scientist) to denote a benign political system in which competing groups exert checks and balances and thereby ensure stability and political freedom. Broadly similar to *pluralism*.

Clientelism Close identity of interest between a government department and client group.

Corporatism Pressure groups incorporated inside the governmental process, economic policy.

Tripartism A form of corporatism associated with Britain in the 1970s when much economic policy was the outcome of negotiations between the government, the Trades Union Congress (TUC) and the Confederation of British Industry (CBI).

sectionalism and the possible exercise of sanctions, which appear to be inimical to ideas of reasoned discussion and the general welfare.

The first major study of pressure groups in Britain was S.E. Finer's *Anonymous Empire*, published in 1958. It demonstrated the existence and operation of such groups within political parties and Parliament and how they influence policy. Finer concluded that the groups were (as far as the general public was concerned) faceless, voiceless and unidentifiable—in brief, anonymous. Yet in practice, liberal democracy should also allow for checks on government and limits to majority rule. The opportunity for pressure groups to operate in the political arena depends, therefore, on the existence of such freedoms as those of association, assembly and speech, and on the acknowledged legitimacy of viewpoints different from those of the government. Recognition and toleration of the diversity of interests in society are necessary conditions for pressure-group activity.

In Britain today, more than half the adult population are members of at least one organisation (this can range from Amnesty International to the Women's Institute) and many

FOCUS 21.2

ressure groups and the decline of mass political parties

One of the features of British society as it evolved in the post-1945 era, is that it has become much less homogenous. Greater diversification in race, class, culture, leisure, work, etc reflect the development of a much more heterogeneous and diverse peoples. This has challenged the more traditional analysis of British society and politics based on a crude dividing line between capital and labour. For political science, in order to analyse many contemporary political issues, class is no longer the main determinant of political attitudes and what people expect of government. Other fault lines have appeared between, for example:

- the educated and knowledge rich and the knowledge poor;
- those that are IT literate, as opposed to those who are electronically disenfranchised;
- those who feel secure and embrace change and those who feel threatened by change;
- those who want maximum freedom for the individual to pursue their own interests and those who desire a society where communities are encouraged to co-operate together to enhance social capital (see Gibbins and Reimer 1999).

These trends have made the task of mainstream, mass political parties that much more difficult. For many, the concept of mass political parties is no longer regarded as the best means by which a person in society can express his opinions or channel a multiplicity of demands. Indeed, in the second half of the 20th century, the rise of single-issue pressure groups became a key feature of society. Increasingly, individuals have come to regard pressure group activity, rather than party political membership, as a more effective means of having a direct impact on a political issue or debate. In particular, mass political parties are increasingly portrayed as being no longer able to voice the concerns and sentiments of an increasingly diverse society.

Thus, at the start of the 21st century, it is argued that the failure of political parties to meet the complexity of demands placed upon them by an increasingly complex and socially diverse electorate has been reflected in a steady decline in party membership and low turnouts at general elections. Conversely, there has been an exponential rise in both the number and membership of pressure groups, as individuals have come to regard pressure groups as a more effective channel for political expression. Post-modernists argue this trend indicates that we now live in an era in which traditional forms of political practice based on mass political parties are in terminal decline, and a new form of politics is now developing (see Chapter 23).

belong to a number of groups (the Royal Society for the Protection of Birds has more members than all of the British political parties put together!). They also belong to other communities of interests based on one's identity which can include homeownership, employment status, students, gender, shareowners, urban or rural dwellers, homosexuals, ethnicity, parents, pensioners, car owners, and so on, even though these interests might not be formally organised. In contrast to the opportunities provided by groups for representing specific interests, voting at a general election may not be particularly effective for expressing and weighing individual views on the issues. Elections provide a rough and ready verdict on the policy packages of the parties, while groups supplement and qualify the representational role of the election by providing for the expression of views on specific issues. Indeed, one of the contemporary debates in British politics and elsewhere is to explain the decline in both voter turnout and party membership. One compelling argument is that we now live in a much more complex, diverse society with numerous competing interests compared to say 40 years ago and this has problematised the way in which political parties can offer a broad package of policies that have a widespread appeal (see Politics in Focus 21.2 and Chapter 22).

The role of pressure groups and political parties

In so far as groups are voluntary associations, containing like-minded members, and attempt to influence policy, they partially resemble political parties. But parties differ from groups in three important respects (see also Politics in Focus 21.3):

- Parties run candidates at general elections and try to capture political office directly. Although some groups support candidates for a political party at elections, only the trade unions sponsor candidates on a considerable scale.

- Parties, as would-be governors, develop comprehensive programmes of policies to appeal to a majority of the electorate: in doing so they have to aggregate and strike a balance between the demands of various interests. Groups, by contrast, seek to articulate a sectional interest—even though they may find it good tactics to present it as identical to the public interest.

- A party in government has to accept responsibility for co-ordinating and implementing a wide range of policies, whereas a group seeks to influence the policy-makers in the area that concerns it.

Critics may reasonably propose qualifications to the above distinctions. Such parties as the Greens or the UK Independence Party have more in common with pressure groups—mainly interested in a single issue—although they operate as a political party. Elsewhere, in both the 2001 and 2005 general elections, Dr Richard Taylor, a retired consultant physician successfully won the Worcester seat of Wyre Forest on an independent platform—the Kidderminster Hospital and Health Concern (KHHC)—over the sole issue of the closure of Kidderminster Hospital. The media dubbed the doctor 'the man in the white coat', a reference to the mantle he had inherited from the journalist Martin Bell, the original 'man in the white suit' who for one term in 1997 was elected MP for Tatton over the single issue of sleaze in politics. But the broad distinction is still useful: the political party seeks office, general influence and, ultimately, responsibility; the interest group primarily seeks access to decision-makers and to exercise sectional influence.

Theory Pressure groups remedy the shortcomings of representative democracy:

- they permit a continuous dialogue between government and the governed
- they provide opportunities for political participation
- they provide government with information and expertise
- they articulate and defend minority interests
- they act as a check on abuse of government power
- they compete with one another to influence policy outcomes

Practice

- not all groups have equal access
- resources and leverage vary between groups
- clientelism may arise and be detrimental to national interest

The growth and impact of pressure groups

Reasons for the growth of group activity in the last century are not hard to find. As we saw in Chapter 3, the role of government shifted from that of a 'night watchman' to one in which its functions dramatically grew as an employer, economic decision-maker, taxer, regulator and distributor of benefits. One effect has been the increasing impact of government on many areas of life. This has politicised more and more human activity, while at the same time making government more dependent on an array of groups for co-operation and compliance. Without continuous consultation and co-operation between groups and government departments, the formulation and implementation of policy would grind to a halt or at least become more difficult. The nature of the relationship between government and groups can, more often than not, be understand in terms of co-dependence—they need each other in order to achieve their goals (see below). Here, governments prefer to negotiate with authoritative and representative spokespeople for interests. Ministers may have policies for housing or education but they do not build houses, set mortgage rates, recruit teachers or build schools. The policies of government consist of initiatives, resources and decisions, which they hope will lead groups and other decision-makers to behave in desirable ways. In this type of relationship, co-operation is more usual than conflict.

Classifying pressure groups

Following Finer's (1958) original study into pressure groups there have been a number of attempts to create a typology of pressure groups. We may distinguish three types of groups that try to influence government without themselves holding office.

Promotional, cause or attitude groups

These types of groups advocate a cause and their potential membership is, in theory, coextensive with the entire population (see Stewart 1958). Among such groups are the Abortion Law Reform Association and the Howard League for Penal Reform. We might also include the 'think-tanks' that have emerged in recent years, promoting ideas and policies, for example, from the New Right—the free market Adam Smith Institute and Institute of Economic Affairs, whilst from the Centre Left—DEMOS or the Institute for Public Policy Research.

Sectional/interest groups

These groups are usually based on an occupation or economic interest, like professional organisations, trade unions and business groups. Their role is to represent the interests of that section and membership is often restricted to that section only (see Jordan and Richardson 1987). Such groups might include, for example, the British Medical Association (BMA) as the voice of the medical profession representing doctors, or the National Farmers Union (NFU) representing farmers.

The distinction between the two groups is not always clear-cut. Some promotional groups may contain supporters who have an economic interest in the cause, and interest groups try as a rule to link their campaign with a wider cause, for example, the Countryside Alliance aver that a ban on fox-hunting will have a widespread residual impact on both the countryside and rural communities. Because promotional groups have few tangible rewards to offer their supporters and few sanctions to wield, they appear to be weaker than interest groups. More importantly, neither of these two categorisations is particularly helpful in analysing the influence that groups may wield. If, at the heart of the debate on pressure groups lies the question, how variable is the nature of their power and concomitantly influence, then a more useful distinction can be made between insider and outsider groups.

Insider/outsider groups

This is the most enduring categorisation of pressure groups. Grant (2000) observes that insider groups enjoy legitimacy from government and are consulted on regular basis, while outsider groups either do not want to or have been unable to establish a consultative role with government, or have yet to gain recognition (see Politics in Focus 21.4). The chances of a group gaining access to the relevant department or decision-makers depend on various factors, but most importantly this is conditioned by the resources it commands and to what extent government is dependent on those resources. The two most important resources a group can possess are—expertise/knowledge and veto power:

(1) Expertise: Many insider groups tend to be experts in their field, for example doctors in the field of health care. They tend to have a monopoly over knowledge in a particular area and so Whitehall is almost wholly dependent on them for access to

POLITICS IN FOCUS 21.4

Insider status

In 1989 Wyn Grant categorised groups as 'insider' and 'outsider' (*Pressure Groups, Politics and Democracy in Britain* (London: Philip Allan, 1989). For further discussion on this, see Wyn Grant's follow-up study, *Pressure Groups and British Politics* (London: Macmillan, 2000).

What is an insider group? A group having direct and regular access to the government department responsible for its particular policy sector.

Why do groups seek to become insiders? In Britain's centralised system of government groups enjoying direct access to Whitehall, where detailed policy is drawn up, have the best chance of influencing policy outcomes.

How do groups become insiders? They have information and expertise the government needs
— they speak with authority for their sector and have a high density of membership
— they have leverage/sanctions
— their aims are compatible with the policy agenda of the government of the day.

Do all groups seek to become insiders? No, it brings constraints on a group's freedom of speech and activity and may involve an expectation of consultation in exchange for the group delivering members' co-operation in the policy that results. In short, constraints are the informal 'rules of the game' (see below).

this knowledge when making policy in the relevant field. This is a vital resource as it conditions a department's reliance on a group for good-quality information and administrative co-operation, as well as functional indispensability.

(2) Veto Power: A group's authority is enhanced where it is representative or has a high-density membership, that is, a high proportion of actual to potential members, as in the case of the National Farmers Union. Only farmers can implement farming policy which results in the National Farmers Union enjoying a powerful insider status, so it is potentially in a position to turn round to government and refuse to implement a particular farming policy it disagrees with. The key word here is compliance, which is vital if legislation is to be effective. Governments recognise the importance of compliance and so they are willing to listen to interest groups who can command an effective veto and are therefore capable of ensuring non-compliance of policy.

Other characteristics expected of an insider group include a reputation for discretion, responsibility and confidentiality. Insider groups are likely to have regular access to the department and exchange information—something which is unlikely to take place without mutual trust. A group's adherence to norms of 'responsible behaviour' or 'rules of the game'—are its leaders reliable to deal with, will they keep confidences, will they avoid controversy, etc—increases the likelihood of its access. Outsiders have few rights of access because they have not established trust and/or have little relevant information to provide. For example, in recent years, the now annual May Day anti-globalisation protests have involved a rainbow alliance of groups including the anarchist organisation Black Flag,

Class War Federation, the republican group Movement Against the Monarchy (MA'M), as well as more disparate organisations such as Reclaim the Streets. None of these groups either wish to be, or are likely to be consulted by governments who view them with deep distrust. Elsewhere, the Howard League for Penal Reform has access to the Home Office; RAP (Radical Alternatives to Prisons), which favours the abolition of prison, does not. Arms manufacturers have long had access to Ministry of Defence officials, but the Campaign for Nuclear Disarmament (CND) does not. It is easy to see how, over time, civil servants in a department and group leaders may come to share a similar outlook about 'sensible' (*sic*) policies.

Although the insider/outsider typology remains the dominant approach for classifying pressure groups, its usefulness has recently come under challenge. In some policy areas, insiders greatly outnumber outsiders and achieving consultative status for example, serving on a departmental advisory committee may signify that the group has been incorporated or been 'tamed' by Whitehall. Elsewhere, some critics have argued that, in view of the large numbers involved, one needs to identify *core* insider groups from others (Maloney, Jordon and McLaughlin 1994; Grant 2000). Nevertheless, the utility of the insider/outsider approach is in its implicit recognition of the influence that different groups either do or do not wield. This then leads to the question—what tools are available for measuring the politics of influence exerted by pressure groups? Here, we can turn to the policy networks approach, which in the last two decades has become one of the most dominant methodologies used in political science for analysing political power and the impact of pressure groups.

The policy network approach

One of the tasks of political science is to explain why certain policy outcomes occur and which actors are responsible for shaping a particular policy. Yet, this is no simple task, for as has already been observed in Chapter 3, the British political system can be broadly characterised as closed, elitist and secretive (see Marsh, Richards and Smith 2003). Even in the light of the introduction of a Freedom of Information Act in 2000, the Official Secrets Act still ensures that information and minutes concerning key discussions involving ministers, civil servants and other interested parties in the formulation of policy are not readily available for analysis. To overcome this problem, the policy network approach is one means by which we can attempt to analyse the relationship between the state and pressure groups.

What is the policy network approach?

The policy network approach is more flexible than broader theories of the state, as it is concerned with explaining behaviour within particular sections of the state or particular policy areas. Therefore, it can account for variations in pressure group/government relations that exist over a range of policy areas. This overcomes one of the problems of traditional macro-theories of the state which, by attempting to analyse the state in its totality (holistically), tend to regard state institutions as fixed or monolithic phenomena. Policy networks provide a mechanism for assessing various conflicts within state institutions and between pressure groups and its focus of analysis is on a particular policy area. By examining the ongoing relationship between government and pressure groups, network analysis can be seen as a useful way of linking micro-levels of analysis pitched at the level of a particular policy decision to macro-level analysis concerned with power in society. Therefore, the network approach argues for the need to disaggregate (or breakdown) policy analysis across different functions in order to provide a more satisfactory understanding of state action. In so doing, the policy network approach can be regarded as being a multi-level tool of analysis, in that having disaggregated, policy networks can then be applied to macro-theories of the state in order to explain the types of relationships between state actors and pressure groups.

The evolution of network analysis

Since the mid-1960s, US political scientists have accepted the notion that policy-making occurs in subsystems. Originally, these subsystems in the US were referred to as 'iron triangles' as they involved three actors: an administrative agency; a congressional subcommittee; a pressure group. Policy was seen to be developed within a tightly knit relationship between the three—hence the phrase an 'iron triangle'. So, policy networks and their importance for understanding pressure group/government relations derived out of this notion of sub-government in the US.

Heclo and Wildavsky

This was a theme developed in Britain by Heclo and Wildavsky's (1974) *The Private Government of Public Money*, a longitudinal study of the Treasury, which led the authors to argue that Whitehall was best understood as a 'village-like community'. Policy was made within this community, by a limited number of actors who regularly interact and have shared values.

Richardson and Jordan

Richardson and Jordan (1979) *Governing Under Pressure* first introduced the notion of a policy community as the key to understanding policy-making in liberal democracies. They regarded policy-making in Britain as taking place within subsystems in which government agencies and pressure groups interact. From this, the notion of policy networks was developed as a means of understanding the relationship between pressure groups and the state. Richardson and Jordan were reacting to what they saw as a problem within macro-state theory, in that it was too monolithic and inflexible to explain individual policy outcomes. Instead, they emphasised the need to disaggregate, arguing that there are many divisions in government and society is fragmented and diffuse.

Rhodes

Networks exist where there is some form of an exchange of resources between the state and pressure groups. This can range from a limited exchange of information to the institutionalisation of a particular group in the policy process. Rhodes' (1981) work emphasises the structural relationships between political institutions as the key terrain of analysis, rather than the interpersonal relations within those institutions. He developed a model that was drawn from a study of relations between central and local government. His framework was based on a theory of power-dependency based on five propositions:

- Any organisation is dependent upon other organisations for resources.

- In order to achieve their goals, the organisations have to exchange resources.

- Although decision-making within the organisation is constrained by other organisations, the dominant coalition influences which relationships are seen as a problem and which resources will be sought.

- The dominant coalition employs strategies within known rules of the game to regulate the process of exchange.

- Variations in the degree of discretion are a product of the goals and the relative power potential of interacting organisations. This relative power potential is a product of the resources of each organisation, of the rules of the game and of the process of exchange between organisations.

In this model, centre-local relations are seen as a 'game' in which both sets of participants are jockeying for position. Each deploys its resources, be they organisational, financial, political, etc to maximise their influence over the outcome. One of the problems with this original power-dependency model was that it failed to distinguish clearly between micro, meso and macro levels of analysis. So, in a latter version, Rhodes (1986) defines a policy network as a cluster or complex of organisations connected to one another by resource dependencies. He distinguished between five types of networks which range along a continuum from at one end tight policy communities to the other end of loosely integrated issue networks. These different types of networks are distinguished by their membership and the distribution of resources between members (see Politics in Focus 21.5).

Marsh and Rhodes

More latterly, Marsh and Rhodes (1992) advanced the network debate by treating policy communities, policy networks and issue networks as types of relationships between interest groups and government. Their approach and the typology they create treats policy networks as a generic term. They argue networks can vary along a continuum according to the closeness of relationships within the network. So, policy communities located at one pole involve tightly bound relationships, while issue networks at the opposing pole involve much looser group interaction (see Table 21.1).

Policy community

If we turn first to a policy community, than the characteristics associated with this type of network would include:

- Limited number of participants with some groups consciously excluded.

- Frequent and high quality interaction between all members of the community on all matters related to the policy issue.

Policy Communities are characterised by stability of relationships, continuity of a restrictive membership, vertical interdependence based on shared service delivery responsibilities and insulation both from other networks and the public more generally. The network is tightly integrated with a high level of vertical interdependence but limited horizontal expression. The policy community will be continuously involved in policy-making on a daily basis, it will set the rules of the game (which you need to abide by or participation will be refused) and it also controls membership, ie acts as a gatekeeper. Policy communities are normally based on major functional interests in government, eg agriculture or policing.

Professional Networks are characterised by the pre-eminence of one particular class of participant in policy-making—the professions. The most frequently cited example of a professional network is the NHS, where one large professional body, ie the BMA largely determines policy outcomes. These networks express the interests of a particular profession and have a substantial degree of vertical interdependence and are insulated against other networks.

Intergovernmental Networks are based on the representative organisations of local authorities. Their characteristics include topocratic membership, an extensive array of interests encompassing all local authority services, limited vertical interdependence as they do not have service delivery responsibilities, but extensive horizontal articulation or, an ability to penetrate many other networks.

Producer Networks are distinguished by the prominent role of economic interests in policy-making. They have fluctuating membership, there is only limited interdependence among the economic interests and the networks are not usually stable.

Issue Networks have a large number of participants and there is a limited degree of interdependence. Stability and continuity are rare and the structure tends to be atomistic.

(See Rhodes 1986: Ch 2)

- Consistency in values, membership and policy outcomes.
- Consensus with the ideology, values and broad policy preferences shared by all participants.
- All members have resources, so the links between them are exchange relationships, interaction involves bargaining between members with resources.
- There is a balance of power, not necessarily one in which all members are equal, but where all members are co-dependent and involved in a positive-sum game.

A good example of a policy community can be found if we look at agriculture policy in the course of the last 50 years or so. After 1945, the Attlee Government and successive governments since have been committed to sustaining high levels of food production on the premise that the country needed to be in a position to be able to feed itself. At the same time, the dominant pressure group in this policy area has been the National Farmers Unions (NFU), who clearly saw it as in their own interest to support this policy position as it ensured continued and guaranteed work for its members and that, at times when the industry faced problems, governments were willing to bail it out. Thus, after 1945, a tight policy community was established between the NFU and the Ministry of Agriculture, Fisheries and Food (MAFF) that was constant over time and the two members shared similar interests. The only substantial change to this policy community occurred in 1973 when Britain entered the European Economic Community (EEC). Yet, the interest of the EEC in the area of farming was to subsidise agriculture production in the shape of the Common Agriculture Policy (CAP). Thus, while a new member entered the policy community, the interests of the members remained predominantly the same and so the new member was easily absorbed. It is only in the last two decades that the policy community has come under stress with the increasing rise in the power and influence of supermarkets, as well as consumer affair associations, environmentalists and the shocks caused by food scandals such as salmonella in eggs, BSE and foot and mouth. Indeed, in the aftermath of the foot and mouth crisis, the present Labour Government abolished MAFF, arguing it had developed an unhealthy client relationship with the NFU. It its place, a new Department for the Environment, Food and Rural Affairs was created in 2001.

Issue networks

At the other end of the continuum is an issue network. The characteristics associated with this type of policy network include:

- many participants
- fluctuating membership and access for the various members
- limited consensus and ever-present conflict
- interaction is based on consultation rather than negotiation or bargaining
- an unequal power relationship in which many participants may have few resources and little access and power is predominantly a zero-sum game.

A recent example of an issue network can be seen in the policy pursued by the Labour Government to ban fox-hunting which passed into law in February 2005. The original policy contained in Labour's 1997 election manifesto stated that: 'We will ensure greater protection for wildlife. We have advocated new measures to promote animal welfare, including a free vote in Parliament on whether hunting with hounds should be banned'. Yet, ever since, the policy has proved constantly problematic to the Government. First, on 3 July 1998 the Labour MP Michael Foster's Wild Mammals (Hunting with Dogs) Bill was blocked in the Commons, and was subsequently voted down by the Lords on three occasions, which finally resulted in the Government resorting to the use of the Parliament Act in order to ensure the passage of the bill into law.

The issue of fox-hunting has proved highly contentious, most obviously because it is a policy on which little common ground can be found between the opposing sides. The ban on fox-hunting can be referred to as a single issue, and it can be characterised as involving two diametrically opposed groups of supporters. On the one side there is the Countryside Alliance formed in March 1997, in anticipation of the proposed ban on hunting. The Countryside Alliance is formally an amalgamation of three groups: the British Field Sports Society, the Countryside Movement and the Countryside Business Group. It perceives its role as fighting to protect what it regards as a traditional, rural way of life that is being threatened by an insensitive, ignorant, metropolitan political elite. Opposing this group are a wide array of animal welfare groups including the Campaign for the Protection of Hunted Animals and the League Against Cruel Sports, which regards the killing of foxes by hunting as an inhumane act. Clearly, the issue of a ban provides little room for consensus (despite the attempts by the Middle Way Group to establish a cross-party group of MPs to seek a workable resolution to the debate about hunting with hounds). Unlike a policy community, where the members have similar/shared goals or interests, in this case, the nature of group participation is predominantly conflictual and power should be understood as a zero-sum game based on the notion that there are those that will win over the issue and those that will lose.

	Dimension	Issue Network	Policy Community
1: Membership	Number of participants	Many	Limited
	Type of interest	Wide range	Economic/professional
2: Integration	Frequency of interaction	Contact fluctuates	Frequent, high quality
	Continuity	Fluctuating access	Membership and values stable
	Consensus	Variety of views	Shared basic values
3: Resources	Distribution of resources within network	Often groups have few resources	All participants have resources to exchange
	Distribution of resources within participating organisation	Varied and variable distribution	Hierarchical
4: Power	Nature of power	Unequal power, zero-sum	Power is positive sum

Source: adapted from Marsh and Rhodes (1992)

The changing nature of policy networks

The post-war period saw the development of a range of policy networks in different policy areas such as agriculture, education, energy, transport and health. The development of these networks were a direct response to the growth of the modern state and the need to intervene in society without developing an enormous and overbearing state bureaucracy. Thus, these networks had considerable advantages for government:

- They created mechanisms for government intervention.
- They simplified the policy process by excluding groups that do not accept the basic values of the policy sector.
- It makes policy-making more predictable. Within a particular policy community, there is a range of solutions possible. For example, in the health policy community, a solution to the problem of health policy was to charge patients.

Nevertheless, different governments have adopted a variety of responses to both networks and the role pressure groups and, in particular, they are not always regarded in an uncritical light.

Thatcherism and pressure groups

With the election of the Thatcher Government in 1979 there was more conflict between interest groups, largely in the public sector, and the Conservative Government than at any other period in the post-war era. As we saw in Chapter 4, the New Right and Thatcherite Conservatives were often suspicious of pressure groups blaming them for overload and exponential state expansion. Most notably, one of the stated aims of Thatcherism was to 'tame the enemy within' (trade unions) which it regarded as one of the key parties responsible for Britain's economic decline (see Politics in Focus 21.6). Interest groups were seen as protecting special interests and, thus, opposed to attempts to extend the market and limit the role of government. Thatcherites accepted the notion that Britain was a corporate society and they saw that as one of the key factors in accounting for Britain's decline. What the Thatcher Government wanted to do was re-establish a direct link between individual voters and a sovereign Parliament rather than work through group representation. The Conservative position was that government, not pressure groups, ran the country (Judge 1993). Richardson (2000: 1010) observes that Thatcher and her ministers:

```
...had their own ideas, policy frames and policy preferences... and
relatively few of the new policy ideas emanated from the plethora of
embedded policy communities around Whitehall that had grown up in
the post-war years.
```

POLITICS IN FOCUS 21.6
Thatcherism and trade unions—taming the enemy within

It is generally accepted that British trade unionism as a political force has been in decline since 1979. This has been illustrated in a number of ways: a decline in the unions policy-making role, or 'no more beer and sandwiches at No 10'. Mitchell (1987) and Marsh (1992) demonstrate that trade unions have experienced an increasing marginalisation from the British policy-making process since the 1980s. This conclusion is reinforced by the fact that the Conservatives abolished a number of tripartite bodies which had previously given unions a role in government policy-making; the decline in the number of strikes; and a decline in union membership which in 1997 reached its lowest level since 1945.

There are two broad competing explanations for the decline of trade unions as a political force: the first argues that the decline was a direct result of the extensive legislative programme of trade union reform introduced by the Conservative Administration. The Thatcher Government introduced six industrial relations Acts that curtailed the rights and powers of trade unions. These were followed by two further Acts under the Major Government. Most commentators accept that the last Conservative Administration presided over a substantial weakening of the legal position of trade unions; the second suggests that the decline of the unions after 1979 was more a result of the autonomous changes in the structure of international economic markets. In so doing, this argument downgrades the real impact of Thatcherism. Instead, the decline of the unions can be explained by the changing nature of employment in the workplace. In particular, three changes are stressed: de-industrialisation which refers to the decline in size and importance of the British manufacturing sector since 1979, and the rise in importance of the services sector (retailing, leisure, information/technology, etc). This argument stresses the decline of full-time, permanent, manual work and conversely, the rise of part-time, temporary, non-manual work. British trade unions have been traditionally heavily represented in manual occupations, eg manufacturing industry. It was these industries which contracted most in the 80s and, as a consequence, union membership suffered; greater flexibilisation which refers to: employees becoming more flexible in the job market through a switch from long-term to short-term contracts. This process has undermined the practice of free collective bargaining, whereby, traditionally, wage levels are decided by unions and employers at the national level, and applied uniformly across the industry. Now, increasingly, the notion of personal contracts and local pay bargaining operates. This process has been strengthened by the increase of sub-contracting in the public sector, where firms compete against each other for short-term contracts to provide government services at both the national and the local level; finally, there has been a process of 'Japanisation' which refers to the increasing trend of firms from Japan (and SE Asia more generally) either agreeing to create new plants and investment in Britain, or taking over existing British firms, but, only on the basis of a Single Union Agreements (SUA), that is, Japanese firms agree to invest in Britain in return for an agreement that they will only have to recognise one union at the plants they create or take over. Moreover, that union must also agree to sign a no-strike agreement. The consequences for union power are pretty obvious here.

Consequently, there was an attempt to reduce the role of groups and undermine existing policy networks. The Thatcherite approach towards pressure groups was therefore conditioned by a number of factors:

(1) The Thatcher Government made no secret of its wish to change the direction of policy in much of the public sector. Groups which had an interest in the status quo were therefore likely to be offended.

(2) Ministers wished to constrain the growth of public spending on many services and to reduce state subsidies; again, it was not surprising that interests dependent on such expenditure, notably on health, social welfare, education and local government, complained. The Major and Blair Governments have continued with policies designed to encourage market disciplines and competition as spurs to efficiency in the public sector.

(3) Ministers finally took seriously claims that the authority and autonomy of an elected government should not be compromised by bargains with sectional interests, particularly the trade unions.

A theme running through the period was a general distrust of producer interest groups, particularly in the public sector. Ministers complained that too often there was an 'unholy alliance' between a department and its client interest group. Interest groups and bureaucrats were allegedly interested in maximising their own advantages—in the form of autonomy, salaries and conditions of work—rather than responding to the consumers of their services. A more elaborate statement of this case is made by Mancur Olson (1982), who has claimed that interest groups ('distributional coalitions') use their power to resist change and slow down innovative policies; their veto power produces an 'institutional sclerosis'. In Germany and Japan, by contrast, the interests were either smashed or severely weakened by the rise of totalitarian governments or defeat in the war, and both countries have enjoyed post-war economic regeneration. Olson claims that the collapse of the regimes destroyed many tradition-bound forces. Innovation was helped by a fresh start. In the case of Britain, the continuity of the regime allowed the interests to become entrenched. Much of this analysis was implicitly accepted by Thatcherites.

The influence and formal powers of two other major interests, local government and trade unions (see Politics in Focus 21.6), have been severely curtailed in the past two decades. Some commentators might point to the partisan factor at work here— Labour-supporting trade unions and left-wing local authorities. But the Conservative Administration also confronted the middle-class professional groups. The claims to self-regulation and possession of professional expertise by lawyers, doctors and teachers were challenged by Thatcherism. These groups claimed to be the expert judges of what is a 'good' service, be it legal advice, health care or education. Schoolteachers found that their pay-bargaining machinery was scrapped and a core curriculum, national testing of pupils and a contract of service imposed on them. University teachers lost tenure and the quality of their teaching and research is regularly assessed by independent bodies. In 1989 the doctors had new contracts imposed on them by the Ministry of Health. These limited their budgets and linked a greater part of their pay to the number of patients they treated. In much of the public sector there was a new emphasis on audit performance, pay and value for money. Not all of the measures enhanced the power of central government. Some of the changes gave more power to the professions, for example, ballots for trade union members, schools opting out of local authority control and managing their own budgets, hospitals and GPs controlling their own funds.

The pace of change continued under the Major Government, whether it was the Citizens' Charter promoting greater power for consumers over the deliverers of public services, or the 1993 Trade Union Reform and Employment Rights Act. When analysing the Conservative Administration's approach to pressure groups, it can be argued it challenged pressure groups in a number of ways:

- It shifted the terms of political debate. As we saw in Chapter 3, a key element of the modern state was the assumption that the state resolved problems and delivered public goods. As the British state is not a totalitarian state, it often had to deliver policies in consultation, or with the assistance, of groups. Thatcherism attempted to change the debate so that the Government was not always seen as the source of problems or solutions. For the Conservatives, solutions could be derived from the market and groups were seen as often distorting the market. Therefore, by shifting the emphasis of public goods away from the state, groups did not need to be involved in the policy process.

- It challenged intermediate and corporate institutions. New Right ideology led the Conservatives to believe in the direct contract between the voter and government and that intermediate organisations such as pressure groups, churches, local authorities, should not have a role in making policy. Therefore, they were committed either to abolishing them or reducing their power. According to Gamble (1994):

> Legitimacy is withdrawn from voluntary institutions like trade unions and from public institutions like the BBC, the universities and state education systems, nationalised industries and local government, until they have reformed themselves or been reformed from outside. A whole range of what we see as corporatist intermediate institutions, such as the National Economic Development Council, the Manpower Services Commission and Wages Council, were abolished by the Thatcher and Major governments.

- The privileging of new interests. Whilst being suspicious of many interest groups, such as trade unions and professional groups associated with the establishment of the welfare state, the Thatcher and Major Governments gave access to a different range of groups. For instance, whilst in the 1970s it was the CBI that had good relations with government, after 1979, the Thatcher Administration was more open to the advice of the more neoliberal Institute of Directors.

- The Conservative Administration also depended more on ideological think-tanks for policy advice rather than interest groups. In policy developments such as the community charge and welfare reform, think-tanks were influential and, in particular, they could be used to 'fly kites'. Here, the Conservative Government would use right-wing thinks-tanks to suggest a radical reform and, then gauge the reaction or get voters use to the idea before the Government proposed and developed the policy (see Cockett 1995; Hay 1996; Kandiah and Seldon 1996a, 1996b).

The Conservatives were also direct in the way they confronted some of the established policy networks. The Thatcherite view was that changing policy often required changing the role of groups in the policy process. Therefore the Conservatives explicitly attempted to break up policy networks in education, health, local government and energy which were seen as major, reactionary forces stalling attempts to change policy. In a number of cases, the Conservatives tried to bypass the networks either by creating different networks or by overriding them. So for example, in education, there was a conscious move to shift decision-making away from the network through creating more direct relationships between the Secretary of State and schools. In health, an alternative network was created to look at reform of the NHS and in energy, privatisation destroyed the networks established for an energy policy based on publicly owned industries. Elsewhere, Dudley and Richardson (1996) have highlighted how the growing opposition to roads (coupled to Treasury opposition to rising costs) led to the loss of power of the pro-roads lobby within the transport policy community.

The Blair Administration and pressure groups

The Blair Administration has gone further in the laying down of targets for the public services. The Government has found itself at odds with various interests, including consumer and environmental lobbies (over genetically modified foods), the Countryside Alliance (over fox-hunting and rural decline) and the Campaign for Freedom of Information (because of disappointment over Labour legislation). However, according to Marsh et al (2001), since Labour's 1997 electoral victory, there is little doubt that there has been both a major increase in pressure group consultation and a change in which groups are being consulted. The Labour Government has different policy objectives and is more committed to consultation. However, at the same time, it has debts to pay to the groups that serviced and advised it in opposition; so increased consultation with such groups is unsurprising. Part of the current exchange relationship involves access in return for services rendered in the past.

There are two important points to make concerning New Labour and interest groups. First, that Labour has probably had much better contacts with business than any previous Labour Government. Since the early 1990s, Labour has been cultivating links with business in order to change the perception that it is an anti-business party. Blair has explicitly stated that he does not wish to punish wealth-creation and has been willing to place business people such as Geoffrey Robinson and David Simon into key places in his administration (see Cohen 1999; Walden 2001; Kavanagh and Richards 2002; Cohen 2003). In addition, in an attempt to reduce reliance on the trade unions, the Government has attempted to encourage businesses to make donations to the Government. Whilst we could not suggest that this buys influence, it clearly gives access. In the case of the Bernie Eccleston affair, the Labour Party received £1 million from the owner of Formula One racing just prior to the 1997 election. Once in government, there was a change in position on banning tobacco sponsorship of Formula One, but of course there is no direct indication of a connection between the two events (see Naughtie 2001; Rawnsley 2001; Toynbee and Walker 2001; Cohen 2003).

Second, whilst Labour was open to pressure groups early on in their first term, it increasingly became more immune to their influence. Once the Government was established and developed new lines of policy advice from officials and task forces, the need for pressure groups diminished. Events, such as protests against changes in disability benefits (1999), the fuel protests (2001), the ban on fox-hunting (2003–05) and changes to the funding of higher education and student fees (2004) often make the Government less willing to listen to interest groups. In addition, the Government was wary about re-establishing the types of relationships that Labour had with the trade unions in the 1960s and 1970s. During the 1997 election campaign, Blair stated:

> We will not be held to ransom by the unions...We will stand up to strikes. We will not cave in to unrealistic pay demands from any one...Unions have no special role in our election campaign, just as they will get no special favours in a Labour Government (quoted in Ludlam 2001: 115).

Since 1997, the Labour Government has had an uneasy relationship with the unions and there has clearly been no return to the days of the 1970s when trade union leaders were involved in almost daily discussions with the Government over national economic policy. Yet, since the early 1990s, the response of the unions to both the Thatcherite reforms and the lukewarm relationship with New Labour has been broadly pragmatic and is captured in what is referred to as 'New Unionism'. The unions, under the recent stewardship of John Monks, and since 2003 Brendan Barber, General Secretary of the Trade Union Congress, adapted to 18 years of Conservative attacks by embracing a 'new realism' in which the unions: recognise they no longer deserve special favours; are willing to work with any mainstream political party; and are prepared to create a new partnership with employer groups such as the CBI and the Institute of Directors. Finally, the unions now often bypass Westminster/Whitehall completely, as they increasingly opt to use the European route as an alternative corridor of power for reasserting themselves on the political stage. This is indicative of the changing era of governance explored in Chapter 3.

Policy networks and macro-theories of the state

As we saw in Chapter 4, general theories of the state have received much criticism for the way in which they tended to regard the state as monolithic. The benefit of the policy network approach is that it is a concept which provides a link between individual studies of specific policy outcomes and broader macro theories of the state. Yet, at the same time, network analysis can be seen as an attempt to put life back into macro-theories of the state. Indeed, on their own, the policy network approach has only limited analytical use. Network analysis requires application to the broader macro-theories of the state, in order to explain the sorts of relationships that develop within networks. For example, why in the post-war period has the NFU dominated the agricultural network? Network analysis on its own struggles to address such questions. What needs to be stressed here is that network analysis needs traditional state theory in order to be of explanatory value. For example:

(1) Marxists would regard the majority of policy networks as being closed policy communities dominated by the interests of capital, eg the Confederation of British Industry (CBI), the City and the Institute of Directors (IoD) have a dominant position within a closed economic policy network. Here, the view is that power is concentrated in the hands of a narrow range of organisations operating in the interests of capital.

(2) Similarly, elitists would see networks as closed and dominated by a clique of social elites with prominent state roles in life that rule in their own interests. Again, power is concentrated in the hands of a narrow range of individuals/groups, which impose their own value-set upon society.

(3) Pluralists would argue that policy networks are continually breaking down into issue networks making it increasingly difficult for any one actor to dominate a particular sector. For pluralists, power in the British political system is dispersed and as such, they reject the notion that policy communities exist because of the intensity of pressure group competition.

 ## Conclusion

The claim that Britain is a pluralist political system rests on the belief that several autonomous groups are involved in policy-making and that no group dominates the process. The late R.T. McKenzie defended groups as an ancillary form of representation, enabling voters to convey more specific views to the government than can be represented by broad party programmes at general elections every four to five years. Democracy, he claimed, includes the: 'right to advise, cajole, and warn [the authorities] regarding the policies they should adopt' (1974: 280). Others suggest that a kind of free market operates and prevents one set of interests being dominant for too long: the government's fear of public opinion, the existence or likely emergence of rival or counter-groups and certain general 'rules of the game' combine to produce over time a rough balance of power among interests. Because citizens are members of different groups and have different loyalties they do not become too closely attached to one interest.

Marxist and elitists, however, make two contrary arguments. One is that interests differ in their organisational strength, resources, leverage over society and access to decision-makers. The group system, in other words, is biased in favour of some interests and against others. The minority who benefit from a policy may be better organised and more articulate than the larger number of non-beneficiaries, for example, the taxpayers. Another matter of concern is the definition and defence of the public interest amid all the sectional pressures. Is the government able to pursue a coherent, long-term set of policies, or does it reflect the balance of pressure-group forces?

What the policy network approach provides is a useful, empirically-based methodology for assessing the role of pressure groups in the British political system. It is best to understand network analysis as a tool for enhancing our understanding of macro-theories of the state. Network analysis is not a theory in its own right. Furthermore, no single view of networks should be taken. State and interest group relations are highly variable both over time and space. Interests that dominate one network can vary and change and so they need to be understood in a political and historical context. As a tool of analysis, it is important to stress that policy networks should be used in conjunction with a range of macro-theories of the state when trying to explain the nature of power in the British political system and the influence of pressure groups.

KEY POINTS

- Interest groups extend opportunities for participation in the state and provide a channel for continuous communications between government and those affected by government policy.

- The growth of group activity accompanied the rise of the interventionist state after 1945. Governments depend upon the expertise of groups, but at the same time governments impinge more extensively on citizens' lives and this prompts citizens to seek to influence the nature of such intervention.

- There are different types of groups, including: promotional groups which advocate a cause; interest groups which are usually based on economic interests; and peak groups which articulate the views of a set of interests.

- The effectiveness of a group at any particular time will depend upon such factors as: the compatibility of its aims with the programme of the government of the day; the prevailing climate of opinion; and the degree of support for the group's demands.

- The policy network approach is a meso-level tool for analysing the role of pressure groups in different policy areas.

- The Marsh and Rhodes continuum based on issue networks and policy communities is a useful means of conceptualising the array of different types of networks that exist.

- Thatcherism rejected the policies of the post-war consensus and the consensual style of policy-making which reduced the Government's authority and restricted the Government's role to that of being negotiator with, or referee between, competing interests.

- The Blair Government has been less conflictual in its attitude towards pressure groups and has been willing to develop much closer relations with business than previous Labour governments.

- Policy networks on their own are an insufficient tool for analysing political power and they need to be applied to macro-theories of the state.

KEY QUESTIONS

(1) Do interest groups enhance democracy?

(2) Interest groups are a mixed blessing. Discuss.

(3) Why have Conservative governments since 1979 been more successful than their predecessors in altering the legal position of trade unions?

(4) Why are some pressure groups more powerful than others?

(5) How does the policy network approach enhance macro-state theory?

(6) 'All citizens have an equal opportunity to influence public policy through interest-group activity.' Discuss.

(7) How has New Labour's approach to interest groups differed from that of the last Conservative Administration?

IMPORTANT WEBSITES

Nearly every major pressure group now has a website. Some examples include:
www.foe. co.uk/
www.charter88.org.uk
www.anl.org.uk/campaigns.htm
www.amnesty.org/
www.tuc.org.uk/

A useful one for looking at the work of new social movements at a global level is www.protest. net/. Also useful is the Reclaim the Streets site: www.gn.apc.org/rts/ and the Make Poverty History site: www.makepovertyhistory.org/. There are also sites for voluntary groups: www.oneworld.net/. For a comparative analysis of social capital see www.cspp.strath.ac.uk/index.html?catalog9_0.html. For an examination of civil society see www.civitas.org.uk/, www.oxfam.org.uk/. For a very useful site on encouraging participation at the local level see www.urbanwebsolutions.com/planning/ and for an example of a participatory organisation see www.napp.org.uk/. Examples of radical groups found beyond mainstream policy networks see: http://flag.blackened.net/blackflag/, www.londonclasswar.org/ and http://members.lycos.co.uk/moveagainstmon/.

FURTHER READING

On pressure groups see: S. Finer (1958) *Anonymous Empire*, London: Pall Mall; K. Middlemas (1979) *Politics in Industrial Society*, London: Andre Deutsch; W. Grant (1993) *Business and Politics in Britain*, 2nd edn, London: Macmillan; D. Marsh (1992) *The New Politics of British Trade Unions and the Thatcher Legacy*, London: Macmillan; W. Grant (2000) *Pressure Groups and British Politics*, London: Macmillan; G. Jordan and W. Maloney (1997) *The Protest Business*, Manchester: Manchester University Press; and P. Joyce (2002) *The Politics of Protest*, Basingstoke: Palgrave. On policy networks see H. Heclo and A. Wildavsky (1974) *The Private Government of Public Money*, London: Macmillan; G. Jordan and J. Richardson (1987) *Government and Pressure Groups in Britain*, Oxford: Clarendon Press; R.A.W. Rhodes (1981) *Control and Power in Central-Local Relations*, Aldershot: Gower; R.A.W. Rhodes (1986) *The National World of Local Government*, London: Allen & Unwin; D. Marsh and R.A.W. Rhodes (1992) *Policy Networks in British Government*, Oxford: Clarendon Press; and J.J. Richardson (2000) 'Government, Interest Groups and Policy Change', *Political Studies*, 48: 1006–25.

CHRONOLOGY

Pressure groups and political power in Britain, 1787–2005

1787   The Abolition Society, one of the earliest promotional pressure groups, was founded by William Wilberforce and Thomas Clarkson, succeeded in abolishing slavery by 1807

1839	Anti-Corn Law League
1903	Women's Social and Political Union, pressing for votes for women
1945	Enormous increase in interest-group activity accompanied the rise of the interventionist Welfare State
1962	National Economic Development Council ('Neddy' or NEDC) created as a forum for tripartite discussions on the economy
1965	Confederation of British Industry (CBI) formed
1974	Heath calls 'Who Governs?' election
1975	Health and Safety Commission created. Labour minority government makes Social Contract with the unions
1976	Advisory, Conciliation and Arbitration Service (ACAS) created
1978	Winter of Discontent—many local services paralysed by unions
1979	Mrs Thatcher introduces a less consensual political culture
1984-85	The Miners' Strike
1988	Edwina Currie resigns her position as junior Health Minister after offending egg producers and the National Farmers Union by claiming that almost all egg production was infected by salmonella
1990	Widespread anti-poll tax demonstrations
1992	NEDC abolished
1995	Animal rights demonstrations against the export of live animals
1998	Countryside Alliance demonstration in London
1999	Protests against changes in disability benefits
2001	Fuel protests
2003	Anti-war demonstrations against military action in Iraq and another Countryside Alliance demonstration in London
2004	Demonstrations in London against changes to the funding of higher education and student fees
2005	Demonstrations against the G8 group meeting in Gleneagles, Scotland and the Live 8 concerts across the world

 Visit the Online Resource Centre that accompanies this book for links to more information on this chapter topic

CHAPTER TWENTY TWO

The decline in representative politics

READER'S GUIDE

The British political system has traditionally limited participation by citizens in the political process. People vote in elections but under the doctrine of the mandate. People vote for what the party has to offer and then it is up to MPs to decide what is in the national interest. This chapter analyses how this limited notion of representation developed and how it seems to have led to a disillusionment with traditional politics. The chapter then examines how the decline in political participation may not be an indication of apathy but of how people are developing alternative ways of participating in the political process.

Introduction

The Westminster model is predicated on a particular and limited type of political participation. Recent times have seen the development of new forms of participation which occur outside the boundaries of the Westminster model. Increasingly people are participating through single issue groups and direct action. The rise of the environmental movement or individual causes such as the fuel protests or against the war in Iraq seem to indicate that people are more willing to protest outside the formal institutions of politics. These movements challenge the traditional conceptions of participation and highlight a growing disjunction between formal political procedures and the way ordinary people think about politics. However, we need to make a careful assessment about whether these protests are new and whether they involve more people. Is it really the case that people are turning from MPs and political parties to other forms of protest? Or is it the case that people are just becoming disillusioned with politics and refusing to engage? As we saw in the Introduction to this book, it appears to be the case that young people are more likely to vote in *Big Brother* or *The X Factor* than in an election. Are young people less political or simply expressing their political views in different ways and in different fora? These are all fundamental questions that relate back to the question of what is politics and how representative and democratic is the British political system. It may be that it is a political act not to participate or it is much more of a political act to demonstrate for a cause than to vote in an election, where one vote will not have an impact on the outcome.

This chapter will look at the development of new forms of participation. It will begin by discussing participation in the Westminster model and outline the limited form that representation has traditionally meant in Britain. It will examine the question of whether we have recently seen a crisis of representation, before looking at the factors which may explain the development of new forms of participation. The chapter will then look at the way people participate now and through a number of case-studies explore the range of ways that politics and representation have changed. It will then evaluate the impact that these changes are having on politics.

Representation in the Westminster model

As we have seen in earlier chapters, the Westminster model has a limited notion of participation based on the notion of representation proposed by one of the founders of Conservatism Edmund Burke. For Burke the MP owes his constituents, 'not his history only, but his judgment; and he betrays, instead of serving you, if he sacrifices it to your opinion' (Burke 1834: 176). Within this model, participation is limited to elections, although the 20th century saw, as Chapter 21 illustrates, the development of pressure group politics. Under the Westminster model people vote in elections for representatives. Representatives are not there as delegates of the electors but to represent voters in the ways which best match the interests of their constituents with the public interest. If they are not seen as representing the interests well they can be voted out at the next election. They are then accountable to the electorate. This conception was codified through the notion of the doctrine of the mandate. This is the idea that politicians put a manifesto before the country, voters choose the best manifesto and then the party has a mandate to govern (see Chapter 20). It is not uncommon to hear a politician saying we have a mandate as a justification for a particular policy. It assumes that people have read manifestos and agreed to allow politicians to do what they contain.

This view of the political process has little resonance with reality. There is much evidence to demonstrate that people have almost no knowledge of the activities of their representative, who is not independent but subject to party discipline, and people vote according to broad party lines and general economic conditions rather than on a judgement concerning the effectiveness of their Member of Parliament. In addition much decision-making in Britain is undertaken in secret and with little regard to public opinion.

However, as Dunleavy (1999) has demonstrated this limited notion of democracy has continued for a number of reasons:

- *Democracy developed in Britain in the context of Empire*. Whilst Britain was introducing the secret ballot and extending the franchise at home, it was imposing colonial rule abroad. Consequently democracy developed within a very limited framework and without any conception of universal rights. The rights of white British males could not be extended to those that lived in the colonies. As Dunleavy (1999: 210) points out, 'Civil liberties and human rights in the mainland state could never be given any codified legal protection; for fear that they would spillover into the imperial realms'.

- *The existence of a club ethos*. Britain's governing class has operated with a limited notion of democracy. Moreover, both Labour and Liberal Parties have been incorporated into government by accepting the existing rules of the game. Neither party has developed an alternative framework for democratic governance. Once in power Liberal and Labour leaders effectively suppressed demands for wider democracy in their own parties (note for example the failure to radically reform the House of Lords or to end the high degree of secrecy in British government). It was only when they were out of power for long periods that they were prepared to consider radical reforms to the British constitution.

- *An absence of an alternative conception of democracy*. The view of most commentators and writers on British democracy up until the 1960s was that the system was more or less a perfect form of democracy. It provided for the democratic election of a government with a clear choice between two parties but at the same time it provided strong government. It was also a government that was constrained by the powers of the House of Commons and the House of Lords and was fair because of British traditions of the rule of law. As a consequence, there was no serious debate concerning the nature of democracy in Britain.

- *The compliance of the British electorate*. There was almost no pressure within the electorate for democratic change. The British electorate has traditionally been seen as deferential and issues of constitutional reform have attracted very little attention amongst the electorate as a whole (this, of course, is not true in Northern Ireland: see Chapter 17).

Throughout most of the 20th century the form of democracy in Britain was limited. Whilst in many ways Britain was a liberal society in the sense that there was freedom of speech, a limited state and certain rights maintained in law, the ability of ordinary people to influence the decision-making process was severely curtailed. However, in recent years people have suggested that there has been a crisis of representation and the development of anti-politics.

The crisis of participation

There is increasingly a concern in Britain, and other Western countries, that levels of participation have been in decline. Turnout in local elections in Britain is about 36% and in the 2004 European elections it was 38%; a significant increase on the 1999 turnout of only 24%. Even in the 2001 general election participation fell to an all time low of 59% which was a decline from 71% in 1997. There was a slight increase in 2005 to 61.5%. In some inner city seats in Northern England turnout was less than 45% and in Liverpool Riverside it was 34.1% in 1997 but increased by 7% in 2005. Turnout in general elections has been in steady decline since the 1950s (see Figure 22.1).

Some see this declining turnout as part of a general disillusionment with politics. In the United States, Robert Putnam (1995) has identified what he sees as a decline in social capital. He argues that people are no longer participating in community affairs, preferring, as he says, to bowl alone. Rather than being involved in the community, people are spending time in their homes watching television. This leads to a decline in social capital which he sees as trust in local and political institutions. As people participate less in the social community, they participate less in politics.

These ideas have had resonance with the Blair Administration and Putnam has been invited to Downing Street to give a seminar on social capital. A report by the Downing Street strategy unit in November 2003 highlighted the high levels of mistrust of politicians and

FIGURE 22.1

Decline in electoral turnout: A democratic deficit?

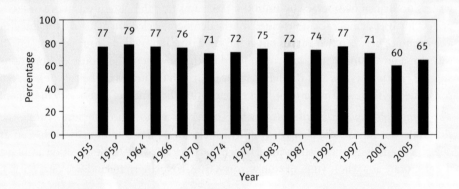

demonstrated that it was higher than in other European countries. The work of the Citizens' Audit conducted by Charles Pattie, Patrick Seyd and Paul Whiteley has extended this work to Britain (Pattie et al 2004). They discovered that whilst people in Britain had relatively high trust in non-political institutions such as the police, courts and Civil Service, they had little trust in politicians and the House of Commons. Out of a score of 11, trust in politicians was only 3.3 compared to 6.3 in the police. A report by British Social Attitudes found that only 16% of people think that governments will put the interests of the country above their own.

However, unlike Putnam the work of Pattie et al found little link between television watching and political activity, or between trust and political activity. The only similarity they found with Putnam was that people who were active socially are more likely to be active politically. There seems little doubt that people are increasingly disillusioned with traditional parties and politics. For example, of 12 elections for the new executive mayors, six went to non-party candidates. There has also been a significant decline in party membership (see Figure 22.2).

There are three ways of looking at this evidence. First, it could be that there are now distinct groups of people who do not participate in politics (see Politics in Focus 22.1) and that is likely to undermine the quality of decision-making and democracy, and can even lead to the rise of extremist parties as people are increasingly disaffected and disengaged from traditional politics. Second, it may be that people are more or less satisfied with the current political and economic situation and see little difference between the parties. Consequently, they feel no need to participate. This does not mean that they do not participate in other social and community activities (see Roberts and Devine 2004), but they are happy enough with the political situation not to participate. However, evidence suggests those who are least likely to participate are the most deprived, not the most complacent. O'Toole (2003) points out that non-participation does not mean that people

FIGURE 22.2
Membership of main British parties 1953–2002

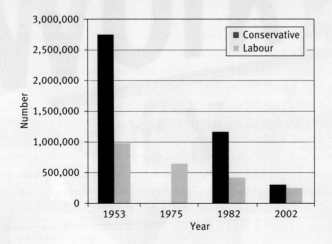

are apolitical. It is often the case that they have strongly held political views but do not have the mechanism for expressing them. Third, the more optimistic conclusion is that people are cynical about traditional patterns of policy which are essentially based on a passive view of political activity—people are expected to vote and nothing else—but they are prepared to organise themselves and to take direct political action. The citizens' audit demonstrates that certain forms of political activity have increased. Indeed, in 1983 only 8% said that they would participate in direct action and by 2000 it had increased to 16%. Before looking at new forms of participation we will examine some of the reasons why the traditionally passive British electorate has changed and why this may have led to new types of politics. Whilst electoral participation is in decline millions of people, for example, are prepared to wear Make Poverty History bracelets, demonstrate at the 2005 G8 Summit and to try to win tickets for the Live8 concerts. They undertake political activity, but not of the traditional kind.

Causes of change

Over the last 20 years traditional patterns of representation have broken down. In the past, people joined political parties or voted, and in some cases joined trade unions and other pressure groups that represented their interest. Politics took place in the parliamentary arena with the public influencing decisions but politicians being the active participants. It appears that in recent years there has been a growing disillusionment with traditional forms of politics and as we have seen a growing distrust of politicians. As Figure 22.2 indicates, there has been a significant decline in party membership.

The key factors in this process are:

(1) The decline and fragmentation of class. In Britain representation has traditionally been through class-based organisation. As we saw in Chapter 18, parties were traditionally supported by particular classes. However, since the 1970s there has been a considerable realignment of voting with a much more fluid relationship between class and voting. In addition, there has been a decline in trade unions. In 1979, 53% of the population were members of trade unions and by 2002 it was 18% (Curtice and Seyd 2003).

(2) The rise of post-industrialism and post-materialism. For many commentators politics has traditionally been organised around issues of production and consumption. Should goods be produced privately or publicly? Should citizens have rights to economic and social security? However, it is argued that Britain is now a post-industrial society. Few people are engaged in manufacturing and the last 30 years have seen the rise of the service and information sectors which have developed with a more highly educated workforce (see Chapter 5). As a consequence Inglehart (1990) suggests that people have developed post-material values. We are now less concerned with issues of production and more concerned with issues of identity and lifestyle. Ulrich Beck, amongst others, has developed this thinking in a different way and argued that late capitalist society is marked by a concern not with economic risk but with environmental risk and, therefore, people's interests are increasingly concerned

with issues of ecological safety relating to the environment, food, transport, and not simple issues of production (Adam, Beck and Van Loon 2000).

(3) The end of deference. With increased education, travel and media sources, people are no longer willing to be passive and deferential. In the past politicians were treated with great reverence. A Jeremy Paxman-like figure would never have grilled Winston Churchill in the way that politicians are interviewed today. As a consequence, and as we have seen above, politicians are much less trusted than in the past. This has partly been exacerbated by the politics of blame which has developed in the context of greater uncertainty.

(4) The failure of politics. The last 30 years or so has seen politics fail in a number of ways. First, there has been what has been perceived as a failure of delivery. Governments have been criticised for failures in terms of economic policy, welfare and education. For instance, in 1992 Britain was forced to leave the European Exchange Rate Mechanism because of economic miscalculations by the Prime Minister, John Major, and the Chancellor of the Exchequer, Norman Lamont. The Labour government has continually presented itself as aiming to improve public services, but many people continue to believe that they are no better. Second, there is a failure of representation. People believe that politicians do not represent them, that they are all the same and they are self-interested. The first past the post system makes it almost impossible for a single voter to affect the outcome and so people see little point in voting. Third, in recent years there have been a number of scandals relating to politicians which have undermined public faith. The last few years of the Government of John Major (1990–97) saw a considerable number of personal scandals involving MPs covering both sex and money. Under Labour these continued, although not at such a rate, and affected senior figures such as Peter Mandelson, Ron Davies and David Blunkett. The questions concerning the personal propriety of politicians links closely to wider issues of trust. The last 20 years have seen a number of issues such as BSE, genetically modified organisms (GMOs) and human genetics where people have either been misled by politicians or lost trust in them.

The crucial issue is whether these factors have led to a decline in participation. Are people less interested in politics and think that the parties make no difference and so focus on private activities? Or is it the case that people are undertaking new forms of political participation which exist outside of the traditional arenas of the Westminster model?

New forms of participation

There is evidence that an increasing number of people are now willing to participate in demonstrations and increasingly to undertake legal and illegal direct action. Curtice and Seyd (2003) indicate that there has been a distinct rise in the level of non-electoral participation ranging from signing petitions to demonstrating. Areas that affect all our lives such as GMOs, the environment, road building and war in Iraq have produced a great deal of political activity. We can identify a number of features of this form of participation:

- The activity occurs in the civil sphere. The rise of new forms of participation are seen by many as the development of a lively civil society. Civil society is a space where people can organise independently of the state.

- The action is often direct in the sense that people themselves are often involved in political activity or getting their voices heard rather than relying on representatives.

- The issues tend to be 'post-material' and concern issues of quality of life rather than pure economic issues, although this is not always the case, as in the fuel protest (see below).

- Often these groups are cross class. Many of these sorts of protests contain a wide alliance of support from different social groups and with different interests. What is interesting about new forms of political activity is that they often involve complex alliances. For instance, the anti-roads protest has involved radical environmental groups like the donga tribe and middle class and traditional homeowners who do not want roads built literally in their backyards (Nimbys). It combines the anti-materialist and the strongly materialist in a political protest.

- There is a tendency for the issues to be single-issue, often focused on a particular event such as the war in Iraq or the building of the road. Nevertheless, for some there is a broader set of goals, the environment or anti-globalisation, or people are involved in a rolling set of single issues. To some extent it is the same group of people protesting about a range of different issues.

- This form of participation uses a range of tactics. The sort of tactics used by protest groups range from low cost actions such as organising and signing a petition to high cost and risk activity such as undertaking illegal activity. Often the aim in these protests is to raise awareness of an issue.

The development of direct action

Direct action is not new, but a development of the new social movements organised around issues such as the environment and identity politics that developed in the 1960s and 1970s. Groups like the women's movement and the environmental movement had some impact on the nature of political debate. However, their political influence was limited and when they seemed to have an impact on politics it was often through traditional mechanisms. The 1970s and early 1980s saw political activity largely revolving around trade unions. One of the major political events of the period was the year-long miners' strike which resulted in defeat for the National Union of Miners and the subsequent decimation of the coal industry. Following the defeat of the miners and the development of a range of legislation restricting the role of trade unions, there was a decline in mass political activity. However, one particular policy seemed to reignite the impetus behind direct action and led to a growing number of direct action causes and that was the poll tax.

The poll tax—officially called the community charge—was a tax introduced to replace the rates and was effectively a fixed rate tax on everyone over 18. There was a high level of opposition to the tax because it was seen as highly regressive—the wealthy paid the same as the poor, and it resulted in large increases in local taxation for most (with a small number of very rich people seeing massive reductions in the level of local tax that they paid). There was widespread opposition in opinion polls to the new tax. At the same time a campaign of non-payment started to develop. In Scotland it was estimated that 15% of people had not paid the tax in the first year and a similar non-payment campaign developed in Britain (Butler, Adonis and Travis 1994). There were also demonstrations council meetings throughout the country which culminated in a major riot in London on 31 March 1990.

Whilst non-payment and the riot were condemned by politicians as illegal activities carried out by a minority, there can be little doubt that they were important factors in Margaret Thatcher being forced out of office and the abolition of the tax. The non-payment campaigns and the riot raised the issue of the rights of citizens to protest against unjust legislation (Butler, Adonis and Travis 1994). Like the new protests that were to develop later, the anti-poll tax protest created an alliance between radical left wing, Trotskyite and anarchist groups with middle England. Those who were hit hardest by the poll tax were those homeowners who had houses around the average price, earning just enough to miss out on rebates and who were not prepared to undertake illegal action like non-payment. Consequently, opposition to the poll tax ranged from Conservative voters to the far left.

The poll tax demonstrated that protest could have an effect on government and it seemed to have an impact on encouraging the development of direct action. As Sanders et al (2003) have demonstrated there is contagion with protest. People seeing successful protests are inspired to replicate direct action. As we will see there are now a growing number of direct action protests (see Politics in Focus 22.1).

FOCUS 22.1

The poll tax riot was one the largest riots in London during the post-war years. Since the introduction of the poll tax there had been a number of demonstrations and a campaign of non-payment against the poll tax. On 31 March 1990, over 100,000 people marched to Trafalgar Square protesting against the tax. A small group began a sitdown protest outside Downing Street which became violent when the police started to remove the protesters. The violence soon escalated into a full-scale riot with looting and the burning of cars. Over 400 people were arrested. Whilst the riot was not the direct cause of the resignation of Margaret Thatcher and the end of the poll tax, it did highlight the feelings against the tax. For a view of the riot from the protesters' perspective see the video, *Battle for Trafalgar*.

Source of picture: marina.fortunecity.com/embankment/108/PTR10.JPG

Anti-road protests

One of the most visible of the direct action issues has been the anti-roads protests. There have been a number of campaigns which have attempted to prevent the development of new motorways. These have included the Winchester and Newbury bypasses and Oxleas Wood. Much of the anti-roads protest was organised by the umbrella group Earth First. This group is committed to direct action as a way of opposing corporate power and has undertaken a number of actions in relations to environmental issues and against corporations such as McDonalds (Doherty, Plows and Wall 2003). Earth First developed a two-pronged strategy. The first was to undertake direct action which attracted media attention. A number of high-profile stunts were undertaken such as creating tree houses in the proposed routes of new roads. The second was to build alliances with more traditional groups who were opposed to road building in their own areas. Consequently, the opposition to road building did not seem to be the views of a limited number of extremists. Is also seems that the action had an impact on road building policy and the Government did move to a position where more roads were not necessarily seen as a solution to the transport problem.

Anti-GMO protest

The protest against genetically modified organisms (GMOs) provides an interesting demonstration of the way in which direct action can have a major impact on policy outcomes. Toke (2002) gives a comprehensive account of the impact of protest groups on GMOs. From the mid-1990s the United States was producing an increasing amount of genetically modified crops and the EU gave permission for the importation of GM crops. In 1996 the Ministry of Agriculture supported the development of GM crop technology and initially did not believe that it was even necessary to make an assessment of the environmental impact. The Friends of the Earth (FOE) then campaigned for a moratorium on the growing of commercial crops. Toke points out that FOE were to an extent excluded from direct policy influence but there was support amongst the general public for their position. As Margetts (2000) highlights, in 1999 polls indicated that 73% of the public did not want GM crops grown. This public support, combined with insider groups (see Chapter 21) like the RSPB and English Nature taking up the issue, resulted in considerable pressure being placed on the Government.

However, perhaps two factors were crucial in a change in policy on GMOs and in a way they are an interesting commentary on how participation has changed because they were different, but very direct forms, of political activity. The first was that some radical groups such as Greenpeace undertook direct action and were prepared to destroy GM crops and face the potential consequences in terms of court action. These activities gave considerable publicity to the issue and created a public sense that there were dangers with GM crops. The second was that the media was prepared to play on these fears and gave considerable attention to what was called 'Frankenstein food'. It is also important to remember that the debate on GM foods was played out in the backwash of the BSE scandal. With Bovine Spongiform Encephalitis (or 'mad cow disease') the Government had tried to convince consumers that there was no risk to eating beef. Subsequent scientific investigation suggested that there were some major risks (Smith 2004). As a result consumers were highly mistrustful of new scientific developments in the area of food policy and consumers were not prepared to buy GM foods. This commercial pressure had an immediate impact. According to Toke (2002: 69):

> In the spring of 1998 the supermarket chain Iceland had announced that it was withdrawing GM foods from its shelves. This gave the company a competitive advantage which allied to the never-ending streams of letters from anti-GM activists, persuaded other supermarkets to follow suit.

A combination of direct action from radical groups, protests from established groups, boycotts by consumers and decisions by supermarkets not to stock GM foods led to the undermining of government policy (and perhaps more spectacularly undermined the export strategy of industrial agriculture in the United States). What is interesting in terms of participation is first, the wide range of actors involved and second, the impact that they had without going through the formal channels of Parliament and government. The Government was following, rather than leading, public opinion and the decision by supermarkets not to stock GM foods effectively changed policy without any government

JS 22.2

cience Review'

Main conclusions:

- If all else remains constant and the three crops are introduced and managed in the way they were in the trials, then for GMHT beet and spring oilseed rape a significant reduction would be expected in weed biomass and weed seed return resulting in fewer nectar resources for pollinators and fewer weed seed resources for granivorous birds. For GMHT maize the opposite is expected.

- These effects arise from the crop management regimes (ie the herbicide applications) associated with these GMHT crops, and are not a direct consequence of the way the crops have been produced.

- These data, and more that will follow, offer modelling opportunities to assess the longer-term and large-scale implications of this work, and will inform debate on broader agricultural issues related to societal choices and the balance of natural resources.

- That the findings of the experiments were different for different crops with GMHT traits reinforces the general conclusion in our First Report that impacts of GM crops must always be assessed on a case-by-case basis.

involvement. The issue of GM foods was highly politicised outside the formal institutional channels of representative government. As a result of the pressure, farming interests and the biotechnology industries agreed to a ban on commercial planting of GMOs until 2003 and the completion of trials.

In January 2004, a report on the trials seemed to produce mixed results but concluded: 'The advisory committee on releases to the environment (Acre) evaluated the farm-scale trials and came to the conclusion that in carefully controlled circumstances the commercial planting of GM crops could go ahead without any risk to the environment' (*Guardian*, 14 January 2004). The conclusion was strongly contested by environmental groups because in their view the report was ambiguous about GMOs (see Politics in Focus 22.2). The Government decided to allow the planting of genetically modified maize but was unable to allow it without agreement from Scotland and Wales, both of which opposed the policy. Likewise the EU has allowed for the use of GMOs under a system of strict regulation.

The 'respectable' cross-class protest

A key feature of both the anti-roads and anti-GMO protests is that they spread outside of the stereotype of the traditional protesters. Even if members of the general public did not participate in illegal direct action, they gave considerable support to the aims of the protest through less dramatic forms of direct action. As we saw above consumers boycotted GMOs and were prepared to participate in demonstrations against new roads. This is an indication of a unique phenomenon: the apparent willingness of a group outside the 'radicals' to participate in direct action. The extent of the change is indicated by two particular examples, the Countryside Alliance and the fuel protest.

The fuel protest is one of the most spectacular forms of direct pressure in recent years. According to Doherty, Paterson, Plows and Wall (2003: 2):

> In September 2000, a network of British farmers and road hauliers
> launched a dramatic campaign of direct action to protest at fuel
> duty...The British protesters blockaded petrol refineries...and
> within days created a fuel crisis that paralysed distribution
> and brought the country to a virtual halt.

What was different about this protest was the tactics they used and the impact it seemed to have on the running of the country and on the Government. The direct cause of the protest was a rapid rise in the price of fuel as a consequence of rising oil prices and increased government taxes. In addition, action in France by road hauliers seemed to have won significant concessions from government. The protest began in June 1998 with go-slows by lorry drivers in Birmingham and Kent, followed by protests in London. The actual fuel blockade began at the Stanlow refinery in Cheshire when 150 protesters blocked the refinery. By 11 September it had spread to most of the refineries in Britain and petrol stations were rapidly running short of petrol and diesel. The fuel protesters appear to have been successful, at least in the short term, in restricting fuel supplies because they seemed to have broad support in the community. Neither the police nor the oil companies tried with much effort to break the picket. Despite widespread public and media support, the protest ended quickly on 14 September with the protesters setting a 60-day deadline for some concessions on fuel taxation by the Government (Robinson 2002; Doherty, Paterson, Plows and Wall 2003).

The protest achieved little but a number of significant factors came out of it:

- It demonstrated the ease by which protest could cause major logistical problems in the United Kingdom.
- It was organised through a range of disparate groupings and independent actions rather than through a formal organisation with a distinct leadership. The form of protest was more like a network than a hierarchy and organised through mobile phones and e-mail, allowing rapid responses and changes of tactics.
- Support for it was widespread and included a large number of middle class and lower middle class protesters who would not normally have participated in such action.
- There was considerable support for the action outside of those who directly took part in the protest.
- 'Ordinary' people were prepared to take part in direct action. It was not something that was restricted to an extremist minority.

Nevertheless, an attempt to develop a similar movement in September 2005 failed to produce widespread support suggesting that the Government had learnt the lessons of the first protest.

A similar complex pattern is provided by analysis of the Countryside Alliance. The Countryside Alliance is a loose coalition of groups concerned with trying to ensure better treatment for rural areas. Unlike, the roads protest it does not have a formal organisation with a leader (see Politics in Focus 22.3). However, one of the key issues underpinning their protest is the legislation passed by the Labour Government to ban hunting. The Countryside Alliance linked the issue of fox-hunting to issues of livelihood and liberty in relation to the Government's overall policy in relation to the rural areas.

The Countryside Alliance has organised two major marches in London in 2002 and 2003. Both have attracted considerable support and seemed to slow the passing of the legislation. Nevertheless, in November 2004 the House of Commons approved the legislation in order to bring in the ban in February 2005 and the hunting of live foxes was made illegal.

In order to placate rural protest, the Government has developed a rural White Paper which has tried to take account of some of the wider concerns of the Countryside Alliance in relation to rural poverty, housing and services. This is a significant change because it represents a shift from the perception of rural concerns and policy being focused almost exclusively on agriculture to one where the wider problems of the rural communities are recognised.

There is considerable debate concerning whether the Countryside Alliance does represent an attempt to develop new forms of political action or whether it is an organisation that has rather cleverly used wider concerns about people in the countryside to support their campaign against hunting. Whilst a large number of people did support the Countryside Alliance marches, it has been suggested that really the organisation is limited

ꓥꓤUS 22.3

What is the Countryside Alliance?

The Countryside Alliance (CA) was formed in 1998 from the British Field Sports Association, the Countryside Business Group and the Countryside Movement.

How many members does it have?

The CA has 100,000 individual members and 350,000 affiliate members.

Who runs it?

The chief executive is Richard Burge, a Labour Party member who lists his recreations in *Who's Who 2002* as 'pigs, theatre, gardening'.

The CA promotes itself as a broad-based rural campaign group that represents a cross-section of the countryside community, many of whom are struggling in poverty, and has 'massive cross party political support'.

Source: The *Guardian* (20 September 2002)

in its aims. Corporate Watch has demonstrated that the board of the Countryside Alliance is dominated by members who have a direct interest in hunting. The alliance has made a number of vocal attacks against gay and black Labour MPs, and in many senses it is engaged in a very traditional struggle between rural, land-owning interests and an urban orientated Labour Party. The *Observer* columnist Nick Cohen has suggested that: 'They are the Tory Party on horseback. The Alliance offices are filled with ex-Conservative officials and MPs who lost their jobs in the 1997 massacre'.

It is important to draw lessons from the nature of these new forms of protest. First protest seems wider and more common than in the past. There is a whole range of policy areas where direct action has been used to influence debate (see Table 22.1 below). Second,

Campaign	Impact
Gun control. Snowdrop campaign following attack at Dunblane	Legislation introducing severe restraint on use and ownership of guns
Anti-roads lobby campaign of road building	Apparently reduced Conservative programme for roads and forced Labour Government to think carefully about road building. However Government's New Deal for trunk roads proposes 37 new schemes
Campaign against second runway in Manchester	Failed
Campaign against nuclear power	Abandonment of any new building of nuclear power stations, although situation being reviewed from 2005
Campaign organised by Greenpeace against dumping of disused oil platforms in the North Sea	Shell agree to recycle rather than dump Brent Spar oil platform
Campaign against GMO led by Greenpeace	Led to Government introducing testing and a large number of retailers and producers not using GMOs
Animal rights movement	Led to Huntington Life Sciences ending public status and decision by Cambridge University not to build new laboratory (although new laboratory to be built in Oxford)
Countryside Alliance — support hunting	Delay in legislation on banning fox-hunting but ban still introduced in 2005
Anti-war protest — opposed war in Iraq	No impact

these protests are by-passing the traditional forms of representation whether they are party, unions, traditional pressure groups or Parliament. Often their concern is not with getting the attention of politicians but of the media. Third, in many cases they are not organised like traditional political organisations. They often lack a clear leader and tend to be networks of a range of different organisations working together rather than a single, uniform and hierarchical organisation. This does raise important question of representation and accountability within the movement. If there is no formal structure or leadership, how are policies decided, goals formulated and leaders appointed? How do we know who these organisations represent? Fourth, these organisations do not follow the traditional boundaries of identity or class that characterised political organisation in the past. Parties in Britain tend to be organised on class lines. Pressure groups often organise around particular groups—the old, poor, consumers. These new movements have no simple patterns of representation. They often included different classes, occupation groups and political interests. The Countryside Alliance combines millionaire landowners with the rural poor. The GMO and anti-roads protest included anarchists, violent protesters and Conservative Party members. What unites all the protestors is usually opposition to something: a new road, GMOs or a tax. Often these organisations are easily divided when it comes to producing more positive proposals or developing the organisation further. For example, a range of divisions over goals and tactics made it difficult for the fuel protest to continue after its first dramatic actions. Likewise, Bob Geldof was criticised by some NGOs for being too close to the leaders of the G8 in July 2005. Finally, the importance of these groups is the way they reshape the political agenda and how they can bring to the attention issues that politicians have previously ignored (such as poverty in Africa). Consequently, we can see the second face of power in operation as issues are pushed on and off the agenda. Or alternatively, these protests could be an indication of the development of a more pluralistic political system. However, as we will see below assessing the impact of direct protest is difficult.

Power and protest

In terms of the politics of the new forms of protest one of the crucial question is whether these organisations and demonstration have any impact on decisions. Do protests mean that power is now more widely spread amongst the population? There are a number of examples where direct action seems to have had an impact on public policy (see Table 22.2). For instance, the oil company, Shell was forced to abandon its plans to sink the oil platform, Brent Spar, in the North Sea. The last Conservative Government also curtailed its roads programme and as we saw above, the present Government has certainly been placed on the defensive in terms of its policy on GMOs because of the attention the issue has raised. The Make Poverty History campaign and Live8 appear to have made Government increase aid to Africa and to do more to relieve Third World debt. There seems little doubt that direct action is an important way of changing the agenda and at the least forcing the Government to take account of, and react to, public pressure. However, there are still questions concerning whether they have any real impact on policy.

Whilst we can see successes in areas of roads, GMOs and Brent Spar, two points need to be taken into account. First, in the case of roads and nuclear power, the reason for the decision to suspend plans was not a consequence of direct action but the Government making decisions for economic reasons. When the Treasury was seeking to cut public expenditure, one of the easy areas to cut was the road programme. It had the advantage that the Government looked like it was listening to protesters. Similarly, the reasons behind the abandonment of nuclear power were not protest but the fact that the privatisation of electricity meant that nuclear power was uneconomic. However, the Government is currently considering the option of building more nuclear capacity, illustrating the weakness of the environmental movement. Second, whilst direct action can cause governments to reconsider policy as an immediate reaction to protest, governments often just delay the implementation of decisions. So whilst the introduction of GMOs has certainly been a long-drawn-out process, the Government still intends to allow the commercial use of genetically modified crops. Likewise with the roads programme which was delayed at the end of the Conservative period in office but has been resumed under Labour. When the Government takes a clear position on a central issue such as the war in Iraq, it seems that direct action has little or no effect. The impact of the direct action movement is still limited in that in most cases it represents a minority and those who protest come from a limited group. The Government can argue that it represents the majority view and the national interest and it does not need to bend to the demands of an unrepresentative minority.

However, the main point is not the influence that these groups have directly but the way that they have changed politics. The Live8 concert in July 2005 was an example of how the political arena has changed from one of putting votes in a ballot box to one of registering protest through attending a concert and putting a name on a website. The Make Poverty History campaign and Live8 forced the politicians at the G8 Summit in Scotland to take the issue of poverty in Africa seriously and to make commitments to future action. Live8 also linked direct protest to mainsteam politics by not using violent or disruptive process, but through issue raising and the leaders of Live8 clearly trying to influence rather than alienate the G8 political leaders. Of course, the willingness of people like Bob Geldof to remain on friendly terms with world leaders caused divisions within the movement demonstrating the difficulties of maintaining unity in these types of organisations.

The globalisation of protest

One important development recently has been the way in which direct action has developed into a global protest movement. The globalisation of protest has occurred in three ways:

- There is a growing international movement against globalisation through the development of what is a global anti-capitalist movement. Much of the global protest is a reflection of, and reaction to, what is seen as the globalisation of capitalism and the belief that it has to be opposed at the global level. The World Trade Organization and the G8 (the organisation that represents the eight most powerful economies in the world) is the focus of much of this protest because they are seen as perpetrating the spread of globalisation through the development of free trade. This movement gained a lot of media attention when it protested against the World Trade Organization (WTO) at the trade talks in Seattle in 1999. The protest at Seattle represented a wide coalition of traditional NGOs such as Oxfam, developing countries, environmental groups, trade unions and anti-capitalist groups. A combination of protests within the WTO and demonstration outside effectively resulted in the failure of the Seattle trade talks and pressure on the WTO to think about how it deals with issues of trade in developing countries. The protest in Seattle was followed with major demonstrations in Prague and the G8 meeting at Genoa, demonstrating the increasingly international nature of the protest. What is interesting is that through the Make Poverty History campaign and the Live8 concerts, protests against the G8 were pushed into the mainstream with many 'respectable' people demonstrating at the St Andrews Summit in July 2005.

- There is an attempt by direct action movements to co-ordinate activity globally. One group that has been particularly active in this has been the Reclaim the Street groups which are trying to oppose the domination of streets by motor vehicles. They link this to wider issues concerning the nature of capitalism and its global development. What the Reclaim the Streets movement has attempted is to expand their protest globally. Through the internet they attempt to co-ordinate protests on a global scale. So for instance the J18 protests in 1999 were an attempt to co-ordinate a Reclaim the Streets protest in financial centres throughout the world (see Politics in Focus 22.4).

- Direct action groups have attempted to attract global attention to the issues they raise. This has always been one of the tactics of Greenpeace and it has been used in campaigns like those against the destruction of the rainforest. Perhaps one of the best examples of the globalisation of protest has been the Zapatistas in Mexico. What is interesting about the Zapatistas is that they were essentially pursuing armed resistance to try to win rights for the indigenous people of the Chiapas. However, in their struggle they have cleverly used the internet to ensure that their views and arguments have been sent around the world. As a consequence, they have achieved a high level of international coverage and been very successful in getting their case widely heard (see Chapter 23).

treets

Bay Area Reclaim the Streets (RTS) is part of a global, decentralised direct action movement. Direct action means that, rather than hoping and waiting for the powers that be to make the world all better, we personally set about the urgent task of reclaiming the streets (and the planet and our lives) from the destructive tyranny of global capitalism. The streets are the arteries of the capitalist system of exploitation and oppression, painful extensions of the military-industrial complex that is destroying the earth. By creating a zone of fun in the streets, we disrupt the normal functioning of that system, thereby opening a space for creative development (revolution). Stepping off the sidewalks and into the street brings us together, and allows us to challenge the dehumanisation of our lives and the sterile world that accompanies it.

Source: http://guest.xinet.com/rts/

Conclusion

We have seen in this chapter that the traditional notion of representation derived from the Westminster model is based on a limited notion of participation. Politics is essentially for politicians who are voted for by the people. Participation is limited to elections every five years or so. However, there has been increasing disenchantment with Westminster as the arena of political representation. The dominance of government makes it very difficult for alternative views to have much influence on public policy. This has led to increasing disenchantment with traditional forms of participation and increasingly it seems that people are turning to direct action. The groups participating in action today vary from those in the past. Often they are not intent on overthrowing the political system and are relatively conservative in their aims, for example the anti-fuel protest. It is also the case that a number of movements like the anti-roads protest are also crossing class lines and can include radical and anarchist movements with middle class, home-owning protesters. It is also the case that these protests are globalising. Direct action is taking on an international character reflecting the rise of global political issues. We have to be careful not to exaggerate the impact of new forms of political action. Whilst direct action has had some notable successes in areas like GMOs, they are still not widely supported and often they result in a delay in government action rather than preventing it. It has to be remembered, however, that demonstrations and social movement are the exception rather than the norm. For the vast majority of people, they either do not participate in politics or participate through elections. Demonstrations may be newsworthy but they are not the most common form of political activity. However, as we will see in the next chapters, there a number of ways in which government at local and national level is attempting to extend the representative process.

KEY POINTS

- There is evidence of increasing disillusionment with traditional patterns of representation.

- Participation in elections appears to be in decline and less people are prepared to join political parties.

- People however are prepared to undertake other forms of political activity.

- Direct action is increasingly used as a mechanism for influencing the political agenda.

- In a number of areas including fuel prices and GMOs, direct action seems to have considerable impact on government policy.

KEY QUESTIONS

(1) What is the traditional pattern of representation in Britain?

(2) Why does there seem to be a growing disillusionment with politics?

(3) What accounts for the rise of direct action?

(4) How much impact has direct action had on public policy?

(5) Has the political system become more pluralistic as a consequence of these types of movements?

IMPORTANT WEBSITES

Many direct action groups have websites which provide considerable information on their tactics and goals. See for example: www.**countryside-alliance.** org. For a more 'radical group' see the site of the Animal Liberation Front: www. animal-liberation.com/ index.html. The Make Poverty History website is: www.makepovertyhistory. org/.

For a site that links various direct action groups see www.direct-action.org.uk/. For the way in which the internet is used to internationalise direct action see: www.ezln.org, the webpage of the Zapatistas in Mexico. An extremely useful site on issues of voting and participation is www.powerinquiry.org/ which contains a number of papers on these issues.

FURTHER READING

The concept of representation in B. Manin (1997) *The Principles of Representative Government*, Cambridge: Cambridge University Press. How the form of representation adopted in Britain shaped the nature of decision-making is illustrated in D. Marquand (1988) *The Unprincipled Society: New Demands and Old Politics*, Fontana: London. Attitudes towards political institutions and issues of why people vote are discussed in H. Clarke, D. Sanders, M. Stewart and P. Whiteley (2004) *Political Choice in Britain*, Oxford: Oxford University

Press. For a comprehensive survey of participation in Britain read C. Pattie, P. Seyd and P. Whiteley (2004) *Citizenship in Britain: Values, Participation and Democracy*, Cambridge: Cambridge University Press. The notion of social capital is explored in R. Putnam (2000) *Bowling Alone*, New York: Simon and Schuster. For examples of direct action see B. Doherty, A. Plows and D. Wall (2003) 'The British Direct Action Movement', *Parliamentary Affairs*, 56(4): 669–86.

 Visit the Online Resource Centre that accompanies this book for links to more information on this chapter topic

CHAPTER TWENTY THREE

New forms of participation

READER'S GUIDE

We saw in the last chapter that as a response to a perceived crisis of
representation, people have started to participate in politics in different ways.
However, this has not been the only change. Increasingly government is
responding to declining electoral participation by developing new forms of
participation. These range from different ways of voting to citizens' juries and
participation in decision-making. This chapter examines these different
processes of representation and assesses their impact on policy-making.

Introduction

As we saw in the previous chapter, the Westminster model is based on a limited notion of political participation. People vote in elections for an MP who is a representative, not a delegate and Parliament, rather than the people, is sovereign. As a consequence decisions are often made in secret by a small elite. Whilst Britain has long been a liberal democracy, the emphasis has been on the liberal rather than the democratic side of the equation. British citizens have a number of freedoms: there is little constraint on political organisations, there is a free media, there is rule of law and an independent judiciary. Nevertheless, the ability of citizens to influence political decisions has often been limited. They have not been actively involved in the decision-making process, there has been an absence of direct democracy. As a consequence, people have looked to alternative mechanisms for trying to influence policy outcomes. However, it is also the case that governments have attempted to respond to the limited forms of representation in Britain and to develop modes of governance that are more inclusive. This chapter will look at the ways in which representation and participation has changed at both local and national level.

In recent years there have been a number of conscious attempts to make British democracy more inclusive and move beyond the regular elections for MPs and councillors. Some of these changes, such as devolution and the reform of the House of Lords, are discussed in other chapters. This chapter will focus on other forms of participation which include referenda, the use of citizens' juries, partnerships in local government and the role of the internet. Government at the national, regional and local level has looked at ways in which it can try to engage with its citizens. New technology is opening up possibilities for participation which have not existed in the past. This chapter will outline these mechanisms and examine how effective they are. It will also examine how these affect our understanding of representation and the extent to which they mean that the narrow Westminster notion of representation is now under challenge. The chapter begins by looking at different understandings of representation and participation.

Rethinking representation

Representation in Britain has been on the basis that we vote for individuals as our representatives to local and national government. We are represented as individuals and it is our representatives who judge how best to act in our interests. This limited form of representation has been challenged by ideas of civil society and exclusion. The concept of civil society, which is increasingly being used to understand the processes of democratisation in Latin American and Eastern Europe, presents a more inclusive notion of representation. Within the concept of civil society is the idea that democracy cannot just be based on formal representation but that democracy must be built through engagement with citizens, both through political activity and through associations or groups in society. The concept of exclusion highlights how people are excluded by the traditional processes of representation.

In many cases, people do not engage in politics because they do not vote or because an individual vote has an infinitesimally small impact on political outcomes. For those of us who are not rich, or not in powerful pressure groups, the impact that we can have on government is limited.

As a result of the decline of trust and turnout in voting, government has thought about ways in which it can re-engage the public and so has developed new forms of representation and political interaction. As Figure 23.1 demonstrates there are a number of ways in which citizens can participate in government that go beyond traditional patterns of representation. These can range from simply providing information such as what is happening in public bodies or informing people of their entitlements. At the next level, it includes consultation on policies and the delivery of public goods. At the higher level, it involves participation when citizens are included in the decision-making process. Finally, it can mean empowerment where citizens are allowed to make decisions themselves and to have control over how public services are delivered. Through organisations like foundation hospitals and tenant control the Government has tried to move to a situation where those people who are actually delivering services (hospitals) or receiving service (tenants) have control over how

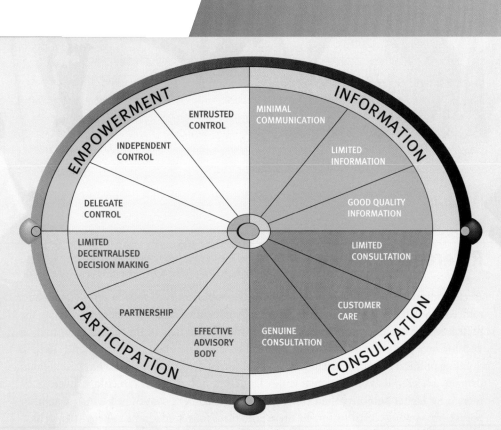

Source: www.step.gb.com/consultation/index.htm

the service is provided. Under the scheme of local management tenants of local authority housing can vote to become self-governing. Once this is done they elect a management committee. It is then the tenants who make decisions about the running and maintenance of the estate (see Extract 23.1). Local management is just part of a process where a range of new mechanisms of representation and participation have been introduced. One new method of representation to have become more important recently is referendum.

Extract 23.1

TENANTS have taken direct control of their homes for the first time since Glasgow's housing stock transfer.

Two groups of tenants have been registered officially as local housing organisations able to take day-to-day decisions on how their communities are managed.

The groups, in Drumchapel and Baillieston, are the first of what will be a network of 64 LHOs in the city to be formally recognised by housing watchdog Communities Scotland.

Eventually similar groups will form the backbone of the city's not-for-profit landlord, Glasgow Housing Association, making key decisions on how £1.5billion of new investment in homes is spent over the next decade.

Some could even break away from the GHA in much-mooted second stage transfers that would put ownership as well as management in tenants' hands.

Communities Minister and Baillieston MSP Margaret Curran said today: "In the five months since the transfer, work has been ongoing to make it a reality.

Source: www.eveningtimes.co.uk/hi/news/5018343.html

Referendums

A referendum is where the electorate is offered the opportunity to vote on a particular issue, rather than vote for a government. It is actually a form of direct democracy whereby the preferences of a majority of the electorate (or more accurately of those who vote) make a decision on a particular issue. In some political systems, referendums are frequently used in deciding political issues. In Switzerland and California, for example, voters have the right to demand a referendum on particular issues. Under the notion of parliamentary sovereignty, there is no higher authority than Parliament and Parliament cannot be bound by another body. Consequently, constitutionally there is no place for referendums in Britain. In principle, any referendum in Britain cannot be binding on Parliament. It is merely advisory.

Nevertheless, there has been increased use of referenda in Britain and the reality is that a government would find it very difficult to ignore or override the result of a referendum.

The rise of the referendum

The first referendum in Britain was the 1975 referendum on the issue of whether Britain should remain a member of the European Union, or as it was at the time, the European Community (although one had been held in 1973 in Northern Ireland on the issue of whether Northern Ireland should remain part of the United Kingdom or not). After a campaign which involved the leading figures in British politics, the result was a clear vote for Britain remaining a member of what was called then the Common Market. This was followed by referendums in 1979 on devolution in Scotland and Wales. Despite the Government supporting devolution, both referendums were lost. In Wales a majority of voters opposed devolution and in Scotland the vote in favour failed to meet the requirement that at least 40% of the electorate supported devolution. Referendums were not used again until after the election of the Labour Government in 1997 which has had referenda on devolution in Scotland and Wales, the Good Friday Agreement in Northern Ireland and on the issue of government in London and over mayors in a number of local government districts and regional government in the North East in 2004. In addition, referenda have been suggested on the issue of proportional representation (although the likelihood of such a referendum seems to have receded), on the new European Constitution (which was to occur after the 2005 general election but was quickly abandoned once French and Dutch voters rejected the new constitution) and on British membership of the Euro (which in principle will occur when the Treasury decides that the conditions are right for Britain's membership but is now unlikely during the 2005 Parliament (see Chapter 26)).

The advantages and disadvantages of referendums

Referendums a have a number of advantages:

- They mean voters can have a say over a particular issue that could have an important impact on the future of the country. All of the referendums held so far have been broadly on constitutional issues, rather than substantive issues of policy.

- They often provide a way of separating particular issues from broad aspects of government policy.

- They often allow governments to pass problems that are divisive within their own party. In 1975 the Labour Government was split over the issue of membership of the European Community and a referendum was an alternative to the Government losing the vote in the Commons. Likewise the Conservative Government opted for the proposal of a referendum on the Euro as a way of avoiding splitting the party.

Nevertheless, there are a number of disadvantages:

- The results are often open to manipulation. The outcome of a referendum depends to a large degree on how the question is phrased. It is also the case that the government is in a strong position to try to influence the outcome. In the run up to the 1975 campaign, the opinion polls suggested that people were opposed to membership of the European Community. However, after the Government put considerable resources behind the Yes campaign (subtly disguised as a neutral position) the final result was strongly in favour. In a number of referendums outside Britain when governments have not got the result they wanted, they have held the referendum again.

- Voting studies suggest that people often vote on issues other than those of the referendum. Consequently, a government is likely to lose a referendum if it is unpopular. This is why Tony Blair decided to have the EU constitution referendum shortly after the 2005 general election (although once the constitution was opposed in France and Holland, the idea of a referendum was abandoned completely). The period just following an election is traditionally the high point of government support. Consequently, through the timing of referendums, governments are able to influence the outcomes.

- Referendums can only deal with simple issues where the question can easily be answered yes or no. Consequently, they may be inappropriate for issues such as membership of the Euro where the arguments are complex and the outcomes of decisions are difficult to know.

- Forms of direct democracy such as referendums can create problems for minority rights. They are a form of majoritarianism when the only outcome that is of interest is how the majority voted and not the intensity of preferences or the fundamental rights of humans. Referendums could easily be used to repress the rights of minorities or to introduce policies such as the death penalty which infringe human rights.

Whatever the problems with referendums, they are a relatively new and recent addition to the British polity. It seems that two issues are likely to lead to referendum—constitutional change and the devolution of power to local levels; and significant changes in relation to the EU. However, they can be highly problematic for government if things go wrong. In November 2004 the Government held a referendum on whether people wanted regional government in the North East. Despite Government support for regional government, the vote was overwhelmingly against (see Table 23.1), and as a result the Government's policy on regional government collapsed.

Referendum	Yes %	No %	Turnout %
Common Market membership 1975	64.5	35.5	65
1997 Scottish devolution	74.3	24.7	60
1997 Welsh devolution	50.3	49.7	50.1
1998 Good Friday Agreement	71	29	80
2004 NE regional government referendum	22	78	48

Citizens' juries

Whilst referenda provide a more direct form of democracy, there is no indication that when people vote in a referendum that they have taken the issue seriously or have a good understanding of the issues. In the case of the Euro, for example, the argument are complex and voters could be faced with playing economic arguments (what is best for the economy) off against political arguments (what is strategically in Britain's political interest). Consequently, it has been argued that if we are to have decisions made in a considered way (rather than being based on prejudice and ignorance), the process of democracy should be more deliberative. Through deliberative democracy participation involves more than just voting. It involves people in thinking and discussing the particular issues that they are voting on. One of the ways in which deliberative democracy has been developed is through citizens' juries.

Smith and Wales (2000: 55) give a succinct definition of citizens' juries:

> A citizens' jury brings together a group of randomly chosen citizens to deliberate on a particular issue, whether it is setting a policy agenda or the choice of particular policy options. Over a number of days participants are exposed to information about an issue and hear a wide range of views from witnesses, who are selected on the basis of their expertise or on grounds that they represent affected interests. With trained moderators ensuring fair proceedings, the jurors are given the opportunity to cross examine the witnesses... Following a process of deliberation amongst themselves, the jurors produce a decision or provide recommendations....

Since 1996 there have been over 100 citizens' juries on issues such as health, education, genetic food and medicine (Delap 2001) (see Politics in Focus 23.1). The point about citizens' juries is that they involve people in decision-making in a much more real way than voting in elections or referenda. The members of the jury are selected randomly (usually from the electoral register) and so they do not represent particular interests or social groups. They are intended to represent the population as a whole. The process of democracy is one of deliberation rather than representation and this means that decisions can be tackled in a considered way on the basis of evidence. For example, if somebody is asked a question in a poll they may respond in a few seconds without any thought. The response is likely to be held on the basis of prejudice or ignorance, rather than knowledge. If people are given time to examine evidence and spend time on the issue they may come to a much more considered view. In addition, it means that 'ordinary people' rather than politicians and policy-makers are involved in policy-making.

23.1

itizens' jury on GM foods

In order to assess views on genetically modified foods, the Food Standards Agency held a three-day citizens' jury in April 2003. The jury was presented with the question, 'Should GM foods be available to buy in the UK?' The jury consisted of 15 members of the public. They were first presented with some of the issues concerning GM foods and then split into small groups to discuss the pros and cons. They were then presented with evidence from a range of experts who supported and opposed GM foods. The jurors were given the opportunity to ask questions and again discuss the issues in small groups. There was also a role play session. At the end of the three days the jurors discussed the evidence and voted on the question. They voted 9 to 6 in favour of GM foods. The proceedings of the jury can be watched on video at www.flyonthewall.tv.foodstandardsagency .

Whilst citizens' juries seem an important and innovative way of changing the process of representation and decision-making, there are number of problems:

- Parkinson (2004) points out that as jurors are chosen randomly they are not representatives for, or accountable to, the people that they are purportedly supposed to be representing. They could in fact come to decisions that the majority of the population oppose and they do not have to answer for those decisions.

- This possibility is made worse by what Parkinson (2004) calls the 'Grandview' problem. The jurors are chosen randomly to provide a cross section of the population. However because the jurors are subject to detailed information and in-depth discussion over an issue, they often go through a process of transformation. Consequently, they 'are no longer representative of the attitudes, beliefs and values of the population' (Parkinson 2004: 380).

- Because the jurors are usually selected from the electoral role this means that about 10% of the population will be excluded.

- The decisions that juries make are usually advisory rather than binding. This may be desirable, considering the problems of representation that have been raised. It does mean, however, that politicians and policy-makers can easily ignore outcomes that they do not like.

- Because the jurors are coming to an issue without any knowledge, they are vulnerable to the way the proceedings are organised. The organisers choose the questions, set the agenda, structure the proceedings and appoint the witnesses. They are in a position to manipulate the outcomes.

- The process is high cost both financially and in terms of time. Therefore, it can only be used in limited circumstances. It may also be the case that those who are prepared to commit the time are not particularly representative, and it leaves the question of how the views of those who are less engaged are evaluated.

The development of e-government

The growth of the internet has developed a new range of ways in which citizens and government interact. Some of these changes are about the delivery of services but others can be related to new forms of representation. The spread of the internet in the United Kingdom has been extremely rapid. In 2000, only 34% of people had internet access at home and at work (Cabinet Office 2000) but as Politics in Focus 23.2 indicates by 2004, 50% of homes had internet access and 68% of small businesses. Consequently, the internet has become a mechanism by which government can interact with citizens. By 2006 it is projected that the Government will have spent £6 billion promoting e-government (Bastow et al 2003) and there is an e-government minister who heads the Office of the e-Envoy with responsibility for ensuring the development on e-government.

There are in fact three levels of interaction:

• Information—the lowest level is providing information and there is now a considerable amount of central and local government information. By 2001 85% of central government agencies had websites and by 2003 all English local authorities had a webpage. As a consequence, much government data and information is now accessible via the web, improving, in principle, communication between government and citizens.

• Transaction—the second level is transaction—that is, the internet can be used for obtaining and delivering services. The Government is committed to a major shift to the on-line delivery of services. The Government aimed to bring all services on-line by 2005, and although that target has not been met there are many services that can be delivered

N FOCUS 23.2

e United Kindom

Internet access

• 59% of UK homes have a PC
• 50% of homes (around 12.5 million) have internet access
• 68% of small businesses have internet access

Broadband

• 3.2 million broadband connections
• 1.82 million DSL connections
• 1.36 million cable modem connections
• 12% of homes have broadband
• DSL is available to 85% of UK homes and businesses

Source: www.internetworldstats.com/eu/uk.htm

on-line (see Politics in Focus 23.3). Local authorities have also moved to providing services through the internet. Facilities such as paying rents, council tax and parking fines on-line exist in a number of councils (Bastow, Dunleavy and Margetts 2003).

- Intereaction—the third level, and perhaps the most important, is the development of the internet as a form of political interaction. This has occurred in number of ways (see below).

On-line voting

Perhaps the most significant political development in terms of the internet is the potential of on-line voting. This may change the whole organisation of elections. Already electronic counting has been used in the London mayoral elections and a number of local authorities have experimented with on-line voting. A number of non-governmental organisations such as PricewaterhouseCoopers, the Scottish Labour Party Executive Committee and universities have used on-line voting for internal elections. On-line voting can be used in a number of ways. People could go to polling stations and vote on-line or there could be voting from home via the internet. There are a number of advantages to on-line polling:

- it could increase turnout as the cost of voting is very low in terms of time;
- with increased use of the internet it is very convenient;
- it could appeal to younger voters;
- it could reduce costs of elections;
- it could lead to much greater interaction, in principle, allowing for on-line consultation on a range of issues.

n-line

Some of the government service on-line include:

- Completing tax assessment
- Applying for a passport
- Making a money claim
- Claiming carer's allowance
- Doing a mock driving theory test
- Searching a database of job opportunities
- Making a planning application
- Claiming child benefit
- Appling for pension credit
- Buying a TV licence

However, the prospect of on-line voting does raise considerable questions regarding security. Electronic polls for *Big Brother* and Radio 4 demonstrate the difficulties of controlling how often people vote. Not only would electronic voting have to ensure that it was the person entitled to vote that did vote, it would also have to be secure from hackers and viruses. One investigation by the US National Science Foundation found that 'remote internet voting systems pose significant risks to the integrity of the voting process' and so should not be used in public elections (Parliamentary Office of Science and Technology 2001). There are also problems in Britain in relation to existing legislation such as data protection.

On-line consultation

The Hansard Society e-Democracy Programme is using on-line consultation methods in order to increase public 'engagement with parliamentary decision making'. They have opened up a number of issues for discussion on the internet including hate crime in Northern Ireland, the Constitutional Reform Bill and Human Reproductive Technologies. The on-line responses are then fed into the considerations of select committees. Whilst this may be a useful mechanism for widening debate, few people respond to these consultations. For example, in the case of the Constitutional Reform Bill consultation, only 53 people posted comments. In addition, many were academics and commentators who were already involved in the debates. As such, it is not clear that these consultations are representative or very legitimate.

Political blogging

Blogsites are essentially on-line diaries that cover a range of activities from the bizarre to the mundane (there are nearly three million on the internet). Recently, there has been the development, particularly in the United States, of political blogs where, for example, politicians provide an on-line account of their activities, and these are seen as an important mechanism for allowing voters to interact more closely with their representatives. The blog, *Salam Pax*, had an impact in terms of informing people of conditions in Iraq shortly before and during the Iraqi war of 2003 when there were no sources of independent information in Iraq. Similar blogs have started to develop in Britain. There are a number of politicians who have weblogs and there was, for example, a blog following the progress of the London mayoral election in 2004. Ferguson and Howell (2004) point out that the key to weblogs is the way in which they build a network of interested internet users around them and this can develop into a sense of community. However, it is clear that their political impact is very limited. First, they do not have a large audience and very few responses to the blog are posted. Second, Ferguson and Howell discovered that there was little attempt at interaction amongst most bloggers. Really, they were just using the sites to put across their own views rather than interact with voters. In addition, as the examples in Politics in Focus 23.4 indicate, the level of debate in the weblogs is not very high or even particularly political. Nevertheless, the weblog does open up a new channel of political communication and allows a more direct contact between voters and politicians. A weblog that came from the Prime Minister may attract considerable attention.

Remember what happened to Scargill

I can remember exactly where I was when I experienced my first spasm of savage Right-wing indignation. It was 1984, at breakfast time—about 10.40am—and I had a spoonful of Harvest Crunch halfway to my lips. The place was the Junior Common Room of my college.

For the previous two decades I had viewed politics with a perfectly proper mixture of cynicism and apathy. Whatever I read under the bedclothes, it certainly wasn't Hansard. Like everyone at my school, I had undergone vague sensations of enthusiasm when the Falklands were recaptured, but otherwise, frankly, I did not give a monkey's.

Occasionally I would glance at the political columnists in the newspapers, and be amazed that anyone could pay them to write such tosh. I hadn't a clue who was in the Cabinet. The world was too beautiful to waste time on such questions.

Music paradise?

Category: *From Tom*

I don't know if I've ever told you that I'm a former deputy treasurer of the all party parliamentary music group (long story for another time). I've pondered on the music industry for years now. It struck me that the industry just didn't have an adequate response to the chasmic leaps in technology that confronted it. Rather like the vain attempts of the French to keep their language frozen in time, the music industry couldn't deal with file sharing and all that clever stuff. They had a problem. I mean we cannot allow the old-napster-style-sites to drive our talented artists into starvation. For every Bono there are a thousand artists trying to pay the bills at the end of the month after all. So what did the industry do? King Canute like, they tried to pretend nothing was happening and started arresting their customers—not a particularly productive exercise in the long run. What they lacked was a new business plan; one that accepted that the online revolution wasn't going away.

I might be wrong but *Radio Paradise* might just be the plan they need. I might also be way behind the times here. But an online radio station, with a varied playlist, that allows you to download the music by the artists playing on the site and gives you helpful info on each track, is a new and welcome development, to me at least. Surely this is the way the industry should be configuring itself? One last thing—this kind of model will probably only work if the music is cheaper than at present. That's a bit of a leap for the industry to make but I have a hunch that we'll all spend the same amount on more varied choices of music—music our peers recommend to us, not the marketing people.

Now, shoot me down in flames for being a; wrong and/or b; way behind the times.

Posted by tomwatson at *10:22 pm* | *Comments (14)* | *TrackBack (0)*

The web as a mechanism for political organisation

For a number of people the internet provides a new site for political organisation. There are 79 registered political parties in Britain with websites. It is increasingly the case that parties are using the web as a means of communicating. For instance Billy Bragg has been involved with a website, www.Theyworkforyou.com, in order to try to encourage tactical voting. However, perhaps the greatest impact of the web is the way in which it allows the development of less traditional political organisations. The web has a number of advantages in terms of political movements. First, it is not controlled by government and is almost completely uncensored. This means that any political view can find a forum on the web. Second, except in the case of North Korea, the internet is accessible almost anywhere in the world. Consequently, even minority political interests can access supporters and bring together like-minded individuals. Third, groups such as the anti-globalisation movement (see Chapter 22) see the web as a mechanism of developing worldwide political activity and developing a global civil society where a range of different actors across the world can interact in order to develop opposition to corporate and state power. Probably the best example of this new type of politics is the way the EZLN has used the internet to publicise their plight in their conflict in the Chiapas region of Mexico against the Mexican government. In particular, their leader, Subcommandante Marcos, has used the internet and other forms of media to bring worldwide attention to this particular part of the world. This has undoubtedly limited the ability of the Mexican government to crush the rebellion. The website of the EZLN has had over 10 million visitors (see www.ezln.org) and changed the perception worldwide of what is essentially a revolutionary guerrilla movement. In Britain the Make Poverty History campaign has been organised in large part through the web.

There is a danger of exaggerating the impact of the internet on politics because of its pervasive influence in society. Hitherto, the internet has had little political impact. It has provided new sources of information and new mechanisms for communication. It is also increasingly being used as a mechanism for obtaining and delivering services. This, of course, is a mechanism for administration rather than politics. The political element is more one of potential than actuality. The internet could be used for voting, informing citizens of policy, interacting with citizens or referenda but a number of problems need to be overcome before such developments occur. One of the problems that continually recurs is the extent to which there is a growing digital divide making the internet a mechanism for exclusion rather than inclusion. For example, whilst in 2001 429 million people used the internet worldwide, that is only 6% of the world's population and 41% of the figure is based in the United States. In Britain access to the internet is much greater amongst the top social classes and access in both terms of having technology and skills is less for women, the poor, ethnic minorities and the disabled. Gibson, Wainer and Ward illustrate that those who engage in on-line political activity are more likely to be male, highly educated and of a higher social class. However they did find:

> . . . [t]hat UK citizens engaging in online participation are significantly different from citizens engaging in existing more traditional forms of politics . . . In particular while female citizens and those from poorer backgrounds are less likely to do more activist politics off line or contact organisations online, they are equally likely to engage in online participation in general as men and high social status individuals (Gibson et al 2005: 578).

Nevertheless, it has to be pointed out that the percentage of their respondents engaged in political activity is very low and so whilst internet usage is high in Britain, and growing, there is a danger that the most needy groups are excluded and that the internet then becomes a tool that misrepresents interests in Britain.

Partnership

One of the key problems of democracy has been the decline of participation in local government. Turnout in local government elections can be very low (see Chapter 15). Consequently, government has looked at new ways to reinvigorate participation at the local level. One of the mechanisms for improving local involvement is through the concept of partnership (see Catney 2004). Tony Blair has set out the importance of partnership:

> The days of the all-purpose authority that planned and delivered
> everything are gone. They are finished. It is partnership with others—
> public agencies, private companies, community groups and voluntary
> organizations that local government's future lies... To enure that the
> shared vision is delivered by bringing cohesion and co-ordination to
> the current fragmented scene... Councils will no longer be defined just
> by lists of statutory responsibilities but by what, in partnership
> with others, they achieve (Blair quoted in Catney 2004: 10).

The traditional model of local government saw people electing councils who then delivered public service to the locality without taking much, if any, notice of the desires of local citizens. In Blair's view they were seen as control and command systems. The notion of partnership is based around the idea that public services are delivered in co-operation with other groups and interests within the locality. Labour undoubtedly built incentives for partnerships forming at local level by providing grants where partnerships were formed (Stoker 2001). In addition, Catney (2004) points out how the Labour Government has used partnership as a mechanism for ending exclusion. Traditionally, local government has been seen as dominated by local elites—particularly business (Saunders 1995). Through partnership the intention is to increase community participation and in particular to ensure that deprived communities, hitherto excluded from participation, are included in partnerships.

In particular, partnerships are seen as a mechanism for delivering urban regeneration, especially in the use of urban regeneration budgets.

A number of questions have been raised about partnerships and whether they are really a mechanism for increased democracy.

(1) It is argued that there is still over-representation of business and that often the inclusion of community groups is symbolic rather than having any real impact on the outcome of decisions.

(2) Partnership is seen by some as a way of bypassing local government and ensuring that the government has direct control over services at local government. Through its control over the budget, central government is effectively able to control local partnerships.

(3) Partnerships are based on group representation and therefore represent only those who are involved in local groups. This excludes a large number of citizens.

Conclusion

The traditional pattern of political participation in Britain has always been straight-forward. People voted for representatives in parliamentary and council elections and it was those representatives who made decisions. In certain policy areas and at particular times people may take part in pressure group activity in order to try to influence policy outcomes. Certain pressure groups developed close relationships with government where they were able to be consulted over a period of time about policy. Both the voting system and the pressure group system excluded the majority of people from government. The last few years have seen an attempt to create mechanisms that are more responsive to the views of people. Through the use of referenda, citizens' juries, e-government and partnerships, government has been building patterns of representation that are less infrequent than elections and less exclusive than policy networks. Many of these new mechanisms are in the early stage. Except for the referendums—which have only been used in a limited number of cases—there has been little impact on major policy decisions. Nevertheless, what there has been is an attempt to rethink the nature of representation and to find ways of bringing government closer to the people. This is a break with the elitism of the Westminster model of representation and whilst it may only be a small beginning it does indicate a process of change. What we have seen is a shift away from politics only being about voting for a representative and looking at ways to engage citizens in politics. This is particularly the case at local levels where the smaller forms of government make it possible to widen the political debate. Moreover developments in the internet and new experiments in participation mean that the limited form of Westminster representation is under challenge and in the future we are more likely to see different patterns of political engagement.

KEY POINTS

- Traditional notions of representation in Britain are based on limited conception of voting for a representative.

- Government has looked to new types of mechanisms to improve representation so that it involves citizens through information and developing policy.

- The internet has developed as a new tool for building relationships between government and citizens.

- There has been an increased use of referendums in British politics.

- Representation has changed at local level through the development of partnerships.

KEY QUESTIONS

(1) What is the impact of the traditional model of representation on democracy?

(2) What are the advantages and disadvantages of referenda?

(3) Are citizens' juries a useful way of improving democratic decision-making?

(4) How have partnerships changed decision-making at the local level?

IMPORTANT WEBSITES

There is useful information on the web and politics at www.governmentontheweb.co.uk.

The electoral commission has information on all referenda in Britain www.electoralcommission. gov.uk/. Information on citizen's juries is available at: www.soc.surrey.ac.uk/sru/SRU37.html. An example of an actual jury can be found at: www.food.gov.uk/gmdebate/**citizens**_jury/. The Zapatistas website is: www.ezln.org. An example of a partnership arrangement at local level can be found at: www.**sheffieldfirst**.net. The government's e-government website is: www.cabinetoffice.gov.uk/e-government/.

FURTHER READING

There is a useful discussion of the concept of representation in A. Birch (1964) *Representative and Responsible Government*, London: Unwin Hyman. Some of the issues surrounding forms of deliberative democracy are discussed in J. Parkinson (2004) 'Hearing Voices: Negotiating Representation Claims in Public Deliberation', *The British Journal of Politics and International Relations*, 6: 370–88 and G. Smith and C. Wales (2000) 'Citizens' Juries and Deliberative Democracy', *Political Studies*, 48: 51–65. For a thorough examination of all the alternative forms of democratic participation see G. Smith (2006) *Power Beyond the Ballot: 57 Democratic Innovations from Around the World*, Report to the Power Inquiry, available at: www.powerinquiry.org/.

 Visit the Online Resource Centre that accompanies this book for links to more information on this chapter topic

The judiciary and rights

READER'S GUIDE

This chapter analyses the interconnections between politics and the law, and the forces leading the judiciary to have a growing impact in the political arena. These include the Human Rights Act, membership of the European Union and judicial review. It discusses the principle of judicial independence and how the Government has tried to draw a line between the judicial and legislative functions by creating a new Supreme Court in which the Law Lords will sit rather than in the House of Lords. It discusses how what critics regard as examples of judicial activism have led to clashes with politicians. It then examines civil liberties and the background to the recent Human Rights Act. Finally, it considers the citizen's opportunities via the Parliamentary Ombudsman and tribunals for obtaining redress of grievances against the administration.

Introduction

The law is often regarded as a *set of procedures* which promotes order, justice and a degree of predictability in relations between individuals, groups and the state. In a free society law also underpins the citizens' freedoms by guaranteeing certain civil liberties and imposing legal checks on the authorities. A second and narrower usage of law may be as a *means of resolving disputes*, and is ultimately backed by criminal sanctions imposed by the courts. Another is the *common law*, derived from precedent and judges' interpretations of the law. Finally, one may refer to *statute law*, that is, an Act which has been passed through Parliament and received the Royal Assent. A consequence of the sovereignty of Parliament is that statute law takes precedence over common law, but even here judges have a role to play, in assessing (and helping juries to assess in jury trials) criminal guilt or innocence, as well as interpreting a statute, and determining its boundaries and application.

As long ago as 1865, in his *The English Constitution*, Walter Bagehot noted the law-abidingness of the British, although claiming that the natural impulse of the English 'is to resist authority', to regard government as 'an extrinsic agency' and legislation as 'alien action'. Respect for law in Britain has depended, in large measure, on people regarding the laws as reasonable and on the restrictions on liberty being limited. There have been occasions when groups have felt it necessary to resort to direct action against a law, or to further a cause outside of the parliamentary process. In the 19th century, the Catholic Emancipation League, the Chartists, parliamentary reformers, Irish Nationalists, and then the suffragettes before 1914 all employed methods of direct action to promote their causes. The violent demonstrations against the poll tax in 1990 followed in a long tradition.

With a few exceptions British political scientists have not shown much interest in the judiciary. Politics and law have usually been seen as separate spheres. Partly this may derive from the lack of a written constitution, partly from the judiciary's subordination to Parliament and partly from the political independence of the judiciary. But this attitude is changing, under the impact of the European Union, growing unease about the power of the executive and the effects of some of the constitutional changes since 1997 (notably the Human Rights Act and devolution). All have contributed to an appreciation of the connections between law and politics and to the growth of judicial activism.

The law and politics

The law is also usually the best-represented profession in the House of Commons: in post-war Parliaments the number of MPs who were or are solicitors or barristers has rarely fallen below a hundred, or a sixth of the House. Margaret Thatcher, Michael Howard and Tony Blair were all barristers before becoming MPs.

Common law   Derived from ancient custom as interpreted in court cases, not codified.

Statute law   Acts of Parliament, which usually take precedence over common law.

European Union law   Takes precedence over British law in areas of EU competence and requires no parliamentary action to become operative in Britain. (See European Court of Justice, below.)

Public law   Law which covers the relationship between the state and the citizen, including both civil liberties and administrative matters, for example, the compulsory purchase of private property or entitlement to benefits. Britain does not have a formally identified body of public law.

Criminal law   Concerned with wrongful acts harmful to the community such as murder and arson.

Civil law   Concerned with rights, duties and obligations owed by individuals towards each other, for example, divorce, debts.

European Court of Justice   An institution of the EU created to ensure uniformity in the interpretation and application of EU law. It sits in Luxembourg.

ECHR   European Court of Human Rights. Britain ratified the European Convention on Human Rights in 1951 but did not incorporate the convention into British law; therefore it did not confer legal rights enforceable in British courts but its decisions were influential, carried moral authority and frequently embarrassed the British government. Now incorporated in Human Rights Act (1998).

Ultra vires   The action of government must be based on law. Courts can declare actions to be *ultra vires*, or 'beyond the powers', if they are not covered by the terms of a statute.

Judical review   Power of a court to review how ministers, government departments and public authorities exercise their powers or carry out their duties.

Rule of law   Relates to law being predictable, not arbitrary. Citizens may only punished for a breach of the law and all citizens are equal before the law.

We observed in Chapter 10 that in the British system there is no higher authority than statute law—with the notable exception of European Union legislation. With this exception, the sovereignty of Parliament refers to that body's unlimited right to make law and the inability of the courts to overturn a statute, which is not *ultra vires*. In addition, decisions involving the use of prerogative powers, such as the award of honours or the power to make treaties, are not subject to judicial review. By contrast, in countries like Germany and the United States, both of which have written constitutions, the courts can rule an act of the government unconstitutional and play a crucial role in making judgments which affect public policy. This does not mean that British judges are entirely passive. They may review of the actions of the executive and rule whether ministers or their agents have statutory authority for their actions. Judges are also competent to rule that an office-holder has been guilty of *ultra vires* (ie acting beyond authority) or of an error of law (ie an improper act). They have, however, been reluctant to go further and decide on the merits or constitutionality of a particular statute, since, by so doing, they might lay themselves open to the charge of attempting to usurp the legislative function. By tradition they have contented themselves with a literal reading of the statute to establish whether a minister or official acted within his statutory powers. Even here judges are bound to some degree by precedent and certain rules of procedure. This is one aspect of the informal separation of powers.

The lack of a written British constitution, or 'fundamental' law, has to date limited the ability of the courts to review acts of the executive. Within the United States the more judicially (and politically) activist Supreme Court has such a role, and the other branches of government are expected to comply with its rulings. But that Court's judgments in several contentious areas in recent years have produced a reaction on the political right against its alleged 'liberal' rulings on civil rights, free speech, school prayers, bussing of schoolchildren to promote racial integration and abortion. At times the line between the law-making powers of elected politicians and the judicial interpretations of non-elected judges is a fine one. Britain may follow this route as the effects of British membership of the EU and of the introduction of devolution and the Human Rights Act work through.

There remains scope for judicial discretion. Statutes may not cover all cases, their wording may be unclear or open to different interpretations, and precedents from common law may conflict. Since the case of *Pepper v Hart* (1992) judges have been able to consult the relevant parliamentary debates, reported in *Hansard*, when the bill was being discussed, in the hope of gaining a better knowledge of the intentions of the framers of the Act. But there is no guarantee that such study will uncover a clear legislative intention. Statutes are usually drawn up by legal counsel who remain anonymous, and voted by a Parliament, many of whose members will not have read the precise wording of the bill. An Act in many instances represents a compromise between different points of view and may be open to different interpretations by its supporters, and one cannot be certain which view or interpretation prevailed when it was enacted.

 # Judicial independence

The judiciary's independence from political control or influence is a key principle of the British constitution. Judges may not be MPs, and MPs who become judges are required to resign their seats. Judges are expected not only to be impartial but to demonstrate impartiality. The salaries of judges are a standing charge on the Consolidated Fund and may not be altered through the annual estimates or be the subject of parliamentary debate. Senior judges are removable from office only as a result of an address to the monarch by both Houses of Parliament; in effect, they have security of tenure. A final safeguard is that judges are, ostensibly at least, appointed and promoted on professional rather than political grounds (before 1914 this was less true). This last feature is striking because, until the creation of the Judicial Appointments Committee in 2005, the Lord Chancellor, himself a politician and member of the Cabinet, was responsible for the appointments. The Prime Minister also has a say in the appointment of the Lord Chief Justice and of the Lords Justice and Lords of Appeal. MPs, even though protected by parliamentary privilege, generally withhold comment on judges and on pending legal cases; these are regarded as being *sub judice* until the proceedings are completed. Until recently, judges and politicians have exercised self-restraint and tried not to intervene outside of their own separate spheres of activity (but see below).

But the separation has never been total. The position of the Lord Chancellor was the most notable breach of the principle of the separation of law and politics. As a member of the Cabinet and the House of Lords, a judge and, until 2005, appointer of judges, he (there has never been a woman) represented a fusion of the executive, legislature and judiciary. The Attorney-General and Solicitor-General, as well as the Law Officers for Scotland (Lord Advocate and Solicitor-General), are members of the government. The Law Lords, the senior members of the judicial branch and sitting in the Lords (until their planned move to a Supreme Court takes place) act as the final court of appeal but have also been legislators, and the Home Secretary has also had the right to intervene in the judicial process. Until 1997, he (again, there has never been a female Home Secretary) could refer convictions back to the Court of Appeal when new evidence became available; this happened, for example, over the 'Guildford Four', 'Birmingham Six' and 'Bridgewater Four', all of whose convictions were later overturned. In 1997 this referral power was passed to the Criminal Cases Review Board.

Ministers of all parties have found it convenient to use judges as 'neutral' figures to preside over commissions, tribunals of inquiry and other investigatory and advisory bodies, to reassure the public that an independent inquiry is being held into politically contentious issues. Examples include; Lord Widgery on 'Bloody Sunday' in Londonderry (1972), Lord Scarman on the Brixton riots (1981), Sir John May on the convictions of the Guildford Four (1989), Mr Justice Scott on arms for Iraq (1996) and Lord Hutton on the circumstances surrounding the death of Dr David Kelly (2003). A danger is that involvement in such extra-judicial activity will undermine the myth of judicial neutrality. Indeed many critics of the Government dismissed the Hutton report, with its strong criticism of the BBC and failure to castigate the Government more severely, as a 'whitewash'. Lord Hailsham, then Lord Chancellor, warned in 1973, 'You cannot keep independent judges in Britain if you constantly expose them to ordeal by public criticism which is not only inevitable but legitimate and proper whenever you ask them to preside over tribunals of inquiry'.

Since the 1970s the role of judges has been debated in increasingly partisan terms. For supporters the judiciary is an essential element in a liberal democracy, buttressing a system of checks and balances and the rule of law, and providing a safeguard against arbitrary government. But critics on the political left have regarded it as part of a 'dominant' political order, usually making judgments in favour of the state or its own social class. In *The Politics of the Judiciary*, Professor John Griffith (1997) vigorously argued that judges have frequently been partial to the interests of the authorities in cases involving private property, free speech, civil liberties and trade unions, and too often have identified the public interest with what the government of the day decided. Judges are also frequently attacked for political 'bias', allegedly stemming from their exclusive social and educational backgrounds and legal training. The higher ranks of the judiciary for long have been overwhelmingly male, white, and drawn from middle class and elite education backgrounds. The Labour Government, in line with its reforms for the senior civil service, has been pressing for judges to be more socially representative of the nation.

The Lord Chancellor: an anomaly rectified

In 2003 Tony Blair decided to tackle the anomalies—to modern constitutional thinking—surrounding the Lord Chancellor's position and to achieve a clearer separation of the executive, legislature and judiciary. Reformers had long called for such a change, but the Human Rights Act lent a fresh urgency to their campaign. Because the Act rules against bias and the appearance of bias there remained the possibility of a challenge to the Lord Chancellor because of his role as both a legislator *and* a judge. Blair and his Number 10 advisers were determined to replace the Lord Chancellor's Department with one for Constitutional Affairs, create a new Supreme Court, separate from the House of Lords (where at the time Law Lords could vote on legislation and then adjudicate on it) and establish a Judicial Appointments Commission (JAC), to take over the Lord Chancellor's responsibility for appointing judges. In 2003 Tony Blair dismissed Lord Irvine of Lairg as Lord Chancellor and appointed Lord Falconer of Thornton. The Government originally announced that the post of the Lord Chancellor would be abolished before it realised that legislation would be necessary to accomplish this. There had been little or no prior consultation with interested parties and the consequences had not been clearly thought through. Lord Falconer, as Secretary of State for Constitutional Affairs, retained the post of Lord Chancellor until the legislation could be brought in to abolish his post. He decided, however, not to sit as a judge before the new Supreme Court was established. In 2005 the Government bowed to opposition and abandoned plans to abolish the office of Lord Chancellor. The new arrangements under the Constitutional Reform Act are:

- The 12 Law Lords will move from the Lords and constitute a separate Supreme Court once a building has been agreed.
- The Judicial Appointments Commission will make recommendations for appointments as judges.
- The Lord Chancellor will continue to a member of the Cabinet but will no longer sit as a judge.

The Act also contained the provision that ministers will uphold the independence of the judiciary.

Judicial activism

Defenders of the judiciary point to its crucial role in upholding the rule of law. More controversially, some have claimed a role for the courts in checking ministers because of the alleged decline of Parliament in relation to the executive (see Lee 1994). Lord Denning,

Master of the Rolls until 1982, often argued that judges should play a more creative role, particularly in cases where precedents conflict or there is no clear legislative direction. In 1949 he stated:

> In the absence of it [ie perfect clarity in the statute] a judge must set to work on the constructive task of finding the intention of Parliament, and he must do this not only from the language of the Statute but also from a consideration of the social conditions which gave rise to it, and of the mischief which it was passed to remedy, and then he must supplement the written word so as to give 'force and life' to the intention of the legislature (cited in Marshall 1971: 88).

In the late 1970s, the courts often ruled against the decisions of Labour ministers. To followers of the Griffiths analysis this showed the bias of the judiciary. They were reinforced by a number of court judgments in the industrial relations field in the 1980s. The Employment Acts of 1980 and 1982 and the Trade Union Act of 1984 increased the opportunities for employers to sue unions for damages arising from unlawful picketing and secondary action. The 1984 Act also made a union liable for damages arising from industrial action not authorised by a ballot of its members. The National Graphical Association was heavily fined for its conduct of the dispute with the Messenger Newspaper Group in 1983. The Court of Appeal upheld the Government's decision to ban union membership for intelligence surveillance workers at the Government Communications Headquarters at Cheltenham in 1984, on the grounds that it was for ministers to decide whether this posed a potential threat to national security. In the same year a group of working miners successfully sought a court ruling declaring unconstitutional a strike called by the National Union of Mineworkers (NUM), because a ballot of NUM members had not been held before the strike was called. The union was then heavily fined for contempt of court because it insisted that the strike was official. It is important to realise, however, that the courts were applying the law as laid down by Parliament.

But over the 18 years from 1979 it was the turn of Conservative ministers to be on the wrong end of court decisions. These included: the rulings that the minister lacked statutory authority for reducing local authorities' rate support grant (1981); that the Government's planned coal pit closure programme was illegal on the grounds that there had been insufficient consultation with affected groups (1992); and, against the minister, that a teaching union's boycott of school tests was not illegal (1993). In the same year the Law Lords agreed that the Home Secretary's disregard of a court order to halt the deportation of a Zairean dissident placed him in contempt of court. A later Home Secretary, Michael Howard (1993–97), also saw many of his decisions overturned by the courts. In 1996 there was a notable ruling when the court stated that he was wrong to take account of a public petition when increasing the minimum sentence served by two minors for the killing of the two-year-old Jamie Bulger. Noting the frequency with which the courts challenged the Conservative governments in 1980s and 1990s Professor Simon Lee claimed: 'Law is overtaking politics as a way in which power is exercised and challenged. It is lawyers more than opposition MPs or the media who call the government to account, the brief as much as the ballot box which constrains government policy' (Lee 1994: 123–4).

Since 1997 it has been the turn of Labour Home Secretaries to complain. David Blunkett (Home Secretary between 2001 and 2004) enjoyed the support of the tabloids when he said he was 'fed up' with what he regarded as the judiciary's 'soft' attitude to sentencing hardened criminals and overturning the thrust of Parliament's will on terrorist suspects, illegal immigrants and asylum-seekers. The Asylum and Immigration Bill in 2004 removed the final decision on asylum and immigration application from the courts—over the protests of many judges.

There is no doubt that conflicts between ministers and judges have been exacerbated by the rise of terrorism and the clashes this has raised between national security and the protection of the public versus civil liberties. In 2001, following the attacks on New York on 11 September the Government rushed through the Anti-Terrorism Crime and Security Act, which allowed the indefinite detention of those suspected of terrorism. In December 2004 the Law Lords, using the Human Rights Act (see below pp 489–91) ruled by an 8–1 margin that the human rights of foreign terrorist suspects who had been held under the 2001 Act in Belmarsh prison for up to three years without charge or trial, had been breached. The Home Secretary Charles Clarke announced that the prisoners would be detained further until Parliament agreed the future of the law. The House of Commons entered into a trial of strength with the House of Lords over the Prevention of Terrorism Bill, designed to replace the previous anti-terror law which would expire on 14 March 2005. A few days before the deadline the bill, following government concessions, became law and the prospect of the prisoners being released the following week receded.

Judicial review of administrative actions has also increased. Decisions of public authorities are more likely to be challenged in the courts by groups and individuals who feel adversely affected; this has particularly so in cases affecting immigration and asylum, employment and discrimination cases. Between 1979 and 2000 there was a ten-fold increase in the number of applications for review per annum. The trend is likely to increase further because of the Human Rights Act.

But not everybody is happy with the growth of activism. Critics like Griffith (see above p 481) dismiss the claim that the courts can compensate for the weaknesses of Parliament; indeed they argue such intervention only further weakens the ability of the elected body to hold the executive to account. They have opposed anything like a Bill of Rights and wish to reverse what they regard as the growing influence of judges on public policy at the expense of the political process.

CHAPTER TWENTY FOUR The judiciary and rights

An assumption of liberal constitutional theory is that in order to guarantee individual liberty and avoid arbitrary government or tyranny, the three main branches of state should be separate. These are:

- legislature: those empowered to make laws
- executive: those responsible for implementing the laws
- judiciary: those tasked with applying the laws

The British constitution pays scant regard to this doctrine. There is some recognition of the need for judicial independence but the British arrangements represent a fusion rather than a separation of powers. The Lord Chancellor, as head of the judiciary, member of the House of Lords (legislature) and member of the Cabinet (executive), is at the centre of three overlapping branches of state.

European influences

British membership of the European Union has also enhanced the scope for judicial intervention. In cases where British legislation has an EU element, or there are disputes about the EU treaties or related matters, or in those which reach the Law Lords, there must be reference to the European Court of Justice (ECJ) for a definitive ruling. Where British domestic law conflicts with EU laws, British judges are obliged to give priority to the latter. The British government had to change social security policy after the House of Lords in 1994 ruled that differences in the protection given to full-time and part-time workers breached the EU's insistence on sexual equality; the bulk of part-timers are women. Other examples include the ending of the ban on gays and lesbians in the armed forces and in 1999 the ending of sex discrimination over winter fuel payments; women and men now both receive the payment at age 60. Equally far-reaching was the impact of the *Factortame* case (1991), by which British courts were empowered to suspend provisions of an Act of Parliament which might appear to breach the law, pending a ruling by the ECJ. The ECJ has been a force for integration and for implementing common laws across member states.

Civil liberties

The British have traditionally prided themselves on the security of their individual liberties. In practice, the liberties and rights of individuals and groups are always qualified because they may conflict with other rights or with a broader social goal, such as public order and, in 2005, protection of the public against terrorism (see above p 484). Individual rights and liberties in Britain have emerged from, and been sustained by, a largely negative view of freedom: individuals may do what they want unless and to the extent that they are forbidden to do it. Despite the 1998 Human Rights Act (HRA) there are few statutory guarantees of rights, but instead a general freedom to do as one wishes, as long as it is not forbidden, that is, as long as the action does not transgress the law or interfere with the rights of others. The HRA does, however, reinforce the rights already present in domestic law.

British freedoms of speech, organisation and demonstration have been supported more by tradition and the political culture than by law. For example, laws against blasphemy, defamation and obscenity qualify freedom of expression. Race relations legislation also makes it a criminal offence to utter or publish statements which are likely to incite racial hatred. For long the dominant view was that British liberties, emerging from the common law and the decisions of the ordinary courts, were better protected than the rights enshrined in a constitution or statute as in other states. What could so easily be given by the state could with equal facility be removed.

There is no absolute freedom of meeting or assembly for British citizens. Meetings and marches are subject to the laws prohibiting obstruction of the highway, public nuisance and trespass, and to local authority by-laws. For example, no march may be held within a mile of Parliament when it is in session, and if the local police have reason to fear that a march may provoke disorder they may insist on rerouting or even banning it. These powers were given to chief constables under the Public Order Act 1936, which was prompted by disturbances surrounding the marches and meetings of the British Union of Fascists.

In Britain the police are bound by laws and rules, and are subordinate to the civil power. The police may not, unless invited, enter a person's premises without a search warrant. A set of 'judges' rules' provides guidelines for police conduct; these require, for example, that a person be brought for trial shortly after his arrest, have access to a friend or solicitor and that no force or other pressure be used to produce an involuntary confession. They uphold the principles of freedom from arbitrary arrest and imprisonment, a person's presumed innocence until proven guilty, the right not to be detained without a trial (that is, if a person is detained he has to be charged with a specific offence) and to be brought before a magistrate within 24 hours if charged, and to a fair trial.

These rights are generally observed but there have been exceptions. During the Second World War, the Defence of the Realm Act empowered the Home Secretary to detain any person whom he had reasonable cause to believe was hostile to the state. It was under this regulation that Oswald Mosley, the leader of the British Union of Fascists, was detained without trial between 1940 and 1943. The continued violence in Northern Ireland (even during a cease-fire) has weakened the rule of law in that province. Under the Internment Act 1971 the authorities were allowed to imprison suspected terrorists or their protectors for an indefinite period and without a trial. In 1974, following bombings in Birmingham, Parliament rushed through the Prevention of Terrorism (Temporary Provisions) Act, which made the Irish Republican Army illegal. Under the Act, any UK citizen born in Northern Ireland could be arrested, detained and then deported to Belfast without any charge being made against him and without a court hearing. The Northern Ireland (Emergency Provisions) Act, renewed annually, also allowed those accused of terrorism to be tried by a 'judge sitting alone, and not by jury'.

An important new legal constraint on personal conduct in recent years has been the growth of anti-discrimination legislation. Traditionally, no special protection has been given to particular sections of the community in Britain. But the growth of 'women's rights' movements, and the influx of immigrants in the 1950s and 1960s from the new Commonwealth states in East Africa, the Indian subcontinent, and the Caribbean challenged that tradition. The widespread evidence of sexual and racial inequalities and discrimination, coupled with demands that they be tackled, provided the stimulus for legislation.

Equal pay legislation requires that women receive the same rates of pay as men when doing similar or equivalent work. The Sex Discrimination Act 1975 forbids discrimination on the grounds of sex and established an Equal Opportunities Commission. Successive Race Relations Acts have prohibited discrimination on grounds of race, religion or national origin in various public places, in the provision of services and sale of goods and in housing, employment and membership of associations. Paradoxically, while the role of the law has been relaxed in many areas of personal relations, such as divorce, abortion and sexual behaviour, it has been used to combat discriminatory conduct on many grounds and the Labour Government has announced plans to extend it to age.

Concerns over human rights

Several countries have a Bill of Rights or some formal statement of the civil liberties of citizens and groups. These provide constitutional guarantees of freedom, for example, speech, freedom from arbitrary arrest, the right to privacy or the freedom to emigrate. In Britain there is no such document. There is a British Bill of Rights (1689) but this deals largely with protecting the rights of Parliament against the monarchy and the Protestant succession to the throne. The British, as noted, have placed less reliance on such formal safeguards and trusted more to a pluralistic political system, independent judiciary, acceptance of limits on what a government may do, and sense of 'constitutional morality' among the population. But civil rights advocates complained in the 1980s and 1990s that liberties were being restricted. They pointed to the banning of broadcast interviews with supporters of terrorism in Northern Ireland, denying trade union membership for employees at GCHQ, imposing a national curriculum on schools, legislating the 'anti-gay' s 28 of the Local Government Act 1988 and increasing police powers. In the era of the 'elective dictatorship', as the power of the executive and the scope of legislation increased, concern grew over Parliament's ability to control the executive, not least to protect individual liberties. There were also cases of miscarriage of justice: the 'Guildford Four', convicted of bombings in Guildford in 1975, were released in 1990, as were the 'Birmingham Six' in 1991, having been convicted of IRA bombings in 1974. These cases, often exposed as a result of campaigns by journalists or freelance groups, prompted unease about the ability of the judicial process to protect individual liberties.

There was therefore growing support for the establishment of a body independent of government to provide more effective protection of individual rights than the traditional safeguards of individual liberties—public opinion, shared political values and self-restraint by the executive. Before 1997 senior figures, including the late Lord Taylor (the then Lord Chief Justice) and Sir Thomas Bingham (Master of the Rolls), advocated the incorporation of the European Convention on Human Rights into British law, and believed that judges should play a creative role in policy-making. Supporters of reform coalesced in Charter 88, a lobby for constitutional reform. In demanding positive civil and human rights in the United Kingdom, modelled on the European Convention of Human Rights (ECHR), Charter 88 called for a constitutional settlement to:

> Enshrine, by means of a Bill of Rights such civil liberties as the right to peaceful assembly, to freedom of association, to freedom from discrimination, to freedom from detention without trial, to trial by jury, to privacy and freedom of expression.

The European Convention on Human Rights 1950 forbids a wide range of discriminatory practices and provides for an equally wide range of freedoms and rights (see Politics in Focus 24.3). A complaint that a signatory state has violated the Convention may result in the government being taken before the Court. The Human Rights Commission, based in Strasbourg, to which the complaint is initially addressed, has to decide if there is a case to answer and satisfy itself that other possible remedies have already been tried. Only when domestic procedures have been exhausted and the Commission's efforts to conciliate have failed is the case referred to the Court. It may take five years or more before a case is resolved and the Commission, not the complainant, takes the decision to refer a case to the Court.

Most of the original signatory states ratified the Convention and recognised the right of citizens to petition it and the Court's jurisdiction. The British Parliament regularly renewed the Convention, so allowing individuals to bring a complaint against the United Kingdom to the Human Rights Commission in Strasbourg. But since Britain was, until 2000, still the only original co-signatory not to incorporate the Convention substantially into its domestic law, its citizens could not use it to appeal to British courts.

Since 1966, when Britain allowed individual citizens to bring cases to the Court, there have been successful appeals by citizens in nearly 40 cases, including those against the closed shop in British Rail (1981) and the use of corporal punishment in schools (1982), and the Home Secretary's right to determine the length of the prison service to be served by the juvenile killers of James Bulger. Paradoxically, the European Court was able to act as a quasi-Supreme Court and judge governments on the criteria of the Convention. Supporters of the Court point out that its judgments declaring unlawful such practices as police telephone tapping, restrictions on prisoners' access to lawyers, inadequate legal protection for detained mental patients and discrimination against foreign husbands of British women have expanded individual liberty.

In 1951 Britain was a co-signatory of the European Convention on Human Rights, which was designed to improve the observance of human rights by European governments. Britain did not incorporate the Convention into British law until 1998; British citizens, therefore, could not appeal to British courts on the basis of the Convention. In 1966, however, governments granted British citizens the right to appeal to the ECHR in Strasbourg. The British government was not bound to act on the Court's verdicts but usually did so since they carry considerable moral authority.

The rights protected (issues raised in cases that have come before the Court).:
Most of the rights and freedoms protected by the Convention are of a civil and political nature. The main ones are:
- restrictions on prisoners' rights of correspondence and rights of access to the Court
- the right to life
- use of the birch as judicial corporal punishment
- the right to liberty and security of person
- detention of vagrants without the opportunity for them to challenge their detention before a court
- the right to fair administration of justice
- delays in bringing those on remand to trial
- respect for private and family life, home and correspondence
- delays in judicial and administrative proceedings
- freedom of thought, conscience and religion
- punishments for breaches of military discipline
- freedom of expression and to hold opinions
- requiring defendants in criminal cases to pay the cost of interpreters' fees
- freedom of peaceful assembly and association, including the right to join a trade union
- a temporary court ban on grounds of contempt that delayed publication of a newspaper article about thalidomide
- the right to marry and found a family
- denial of access to a court where no legal aid is available

Further protection in the protocols covers:
- trade union freedoms to bargain collectively
- seizure and forfeiture of an obscene book
- the right to peaceful enjoyment of possessions
- compulsory sex education in schools
- certain rights to education
- controls on telephone tapping

Prohibited under the Convention and its protocols are:
- rights of transsexuals to change their status
- torture and inhuman or degrading treatment and punishment
- the legality of a trade union 'closed shop'

- slavery, servitude and forced labour
- corporal punishment in schools
- criminal laws that are retroactive
- rights of mentally abnormal offenders to have their detention reviewed
- discrimination in the enjoyment of rights and freedoms guaranteed by the Convention
- discrimination against homosexuals

Some examples of cases: the following are some brief examples of issues raised in cases that have come before the Court:
- corporal punishment in schools
- discrimination against homosexuals
- controls on telephone tapping
- disciplinary proceedings against doctors
- trade union rights to bargain collectively

The Convention sensibly recognises that most of these rights cannot be unlimited in a democratic society and that restrictions may be necessary on grounds of public safety, national security, the economic well-being of a country, public health and morals, the right and freedoms of others or the prevention of disorder and crime. It also permits states to suspend their obligations in time of war or other public emergency. But no state can avoid its obligation to respect the right to life and the bans on torture, slavery and the retroactivity of the criminal law.

Source: M. Zander, 'UK Rights Come Home' (1998) *Politics Review*, 7(4): 19

Human Rights Act

Parliament passed the Human Rights Act in 1998 and it came into effect on 2 October 2000. However, it had already operated from the start of the life of the new legislatures in Scotland and Wales. A consequence is that UK litigants no longer need to go directly to the Court to enforce Convention rights which have been incorporated. They may, however, still petition the Court over the few non-incorporated rights or over cases where they remain dissatisfied with the decisions reached by UK courts. Courts, tribunals and public authorities (eg government departments, local authorities and police authorities) are bound to act in accordance with Convention rights. However, the Parliament at Westminster is not so constrained—the principle of parliamentary sovereignty again! The Act has sought to strike a compromise between upholding the authority of Parliament and the Convention. It requires that every bill will have to contain a statement by the sponsoring minister that its provisions are compatible with the Rights Act. The remit of a Parliamentary Joint Committee on Human Rights is to ensure that legislation is compatible. If a higher court finds that a provision is incompatible with an incorporated Convention right, then it may issue a 'declaration of incompatibility' (only the higher courts have this power). It is then up to Parliament, which remains supreme on matters of primary legislation, to find a remedy if it so wishes. The Act continues to operate until Parliament has repealed or amended it. The minister may use a special 'fast track' procedure for introducing the new legislation. However, measures passed by a Scottish Parliament or Welsh and Northern Ireland Assemblies—which deal with subordinate legislation—can be ruled invalid.

The Human Rights Act, because it deals with so many sensitive issues, will put judges even more in the spotlight than in the past. The ECHR guidelines that limits on human rights should not be 'unreasonable' or 'arbitrary' leaves scope for the judges to exercise their own judgement. Section 3 of the Act invites the courts to give effect to the legislation in ways compatible with the ECHR. In making a ruling, for example, over privacy, or school admissions policy, or a Health Authority's decisions about patients' right to treatment, judges may have to balance competing rights of groups and individuals. It will no longer be sufficient to examine the letter of the law and precedent; they will have to examine the actual merits of the law. In doing so, they are likely to refer to Strasbourg decisions for guidance. The backgrounds of the judges are also likely to be researched and used as evidence of 'bias' by campaigning groups. In a recent ruling by the Law Lords over the Home Secretary's right to extradite the former Chilean dictator General Pinochet to Spain in connection with alleged abuses of human rights Lord Hoffmann, who was part of a 2:1 majority for the right to extradite, was subsequently revealed to be associated with the human rights group, Amnesty International. The ruling was subsequently overturned on the ground that Hoffmann should have been disqualified because of the appearance, at least, of potential bias.

A major test for the Act—and indeed for how societies strike the balance between civil liberties and protection against threats to national security—will be posed by the authorities' measures against the threat of terrorism. The Government had to exempt itself from the provision of the HRA for its Anti-Terrorism, Crime and Security Act 2001, empowering the Home Secretary to detain suspected terrorists without trial and be deported from the UK, subject to limited safeguards. The legislation had been hurriedly passed in the aftermath of 9/11 because the Government claimed that it need extensive new powers. The Law Lords' verdict in December 2004 that the Home Secretary's use of the above Act to detain indefinitely foreign terrorist suspects without trial was in breach of the HRA dramatically underscored how the HRA had changed relations between the judges and ministers. The Government was also taken aback because the powers were the centrepiece of the Government's so-called war on terror.

Some Conservative critics of the HRA have complained that the effects have been an increase in litigation, the encouragement of a 'compensation culture' (eg the prisoner who successfully sued the Government after falling off a roof while trying to escape), and that it is a further step in reducing the role of Parliament. On the other side supporters of the Human Rights Act go further and call for the establishment of a Human Rights Commission, which will promote public awareness of human rights and encourage good practice. To date, however, the Government has not established such a body.

Administrative justice

An Act frequently delegates to a minister (or his officials) or a local authority certain law-making powers which are implied in the substance of the Act. The authorities are given powers to work out details, amend legislation to bring it up to date or create machinery to administer it—all within the framework of the Act. These delegations obviously assist the speed and flexibility of the legislative process, but there have been frequent complaints that the growing use of such *delegated legislation* amounts to a form of executive dominance of Parliament.

In a powerful tract, *The New Despotism* (1929), Lord Hewart argued that the delegation was a form of lawlessness, because of the absence of 'known rules and principles, and a regular course of procedure'. The Government subsequently set up the Donoughmore Committee to review the powers of ministers. The Committee's report (1932) did not wholly share Hewart's alarm, and only in 1944 did Parliament set up a Statutory Instruments Select Committee to review such Acts. There is now a joint committee of the House of Commons and House of Lords whose task is to review the operation of instruments and draw the attention of Parliament to any instrument that appears to make unusual use of the power conferred by the original statute.

In the 20th century, the greater role of the government, for example in managing the economy, the rise of the welfare state and the complexity surrounding the duties and rights of citizens have added a further dimension. Disputes arise about administrative decisions in areas ranging from planning permission for building motorways and extending houses to slum clearance, hospital treatment, allocation of housing and level of rents, dismissal from work, and pensions, unemployment and national insurance benefits. Such disputes raise problems of administrative justice, but if the ordinary courts dealt with them they would be overwhelmed with work. Hence the need for procedures which were simpler, speedier and less intimidating than a court of law.

Public inquiries and tribunals provide a quasi-judicial review of the actions of administrators and the possibility of redress for aggrieved persons. The tribunals and inquiries were set up to examine a class of disputes which were not referred to courts of law. Public inquiries are set up ad hoc, as and when the government considers they are needed or when there is an appeal against a government decision. In a public inquiry into, for example, the use of land, an inspector from the Department of the Environment, Transport and the Regions will hear the views of different parties—the house owner, a developer and the local authority, say. Eventually, the inspector submits a report and a recommendation to the minister, who makes a decision.

Tribunals deal with more specialised matters. For example, an industrial tribunal may consider a worker's complaint of unfair dismissal and award compensation or even order the reinstatement of the complainant. In contrast to inquiries, these are standing bodies and make decisions.

Continued dissatisfaction with the tribunal system and concern at the lack of effective redress against administrative injustice led reformers to look abroad. In France, a powerful

Conseil d'État sits as a court of administrative justice to which aggrieved citizens may appeal and French ministers may be summoned and forced to justify their conduct. In Scandinavian countries and New Zealand, a Parliamentary Commissioner, or Ombudsman, is available to examine complaints of maladministration or cases of harsh or unreasonable decisions. In 1967 a Parliamentary Commissioner for Administration (PCA) was established in Britain; the Commissioner, now called Parliamentary Ombudsman, is appointed by the Crown but is the servant of the House of Commons.

The Ombudsman deals with private citizens' complaints that the authorities have failed to carry out the law, observe proper standards of conduct or follow established procedures. Examples of maladministration by officials include bias, incompetence, delay and arbitrariness in making a decision. The Ombudsman was precluded from investigating complaints against local authorities, hospital boards, the police, armed forces and nationalised industries. Many of the complaints originally received concerned these groups and thus were outside his terms of reference. Subsequently, Ombudsmen have been established for Northern Ireland, local government and the National Health Service, as well financial and pensions services among others. Under John Major's Citizen's Charter most public services also introduced complaints procedures for customers.

If the Ombudsman decides that a case falls within his remit, the first step is to invite comments on the complaint from the department. The Commissioner is empowered to call for the relevant files of the department concerned, although he lacks any executive authority of his own. If he finds a case of maladministration, the department is invited to rectify it. If the department refuses to act on his report then he lays it before Parliament and a select committee will consider the case and issue a report. Of the cases examined each year, some maladministration is found in about 20% of them. Most of the complaints upheld have concerned the Departments of Inland Revenue and Health and Social Security (particularly the Child Support Agency), departments heavily used by members of the public.

The Commissioner's effectiveness has been limited by the terms of reference. Alleged cases of maladministration must have been committed in the United Kingdom and by a department of central government. The complainant has no right to appeal to a court or tribunal against the verdict. The Commissioner is also precluded from questioning policy, or the merits of discretionary decisions, as long as these were taken legally. The concern with maladministration alone, that is, with cases of unfairness arising from the official not following rules and procedures, has disappointed those who feel that injustice may also result from an official following the law. The indirect method by which citizens' complaints are made to the Commissioner probably reduces the public perception of his role. Citizens' complaints must be forwarded in the first instance through an MP. The Commissioner reports the results of his investigation to the MP and is required to submit an annual report on his work to Parliament. The number of cases referred to the Commissioner has been limited by the preference of most MPs to write directly to the minister concerned if there is a problem. In Sweden administration is more open to public scrutiny and citizens have the right of direct access to the Commissioner. But such a move is likely to be resisted by those MPs who would resent being bypassed.

...4

...ppeal

A network of semi-judicial bodies adjudicate in an informal system of 'administrative' or 'public' law. There are two main types:

Administrative tribunals These are numerous and cover a wide range of topics, for example, industrial tribunals hear claims of unfair dismissal, redundancy, etc; education tribunals hear claims against allocation of school places, expulsions, etc.

Composition: usually a legally qualified chairman plus two lay members representing the interests in question; for example, industrial tribunals include one representative of unions and one representative of employers.

Appeal: some tribunals allow appeals to higher court; in others, eg NHS tribunals, there is no appeal.

Statutory inquiries These are usually ad hoc, often set up in connection with planning and compulsory land purchase.

Composition: the chairman is appointed by a minister and advises the minister of his findings. The relevant departmental minister usually takes the final decision. Procedures are regulated by the 1971 Tribunals and Inquiries Act.

Citizens' rights against public authorities are upheld by various other non-political and non-legal mechanisms. The Citizen's Charter (set up by John Major in 1991) was an attempt to make providers of public services more responsive to the users of the services and extend complaints procedures for the latter. The Labour Government developed the idea with its Service First (1998) programme which announced new guidelines for service providers, including standards of performance and the provision, in some cases, for compensation in the event of service failure. Greater use is also being made of regulatory bodies in the formerly nationalised utilities, which are now privatised. Because the scope for direct competition in those services has been limited, the Government established independent regulators. Such bodies as Ofwat (for water) and Oftel (for telecommunications) exercise quasi-judicial powers in regulating prices, profits, quality of service and consumer satisfaction for their respective utilities. For schools, Ofsted is charged with maintaining standards in education.

Conclusion

The connections between politics and law have grown in recent years and are likely to grow in the future, not least because of the growing impact of Europe and the Human Rights Act on British politics. Individuals and groups have become more litigious, resorting to the courts for redress. Applications for judicial review have increased and public authorities, including ministers, departmental officials and Quangos have become increasingly aware that judges are metaphorically looking over their shoulders. Although in some respects the courts have become an alternative to the political arena they are still likely to be drawn into political controversy, not least because government policies on terrorism and immigration and asylum have raised important issues of civil liberties. Interestingly, if it has been the political left that traditionally attacked judicial intervention, in the past two decades it has been the government of the day (which includes Labour Home Secretaries since 1997) that has more often expressed concern that the courts are hampering its attempts to combat crime and terrorism and safeguard borders and in some cases may be 'over reaching' themselves.

KEY POINTS

- Traditionally, British judges have not reviewed the merits or constitutionality of a government's actions or laws but they could rule that a minister or official has acted beyond his statutory powers.

- Since the 1970s the political role for the judiciary has increased: a more activist judiciary; a greater willingness for those aggrieved by legislation or rulings to seek redress through the courts; and the nature of some policies and legislation relating to workplace rights, human rights and immigration, asylum and terrorism has drawn judges into a more conspicuously political role. Determining the compatibility of British with EU law and with the Human Rights Act has also contributed to this process.

- In an attempt to ensure judicial independence a mutual exchange of self-restraint exists between politicians and judges. As a rule, judges refrain from public comment on politically contentious issues and MPs avoid commenting on cases before the courts. Judges may not be MPs, their

salaries are not debated in Parliament, they have security of tenure and are appointed and promoted on professional grounds.

- In Britain civil liberties are now enshrined in the Human Rights Act, and citizens still remain theoretically free to do anything not specifically forbidden by law.

- Parliament delegates much detailed law-making to the executive in the form of enabling statutes. The Statutory Instruments Select Committee reviews the operation of these laws.

- The Parliamentary Commissioner for Administration provides citizens, via their MPs, with a means of redress in specifically defined cases of maladministration. But the PCA can only rely on moral suasion to enforce his rulings.

- The line between politics and law is becoming increasingly blurred and the role of the judiciary has become more controversial in recent years.

KEY QUESTIONS

(1) How effectively are individual rights protected in Britain?

(2) Discuss the view that the rule of law is a theoretical concept that has no practical application.

(3) 'Judicial independence is guaranteed by a mutual exchange of self-restraint between politicians and judges.' Discuss.

(4) Examine the factors that have contributed to an increasing politicisation of the judiciary in recent years.

IMPORTANT WEBSITES

On human rights see European Court of Human Rights www.echr.coe.int; for legal and constitutional aspects of the EU see European Court of Justice www.europa.eu.int/cj/en/index.htm; on recent legal and constitutional development see Lord Chancellor's Department www.lcd.gov.uk. The Crown Prosecution Service www.cps.gov.uk/ and the Law Society www.lawsociety.org.uk/home.law are other useful sites.

FURTHER READING

For an overview, see J. Rosenberg (1997) *Trial of Strength. The Battle Between Ministers and Judges over Who Makes Law*, London: Richard Cohen. For criticism of the judiciary see J. Griffith (1997) *The Politics of the Judiciary*, Oxford: Clarendon Press. On constitutional aspects see R. Blackburn and R. Plant (eds) (1999) *Constitutional Reform*, London: Longman. On connections with politics see L. Foster (2000) 'The encroachment of the law on politics' *Parliamentary Affairs*, 53(2); D. Woodhouse (2002) 'The law and politics: in the shadow of the Human Rights Act', *Parliamentary Affairs*, 55(2); and S. Lee (1994) 'Law and the Constitution', in D. Kavanagh and A. Seldon (eds) (1994) *The Major Effect*, London: Macmillan, 122–44. Also see M. Senvirante (2002) *Ombudsmen and Administrative Justice*, London: Butterworths; and L. Blom-Cooper (2005) 'Government and the Judiciary' in A Seldon and D Kavanagh (eds) *The Blair Effect 2001–2005*, Cambridge: Cambridge University Press, ch 11.

CHRONOLOGY

The role of the judiciary in UK political life

1951	Britain ratifies the European Convention on Human Rights
1967	A Parliamentary Commissioner for Administration is appointed
1971	Tribunals and Inquiries Act: regulates procedures of administrative judicial bodies
1972	European Communities Act: EU law takes precedence over British law in areas of EU competence. Lord Widgery chairs an inquiry into 'Bloody Sunday'
1974	Parliament passes the Prevention of Terrorism Act in 24 hours. The local government ombudsman is appointed
1975	The Court of Appeal rules that the Home Secretary had no right to prevent people from buying TV licences in advance to avoid increased fees
1976	The Court of Appeal rules that the Secretary for Education could not force the Tameside Local Education Authority to adopt comprehensive schooling
1977	The National Health Service ombudsman is appointed
1981	Lord Scarman's inquiry into the Brixton riots
1982	The ECHR upholds the case against corporal punishment in schools
1984	The Court of Appeal and House of Lords uphold the Government's decision to ban unions at GCHQ

1988	Charter 88 calls for Bill of Rights
1989	Sir John May's inquiry into the conviction of the Guildford Four
1990	Courts and Legal Services Act: deregularises some rules in respect of solicitors and barristers; creates Legal Sevices ombudsman
1991	*Factortame* case: Lords rule that the 1988 Merchant Shipping Act is incompatible with EU law
1994	Criminal Justice and Public Order Act: curtails some civil liberties
1996	Report of Scott Inquiry into arms for Iraq, Nolan Committee Inquiry into standards in public life; Scottish courts rule that the *Panorama* interview of PM cannot be shown before local elections. The ECHR rules against the British government over killings of members of the IRA in Gibraltar
1998	Human Rights Act incorporates ECHR into British law
2001	Anti-Terrorism, Crime and Security Act
2003	Announcement of plans to end Lord Chancellor's Office and create a Supreme Court
2005	Prevention of Terrorism Act
2005	Constitutional Reform Act

 Visit the Online Resource Centre that accompanies this book for links to more information on this chapter topic

CHAPTER TWENTY FIVE

The mass media and politics

READER'S GUIDE

The relationship between politicians and the media is symbiotic: politicians need the media to get their message across; the media need 'copy'. Much political activity is 'mediated', that is, it comes to us via the media. The chapter begins by establishing what constitutes the media and then addresses the following topics: the influence of the media, setting the agenda, the media's role in election campaigns and the impact of television on British politics. It concludes by noting that although the media may act as a check on politicians there seem to be few checks on the media themselves.

Introduction

Most people gain their information about politics from the mass media, from press, radio and television. The media report and interpret events, help to set an agenda—by highlighting certain issues and neglecting others—and shape popular perceptions and images, for example, a 'wimpish' John Major or a 'presidential' or 'untrustworthy' Tony Blair. Indeed, many politicians are so convinced of the influence of the media that they think that, in effect, what the media reports is, virtually, political reality. Politics is largely a *mediated activity*, in which the voters and politicians learn about each other through the media. According to Peter Riddell of *The Times*:

> The main arena of British political debate is now the broadcasting studio rather than the chamber of the House of Commons—and the most important aides to political leaders are now media advisers, rather than parliamentary whips (Riddell 1998: 160).

The media are therefore more than a neutral channel of political communication. They are pervasive, persuasive and influential participants in the political system.

A free media, that is, one not state-owned or directed, is a key feature of a liberal democracy and underpins free speech and open debate. In Britain one may point to the diversity of newspaper and magazine titles, the competition between them for sales and readers, and their independence from any political party although they may support a party. As we will see below, a newspaper's support for a party may be conditional and papers often have their own agendas, which may be separate from that of the party they may support at elections. During the Iraq war, for instance, Labour-supporting papers such as the *Mirror, Guardian* and *Independent*, were vigorous critics of Blair and the war. Pluralists welcome this variety and looseness of attachment to parties and claim that it serves the public interest.

Some critics of recent media developments argue that the media have to some extent usurped the role of the opposition and Parliament. *Question Time* on the TV; radio and TV in-depth political interviews; documentaries; polemical articles in the quality press serve as watchdogs to alert the electorate and to keep the government on its toes. Politicians are less fazed by a gruelling session at the parliamentary dispatch box than by a 'grilling' from political interviewers like Jeremy Paxman and John Humphrys. Politicians complain that the adversarial culture of much current affairs coverage encourages cynicism about politics and breeds a distrust of politicians and the political process among viewers and readers (Lloyd 2004). They also charge that sections of the press have their own agenda, are unelected political actors, and operate free from effective regulation, apart from that provided by the Press Complaints Commission (established in 1990, replacing the Press Commission), and the recently created communications regulator, Ofcom, or the Office of Communications. For such critics the media's power is a problem for democratic politics.

The media are also a powerful interest group in their own right. For example, in Britain Rupert Murdoch's multinational News International Corporation owns BSkyB Television as well as *The Times, Sun, News of the World* and *Sunday Times*. There may be a diversity of titles but press ownership is concentrated. In addition to News International, there are also conglomerates like the Rothermere Press and United Business Media. As commercial enterprises the media have a vested interest in the success of the capitalist system in so far as it affects their profits. Indeed, Marxist analysts argue that the media reflect and promote the class interests of the dominant groups in society and legitimise inequalities and the status quo.

Press and television

Britain has 11 national daily newspapers (see Table 25.1). Some three-quarters of British households take a daily paper and a similar proportion of the population aged 15 or more claim to read one. These figures have been declining for some years but are higher than those in many other comparable states. In 2005, 8.8 and 4.5 million respectively, read the mass circulation dailies, the *Sun* and *Daily Mirror*. There is a division between the five popular papers or tabloids (eg the *Sun* and *Daily Mirror*), and the five broadsheet papers (eg *The Times* and *Guardian*). In 2005, the former had daily sales of around 9 million, the latter of 2.3 million.

The tabloids often present a simplified, exaggerated and personalised view of politics. Pictures and graphics appear to have driven out words, and partisanship is blatant in elections. The broadsheets (including *The Times, Independent* and the *Guardian* from September 2005, which have moved to a compact format) provide a more extended and serious coverage of politics and current affairs and also have a more middle-class and well-educated readership; the *Express* and *Mail* draw their readers fairly evenly from across the social spectrum. The readerships differ in their evaluation of the media. Broadsheet readers are likely to regard the press as their main and most reliable source of news, while readers of the tabloids regard television as the main and most reliable source of news.

The regions have some important local newspapers, like the *Scotsman* in Edinburgh, the *Telegraph* in Belfast, and the *Western Mail* in Cardiff. But the press has, on balance, been a force for political nationalisation and centralisation. Virtually every household in Britain can receive a daily paper which has been printed overnight in London or Manchester.

The Press Complaints Commission was established as a voluntary body in 1990 to receive and adjudicate on complaints about press intrusions on privacy. Newspapers are represented on the Commission and to that extent it is a form of self-regulation. It is, however, widely seen as a toothless body. Some reformers have advocated the introduction of a privacy law, but this has proved difficult to frame, most of the newspapers are strongly opposed, and governments to date have been fearful of offending them. In their defence the media claim that many of the politicians who complain about how they are covered have usually brought many of their troubles on themselves by their incompetence or

Name of paper Ownership group (Chairman) Editor Preferred result	Circulation[1] (2001 in brackets) (000s)	Readership[2] (2001 in brackets) (000s)	% of readers in social grade[3] (2001 in brackets)	
			ABC1	C2DE
Mirror Trinity Mirror (Sir Victor Blank) Richard Wallace Labour victory	1602 (2056)	4657 (5733)	38 (34)	61 (67)
Express Northern and Shell (Richard Desmond) Peter Hill Conservative victory	884 (929)	2132 (2168)	60 (64)	40 (37)
Sun News International (Rupert Murdoch) Rebekah Wade Labour victory	3098 (3288)	8825 (9591)	37 (33)	63 (67)
Daily Mail Daily Mail and General Trust (Viscount Rothermere) Paul Dacre Not a Labour victory	2278 (2337)	5740 (5564)	66 (64)	34 (36)
Daily Star Northern and Shell (Richard Desmond) Dawn Neesom No preference declared	735 (585)	1965 (1460)	33 (27)	67 (72)
Daily Telegraph Telegraph Group (& The Business) (Barclay brothers) Martin Newland Conservative victory	868 (989)	2181 (2235)	87 (86)	13 (14)

Name of paper Ownership group (Chairman) Editor Preferred result	Circulation[1] (2001 in brackets) (000s)	Readership[2] (2001 in brackets) (000s)	% of readers in social grade[3] (2001 in brackets)	
			ABC1	C2DE
Guardian Scott Trust (Paul Myners) Alan Rusbridger Labour victory[4]	327 (362)	1068 (1024)	89 (88)	11 (12)
The Times News International (Rupert Murdoch) Robert Thomson Labour victory[5]	654 (667)	1655 (1575)	87 (88)	13 (13)
Independent Independent Newspapers (Tony O'Reilly) Simon Kelner More Liberal Democrats	226 (197)	643 (571)	87 (89)	13 (12)
Financial Times Pearson (Lord Stevenson) Andrew Gowers Labour victory	132 (176)	453 (598)	92 (92)	8 (7)

Source: M. Scammell and M. Harrop in Kavanagh and Butler (2005: 120–2).

[1] Average net total circulation in the United Kingdom. *Source*: Audit Bureau of Circulation (April 2005).

[2] *Source*: National Readership Survey (January–December 2004).

[3] Calculated from National Readership Survey (January–December 2004), which classifies the population 15 or over as follows:

ABC1 (professional, administrative, managerial and other non-manual)—54% (2001: 50%).

C2DE (skilled manual, semi-skilled or unskilled, and residual)—46% (2001: 49%).

[4] Also increased number of Liberal Democrats.

[5] Also a larger Conservative opposition.

indiscreet or improper behaviour. They also warn of a possible return to the silence of the British media about Edward VIII's affair with the divorced Mrs Simpson in the 1930s. But some public figures, in entertainment and sport, have been able to use the Human Rights Act to prevent publication of potentially embarrassing material about themselves.

	Preferred 2005	Winner (2001)	Circulation[1] (000s)	Readership[2] (000s)
News of the World	Lab	(Lab)	3417	9490
Sunday Mirror	Lab	(Lab)	1441	4851
The People	Lab	(Lab)	870	2217
Mail on Sunday	Not Lab	(Con)	2336	6329
Sunday Express	Con	(Lab)	866	2214
Sunday Times	Con	(Lab)	1197	3272
Observer	Lab	(Lab)	405	1163
Sunday Telegraph	Con	(Con)	660	2045
Independent on Sunday	Lib Dem[3]	(Lab)	176	666

Source: M. Scammell and M. Harrop in D. Kavanagh and D. Butler (2005, pp 120–2).

[1] *Source*: Audit Bureau of Circulation (April 2005).

[2] *Source*: National Readership Survey (January–December 2004).

[3] But 'where the realistic choice is between Labour and Conservative, we prefer Labour' (*Independent on Sunday*, 1 May 2005).

Television

The British Broadcasting Corporation (BBC) was established as a public corporation in 1926, and is financed by fees from the sale of licences to owners of radios and televisions. It held a monopoly in the field until in 1954 the government established an Independent Broadcasting Authority (later Independent Television Commission), with companies financing programmes out of advertising revenue. Although the two major broadcasting authorities are independent of the government, the latter possesses important levers. It decides on the size of the BBC licence fee, and so determines much of the BBC's finances, and the Prime Minister appoints the Board of Governors which in turn appoint the Director-General. Both bodies operate under charters which are subject to review and renewal by the government. Both also accept that they are under an obligation to be impartial in their political coverage and balanced in their treatment of the parties. The satellite and cable channels are free from such requirements.

Broadcasters, partly because of their subservience at the time to politicians, were slow to cover politics. In the 1950s they adhered to a so-called 14-Day Rule, under which they did not cover topics likely to be discussed in Parliament in the next fortnight. Until 1959 they also ignored the general election campaign apart from carrying party election broadcasts, although news of the general election dominated the national press. Only in 1989 were proceedings in the House of Commons televised.

POLITICS IN FOCUS 25.1

Theory and practice: a free press and independent broadcasting freedom

Freedom

Freedom of the press and independence of broadcasting are defining characteristics of liberal democracy. Voters require independent information about politics and government in order to make an informed choice.

Constraints

(1) **Charter** Broadcasters, although not journalists, are required to adhere to the strict impartiality code set out in their charters.

(2) **Legislation** Official Secrets Acts 1911 and 1989; laws on libel, slander, obscenity, race relations, sedition.

(3) **Culture** The habit of secrecy is deeply ingrained in British government. Whitehall and Westminster collude to ensure that the mysteries of government remain just that. This tradition is reinforced by the Official Secrets Acts. More intensely competitive journalism, and a declining willingness to play by the rules on the part of journalists, politicians and officials indicate signs of a cultural change taking place.

(4) **Appointments, funds and franchises**—The Director-General and Board of Governors of the BBC and the Independent Television Commission are government appointments

— The government sets the BBC's licence fee

— The government also oversees the allocation of independent television franchises

All of these offer opportunities for informal pressure.

(5) **Regulatory bodies**—Broadcasting Complaints Commission

— Advertising Standards Authority

— Broadcasting Standards Council

— Ofcom

— Radio Authority

— Press Complaints Commission

All perform a watchdog role over the media. Their terms of reference, composition and powers are largely a matter for the government.

(6) **Rules of the game** —'D' notices: voluntary restraint on publishing on advice of the government

— Lobby system: information in exchange for non-disclosure of sources

Members of the media who break the 'rules' are punished by exclusion.

(7) **Shared agenda** The existence of interlocking relationships between media moguls and the establishment imposes the intangible constraints of a shared socialisation and shared agenda.

(8) **The market** Advertisers and consumers themselves may impose restraints. In the 1980s Wills tobacco withdrew £500,000 of advertising from the *Sunday Times* because it published an anti-smoking article.

Political influence

The political influence of the media is often misunderstood. Newspapers and television are certainly important as sources of information about politics. They are, however, only one among several shapers of political attitudes. Attempts to impose direct pressure on government usually fail. The efforts of the press lords Beaverbrook and Rothermere to shape Conservative Party policy in the inter-war years failed spectacularly. Lord Rothermere's demand in 1931 that he have a say in the choice of Stanley Baldwin's future Cabinet in return for his press support was contemptuously dismissed by the latter as a demand 'for power without responsibility, the prerogative of the harlot through the ages'. Much of the Conservative-inclined press campaigned for the unseating of John Major in the party's leadership election in 1995—the *Mail*, *Telegraph* and *Sun* strongly so. Conservative MPs and, according to surveys, Conservative supporters disagreed.

Claims about the media's political impact should be made with care. The media have different effects on different people; readers, listeners and viewers have their own predispositions. Early academic research suggested that the media more often reinforced than changed political views. The *selectivity* thesis argued that users of radio and press interpreted what they heard and read to *reinforce* existing loyalties. People seemed to be selective in their *exposure* to political communications, selective in their *interpretation* of them and selective in their *retention* or recall of them.

POLITICS IN FOCUS 25.2

...sures for change: press regulation

Issue	Proposed reform
Press intrusion: intensified competition plus changes in technology have resulted in the press becoming increasingly intrusive	Statutory control in the shape of privacy laws similar to those of some European countries, eg France
Inadequacy of regulation under the auspices of the Press Complaints Commission	Give existing regulatory bodies more teeth/sanctions and greater independence — insufficient sanctions — insufficiently independent — partly self-policing
Concentration of ownership of the press plus broadcasting, eg Murdoch's News International empire, raises questions about control and potential influence	Close scrutiny by Competition Commission
Excessive government secrecy v the need for greater openness and freedom of information	Freedom of Information Act

Extract 25.1: role of the Number 10 Press Secretary

Bernard Ingham, press secretary to Mrs Thatcher (1979–90) reflects on the art of news management:

> I would deal with only one aspect of the relationship with journalists: news management. This is a most heinous offence in journalists' eyes and is the crime—I do not jest—with which press officers, and not least Chief Press Secretaries, are most frequently charged. Journalists see us all as consummate Machiavellis. I plead utterly, completely and wholeheartedly guilty. Of course, I tried to manage the news. I tried—God knows, I tried—to ensure that Ministers spoke with one voice, if necessary by circulating a standard speaking note which I wrote myself. I was hit by all kinds of journalistic avalanche if they spoke out of turn. I tried to ensure that Ministers were aware of what each other was doing and whenever they were likely to cut across each other. Dammit, that was what I was supposed to do. And if I failed, then the media would fall like wolves upon Government and condemn it as useless. I tried—hell's teeth I tried—to make sure that the media had early, embargoed copies of important documents so that they had plenty of time to digest them and prepare their stories before publication.

But he (the information officer) is not in charge of events, or journalists. Nor has he any influence over a minister who suddenly goes ape and commands the front pages. Unfortunately, he is not in command of other events in the global village in this age of instant, telephonic and, more important, televisual communications. An earthquake here; a famine there; an horrendous aircrash elsewhere; or quite simply some appallingly visual event anywhere— and his news management cause is lost. The real news managers today are the media themselves. It is television which predominantly dictates news values for the masses: either there are pictures or there are not, and if there are no pictures there is no news. It is the editors of this world who receive the raw material in the form of reports from the journalist on the spot. Then they get to work on it: developing it, exploiting it, angling it, massaging it and eventually presenting it as polished fact and unvarnished truth. And they dare to accuse Government press officers of news management?
Bernard Ingham, *Kill the Messenger*, London: HarperCollins, 1991: 187–8)

Later studies of the new medium of television adopted a *uses and gratifications* approach (Blumler and McQuail 1968). This showed how voters' values and expectations led them to use the media for, variously, information, reinforcement of values, voting guidance and entertainment. More recently, both theories have been challenged on the grounds that declining partisanship means that fewer voters have firm party loyalties to reinforce, and the media therefore may have more scope for forming and changing views. According to Norris et al (1999: 7):

> Lacking stable social and partisan anchors, voters may become more open to the influence of campaign factors: valuations of the government's record, particularly on the economy, preferences about Party policies, perceptions of party and leadership images, and the way all these factors are communicated to the public.

A third, so-called *radical*, model argues that the media reflect the assumptions and values of dominant groups in society and are biased in particular against parties of the left and trade unions which question those assumptions. The Glasgow University Media Group (1982), in its coverage of industrial disputes, claims to detect a bias for employers and against trade unions; the latter are often presented, unfavourably, as making 'demands' and 'threatening' to strike. The Group regards the mass media as part of the ruling order in a capitalist society. Its analysis of coverage on industrial relations, however, has been subject to damaging reassessment (Harrison 1985).

Politicians frequently express concern about *political bias in the press*. Complaints have most often come from the left, for most national newspapers have long supported the Conservative Party. The pro-Conservative bias increased in the 1970s. In 1970, the Conservative Party had been supported by papers which had 57% of the national daily circulation, Labour by papers which had 43%. By 1992 the figures had shifted to 70% and 27% respectively. The switch of the popular *Sun* newspaper in 1974 to the Conservatives accentuated the imbalance. As long as 80% of the working class read a tabloid, many Labour voters were exposed to a Tory-supporting paper. After the 1992 general election, many formerly staunchly pro-Conservative papers became highly critical of John Major's Government and the *Sun* switched to Labour in 1997. In the general election of that year Labour, for the first time ever, had the support of most of the national daily newspapers. By 2001 its advantage had increased; the circulation of pro-Labour dailies was 72% and of pro-Conservative papers only 28%. In 2005 Labour support fell but it still ran ahead of that for the Conservatives.

There is the problem of untangling cause and effect in this area. How many readers choose a paper because it broadly represents their political leanings rather than switching their views to accord with those of the paper? Early studies reported that people often chose newspapers to fit in with their existing party loyalties, in line with the *selectivity* thesis. Martin Harrop (1986) doubted that the press could have much effect in the four weeks of a campaign and thought that on balance the support of the press was worth only a 1% advantage (or some 10 seats) to the Conservatives. Other work, however, allows that over the long term the press can influence attitudes. The continued imbalance in press parti-sanship and the steady diet of anti-Labour propaganda in the 1970s and 1980s may have helped to make voters more resistant to the party's policies, reinforcing negative images of the party and putting party spokesmen on the defensive by raising 'scares'.

The questions of press bias and influence came to a head in 1992. After the election the *Sun* newspaper proclaimed 'It's the sun wot won it'. That paper had campaigned ruthlessly against Labour and Neil Kinnock and on polling day ran a nine-page special, with the front page reading 'Nightmare on Kinnock Street'. The paper's boast was endorsed by Lord McAlpine, a former Treasurer of the Conservative Party, and by Neil Kinnock, who attacked the bias of sections of the press when he announced his resignation as Labour leader.

Subsequent analysis, however, has cast doubt on the *Sun*'s claims that it produced the alleged late swing to the Conservative Party. The pro-Conservative swing occurred across readers of most papers, including those of the Labour-supporting *Mirror*. A careful study of the subject in 1992 concluded that partisanship, however attenuated, still operates, lead-ing most voters to screen out unwelcome or divergent political messages. In other words, selectivity still operates (Semetko, Scammell and Nossiter 1994). The subsequent switch of the *Sun* to Labour in 1997 and the lukewarm support of many traditional Conservative papers for that party was due, in part, to disillusion with John Major and partly to the moderation and popularity of Tony Blair's new Labour Party. No editor could ignore for long the widespread unpopularity of the Conservative Party and Labour's long-standing and huge lead in the opinion polls. A newspaper that persists in advocating a course rejected by most of its readers runs the risk of losing circulation. It is plausible to argue that the *Sun* followed it readers and the voters in deserting the Conservative cause. Newspapers, in part out of their commercial interests, generally reflect the party loyalties of readers.

A slavish support for a political party may not be good business at a time when party politics appears to be in decline. Papers are mounting their own campaigns and these may or may not coincide with support for a party. The *News of the World* campaigned to 'out' convicted paedophiles, the *Mail* for traditional family values, and it and the *Sun* against British membership of the Euro, and the Labour-supporting *Mirror* campaigned vigorously against British participation in the war against Iraq. The *Mirror* lost sales during the campaign and its editor Piers Morgan was sacked when he acknowledged that the paper had published fake pictures of British soldiers torturing Iraqi prisoners.

Some of the increasing polarisation in the press in the 1980s may have been a consequence of Mrs Thatcher and her determination to break with consensus politics and the divide between the Conservative and Labour Parties. The Conservative papers had been less partisan when Edward Heath was Prime Minister (1970–74) and were unhappy with John Major after his 1992 election victory. The tabloids strongly supported Mrs Thatcher's 'tough' stand on law and order, vigorous advocacy of the British cause in the EC and campaigns against the trade unions and left-wing local councils. Tony Blair's acceptance of many Conservative policies, and the broad agreement on a 'wait and see' approach to Britain's membership of the European single currency reduced the ideological divide. Many tradi-tional Conservative newspapers, particularly those from the News International stable, as well as the *Telegraph* and *Daily Mail*, demanded outright rejection of membership. No major political party promised this, although the Conservative Party contained a large number of declared Eurosceptics. In the absence of clear Labour–Conservative differences, press partisanship has been less in evidence since 1997.

In recent general elections newspapers have become more pragmatic and businesslike in making endorsements of parties. Dealignment has affected papers as well as voters. A verdict on the press's role in the 2005 general election was:

> Traditional displays of press partisanship seem out of place in an era in which many electors (including newspaper readers) no longer even take the trouble to vote. Furthermore, newspapers are preoccupied by the problems of their own declining but competitive market. They have little choice but to become more commercial in outlook, a goal which is difficult to reconcile with the pursuit of traditional Party politics (Scammell and Harrop, 2006).

New Labour, agenda-setting and spinning

In spite of the many tensions between politicians and the media there is also a mutual dependence. The former need publicity for their policies, speeches, and initiatives, while the latter need the co-operation of political actors to write their stories. Political parties, groups and government departments have media officers who are specialists in liasing with the media, trying to set the agenda and put a favourable 'spin' on relevant news items. Agenda-setting assumes that what is carried in the media determines what the public regard as the most important issues.

Politicians, parties and governments stage media events and photo-opportunities exclusively for the media; these events would not take place unless they were present. The media, particularly television, want pictures and these sometimes drive the story. Mrs Thatcher held a calf in a Norfolk field for over 15 minutes for the benefit of photographers in the 1979 election campaign. It was a good 'visual' and therefore virtually guaranteed press and television coverage and it would, Tory campaign managers calculated, soften her image. Parties may decide not to supply party representatives to a programme if the subject is potentially embarrassing, or try to deflect coverage by running another story. A gruesome example was the e-mail from Jo Moore, the Labour special adviser at the Department of Trade and Industry on '9/11' in 2001 when the terrorist planes were crashing into the World Trade Center twin towers that it was 'a good day to bury bad news'. During election campaigns, party strategists often seek to confine media questions to and grant interviews on the party's chosen themes of the day.

Once Tony Blair became leader, Labour raised spinning and communication to another level. The party recruited a number of spin doctors whose job was to suggest stories and lines to follow for journalists which would reflect favourably on the party or leader. More negatively, they bullied or denied access to those journalists who showed a lack of sympathy to the party (Jones 1997; Oborne and Walters 2004; Price 2005). Alastair Campbell disapproved of the *Guardian*'s critical support for the Government and threatened to launch a boycott of the paper by party supporters. Labour ministers, no doubt influenced by the success of their communications strategy in opposition and the stunning election triumph were determined to carry on with this approach. From the start, Number 10 and some ministers have at times seemed obsessed with presentation and spin, repackaging and relaunching earlier policy statements and spending plans, all to give the impression of new initiatives and additional money. Even a Labour-dominated Trade and Industry Select Committee complained in September 1999 about ministers' bogus claims of an increase in funding to a small business award scheme: 'We have noticed a regrettable habit of such relatively prosaic ministerial announcements being dressed up in ministerial statements with potentially misleading figures.'

Labour and communications

Why was the Blair-led Labour Party so preoccupied, even obsessed, with the media? One explanation lies in the changes in the media—the increase in the number of radio and television outlets and increase in the size of the newspapers; the 24-hour media, hungry for new stories and new angles on stories; the increase in the number of political reporters and size of the lobby; and the trends to a more aggressive, adversarial and sensational style of reporting. Politicians, political parties, government departments and interest groups had to be equipped to cater for and cope with this. A New Labour mantra is that good policy is inseparable from good presentation; the policy must be capable of being communicated in a clear and persuasive manner.

A second was the memory of the 1980s and the relentless and at times crude attacks from some tabloids on the party and its leaders, particularly Michael Foot and Neil Kinnock. The party was regularly placed on the back foot as some papers portrayed it as 'loony' and 'extreme'. During general elections Conservative ministers regularly briefed friendly press proprietors and editors with anti-Labour material. Blair and Campbell regarded as a priority, combating this hostility and winning over, or at least moderating the negativism, a tabloid, say the *Sun* or *Mail*. They wanted to catch up with the Conservatives. This was one reason why they accepted an invitation to travel half way round the world in 1995 to address News International executives and reassure them about New Labour.

A third was the lesson learnt about the importance of communications in the successful Clinton campaign for the US Presidency in 1992. Attacks and criticisms should be immediately refuted. Labour borrowed the idea of the Rapid Rebuttal Unit; this enabled it to make computer-generated responses to attacks and the media could carry them along with the original charge. The Conservatives quickly followed.

The importance of the media and communication was reflected in Blair's decisions about staffing and organisation as leader of the party and then as Prime Minister. His first and most influential appointment was of Alastair Campbell as his Press Secretary. In government, only Campbell (along with Blair's Chief of Staff) among the political appointments was given the power to instruct civil servants and to attend meetings of full Cabinet. Both powers were unprecedented. His authority and closeness to Blair led to him being called 'the real deputy Prime Minister'. To ensure that the Government remained 'on message', disciplined and united *vis-à-vis* the media ministers were instructed that all requests for media interviews and announcements were to be cleared in advance with Number 10. The Government should speak with one voice, otherwise the media would report 'splits'.

The new outlook was quickly felt across Whitehall as it was reported that ministers were unimpressed with the quality of departmental information officers. There was a large-scale turnover of staff and in 1998 the Government and Information Service (GIS) was renamed Government and Information Communication Service (GICS), to reflect the new role of information officers—to put government announcements in a political context. The change gave rise to accusations that the service was being politicised. Inside Number 10 the Press Office was expanded and a number of sympathetic journalists appointed. A new Strategic Communications Unit was established, again staffed by a mix of civil servants and sympathetic journalists, with responsibility for briefing, writing articles and speeches for ministers and the Prime Minister, and co-ordinating the news agenda of departments. Also new was a Research and Information Unit with a remit to collect information for Prime Minister's Questions and analyse material about the Government's record by regions and constituencies for campaigning purposes.

The result has been a substantial increase in Tony Blair's staff in Number 10 with a media or communications-related background and who are politically appointed. No other Prime Minister has been as aware of the media as Blair. He has written (and had written for him) hundreds of newspaper articles and held regular press conferences. In a leaked memo in 2000, he was seen asking staff to suggest 'headline catching initiatives' and that he should be personally associated with them. Labour has defended this emphasis on the grounds that the Government and the Prime Minister have to communicate their achievements and agenda to the public. But ministers gained such a reputation for spin and 'overclaiming', that Philip Gould, Blair's pollster, warned that the New Labour 'brand' had become 'badly contaminated' and suffered a loss of trust.

Tensions

A by-product of the more continuous, intensive and competitive coverage of politics seems to have led to more concentration on crises, scandals, personal rivalries and divisions. In the past decade politicians have been casualties in a number of press stories. In the 1990s 'sleaze' did untold damage to the standing of the Conservative Party.

But in government Labour was vulnerable because it had claimed that it would 'clean up' politics and be 'purer than pure'. Its reputation was quickly harmed by the revelation that Bernie Ecclestone, of Formula One motor racing, had apparently used his donation of £1 million to Labour to change Government policy. He held a private meeting with Tony Blair in Number 10 and soon afterwards the Government policy of supporting a Europe-wide ban on tobacco advertisements and tobacco sponsorship was amended to exempt F1. The press also revealed that Geoffrey Robinson, a Treasury minister, was involved in a tax-avoidance scheme even though the Treasury was trying to clamp down on such schemes. There were cases of secrecy over large donations to party funds and Labour MPs being suspended from the Commons for failing to declare relevant financial interests.

The press targeted other ministers with allegations of improper conduct. The Secretary of State for Wales Ron Davies, resigned following media coverage of his 'moment of madness' on Clapham Common. Peter Mandelson twice faced a media onslaught when it was revealed, in one case probably wrongly, that he had infringed ministerial rules and was forced to resign. David Blunkett's resignations from the Cabinet in 2004 and 2005 were both driven by media 'frenzies' about his personal behaviour. Politicians, as far as much of the press was concerned, were a rich source of copy for scandal. In turn, Labour politicians complained that they were being unfairly singled out, that the press was undermining popular respect for the political process, and that the media was arrogating to itself the role of being the political opposition. A survey among MPs in 2005 reported that many Conservative and Labour MPs considered that the BBC was biased in its political coverage.

Difficulties arise between politicians and journalists simply because they have different agendas of professionalism and because of the close and sustained relationship between them. For the politician, being professional means trying to shape, directly and indirectly, the news agenda. For the journalists, being professional means achieving a healthy degree of autonomy and discretion, and reporting according to their own criteria of objectivity and newsworthiness. Not surprisingly, each side often cries 'foul' self-righteously at alleged misdemeanours by the other. But as Enoch Powell observed, politicians who complain about the press are like sailors who moan about the sea.

Both Labour and Conservative ministers have long complained that so-called good news is ignored or under-reported by the broadcasters, whereas so-called bad news, is prominently reported. For example, ministers of any party in government, regularly complain that hospital closures or job losses appear to be more prominently reported than the opening of a new hospital or a new factory. BBC coverage of the Falklands War in 1982 offended Conservative leaders who did not think that this was the time to be even-handed between 'our' side and Argentina. Pressure on the BBC under the last Conservative government also took the form of pre-emptive attacks prior to a general election. Before the 1992 general election, the party Chairman, Chris Patten, urged Conservative viewers to protest about unfair coverage by the BBC.

This mix of sensitivity and bullying is not confined to Conservative ministers. Before and after the 1997 general election, Labour spin doctors regularly harassed BBC reporters and executives about their political coverage, including choice and running order of stories, political balance and selection of interviewees. One claimed: 'Of course, bullying the BBC works. That's why we do it. We know it works. Obviously, in the end, the newsrooms give in, that's why we keep it up' (Jones 1997: 249). The aggressive attitude may then have been understandable because Labour had been out of office for so long.

But in government there was no let up. Alastair Campbell and his team frequently complained about the decline in the quality of political journalism, that there was too much comment and less straight reporting, too much concern with personality, trivia and scandal and too little on policy. 'The journalists are the real spin doctors', he said. Many of Campbell's complaints were addressed to the BBC and its flagship programmes, *Today* and *The World At One*. The bad feeling between the party and the BBC eventually came to a head over Iraq. During his appearance before the Foreign Affairs Select Committee in June

2003, Campbell attacked the BBC for 'having an agenda', particularly in its coverage of the Government's position over the Iraq war. The later Hutton inquiry into the circumstances leading to the death of the government scientist Dr David Kelly (see p 208) reported the avalanche of complaints from Number 10 to the BBC over reporter Andrew Gilligan's claim that Campbell had 'sexed up' an intelligence dossier on Iraq's weapons. It became highly personal as Campbell admitted in his diary that he wanted to 'fuck Gilligan'.

The BBC is more exposed than any other media outlet because it is so heavily dependent on the licence fee, the level of which is set by the government of the day. Interestingly, BBC executives had concluded that the organisation had been too compliant in following the main parties' agendas during the 1992 general election. They felt that the manipulation and hectoring by party managers had been so blatant and so persistent that journalists and producers had to take steps to be seen to be independent of them. They therefore urged their reporters to be bolder and more open in their interpretative role—a clear encouragement to the broadcasters to referee the political process and even, perhaps, to shape the agenda (Blumler and Gurevitch 1998).

The media and election campaigns

Both politicians and reporters are in the business of persuading the voter and reader/ viewer. They feed off each other. They mix frequently in the Lobby, in which journalists are briefed twice daily by the Number 10 press secretary when the House of Commons is sitting, and at many policy launches, party conferences, receptions and other social occasions, sometimes referred to disparagingly as the 'Westminster hothouse'. Politicians are keenly interested in how they are reported and journalists depend on access to key party figures for information. At the same time the relationship is fraught with tension, as each side often comes to feel aggrieved. Politicians and press secretaries reward 'friendly' journalists with information and access, and deny the same to journalists who display insufficient sympathy or understanding. Journalists in turn often resent the sense of being used or manipulated by the party spin doctors, or being supplied with misleading and self-serving information. They may also 'unmask' the hidden agendas that lie behind politicians' activities and speeches. One former BBC political reporter, Nick Jones, has written a number of books exposing the manipulative activities of Labour's spin doctors, under such titles as *Soundbites and Spin Doctors* and *Sultans of Spin*. Surveys also reveal a disjunction between the voters' agenda and that of the media. In 1997 and 2001 the media gave great coverage to 'Europe' and tax but the voters did not rank them highly. In the 2005 general election Labour leaders were furious at the heavy amount of coverage the media gave to Iraq, although surveys suggested that voters ranked the issue well behind health, education and immigration.

Analysis of media coverage of elections shows that accounts of party strategy and of opinion polls are usually among the top three front-page stories in the newspapers during general elections. Surveys, however, show that voters are not much interested in this type of reporting. A major study of media coverage of the 1997 general election, *On Message*, revealed that whereas the parties' messages concentrated on policy issues, the media gave more coverage to matters of campaign strategy and the election horse race—who was winning (Norris et al 1999: 181–2). In the 2005 general election, Iraq was the most heavily covered issue in the media but it hardly registered among voters when they were asked about which issues most concerned them.

The interdependence between politicians and media is at its closest during elections. The parties recruit experts from the public relations, media and advertising industries to assist with campaign publicity and media presentation in general. Established film producers and writers are also involved in the filming and writing of party election broadcasts. Much of the leading politicians' campaign day—the morning press conference, walkabout, and even rally—is now largely shaped by the requirements of the media, particularly television. Setting the election agenda for the mass media is the main purpose of a party's communications strategy. Within the political parties people with communication skills have risen in importance, particularly with regard to election campaigns. In parties, and to some extent interest groups and other political organisations, those with a record in the media are now likely to occupy key communication posts; the skills are assumed to be transferable. Parties are also now more likely to employ an advertising agency (the Saatchi and Saatchi agency worked on all Conservative general election campaigns from 1979 to 1997), opinion pollsters and film directors to help make political broadcasts. In 2003, Maurice Saatchi became co-Chairman of the party.

An election is also a period when tensions between the two groups are particularly intense and fraught with the possibility for rows and misunderstandings. All parties scrutinise broadcast coverage for signs of deliberate or accidental bias or unfairness, and put pressure on the broadcasters. The latter strive to satisfy the parties' demands for balance and fairness while also seeking, as professionals, to report items on the basis of their newsworthiness. Usually this means appearances of party splits, gaffes, personal attacks and shifts in the opinion polls. Tensions arise from the different role of newscasters and politicians. For the former, 'communication was a tool of public enlightenment, to the latter (politicians)—against rival parties *and* professional journalists' (Blumler, Gurevitch and Nossiter 1989: 159).

Campaign managers draw up a daily 'grid' of activities and try to ensure that the media cover the party's agenda for the day or days, by:

- holding a number of press conferences on the same topic on the same day;
- putting forward only one or two major speakers on the hustings to discourage cameras from reporting somebody who does not voice the chosen issue of the day;
- co-ordinating the party leader's activities during the day so that the same theme is reflected in what he says and does;
- declining interviews on subjects not on the party's agenda.

In their turn, journalists as professionals try to create a role for themselves in shaping the campaign agenda. They concentrate on the 'horse race' (using opinion polls to report which party is in the lead) or provide 'state of play' interpretations of the campaign, and perhaps ask the questions of party leaders that the latter would rather not have posed. The 2005 general election was an interesting test for students of agenda-setting. The most covered topics across press and television were Iraq, Blair (and lack of trust in him) and immigration, all issues the Labour Party did not want to emphasise and, except for Iraq, played to Conservative strengths. But the media agenda did not, according to surveys, reflect the major interests of voters and the salience of Labour's agenda of public services and the economy actually increased for voters during the course of the campaign (Kavanagh and Butler 2005: chs 8 and 9).

Television effects

The politicians are increasingly concerned with agenda-setting, and this is another cause of their sensitivity over television. A feature of the more 'permanent' or lengthy campaign is that a party's communications officers and public relations advisers are regularly developing media strategies for the politicians. At times, it may appear that at least as much attention is paid to the presentation as to the substance of politics. The government of the day has many opportunities to shape the news agenda by exploiting its use of office, via ministerial announcements, policy initiatives, the budget and Prime Minister's Question Time, to dominate the airways. What Prime Ministers do is newsworthy. Party conferences, like American party conventions, have increasingly become stage-managed for the televised projection of the positive party image and strong leadership. Press coverage of Parliament has steadily declined and it is no surprise that MPs queue up to be interviewed on the *Today* programme or television, rather than speak in Parliament. One MP complained that the best way to keep a secret was to announce it in the Commons. The local and regional media provide opportunities for media-oriented backbench MPs to become well-known figures. The broadcasting of debates in the Commons has not lessened the desire for politicians to be interviewed outside Parliament. On major occasions like a leadership election, Cabinet reshuffles, ministerial resignations or the Budgets, the strip of turf opposite Parliament on College Green resembles a crowded marketplace.

How the media cover politics is increasingly becoming an issue in its own right. Political parties now routinely make charges of bias, for example, over the amount and tone of coverage, the running order of stories, and the selection of interviewers. Politicians speak in soundbites or insist on being interviewed live, to reduce the likelihood of being edited and their 'message' being lost. They impose control over media access to a party's spokesperson, in an attempt to screen out those who are not 'on message'. They recruit professionals in media and public relations who can play the journalists at their own game.

Ministers try to avoid aggressive interviewers like Jeremy Paxman and seek less adversarial forums in the popular and less political programmes. Blair has appeared in programmes like the *Des O'Connor Show* or *Richard and Judy*, where he can field 'soft' questions and allow himself to appear as a 'regular guy'. As noted, no British Prime Minister has taken the role of communicator-in-chief as seriously as Tony Blair, and no Government has so assiduously sought to convey its messages through news outlets as the present Labour Government.

Despite the politicians' complaints about television bias, survey evidence consistently fails to support the claims. Some four-fifths of people detect no bias in election coverage and regard television as trustworthy and truthful, compared with less than a quarter thinking the same of the press. At the time of the conflict between the Labour Government and the BBC over coverage of the Iraq war, a majority of voters trusted the BBC more.

Television has encouraged a presidentialism, or personalisation, in politics in so far as it focuses more on the activities of party leaders. Between general elections something like one-third of television coverage of a party's politicians is of the leader and more than half during an election. This means that a party's campaign messages are carried largely through the leader. The concentration is partly a consequence of television resources. Camera crews and major reporters are assigned to follow each party leader—hence there is more film of the leader. Michael Foley (1993: 121) has commented on the relationship between party managers and media: 'television's inclination to personalising the treatment and presentation of politics has been matched by the willingness of parties to provide their leaders with the prominence and license to fit the party product to the optimal form of communications.'

Television to date has not influenced the political careers of politicians, although this may be changing. Mrs Thatcher, Michael Foot and Mr Heath were not particularly skilful at public relations and presentation, certainly not when they were elected as party leader. In Britain politicians usually get to lead the party by displaying parliamentary skills, being acceptable to all or most strands of the party, and being regarded as an election winner. Political leaders now work hard to develop their television skills, something increasingly regarded as essential for a would-be leader. Alternatively, lack of presentational skills (being 'bad' on television) is now probably a barrier to political advancement. One wonders if Clement Attlee, generally regarded as one of the more successful premiers but also thought to be colourless, could have got to the top today.

 ## Conclusion

British politicians have had to adjust to a more media-saturated political world. Given the explosion of media outlets and 24-hour coverage they have developed more media-centred publicity strategies, adapted much of their political rhetoric and activities to the format imperatives of television (eg soundbites and photo-opportunities) and made elections into political marketing campaigns. They and the media compete in setting the political agenda.

One consequence of these trends has been an increase in short-termism. Politicians increasingly seek to be proactive and launch initiatives to attract coverage. As Labour's chief public opinion adviser, Philip Gould, has explained: 'You must always seek to gain and keep momentum, or it will pass immediately to your opponents. Gaining momentum means dominating the news agenda, entering the news cycle at the earliest possible time, and repeatedly re-entering it, with stories and initiatives so that subsequent news coverage is set on your terms' (1997: 294). Governing is akin to campaigning; hence 'the permanent campaign'.

The shortening of time between an event or incident and coverage of it reduces the time which politicians have for making decisions. Coping with the immediate news coverage imposes time pressures. Seeking to gain favourable short-term media coverage can crowd out the energy and resources devoted to good policy. Effective policy requires time to collect information, consider different policy alternatives, conduct pilot studies and assess other factors, all of which preclude speedy decision-making.

In the United States many media scholars have complained that the style of media coverage makes the tasks of government more difficult as voters are encouraged to be more cynical and in turn depressing levels of political participation. There is certainly evidence of an increase in negative coverage of politics. Scammell and Semetko (1998) considered the balance of negative/positive press evaluations of the parties and candidates in the 1992 and 1997 general elections. They found that all newspapers were more negative than positive in coverage in 1997 and the broadsheets significantly so. In the 1960s and 1970s newspapers consistently gave more space to the parties they supported editorially. Since 1979, however, they have given more space to parties they opposed, one explanation for the increase in 'knocking' copy. Another consequence is for the quality of political debate. Today, leading politicians can hardly speak spontaneously, speculate aloud, or disagree even slightly from colleagues because journalists will instantly pounce and describe such actions as evidence of indecisiveness or party divisions.

KEY POINTS

- Politics is largely a mediated activity. Media provide information about politics but they are also influential in shaping opinions and an interest group in their own right.

- The extent and nature of the political influence of the media are keenly debated by both academics and politicians. Some argue that the media serve to reinforce rather than change political views. Others argue that declining partisanship has increased the political influence of the media. The radical model asserts that the significance of media influence is not in persuading voters to support one or another party, but in reinforcing the status quo, making radical alternatives seem dangerous, 'un-British'.

- A traditional pro-Conservative bias in the press has been overturned in the general elections in 1997, 2001 and 2005, as papers have endorsed Labour. The broadcasting authorities are required to adhere to a strict code of political impartiality. Politicians from both sides, however, frequently accuse broadcasters of bias.

- There is a mutual dependence between politicians and the media. Many political events are staged for, or geared towards facilitating, media coverage. The 'political' leak has become a commonplace of political communication. Inevitably 'bad' news and political indiscretions attract the greatest coverage. The media largely determine 'what's news', and there is a growing trend towards media coverage itself forming part of that news.

- Election campaigns are increasingly media events, reflected in the parties' increased reliance on media and public relations experts. Daily press conferences and campaign events are co-ordinated with media coverage.

- Television has helped to presidentialise election campaigns and personalise politics. The political role of television and the question of potential bias have become issues.

- As relations between politicians and the media have deteriorated, so regulation of the media is itself a controversial issue.

KEY QUESTIONS

(1) To what extent do the media set the political agenda?

(2) A free press is a myth. Discuss.

(3) The media enhance democracy. Discuss.

(4) What kind of problems are associated with attempts to regulate the mass media?

(5) Why is regulation of the media frequently on the agenda?

FURTHER READING

For a good introduction see R. Negrine (1998) *Television and the Press since 1945*, Manchester: Manchester University Press; J. Tunstall (1996) *Newspaper Power: The National Press in Britain*, London: Routledge; and C. Seymour-Ure (1996) *The British Press and Broadcasting since 1945*, Oxford: Blackwell. On press and television during a general election see the chapters by M. Scammell and M. Harrop and by M. Harrison in D. Kavanagh and D. Butler (2005) *The British General Election of 2005*, London: Palgrave; C. Seymour-Ure, 'New Labour and the Media' in A. King (ed) (2001) *Britain at the Polls 2001*, London: Chatham House; and P. Norris et al (1996) *On Message*, London: Sage. More generally see B. Franklin (1994) *Packaging Politics*, London: Arnold. On spin see P. Oborne and S. Walters (2004) *Alastair Campbell: New Labour and the Rise of the New Media Class*, London: Aurum; N. Jones (1999) *Sultans of Spin*, London: Gollancz and his (2002) *The Control Freaks*, London: Politicos; and B. Ingham (2003) *The Wages of Spin*, London: John Murray. On broader issues see J. Lloyd (2004) *What the Media are Doing to our Politics*, London: Constable.

CHRONOLOGY

The increasing role of the media in politics

1912	'D'-notice system begins: voluntary suppression of information on government advice
1924	First party political broadcast on radio
1926	BBC created
1936	BBC begins TV broadcasting
1947	Hugh Dalton, Chancellor of the Exchequer, resigns; disclosed budget secrets to press before Parliament
1950	BBC's first transmission of general election results
1951	First party election broadcast on TV
1954	Independent Broadcasting Authority established—commercial TV
1963	Press Council set up
1973	Commercial radio broadcasting
1981	Rupert Murdoch buys *The Times*; Lonrho buys the *Observer*
1982	Launch of Channel 4

1986   The *Independent*, a new quality daily, launched; also *Today*, a new tabloid. Leon Brittan, Secretary of State for Trade and Industry, resigns, taking responsibility for press leaks of his department's officials

1987   The Government obtains an injunction to prevent BBC showing a programme about the *Zircon* spy satellite

1988   Broadcasting Standards Authority created

1989   House of Commons televised, ban on broadcasting interviews with Irish extremists

1990   Press Complaints Commission established

1992   David Mellor, Arts and Heritage Secretary, resigns amid media coverage of his private life, and complains that the media have become almost another criminal justice system

1994   The *Sunday Times* reveals the 'cash for questions' scandal

1997   Labour for first time is supported at a general election by bulk of press

1998   Labour Government greatly strengthens communications presence in Number 10

2003   Ofcom established. Combined BSC, ITC and Radio Authority with telecommunications and radio communications to regulate communications

2003   Hutton inquiry clears Number 10 of 'sexing up' intelligence about Iraq weapons

 Visit the Online Resource Centre that accompanies this book
for links to more information on this chapter topic

PART THREE
Policy

CHAPTER TWENTY SIX

Economic policy

READER'S GUIDE

Economic policy is one of the most important policies for government. There is a strong relationship between economic success and electoral success. However, economic policy has often been a considerable problem for British government. The period from 1945 was characterised as one of economic decline. The 1970s saw a period of sustained economic crisis. This chapter examines how governments have responded to economic problems and assesses the extent to which the present Government has resolved the problems of economic decline. It also examines the extent to which government has lost control over economic policy as a consequence of globalisation and membership of the European Union.

Introduction

Economic policy is one of the most important policy areas for government. There is strong evidence that success in economic policy leads to success in elections. However, one of the problems for government is that whilst they like to present themselves as making crucial decisions that will affect Britain's economic future, and often build elections around their management of the economy, it is questionable how much control they actually have over economic outcomes. Again, it is a question of structure and agency; is economic policy determined by the structure of the world and the domestic economy or is it a consequence of decisions taken by individual actors? It may be that economic outcomes are determined by events that governments do not control rather than policies created by governments. With the apparent globalisation of the economy the degree to which government can affect economic outcomes may be less than ever.

This chapter will outline the history of economic policy in Britain. Economic policy has been one of the most important and difficult aspects of policy-making in the post-war years. Whilst Britain relatively easily became a leading economic power in the 19th century, coping with decline in the 20th century was highly problematic. There was an almost constant debate concerning whether the best solution to economic decline was state intervention or free markets. Whilst in the 1950s and 1960s there appeared to be a consensus that some degree of intervention was desirable, from the 1980s onwards the predominant view was that the state has a limited role in the economy. The Thatcher Government seemed to create a new consensus concerning the direction of economic policy and it has been argued that New Labour's economic policy is a development of Thatcherism. Therefore this chapter will examine the unfolding of Britain's economic policy and examine whether the policies that have developed since the 1980s have resolved the issue of decline. It will also focus on how economic policy is made under New Labour, the mechanisms that are used and the success they have had and, in particular, the extent to which their economic policy is or is not Thatcherite. Finally, the chapter will examine the debate concerning the impact of globalisation on economic policy-making.

Economic policy in historical context

British economic policy has been subject to considerable controversy over the last 30 years. It is impossible to understand the nature of economic policy without understanding how the past has shaped current economic policy. Britain was the first industrial nation and by the middle of the 19th century it was by far the most dominant economic power in the world. As a consequence, economic growth developed without much intervention from the state. The British economy developed on the basis of what is called laissez-faire or non-intervention. The role of the state was not to positively encourage economic development but to enable the British economy to grow by removing the constraints on free market activity. After much political conflict, which in effect split the Conservative Party, the decision was taken in 1846 to repeal the Corn Laws. This essentially created free trade in Britain where goods could be brought into Britain without duty and therefore relatively cheaply. As a consequence, British manufacturers were able to import cheap raw materials and process them into expensive manufactured goods. At the same time the British state followed a policy of imperial expansion which enlarged both the sources of raw materials and ensured a captive market for British goods. In this sense the British state played a key role in economic policy but the role was political: an aggressive imperial policy. This combination of free trade and imperialism led to the British economy becoming the largest in the world, producing 33% of world exports in 1899 (Gamble 1990).

Underpinning this economic growth was an economic policy based on the notion of sound money, free trade and laissez-faire. The pound was linked to the value of gold which meant that the price of sterling was fixed and this was a way on ensuring that inflation was tightly controlled (if a currency is linked to gold, the government cannot easily print more money). The government attempted to maintain and export free trade in order to ensure that it had access to markets throughout the world. Finally, the underlying philosophy was that the market knows best and that there was little government could do apart from ensuring order, protecting private property and allowing capitalism to operate in an unrestrained way. This policy worked well when the economy was growing and Britain was economically dominant. It was less attractive when, in the late 19th century, Britain began to face serious economic competition from the United States and Germany and then, in the inter-war years, a prolonged period of depression.

Depression and changing patterns of economic intervention

The First World War saw the Government's first significant intervention in the economy. The Government fixed the price of a number of goods, oversaw the production of certain industrial and military goods and developed a system of agricultural support. However, the prevailing economic view was that war was exceptional and that there was a need to return to the principles of laissez-faire when it finished. Consequently, following the war the Government dramatically cut public expenditure and returned sterling to the gold standard (in other words the value of the pound was fixed again to the price of gold). The reassertion of classical economics, combined with a downturn in world economic activity, led to a depression that affected many countries in Europe and the United States.

One of the consequences of the depression was that it ignited a debate over the ability of laissez-faire policies to resolve Britain's economic problems. A number of politicians and economists such as Harold Macmillan and John Maynard Keynes suggested that there may be a middle way between free market capitalism and full blooded socialism. In particular, Keynes published his general theory of employment in 1936, which argued that governments could reduce unemployment through deficit spending. Such a view was in direct opposition to the classical market economics which emphasised the need to balance budgets.

Such was the extent of the inter-war depression that the ideas of those who proposed a more interventionist approach to economic policy started to have an influence. The

Government did introduce a limited number of measures in an attempt to bring Britain out of recession including some public works and low interest rates. However it was only really during and after the Second World War that Keynesian ideas took hold.

Establishing the post-war consensus

The Second World War was a total war. The state effectively took over all aspects of society in order to direct activity at the single goal of winning the war. The state therefore took on the role of planning of the economy. It rationed goods, fixed prices and controlled labour and production. The apparent ability of wartime planning to produce economic and military success reshaped the economic policy agenda. The hitherto dominant laissez-faire paradigm was discredited. There was a belief that Britain could not return to the mass unemployment that had characterised the 1930s. As a consequence, both Labour and Conservatives seemed to accept the foundation of a post-war economy. They recognised that the government had responsibility for the level of employment and could intervene in the economy to achieve full employment. Likewise they accepted the need to ensure minimal welfare standards and, as a consequence of the Beveridge report, set up the NHS and a system of benefits for the unemployed (see Chapter 28). Both Labour and Conservatives acknowledged the need for government intervention and to increase public expenditure, and that trade unions had a role in economic policy-making. Nevertheless, there were considerable differences on economic policy (see Politics in Focus 26.1).

Britain's relative economic decline and stop-go policy

Whilst Britain was militarily victorious in the Second World War, a number of problems soon became apparent in the economy. The war was extremely expensive and the British economy was almost bankrupt. Initial attempts to return sterling to pre-war parity failed

It has been argued that when the Conservatives were re-elected in 1951 they accepted most of the policy changes that had been introduced by the post-war Labour Government. Consequently, it was seen by a number of commentators that there was a post-war consensus based on the notion that the government had some responsibility for the economy, that Keynesianism was a useful tool of economic management, that the government should try to maintain full employment, that a degree of public ownership of major utilities like water and energy was acceptable and that the unions should have a role in the policy process.

However, others have suggested that the consensus was not very substantial. That there were in fact major disagreements between the parties on public expenditure and nationalisation and that where similar policies were followed by Labour and Conservative governments it was the result of external factors forcing convergence rather than any deep-seated ideological consensus.

and Britain was forced to ask for US support in order to avoid economic catastrophe. Many of the strictures of the war-time economy continued throughout the 1940s and despite the relatively high level of economic intervention by the Labour Government, the economy took a considerable time to recover from the impact of the war.

Nevertheless, by 1958 the Prime Minister, Harold Macmillan was able to say that 'You have never had it so good'. By the end of the 1950s, Britain had benefited from a considerable period of economic growth. For the first time ordinary people were able to purchase material goods such as cars, fridges and televisions. Many people moved from poor inner-city housing to new council houses and flats.

Economic growth, however, was hiding a series of underlying economic problems. The first was Britain's relative economic decline. Whilst Britain's economy was growing rapidly in the post-war period it was not growing as fast as her competitors. France, Germany, Japan and the United States all saw much greater increases in their national wealth during the Second World War (see Chapter 7 and Politics in Focus 27.2).

The second problem which may have been both a cause and effect of decline was that governments were forced into following a policy that was called stop-go. According to Keynesian theory, governments could increase demand through extra spending and this would increase economic growth. If economic growth resulted in an increase in inflation, government could cut expenditure and dampen down the economy. The trick was to get the right balance between inflation and unemployment. However the problem with the British economy was that every attempt at expansion quickly produced an increase in imports and higher inflation. The influx of imports unsettled the currency markets and so there was pressure on governments to devalue sterling, which they generally opposed fearing that it would produce more inflation. Therefore, governments were forced into a

27.2

ative economic decline

A whole range of explanations have been developed to explain why the British economy did not grow as quickly as her competitors in the post-war period. Often these explanations have an ideological tinge with those on the Left and Right focusing on different factors. Explanations include:

- The power of the unions
- The level of public expenditure
- The power and dominance of the City of London
- Too much government intervention
- Too little government intervention
- Too much taxation
- The adversarial nature of British politics
- The post-war consensus
- The anti-industrial nature of British culture.

stop phase in order to curtail economic growth, so that inflation and imports could be controlled. This pattern of stop-go persisted well into the 1970s.

Stop-go was a consequence of two structural problems. The first was that sterling was in a precarious position because of the sterling area. The sterling area was an overhang of Empire. Most of the countries that had been or were still in the Empire were in the sterling area, that is, they used sterling as the mechanism of exchange in trade within the area. As a consequence all these countries held their reserves in the Bank of England in sterling and so Britain had tremendous financial liabilities. If all of the countries of the sterling area tried to withdraw their money, Britain would have been unable to pay. Overseas holders of sterling had to be assured that the value of the currency would be maintained. Consequently, the British government was always vulnerable to currency speculation and had to continually reassure the financial markets that it was acting responsibly.

The second problem was that British industry suffered from relatively low levels of investment, industrial production remained outdated and productivity was low. While Japan, France and Germany had renewed their plant in the post-war period, Britain, cushioned by its economic dominance and the assured Empire markets, failed to modernise. As a consequence, when the government increased demand in the economy, British industry could not supply the extra production and so goods had to be imported and/or prices rose as more money chased a limited number of goods. Again this unsettled the currency markets.

Stop-go was also exacerbated by a number of decisions made by policy-makers and other economic actors—it was not all a matter of structure:

- The Government avoided the detailed intervention that occurred in France, Germany and Japan, which encouraged the development of industry. There was an absence of a state-led attempt to resolve the supply side problems that were leading to stop-go (see Politics in Focus 26.4).

- There was a failure to develop the close and consensual relations between unions, business and government which occurred in much of Europe. Whilst for most of our competitors national economy strategy was uncontroversial, in Britain there was considerable conflict between business, unions and political parties over the main elements of economic policy. Consequently, attempts at intervention by government were often resisted. Economic policy in Britain was adversarial and subject to continual change.

- There was a failure to develop a close relationship between banks and industry. In Germany and Japan banks invested in national industry and as a consequence there were long-term investment relationships which allowed for the renewal of the economic base. In Britain the City of London was given considerable autonomy and tended to invest overseas. Moreover its interests were in shareholders rather than producers and often investment decisions were short term.

- The Government failed to devalue the pound, ensuring that imports were relatively cheap.

Post-war economic policy in Britain can be described as a limited form of Keynesianism. There was an attempt to maintain full employment through demand management. However, this demand management was severely restricted by the desire to ensure the value of sterling and control inflation. There were few and limited attempts at detailed planning. In many ways the laissez-faire ethos that had dominated 19th century Britain continued to exercise a hold on policy-makers who were not prepared to challenge the power of the City or the currency markets. In this sense Britain's economic growth in the 1950s and 1960s was not a consequence of decisions to adopt Keynesian policy but was the result of the external context. A worldwide economic expansion driven by US expenditure led to a period of long-term growth.

POLITICS IN FOCUS 26.3
Economic myths

Post-war British economic policy is surrounded by a number of myths many were propagated by the Conservatives in the 1980s and by New Labour. The myths include:

- *There was a post-war consensus*. There were significant disagreements over policy.

- *That adversarial politics produced numerous changes in policy*. There were significant changes in policy but they tended to be within governments rather than between them and they were a result of economic problems not politics.

- *Government policy was interventionist*. British economic policy was not particularly interventionist especially compared to most European states. Intervention was often half-hearted. Britain never developed the detailed economic planning that occurred in France or Japan.

- *Post-war policy was dominated by the unions*. For most of the post-war period the unions had very little role in economic policy. Particularly in the 1950s and 1960s they adopted a voluntarist strategy, preferring to keep out of politics and economics if the Government kept out of their affairs.

- *Government policy made a difference*. The roller-coaster of economic policy in the post-war period was a consequence of the impact of the Second World War, US foreign economic policy and structural readjustment as a consequence of the loss of Empire. Government action made little difference to these events.

- *A managed devaluation of the pound would have resolved Britain's economic difficulties*. Many people argue that had Britain not tried to retain the value of the pound many of the post-war economic problems would have been avoided. However, devaluation would have created a new set of problems including higher inflation and a further loss of confidence by the financial markets. Continual devaluation tends to exacerbate, rather than resolve, problems.

- *The level of taxation was high*. Britain's taxation rates were no higher than those of most competitors.

0s and 1960s

During the 1950s and 1960s both Labour and Conservative governments introduced a range of policies in an attempt to modernise the British economy. These included:

- Attempts to increase competition and reduce restrictive practices
- Attempts at economic intervention through the National Economic Development Council, the creation of the Department of Economic Affairs and the National Plan
- Attempts at controlling wages through the National Income Commission
- The creation of the Industrial Reorganisation Corporation as a mechanism for encouraging rationalisation in British industry
- Post-war policy was not really a failure to intervene but a failure of the intervention.

The collapse of Keynesianism

As we saw above, the form of Keynesianism adopted in Britain was based on limited intervention in the economy. There were from the 1950s through to the 1960s a whole range of half-hearted attempts at economic interventions. This limited intervention meant that there was a failure to modernise the British economy. As a consequence the problems of low growth, increased union militancy, rising inflation and unemployment were becoming endemic within the British economy. Initially the 1970–74 Conservative Government, led by Edward Heath, attempted to resolve these problems through a return to market-based policies and by seeking to disengage from industry. In a prototype of Thatcherism, Heath believed that the market was a solution. However, with rising unemployment and growing industrial relations problems the Heath Government rapidly reversed its policy and introduced what was probably the most interventionist raft of economic policies in Britain's post-war history. The Government combined industrial intervention with a massive increase in public expenditure in order to try to blast Britain to modernisation. This policy failed because of a combination of industrial unrest, in particular the 1973 miners' strike which forced Britain into a three-day week, and the OPEC oil crisis which saw the quadrupling of oil prices in a few months (Gamble 1995).

The Conservatives were defeated in 1974 and replaced by a Labour Government which initially attempted to resolve the problems of the British economy through building on Heath's interventionist framework. The Labour Government introduced the National Enterprise Board to buy up key industries, and through Sector Working Parties the Government developed detailed plans to improve efficiency and productivity in British industry. However, again modernisation was wrecked by industrial relations problems and a sterling crisis which forced the British government to request a loan from the International Monetary Fund (IMF). The impact of the loan was that the Government was forced to cut public expenditure, attempt to control the money supply and sell part of the nationalised oil industry. The failure of an interventionist strategy led to a shift towards a more market-orientated policy. The roots of Thatcherism were developed in the soil of a Labour government.

Thatcherism and the return to the market

In terms of economic policy, the 1970s revolved around a range of attempts to save a failing Keynesian welfare state. Whilst, as we saw above, the Labour Government developed a more market-orientated policy, it was still committed to maintaining the welfare state and an economic role for government. The Conservative Government elected in 1979 was fundamentally different because it believed that the Keynesianism welfare state was not something to save, but the cause of the problems. For the New Right the state was inefficient and state actors self-interested. State policies created more problems than they resolved. In their view, the Government could not control the level of employment (although ironically it could control the level of inflation) and state activity was parasitic on the private sector, thus sucking initiative and investment from efficient market activities to support inefficient state activities. Finally, the state restricted individual freedom. Consequently, the basis of Thatcherite economic policy was the attempt to set the economy free. There was no simple Thatcherite blueprint which was immediately implemented when the Conservatives came into power in 1979. There were many contradictions and problems. With unemployment rising rapidly, it was difficult for the Government to disengage swiftly from industry and with increased benefit payments to the rising number of unemployed it was almost impossible to control public expenditure.

Nevertheless over the 11 years of the Thatcher Government a range of policy instruments were developed which were very different to those used in the Keynesian years. These included:

- Monetarism—a policy based on controlling inflation through controlling the amount of money in the economy
- Cutting the levels of personal and corporate taxation
- Abandoning the goal of full employment
- Cutting public expenditure
- Encouraging enterprise
- Privatisation of state-owned industries
- Reforming industrial relations legislation and effectively reducing the power of the trade unions.

Did Thatcherism end Britain's relative economic decline? There can be little doubt that the Thatcher years had a major impact on the structure of the British economy. Many policies concerned with intervention disappeared, the budget of the Department of Trade and Industry was cut substantially (and there was even talk of its abolition), large swathes of industry particularly heavy manufacturing like steel and shipbuilding, and primary industries like coal disappeared, others like telecommunication and car production were significantly restructured, trade union membership declined and inflation fell from the high levels of the 1970s. The 1980s also saw sustained periods of high economic growth. The Thatcher

Government did resolve some of the problems of the British economy but it did so at a very high price to those who were the losers in the process; the people who lost their jobs, the industries that disappeared and the regions of the country which were consigned to a long period of stagnation. The Thatcher years increased inequalities and removed life chances for large sections of the population. The impact on inner city areas and the loss of a sense of community is still felt in many parts of Britain today.

After Thatcher

John Major replaced Thatcher as the Prime Minister in 1990. The economic policy that he and his Chancellor, Norman Lamont, followed shared the basic framework of the Thatcher years. They were committed to controlling inflation. However, their tight monetary policy resulted in recession and the Government then relied on the European Exchange Rate Mechanism to produce recovery (see Thompson 1996). The intention of Lamont and Major was to use linking sterling to the Deutschmark at the rate of 2.95 as a mechanism for ensuring discipline in the economy. However, the markets saw the pound as overvalued and a series of currency speculations forced Britain to withdraw from the ERM. The Government's economy strategy was in tatters but ironically the devaluation of the pound resulting from the ERM exit acted as a boost to the British economy and gradually the economy came out of recession.

New Labour and economic policy

New Labour came to power in 1997 conscious of Labour's reputation with regard to economic management. The belief within the Labour Party leadership was that Labour's economic failures in government had resulted in its inability to ensure a sustained period in government. The financial power in the City of London and international markets regarded Labour as profligate in spending and too willing to raise taxes, which were seen as a disincentive to economic activity. Therefore, one of the main elements in Labour's economic policy was the need to reassure the markets that they could run the economy. As a consequence, underpinning Labour's policy was a commitment to macroeconomic stability. What this meant was that Labour would aim for low inflation and sound public finances (in other words they would not borrow excessively). The party also committed itself to not raising income tax and rejected any return to public ownership or the national economic planning that had existed in the 1970s.

The new Government attempted to institutionalise its new economic seriousness and it did this in three ways:

- In a radical and bold move Gordon Brown, the Chancellor of the Exchequer, announced on taking office that he would give independence to the Bank of England. This means that the Bank can now set interest rates according to economic criteria rather than the decision being made by the Chancellor and/or the Prime Minister on political grounds. What happens now is that the Chancellor sets an inflation target and the Bank has to set a rate which it believes is appropriate for achieving the target.

- The Government, in order to reassure the markets on public expenditure, committed itself to keeping spending within the plans set by the Conservative Government for the first two years.

- Gordon Brown announced that the aim in terms of public expenditure was to ensure that expenditure and income were in balance over the economic cycle. In addition, he introduced the golden rule; borrowing would only be for investment and not for current expenditure such as benefits, salaries, etc. However, in 2005 Brown decided to change the length of the economic cycle which to many critics appeared as a cynical attempt by Brown to avoid missing his original golden rule. As an *Independent* editorial stated on 20 July 2005:

> Gordon Brown's announcement that he is now of the opinion that the present economic cycle began in 1997—not 1999—lacked the fanfare with which the chancellor usually heralds his decisions. He slipped it out in his testimony to the Commons' Treasury select committee [on Monday]. The reason is not hard to discern. Mr Brown has opened himself up to the accusation that he has tarnished his 'golden rule' for managing the public finances.

Labour and public expenditure

Whilst the Government did stick to the Conservatives' levels of expenditure in the first two years, it redistributed money within the budget (so, for example, defence spending was cut but health expenditure was increased) and after the two-year moratorium it increased expenditure significantly (see Table 26.1).

	Long-term trend	April 1979 to March 1997	April 1997 to March 2003	April 2003 to March 2006
Social security	3.7	3.5	1.7	2.0
NHS	3.6	3.0	5.6	7.3
Education	4.0	1.5	4.1	5.8
Defence	−0.3	−0.3	−0.5	0.8
Transport	N/A	0.5	1.8	4.9
Law and order	N/A	4.0	4.8	1.1
GDP	2.4	2.1	2.8	2.8

Source: Emerson, Frayne and Love (2003)

Table 26.2 illustrates a number of interesting things about public expenditure. The first is that both Labour and Conservative governments have cut expenditure on defence. Indeed, defence spending has declined from 5.6% of GDP in 1963–64 to 2.4 in 2002–03. Second, despite the apparent antipathy of the Conservatives to the public sector and aspects of the welfare state, they increased public expenditure in health, education and social security. However, in both cases they increased at a slower rate than the general trend. Education in particular saw a much smaller growth. Labour, on the other hand, has increased spending on health and education well above trend. There can be little doubt that Labour has significantly shifted resources towards health and education in the period since 1997. For most governments in the post-war period, expenditure is close to trend. In other words, there has been a steady rise in public expenditure in the post-war period regardless of which party has been in power. However, Labour has significantly increased expenditure on health and education above trend. It is important to point out that expenditure on health in Britain is below that of comparable countries like France, Germany, Italy and the United States but over the next few years it will match and overtake the average of European spending.

The Labour Government has also changed the way that public expenditure policy is made. Public expenditure policy-making has long been a problem for government. The departmental nature of British government means that departments tend to have a lack of concern for the overall budget. Whilst they may be committed to government policy of restraining public expenditure, they tend to believe that the budget of their own department should increase. Their aim is to ensure that they receive the largest possible budget, and there is an incentive to do so because success as a minister is measured in terms of the ability to increase the budget. This leads to a situation where departments bid to the Treasury in excess of what they need. For many the process has become little more than a game (see Politics in Focus 26.5). Where departments overbid the Treasury, knowing that this is what department do, will only meet part of the bid.

Governments from John Major onwards have attempted to resolve the problem of over-bidding. John Major's Administration introduced the notion of a cash-limited spending

Lord Parkinson who was a Cabinet minister in the 1980s revealed what few ministers have been prepared to say:

I felt that the whole public expenditure round was a waste of time, and that if the spenders put in meaningful bids in the first place, and the Treasury behaved reasonably, the whole process would be a good deal shorter, much less acrimonious and would leave ministers free to concentrate on getting value out of their current programmes rather than spending so much time arguing about next year's. When I put the case at a meeting of ministers and senior officials, it was regarded as heresy.

Source: Smith (1998: 154–5)

round so that if a department wanted more money it could only come from the spending of another department, not through increasing the overall level of spending. Gordon Brown has sought to institutionalise this mechanism of public expenditure control through the Comprehensive Spending Review (see Politics in Focus 26.6).

Whilst Labour has attempted to control and plan public expenditure Labour's policy on public expenditure has been significantly different to that of the Conservatives:

(1) They have made an explicit commitment to increasing public expenditure. It is seen as a good, rather than a bad, thing.

(2) They have focused spending on welfare policy, particularly education and health.

(3) A large amount of the expenditure has gone into increasing jobs and pay increases, this has acted as a boost on the economy.

(4) The extent of expenditure is probably starting to stretch the boundaries of prudence. The deficit is outside the rule of the European Stability Pact and if Britain goes into recession, the Chancellor will face great difficulties.

Whilst Labour leaders have distanced themselves from the Thatcherite agenda on public spending, they have attempted to be closer to the Conservatives on taxation.

~~FOCUS~~ 26.6

~~Comprehensive Spending Review (CSR)~~

The Comprehensive Spending Review reviews spending over a three-year cycle. So that in year one the global totals for spending are set for the following three years. Departments have to plan their spending for the next three years in accordance with the totals set by the Treasury. According to Gordon Brown: 'By looking not just at what Government spends but at what Government does, the Review has identified the modernisation and savings that are essential. The first innovation of the Comprehensive Spending Review is to move from the short-termism of the annual cycle and to draw up public expenditure plans not on a one-year basis but on a three-year basis' (statement by the Chancellor of the Exchequer, 14 July 1998). Within the review, departments are also expected to make efficiency savings. Departments have to set public service agreements with the Treasury, which lays out the savings the department has to make over three years and the process of these savings is continually reviewed. Perhaps most importantly the CSR allows the Treasury to set the priorities in public expenditure. Under Gordon Brown, as we will see in Table 26.2, education and health have been given priority and therefore the money to fund expansion here reduces what is available to other departments within the global total. The process begins when in the budget the Chancellor sets 'a firm overall envelope' for total spending. In 2002 he set the total as a 3.3% increase in 2004–05 and 2½% in 2005–06. The total managed expenditure (TME) is split into two components: the Departmental Expenditure Limits (DEL) which are the fixed limits of spending for departments over the next three years and Annually Managed Expenditure (AME) which is spending that is not easily fixed over the next three years because it may be volatile or demand-led such as social security.

	2002–03	2003–04	2004–05	2005–06	Annual average growth rate 5
Education and skills	23,170	25,600	27,750	31,140	7.6
Health	58,000	63,930	70,260	77,250	7.3
Transport	7,660	10,690	11,200	11,640	12.1
Office of the Deputy Prime Minister	6,030	6,730	7,230	7,570	5.2
Home Office	10,680	12,280	12,730	13,530	5.6
Defence	29,330	30,920	31,760	32,780	1.2
Foreign Office	1,350	1,450	1,500	1,590	2.8
International Development	3,370	3,700	3,840	4,590	8.1
Trade and Industry	4,740	5,110	5,130	5,540	2.8
Environment, Food and Rural Affairs	2,520	2,900	2,890	2,940	2.7
Work and Pensions	7,020	7,530	7,800	7,820	1.1
Scotland	18,210	19,720	20,880	22,320	4.4
Total departmental limits*	239,710	263,740	279,820	300,990	5.2

*Columns do not add to totals because some departments have not been included in Table.
Source: HM Treasury

Labour and taxation

Government, of course, has to pay for public expenditure and the way that it does this is through taxation. In 2003–04 the Government received £9,020 for every adult in Britain and the largest source of this was through income tax (28.5%) (Adam and Shaw 2003).

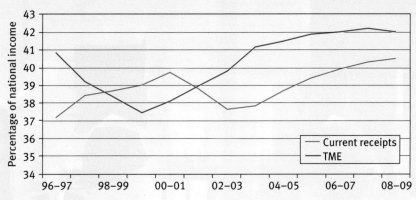

FIGURE 26.1

Receipts & spending as % GDP

Source: Institute of Fiscal Studies

Labour was keen to distance itself from the tax and spend policies that were seen as the core of the Keynesian welfare state. Labour committed itself explicitly to not increasing income tax and appeared to have abandoned the tax system as a mechanism for redistribution. However, despite the rhetoric Labour did raise extra income through the tax system. The first budget included £5.2 billion windfall tax on privatised utilities and the taxes on pensions were changed raising a further £5.4 billion. Through abolition of the married couple allowance and mortgage tax relief, and with increased national insurance, the Chancellor managed to raise extra money without increasing income tax. What is clear is that the tax burden has increased under New Labour, although they have not raised income tax. The IFS table demonstrates that government receipts through taxation have increased from about 37% of GDP to nearly 41% of GDP. If we take taxation and public expenditure together, the Labour Government has increased both spending and taxation. However, because of slower than predicted economic growth, there has been a decline in tax revenues and therefore the Public Spending Borrowing Requirement—the amount the government needs to borrow to meet its spending commitments—is predicted to grow over the coming years.

An important development in recent years has been the introduction of tax credits. Rather than government just using the taxation system to take money from people they have also used it as a mechanism for giving money; in other words it has become part of the welfare system. Since April 2003 there have been two tax credits: the child tax credit and the working tax credit. In the case of the child tax credit, families receive credit in the tax for children, which is adjusted according to income. The working tax credit provides support for people working on low incomes. It is a way of encouraging people on low incomes to work rather than to claim benefit. However, there have been problems with the

Source of revenue	2003–04 (£billion)	Proportion of total (%)
Income tax	122.1	28.5
National insurance	74.5	17.4
Value Added Tax (VAT)	66.6	15.5
Fuel duties	23	5.4
Tobacco duties	8	1.9
Alcohol duties	7.4	1.7
Betting and gaming duties	1.3	0.3
Vehicle excise duty	4.8	1.1
Air passenger duty	0.8	0.2
Landfill tax	0.7	0.2
Insurance premium tax	2.2	0.5
Climate change levy	0.9	0.2
Customs duties and levies	1.9	0.4
Capital gains tax	1.2	0.3
Inheritance tax	2.4	0.6
Stamp duties	7.9	1.8
Corporation tax	30.8	7.2
Petroleum revenue tax	1.5	0.4
Business rates	18.6	4.3
Council tax	18.6	4.3
Other tax and royalties	11.9	2.8
Interests and dividends	4.0	0.9
Gross Operating Surplus and other receipts	17.2	4.0
Current receipts	428.3	100

Source: Adam and Shaw (2003: 4)

calculation of tax credits and a large number of people have found their credits cut without notice.

Supply side policy

The other element of economic policy which has been important to government has been improving the supply side of the economy. In other words, attempting to improve the efficiency and productivity of the economy. The Government has been concerned to encourage investment and to improve the infrastructure and the use of technology. The Government has also tried to reduce the red tape on business and through its taskforce on regulation it has attempted to prevent new controls acting as a disincentive on business. For many commentators the Government developed a policy which is pro-business. In many ways it has followed Conservative policy of allowing business to operate as freely as possible within the market.

Labour has thus combined both elements of Conservative policy and traditional Labour policy in its economic approach. It has adopted Conservative prudence and is committed to a balanced budget (despite the problems of actually balancing the budget). It has promised not to increase income tax. On the other hand it has increased public expenditure and, through a range of mechanisms, it has increased the tax return to government. Nevertheless, Labour is pro-market and apart from the unusual case of the railways it is not committed to the public ownership or economic intervention of its predecessor. The crucial question though is has new Labour had a successful economic policy?

Has Britain's relative economic decline ended?

The issue of Britain's relative economic decline shaped Britain's economic policy for most of the post-war period (see Chapter 7). The question at the beginning of the 21st century is whether that relative decline has now ended. Table 26.4 demonstrates that Britain has done relatively well in recent years. For most years since 1993 Britain has grown faster than its competitors. The economy has, in particular since 1997, seen a significant growth rate when most of Europe has suffered a period of decline, or at least stagnation. In addition, what was one of the main problems of the post-war economy, inflation, seems to have disappeared. According to the Adam Smith Institute, 'Since 1960, annual inflation (measured as RPI-X) has averaged 6.7%. But since 1993, the average has been 2.6%—the same as in the United States and only marginally higher than the 2.1% average for Euro land over the same period.' Under Labour inflation has improved even more dramatically in 2003. The headline rate of inflation which includes all the items in the inflation index was less than 3%, the consumer price index, which excludes house prices, was 1.3%. Whilst Britain has seen marginally higher rates of inflation than some EU competitors, many European economies have been in recession. The period since 1997 has been one of sustained growth (see Tables 26.5 and 26.6).

Under Labour one of the key problems of the post-war era—the inability to combine economic growth and low inflation—seems to have been resolved. Economic growth has not been followed by a period of stop in order to control inflation. In 2004 economic growth remained at the relatively high rate of 3.25%. In addition, Labour seems to have removed unemployment as a problem. In the 1980s and 1990s it became general wisdom that high levels of unemployment, due to changes in technology and the labour market, would be a permanent feature of the economy. Even in the boom years

FIGURE 26.2
UK inflation (RPI-X), % average annual

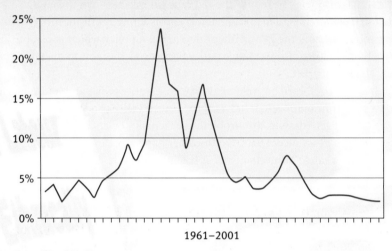

1961–2001

Source: Institute of Fiscal Studies

Country	Unemployment rate %
UK	4.8
Japan	4.9
US	5.7
Canada	7.4
Italy	8.5
Germany	9.2
France	9.5

Source: BBC http://news.bbc.co.uk/1/hi/business/3652269.stm, 27 April 2004

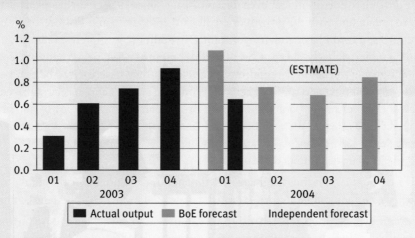

Source: BBC http://news.bbc.co.uk/1/hi/business/3652269.stm, 27 April 2004

of the 1950s it was believed that inflation and unemployment were trade offs. According to the Phillips curve low inflation would mean higher unemployment because with more unemployed people the price of labour would fall. However by March 2004 those claiming job seekers allowance was 882,200, the lowest since 1975. By 2004, Britain had the lowest level of unemployment amongst the G7, the seven largest economies in the world. However, there were significant regional disparities. Whilst unemployment in 2004 was 3.1% in the South East, it was 5.6% in the North East. However, two points need to be noted. First, the decline in unemployment is partly a change in definition and how unemployment is counted. Second, it seems in many areas of high unemployment large numbers of people have been reclassified as being long-term sick and so removed from the labour market.

What factors account for Britain's apparent economic miracle?

- The impact of the Thatcher years. Whatever the costs of Thatcher's economic policies they did have a major impact on the structure of the economy. Many of the inefficient British industries went bankrupt and the tax breaks and incentives introduced by Thatcher led to the development of high tech and service sector industries.

- Perhaps the most important change of the Thatcher period was the creation of a more flexible labour market. By weakening the position of the unions and making it easier to sack workers, the Thatcher Government effectively forced down the price of labour. Even with the minimum wage, the low paid are earning relatively less in the 21st century than they were in the 1970s. With a flexible and cheap labour force, employers are able to out-compete countries in the rest of Europe. In addition, social security benefits have declined relatively increasing the incentives to work for low paid jobs.

• The other important change was the deregulation of credit. Until 1979 it was actually quite difficult to borrow money even for a mortgage. Since 1979 credit has been relatively easy to obtain and with the growth of credit card companies and in-store credit cards, the sources of credit have grown significantly. In addition, low interest rates mean that credit is now relatively cheap. Cheap credit combined with rising house prices has allowed people to take out second mortgages which they have used to buy consumer goods. As a consequence, much of Britain's economic performance has been driven by a credit-fuelled consumer boom. The average British person now has over £4,000 in debt on credit cards, overdrafts and personal loans. There has been the development of private sector Keynesianism. Private borrowing rather than public borrowing is being used to stimulate demand in the economy.

• Increased public spending has increased the amount of money in the public sector creating a boom in public sector jobs which has created more demand in the economy.

• Gordon Brown's economic prudence and commitment to the golden rule on borrowing (money will only be borrowed for capital investment and the budget will balance across the cycle) has reassured the City and the currency markets and Labour has avoided the economic crises which have affected previous British governments. Britain has managed to retain the pound at a relatively high level, which has the effect of controlling inflation and forcing exporters to improve productivity.

How much of this success can be put down to the actions of Gordon Brown? It seems that Gordon Brown has made a number of astute decisions. In particular his decision to demonstrate prudence in the early years of the Labour Government has resulted in a high level of economic confidence. However, much of the success of the Labour Government has been the result of the flexible labour market and the credit boom created during the Conservative years. It is clear that the British economy has been more flexible than its European competitors in recent years and this has enabled it to adapt to changing economic conditions. Much of the success is a result of structure rather than agency.

The Euro

One of the key economic decisions which has hung over the Labour Government has been whether Britain should join the Single European Currency, the Euro (see also pp 166–8). In principle the Government is committed to joining the Euro if there is a referendum vote in favour. The argument for joining the Euro is that the British economy is closely tied to the EU now and that it should be at the heart of economic decision-making. It is also argued that the Euro area is now well-established and, after a shaky start, it has become a strong currency, particularly in relation to the dollar. Through the control of the European Central Bank, it is argued that the Euro will deliver long-term macroeconomic stability.

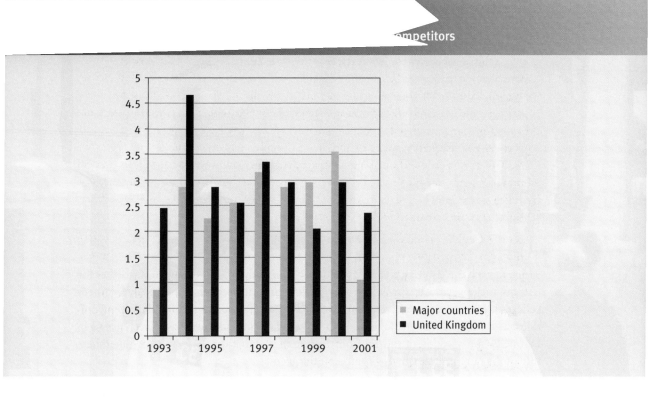

The arguments against the Euro are that it would end Britain's control over its own economic policy with interest rates being set in Europe rather than Britain. Many economists suggest that Europe is such a diverse economy that one interest rate for the whole area is too crude an instrument of economic control. It is also argued that whilst Britain has remained outside the Euro area, its economy has performed much better than those within the Euro. It is also suggested that the Euro area has failed to rigidly enforce the Stability Pact which has meant that certain countries have been borrowing more than they should. This means that the promised long-term stability may not survive.

The Labour Government has managed to avoid making a decision on the Euro through the use of the five conditions. The Government's position is that Britain will only join monetary union when five conditions are met. These are:

- British and EMU members' business cycles and economic structures have to be compatible.

- That there is sufficient flexibility to deal with problems.

- Would the EMU create better conditions of making long-term decisions concerning investment in Britain?

- What impact would EMU have on the competitiveness of the financial services industry?

- Will EMU promote higher growth, stability and stable employment?

In 2003, a statement by the Treasury on whether Britain had met the tests said:

> Overall the Treasury assessment is that since 1997 the UK has made
> real progress towards meeting the five economic tests. But, on
> balance, though the potential benefits of increased investment,
> trade, a boost to financial services, growth and jobs are clear, we
> cannot at this point in time conclude that there is sustainable and
> durable convergence or sufficient flexibility to cope with any
> potential difficulties within the euro area. So, despite the risks
> and costs from delaying the benefits of joining, a clear and
> unambiguous case for UK membership of EMU has not at the present
> time been made and a decision to join now would not be in the
> national economic interest (HM Treasury 2003:7).

Seeing that it is the Treasury, and ultimately the Chancellor, which is the judge of whether the tests are met, provides a convenient tool for delaying any decision until the Government believes that it can win a referendum. In the 2005 general election, Tony Blair seemed to rule out a referendum for the lifetime of the Parliament and the uncertainty created in Europe by the rejection of the EU Constitution means that the issue of British membership of the Euro is increasingly slipping off the agenda.

The globalisation debate and economic policy

One of the arguments which has been propagated by the Government is that as a consequence of globalisation, the Government has little option but to pursue market-led economic policies which enhance competition and provide a cap on wages. They suggest that in a global market, a lack of competitiveness will mean that Britain will lose jobs and investment to other countries. This suggests that economic policies are converging in the West and that we have effectively seen the end of any attempt to manage markets or develop a distinctive social democratic approach. The Government has pursued the de-regulation of the labour market as a response to what it suggests are the forces of globalisation. Likewise the Government has argued that it needs to lower corporation tax or companies are likely to move elsewhere. This is essentially a structuralist argument. The nature of the world economy has forced the Government to adopt a certain set of policies.

Hay and Rosamond (2002) demonstrate that there has not been convergence in economic and welfare policies and, indeed, there is considerable evidence to illustrate that globalisation is not a strong determining force in economic policy. They suggest:

- that patterns of social spending are very different throughout Europe; and
- there is little evidence that trade and investment are becoming more global. Indeed it is the case in Europe that trade and investment are increasingly European.

The conclusion is that there is little evidence of globalisation determining economic policy and that following liberal economic policies is a consequence of choice rather than structure. The Labour leadership has, in Hay's view, found it convenient for political reasons to pursue an economic policy that replicates the key principles of Thatcherite economic policy.

Conclusion

Economic policy in Britain has changed considerably since the 19th century. Yet what is apparent is that a number of themes remain constant. One of the central issues has been to what extent should the state intervene in the economy. For much of the 19th and early 20th century, the view has been that economic policy is best left to the market. However, the inter-war depression and the Second World War led to the development of much more interventionist policies. Intervention was combined both with a worldwide economic boom and relative economic decline. With the intensification of decline and the end of the period of growth, the British economy faced crisis in the 1970s. The response to this crisis was the reassertion of market principles by the Thatcher Government. The economic restructuring of the Thatcher years seems to have ended Britain's relative economic decline. New Labour has adapted some elements of Thatcherism. It continued the strategy of avoiding direct intervention in the economy and has attempted to maintain a balance between expenditure and income. Nevertheless, Labour has elements of policy that are distinctive from Conservative policy. Labour has continued to increase public expenditure and taxation and it seems to accept that the state does have a role in economic development, even if it is not committed to detailed intervention or bailing out bankrupt companies. Under Labour, economic growth has been fuelled by a credit boom and high levels of public expenditure. What is unclear is how long this can be sustained. Moreover, it is also apparent that economic policy is conducted within an international environment and whilst governments can affect domestic economic conditions, they can only do so within the context of the situation within the world economy. It is also clear that whatever the ideological position of governments, they will always see economic success as crucial for their survival and so will always have an economic policy that affects the lives of British citizens.

KEY POINTS

- Britain's Empire-led economic development resulted in limited state intervention in the economy.

- The problems of depression and the Second World War led to a rejection of a laissez-faire economic policy.

- The post-war period saw the adoption of Keynesian economic policy with increased economic intervention.

- Keynesian policies failed to halt the relative economic decline of the British economy and the end of the post-war boom revealed underlying structural weaknesses in the British economy.

- The Thatcher Government returned to a laissez-faire approach and initiated a process of deregulating the economy.

- Labour has continued the broad thrust of Thatcherite economic policy whilst at the same time increasing public expenditure and taxation.

- The period since 1997 has seen sustained economic growth and low inflation.

KEY QUESTIONS

(1) Why have British governments been reluctant to intervene in the economy?

(2) Why did Britain's economy declined relative to other European countries?

(3) Was Keynesianism a successful policy?

(4) To what extent did the Thatcher Government change the direction of economic policy?

(5) What accounts for the apparent success of Labour's economic policy since 1979?

IMPORTANT WEBSITES

Two excellent websites on economic policy are the Government's official one www.hm-treasury.gov.uk/index.cfm, which has a wealth of information and statistics. A perhaps more independent site is the Institute of Fiscal Studies www.ifs.org.uk which again has a lot of information on taxation and public expenditure policy. Information on international political conditions can be found at www.cepr.org/default_static.htm. For information on the Euro see http://europa.eu.int/ euro/entry.html and www.**euro**.gov.uk/.

FURTHER READING

A very useful account of Britain's economic policy and economic decline over the past hundred years can be found in A. Gamble (1990) *Britain in Decline*, London: Macmillan. All sides of the decline debate are reviewed in M. Kenny and R. English (2000) *Rethinking British Decline*, London: Macmillan. Different perspectives on Thatcherite economic policy can be found in A. Gamble (1988) *Free Economy and Strong State*, London: Macmillan and D. Smith, *From Boom to Bust*. Conservative economic policy in relations to sterling is well reviewed in H. Thompson (1996) *The British Government and the European Exchange Rate Mechanism, 1979–1994*, London: Pinter. Labour's economic policy is reviewed in C. Annersley and A. Gamble (2004) 'Economic and Welfare Policy' in S. Ludlam and M.J. Smith (eds) *Governing as New Labour*, London: Palgrave Macmillan. E. Balls and G. O'Donnell (2002) *Reforming Britain's Financial and Taxation Policy*, London: Palgrave provides a New Labour perspective on economic policy. A. Gamble and G. Kelly (2002) 'Britain and EMU' in K. Dyson (ed) *European States and the Euro*, Oxford: Oxford University Press provides an insightful account of Britain's relationship with the Euro.

Visit the Online Resource Centre that accompanies this book for links to more information on this chapter topic

CHAPTER TWENTY SEVEN

The welfare state

READER'S GUIDE

This chapter explores the politics of the welfare state in Britain. Welfare issues
such as education and health care have not only been key themes in recent
general elections, but illustrate some of the most important topics in
contemporary British politics such as the role of the state, ideas about
citizenship, rights and entitlement, and the challenges of providing welfare
services as both the demand for these services and welfare state expectations
rise. To explore these issues we look at the development of the welfare state and
at important aspects of welfare provision. We pay particular attention to the
welfare state under the Conservatives between 1979 and 1997 and under New
Labour since 1997. What has changed? What has remained the same?

Introduction

The welfare state is usually taken to be policies and spending on education, health care, social security, housing and personal social services such as care for the elderly. Table 1 shows welfare state expenditure between 1992 and 2002. This consistently amounted to around a quarter of national income. This spending has remained fairly constant since the 1970s, despite the Conservative Government's intention between 1979 and 1997 to 'roll back the frontiers of the state'.

While money is obviously of central importance to politics, there is more to the politics of the welfare state than spending. While it is necessary to explore the organisation of welfare and see where the money goes, we also need to recognise that there are important *ideas* about welfare that are both deeply embedded and strongly contested in British politics. These ideas relate to notions such as belonging and entitlement, as well as to the proper and legitimate role of the state in human life. We will see that debates about welfare have contained both *organisational* and *ideological* elements and that the two are, in fact, closely linked. These have become particularly clear in the first years of the 21st century as New Labour has sought to change some core aspects of the welfare state by, for example, seeking an increased role for the private sector in the delivery of public services. This has led to allegations that the Government is 'privatising' the welfare state, which is usually taken to mean that a commercial rather than public service ethos is corroding core welfare state values. The stakes are high for any government in this debate about welfare and public services because, while they are held dear by many electors, the costs of and demand for welfare state services remains enormous.

This chapter explores both the organisation of the welfare state and the ideas that underpin it. By doing so we can assess the main welfare and social policy objectives that have been pursued by British governments since the end of the Second World War, examine how these have changed, ask why these changes occurred and look at the ways in which financing and provision of public services have shifted.

The birth of the modern welfare state

At the creation of what could be called the modern welfare state by the Labour government of Clement Attlee (1945–51) the prevailing ideas informing welfare and social policy were social democratic. As Harris (1996: 122) puts it:

```
The rhetorical hallmark of the early years were the replacement of
'charity', 'dependency', 'moralism' and bureaucratic surveillance of
private lives by a new ethic of social 'citizenship'. The principle
would be universalism as opposed to selectivity, entitlement rather
than discretion, and benefits paid on the basis of needs rather than
means tests.
```

TABLE 27.1

Government welfare expenditure, 1992–2002

	1992 /93	1993 /94	1994 /95	1995 /96	1996 /97	1997 /98	1998 /99	1999 /00	2000 /01	2001 /02
Education	31,576	33,544	35,367	36,810	37,953	39,078	38,981	40,895	44,176	49,354
National health service	35,413	37,259	39,879	40,691	42,383	43,878	47,194	48,362	53,039	59,852
Welfare services	6,683	7,700	9,016	10,312	11,521	11,713	11,984	12,168	12,995	13,910
Social security benefits	78,846	85,805	87,941	90,534	92,217	92,146	93,929	95,586	98,899	105,992
Housing	6,984	5,919	5,634	5,445	4,593	3,415	3,605	2,825	2,947	2,973
Total government expenditure	159,502	170,227	177,837	183,792	188,667	190,230	195,413	200,051	211,988	232,081
Current expenditure	151,010	163,289	171,277	177,667	183,842	186,640	191,603	196,240	206,380	226,309
Capital expenditure	8,492	6,938	6,560	6,125	4,825	3,590	4,090	3,596	5,676	5,772
Total government expenditure	159,502	170,227	177,837	183,792	188,667	190,230	195,413	200,051	211,988	232,081
Central government	116,304	126,371	130,819	134,954	137,487	142,132	155,510	159,791	169,168	185,167
Local authorities	43,198	43,856	47,018	48,838	51,180	48,100	40,183	40,045	42,888	46,914
Total government expenditure	159,502	170,227	177,837	183,792	188,667	190,230	195,413	200,051	211,988	232,081
Total government expenditure on social services and housing as percentage of GDP	25.86	26.11	25.72	25.22	24.41	23.08	22.47	21.92	22.16	23.12

Source: Office for National Statistics

Although as Harris then goes on to point out, there was considerably more ambiguity at the time of the creation of the modern welfare state regarding both organisation and principles, there was also an emphasis on equality, social justice and social mobility measured through commitments to full employment and universal health care. These ideas and principles became components of what was seen as a form of consensus politics linking the two main political parties during the 1950s and 1960s, known as Butskellism. In the 1970s levels of welfare state expenditure came under attack as a result of economic problems and then after 1979 the rise of the New Right prompted a challenge both to the financial basis of the welfare state and to the ideas that had informed its development. For the New Right the welfare state was not a solution to Britain's ills, it was part of the problem because of the high costs it entailed and the culture of dependency that it generated among the recipients of welfare state benefits.

Pierson (1996: 139) notes that one of the strongest areas of contrast in British politics is between the social policy of the 1940s and that of the 1990s. New Labour came to power in 1997 with a welfare state that in terms of its organisation and underlying ideology had changed in important respects during the Conservative years. The New Labour Government was keen to portray itself as the saviour of the welfare state. But to what extent have the welfare state policies pursued by New Labour marked a break with the Conservative past? To answer this question requires that we explore the development of the British welfare state.

The development of the welfare state

While we may think of the welfare state as a creation of the period since the end of the Second World War, this would be a mistake. 'Folklore has it', wrote Pierson (1996: 142) 'that the British welfare state was sprung, pristine but fully formed, from the capacious mind of the great reformer [William Beveridge]' but there were significant innovations by the Liberal government of 1906–11 and by the Conservative governments of the late 19th century and between the wars. There are examples of nascent forms of welfare and social policy in the 19th century. The 19th century poor laws, for example, offered some protection while by the turn of the 20th century there were around 25,000 Friendly Societies with nearly seven million members that, on the basis of small contributions from their members, provided support in times of unemployment, sickness or in case of bereavement. However, the prevailing themes in welfare provision at this time were minimalism and voluntarism with the stigma and intrusiveness associated with means testing. Lacking too was a strong and coherent notion of social rights addressed to the state.

This changed after the Second World War, for a number of reasons. One reason was humanitarian. There were real concerns about poverty and need that were seen to blight the nation and contradict notions of building 'a land fit for heroes' for soldiers returning from the war. There were also instrumental concerns that a strong and healthy workforce was necessary to secure economic and social reconstruction. In tandem with these humanitarian and economic concerns were the links made between democratic and welfare rights because the denial of educational opportunity or decent health care would deny opportunity to some members of society. If the provision of services such as health and education were to be based on ability to pay then inequalities would be likely to persist across the generations. The social thinker T. H. Marshall, in his important work on the concept of citizenship, saw clear and important linkages between democracy and welfare. In *Citizenship and Social Class* Marshall composed a grand historical narrative within which the creation of modern citizenship would be the key and would contain three elements that would be a common possession for all members of the community.

- **Legal rights**
  Equality before the law
  Extended between the Glorious Revolution of 1688 and the 1832 Reform Act

- **Political rights**
  Political rights for all
  Enfranchisement for the working class and women between the 1832 Reform Act
  and the 1920s

- **Social rights**
  The creation of the welfare state
  Early development in the 19th century, with modern welfare state built after
  the Second World War.

The recently created welfare state was central to this vision of citizenship put forward by Marshall. Indeed, Marshall's concern was that citizenship would provide a vehicle for the integration of the working classes into a national culture that would be a common possession for all members of the community, not for the rich and privileged. Humanitarian and democratic concerns combined with an interest in economic reconstruction to motivate the work of Sir William Beveridge, who, in 1942, produced a report on Social Insurance and Allied Services that was to lay the foundations of the modern welfare state through an attack on the five giants on the road to reconstruction of Want, Disease, Ignorance, Squalor and Idleness. Beveridge was a Liberal and other prominent welfare state measures such as the 1944 Education Act had some Conservative contribution, but the main development of the welfare state was to occur during the Labour government led by Clement Attlee (1945–51). Both the Labour and Conservative Parties supported the Beveridge report, which helped it become a powerful component of the post-war political consensus. We can now look at the main pillars of the welfare state as it was put in place after 1945.

Extract 27.1: Social Insurance and Allied Services, Report by
Sir William Beveridge, presented to Parliament by Command of His
Majesty, November 1942, HMSO CMND 6404

The first principle is that any proposals for the future, while they
should use to the full the experience gathered in the past, should
not be restricted by consideration of sectional interests
established in the obtaining of that experience. Now, when the war
is abolishing landmarks of every kind, is the opportunity for using
experience in a clear field. A revolutionary moment in the world's
history is a time for revolutions, not for patching.

The second principle is that organisation of social insurance
should be treated as one part only of a comprehensive policy of
social progress. Social insurance fully developed may provide
income security; it is an attack upon Want. But Want is one only of
five giants on the road of reconstruction and in some ways the
easiest to attack. The others are Disease, Ignorance, Squalor and
Idleness.

The third principle is that social security must be achieved by
co-operation between the State and the individual. The State
should offer security for service and contribution. The State in
organising security should not stifle incentive, opportunity,
responsibility; in establishing a national minimum, it should
leave room and encouragement for voluntary action by each
individual to provide more than that minimum for himself and his
family.

The pillars of the welfare state

Health care

In 1944 a government White Paper entitled 'A National Health Service' was published. The three core aims were to ensure that all people 'irrespective of means, age, sex or occupation' could secure the medical care they needed through a comprehensive health system covering all aspects of preventative and curative medicine with health care separated from personal means, that is, free at the point of delivery. The National Health Service Act of 1946 proclaimed that health care would be 'free to all who want to use it'. The British Medical Association representing doctors strongly opposed this form of socialised medicine and some concessions were made to their interests, but by July 1948 Health Secretary, Aneurin Bevan, had steered the legislation through Parliament. In 1951 the

Labour Chancellor of the Exchequer, Hugh Gaitskell, introduced a charge of a shilling (5p) for every prescription and introduced charges for dentures and spectacles. Bevan resigned from the Government. In his resignation letter Bevan wrote that 'It is wrong [to impose national health charges] because it is the beginning of the destruction of those social services in which Labour has taken a special pride and which were giving to Britain the moral leadership of the world'.

Education

The Education Act 1944 created the Ministry of Education, raised the school leaving age to 15, and introduced a system of grammar, technical and 'modern' schools based on selection at the age of 11. The system was described by historian and Conservative MP Robert Rhodes James (1986: 281) as 'the single most important piece of legislation during the War'. The Act was significant in other ways too. It was supported by both main parties and also acquired—as did many other events of this time—a huge symbolic significance because, as future Labour leader Michael Foot was to put it at the time: 'the people's voice seemed to be expressed more powerfully and passionately and persistently then ever before'.

National insurance

The National Insurance Act 1946 guaranteed a minimum income based on contributions by those in employment (except married women). Alongside general taxation, national insurance was to provide the basic financial structure of the welfare state and was to cover unemployment, sickness, maternity, widows' benefits and old age pensions. People paid 4s 11d a week in contributions, which amounted to around 5% of the average wage. James Griffiths, the Minister of National Insurance, described it as 'the best and cheapest insurance policy offered to the British people, or any people anywhere'. The emphasis upon contribution blurred the notion of citizenship and entitlement. Also, the main contributors would be men which meant that social citizenship was seen in male terms with the contribution of women at work and in the home devalued (see Chapter 5). Contributory benefits would be paid from the national insurance fund. A conditions of entitlement to contributory benefits is that the claimant has paid sufficient national insurance contributions. These include unemployment benefit or disability benefits. Non-contributory benefits are those that do not require any national insurance contributions to have been made in order to receive them. These include carers' allowances.

Housing

The 1949 Housing Act led to major house building programmes with a major role played by local councils in the building of large council estates.

Challenges to the welfare state

At its foundation, we can see the influence of social democratic ideas on the welfare state (although Beveridge was a member of the Liberal Party) with the state playing a leading role in promoting social change because other institutions such as the market were unlikely to do so. The welfare state was founded on the ideas of 'reluctant collectivists' such as William Beveridge and the economist John Maynard Keynes and democratic socialists such as T.H. Marshall, Richard Titmuss and Anthony Crosland. In his book *The Gift Relationship*, Titmuss sought to explain why it was necessary for the state to intervene in welfare and social policies:

> The private market... narrows the choice for all men—whatever
> freedom it may bestow, for a time, on some men to live as they like.
> It is the responsibility of the state, acting sometimes through the
> processes that we call 'social policy', to reduce or eliminate or
> control the forces of market coercions which place men in situations
> in which they have less freedom or little freedom to make moral
> choices, and to behave altruistically if they so will.

The welfare state was to become a powerful part of the political consensus between Labour and the Conservatives. Historians have, however, pointed out that when we probe beneath the surface, notions of consensus can be more problematic than at first they seem. There was a broad measure of consensus between the Conservative and Labour Parties on the basic framework of the welfare state, the mixed economy, a commitment to full employment, and a minimum level of social security, but the parties remained divided over the appropriate level of state intervention (Lowe 2005). As is well known, this political consensus was to be challenged by Thatcherism, although the door had been opened by the attempts to rein in public expenditure by the previous Labour government (1974–79). Even so, as we shall see later total welfare state expenditure remained fairly constant during her time in office.

A key challenge from the new right was to the ideological foundations of the welfare state. In order to explore how and why this challenge to welfare came about and to think about some of its effects, it is worth exploring the contrasting ideas of two politicians whose views were central to the politics of the welfare state from the 1950s until today. On the Labour side, we will look at the ideas of Anthony Crosland and on the Conservative side at Sir Keith Joseph. These two prominent politicians are chosen because they both thought very seriously about the purposes, form and effects of welfare state provision. Their ideas were also to have an important effect on debates about welfare. We will see that the views of Joseph and of the New Right strongly influenced the Conservative governments between 1979 and 1997. The relationship between the ideas of Crosland and the ideas and governing practice of New Labour are a bit more distant, which also highlights some tension between what are called 'Old' and 'New' Labour.

Anthony Crosland (1918–77) in his book *The Future of Socialism* (1956) was to be a leading exponent of revisionist social democracy long before Neil Kinnock, John Smith and Tony Blair (see also Jefferys 2000). Crosland wrote that:

> [F]or all the rising material standards and apparent contentment, the area of avoidable social distress and physical squalor...are still on a scale which narrowly reflects the freedom of choice and movement of a large number of individuals. Secondly (and perhaps more intractable), we retain a disturbing amount, compared with some other countries, of social antagonism and class resentment, visible in both politics and industry, and making society less peaceful and contented than it might be. Thirdly, the distribution of rewards and privileges still appear highly inequitable, being poorly correlated with the distribution of merit, virtue, ability or brains; and in particular, opportunities for gaining the top rewards are still excessively unequal (Crosland 1956: 116).

Crosland looked to other countries such as the US as an example of a country with far greater social mobility than the UK or to Sweden where a comprehensive education system had helped build a society with more social consensus and solidarity. For Crosland education, or rather comprehensive education, was a central issue. This provides an interesting parallel because Blair came to power in 1997 proclaiming that his three priorities would be 'education, education and education'. Crosland though advocated a comprehensive system in the name of egalitarianism while the New Labour agenda has centred on quasi-markets (more of which later) and choice. For Crosland:

> Gradually the schools to which children will go will become, as in the United States, not an automatic function of brains or class location, but a matter of personal preference and geographical accident. The system will increasingly, if the Labour Party does its job, be built around the comprehensive school. But even in the large non-comprehensive sector, all schools will more and more be socially mixed; all will provide routes to the universities and to every type of occupation, from the highest to the lowest; and it will cease to occur to employers to ask what school job-applicants have been to. Then, very slowly, Britain may cease to be the most class ridden country in the world (Crosland 1956: 277).

For Crosland, the goals of the welfare state should be equality and redistribution. This, he argued, could lead to a future where economic growth and welfare were balanced and where attention could then turn to personal freedom with more emphasis on 'culture, beauty, leisure and even frivolity. Total abstinence and a good filing system are not now the right signposts to the socialist Utopia; or at least, if they are, some of us will fall by the wayside' (Crosland 1956: 524). These were no idle thoughts dispatched from an academic ivory tower because in January 1965 Crosland became Secretary of State for Education in Harold Wilson's Government. He introduced comprehensive education, but was unable to tackle the private schools.

Sir Keith Joseph (1918–94) adhered to some of the tenets of the post-war consensus labelled as 'Butskellism' after leading Conservative R.A.B. Butler and Labour leader Hugh Gaitskell. Joseph did, however, come to reflect very seriously on the relationship between them and his understanding of Conservatism. As he did this we see a strong contrast between his views and those of a social democrat such as Crosland. Joseph's view was that there was a tension between the welfare state as a device designed to promote equality and what he saw as people's desire for individual improvement. People did not want equality, thought Joseph, they wanted more (meaning pursuit of their own self-interest and material benefits). Joseph turned away from consensus politics which he saw as contributing to the inexorable increase of state power and erosion of individual freedom. This, following Hayek, could be labelled as a ratchet effect of collectivism. In 1975, in what amounted to a confession of error, he stated that 'I had thought that I was a Conservative, but now I see that I was not really one at all'. A particular target was the welfare state and its erosion of personal responsibility. Joseph distinguished between the 'worthy' and 'feckless' poor and advocated a Conservative approach that was both more selective and less dependent on the state:

```
We desperately want to end hardship, but because our resources are
limited we shall end it sooner if we concentrate our efforts and the
taxpayers money on those in need and if we try wherever possible to
help more people help themselves. To us self-help and voluntary
action are more desirable and more likely where practicable to be
effective than state intervention. We can state our objectives: to
strengthen the family, thrift and self-reliance; to strengthen
voluntary service; to remove crutches from those who can walk; to
strengthen the social network; to help those in need better than
ever before, setting to work forces that will of themselves reduce
the need for poverty, particularly in old age; to reduce
delinquency, boredom and purposelessness; to reinforce the
growing volume of voluntary effort so as to give far more people
the grace of helping others (Joseph 1966 cited in Denham and
Garnett 2002: 65).
```

In parallel with Joseph's view we can also point to an important development in academic analysis of the state with the rise of public choice theory (see Chapter 2). This developed in the 1950s with the work of Nobel prize winning economists James Buchanan and Gordon Tulloch (Buchanan and Tulloch 1962). Although there are many strands of thinking and it would be wrong to characterise public choice or variants of it as necessarily right wing or libertarian there was a strong influence of public choice theory on New Right thinking (Dunleavy 1991). The basic assumption is that individuals are self-interested and that this affects both economic and political behaviour. For Buchanan, public choice theory replaced 'romantic' notions about the workings of government based on altruism or ethics of service with an approach that was more sceptical. Public choice theory also identified the potential for interest groups with a strong incentive to organise to dominate the political process at the expense of the general public who possessed neither the same specialist knowledge of the insider groups nor the same incentive to organise. These specialist interests can thus capture government. What could be needed, from this point of view, was a complete reorientation of state activity to break the monopoly of special interests and to promote the interests of the users of services. This could mean reducing the power of public sector trade unions or expanding the role of the private sector in both the financing and provision of public services. With their views on special interests and the role of the market public choice theory has exercised some influence on the approaches of British governments to welfare.

We can now try to draw out some of the distinctions between a social democratic (or what might perhaps nowadays be called an 'Old Labour') view of welfare and the neo-liberal views of the New Right. Table 27.2 draws out distinctions on the basis of perceptions

	Social Democrats	**Neoliberals**
Ends	Social justice	Individual liberty
Means	State intervention	Market forces
Main threat	Inequalities and unfairness of the market	Ratchet effect of state intervention eroding personal freedom
Motivations	Co-operation is better than competition	Self-interest can promote the greater good
Agency (capacity for autonomous action)	Limited because of the power of environmental factors to shape behaviour	People do and should have choices
Role of state	Enabler	Safety net

Source: Adapted from Bevir and O'Brien (2001: 537) and Le Grand (2003: 11–16)

of ends and means, the motivations and agency of actors and perceptions of the state's role. The distinctions between social democratic and neoliberal thinking are, of course, broad and it is important to recognise that when we explore the meaning of political ideologies they are not closed systems, but instead are a: 'set of contrary themes, which continually give rise to discussion, argumentation and dilemmas' (Billig 1990: 6).

Comparing the welfare policies of the Conservatives and Labour

Table 27.2 attempts to draw out some of the broad distinctions between a social democratic and neoliberal understanding of the welfare state. This allows us to move the discussion on and explore some of the contemporary dilemmas that are central to welfare state politics. A tension can be seen between social democratic or what is sometimes called 'Old Labour' views of the universal welfare state with a bureaucratic mode of service delivery and a New Labour approach that modifies this in the light of some dilemmas highlighted by the New Right (Bevir and O'Brien 2001: 536). The conceptual language used to express these differences can be rather unclear. New Labour has seized upon terms such as the third way, stakeholding and community as expressions of its difference both from Old Labour and from the New Right. If we are to make sense of these kinds of concepts, their application and their usefulness then we need to explore the evolution of welfare policy since the mid-1970s. Following Hills (1998) we can do this by examining debates about public expenditure, privatisation, means testing/targeting and inequality.

Public expenditure

For Margaret Thatcher high public spending was a cause of Britain's social, political and economic woes. Yet, despite this, after 18 years of Conservative government between 1979 and 1997 the level of public expenditure devoted to the welfare state remained fairly constant at around 25% of national income. Overall, the level of government spending as a proportion of national income fell, but this was because of cuts in other areas of the budget such as on longer-term capital expenditure and defence. What did change was the distribution of spending within the welfare state budget. More was spent on health and social security and less on housing and education. For example, between 1975 and 1995 expenditure on education fell from 6.7% to 5.2% of national income. The date 1975 is also significant because it was not the election of Margaret Thatcher that heralded the onset of a new era of public expenditure management; rather it was the economic problems of the Labour Government between 1974 and 1979 and the economic constraints imposed by the International Monetary Fund after 1976 (see Chapter 26; also Burke and Cairncross 1992). There were also attempts to rein in the level of social security expenditure, which increased as unemployment soared in the 1980s. The main device used to do this was to break the link between benefits and earnings, which mean that the real value of benefits fell. Overall, however, the story of the Conservative years in power was 'not that of the continuous rolling back of the welfare state which many of its supporters might have portrayed at the time—or, indeed, which its supporters might have hoped for on its election' (Hills 1998: 2). The level of taxation remained at a fairly constant level too. Here, again, the major shifts were within the overall system with a move from direct taxation to indirect forms of taxation, such as increased VAT. Governments may claim to 'cut tax' but what they give with one hand (income tax cuts) they often take with another (VAT increases). Why wasn't the state rolled back? Why did the Conservative rhetoric not translate into action? A key reason for this is that the demand for welfare services has grown and, despite, some flirtations with privatisation, it was (and still is) to the state that most people looked to address their welfare needs. There were large increases in unemployment in the 1980s, which even after the breaking of the link between benefits and earnings increased the social security budget, while an ageing population placed additional strain on the health care system. Indeed, these underlying population dynamics are an important aspect of debates about the welfare state, particularly health care and pensions. British

IN FOCUS 27.2

ange and the welfare state

The UK population is projected to increase from 59.6 million in 2003 to 65.7 million in 2031 with a peak of around 67 million in 2050 after which it is expected to fall.

Of the projected 6.1 million increase between 2003 and 2031, 2.5 million (41%) is projected natural increase through births while 3.6 million (59%) is attributed to immigration.

As the population grows it is also expected to get older. The number of people of state pensionable age has been projected to rise from 11 million in 2003 to 12.5 million in 2020 and 15 million in 2031. This has implications for the demographic support ratio because in 2003 there were 3.34 people of working age for every pensioner, while by the 2040s the figure is projected to fall to around 2.30.

That immigration will be an important component of population change is clear, what is also clear is that immigration is not a magic bullet that will resolve issues of population change because immigrants get older too, which means that continuous, sustained and probably infeasible levels of immigration would be necessary to maintain support ratios. Only high immigration can produce more than a trivial reduction in the projected dependency ratio over the next 50 years. Net inward migration at +300,000 per year could bring the 2040 old-age dependency ratio down from 47.3% to 42.1%. But it is important to realise that this would only be a temporary effect unless still higher levels of immigration continued in later years, or unless immigrants maintained a higher birth rate than the existing population, since immigrants themselves grow old and become pensioners who need workers to support them.

Source: *Population Trends*, Winter 2004

people are living longer, which is not in itself bad news. An ageing population does, though, mean more retired people with fewer people in work to support them.

Labour under Tony Blair after 1994 were keen to shed their 'tax and spend' image. This meant that they committed themselves for their first two years in office to Conservative spending plans. They did so because of their fear that the Conservatives would exploit the tax issue as they had done at the 1992 general election with their 'tax bombshell' advertising campaign.

Analyses of the 1992 general election suggest that New Labour may have been unduly cautious because, as Heath, Jowell and Curtice (1994: 292) argue: 'there is no evidence that they [voters] were particularly averse to high taxation; rather they seemed to be people who had relatively little faith in Labour's ability to improve services like health and education'. Labour's only spending increases when it came to power were the 'New Deal' welfare to work programmes for the young unemployed, long-term unemployed and single parents funded by a £5.2 billion windfall tax on the profits of the public utilities privatised by the Conservatives.

Privatisation

Few issues are more controversial than the role of the private sector in the provision of public services (Pollock 2004). It is important, to distinguish between the *financing* of these services and whether that is by the private or public sector and the *provision* of these services by the public, private sector or voluntary. It could be argued that the real growth in the role of the market in the welfare state has been in the provision of public services and the development of 'quasi-markets' where the state retains responsibility for financing, but the private and voluntary sectors play an increased role in provision (Le Grand and Bartlett 1993). The next chapter shows how *quasi-markets* have been central to developments in health and education. Hills (1998: 10) pointed to greater private sector involvement in service provisions (which increased from 41 to 49% during the Conservative time in office) than finance (private sector finance only increased from 27 to 31%).

Probably the most significant change of the Thatcher years occurred in housing policy with the 'right to buy' policy seeing 1.7 million council houses sold to their tenants between 1981 and 1995. The 1979 Housing Bill gave those who had lived in their home for up to three years a 33% discount on the market value of their home, increasing to 50% for a tenancy of 20 years. A further incentive was offered to buyers with 100% mortgages from local authorities also on offer. Those who could not afford to buy their house could pay a £100 deposit and postpone the sale for two years at which point they could buy the house at the original price. The intention was to create a property owning democracy in the belief that people who owned their own home were more likely to vote Conservative. The role of the private sector increased in pensions too, but of the 5 million people who contributed to private pensions, it turned out that around half had been given bad advice in a mis-selling scandal that badly undermined confidence in the private sector (Hills 1998: 8).

Means testing

Traditionally the left have favoured universal welfare provision. Means testing was hated by many because of demeaning and intrusive tests that were seen as an affront to personal dignity. Means testing can facilitate the targeting of social security, but it is difficult to get public support for generous means tested programmes and means testing is stigmatised because individuals may face intrusive questioning. During the Conservative years there was increased targeting of welfare benefits. New Labour has preferred to 'target' benefits too through use of means tests.

Inequality

Inequality increased during the Conservative time in office because, although real incomes increased by an average of 40% in real terms between 1979 and 1997, this growth was particularly concentrated at the higher end of the income scale.

Of particular importance to the debate about poverty and welfare is the idea of deprivation. Absolute poverty is the level of income below which it is impossible to lead a healthy life. Relative poverty is a comparative measure that shifts over time. It is the level of income below which it is impossible to lead a normal life compared to other members of society.

During the Conservative years in government there was no official measurement of poverty, although there were unofficial studies. Research conducted for the Joseph Rowntree Trust published in 1999 provided a comprehensive and systematic overview of poverty in the UK. Far from diminishing it actually seemed to be increasing. According to the Rowntree research, in 1983 14% of households lacked three or more necessities because they could not afford them. That proportion had increased to 21% in 1990 and to over 24% by 1999. Items that were defined as necessities are those that more than 50% of the population believes 'all adults should be able to afford and which they should not have to do without'). By 1999, 26% of British population were living in poverty, measured in terms of low income and multiple deprivation of necessities.

While the Conservatives were keen to point to rising incomes, New Labour was keen to talk about poverty. They also brought new terms such as social exclusion and inclusion to the policy debate that reflected a more European take on welfare and social rights. A Social Exclusion Unit was set up in 10 Downing Street. There are, though, alternative readings of the term 'social exclusion' as Levitas (1999) has shown (see also Benn 2000: 311):

- The Radical Egalitarian Discourse (RED) would imply redistribution to tackle the many causes of social exclusion.

- Social Integrationist Discourse (SID) with paid work as the route to social inclusion. This is most closely linked to the New Labour take on social inclusion. Linked to it too has been a shift in the language employed to describe welfare provision from state-citizen to provider-client (Freeden, 1999: 43).

- The Moral Underclass Discourse (MUD) that links poverty to the behaviour of the poor and their 'dependency'.

Levitas (1999: 14) succinctly identifies the underlying differences between the three approaches: 'In RED [the poor] have no money, in SID they have no work, in MUD they have no morals'.

Conclusion

The welfare state is a complex creature. It contains a huge number of programmes and consumes a vast amount of money. It has been central to political debate in Britain and will remain so, because it touches upon those matters such as education, health care and social security that are central to most people's lives. In this chapter we have explored some of the organisational features of the welfare state, but also tried to look at some of the ideas that animate these practices. These ideas centre on notions of those who are deserving and entitled to welfare state benefits. These ideas are not always universally applied. Pensioners, for example, tend to be seen as fully deserving recipients of welfare state benefits, while attitudes towards lone parents can be far more ambivalent. Similarly, many people may hold the idea that the welfare state is a vehicle for redistribution from the richer to the poorer members of society. This Robin Hood model of welfare does not always hold true. In fact, it has been shown the some aspects of the welfare state such as university education have been fairly effective ways to transfer resources from poorer to richer members of society. This may be one reason why Conservative governments have retained a commitment to the welfare state because it has rewarded those middle class people they see as their natural supporters (or 'hard working families', as they were labelled by both the Conservative and Labour Parties during the 2005 general election campaign). For New Labour the core dilemma has been the role of the state and the role of the market. We explore this dilemma in the next chapter. As well as embodying a set of ideas about belonging and entitlement, the welfare state also has an organisational dimension. Here too the scope and extent of provision is vast. Two key issues are, however, the funding basis of welfare and the modes of delivery. In the next chapter we look at funding and delivery far more closely when we explore health and education policy.

KEY POINTS

- Discussion of the welfare state centres on both its organisation and the ideas that underpin it.

- The ideas informing the development of the welfare state had a strong social, democratic influence.

- The pillars of the welfare state were the NHS, education, national insurance and housing.

- The welfare state became a powerful component of the post-war political consensus.

- From the 1970s the ideas of the New Right challenged the welfare state consensus.

- New Labour, in power since 1997, has sought to combine a commitment to the welfare state with some elements of the New Right critique.

- A key feature of current debates about the welfare state is the role of the market and the development of 'quasi-market' relationships.

1 What are the key features of the British welfare state?

2 To what extent did the welfare state reflect social democratic thinking?

3 What were the main elements of the New Right critique of the welfare state? How justified were they? What effects did they have?

4 In what ways do the welfare state and social rights fit with understandings of citizenship?

5 What role, if any, should the market play in delivering public services?

IMPORTANT WEBSITES

To get more information about the historical development of the welfare state then see the websites of the Institute for Contemporary British History www.icbh.ac.uk and Institute for Historical Research www.ihr.ac.uk. On the functioning of the welfare state then see the websites of key government departments such as the Department for Work and Pensions www.dwp.gov.uk, Department for Education and Skills www.des.gov.uk and the NHS website at www.nhs.gov.uk.

FURTHER READING

There are a number of good books that survey the historical and political development of the British welfare state. See D. Gladstone (1999) *The Twentieth Century Welfare State*, Basingstoke: Macmillan; H. Glennester (1995) *British Social Policy Since 1945*, London: Blackwell; D. Hirst (1999) *Welfare and Society 1832–1991*, Basingstoke: Macmillan; G. Lewis (ed) (1998) *Forming Nation, Framing Welfare*, Basingstoke: Macmillan; R. Lowe (ed) (2000) *The Welfare State in Britain*, Basingstoke: Macmillan; N. Timmins (1995) *Five Giants: A Biography of the Welfare State*, Hemel Hempstead: Harvester Wheatsheaf.

CHRONOLOGY

1942	Beveridge Report
1944	Education Act
1944	White Paper on a National Health Service
1945	Labour government led by Clement Attlee elected
1946	National Health Service Act
1946	National Insurance Act
1949	Housing Act

 Visit the Online Resource Centre that accompanies this book for links to more information on this chapter topic

CHAPTER TWENTY EIGHT

Health and education policy: the welfare state we're in

READER'S GUIDE

Health and education demonstrate the ways in which politics and political decisions really matter to people's lives. For this reason, health and education have been, are and will continue to be key election issues. Spending on health and education also consume an increasing amount of people's tax contributions. This chapter takes forward the themes developed in the previous chapter about welfare state development and applies them to the funding and provision of health care and education. Our particular interest is on the respective roles of the state and market in the health and education policies of the Conservatives between 1979 and 1997 and those pursued by New Labour in power since 1997.

Introduction

Have New Labour created a new welfare state? When they came to power their rhetoric was grandiose as they spoke of saving the welfare state from the clutches of Conservative government. At the 2001 general election the perceived failure to deliver was one reason why people may have stayed away from the polls, disillusioned by a culture of spin and a perceived failure to 'deliver'. After the 2005 general election, Tony Blair declared that he wished he had actually gone further with many of his welfare state reforms. This provoked cries of anguish from opponents on the left who argued that the introduction of market forces into the welfare state had already gone far enough. In this chapter we ask what is old and what is new in the education and health care policies of New Labour. These are key aspects of welfare provision where we see a huge role played by the state and debates about creeping privatisation of public services. We see that in terms of spending there was some break when New Labour came to power because, after initially adhering to Conservative spending limits, after 1999 spending on health and education increased, but in terms of the role of the market in the delivery of public services we see elements of continuity with the policies of previous Conservative governments. As a result, the welfare state remains a powerful presence in British society and politics, but the ways in which it is organised have changed with a greater role for the market and commercial influences. This chapter begins by exploding some welfare state myths in order to show the continued relevance of the welfare state. The chapter then looks at the health and education policies of the main national political parties in 2005 to identify the key issues. This is followed by an exploration of some ideas that have influenced recent government policy, particularly the prominent role of quasi-markets in health and education and the rise of targeting and an audit culture. The chapter then looks more closely at health and education policy. The aim is to explore what is old and what is new in the welfare state politics of New Labour and to show that while funding has increased there is a strong element of continuity in terms of the emphasis on market mechanisms for the delivery of key public services such as health and education. Through their emphasis on public services New Labour have helped reshape the political agenda, but have done so in a way that changes the ways in which these services are delivered.

Welfare state myths

There are certain myths about British politics that can acquire real influence on the way some issues are understood. The welfare state is one area where these myths have burrowed their way into the political consciousness. One such myth is that the Conservatives in power 'rolled back the state'. We have seen in the previous chapter that in terms of size and expense the welfare state remained at basically the same level throughout the Conservatives' period in office. What changed were less visible—albeit no less important—shifts in ideas about the ways in which these services should be provided with a greater role for the market and market forces. A second is that a strong aversion to paying increased taxes to fund improved public services was a central factor explaining Labour's defeat in the 1992 general election. An aversion to then Labour leader Neil Kinnock being in charge of actually spending tax payers' money seems to have been a stronger motivational factor for many voters rather than a reluctance to fund improvements in key public services such as health and education. A third is that globalisation erodes the welfare state. Here, globalisation refers to the ways in which linkages between societies and economies have intensified. A problem with the view that globalisation inevitably erodes the welfare state is that, first, when we look at welfare state spending the empirical evidence for this assertion appears weak. Furthermore, it also subscribes to a rather narrow 'there is no alternative' perspective that see states and their governments as powerless in the face of globalisation. Evidence from across the EU shows welfare states to be under pressure for a variety of reasons, of which globalisation may well be one, but we should be cautious about ascribing such causal power to the sometimes rather nebulous notion of globalisation.

The welfare state myths to which we have referred relate to the role of the state and elected governments to manage welfare states and change their direction. These are the core themes that we take forward in the remainder of this chapter. Despite overblown talk of the state being rolled back, the welfare state is still with us and the services it provides are highly valued by most people. It will also remain a key political issue. However, the debate about welfare state services such as education and health has shifted over the last 50 years. Indeed, as we noted in the previous chapter, it is in the area of social policy that we see the biggest contrasts between the situation in the 1950s and that at the turn of the 21st century. The main debate is not so much about funding, but about the role of the market and market mechanisms in the delivery of public services.

The welfare state and the market

The market is central to social and political relations because Britain has an economy within which private ownership is a key feature and the market a core mechanism for the allocation of goods and services. A feature of capitalist societies such as Britain—and a fundamental component of a 'welfare state' critique of them—is that inequalities can emerge and that market forces may actually perpetuate and exacerbate rather than diminish these inequalities. This is where the welfare state steps in to redistribute and moderate market-produced inequalities, or at least this is the theory. The market does, however, play a role in the delivery of public services such as health and education and this role has increased over the last 30 years. One reason for this is that the creation of markets or market-like mechanisms in public service provision can change the incentive structure for public service providers in ways that improve the quality of services for users of services. In turn, this touches upon a broader debate about the motivations of those who provide public services such as teachers, doctors and nurses and the rest of us that use them. It is, therefore, useful to think a little more deeply about the motives of public service providers, how these are understood, and how these understandings of motivation affect health and education policy.

Before we do this, though, we can survey the policies of the three main national parties in the areas of health and education to get a sense of what the key issues were in the first decade of the 21st century. It is also worth noting that devolved power to Scotland and Wales has seen the Scottish Parliament and Welsh Assembly acquire powers over health and education policy. Health and education policy have been subject to changed patterns of governance in the sense that we see an increased role for the market and also some multi-levelling of policy with a greater role for sub-national political authorities.

The debate between the political parties at the 2005 general election was not so much about funding because the Conservatives too proclaimed a desire to spend on health and education. The differences occur when the respective roles of the state and market are factored into the analysis. The difference is not about whether or not the market should be involved in public services, but about how strong this role should be. The role of markets in provision of public services has undoubtedly increased, or to be more precise, the role of the quasi-market has increased. This is where the state provides the funding, but provision may be arranged by the private, public or voluntary sectors (see Chapter 13). When we look at current debates about health and education policy we see that much of them centre on the shape, form, content and effects of these quasi-markets.

This enthusiasm for market mechanisms in the delivery of public services does mark a change for the Labour Party. This is most obvious if we contrast current policies in health and education with that strand of social democratic thinking on welfare evident in the 1950s in the work of those such as Richard Titmuss in his book, *The Gift Relationship* which saw the market as inducing inequalities. Market forces from this perspective were the road to inequality. It was the role of the state to correct these. New Labour are much more relaxed about market forces and see them as a way to deliver the new public service buzzword 'choice' for the consumers of public services.

Health, education and party politics

In this section we look at where the three main national parties stood following two terms of Labour government. It gives us a sense of what the three main parties' policies were during the first decade of the 21st century on health and education policy. The sections that follow then seek to explain these policy directions in terms of what they tell us about the ideas concerning the delivery of public services. We then look more closely at the ways in which health and education policy has evolved over the last 30 years.

By 2005 there was a fairly widespread agreement amongst the parties that health and education spending should remain priorities and that the increases initiated by New Labour should basically be maintained (and whose promises were seen as most credible by the electorate). The points of disagreement between the parties concerned the respective roles of the state and private sector with some division between Labour and the Conservatives about the extent of choice, the use of targets and tests and the scope for local political control.

FOCUS 28.1
...rty and the welfare state at the 2005 general election

Health

- Increased spending on health by £34 billion and education by £15 billion a year by 2009–10
- Reduced waiting times
- Increased ability for patients to choose any healthcare provider in the NHS.

Education

- 3,500 pre-school children's centres by 2008
- 85% of children in primary school should be reaching expected level of literacy and numeracy at age 11
- Creation of 200 independently managed city academies by 2010 or soon after
- Higher education tuition fees of up to £3,000 a year to help fund an expansion of the system so that 50% of people between the ages of 18 and 30 would go into higher education.

Labour summary: In 1997 New Labour came to power making bold claims they would save the welfare state. By 2001 there were allegations that spin had triumphed over delivery. After two years of spending restraint, Labour began the 21st century with large increases in health and education expenditure. This increased expenditure was tied to a welfare state reform agenda. For New Labour, the idea of 'choice' and the attempt to empower welfare state users has become a key element of welfare state policies. This has been balanced by a concern to set targets and monitor performance from the centre.

POLITICS IN FOCUS 28.2
...rvative Party and the welfare state at the 2005 general election

Health

- A greater role for the private sector in health care
- Pledged to match Labour's health care expenditure
- Abolish all waiting for treatment within five years
- Patients able to choose any private or NHS hospital with a patient using the private sector having 50% of the costs covered by the public sector.

Education

- Parents able to take state funds to spend on any school whether state or independent
- Schools able to set their own admissions policy, which could include academic ability tests
- No higher education tuition fees.

Conservative summary: Public services have long been Labour Party territory. The Conservatives have lagged far behind Labour in public opinion polls on these issues. In the 2001 general election the Conservative campaign barely mentioned these issues, although they were core concerns for many voters. During his time as party leader, Michael Howard tried to correct this. The Conservatives have sought to match Labour commitment to education and health funding, but see a greater role for the market in health and education.

From this overview of key themes in the health and education policies of the three main national parties we can begin to get a sense of the parameters of the debate. At the heart of this are two core issues: the first is the level of spending. The second is the mode of provision and the balance of power between the central state, the local state, the private

Health

- Favoured increased health spending
- No ideological objection to giving people a choice of health care providers
- Local management of hospitals by giving more powers to local government.

Education

- Favoured increased education spending
- Abolish all schools targets, which they claimed had a distorting effect on schools' priorities
- Abolish higher education tuition fees.

Liberal Democrat summary: The Liberal Democrats were the only one of the three main parties that said they would increase income tax for high earners in order to fund spending on public services. The Liberal Democrats also sought a greater role for elected local government as part of their 'small f' federalism centred on decentralisation of power.

sector and voluntary organisations. It is in this latter area that we see most evidence of change over the last 30 years or so. To understand why this has been the case requires that we delve a little more deeply into some of the key ideas that have informed welfare state policy. In the previous chapter we contrasted the thinking of those such as Anthony Crosland who can be linked with a social democratic strand of welfare state thinking and Sir Keith Joseph who was central figure in the new right critique. In the section that follows, we look at welfare state thinking as it has developed since the 1990s with particular interest in the location of New Labour welfare policy in relation to what could be seen as more traditional social democratic strands of thought and to the New Right.

 # Thinking about the welfare state

The reference point for discussion of welfare tends to be 'the state'. People tend to see a key role for 'the state' in the provision of welfare services. In some senses too they expect 'the state', impersonal as it is, to care about them. It is, though, difficult to analyse the state as a single homogenous entity (see Chapter 3). This becomes clear when we look at the welfare state. By thinking about the diversity and heterogeneity of the welfare state we can also begin to get a sense of some of the dilemmas that confront those who make and implement health and education policy. In health and education policy we do see a key role for the central state, in particular the control of the purse strings. We also see a role for devolved and local government, as well as the private and voluntary sectors.

If we look at health care more specifically, for example, we see a role for central government, local authorities, health authorities, professional associations, trade unions, patients groups, charities, universities and the private sector. Each of these groups has different clients and may well see things differently. The motivations of those central to the provision of public services, as well as the capacity of the users of these services to express their views has become a key issue in debates about the welfare state.

Does one size fit all?

There has been a strong critique of the 'one size fits all' welfare state which, in the NHS, for example, meant that 'it was the expert who would determine the need for health care' (Klein 1995: 248).

The New Right critique questioned the motives of providers and, drawing from public choice theory argued that they would pursue their own interests rather than those of the users of services. The users of services would be treated as passive recipients getting what was best for them, whether they liked it or not. David Marsland (1996: 85–6) criticised an 'extravagantly excessive' welfare state that was 'driving Britain into bankruptcy'.

The bankruptcy was both economic and psychological because of a 'dependency culture' that would erode the sense of individual responsibility. From this point of view the providers of public services were likely to be motivated by self-interest that did not serve the public good, while the welfare state would erode self-reliance. Some have argued that the welfare state should be dismantled in order to return to the voluntary and charitable provision of the 19th century (Bartholomew 2004).

New Labour has certainly not advocated the dismantling of the welfare state; far from it, in fact. What they have done, however, is take on board some ideas from the New Right about the role of the market. A real insight into the thinking behind Labour's health and education policies since 1997 is provided by LSE professor and New Labour welfare advisor, Julian Le Grand, in his book, *Motivation, Agency and Public Policy: Of Knights and Knaves, Pawns and Queens* (2003). He argues, using a chess metaphor, that the welfare state settlement as it developed after the Second World War was based on the view that the providers of welfare states services were *knights* motivated by the interests of the people they were serving while the users of services were *pawns* compelled to take what was on offer as decided by experts such as teachers and doctors. Le Grand argues that at times more *knavish* motivations of self-interest might enter the calculations of service providers, while he also argues that a key challenge for the 21st century welfare state is how to give the users of welfare services real power, that is, to turn them into *queens*, the most powerful piece on the chess board. This would require an alignment of knightly and knavish incentive structures, which to some extent would require competition in the provision of public services. Without this then, drawing from the work of Hirschman (1970) on voice, exit and loyalty, the wealthier members of society may find that they have little chance to express their opinions, to use voice, and so would exit the public sector and seek private health care and education. One example of this could be in education where, Le Grand argues, children from poorer areas could receive a larger educational budget so that schools would compete to take them. Those schools with more children from poorer backgrounds would have larger budgets, be able to afford better equipment and employ the best teachers. This would also counteract a nagging concern that many supporters of the welfare state have had about its effects on the distribution of income and opportunity. Rather than redistributing from the richer to the poorer members of society, welfare states have sometimes redistributed from the poor to the middle classes.

A commercial ethos

The introduction of a commercial ethic to the provision of public services has though attracted criticism. Crouch (2003: 59) argues that mechanisms that encourage participation by the users of pubic services do make sense because it challenges an assumption 'that a central administrative class could determine the needs of the public without much interaction other than that provided by the formal parliamentary process'. Commercialisation, according to Crouch, may not be the answer because the rationale for commercialisation is that the 'quality of public services will be improved if the existing practices and ethos of the public service are replaced by those typical of commercial practices'. The main weakness of this approach, he then argues, is that commercial logic would lead to a focus on those areas of public service that are good for business and that this would corrode the universal value of citizenship. He argues that this is most evident in education where a regime of testing for schoolchildren means that teachers concentrate on those aspects of activity that are rewarded by tests and neglect those that are not. This is because the test results inform the league tables and thus whether a school is 'good' or not. We can now move on to look more closely at developments in the provision of education and the extent to which this sector has been commercialised.

Education policy

For Anthony Crosland, the Labour politician and former Secretary of State for Education, one of his main achievements was to end the divide between grammar schools and 'secondary moderns' and the introduction of comprehensive education. For many on the left this divided system had been a source of much disappointment. As Clyde Chitty put it:

> The realisation among sociologists that in the post-war divided system, grammar schools were largely middle-class institutions while children from working class families invariably found themselves relegated to second-class secondary moderns schools seemed to offer a compelling reason for supporting the reorganisation of secondary education along comprehensive lines.

Since 1979 the idea of comprehensive education has been eroded. In 1988 the Conservatives Education Reform Act made major changes to the schooling system:

- **Perceived failing: students not learning the basics**
  Conservative answer: a national curriculum—a government-sanctioned common curriculum for pupils aged 5–16 shifted responsibility for what was to be taught from teachers to central government.

- **Perceived failing: poor pupil performance**
  Conservative answer: testing—national tests at the ages of 7, 11 and 14 (SATS) with results published annually in league tables (along with GCSE/A level results and truancy statistics).

- **Perceived failing: poor local management of education**
  Conservative answer: local management of schools with management responsibility shifted from Local Education Authorities and given to individual schools. Some schools would be able to opt out of LEA control.

- Perceived failing: failing inner city schools
  Conservative answer: City Technology Colleges specialising in technology, the arts, maths and science set up in inner city areas.

- Perceived failing: lack of accountability
  Conservative answer: the creation of the Office for Standards in Education (OFSTED) with a new inspection regime for schools, inspections every six years and the naming and shaming of 'failing' schools.

New Labour and education policy

The Labour Government after 1997 made it clear that education—or education, education, education, as Blair listed his three top priorities—would be central to the actions of the new government. Education was, though, strongly liked to employability and to the demands of what is called 'the knowledge-based economy'. As the Government's 1997 White Paper on education put it: 'We are talking about investing in human capital in the age of knowledge'. As a New Labour thinker put it summoning the ghost of Charles Dickens: 'education needs to leave behind the organisational models inherited from the nineteenth century' (Leadbetter 1999: 10). When New Labour came to power they inherited and maintained the Conservative focus on numeracy and literacy and maintained both the testing and inspection regimes. New Labour also abolished the 'assisted places' scheme which had allowed small numbers of pupils from state schools to attend private schools.

It is also useful to think comparatively about these developments. Labour also inherited some common features that have been evident in the education policy of many economically developed countries. Bevin (1998) likens these pressures for education policy change to an epidemic, by which he means phenomena that move across populations, but happen to people rather than being things that people cause to happen.

(1) Economic pressures have led to pressure for educational change. Education has become part of the quest for so-called 'national competitiveness'. For much of the post-war period education was more closely linked to equality and social mobility. In some ways the UK could be seen to be doing well in international terms. A report for the rich nations' think-tank, the Organisation for Economic Co-operation and Development (OECD) showed Britain to rank seventh in reading, eighth in maths and fourth in science. By these measures, Britain was doing better than Germany, Italy, France and the US. What got less attention was a statement later in the report that high performance in Britain was combined with above average inequality: 'students are highly segregated along socio-economic lines, in part because of residential segregation and economic factors, but also because of features of the education system itself' (OECD 2000: 196, cited in Chitty 2002: 210).

(2) Criticism of schools and teachers for 'failing' legitimises change.

(3) Change has not necessarily been matched by funding.

(4) Changed patterns of governance with more emphasis on devolved management, plus accountability through league tables and parental choice.

(5) Education becomes more like a commercial commodity through extended choice.

(6) Emphasis on standards, accountability and testing. In 2004, testing at what are called Key Stages 1, 2 and 3 (at ages 7, 11 and 14) showed improved performance in maths and English, but a decline in science results in primary and secondary schools. The test results fell short of government targets. The National Union of Teachers argued that the obsession with testing gave parents and pupils the impression of poor performance and failing when the story as they saw it was one of success and improvement.

Education is one area where the urge to 'deliver' has led to a culture of targeting. At the centre of government is the Prime Minister's Delivery Unit, which was established in June 2001 after the second Labour election victory when low voter turnout was linked to a failure by the Government to deliver on public service reform. For the Department for Education and Skills there is a Public Service Agreement that specifies targets and the time by which they are to be met.

POLITICS IN FOCUS 28.4

Help build a competitive economy and inclusive society by: creating opportunities for everyone to develop their learning; releasing potential in people to make the most of themselves; achieving excellence in standards of education and levels of skills.

Objectives and performance targets

Objective I: sustain improvements in primary education.

1. Raise standards in English and maths so that:
   - by 2004 85% of 11 year olds achieve level 4 or above and 35% achieve level 5 or above with this level of performance sustained to 2006; and
   - by 2006, the number of schools in which fewer than 65% of pupils achieve level 4 or above is significantly reduced.

Objective II: transform secondary education.

2. Raise standards in English, maths, ICT and science in secondary education so that:
   - by 2004 75% of 14 year olds achieve level 5 or above in English, maths and ICT (70% in science) nationally, and by 2007 85% (80% in science);
   - by 2007, the number of schools where fewer than 60% of 14 year olds achieve level 5 or above is significantly reduced; and
   - by 2007 90% of pupils reach level 4 in English and maths by age 12.

Objective III: pupil inclusion.

3. By 2004 reduce school truancies by 10% compared to 2002, sustain the new lower level, and improve overall attendance levels thereafter.

4. Enhance the take-up of sporting opportunities by 5–16 year olds by increasing the percentage of school children who spend a minimum of two hours each week on high quality PE and school sport within and beyond the curriculum from 25% in 2002 to 75% by 2006. Joint Target with DCMS.

28.4

Objective IV: raise attainment at 14–19.

5. Raise standards in schools and colleges so that:
    - between 2002 and 2006 the proportion of those aged 16 who get qualifications equivalent to 5 GCSEs at grades A* to C rises by 2 percentage points each year on average and in all schools at least 20% of pupils achieve this standard by 2004 rising to 25% by 2006; and
    - the proportion of 19 year olds who achieve this standard rises by 3 percentage points between 2002 and 2004, with a further increase of 3 percentage points by 2006.

Objective V: improve the skills of young people and adults and raise participation and quality in post-16 learning provision.

6. By 2004, at least 28% of young people to start a Modern Apprenticeship by age 22. A wider vocational target for 2010, that includes learning programmes in further education preparing young people for skilled employment or higher education will be announced in the 2002 Pre-Budget Report.

7. Challenging targets will be set for minimum performance and value for money in FE colleges and other providers by the Government and the LSCs. (This is also the department's **value for money** target.)

8. By 2010, increase participation in Higher Education towards 50% of those aged 18 to 30. Also, make significant progress year on year towards fair access, and bear down on rates of non-completion.

Objective V: tackle the adult skills deficit.

9. Improve the basic skill levels of 1.5 million adults between the launch of Skills for Life in 2001 and 2007, with a milestone of 750,000 by 2004.

10. Reduce by at least 40% the number of adults in the UK workforce who lack NVQ 2 or equivalent qualifications by 2010. Working towards this, one million adults already in the workforce to achieve level 2 between 2003 and 2006.

Who is responsible for delivery?

The Secretary of State for Education and Skills is responsible for delivery of the PSA. The Secretary of State for Culture Media and Sport is jointly responsible for delivering target 4.

The end of 'bog standard education'?

An important development in New Labour education policy was the challenge to what the Prime Minister's press spokesman Alastair Campbell called the 'bog standard' comprehensive school. By 2005 nearly 70% of secondary schools with over 2 million pupils had achieved specialist status. These are schools that have a special focus on particular subject areas such as sport, music or science, for example. The best of them can have admissions policies that are tantamount to selection, albeit without using that highly controversial word. Indeed, former Secretary of State for Education, David Blunkett, had paraphrased George Bush Senior to state: 'read my lips, no selection'. Schools may not run tests, but the admissions policies that they employ may select socially as evidence suggests that middle class parents may be more likely to push their children towards the 'good' schools. The point then becomes how to close the gap between the 'good' and 'failing' schools if that gap is also one based on social background. It is here that the language of choice encounters longer-standing welfare state themes associated with opportunity and social mobility.

Health care

As the Conservatives discovered when they were in government, the costs of the NHS continued to increase because people live longer, medical technology has improved but become more expensive, while poor public health and health inequalities produce demands on the system. At the risk of being called 'the nanny state' government can try to stop people smoking and reduce levels of obesity, but there is little that it can do about an ageing population.

Labour's room for manoeuvre after it came to power in 1997 was constrained because of the application of the spending commitments of the previous Conservative Government. The first step by the new Labour Government in its 1997 White Paper, *A New NHS* was to curtail the NHS 'internal market' set up by the Conservatives that introduced market mechanisms into the health care system through a distinction between the purchasers of health care and the providers. A 1999 Government White Paper set targets for improving public health and, for the first time, spoke of the need to reduce health inequalities, not least because of the stark evidence of major differences in life expectancy between the poorer and richer parts of Britain. By 1999, though, the spending restraints were shown to be causing real problems in the NHS as the flu epidemic during the winter of 1999–2000 highlighted an NHS at the maximum of its capacity.

In January 2001, in the wake of this evidence that the health system was under real pressure and as perceptions grew that the Government was failing to 'deliver', Tony Blair pledged to bring spending on health care in the UK to the EU average. By 2003 total health expenditure amounted to £91.4 billion, around 8.3% of GDP. This was a huge increase from the 5.5% of the previous Conservative Government, but still lagged behind Germany, France and Italy.

One of the most controversial issues within the welfare state and for health care in particular has been the Private Finance Initiative (PFI) designed by the Conservatives as a mechanism to get private money into the public sector (Pollock 2004). The use of PFI has greatly accelerated under New Labour as Politics in Focus 28.5 shows.

FOCUS 28.5

The Private Finance Initiative

- Introduced by the Conservatives after 1992.
- In 2001 equalled 9% of public investment.
- One of the most controversial measures introduced by the Labour Government.
- Highlights the role of the market in public service provision.

Key features

- Private sector involvement in public services.
- Governed by a legal contract that involves involving private companies in the provision of public services, particularly the construction of public buildings such as hospitals.
- A typical PFI scheme is for a capital project such as building a school, hospital or housing estate. This is designed, built, financed and managed by a private sector consortium with a contract of usually 30 years.
- The private companies are paid from public money depending on performance. If performance targets are missed then it is paid less.
- The contracts are mind-bogglingly complicated.

What are the issues?

- For its opponents, PFI equals privatisation, 'savings' are usually cuts in staff and wages for employees. The National Audit Office called some of the claims made in support of PFI 'pseudo-scientific mumbo jumbo'.
- For its supporters in government, the PFI delivers increased efficiency and improved public services without tax increases. PFI does not show up as government borrowing.

Is it better value?

- The Edinburgh Royal Infirmary cost £180m to build and will cost £900m to pay for over 30 years including operating costs. Would it have been cheaper to build and manage from more traditional forms of public funds? We will not know the answer for 20 years. The politicians who put it in place will be gone by then.

New Labour have also sought a particular route to what they see as the empowerment of local communities through the creation of 'foundation' hospitals, which in the language of 'third way' theorists could be seen as an example of 'stakeholding' (Prabhakar 2004: 576). Foundation hospitals are the quasi-market exemplified. They are NHS hospitals that had attained a top three-star rating. This allows them greater freedom to act outside the control of government. The local stakeholders are patients, the local community, staff and partner organisations such as local authorities. Foundation hospital managers will:

• be given more autonomy;

• not be managed by the Department of Health;

• undergo less inspection and monitoring;

• be able to borrow money from the private sector;

• be able to keep the proceeds of land sales for reinvestment;

• be able to pay staff over nationally agreed terms and conditions.

Foundations hospitals

Pros

• Give people a stake in the services they use

• Promote 'localism' rather than central control

Cons

• Create a two-tier health system with an elite and the rest

• Will fuel health inequalities not reduce them

• Foundation hospitals can poach staff from non-foundation hospitals

The Conservatives said at the 2005 general election that they would match government spending on the NHS, although they would introduce a greater role for the private sector by allowing individuals to access private care with the state paying 50% of the cost and the patient finding the other 50%. The NHS has become such an important element of the NHS that the Conservatives and Labour are open to allegations of privatisation. While it is true that they see a greater role for the market, the difference between Labour and the Conservatives is more one of degree. Labour too has maintained the role of quasi-markets in the health care system.

Conclusion

We began by asking whether we can say New Labour, new welfare state. The answer to this question depends on a distinction being made between the funding of the key public services such as health and education and their provision. If we look at funding then we see a continued central role for national government that continues to hold the pursue strings, although we do see the PFI as a significant route for private money to enter the public sector. Indeed, levels of spending on health and education have increased. When we explore the provision of services then we see a greater role for market forces, or to be more precise the quasi-market. The belief is, to return to the metaphors used earlier, that the users of welfare state services need to be queens, not pawns. The idea is that they be empowered and be given more choice. A key question is whether this emphasis on choice delivers welfare state benefits for all or whether inequalities within education and health care remain stark. Another is whether the urge to promote the delivery of services that are closer to the needs of local communities has actually been a vehicle for new and intense levels of government scrutiny. A vast array of targets, standards, benchmarks and other forms of government intervention have been introduced that seek to ensure that public money is spent as intended. In some senses the objectives are laudable, but it has been asked whether this increase in targets and benchmarks has reduced the ability of teachers, doctors and nurses to actually make professional decisions because their behaviour is dominated by government standards and a fear that funding will be hit if these are not met. The role, function and purposes of the state are obviously central to any discussion of the welfare state we're in. What we can see is that far from withering away or being hollowed out, the state seems to be heavily involved, perhaps even to a greater extent than before, in the delivery of public services.

KEY POINTS

- Despite some of the rhetoric the state has not been 'rolled back'.

- The welfare state and delivery have been key political issues since 1997.

- The role of the market in the delivery of public services has been a particularly controversial feature of debates.

- Both health and education have experienced major changes in terms of, for example, their organisation and the imposition of targets.

- Many of the changes have been informed by the view that the citizen or consumer should have more power over key public services such as health and education.

- There have been big increases in welfare state spending, but some of this has been controversial because of the use of the Private Finance Initiative.

KEY QUESTIONS

(1) Has globalisation eroded the welfare state?

(2) Do targets help deliver better public services?

(3) What are the main differences in the welfare state policies of the Conservatives between 1979 and 1997 and Labour since 1997?

(4) Can the choice agenda within the welfare state deliver higher quality services for all or just for some?

IMPORTANT WEBSITES

To get more information about the historical development of the welfare state then see the websites of the Institute for Contemporary British History www.icbh.ac.uk and Institute for Historical Research www.ihr.ac.uk. On the functioning of the welfare state then see the websites of key government departments such as the Department for Work and Pensions www.dwp.gov.uk, Department for Education and Skills www.des.gov.uk and the NHS website at www.nhs.gov.uk.

FURTHER READING

On the NHS see R. Klein (2001) *The New Politics of the National Health Service*, 4th edn Harlow: Prentice Hall; on education see C. Chitty (2004) *Education Policy in Britain*, London: Palgrave; J. Demaine (ed) (2002) *Education Policy and Contemporary Politics*, London: Palgrave. On New Labour and the welfare state see M. Powell (2000) *New Labour, New Welfare State?*, Bristol: Policy Press.

 Visit the Online Resource Centre that accompanies this book for links to more information on this chapter topic

CHAPTER TWENTY NINE

The politics of immigration, asylum and ethnic diversity

READER'S GUIDE

This chapter analyses why, when and with what effects immigration, asylum and ethnic diversity have at times been emotive, controversial and combustible issues in British politics. The capacity for controversy stems from links between immigration, asylum and ethnic diversity and four basic political questions: first, the power and authority of the British state to regulate access to its territory; second, the state's ability to determine access to important social and political institutions such as the welfare state, labour market and national citizenship; third, political participation and representation by immigrants and their descendants; and, fourth, the impact of supranational and international developments such as European integration and international human rights laws on British politics. Through these issues immigration raises questions about who 'we' are, the kind of society in which 'we' would like to live, and the links between the UK and other parts of the world.

Introduction

In February 2003, Tony Blair appeared on BBC2's *Newsnight* programme. The numbers of asylum-seekers entering the UK had been dominating the news agenda for weeks and Mr Blair knew full well that the programme's presenter, Jeremy Paxman, would want to grill him on this topic. The 2002 asylum statistics showed that 110,000 people had sought asylum in the UK, compared to 32,500 in 1997 when New Labour took office. A bold statement of the Government's intention to allay public anxiety was required, decided Mr Blair, who declared that: 'I would like to see us reduce it [the asylum figures] by 30 per cent to 40 per cent in the next few months, and I think by September of this year we should have it halved'. Yet, the fact that by September 2003 this target was attained did little to soften the tone of the debate about asylum or immigration more generally. The same thing happened during the 2005 general election campaign when Mr Blair was asked by Jeremy Paxman whether he knew how many illegal immigrants were in the UK. He responded by saying that he did not know and that no Government could know the precise number. Critics led by the Conservative opposition alleged that these events showed a Government that had lost control of the immigration system. Indeed, immigration was a key Conservative campaign theme at the 2005 general election (Geddes and Tonge 2005). The Conservatives alleged that the immigration figures were at best unreliable or at worst fiddled, the immigration system was a shambles and that the Government was losing control of immigration. From the other side of the fence, civil liberties and pro-migrant organisations protested that immigration and asylum rules were too draconian and breached national and international human rights standards. While all this was going on, the Government looked nervously over their shoulder at the lurking menace of extreme right-wing parties such as the British National Party eager to play on anti-immigration sentiment.

Why the anxiety?

Why do immigration, asylum and ethnic diversity induce such anxiety? There are historical and political explanations for this. Historically, while Britain has been shaped by migration, there tends not to be the self-understanding as a nation of immigrants that prevailed in settler societies such as the US, Australia and Canada (on Britain's immigration history see, for example, Holmes 1988; Winder 2004). The second explanation focuses more specifically on four issues that are fundamental to the study of politics and that will be this chapter's main focus. These are:

- *State power*. The regulation of immigration at its most basic is about state power and authority as British governments strive to regulate the numbers of people entering Britain. Immigration goes to the heart of debates about the sovereign power, authority and capacity of the British state and the ways in which these change as Britain's place in the world changes.

- *Membership and citizenship.* The conditions governing access by immigrant newcomers to key social and political institutions such as the labour market, the welfare state and national citizenship. If people move from one state to another they then make contributions to and claims on their new country. This may involve access to the labour market, to health care, to schools or to universities. How, then, has Britain, with its long history of immigration, made decisions about rights, entitlements and obligations for immigrant newcomers? To what welfare state benefits should newcomers be entitled? Should newcomers be expected, for example, to learn English and swear loyalty oaths before becoming British citizens? What protections should be offered to immigrant newcomers and their families against racist, ethnic-based or religious discrimination?

- *Participation and representation.* Immigration has changed the social, ethnic and cultural make-up of Britain, but have British political institutions responded to this diversity? Are immigrants and their descendants properly represented in our political institutions? What, in fact, would 'proper' representation mean? Are there gaps and deficits in levels of representation that mean that the voices of some members of British society whose origins lie in immigration are not heard?

- *Globalisation.* While British governments have tended to be enthusiastic advocates of domestic and international economic liberalisation, this enthusiasm has not extended to free movement for people. Why has this been the case? More specifically, what impact has European integration had on the capacity of the British state to regulate migration?

The remainder of this chapter is structured around these four themes. By taking each in turn, immigration, asylum and ethnic diversity can be seen to raise important, pressing and powerful questions about who 'we' are, the kinds of society in which 'we' live or would like to live, and the links between British politics and the international system.

---

005 general election

Immigration was at the top of the campaign agenda at the 2005 general election.

The Conservatives called for an annual immigration and asylum quota set by Parliament; round the clock surveillance at ports of entry (although when pointed out that there were 650 of these it was soon cut back to the 35 or so main ports of entry); a British border control police force; and a points system for work permits.

In its 2005 strategy paper on immigration and asylum, the Labour Government proposed a points system for new economic migrants, but rejected the idea of quotas.

State power and the regulation of migration

In 2003, around 90 million people crossed the UK's borders. Most of these were either British or EU citizens, but around 12 million came from non-European Economic Area (EEA) countries. Of this 90 million around 270,000 people moved to the UK to work, 320,000 to study and just under 50,000 to seek asylum. Many of the remainder were tourists or people passing through the UK to another destination. These figures provide some idea of the scale of movement into the UK. What this snapshot can also do if we drill down more deeply is provide some idea of the diversity of this movement as people enter to work, to study, to seek refuge, for a holiday or to join with family members. While the numbers of people crossing UK borders is very high—and the numbers of those entering for work has increased dramatically since the 1980s and 1990s—there are many different reasons why people enter and the duration of their stay can vary enormously. The scale of movement and its diversity should be borne in mind when considering UK immigration policy. It would be wrong to see 'immigration' as a single, compact event. In fact, bearing in mind this diversity gives a better idea of the policy challenges that British governments face as they seek to regulate immigration.

While arguments for open borders and unconstrained free movement of people have been made (see, for example, Barry and Goodin 1992), British governments have not accepted them. Instead the core dilemma for government can be quite simply stated: regulating access to the state territory is an important component of a state's sovereign authority while being seen to lose control challenges state authority and the legitimacy of elected governments.

The remainder of this section analyses the contemporary history of British immigration policy. Two points are central to the analysis that follows. First, the ways in which British immigration controls were 'racialised', which means that they were represented in social and political terms as involving 'race' and 'racial difference' (Solomos 2004). Second, since the 1990s there has been renewed openness to labour migration coupled with attempts to drive down numbers of asylum seekers.

The decline of the imperial state

The basis for immigration after the Second World War from Britain's former colonies in the Caribbean, south Asia and Africa was an imperial conceptualisation of British citizenship enshrined in the 1948 British Nationality Act. Technically this entitled between 400 and 500 million subjects of the Crown to move to the UK, although it was far fetched in the extreme to imagine that this many people would move.

The ways in which immigration was understood as 'a problem' is central to understanding the politics of immigration, asylum and ethnic diversity in the UK. The important point is that the regulation of immigration was linked to ideas about 'race' and 'racial' differences between newcomers and the host society. If 'the problem' was 'race' then the solution to the problem as defined was controls on immigration from the 'New

Commonwealth' (former colonies in south Asia, Africa and the Caribbean) and Pakistan. Scholars who have studied the responses to immigration have focused on the ways in which these responses were 'racialised' in the sense that immigration was represented socially and politically as involving 'race' and 'racial' difference (Layton-Henry 1992; Saggar 1992; Paul 1997; Spencer 1997; Joppke 1999; Hansen 2001). The words 'race' and 'racial' are placed in inverted commas to indicate that they are very problematic. No credible scientific evidence exists to support the view that people's social or political behaviour can be explained by their 'race'. Some of the worst and most hideous experiences in human history have arisen from the actions of those such as the Nazis who thought that they could. There is actually as much variation within as between so-called racial groups while arguments that people are any more or less human dependent on physical characteristics such as skin colour are deeply repugnant. Yet, in the UK there is a public discourse linked to the discussion of migration that refers to 'race', 'race relations' and 'racial equality'. The point to bear in mind is not that races are real in any scientific sense, but that the British politics of immigration, asylum and ethnic diversity has been socially and politically represented as involving 'race'. Moreover the insidious effects of racism where putative racial characteristics are used as a basis for presumptions of inferiority and superiority have had corrosive effects on British politics.

The 1962 Commonwealth Immigrants Act was the first step in the direction of controls on what at the time was called 'coloured' immigration. The Government was reluctant to admit that this was the intention because it did not want to be labelled as racist, but as a member of the Conservative Government of that time put it: 'The Bill's real purpose was to restrict the influx of coloured immigrants from the Caribbean and Indian subcontinent. We were reluctant to say as much openly' (Deedes 1968: 10).

Politics in Focus 29.1 outlines the main pieces of legislation introduced in the 1960s that reflected the retreat from Empire and a downsizing of the idea of Britain and British citizenship. The 1981 British Nationality Act completed this post-imperial downsizing.

Immigration legislation can be linked to other debates concerning relative political and economic decline (see Chapters 6 and 7).

Debates since the 1990s

Immigration controls are based upon placing people into categories which then determine their right to enter, to reside, to work, to access welfare state benefits and so on (asylum is a rather different issue and needs to be kept separate, as will be discussed more fully below). At the same time, the British state faces constraints on its capacity to control immigration. Initially this was because of the open door to Commonwealth immigration symbolised by the 1948 British Nationality Act. When this door was closed from 1962 onwards, constraints were also faced when secondary migration by family members occurred because this migration was protected by national laws and international legal standards. More recently, the UK government has encountered constraints from international human rights standards that seek to guarantee the rights of asylum-seekers. There are thus some limits on the sovereign authority of the British state to

Commonwealth Immigrants Bill 1962

This distinguished between citizens of the UK and its colonies and citizens of independent Commonwealth countries, such as India. The latter were then subject to immigration controls and would need an employment voucher to enter the UK. The number of these vouchers available was then reduced as a way of limiting labour migration. The aim of the legislation was to reduce what at the time was called 'coloured' immigration, although the Conservative government of the day officially denied that this was the case.

Commonwealth Immigrants Bill 1968

This second measure, designed to limit immigration from Commonwealth countries, was targeted at British citizens of Indian origin residing in African states that were pursuing Africanisation policies in Kenya and Uganda that discriminated against their Asian-origin populations. A patriality rule specified that for anyone to enter the UK they needed a least one parent or grandparent who was born, adopted or naturalised as a British citizen. Many Labour MPs were strongly opposed to this legislation, which they saw as a shabby attempt to withdraw rights from British citizens facing persecution.

Immigration Act 1971

This measure essentially rounded off the controls on labour migration that were introduced in the 1960s. The legislation replaced all previous legislation. It distinguished between citizens of the UK and its colonies who were patrial (the one grandparent rule mentioned above) who could enter the UK and those citizens of independent Commonwealth countries that could not. The basis for admission by non-patrials was a work permit scheme. Immigration policy since has been based on this distinction.

British Nationality Act 1981

This measure completed the post-imperial downsizing by bringing patriality into nationality law by distinguishing between full British citizenship, British Dependent Territories citizenship and British Overseas citizenship. This latter category offered no right to enter the UK and was designed to encourage people in countries such as Malaysia to acquire citizenship in their country of residence. Family-related migration for reunification or formation remained the main immigration route to the UK through the 1970s, 1980s and into the 1990s.

regulate migration. To this can be added the growing influence of the EU, more of which later.

Immigration policies tend to focus on the regulation of immigration channels. These immigration channels may be widened or narrowed, but could never be fully closed. There is a channel for labour migration, another for students, one for family migration and another for asylum-seekers. The categories that are developed to define into which category an immigrant should be placed can be arbitrary and unfair because categories are less to do with the individual qualities of a person than they are to do with official views of the motives for immigration and the possible consequences of it. Once again, the practical development of immigration policies cannot be separated from the ethical basis for the population sorting that they involve. These dilemmas have been particularly acute in the UK since the 1990s as there has been an opening to new labour migration coupled with closure towards those forms of migration that the state has decided are 'unwanted', particularly asylum. It is to the politics of asylum that we now turn.

Tackling asylum-seeking migration

Responses to asylum are a key element of the British politics of immigration, asylum and ethnic diversity. An important distinction needs to be made between *economic migration* governed mainly by national laws and *asylum-seeking migration* protected by a set of international legal standards put in place after the Second World War and which are supposed to bind the behaviour of states. Yet, while asylum-seeking should be kept separate, it is common for economic migration and asylum-seeking to be confused.

The international standards covering asylum and refugee status are to be found in the United Nations' 1951 Geneva Convention.

> **Extract 29.1: Geneva Convention Article 1(A)**
>
> A refugee is a person with a 'well-founded fear of being persecuted for reasons of race, religion, nationality, membership of a particular social group or political opinion'.

While the UK was top of the European league in 2003 in terms of overall numbers of asylum-seekers, when these figures are weighted to account for the total population then the UK is a mid-ranking European country of asylum with one asylum application per 1,000 of the total population, which puts Britain ninth in an EU league table of asylum applications.

The asylum system represents a point at which the sovereign authority of states to regulate access to their territory encounters international human rights standards that may constrain this power. On the one hand are a domestic politics of asylum and migration in the UK that may not be accommodating of new migration, but these encounter a symbolically powerful set of arguments about 'international human rights'.

If we judge Conservative and Labour governments by their actions on asylum-seeking migration since the 1990s then we see a presumption that many asylum-seekers are in fact 'bogus' in the sense that they entered the UK for economic reasons or in pursuit of welfare state benefits. In turn this generates a critique of international legal standards that seek to

FIGURE 29.1

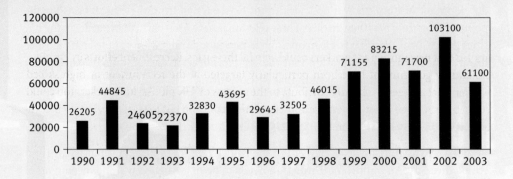

Asylum applications in the UK, 1990–2003

guarantee the rights of asylum-seekers. Both the Labour Government and the Conservative Party have questioned the continued relevance of the Geneva Convention. Such moves are, of course, deeply controversial. They could be seen to stigmatise asylum-seekers and attack basic international human rights standards. At the same time, governments have been fully aware of strong anti-asylum sentiment amongst the general public and a strong campaign against asylum and asylum-seekers in some sections of the press. That said, the statements and actions of governments have done little to portray asylum-seekers in a more positive light and may well have contributed to negative public perceptions and anti-asylum campaigns in the media.

From their actions (legislation in 1993, 1996, 1999 and 2002) we can see that successive governments (both Conservative and Labour) have assumed that the increase in asylum-seeking migration has been linked to people in some way seeking to exploit or abuse the system by using the asylum channel when their real motive for migration is economic. Whether this is right or wrong (and evidence suggests that there are grounds for doubting this presumption), the effects on legislation are clear. What can be seen is a series of measures since 1993 that have changed the relationship between asylum-seekers and the welfare state. Based on the (questionable) assumption that they are 'bogus', governments have sought to alter their rights to welfare state benefits. This has placed asylum-seekers in a more tenuous position and also, more cynically, it could be argued, reduced the likelihood, through the introduction of measures such as special accommodation centres, that asylum-seekers can be integrated into British society and thus ultimately more diffi-cult to deport should their application for asylum fail. As will be seen later in this chapter, the British government has also seen co-operation with other EU member states as a way of reducing asylum flows into the UK. In this instance, European co-operation and integration may actually enhance the ability of states to regulate access to their territory rather than necessarily weakening it.

New labour migration

The efforts to restrict asylum-seeking migration are not the whole story. Since the end of the 1990s, British governments have shown an increased interest in new labour migration to fill labour market gaps in important economic sectors such as health care, education and construction. In 2003, around 270,000 migrant workers entered the UK. In September 2004 the Trade and Industry Secretary Patricia Hewitt identified 250,000 labour market vacancies and argued that new immigrant workers could help fill these gaps. Recruitment efforts by employers and by government have been particularly targeted at the recruitment of high skilled workers that are seen as able to contribute to the success of 'UK plc'. Asylum-seekers too could contribute because many have skills and talents that could be put to good use, but their categorisation as asylum-seekers means that they cannot work. Irrespective of their skills, asylum-seekers are more likely to be perceived as a drain on resources rather than contributors to economic growth. This is not because of an assessment of the individual qualities and talents of asylum-seekers, but because of the effects of categorisation that are the basis for an immigration policy that seeks to sort between different groups of people seeking to enter the UK.

The basis for UK policy since the end of the 1990s has been the view that new labour migration can help resolve labour market shortages and enhance the competitiveness of the UK economy. This has involved a more liberal approach to issuing work permits and, since January 2002, a specific Highly Skilled Migrants programme. The UK has not been alone in seeking to recruit highly skilled migrants. Other European countries too, as well as more traditional immigration countries such as Canada and the US, also compete in the global marketplace for skilled workers. The Labour Government has favoured a market-driven approach rather than having quotas for new immigrants. Former Home Secretary David Blunkett reflected this market-driven approach when he argued that he could see no obvious upper limit to the numbers of labour migrants entering the UK. This was not so much an abrogation of responsibility as an admission that the state attempts to regulate immigration through the imposition of quotas or other limits on new immigration may actually confound the needs of employers and that the market may be a better device for regulating migration than the state.

To conclude, the UK developed 'racialised' immigration controls designed to deal with the legacy of imperialism, which has given way since the 1990s to a twin-track and highly differentiated approach to asylum-seeking migration defined as 'unwanted' and skilled labour migration that has been actively solicited. The chapter's next section demonstrates how the shifting sands of debates about migration have had important effects on debates about membership and citizenship in the UK.

Membership and citizenship

In 2002, more than 100,000 people acquired British citizenship, but were required only to visit a local solicitor and swear a 28-word loyalty oath. This changed in 2003, since when new British citizens have been obliged to attend a ceremony at which they publicly proclaim their loyalty to Britain. Prince Charles attended the first of these ceremonies held in Brent Town Hall at which two Indians, a Pole, a New Zealander, an Australian, five Afghanis, two Kenyans, a Somali, two Sri Lankans, a Nepalese and a South African paid £68 and pledged that: 'I will give my loyalty to the United Kingdom and respect its rights and freedoms. I will uphold its democratic values. I will observe its laws faithfully and fulfil my duties and obligations as a British citizen'. The Government also envisaged classes for immigrants where they could learn English, find out something about the country's history and take a 'Britishness test' before receiving their nationality certificates, although whether or not this happens depends on whether money can be found to fund the scheme.

The focus of UK integration policy has been 'ethnic minorities' whose family origins lie in immigration. 7.9% of the UK population belong to an ethnic minority group. Table 29.2 shows the breakdown of the UK ethnic minority population.

Most immigrants who came to the UK in the period of post-imperial migration during the 1950s and into the 1960s arrived either from the Republic of Ireland (with whom the

	Total population		Minority ethnic population
	Count	%	%
White	54153898	92.1	N/A
Mixed	677117	1.2	14.6
Asian or Asian British			
Indian	1053411	1.8	22.7
Pakistani	747285	1.3	16.1
Bangladeshi	283063	0.5	6.1
Other Asian	247664	0.4	5.3
Black or Black British			
Black Caribbean	565876	1.0	12.2
Black African	485277	0.8	10.5
Black other	97585	0.2	2.1.3
Chinese	247403	0.4	5.3
Other	230615	0.4	5.0
All minority ethnic population	4635296	7.9	100
All population	58789194	100	N/A

Source: Census 2001

UK has a Common Travel Area guaranteeing free movement and the right to vote) or as subjects of the Crown from former colonies, clutching British passports and able to claim *civis Brittanicus sum* (I am a British citizen). In contrast with other European countries such as the Federal Republic of Germany the focus for debate in the UK was not so much access to rights for 'foreigners' but the utilisation of rights by 'ethnic minorities'. This prompted the enactment of legislation designed to tackle racist and ethnic-based discrimination that embodied an immigration policy trade-off formulated by Roy Hattersley thus: 'Integration without control is impossible, but control without integration is indefensible'.

The link between immigration and integration was clear: if integration were to be successfully attained then it required some efforts to limit newcomers. This still leaves hanging the meaning of 'integration'. We tend to understand it as a process rather than an end state because it is far from clear what a fully integrated society would look like or even whether it would be desirable: would we all be the same? Integration as a process of interaction between newcomers and the host society centres on two issues, noted in Politics in Focus 29.3.

How have these questions of entitlement and belonging been given meaning in debate, law and policy? To get a sense of the debate we first have to go back to the 1960s when measures were introduced to tackle discrimination on grounds of race and ethnic origin. Race Relations Acts in 1965 and 1968 put in place measures to tackle discrimination, but were seen as having serious weaknesses. These weaknesses were addressed by the Race Relations Act 1976 which amongst its provisions did two important things:

- It introduced measures to tackle both *direct* and *indirect* discrimination. Direct discrimination was the target of the 1965 and 1968 legislation. This is where individuals are blatantly discriminated against because of their racial or ethnic origin. The 'no blacks' or 'no Irish' signs that were sometimes used when houses were available for rent are examples of direct racist discrimination. Indirect discrimination is more insidious. This occurs where treatment is formally equal but outcomes are discriminatory against a group because of their ethnic or racial origin. The Race Relations Act 1976 dealt with both direct and indirect discrimination.

- It established the Commission for Racial Equality with investigatory powers to monitor implementation by public and private sector organisations of the legislation. The police

1. Redefining the organisational borders of Britain.

Key question: 'who is entitled?' which then defines access to the labour market, the welfare state and other important institutions.

2. Redefining the conceptual borders of Britain.

Key question: 'who belongs?' which is much more nebulous but links to very important themes in the immigration debate that are associated with culture and identity.

were excluded from the scope of the legislation, but in 2000, following the inquiry into the racist murder of Stephen Lawrence and the deeply flawed police investigation that failed to bring to justice any of the perpetrators of this crime, the police were included within Race Relations legislation.

The debate about the 'integration' of immigrant newcomers thus focused on (i) regulating entry in order to protect 'good race relations' and (ii) introducing measures to tackle racist and ethnic-based discrimination.

This brings us back to the point raised at the start of this section when the new citizenship ceremonies were discussed. Why were these seen as necessary at the turn of the 21st century? There are two answers to this question. The first is the official Government line: the countries of origin of immigrants coming to the UK were becoming more diverse. This meant that immigrants might not possess the understanding of British society seen as necessary if they were to make a success of their lives in the UK. Courses and training could help them do this. The second explanation has less to do with immigration and more to do with the kind of society in which we now live where the bonds of citizenship and collective identity have been seen as weakened by more individualised lifestyles. Anxiety about the integration of immigrant newcomers may therefore be a reflection of a broader debate about integration as it affects all of us. In an article on immigration and the welfare state, David Goodhart (2004) called this a 'progressive dilemma', that is, how to maintain bonds of solidarity with people to whom we do not feel a sense of attachment. The point here is that this is not simply an immigration issue. It is in fact a much broader debate about 'integration' as it affects us all because the people to whom we do not feel a sense of attachment may not simply be the immigrant 'other' but also the 'other us' meaning our co-nationals whose lifestyles may differ very much from our own. The debates about this 'progressive dilemma' can be at their most intense when immigrants are the subject, but the debate about immigration may be a cipher or code for a deeper reflection on the changing nature of British society. Put simply, society has changed, so it is not a surprise that expectations for immigrant newcomers have changed too. The point is that we must sort out cause and effect. It is not necessarily immigrants who have driven these changes in British society. In fact, given their numbers (around 4% of the British population) this appears implausible. Rather debate about the integration of newcomers is an effect of a deeper debate about the kind of society in which 'we' would like to live and of a continual process of reshaping the organisational and conceptual borders of that community. This now leads us to the section of this chapter that looks at participation and representation, and the ways in which political institutions have responded to changes in the UK population resulting from immigration.

Participation and representation

Discussions of 'integration' are flawed if they focus only on adaptation by immigrant newcomers as though the onus was entirely on them. Integration is a two-way process involving mutual accommodation by newcomers and the host society. We can develop this point further as we consider the extent to which British political institutions have responded to forms of diversity rooted in the presence in Britain of immigrants and their descendants. The discussion here turns to immigrants and ethnic minorities as political actors with a capacity to articulate their interests and shape British politics.

There is a widespread perception that people from ethnic minorities are excluded from British political institutions and that this is a flaw that strikes at the heart of the representativeness of the system. But what do we mean by representation? Would we expect British political institutions such as the House of Commons or local authorities to 'look' like the British people? Some would argue that they should and that there should be more women, ethnic minority, disabled and gay MPs to reflect the diversity of the population. At the same time, others may point out that political institutions that 'look' like the British people in the sense of being a precise statistical breakdown of the social composition of the British people may not actually represent their interests particularly well. Does a politician need to share the personal and physical characteristics of his constituents in order to represent their interests? Some would argue that it is not necessary and that if we follow this argument to its logical conclusion then no-one could represent anyone else because no person would share the same exact personal or physical characteristics with another. Others would contend that there are distinct experiences too which people may be subject because of, for instance, the colour of their skin and the experience of racism, that mean that only others with some knowledge and experience of this form of oppression could have a real understanding of their interests. This discussion highlights a distinction between *descriptive* representation and *substantive* representation, or, put another way, between political institutions that 'look' like the population they are supposed to represent and political institutions that substantively represent the interest of the population they are supposed to represent.

Levels of ethnic minority participation and representation in politics have improved, although the term 'ethnic minorities' is a very broad category and there is little evidence to suggest a distinct set of 'ethnic minority' political interests that unite groups with very diverse origins (Saggar 1999). Historically there has been a strong alignment between ethnic minorities and the Labour Party. The implication of this is that it is within the Labour Party that debates about ethnic minority representation have been most intense.

In 2005, one of the 23 Cabinet members was from an ethnic minority (Baroness Amos). Of all other Government ministers, David Lammy MP (Tottenham) was the only ethnic minority Commons minister. In total, therefore, three of the 89 Government ministers were from ethnic minorities. The roots of ethnic minority representation in the House of Commons can be traced back to the late 19th century when Dadabhai Naoroji was elected as Liberal MP for Finsbury Central from 1892 to 1895. The first Conservative ethnic minority MP to be elected was Mancherjee Bhownaggree for Bethnal Green North-East from 1895 to 1905. Between 1922 and 1923 Shapurji Saklatvala represented Battersea North for Labour and then between 1924 and 1929 for the Communist Party. It was not until 1987 that the first MPs from ethnic minorities were elected. The four elected then were Diane Abbott (Hackney North & Stoke Newington), Paul Boateng (Brent South), Bernie Grant (Tottenham) and Keith Vaz (Leicester East). Diane Abbott was the first black woman MP. There has been a slow and steady increase in representation. After the 2001 general election, there were 12 MPs

2004

	Per cent from minority ethnic group
Cabinet	9.5%
Other Government ministers and whips	3.4%
House of Commons	1.8%
House of Lords	c.4%
MEPs	4.6%
Local councillors (England and Wales)	2.5%
Public bodies	4.4%
Scottish Parliament and Welsh Assembly	Nil
Greater London Assembly	4.0%

Source: DOD's Parliamentary Companion

(1.8% of the total) from ethnic minorities, all representing the Labour Party. By 2005 the number of MPs of ethnic minority origin had reached 15, including two Conservatives.

This discussion of participation and representation has sought to explore the ways in which British political institutions reflect the ethnic diversity of modern Britain. There have been changes, but change has been slow and piecemeal. We also saw that it important to focus on what is meant by the term 'representation' and to distinguish between descriptive and substantive forms of representation. Do we want political institutions that look like the British people? Do we want political institutions that effectively represent their interests? This is not necessarily an either/or choice. There is a fairly wide consensus across the political parties that descriptive inadequacies need to be addressed and that this can lead to more sense amongst the general public that political institutions reflect British society. It would be glib, however, to assume that this means that the interests of highly diverse ethnic minorities are properly represented.

Globalisation and European integration

Immigration and asylum are not solely domestic concerns to be addressed by British political institutions alone. They signify links between the countries people move from and the countries they move to. They signify global inequalities of wealth and power that motivate migration and that link migration to broader global responsibilities. They signify

	Constituency	Party
Abbott, Diane	Hackney North and Stoke Newington	Labour
Afriyie, Adam	Windsor	Conservative
Butler, Dawn	Brent South	Labour
Dhanda, Parmjit	Gloucester	Labour
Hendrick, Mark	Preston	Labour
Khabra, Piara	Ealing Southall	Labour
Khan, Sadiq	Tooting	Labour
Kumar, Ashok	Middlesborough South and East Cleveland	Labour
Lammy, David	Tottenham	Labour
Mahmood, Khalid	Birmingham Perry Barr	Labour
Malik, Shahid	Dewsbury	Labour
Sarwar, Mohammed	Glasgow Govan	Labour
Singh, Marsha	BradfordWest	Labour
Vara, Shailesh	North West Cambridgeshire	Conservative
Vaz, Keith	Leicester	Labour

Sources: DOD's Parliamentary Companion, various internet sources

the role of international organisations, such as the United Nations High Commission for Refugees, the International Organisation for Migration and the European Union in policies concerning immigrants, asylum-seekers, refugees and ethnic minorities.

Migration and globalisation

Even though international migration is made visible by states and their borders, migration can be linked to that modern day buzzword 'globalisation'. Countries such as Britain in the prosperous and developed parts of the world are often keen to maintain their ability to regulate access by people to their territory. British governments express their support for international economic liberalisation, but this has not extended to supporting free movement of people. If economic liberalisation is advantageous—as British governments assert—then why are arguments not made for freer movement by people?

The reason for this can be seen if we compare free movement for widgets and free movement for people. Both widgets and people can be vital components in the production process. The skills and learning abilities of humans will of course far surpass those of the humble widget. Yet widgets cross national borders much more easily than people. The reason for this is that a widget does not make claims on the society to which it moves. We do not tend to worry about the education of widgets, their housing or their access to health care. Nor do we tend to concern ourselves unduly with the question of whether widgets are properly represented in our political institutions. The key point is that immigrants to the UK have rights, that those rights and entitlements tend to increase as a result of residence, and that the possession of rights means that migrants can legitimately make claims on the institutions of British society (and, reciprocally, these institutions can make demands on them). The result is that while British governments are keen advocates of economic liberalisation as the organising principle of the international economy, this enthusiasm does not extend to free movement of people. This does not negate economic and ethical arguments in support of the free movement of people. Rather, it helps explain why these arguments have thus far had limited effects.

Migration and European integration

European integration has an ambiguous relationship with globalisation. Is European integration driven by globalisation? Perhaps European integration is a reaction against globalisation? Maybe it is both a reaction to and a response against globalisation? This dual identity of the EU—possessing both globalisation-enhancing and globalisation-defying attributes—becomes clear when we look at EU immigration and asylum policy. Here we see a distinct UK response centred on opt-outs from key EU provisions regarding migration and asylum. The reason for these opt-outs is quite straightforward. The UK relies on external frontier controls exercised at points of entry to the UK. Other EU member states tend to share land borders with their neighbours and have developed different systems for regulating movement of people cross their borders. As an island, the UK has developed an alternative approach. The UK has therefore opted out of those provisions which move the EU in the direction of a frontier free area insofar as this relates to the free movement of people. So, if someone were to fly from the UK to Paris then they would need to show their passports when entering French territory, but if that person were then to fly on to Italy from France they would not need to show their passport again because that would be classed as an internal flight within a frontier-free EU. It is this different system for the regulation of population movement based on the UK's island position that has led to a difference between the UK and the rest of the EU on border controls.

This does not mean that the UK has not been interested in EU developments. Since 1997, UK governments have seen scope for the EU to help the UK reduce numbers of asylum-seekers. This has meant that the UK has been to the fore in proposing schemes for the external processing of asylum claims, which would mean that claims for asylum would be processed in camps close to the countries of origin of asylum applicants, that is, a long way from Britain. If such schemes were to come to fruition then European integration could be sovereignty enhancing in the sense that it would allow the UK government to achieve a domestic policy objective through the EU rather than sovereignty-diminishing. It may appear counter-intuitive to suggest it, but European integration could actually enhance the sovereign power and authority of member states if it helps them resolve domestic issues.

Conclusion

International migration is not a political side-issue because it goes to the heart of four very important political questions that tell us important things about the role and power of the British state. These four questions are the power and capacity of the state to regulate access to its territory; the ability to regulate access to key social and political institutions; the representation of ethnic minorities in political institutions; and the relationship between national migration policies and important international developments. The capacity of the state to regulate migration remains formidable, but perceptions of loss of control were a key issue at the 2005 general election. It is also accurate to say that there have been large increases in net migration to the UK. It would, however, be a mistake to ascribe huge causal significance to migration and to imagine that it drives welfare state and labour market changes. In fact, international migration is likely to be an effect rather than a cause of these changes. By this is meant that the ways in which the UK economy and welfare state works can create spaces for new migrants. So, for example, a dynamic, liberalised and deregulated UK economy can create spaces for economic migrants at the top and lower ends of the labour market. If we think about the issue in this way then we can see that international migration in its various forms provides a lens through which we can view all these issues and acquire important insights into British society and politics and also to debates about Britain's place in the world. This became clear at the 2005 general election when immigration and asylum were central to the Conservative campaign. Population ageing and labour market needs seem likely to mean that migration will remain an important and controversial feature of British and European politics in the years to come.

KEY POINTS

- Immigration to Britain increased after the Second World War.

- The bulk of migration to Britain was related to colonial ties between sending countries and Britain.

- Immigration became politically contentious in the 1950s and 1960s.

- The political contention of immigration was based on ideas about 'race' and supposed 'racial difference'.

- Tough controls on immigration were introduced between 1962 and 1971.

- British citizenship was changed in 1981 to mark the retreat from Empire.

- Migration came back onto the political agenda in the 1990s when asylum-seeking migration increased.

- Labour governments have often felt vulnerable to attack from the Conservatives on immigration issues.

KEY QUESTIONS

(1) Why did immigration to Britain increase after the war?

(2) Why and with what effects were British immigration controls 'racialised' in the 1960s and 1970s?

(3) Why and how was British citizenship legislation changed in 1981?

(4) Why did the numbers of asylum-seekers coming to Britain increase during the 1990s and at the beginning of the 21st century?

(5) Should Britain have a more open or a more restrictive approach to migration?

IMPORTANT WEBSITES

A useful (and free!) global email newsletter Migration News is available from Migration Dialogue, UC-Davis, California, http://migration. ucdavis.edu/mn/index.html. The Migration Research Unit, University College London contains the European Migration Information Network, which is an information network on immigration funded by the EU www.geog.ucl.ac.uk/mru. The Migration Policy Group in Brussels is a leading Brussels-based think-tank that keeps a close eye on migration in Europe www.migpolgroup.com.

Statewatch is a European civil liberties group that monitors EU developments in the area of immigration, asylum and racism (as well as other internal security issues) www.statewatch.org. The following are the sites of leading international organisations active in the area of migration: the International Organization for Migration www.iom.int, the United Nations High Commission for Refugees www.unhcr.ch. For UK migration data see the UK national statistical office at www.statistics.gov.uk.

FURTHER READING

A very good source is R. Hansen (2000) *Immigration and Citizenship in Post-War Britain*, Oxford: Oxford University Press. A little dated but still useful for their historical overviews are Z. Layton-Henry (1992) *The Politics of Immigration*, Oxford: Blackwell and S. Saggar (1992) *The Politics of Race in Britain*, London: Harvester Wheatsheaf. On race and politics in Britain see J. Solomos (2003) *Race and Racism in Britain*, 3rd edn, London: Palgrave Macmillan. On comparative European immigration politics see A. Geddes (2003) *The Politics of Migration and Immigration in Europe*, London: Sage.

 Visit the Online Resource Centre that accompanies this book for links to more information on this chapter topic

CHAPTER THIRTY

The politics of law and order

READER'S GUIDE

This chapter examines the politics of law and order policy by first analysing the philosophy framework underpinning this policy area. Here, we argue that all governments need to grapple with the boundaries between civic order and individual liberty. The chapter then considers change and continuity in the nature of the politics of law and order through an approach based on examining different epochs of social conservatism and social liberalism. The policies of various governments towards law and order are reviewed from the 1945 Attlee Government to the present Labour Government. The chapter concludes by addressing issues concerning both structure and agency and continuity and change.

Introduction

In liberal democracies such as Britain, the principle of the rule of law is one of the fundamental tenets that underpins the political system. The idea that the 'law' should 'rule', establishes a framework that conditions the way each citizen, no matter what their social status, conducts themselves and behaves within the sovereign territory of the state. The rule of law demands that individuals must conform, as an essential prerequisite for a civil and orderly society. Yet, questions concerning the relationship between law and politics, and the balance between state authority and individual liberty are a highly contested area of public policy. Since the terrorist attacks in the United States on 11 September 2001 to the suicide bombings in London on 7 July 2005, the parameters within the debate between individual liberty and state authority have shifted. The Government's stated concerns over national security have made this one of the most highly complex and politically contentious issues in British politics today. Yet, the themes being debated and contested between government and different actors in civil society at present are far from new. In the last three decades, British and Irish governments have had to address the spate of terrorist attacks both in mainland Britain, Northern Ireland and the Irish Republic—Belfast (1969–2005), Dublin (1974), Birmingham and Guildford (1974), London (1982), Brighton (1984), Enniskillen (1987), Omagh (1992), Warrington (1993), Manchester (1996)—by both Republican and Loyalist para-military organisations (see Chapter 17).

Numerous eminent political philosophers throughout the ages—Aristotle (3rd century BC), Thomas Hobbes, John Locke (17th century), Jean-Jaques Rousseau (18th century), John Stuart Mill, Karl Marx (19th century), Friedrich von Hayek, Herbert Marcuse, Eduard Bernstein, Hannah Arendt, Robert Nozik and John Rawls (20th century)—have grappled with philosophical issues concerning individual liberty and the state. Indeed, it is one of the defining themes in politics and has shaped both the nature of individual nation-states, from authoritarian to liberal regimes, and the nature of social relations, structuring the way in which individuals within society are able to socially interact with one another. As we see below, the imprint of this vexed issue—the balance between authority and liberty—can be amply illustrated if, for example, we examine the politics of law and order in Britain in the last half-century. Our focus in this chapter is an institutional one, an examination of the role of the Home Office, the department whose main functional responsibility has been for the maintenance of law and order in Britain.

Law and order in Britain: a Home Office perspective

The Home Office is more defined by its philosophical base than that of any other Whitehall department. It is a department whose fundamental concern is the problem of public order and its culture revolves around the issues of the individual versus the state and liberty versus order. Of course, such philosophical concerns are reflected in its functions, namely immigration, prisons, law and order. The task facing all Home Secretaries is to find a balance between maintaining civic order and ensuring the liberty of the individual. James Callaghan (1982: 11), a former Labour Home Secretary (1967–70) amply illustrated this point:

> The Home Office occupies the politically charged ground marking the boundary between the role of the state and the liberty of the citizen. It is this function that makes the Home Office both politically and constitutionally one of the great departments of state. It deals with fundamental issues at the very heart of a complex democratic system. 'Rights', 'duties', 'equity', 'punishment', the concepts which political theorists and philosophers write about, are the essence of the daily work of its ministers and officials.

In the last 60 years, two values, those of state intervention to ensure social order and libertarianism to defend individual liberty, have been fundamental precepts around which the work of the Home Office has evolved. During the post-war period, these two values have sometimes appeared complementary and at other times contradictory. As a former serving Home Office official observed:

> The Home Office has always been concerned, ever since it was founded in the eighteenth century, with how to reconcile the interests of the state with the rights of the individual. You can boil down virtually everything that has gone on in the Home Office to the central dilemma of balancing those two conflicts. Despite being regarded as reactionary in some quarters, I think we have always been conscious of the need to encroach on the rights of individuals, with regard to rights of the state, as little as possible. We have always been preoccupied with that central question.[1]

The balance of liberty versus order has been influenced by a number of factors, namely the ideological position of governments, external pressures and internal conflicts. For example, in recent years, there have been a number of occasions when British governments have opted to pursue a more authoritarian approach, in response to what they have argued has been a *real* rather than a perceived threat to law and order: in 1978–79, the Conservative Party in opposition pursued a successful strategy of claiming that, in the

---

[1] Private information.

light of the winter of discontent and the associated industrial unrest, the rule of law was being fatally undermined; again, in 1984 in the year of the miners' strike, the Conservative Government passed a number of emergency laws in order to combat what it perceived as a threat to law and order; in 1994 the Criminal Justice and Public Order Act was passed in response to what the Government perceived as a threat to social order from the rapid rise in the number of un-licensed 'rave gatherings' across Britain in the early 1990s; and finally, perhaps most dramatically, the response of the Labour Government in its review of both internal and external security following the 9/11 attacks on mainland America in 2001 and the London bombings in July 2005. These periods contrast with the more liberal environment that permeated the Home Office in the late 1960s, when a series of legislative bills were passed concerning social relations, for example, the legalising of homosexuality between consenting males over the age of 21. The point here is that it is important to recognise that it is a combination of exogenous (eg 11 September 2001) and endogenous (eg The 7/07 suicide bombings on London's transport system) factors coupled to the ideological outlook of the of the day (see Politics in Focus 30.1 and 30.2) that affects the politics of law and order in Britain.

Law and order in the post-war period

If one looks at the post-war period, what has determined the balance between individual liberty and the need to protect civic order has been the adoption, by various governments, of either a socially-conservative or a socially-liberal approach. Over time, the balance between these two contrasting values has fluctuated. Yet, it is important to recognise that, perhaps surprisingly, where a paradigm shift takes place in the policy field of law and order, it does not necessarily coincide with a change in government. Indeed, law and order provides a useful case-study of the theme of continuity and change that permeates British politics (see Chapter 1, Politics in Focus 1.2). But also, the oft-found occurrence of governmental change does not necessarily lead to an explicit change in policy direction. In the next section, we examine the various eras of law and order policy since 1945, highlighting that both Labour and Conservative governments have often continued to pursue similar policy goals in this field. When policy change does occur, it is often well into the lifetime of a government rather than at the onset of a new administration.

1945–late 50s: an era of social conservatism

From 1945 up to the late fifties, social conservatism was the dominant perspective conditioning both the views and policies of governments, both Labour and Conservative. For example, the Attlee Government, often viewed as the most radical reforming Labour government of the post-war era, was nevertheless cautious when it came to law and order policy. So while its 1948 Criminal Justice Act contained a number of liberal measures, most notably the abolition of hard labour within the existing penal system, at the same time, the

The political thought underpinning the Conservative Party is wide-ranging, drawing on different philosophical traditions and at times this plurality of views has caused tension within the party. This can be clearly seen in the growth of the New Right in the second half of the 20th century as a counter to Keynesian social democracy and a growing concern about issues of social breakdown and the perceived decline in authority. The New Right was a merging of two distinct traditions—neoconservatism and neoliberalism. Neoliberalism is derived from classical political economy from the writings of free-market economists from Adam Smith to Friedrich von Hayek and based on the primacy of the market. Here, the state is viewed as a malign force stymieing initiative, enterprise and distorting the efficiency of the market. Neoliberals therefore advocate the reduction of state activity to a minimum believing the free-market to be the most effective means of delivering an efficient and prosperous economy. The emphasis here is on self-help, individual responsibility and entrepreneurialism. In contrast, neoconservatism draws from 19th century conservative social principles—reflected in the writings of among others Edmund Burke, Michael Oakeshott and Roger Scrutton. As a reaction to the perceived growth of permissiveness and deviancy in society, it advocates the restoration of authority and traditional values of respect and moral decency based on the nuclear family, religion, national self-pride and social hierarchy. Here, the state needs to take an active role as part of a project based on the restoration of authority and traditional family values. The tension between these two positions can be demonstrated if, for example, we take the issue of drugs in society. Neoliberals would advocate the removal of any legislation limiting the availability of drugs within society, believing it is the individual and not the government's role to determine whether or not to engage in drug-taking. Neoconservatives would argue for the imposition of the strongest possible legislation regarding the availability of drugs, believing they pose a threat to the moral fabric of society, as their consumption leads to deviant behaviour.

In government, the Conservative Party has tended to advocate the need for the protection of the individual and the need to maintain the primacy of the rule of law. Thatcherism in particular, believed in the foibles of human nature and the need for the maintenance of the traditional family unit and the importance of the Church, school and community, in order to preserve the social fabric of society and respect for the rule of law. But Thatcherism went further by trying to impose a Conservative moral agenda in response to what it saw as alarming trends in society concerning the rise in teenage pregnancies, abortion, pornography, open homosexuality, etc. Here the state was to take an active role in, for example, the introduction of Clause 28 of the 1988 Local Government Act that banned local authorities from intentionally promoting homosexuality, publishing material with the intention of promoting homosexuality, or promoting the teaching in any state school of the acceptability of homosexuality as a pretended family relationship. The final phase in the Conservatives reactionary moral agenda was John Major's much maligned 'back-to-basics' campaign, where the then Prime Minister conjured up images of a return to a country of 'nannies pushing prams in parks, warm beer and cricket'. The programme lost both its impetus and political legitimacy following various sexual and financial wrongdoings by an array of Conservative politicians throughout the mid-90s.

CUS 30.2

nd law and order

The Labour Party's changing position in relation to the issue of law and order provides a useful cari-cature of what can be referred to as 'old' and 'new' Labour. Both traditions within the Labour Party believe in an active role for the state in order to tackle the issue of crime, but it is their interpretation of the causes of crime that differ.

Traditional or 'old' Labour embraced a predominantly structural explanation in its understanding of the seeds of lawless behaviour. That is to say poor social or environmental conditions were the primary explanation as to why crime occurred in society. Therefore, the most effective means to eradicate crime lay in tackling the issue of social deprivation, whilst also pursuing programmes of social rehabilitation for existing offenders. This view was perhaps best reflected in the 1964–70 Labour Government which identified the roots of crime in poverty and family breakdown. As the party's 1964 manifesto observed, those on lower incomes were more susceptible to crime because: '. . . the strain of their living conditions must tend to weaken their resistance to such temptations' (Labour Party 1964: 5). The party's solution then was to pursue: '. . . social measures designed to remove or reduce the factors which predispose people to crime' (ibid).

The most oft-heard mantra associated with New Labour on the issue of law and order is 'tough on crime, tough on the causes of crime'. This is perhaps a more subtle approach towards the under-standing of crime, as it brings in the role of agency. For what New Labour is suggesting is that it is not simply social or culture factors that are responsible for crime, but that individuals must also take responsibility for their actions. As New Labour observed in its 1997 manifesto, the party promised to: 'insist on individual responsibility for crime' (Labour Party 1997: 220). Moreover, New Labour's approach appeals to old or traditional Labour sentiments, but its policies here were revised, it is sug-gested, for expedient or political reasons. The 'old' Labour theme is re-echoed in the latter couplet of the sentence 'tough on the cause of crime'. This avers that Labour government should have an active 'social' role in addressing the symptoms of crime—social dislocation, poverty, etc—classic, traditional Labour rhetoric. Yet, the first couplet 'tough on crime' in many ways sees New Labour commandeering natural Conservative political territory by suggesting the party is not going to be an 'easy touch' on crime and public order. For the Conservatives have traditionally found great political mileage by claiming the Labour Party to be 'soft' on the issue of law and order. New Labour argues it is going to be tough on crime—which can be interpreted as coming down hard on offenders—and so encroaching on what has traditionally been regarded as Conservative territory.

In government, the logic of Labour's position on crime and order can be witnessed first, for example, in its New Deal for Communities programme—investing in jobs, training, etc—in order to alleviate social deprivation. At the same time, the present Government argues that: 'crime runs in certain families and that antisocial behaviour in childhood is a predictor of later criminality' (Muncie 2002: 146). Here, Labour argues that poor or irresponsible parenting is a key factor in causing crime. The response has been to introduce a series of punitive measures such as anti-social behaviour orders (ASBOs) for young offenders and fines or sometimes even custodial sentences on the parents of persistent school truants. Together, these examples show the reality of New Labour's approach towards both crime and its causes.

Act was a: '... penological dinosaur in so far as it sought to combat recidivism via penetrative detention, corrective training for young offenders, and the creation of detention centres designed to administer a short, sharp shock' (Randall 2004: 180). In the course of the subsequent Conservative Administration (1951–64), there was no clear divergence from the existing value-set underpinning law and order. R.A. Butler, the Conservative Home Secretary from 1957–62, fought a fierce battle in resisting Tory back-bench demands for the reintroduction of corporal punishment (see Butler 1971: 200). Nevertheless, he did oversee, with the then existing laws on capital punishment, more executions than any other post-war Home Secretary (although this is mainly explained by the length of time he was in this post). However, even during Butler's time, the mood of the nation was changing and this was reflected in the cultural transformation that the field of law and order was about to undergo. At the same time, it must also be recognised that there did exist a broad bi-partisan agreement that a causal relationship existed between 'anti-social conditions' and 'anti-social behaviour'. Thus, the reformist Attlee Labour Government, alongside the subsequent Conservative Administration, whose front bench was predominantly made up of One-Nation Tories, were willing to undertake an active role in the field of social-welfare polices in an attempt to alleviate poverty. This, it was argued, would in turn reduce crime. What we see in this era is a degree of policy continuity whilst also, at the same time, providing substantive evidence to the existence of a 'post-war consensus' (see Chapter 4).

1960s: an era of social liberalism

The 1960s is often portrayed as a decade of both political and social change. An era in which respect for authority and the existing order were increasingly challenged. A new liberal wind was blowing through society removing the shackles of austerity and self-denial that had characterised the immediate post-war years. Popular labels often attached to this decade include: 'the psychedelic years', 'the swinging sixties', 'the decade of sex and drugs and rock and roll', 'turn on, tune in or drop out' and 'if you remember the sixties, you weren't there!' This was the era that witnessed the rise of the civil rights movement in America, the Kennedy Administration (and assassination), the Prague Spring, the anti-Vietnam war movement, Woodstock, student rebellions that paralysed France in 1968, the growth of the women's movement, etc (see Kurlansky 2004). At the same time, it must also be recognised that this is one particular and contested narrative of the sixties. Alternatively, it is suggested that the impact of the 1960s on day-to-day life was less than many popular accounts allow for. For example, despite the lifting of the ban on D.H. Lawrence's *Lady Chatterley's Lover* (1960), the Beatles' ground-breaking *Abbey Road* album (1969) or Anthony Burgess's subversive novel, *A Clockwork Orange* (1962),[2] the

---

[2] The novel, *Clockwork Orange* was turned into a film by Stanley Kubrick in 1971. At the time, the film was controversial for its high level of violence, with the media in particular blaming the influence of the film for a spate of what appeared to be random physical assaults on people. The film was subsequently withdrawn from distribution. The reason for its withdrawal was subsequently revealed in a television documentary made after Kubrick's death in 1999. His widow Christiane confirmed rumours that Kubrick had asked for the film's withdrawal following police advice after death threats were made against him and his family.

largest selling album of the decade (and most popular film) was *The Sound of Music*! Nevertheless, the 1960s was undoubtedly a decade in which existing social and political norms and values were increasingly questioned and, in some cases, rejected.

The progressive spirit of the 1960s left its mark on debates concerning law and order, most notably in the area of social relations. Yet, when explaining the subsequent paradigm shift in this policy area there is a problem of causation. Was it public pressure for a more permissive moral code that created the opportunity for political elites to overturn the socially conservative agenda of the 1950s? Here, the interpretation would suggest that ministers and civil servants acted as the bearers of public expression. Alternatively, was it the political elites who acted as agenda setters, expressing a need for change, which then received popular support from a public ready to move on from the more austere years of the 1950s?

In terms of actual change, it was in the course of the Wilson Labour Government (1964–70) that a new approach to law and order policy was first evidenced. The 1964 Labour manifesto clearly espoused traditional Labour values (see Politics in Focus 30.2; Labour Party 1964: 5) advocating the need to eradicate social deprivation, in order to reduce the likelihood of individuals falling into a life of crime. This was addressed by the 1967 Criminal Justice Act that aimed at transforming prisons into 'institutions of social learning', introduced the parole system and extended the use of fines rather than custodial sentences. As important was the 1969 Children and Young Persons Act which has been: '. . . recognised retrospectively as the apotheosis of progressive criminology, with its removal of all children under the age of fourteen from the jurisdiction of the courts' (Randall 2004: 180).

One of the central figures in this more progressive approach towards law and order policy was Roy Jenkins who had two spells as Home Secretary (1965–67, 1974–76). The combination of greater liberalism in society and Roy Jenkins' liberal outlook resulted in an important cultural change in the department. Throughout both his spells as Home Secretary, Jenkins influenced Home Office attitudes in favour of liberalising laws affecting human behaviour. As one official, who served in the Home Office for over 30 years, observed: 'Jenkins not only liberalised the criminal justice system, but was responsible for changing the culture of the whole Department with his progressive approach in the field of abortion and the treatment of homosexuals.'[3] It has been argued that Jenkins' periods in the Home Office shaped the thinking and attitudes of the officials in that department for the next 25 years (see Marsh, Richards and Smith 2001).

1970s–80s: continuity and consensus

Social liberalism remained in the ascendancy, throughout the 1970s and even after the election of the Thatcher Government in 1979. Not only is it possible to trace a broad consensus and continuity in policies from Merlyn Rees (Labour Home Secretary 1976–79) to William Whitelaw (Conservative Home Secretary 1979–83), but social liberalism continued to inform and influence Home Office thinking in the policy-making process.

---

[3] Private information.

Effectively, the culture of social liberalism became embedded as the dominant 'world view' of the Home Office during this era. Officials were socialised into the view that their role was to project the rights of individuals and this provided the framework, influencing the advice they offered to ministers.

Yet, with the onset of the new Thatcher Government in 1979, it is important to recognise the political context surrounding issues of law and order. First, despite the more liberal agenda established since the late 1960s until the 1970s, the issue of crime lacked political salience. As Downes and Morgan (1997) observe, it was the New Right attacks in the 1970s on what it regarded as the poor record on law and order by post-war governments, both Labour and Conservative, that saw crime emerge as an important political (and electoral) issue. Moreover, elements within the print media, receptive to the increasing salience of law and order as an issue, increasingly generated a variety of 'moral panics' (see Politics in Focus 30.3) around issues of crime and race, in order to counter the existing liberal consensus.

It is important to recognise that although a socially liberal view remained the dominant outlook of the Home Office, despite the change in government in 1979, this view did not always concur with the rhetoric of the newly elected Conservative Government. Central to Thatcherism was first a belief in law and order and the need to reject the progressive penal policies that were seen as a feature of British society since the 1960s. There was also the need to re-establish the primacy of the rule of law which the Conservatives argued had been severely damaged during the course of the 1978–79 winter of discontent. Furthermore, in the early 1980s, rising crime figures (see Politics in Focus 30.4), a concern with public order resulting from problems in Northern Ireland, and riots in Bristol, Birmingham, Liverpool and London provided the Conservative Government with the potential political space to pursue more authoritarian police and criminal legislation, if it so wished. Yet, interestingly, until the late 1980s, there was a lack of Home Secretaries with the political will to challenge the established socially liberal culture in the Home Office. So, despite the consistent use of vitriolic rhetoric on crime by various Conservative Home Secretaries (most often heard at the annual party conferences) there was little in actual policy content to distinguish the 1980s from the previous era. As one senior Home Office official noted:

> One has to emphasise the surprising degree of continuity between the two different governments, which, despite the Thatcherite approach, remained unbroken up until Douglas Hurd left the Home Office in 1989. Indeed, the continuity remained intact from Jenkins in the sixties, all the way through to Hurd.[4]

The first socially conservative and pro-capital punishment Home Secretary was David Waddington, appointed by Margaret Thatcher in 1989, 10 years after the Conservatives

---

[4] Private information.

In 1972, Cohen's *Folk Devils and Moral Panics: Creation of Mods and Rockers* (revised in 2002) was a ground-breaking study of 'deviant' subcultures and the 'moral panic' they generated in the media and in public debate. His analysis of Mods and Rockers in the 1960s provided a new analytical framework for understanding the nature of sub-cultural groups in society, whilst also identifying the concept of a 'moral panic' generated by a reactionary print media. Cohen argued that this led to groups being vilified in the popular imagination, and restricted rational debate about solutions to the social problems presented by sub-cultural groups. In the 2002 revised edition, he contemporaries these arguments by analysing more recent moral panics including the demonisation of young offenders, asylum seekers and the *News of the World*'s name and shame campaign of paedophiles in response to the death of Sarah Payne and the paper's demand for 'Sarah's Law'.

   The central theme of Cohen's narrative is that agents of social control, particularly governments and the police, 'amplify' deviance. He also argued that the nature of the media had changed from once being the messengers of an event to now engaging in a new ideological role of 'constructing' meanings from events. Neo-Marxists used Cohen's analysis to argue that the mainstream media play an active role in helping avoid wider conflict in society by focusing attention on the supposedly deviant behaviour of outsider groups, such as new age travellers, teenage mothers, welfare scroungers, 'militant' trade unionists, asylum seekers and, most recently, so-called 'Islamic extremists'. Here, the suggestion is that by drawing attention to such groups, the media undertakes a powerful role in creating and underpinning the social consensus of society's core values. As Fowler (1991: 53) observes:

> Law and public opinion stipulate that there are many ideas and behaviours which are to be condemned as outside the pale of consensus: people who practise such behaviours are branded as 'subversives', 'perverts', 'dissidents', 'trouble-makers', etc. Such people are subjected to marginalization or repression; and the contradiction returns, because consensus decrees that there are some people outside the consensus. The 'we' of *consensus* narrows and hardens into a population which sees its interests as culturally and economically valid, but as threatened by a 'them' comprising a motley of antagonistic sectional groups: not only criminals but also trade unionists, homosexuals, teachers, blacks, foreigners, northerners, and so on.

The arguments of Cohen have also been adapted by McRobbie (1994: 199) to suggest that the last Conservative Administration actively created moral panics in order to provide it with the political space to pursue a programme of social control and the restoration of traditional values and authority. McRobbie observes: '. . . the extent that the panics are no longer about social control, but rather about the fear of being out of control' (McRobbie 1994: 199).

had come to power. Waddington's appointment is interesting, as it can be interpreted as a desire by Thatcher to counter the dominance of social liberalism within the Home Office. Waddington recognised the strength of the Home Office, observing that on entering the Home Office:

> You were very much given the impression, when you went to the Home Office, that governments came and went and ministers come and go but things went on as they had always done. That they had responsibilities which went far wider than the political concerns of ministers who were here one day and gone the next and they had to operate grand empires whether it was the Prisons or the Immigration Service and it was a fair assumption that whichever party was in office they would expect those functions to be performed in very much the same way.[5]

Waddington was never able to leave a mark, as events in the shape of the Strangeways prison riot in 1989 followed by Margaret Thatcher's resignation in November 1990 meant he lacked the time and institutional support to make any real impact on the department. Kenneth Baker (a Thatcherite) and then the more liberal Ken Clarke succeeded Waddington in the early 90s, yet neither left any significant mark during their spells in office.

1993–79: changing the agenda: Michael Howard's social conservatism

In 1993, Michael Howard was appointed Home Secretary. He was the first Conservative Home Secretary to have both the inclination and time in office to challenge the existing agenda. Moreover, Howard felt he had a political mandate to affect change as, by June 1993, crime levels had soared to a record level—5.7 million reported crimes as opposed to 2.4 million in 1979. The Conservatives, the avowed party of law and order had presided over an unprecedented rise in crime, while clear-up rates for offences had fallen from 41% to 26% in the same period (see also Figure 30.1). These figures increased the perception that penal policy was in crisis and an opportunity for change existed. From Howard's perspective, there was much to do: 'The Home Office together perhaps with the Department of Education seemed completely untouched by all the changes that had affected other departments in the period since 1979. It just had not changed'.[6] Here, what is of interest is that despite the arguments associated with the radicalness of Thatcherism (see Chapter 4), it can be argued that the New Right project pursued after 1979 was slow to penetrate the policy areas of both education and law and order.

---

[5] Interview with the authors.
[6] Interview with the authors.

981–2004

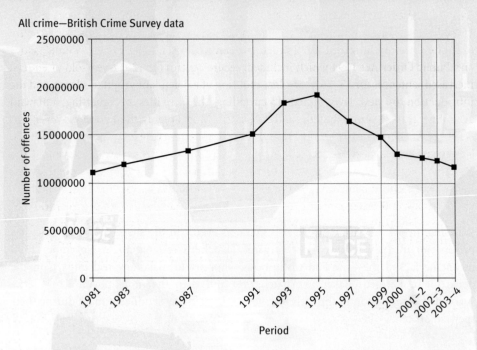

All crime—British Crime Survey data

Source: British Crime Survey (BCS)

How the British Crime Survey (BCS) works:

- For a variety of reasons, people do not always report crimes to the police—which means they don't get reflected in police recorded crime figures.
- The British Crime Survey (BCS) asks people about their *actual experiences*—and so gives us a more accurate picture of crime levels and trends across England and Wales.

Note: The BCS does not include crimes against businesses or commercial property.

According to the BCS:

- In 2003–04 the total number of crimes in England and Wales was around 11,716,000.
- Total crime peaked in 1995, and has since fallen by 39%.
- In 2003–04 nearly 26% of the population were the victim of some type of crime.
- This has fallen from a high in 1995 of nearly 40% of the population.

Source: Home Office

Howard embraced a number of the themes tentatively outlined during the Waddington era, in order to shift the priorities of the Home Office away from individual liberty towards civic order. He believed his predecessors had been soft on crime, the police were demoralised and the criminal justice system was weighted too heavily in favour of defendants. Howard argued the Conservatives had failed as they had not been tough on criminals. Indeed his new line was best encapsulated in the phrase: 'Prison works'. During his tenure as Home Secretary, he introduced a range of measures most notably in the Criminal Justice and Public Order Act 1994 which included: secure centres for 12–14-year-old offenders; increased sentences for 15–16-year-olds; abolition of a defendant's right to silence; and the introduction of new laws aimed at curtailing the activities of squatting, unlawful assemblies (raves), hunt saboteurs and trespassers. Most notably, the 'Prison Works' motto was acted on. Between 1993 and 1997, the prison population rose by 20% (see Figure 30.2). The measures Howard pursued can be seen as an attempt to restore the image of the Conservatives as the party of law and order. He differed from his immediate predecessors in the Home Office by having the political will to introduce a series of illiberal, perhaps populist, law and order reforms. Yet, again, it is important to recognise structural and agency explanations as to why Howard succeeded where, for example, Waddington failed. Howard had the time (nearly five years), the support (in terms of the party, the Cabinet and many elements of the print media) and empirical data in the form of rising crime statistics to assist his arguments for a programme of reform.

FIGURE 30.2

The prison population of England and Wales, 1979–2005

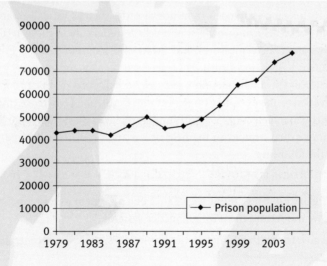

Source: Figures compiled from official statistics released by the Home Office

New Labour and law and order: having it both ways?

Since the Labour Party came to power in 1997, a number of critics have argued that in the field of law and order, the present Government has further embedded the trend established in the Howard era of social conservatism, but in a less explicit fashion. The present Labour Government has had three Home Secretaries, namely Jack Straw (1997–2001), David Blunkett (2001–04) and Charles Clarke (2004–to date). Jack Straw's remit was to pursue an explicit set of promises laid out in the 1997 party manifesto.

- Fast-track punishment for persistent young offenders.
- Reform Crown Prosecution Service to convict more criminals.
- Police on the beat not pushing paper.
- Crackdown on petty crimes and neighbourhood disorder.
- Fresh parliamentary vote to ban all handguns.

(Labour Party Manifesto 1997)

As we saw above (see Politics in Focus 30.2), underpinning Labour's thinking on law and order were themes associated with both traditional social conservatism in the form of being 'tough on crime', but also traditional left views of the causal relationship between crime and social circumstances, in the form of being 'tough on the causes of crime'.

In the course of Labour's first term, Jack Straw pursued an active legislative programme, introducing the Crime and Disorder Act 1998, Youth and Justice and Criminal Evidence Act 1999, the Regulation of Investigatory Powers Act 2000 and the Criminal Justice and Police Act 2001. These Acts together addressed issues concerning the gathering and surveillance of data in particular on the internet, the need to increase police powers against terrorism, drug-testing in prisons, a zero-tolerance approach to minor disorder such as vandalism and graffiti (by introducing anti-social behaviour orders) and calls to reduce the right to trial by jury—all broadly socially conservative measures. But Straw also incorporated the European Convention on Human Rights into British law, increased literacy and numeracy programmes for prison inmates aimed at rehabilitation, and demanded action on institutionalised racism in the police revealed by the Macpherson Report into the Stephen Lawrence case.

After the 2001 general election, David Blunkett replaced Straw as Home Secretary and continued Labour's dual strategy in the field of law and order. The 2001 party manifesto had promised the following.

10-year goals:

- Halve the burglary rate and double the chance of a persistent offender being caught and punished, as we modernise the criminal justice system.
- Reform local government with higher-quality services, as we decencentralise power.

Next steps:

- An extra 6,000 police recruits raising police numbers to their highest ever level.
- Double the amount of assets seized from drug-traffickers and other major criminals.
- Increased sentences plus education and drug treatment for persistent offenders.

- A bill of rights for victims.
- New freedoms with new targets for local government.

(Labour Party Manifesto 2001)

The commitments the party made included:

- Burglary rates would be cut by 50% by targeting 100,000 persistent offenders.
- 6,000 extra police would be employed.
- Those who offend while on parole will return to prison without a trial.
- 'Yob culture' will be cracked down on.

(Labour Party Manifesto 2001)

Yet, the issue of immigration and asylum became the central issue that Blunkett had to address (see Chapter 29). But elsewhere, he announced an extension to the Regulation of Investigatory Powers (RIP) Acts, which some elements of the media labelled as a 'snoopers' charter'. His Criminal Justice Bill 2003 reduced legal safeguards such as the right to trial by jury and double jeopardy rules. Blunkett also attempted to use the new political agenda created by the 9/11 attacks to introduce compulsory national identity cards.

Following David Blunkett's resignation in 2004, the present Home Secretary, Charles Clarke, has continued to pursue a similar policy agenda—combating crime and anti-social behaviour, strengthening national security, reforming the criminal justice system, introducing identity cards, tackling immigration abuse and cutting re-offending. After a year in office, Clarke's agenda became dominated by the terrorist attacks carried out in July 2005 and the need to be seen to be dealing effectively with the potential threat of further attacks. Yet, in one of his first interviews as Home Secretary, prior to the 7/07 attack, Clarke reflected on the extent to which he would continue his predecessor David Blunkett's agenda, prioritising civic order over individual liberty in the post-9/11 era:

I think I'm closer to him in his view of the importance of collective security, than some people have acknowledged... I look at the challenges that the country faces, the challenge of highly organised international crime, in areas like people trafficking and drug dealing, the challenges of international terrorism from organisations seeking to bring down every aspect of our democratic liberties, and I think it's the prime responsibility of the Home Secretary, any Home Secretary actually, certainly I take it in this role as my prime responsibility, to do what I can to protect the country, to protect the civilization, even against those kinds of threats, to create a secure country in which everybody can live at peace, and that is my priority at this time. (BBC *Newsnight*, 17 December 2004).

His time as Home Secretary has not been without controversy: in February 2005 he advocated the introduction of control orders which would provide powers to the police to detain terror suspects under house arrest without trial, so conflicting with the principle of *Habeas Corpus*;[7] after the 2005 general election, the Home Secretary again renewed Labour's commitment to introduce identity cards, despite widespread criticism; and, in response to the July 2005 terrorist attacks, Clarke not only continued the Metropolitan Police Force's policy of 'shoot to kill', despite the mistaken killing of the young Brazilian, Jean Charles de Menezes by plain clothed policeman at Stockwell tube station on 22 July 2005, he also pursued a range of anti-terrorist measures, including a controversial new offence of 'indirect incitement to terrorism'.

As Politics in Focus 30.4 and Figure 30.1 show, during the first two terms of the present Labour Government, the overall crime rate has fallen, but at the same time the size of the prison population has continued to grow. Labour also increased the number of police officers in England and Wales, reaching a record high of 138,000 in March 2004 (see also Figure 30.3). In July 2004, Labour unveiled its five-year 'anti-crime' drive which reinforced the twin strategy of being tough on crime but also tough on the causes of crime. On the one hand, Labour overtly rejected the notion, embraced by Michael Howard that 'prison works', by placing an upper limit of 80,000 on the jail population of England and Wales and argued that prison would be reserved only for the most serious and dangerous offenders who would forthwith receive longer sentences. In the same month, Blair (2004) made a speech at a Community Centre in London in which he declared:

> People do not want a return to old prejudices and ugly discrimination... But they do want rules, order and proper behaviour... The 1960s saw a huge breakthrough in terms of freedom of expression, of lifetstyle, of the individual's right to live their own personal life in the way they choose... But there was a resigned tolerance of failure, a culture of fragmentation and an absence of any sense of forward purpose across the whole criminal justice system. And anti-social behaviour was a menace... The purpose of the reforms... is to rebalance the system radically in favour of the victim, protecting the innocent but ensuring the guilty know the odds have changed.

In the five-year plan, the Labour Government proposed to overhaul the criminal justice system, introduce satellite tracking of persistent offenders, double the numbers of

---

[7] *Habeas Corpus* is a writ which requires a person detained by the police to be brought before a court of law so that the legality of the detention may be examined.

offenders electronically tagged, increase the number of police officers by 20,000 and continue and strengthen its programme against anti-social behaviour. The rhetoric used by Labour in unveiling these proposals during the lead-up to the 2005 general election was clearly aimed at rejecting the Howard ethos, while at the same time presenting Labour as being strong on the issue of law and order.

Analysing New Labour's approach to law and order is a complex task, as their policies have drawn from an array of traditions ranging from 'old' Labour themes emphasising rehabilitation and the need for tackling socioeconomic deprivation to much more authoritarian themes concerning, for example, the transfer of responsibility to parents (and the imposition of custodial sentences) for school truancy. To return to the theme of continuity and change, it would be misleading to conclude that the present Labour Government has simply continued to pursue the socially conservative agenda established during the Michael Howard era. Randall's (2004: 182) conclusions are probably the most perceptive in summing up the post-1997 era,

FIGURE 30.3
Police numbers in England and Wales, 1979–2005

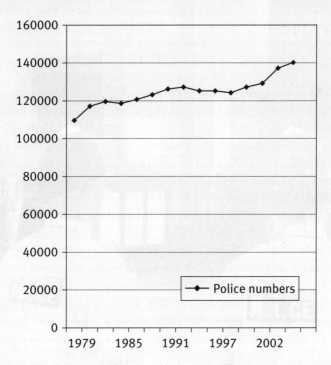

Source: Figures compiled from official statistics released by the Home Office

arguing that Labour's approach has embodied a:

> . . . conservative and confirmist communitarianism. Yet, while this
> configuration may be novel, their underlying rationale is not
> entirely alien to the Labour Party. At the heart of these policies
> lies a distinction between the respectable working classes, who
> deserve the state's support, and an irresponsible, undisciplined
> 'underclass'. In many respect this is not far removed from the
> Attlee Government's defence of the 'morality of the nuclear family,
> dominated by the respectable working man'.

Conclusion

The politics of law and order go right to the heart of some of the most important issues concerning both political science and political philosophy. What is the role of the state? How do we define liberty? What should the relationship be between the needs for social order and the protection of individual rights? Law and order is also a policy field that is affected by the ideological outlook of the incumbent government, alongside both endogenous (eg growth in juvenile crime or the rising rate of mobile phone thefts) and exogenous (eg 9/11 attack in the US) forces. What is interesting is that up until the 1970s, the issue of law and order was not high on the political agenda. It was only the success of the Thatcherite critique after 1979 on what it saw as the failure of post-war governments to confront the issue of crime and the decline in respect for authority and the rule of law which made it an issue that mainstream political parties took much more seriously. It is also a policy area where we can depict a seam of continuity, despite changes in government. Social conservatism dominated the initial post-war era. This was to be replaced by a more socially liberal approach by governments from the late 1960s onwards until the Howard era of the 1990s. Thus, law and order presents an interesting case-study in relation to the debates surrounding the contested nature of the 'post-war consensus' and 'Thatcherism' (see Chapter 4). It also presents an interesting insight into interpreting what is and is not new about the present Labour Government. What we have seen is that Labour's approach to combating crime is a complex or multi-dimensional strategy based on: an authoritarian approach to the issue of crime (and, in particular, terrorism); a willingness to embark on rehabilitation programmes for offenders; and attempts to alleviate social deprivation in society, with the hope that one effect will be to reduce in number those tempted to pursue criminal activities. Finally, one of the most challenging tasks facing political science in analysing change in the field of law and order is the issue of structure and agency. Can change in this policy area be explained predominantly by changes in society and the emergence of new popular pressures which the elite political classes then respond to? Alternatively, is it the political elites who are acting as agenda setters, that in turn engender broad popular support, allowing the political class to then pursue policy change? The issue of course is a dialectical one, but it is important that as students of political science, we are aware of it when attempting to explain the politics of law and order in post-war Britain.

KEY POINTS

- At the heart of the debate on law and order is the balance between the need to maintain civic order and protect the rights of the individual.

- Until the 1970s, the issue of law and order lacked high political salience.

- In the post-war era there has been a number of paradigm shifts in governments' approach to law and order switching from a socially conservative to a socially liberal perspective.

- There has been a degree of continuity in law and order policy, despite various changes in government, for example, 1951, 1970 and 1979.

- In explaining where change in law and order policy occurs, it is important to recognise the importance of the issue of structure and agency.

- New Labour has attempted to reconcile both a socially conservative and socially liberal approach to law and order, as reflected in one of its most well-known mantras 'tough on crime and tough on the causes of crime'.

KEY QUESTIONS

(1) Explain the problem of structure and agency when analysing the politics of law and order.

(2) To what extent does law and order provide a useful case-study when analysing the contested nature of the post-war consensus, Thatcherism and New Labour?

(3) Explain the extent to which political ideology affects the way that both main parties have viewed the issue of crime between 1945–2004.

(4) Would you regard New Labour's approach towards law and order as drawing more from a socially conservative or a socially liberal position?

IMPORTANT WEBSITES

For websites on the the main political parties and their positions on law and order see: Labour www.labour.org.uk, for the Conservatives www.conservative-party.org.uk, for the Liberal Democrats www.libdems.org.uk, then SNP www.snp.org.uk and Plaid Cymru www.plaid-cymru.wales.com. For details on the work of the Home Office go to www.homeoffice.gov.uk/ and for prime ministerial announcements www.number-10.gov.uk. Other useful websites include the British Crime Survey statistics www.data-archive.ac.uk, the Association of Chief Police Officers www.acpo.police.uk and the Howard League for Penal Reform www.howardleague.org/.

FURTHER READING

A useful institutionalist account of the politics of law and order and the role of the Home Office is D. Marsh, D. Richards, and M.J. Smith, (2001) *Changing Patterns of Governance: Reinventing Whitehall*, Basingstoke: Palgrave. Accounts of change under New Labour can be found in N. Randall (2004) 'New Labour's Home Office' in S. Ludlam and M.J. Smith, *Governing as New Labour*, Basingstoke: Palgrave and from a more critical perspective: N. Cohen, (2003) *Pretty Straight Guys*, London: Faber and Faber. Numerous Home Secretaries have published their memoirs including: Lord Butler (1971) *The Art of the Possible: The Memoirs of the Late Lord Butler*, London: Hamish Hamilton; J. Callaghan (1987) *Time and Chance*, London: Harper Collins; R. Jenkins, (1991) *A Life at the Centre*, London: Macmillan; and D. Hurd (2003) *Memoirs*, London: Little Brown. Other reading on issues relating to crime and culture include M. Maguire, R. Morgan and R. Reiner (eds) (1997) *The Oxford Handbook of Criminology*, 2nd edn, Oxford: Oxford University Press and S. Cohen (1972) *Folk Devils and Moral Panics: The Creation of the Mods and Rockers*, Oxford: Martin Robinson (reprinted 2002).

Visit the Online Resource Centre that accompanies this book for links to more information on this chapter topic

CHAPTER THIRTY ONE

Foreign and defence policy

READER'S GUIDE

Since the end of the Cold War the meaning of security has changed. Issues such as terrorism, drugs trafficking, organised crime and illegal immigration have become part of the Foreign Office agenda. These changes intensified after the attacks on New York and Washington on 11 September 2001. The 'war on terror' lies behind major domestic changes such as proposals for ID cards, the detention without trial of terror suspects and the development of what has been called the 'surveillance state'. This chapter explores how the meaning of security has changed and how the boundaries between domestic and international politics have become blurred. This has meant that ostensibly foreign policy issues such as the 'war on terror' and the invasion of Iraq have also had domestic impacts. This chapter analyses the changing context of defence and security policy and the growing importance of intelligence in the face of global terrorism.

Introduction

In December 2003 the Foreign and Commonwealth Office produced a strategy document that sketched British strategic priorities and challenges for the next 10 years. In this document was an interesting and revealing sentence from Foreign Secretary Jack Straw who wrote that 'foreign affairs are no longer really foreign. What happens elsewhere increasingly affects us at home'. Straw argued that issues such as terrorism, drugs, crime and illegal immigration all indicated how the boundaries between domestic and international politics—and thus the meaning of foreign policy—have shifted. During the Cold War, international politics had been dangerous, of course, but rather more straightforward. Britain knew where it stood with the USA in a nuclear stand-off with the ex-USSR. The geopolitical shake-up since the end of the Cold War has introduced new uncertainties that challenge traditional ideas about foreign policy, about the role of the state and about Britain's place in the world. One thing that has remained constant is the close alliance with the US. No student bedroom could be complete in the 1980s without a spoof *Gone with the Wind* film poster showing Margaret Thatcher and Ronald Reagan locked in an embrace. By the first decade of the 21st century, this image had been replaced by Prime Minister Blair as President Bush's poodle.

The context of foreign and defence policy

At its most basic, British foreign policy concerns Britain's relations with other states. These relations can be quite complex. One element of this complexity is Britain's post-imperial connections that still give it a global role. We have also seen that European integration has altered British relations with other European countries, but this cannot be understood as a foreign policy issue because it encroaches on many areas of domestic politics such as competition, regional and agricultural policy. Traditional understandings of foreign policy focus on the way in which the classic purpose of foreign policy is to protect the state against attacks from without and increasingly within, and developing Britain's influence *vis-à-vis* other states. As such it can be considered an essential or defining task of a state. While the state remains the building block of the international order and it would be foolish to try and write the state out of our analysis, it is also the case that the context in which foreign policy is made has changed. Part of this change is linked to European integration, but other factors have made a difference too, such as the end of the Cold War and more recently the 'war on terror'.

At first sight, foreign policy would seem to be very different from domestic policy. In real life the distinction between the two is often less sharp. Northern Ireland, for example, is in the United Kingdom and policy affecting it is clearly part of the domestic agenda. But Britain also recognises the right of the Irish Republic to shape policy and the future government of the province and the United States has been heavily involved in shaping policy.

The Department of Trade and Industry is closely involved in arms sales. Increasingly British political parties look abroad for best practice in such areas as education, training, labour relations and social policy. Reforms in these areas have been motivated in part by the politicians' concern for Britain to be internationally competitive—winning and not losing markets and jobs to competitors. Richard Rose (2001) has referred to the increasing overlap between the two as 'intermestic politics'.

Britain's international position has changed greatly since 1945. As we saw in Chapter 6 Britain was then a world power, the head of a vast empire, emerging as one of the 'big three' victorious states (Britain, the US and the USSR) from the Second World War and the only one of the three to have fought against Germany from the start of the war in 1939. Winston Churchill spoke of Britain uniquely being at the centre of 'three interconnecting circles'—the Commonwealth, the special relationship (dating from the entry of the US to the war in 1942) between Britain and the US, and Europe. That wide range of interests has often been advanced as an explanation for Britain deciding not to join the European Economic Community in its formative years. To choose Europe would have meant Britain turning its back on its relations with its other friends. Yet, as we also saw in Chapter 6, the US was keen that Britain should join the EC in order to bolster this capitalist bloc and steer it in a direction favourable to US interests.

The problem was that Britain was only a medium-sized power compared with the US and the USSR. It had emerged victorious in 1945 but economically drained; it had lost markets, and the onerous conditions attached to a US loan in 1946 were a further constraint. Britain continued its steady relative economic decline for much of the second half of the 20th century. It was no longer able to carry out its far-reaching defence commitments. It had troops stationed in Germany and east of Suez and the military budget was much higher than those of comparable Western states. In truth the costs were too heavy for it to bear; a classic case of military overstretch and of great power delusions. In an increasingly bi-polar world, Britain settled for a role as a subordinate partner of the United States.

The weakness was clearly seen over the Suez episode in 1956 when Britain invaded Egypt after the Egyptian government had seized the Suez Canal. However, it had to abort the operation after the US exerted financial pressure. In many respects, Harold Macmillan's application to join the EEC in 1961 recognised that Britain could no longer be a great power on its own; it was dependent on the US and that support could not be guaranteed. The EEC seemed to be the preferred route. The application was rebuffed and Britain only finally joined in 1973. As we saw in Chapter 8, by the time Britain joined the EEC, the rules that had been established by the other member states were not necessarily in Britain's best interests. Indeed, the budget mechanisms and rules for the Common Agricultural Policy still haunt the British government in the first decade of the 21st century. As of 2006 a there is a stand-off between Britain and France over the CAP and Britain's budgetary contribution.

Yet it is worth remembering that throughout the post-war period Britain remained a major player. It was one of the five permanent members of the Security Council of the United Nations set up in 1946; this gave it the right to veto UN resolutions. It was a founder member of NATO, set up in 1949 as the shield for the Western powers in the Cold War, possessed nuclear weapons, was a member of the G8 countries and remains a member of over 150 international organisations. At the same time, there was a powerful feeling that Britain had declined (see Politics in Focus 31.1). As we saw in Chapter 7 this sense of relative decline—and remedies that were proposed for it—was a central feature of British politics from the 1960s until the 1980s. Margaret Thatcher was determined to put the 'great' back into Great Britain, based on a particular understanding of the causes of social, economic and political decline.

The organisation of foreign policy

The key departments in foreign policy are the Foreign and Commonwealth Office, the Ministry of Defence, Number 10 and the Department for International Development, first created in 1964 as the Department of Overseas Development. The Department of the Environment, Food and Rural Affairs and the DTI, not least on arms trade, also often become involved. The Cabinet usually receives a weekly oral report from the Foreign Secretary and much of the policy is considered in the Cabinet committee, the Defence and Overseas Policy Committee (DOPC). In Number 10, the Prime Minister traditionally relied on a single private secretary, usually seconded for about three years from the Foreign Office. Because of the pressure of work (involving the EU, Northern Ireland, the Balkans and Iraq) a second secretary was appointed in 1994, and under Blair a further two have been added. The task of the private secretaries is to keep the Prime Minister aware of what is going on in Defence and the Foreign Office and to inform these two departments of the Prime Minister's views (see Politics in Focus 31.2). Blair, in his determination to make Number 10 something of a powerhouse has increased his staff. After the 2001 general election he created a new Overseas and Defence Secretariat in Number 10, drawing functions from the Cabinet Office, a new European Secretariat, again drawn from the Cabinet Office, and appointed two senior civil servants to head them.

A Prime Minister's interest in foreign affairs varies with the incumbent and circumstances. Neville Chamberlain, forever associated with the appeasement of the dictators in

We persist in regarding ourselves as a Great Power capable of everything and only temporarily handicapped by economic difficulties. We are not a Great Power and never will be again. We are a great nation, but if we continue to behave like a Great Power, we shall soon cease to be a great nation (Sir Henry Tizard, chief scientific adviser, Ministry of Defence, 1949).

Source: M. Gowing, *Independence and Deterrence: Britain and Atomic Energy, 1945–52* (1974, London: Macmillan, vol 1: 229)

the 1930s, took virtual command of foreign policy soon after he became Prime Minister in 1937. Mrs Thatcher took an increasing interest in international affairs, favoured an assertive foreign policy, not least with the USSR and the EC, and at times was unimpressed with the advice she received from the Foreign Office. She disagreed with her Foreign Secretaries over such issues as Rhodesia-Zimbabwe, the Falklands, EC, South Africa and the US defence system, 'Star Wars'. John Major was willing to leave great leeway to the more experienced Douglas Hurd and Malcolm Rifkind. Tony Blair has also been heavily involved (see below).

Over time Prime Ministers seem to become more interested in 'abroad' than 'home'. Abroad they are treated as statesmen, given a red carpet treatment, and escape from pressing and complex issues at home. When Mrs Thatcher was first informed in November 1990 that she had failed to win the first ballot of the leadership election against Michael Heseltine in November 1990, she was 'abroad', in Paris attending a conference on European Security and Co-operation, to celebrate the end of the Cold War. It is interesting that the autobiographies of Prime Ministers Margaret Thatcher and James Callaghan contain so many pictures of them on overseas tours or in the company of foreign leaders.

Ted Heath has perhaps been the only post-war British Prime Minister who has not placed British relations with the US ahead of Europe in conducting foreign policy. Margaret Thatcher, like Harold Wilson and James Callaghan before her, was an Atlanticist, and appreciated the support of the US at the time of the war over the Falklands and, controversially, allowed US bombers to use British bases to launch attacks on Libya in 1986. She supported the Reagan's 'Star Wars' initiative to protect the US from a nuclear attack, co-operated in the substantial increase in expenditure on defence, a battle the economically weak USSR could not win, and both were determined to resist what they regarded as USSR military expansion. Once US President Ronald Reagan retired in 1988, the US appeared to be more interested in West Germany and Japan, and encouraged Britain to advance its views through the European Community.

The relationship between Britain and the US became special again during the Gulf War. British troops supported the US military action against Iraq in 1991 following the latter's

... the Foreign Secretary

Only four times since 1945 (up to 1997) has a Prime Minister been saddled with an uncongenial Foreign Secretary. None lasted long. Eden and Macmillan rapidly fell out, and a reluctant Macmillan was soon transferred to the Exchequer. Wilson appointed George Brown because there was no other post senior enough for him, but Brown, with justification, resented Wilson's high-handed behaviour, such as his despatch of personal envoys to Vietnam and Rhodesia. After innumerable rows, the mercurial Brown resigned. When Carrington resigned after the Falklands invasion, Mrs Thatcher had no senior replacement except Francis Pym. (She fell out with him and dismissed him after the 1983 election.) Before many more years elapsed, she had similarly fallen out with his successor Howe . . .

Source: S. James, *British Cabinet Government* (1999, London: Routledge, 2nd edn: 143)

seizure of Kuwait, and under Blair in Kosovo and Iraq again. The special relationship is not one of equals; the US's hard-headed calculations of its own interest were seen when it informed rather than consulted Britain when invading Grenada, a British colony in the West Indies, in 1985 to restore a regime just deposed in a military coup. At the time, the Prime Minister was Mrs Thatcher, who appeared to be a jealous guardian of British sovereignty, but this appearance can be questioned. She allowed British bases to be used for the US raids on Libya, with the Cabinet and Parliament being informed after the event. It is worth recalling that in the mid-1980s Margaret Thatcher was also involved in the negotiation of the Single European Act, which proposed widespread deregulation in pursuit of a single European market with free movement for goods, services, people and capital to be attained by the end of 1992. Coupled with a domestic economic programme that sought deregulation and liberalisation, these kinds of developments at European level, which Thatcher strongly supported, had major implications for state sovereignty because key economic and financial tools were taken out of the hands of the British government and given to 'the market'.

The end of the Cold War also had major implications for defence, foreign and security policy. This was a particular problem for Thatcher who had seen the EEC in Cold War terms as a Western bloc in the face of Soviet communism. A series of new challenges arose. For example, many of the asylum seekers and refugees who came to Britain in the 1990s came from ex-Yugoslavian countries such as Bosnia and Kosovo. The post-Cold War fall out and subsequent geopolitical re-ordering had major implications for perceptions of security. New kinds of challenges came onto the agenda such as migration and organised crime that had previously not been within the remit of the Foreign Office. As Straw pointed out in the Foreign Office strategy document, foreign policy is not really foreign anymore. This is marked, for example, by much closer co-operation with other EU member states on issues that have ascended the security agenda, such as illegal immigration, drugs trafficking and organised crime. The EU has moved into what the distinguished American political scientist Stanley Hoffmann has called areas of 'high politics'. This has important implications for traditional understandings of state sovereignty. Hoffmann argued that states would tend to shy away from integrating in those areas that were most closely linked to their sovereignty, such as defence, security and foreign policy. As the EU proposed to move into areas of 'high politics' since the Maastricht Treaty (1992), interpretations of sovereignty have been central to British politics.

New Labour's foreign policy

Labour tried to set a new course in foreign policy in 1997. The first Foreign Secretary, Robin Cook, spoke of an 'ethical dimension' rather than an ethical policy when he laid out the values guiding the new Government's stance in international affairs. Britain, it appeared would take account of human rights, civil liberties and democracy in its dealings with other countries and assume a more moral stance on the arms trade. There would also be a more positive approach to the EU, although this was not saying much compared to the frigid atmosphere of much of the Thatcher and Major years. Indeed Blair spoke of a determination to 'lead' and 'modernise' the EU. Where Thatcher thought that sovereignty was based on the sanctity of the nation-state, Labour started out with an orientation to interdependence and co-operation. The former had a *realpolitik* or 'realist' view of international affairs in which Britain's national interest would be the determinant of foreign policy. Labour started with a more 'idealist' view of international relations.

The promises, however, soon fell foul of events. The Foreign and Commonwealth Office approved the shipment of arms by Sandline International, a British company, to Sierra Leone, despite a UN embargo, instigated at Britain's request, on such deals. In this 'arms to Africa' affair President Kabbah had been ousted in a military coup and the new rulers showed little respect for human rights. Britain also exported arms to Indonesia where the regime brutally repressed opposition in East Timor and suppressed student protests. The Labour Government has also expressed support for attempts to fashion an EU foreign and defence policy. But Blair's support for US military involvement in the Balkans and in Iraq has tried the patience of many of the EU governments. Many have resented Blair's role of regarding Britain as a bridge between Europe and the US rather than as a member of the former, and his readiness to support the US rather than help to formulate an independent EU policy. He, like Thatcher, was frustrated at the slowness with which European countries developed united and effective policy stances in the Balkans and on Iraq.

Blair spelt out his foreign policy approach in April 1999 in a speech in Chicago. In this he talked about what he regarded as the doctrine of the international community; the circumstances in which it could be legitimate for an outsider to intervene in the internal affairs on a sovereign state or to attempt to change a regime. He posed five criteria for a just intervention, namely:

(1) Are we sure of our case?

(2) Have diplomatic means been exhausted?

(3) Are our national interests involved?

(4) Can the military operation be prudently executed?

(5) Is there a will to hold out for the long term (if this is necessary)?

Blair and his supporters regarded British involvement in the war over Kosovo as an example of an ethical stand. The war did not involve any British interest but was fought on humanitarian grounds. President Milosevic of Yugoslavia was persecuting the Muslim majority in Kosovo and Blair was a leading 'hawk' for NATO intervention. When negotiations with Milosevic for a settlement broke down, over his rejection of the idea of a NATO peacekeeping force, NATO mounted air attacks on Serbia in March 1999. Milosevic was eventually forced back to the negotiating table.

The war in Iraq

British involvement in the war on Iraq in 2003 divided public opinion more than on any military issue since Suez. Britain went to war in support of US action without a Security resolution in favour of the action, although it invoked UN Resolution 687 calling for the removal or destruction of Iraq's biological and atomic facilities and weapons. Once the completion of that process had been approved by UNSCOM inspectors, economic sanctions imposed by the UN would be lifted. The inspectors failed to find such weapons and the British and US governments alleged that this was because the Iraqi government had managed to hide them.

Blair believed that it was important for Britain to support strongly the United States after 9/11. He feared that that in its war on terror the United States might retreat into isolationism. Although the US provided over 90% of the manpower in the operation the involvement of Britain, and some other states, notably Spain and Australia, in the war was important in enabling President Bush to talk about 'a coalition of the willing' fighting against Saddam. Although Blair persuaded the US to delay invasion and allow time for diplomats to win UN approval, it seems clear that a year earlier he had already pledged British military support. Not only did he regard the removal of Saddam as worthwhile in itself, regardless of weapons of mass, destruction, but he feared that if the US acted alone it might retreat into isolationism.

Apart from the questions raised about his judgement of the case for going war the event and its aftermath has had a considerable downside for Tony Blair (see Politics in Focus 31.3), notably:

(1) It damaged his standing with his own party, including MPs, party members and voters. In March 2003 139 Labour MPs voted against going to war. They were influenced by the lack of a UN resolution in support of the war and Blair's close relationship with a US neoconservative President. He suffered the resignation of two Cabinet ministers and a number of junior ministers. Labour was the only social democratic party in Western Europe to support the war.

(2) It provoked mass demonstrations against the war and public opinion eventually tuned against it, according to the polls.

(3) It raised doubts about Blair's integrity, because he appeared to many to have over-interpreted the intelligence assessment and exaggerated the military threat—particularly his claim that Iraq could mobilise weapons of mass destruction within 45 minutes.

(4) It strained relations with some EU members, particularly France and Germany, although Spain, Italy and some of the newer members supported the action.

(5) It weakened the case for military action against other 'rogue' states (Iran, Syria and North Korea were sometimes mentioned in this context) who might supply weapons or sanctuary to terrorists. Certainly the doctrine of pre-emptive action, or military intervention against a state that is not an immediate threat but may become so was no less contentious after the Iraq conflict.

(6) Labour and Blair paid a price in the 2005 general election. Surveys report that a quarter of Liberal Democrat voters switched from Labour because of Iraq and Blair was no longer the electoral asset he had been in 1997 and 2001.

Blair's critics complain that his whole-hearted support for the United States made Britain appear as an American lapdog and that he should have insisted on more leverage over the United States. For example, they suggest, he should have pushed for a firmer commitment of US engagement in the search for peace in the Middle East and support for the Kyoto agreement on climate change.

Defence

Defence has rarely been an issue between the main political parties. In government both parties were committed to NATO as the guarantor of collective security and to nuclear deterrence. It was a Labour government that decided in 1947 to develop a nuclear bomb; leaders of both Labour and Conservative Parties calculated that Britain needed its own deterrent in case the United Sates withdrew from Western Europe and that the bomb ('a British finger on the trigger') was essential if Britain was to continue to have a seat at the top table in international affairs. Deterrence seemed to work insofar as there was no war with the USSR and no nuclear conflict.

But defence has been a recurring cause of dissension in the Labour Party. The party has always contained an anti-war section and many of its leading politicians were prominent in the Campaign for Nuclear Disarmament (including, Michael Foot, the party leader between 1980 and 1983). The party conference vote to give up nuclear weapons unilaterally in 1981 broke the longstanding consensus between the party frontbenches on defence. Politically it was important in triggering the decision of some Labour MPs to leave the party and found the SDP. Labour's non-nuclear defence policy—involving the cancellation of Trident and refusal to allow Cruise missiles to be sited in Britain—was a major handicap in the 1983 general election. During the election the daily newspapers had more lead stories on defence (overwhelmingly negative) than on any other issue. Labour gradually abandoned the policy and by the 1992 general election was pledged to support Trident. Blair knew that it was important for the party to be seen as 'standing up for Britain'. The Conservatives, particularly under Mrs Thatcher, were widely regarded as staunch defenders of Britain.

In government again in 1997, Labour launched a Strategic Defence Review (SDR) and this reported a year later. It took account of the changed world, notably the break-up of the

...lligence and the case for war with Iraq

In a critical examination of how Tony Blair and his aides handled intelligence, Butler noted that although 'excellent-quality papers' were written by officials, they were not discussed by the Cabinet. He continued: 'Without papers circulated in advance, it remains possible but is obviously much more difficult for members of the Cabinet outside the small circle directly involved to bring their political judgements and experience to bear on the major decisions for which the Cabinet as a whole must carry responsibility . . . We are concerned that the informality and circumscribed character of the Government's procedures which we saw in the context of policymaking towards Iraq risks reducing the scope for informed collective political judgement.'

Source: Lord Butler, *Review of Intelligence on Weapons of Mass Destruction* (2004: 147–8)

USSR and the possible need for British involvement in conflicts around the world. The review paved the way for the creation of a rapid reaction force of the three services, to be deployed on various military, peacekeeping and relief operations around the world.

Britain's arms industry provides a significant number of jobs and is important in trade. Firms like GEC and British Aerospace depend heavily on the British government for orders or support for sales abroad. Although the government has an obvious interest in encouraging and sustaining a national defence industry, ministers, particularly from the Treasury, often complain at the cost of orders and even more at the occasional large cost overruns. Export deals are sometimes clouded in murky political arrangements. The loan in 1994 to Malaysia on generous terms to build the Pergau Dam was linked to the purchase of British arms and was made in spite of Civil Service advice that it was poor value for money.

Foreign and defence issues have rarely been prominent in recent general elections, in large part this is because of broad agreement between the parties. The reason defence was such an important issue in the 1983 general election was that Labour's unilateralist stance was a divide between the main parties. Even Europe has been a low profile issue, partly because of public (although not press) indifference, and partly because of divisions within each of the Labour and Conservative Parties. Yet foreign affairs have caused problems for Prime Ministers. Eden resigned soon after the Suez failure in 1956. Mrs Thatcher's position was fatally weakened by her outbursts against greater European integration in October 1990; it led to the resignation from her Cabinet of Sir Geoffrey Howe and this in turn prompted Michael Heseltine to challenge Mrs Thatcher for the leadership and force her resignation. John Major's premiership was from September 1992 effectively broken by Britain's forced withdrawal from the ERM and the battle to carry the Maastricht Treaty through Parliament. As noted, Tony Blair's decision to go to war with Iraq and its aftermath greatly damaged his standing with his party and the public.

Security and intelligence

Intelligence backs up foreign policy and the military arm in protecting the state. The devastation of the twin towers in New York in September 2001 showed that even the most powerful and best armed state in the world is vulnerable to new forms of threat, facilitated by permeable borders, open societies and sophisticated high tech weaponry. Massive armies and elaborate security precautions are ill-equipped to combat terrorism. 'The war on terror' has replaced the Cold War.

Britain has a well-developed intelligence machinery. So much is shrouded in secrecy that it is sometimes a secret state. National security matters are exempt from the provisions of the Freedom of Information Act; ministers may refuse to answer questions in Parliament on the grounds that to do so would imperil national security; and Prime Ministers have always refused to allow the head of MI5 to appear before the Home Affairs Select Committee.

MI5, or the secret service, deals with domestic intelligence (including Northern Ireland) and serious crime and is under the jurisdiction of the Home Office. MI6, or the Secret

Intelligence Service, deals with foreign materials and is under the Foreign Office. GCHQ or the Government Communications Headquarters at Cheltenham monitors communications around the world. These bodies provide intelligence and counter intelligence services, frustrate hostile intelligence services and penetrate terrorist groups.

The Prime Minister receives a weekly report, often sifted beforehand by his Principal Private Secretary, from the JIC or Joint Intelligence Committee. It meets weekly and consists of the heads of MI5, MI6, GCHQ and senior officials of the Foreign Office, Defence and the Treasury. Following a post-Falklands review of operations it was decided in 1983 that the JIC would be based in the Cabinet Office and that the Prime Minister would appoint the chairman, who would report directly to the Prime Minister rather than the Chiefs of Staff. After 9/11 security moved from being a minor part of the Cabinet Secretary's remit to a major one and it was decided in 2002 to create a new post in the Cabinet Office of Security and Intelligence Coordinator.

Security and the battle against terrorism had risen sharply up the political agenda even before the bombings and loss of life on the London underground and a bus in July 2005. They raise crucial issues of balancing Britain's tradition of civil liberties and an open society with the need for security. In 2005, the Labour Government tried to legislate for the introduction of ID cards and the courts have ruled against its attempts to detain suspected terrorists indefinitely on the grounds that they infringe the Human Rights Act.

Conclusion

There has been a good deal of continuity and cross party agreement on the broad objectives of foreign and defence policy. Some of this bipartisanship emerges from a belief in the national interest and that wars involving the lives of British troops should be 'above' party or 'above' politics. But there are also more constraints in the form of treaty commitments and pressures to adhere to the policies or values of the many international bodies to which Britain belongs. For most of the time voters are more concerned with domestic than foreign issues. Partly because of the end of the Cold War, and with it the fear of an external military threat, defence spending as a share of GDP has been shrinking. But in the new millennium security issues and the 'war on terror' has become of major importance to the Government and the public.

KEY POINTS

- Britain from 1947 regarded the possession of nuclear weapons as essential for great power status.

- Britain has managed a relatively peaceful (compared to other former colonial powers) handover of power to its colonies.

- Involvement in wars in the Balkans and Iraq since 1990 has deepened and strengthened Britain's alliance with the United States.

- Foreign and defence tend to be areas of great continuity in government policy.

KEY QUESTIONS

(1) Has Britain resolved the tensions in its dual loyalties to the US and the EU?

(2) What are non-military sources of international influence?

(3) How might a united European foreign and security policy affect Britain's position in the world?

IMPORTANT WEBSITES

On defence and security issues see NATO www.nato.int and Ministry of Defence www.mod.uk. On foreign and EU issues see Foreign and Commonwealth Office www.fco.gov.uk and European Union www.europa.eu.int.

FURTHER READING

For critical analysis see D. Sanders (1990) *Losing an Empire, Finding a Role*, Basingstoke: Macmillan. On defence and security see D. Keohane (2000) *Security in British Politics*, Basingstoke: Macmillan, L. Freedman (2001) 'Defence' in A. Seldon (ed) *The Blair Effect*, London: Little, Brown, and L. Freedman (1999) *The Politics of British Defence 1979–1998*, Basingstoke: Macmillan.

 Visit the Online Resource Centre that accompanies this book for links to more information on this chapter topic

CHAPTER THIRTY TWO

Conclusion: continuities and change in 21st century British politics

READER'S GUIDE

One of key themes of this book has been the extent to which the British polity has changed over the past 30 years. The book has highlighted myriad changes in terms of international relations, the constitution, participation, the structure of government and policy. Nevertheless the book has also highlighted that these changes, although radical, have also had considerable continuities. This chapter examines the degree of changes that have occurred within Britain, and makes an assessment of whether the Westminster model still exists. It also reflects on where power lies today.

Introduction

This book has outlined the way the British political system works and how it has changed. One of the central themes of to emerge is that British politics is radically different from 30 or 40 years ago. Nevertheless, despite these changes the political system continues to retain many of the imprints of the past. The traditional conception of British political development contained in the Westminster model is a Whig notion of history. From this perspective, change is a gradual process which takes place within the confines of British political tradition and ensures that the constitution remains in balance. For example, if we look at the role of the monarchy, it could be argued that it has adapted over time to the political circumstances that it has faced whilst retaining a central role within the British political system. At the same time it has not compromised the basic democratic principles of the system. However, it is possible to suggest that whilst the nature of British society today cannot be understood without understanding its history, the changes that have occurred in the last three decades have indeed been radical. What we have seen since the 1970s is a transition from the post-war period and the development of a different sort of polity, economy and society in the new millennium. In this concluding chapter we try to pull together the key themes that have been outlined throughout the book and make some assessment of the nature of the British polity in the 21st century.

Epochs in British politics

Any attempt at breaking up society in to stages or epochs is bound to be false. Descriptions such as the Elizabethan age or the post-war era are post-hoc rationalisations on a period of history that has gone. It is an attempt to tidy up what is a confused reality that does not have a definitive start or finish. Nevertheless, periods allow us to apply a framework for looking at how politics has changed and how an array of forces may shape the lives and politics of a country. Politics in Britain between 1945–75 can be seen as the post-war era. Many of the political issues of the day and the political solutions on offer were a response to the impact of the Second World War and its aftermath. The people who ran the country, and many of those who voted, had lived through and fought in the war. The experience shaped how they thought about politics and the state. Even in the 1960s and early 1970s, school boy comics were about the Second World War and playground games would normally include Germany as the enemy. The war and its consequences provided the shape of the post-war world.

The war shaped politics in many ways:

- It demonstrated that the state could be a positive force in society. The British government had successfully organised a victory; it did this through planning nearly every aspect of British society. Consequently, the state was seen to have succeeded in wartime, whereas the laissez-faire policy of peace time had failed to solve the economic problems of the interwar years.

- Politicians were convinced that Britain finished the world war as a leading world power. It was the only major country that had been undefeated and had not been invaded throughout the duration of the war. Even the prominent left-wing politician Aneurin Bevin said in a speech to the House of Common:

> His Majesty's Government does not accept the view... that we have ceased to be a great Power, or the contention that we have ceased to play that role. We regard ourselves as one of the Powers most vital to the peace of the world... I am not aware of any suggestion, seriously advanced, that by a sudden stroke of fate, as it were, we have overnight ceased to be a world power (quoted in Vickers 2003:168).

Britain in the post-war era

Under the subsequent Attlee Labour Government (1945–51), Britain remained an Empire state and this shaped Britain's conception of its place in the world and also the understanding of the nature of the domestic state. Post-war Britain was shaped by:

- Dependence on the United State. Despite the self-belief that Britain was a world power it ended the war with a high degree of dependence on the United States. The war was only won with US support and lend-lease (where the US effectively lent Britain equipment for the war) ensured that Britain could continue its wartime efforts. At the end of the war, Britain was in considerable debt. The national debt had trebled during the war from £7,247,000 in 1938 to over £21 million in 1945 (Vickers 2003). Britain's world role could only exist within the context of United States hegemony.

- 'A land fit for heroes'. There was a feeling that the First World War was futile and that many of the soldiers who fought in the war had been betrayed because they returned to economic depression and essentially the continuation of Edwardian England. After the First World War, the Government had failed to provide 'homes fit for heroes'. In the 1940s, party leaders could not again be seen to let down returning soldiers. There was a strongly held view that the same mistake could not be made again and post-war Britain had to be a better place (Hennnessy 1992; Addison 1994). There was a growing acceptance by the political elites for the need for social improvement following the war. So, as we saw in Chapter 27, many elements of the post-war welfare state were established during the Second World War. Moreover, many of the propaganda films made by the Government during the Second World War emphasised the need to build a better, fairer society after the war.

- The growth of working class power. Until the interwar years the working class had little power in British society. The unions had a limited impact on politics and the Labour Party until the 1920s was the third party in British politics. In the interwar years there had been considerable conflict between business and labour, perhaps best illustrated by the General Strike of 1926. The unions were to a large extent seen as a disruptive or even a revolutionary force. The war saw the coming of age for the Labour Party with the acceptance that the party could form part of the war time coalition. The trade unions also became part of the polity because of their crucial role in controlling the labour market during the Second World War. There was a sense that politicians had for the first time really responded to the demands of the working class. There was an accommodation between labour and business. During the war, government needed the unions in order to control labour costs and to avoid strikes. As a consequence they were drawn into the governing process (Middlemas 1979). From the Second World War onwards both the Labour Party and the Conservatives accepted that the unions had a legitimate role in government.

• Faith in the British political system. The Second World War was fought on the basis that it was protecting British democracy against German fascism. The war established the belief that British parliamentary democracy was the best form of democracy in the world. Moreover, after the instability in interwar Europe, the fact that Britain had come through the first half of the 20th century with its parliamentary democracy intact, demonstrated further the resilience of the British political system.

The point of all the above factors is that they structured and shaped the nature of post-war British politics. To return to the question of structure and agency, the war provided the framework within which decisions were made. Britain after the war was a relatively homogenous society. Despite being highly class bound—there were clear distinctions between the classes—there was a high degree of deference and a general acceptance concerning the nature of the British political system. Unlike other European countries, there was no strong Communist Party, there was an absence of religious parties and a general acceptance of the relationship between the state and the market. This relationship was established during the course of the Attlee Government and embedded by the subsequent Conservative Administration (1951–64), despite a number of critics on the right who called for the return to laissez-faires and a small number on the left who demanded the extension of nationalisation to the majority of the economy. Likewise, there was a broad acceptance across the parties of the key features of the welfare state. Even if the Conservatives did have reservations about its form and nature, they knew by the time that they formed the government in 1951 that they could not dismantle the welfare system that they had inherited from Labour, the framework of which had been established during the Second World War.

The political system was stable and elitist, but legitimised through the process of elections which allowed the electorate to change the elite; between one broadly favourable to capital and one favourable to labour. Moreover, both parties were prepared to accommodate the interests of a range of classes; there was a sense in which they were both prepared to play by the rules of the game. As we saw, Britain was also a relatively white society with an apparent consensus about how society should be organised and ruled. It has to be remembered that during this period much of Europe was recovering from the impact of total war and were establishing, in some cases for the first time, liberal democracy. In other parts of the world, many colonial countries were becoming independent. Consequently, a country like Britain which could build politics around some sort of compromise, and which was able to easily secure a transition from one party to another (for some there was even a natural continuity to the process with the Labour Party and Conservative Party taking turns in power to ensure that the system could be neither too socialist or too capitalist), was seen as a beacon of how a political system should operate. The Westminster model was used as an example of what today would be called good governance.

There were also three closely related external factors which were important in shaping British politics.

The Cold War

The first was the Cold War (see Chapter 31). The Cold War developed as a consequence of the power blocs that developed following the Second World War which in effect created separate spheres of influence for the United States and the Soviet Union. These separate spheres were effectively in conflict from 1948 onwards and created an ever present danger of actual conflict at some point. The Cold War questions the notion that globalisation is a new phenomena. Such was the power of the United States and the Soviet Union, and so great were the implications of the conflict, that the Cold War effectively shaped politics around the world. In the case of Britain, a whole range of areas such as foreign and defence policy, internal security, the process of decolonisation, industrial relations policy, and relations with Europe were shaped by the Cold War. The Cold War was a prism through which a whole set of social, political and economic relations were viewed. There was what some international relations theorists see as an 'international regime', dominated by the United States, which effectively limited 'the discretion of their constituents units to decide and act on issues that fall within the regimes domain' (Ruggie 1998). The Cold War regime dominated by the United States limited what British governments could do in terms of international trade, foreign policy and key elements of domestic policy.

Decolonisation

The second external factor was the process of decolonisation; which of course was not unrelated to the first (see Chapter 6). At the end of the Second World War, the Labour Government recognised that certain countries should be given independence. Whilst Britain withdrew rapidly from India, it withdrew rather more slowly from other colonies, and it was only really in the 1950s and 1960s that the process of decolonisation developed with any pace (and, or course even today, there are still small parts of the world which are British colonies such as Gibraltar, the Falkland Islands and the Bahamas). However, this process of decolonisation was traumatic, at least for the ruling elite. Britain was defined as an Empire state; it was the Empire that had shaped the nature of the British state and its view of itself (see Gamble 2003). Therefore, the loss of the Empire was traumatic and disorientating. Britain lost its world role to the United States but continued in its desire for an international role (see Chapter 6). Even with the Empire gone, throughout much of the

1960s and into the 1970s, Britain saw its key international alliances through the Commonwealth, the organisation of ex-colonies, and was therefore reluctant to embrace the European route.

Europe

Nevertheless, the pull of the continent was the third external factor and it became more so with the loss of Empire. Despite Britain's problematic relations with Europe, Britain could not ignore the continent. Within a 25-year period Britain has fought two wars with Germany. The problem for Britain was that it saw itself as the leader of Europe, not a partner. Through the eyes of its political elites, it had on behalf of the rest of Europe vanquished Germany twice and so Britain's importance should be recognised. Therefore, Britain would not become involved in the early development of the European Union (see Chapter 6). However, the decline of the Empire, Britain's continuing economic problems and the increasing levels of trade with European countries forced Britain's political elites to decide its future lay with the European project. That the rules of the Union were established before Britain joined in 1972 meant that it has never been comfortable with the European framework.

Post-war British government was defined by the two-party systems, a degree of agreement between the parties about the nature of British politics, an accommodation of class divisions and a coming to terms with the end of Empire within the context of the Cold War and closer relations with Europe. Above all, the post-war polity was conditioned by the Westminster model which meant that the source of economic and social reform after the war was directed by the executive and Whitehall in a way which allowed the electorate a say over which party was in power, but no direct control in the decision-making process. This system of what might be called elite democracy underpinned the Keynesian welfare state; the belief that the government could use economic levers to manage the economy combined with free education, health and a degree of social security.

The crisis of the Keynesian welfare state and the end of the post-war era

Despite perceptions, this relatively stable and broadly consensual system lasted for a short period of time. The agreement between unions and government and between the major political parties about appropriate political arenas was starting to break down in the 1960s. There was considerable conflict between the unions and the government over industrial relations reform and wage control. Moreover relative economic decline as discussed in Chapter 7, made it difficult for the social aspirations of government to be achieved. The problems of the 1960s developed into a narrative, or

perception, of a 'crisis' in the 1970s. This 'crisis' was seen to be the directly related to rising oil prices. But, it was more broadly related to the end of the post-war boom. The post-war boom was sustained by US expenditure, much of it military. With the escalating costs of the Vietnam War and the decision of the US to cut spending, the period of prosperity came to an end.

The perceived crisis of the 1970s undermined many of the certainties of the post-war era. The Keynesian welfare state had promised full employment and social (in the broadest sense of the word) security. However, the 1970s saw rising prices along with increased unemployment (stagflation) and considerable industrial relations conflict ranging from the three-day week in 1973–74 to the winter of discontent in 1978–79. A debate emerged in academic, political and media circles that Britain was becoming ungovernable and that the Westminster model of two-party, strong government was coming to an end. In a sense, narratives of crisis in the 1970, allowed critics to de-legitimise the perceived political consensus established in the post-war era and in so doing create a political vacuum that needed to be filled. For the New Right in particular, the party was over and it was time for Britain to cut back public expenditure and turn away from the idea that the state could resolve all problems.

Retrospectively, the 1970s can be seen as the end of the post-war period in British politics and it led to a major debate about the future direction of British society. There were, to simplify, three main positions.

(1) **Socialist:** For socialists the way out of the crisis was to increase the level of public ownership, state planning and redistribution. It suggested that post-war social democracy was a halfway house between capitalism and socialism which was destroyed by its own contradictions and therefore Britain should move to a full blooded socialism. This was the position that was adopted by Tony Benn and Stuart Holland on the left of the Labour Party.

(2) **Social democracy:** It was argued that social democracy had been compromised by both business and labour (and by the Conservatives) and what was needed was a return to real social democracy. The argument, particularly as developed by Tony Crosland (and his supporters such as Roy Hattersley and Shirley Williams) was that Labour never really developed a social democratic programme and spent too much of its time attempting to assuage the unions and business. Therefore, the development of targeted economic intervention and economic redistribution through the tax system could save Britain.

(3) **The New Right:** The third alternative was that offered by the New Right and proselytised in the Conservative Party by the likes of Margaret Thatcher, Keith Joseph and Geoffrey Howe. This was the view that Britain's problems derived from the post-war consensus which had led to an overbearing state that had taken too much money in taxes and given too much power to the trade unions. The argument put forward by the New Right was that the government had to reduce the size of the state, free the market and give people back their freedom.

The impact of Thatcherism

What became known as Thatcherism was attractive for a number of reasons:

- It provided an explanation of Britain's failures which resonated with people's own experiences.
- It offered clear and simple solutions, and provided a coherent alternative to the Keynesian welfare state.
- It was economically liberal and socially conservative. Thus it could appeal to people's desire to better themselves but at the same time try to ensure moral security.
- It was something new in the sense that it differed from that which had been offered by both Labour and Conservatives in the post-war years, yet the ideas of the small state and free market economic harked back to the days of Britain's 'greatness' in the 19th century.

In the period between 1979 and 1990, the Thatcher Administration made a number of significant changes to the British polity, which undermined key elements of the post-war settlement. It constrained the influence of trade unions in the policy-making process; it privatised most of the state-owned industries; it introduced managerial reforms into the operation of the state; it increased the number of people that owned their own homes; it reduced the powers of local government; and it transformed, at least for some people, the perception of Britain internationally. There is little doubt that the market became a more important factor in Britain. However, what did not happen was a reduction in the size of the state. Whilst the state's role was reduced in certain spheres and there were public expenditure cuts in areas such as industrial aid and housing, expenditure remained the same or increased in health, welfare and education. Whilst much about Britain changed, British citizens retained free access to health care and education, and whilst certain benefits were cut, people continued to receive welfare payments for unemployment or sickness.

Thatcherism changed the balance of political forces in Britain but it did not undermine key aspects of the welfare state partly because many voters, including large sections of the middle class, relied on free health care and education. It was not politically or electorally expedient for the Conservatives to undermine education and health care. Nevertheless, what Thatcherism did do was create the framework for the post-war period in British society. It introduced new mechanisms of governance and new sets of relationships between the state and the individual. Thatcherism was radical and conservative. It wanted to change the nature of the relationship between the state and the individual, and free the market, but at the same time it wanted to preserve what it saw as traditional, values in terms of law and order, the family and morality (Gamble 1994). The problem, for the Conservatives, was that they opened Pandora's box. Through deregulating the economy and emphasising individual choice, in many ways they allowed rapid access to new international forces and new technologies, and so they undermined the traditional basis of British society. Thatcherism promoted individual responsibility over the state; that is fine if people do what you want, but if they choose to exercise that responsibility by spending

rather than saving or being indolent rather than working hard, the state cannot then say you made the wrong choice. The *Guardian*, always a critic of Thatcherism, summed up Margaret Thatcher's legacy on her 80th birthday:

> Free markets and globalisation, the close alliance with the US, the Thatcher legacy endures, albeit with humane modification. Her severest critics are yet to provide a model which works better. That is one of her many crimes and she is still loathed for it (The *Guardian*, 14 October 2005).

It is this legacy that has shaped British politics in the new millennium.

Politics in the new millennium: the challenges for the Labour Administration

If we look at the last 30 years in a broader context, it is clear that a number of external changes have occurred. First, the process of decolonisation has finished and Britain, even if leaders seldom state this explicitly, is now clearly a nation deeply enmeshed into the European Union. Second, the end of the Cold War has significantly changed the external context and had a considerable impact on defence and foreign policy. It opened up the opportunity of peace in Northern Ireland, humanitarian intervention in Bosnia and Kosovo, and the war in Iraq would never have happened within the context of the Cold War. It also opened up new markets in Eastern Europe and China. Thirdly, there was the growth of new sets of forces that are often referred to under the catch-all label of globalisation; the apparent greater global integration of markets, politics and cultures. In the case of Britain, the increasing size of international trade provided the justification and impetus for increased labour market deregulation and fiscal conservatism (see Chapter 26).

External challenges

The external changes were coterminous with the development of new technologies such as computers and telecommunications which have rapidly changed the relationship between time and space and created vastly expanded, easily accessible, reservoirs of knowledge. The development of new technology, particularly in relation to capital markets, was essential to the development of global markets.

These social, technological and international changes have affected people's aspirations. Through new technologies people have access to a broader range of information concerning what goods and lifestyles are available. Whilst inequality remains a core component of British society, people's expectations are shaped much less by class than in the past (see Chapter 5). Even 40 years ago, few people owned cars, many people did not have telephones, and only the well-off went on holidays abroad, and only a small percentage of the population went to university. Today, a DVD player, an iPod or a mobile phone are regarded as lifestyle necessities and those who do not own one are regarded as not conforming to the norm. Expectations about life have greatly changed over the last 40 years. With these material changes, there have been changes about expectations in politics.

Domestic challenges

Managing expectations and complexity

In the post-war period, politics and in particular people's political outlook appeared relatively straightforward. People tended to vote according to their class. The Labour Party were broadly seen as the party of the working class and had strong connections with the trade unions. The Conservative presented themselves as the party of the nation attracting a significant working class vote. There were two main parties that alternated in power. There was, according to some, a clear difference between the parties but enough agreement to ensure stability in the political system. Today, in some ways, politics appears to have become less important. People seem to have less attachment to the two main parties, they are more cynical about politics and appear to be less willing to vote (see Chapter 22). However, at the same time whilst people are disillusioned about the parties and politicians, many are still prepared to protest about the war in Iraq, or fuel prices or new roads. Westminster is no longer the single site of political protest in Britain.

New arenas of politics

Another key change that has occurred in British politics is the development of new arenas of politics. Whilst in the past, politics was defined almost solely by Westminster, this is no longer the case. As we saw in Chapter 22, many people are now prepared to protest outside formal politics, through demonstrations and self-organisation. Even within the formal political arena, both central and local government are developing new forms of representation through mechanisms such as referenda, citizens' juries, partnership and direct participation. Through membership of the European Union and the incorporation of the European Convention on Human Rights new political arenas have been developed that exist above the level of the nation-state, and through devolution to Scotland and Wales, there are new arenas, which exist below the level of the nation-state.

Controlling new forms of the state

The other major change that has occurred is the way in which the state operates. In the post-war period, a vast array of services were provided by central government ranging from education through to telecommunications. Many of these services were provided in standardised ways; the structures of government departments were similar and the roles and functions of civil servants were clear and uniform. Civil servants of the same grades worked under the same conditions with standardised rates of pay. At the elite levels, the constitutional relationship between ministers and officials was symbiotic—officials advised and ministers decided. The reality was that these roles were not easily separated and that officials often had considerable influence over the direction of policy

(see Chapter 12). Moreover, what was clear was that officials had a monopoly of policy advice and that ministers were highly dependent on them in terms of running departments (see Chapters 12 and 13).

Today, many of these features of the state have changed. The example of telecommunications illustrates clearly the sort of political/economic changes that have occurred. If you had wanted a telephone in 1978, you would have had to wait months for a line and once the line was available there was a choice of two telephones that you could hire from the monopoly supplier—the state-owned British Telecom. You could not use your own telephone and you had no choice over who would provide your line. For most families, the telephone was expensive and used relatively infrequently. Today, there are multiple telephone service providers, there is an infinite variety of phones available and a vast array of telephone packages in terms of the tariffs that exist. Telephones now carry out a wide range of functions and it is unlikely that these developments would have occurred within the context of a state-controlled telecommunications industry. The degree of choice that exists in the private sector is being used as a model which is being slowly transferred to the remaining elements of the public sector in areas like health and education. The Government is attempting to create a market of suppliers, so that consumers have choice and they see this as a mechanism for improving public services. In October 2005 Tony Blair stated that in 2001 the Government, 'started to open the system up to new influences and introduced the beginnings of choice and contestability'. Perhaps most boldly he said:

> In both the NHS and in education, there will in one sense be a market. The patient and the parent will have much greater choice. But it will only be a market in the sense of consumer choice, not a market based on private purchasing power. And it will be a market with rules. Personal wealth won't buy you better NHS service. The funding for schools will be fair and equal no matter what their status; and there will be no return to selection.

What is interesting about New Labour is that it regards the market and choice as a way of improving, not replacing the public sector.

Managing Whitehall

The role of civil servants has also changed. Most civil servants now work in agencies outside London rather than departments in Whitehall, and there is more flexibility over working arrangements between agencies. At senior levels the relationship between ministers and officials has changed. Ministers are more likely to be policy activists and less likely to look to officials for advice. Ministers have many sources of advice and officials are likely to be concerned with management rather than policy. Moreover, the work of both officials and ministers is increasingly shaped by Europe rather than by domestic politics and in matters of trade, pollution, foreign policy and immigration, the key determinants of policy are global rather than European.

The response of the Blair Administration

It is within this context that we need to understand New Labour and the Blair Government. New Labour can be seen as Labour's response to the political and social changes of the new millennium. Historically, the Labour Party developed within, and did much to develop, the Keynesian welfare state. Yet, the crisis of the 1970s was traumatic for Labour, it undermined its core conceptions of how the world and the economy worked (see Chapter 3). It had great difficulty adjusting to new economic and political conditions which led to considerable conflict within the party (see Chapter 18). New Labour was in many ways a realisation that a return to post-war social democracy was not possible. Therefore, the Labour Party abandoned for both electoral and practical reasons many of its key policies such as state intervention and nationalisation. For good or ill, New Labour accepted finally that the market was the primary mechanism for organising the economy and that there were limits to what the state could do. Labour perceived a structural framework which would not allow anything other than fiscal neo-liberalism (see Chapter 26). First, Labour believed that the liberalised financial markets would not allow Labour to follow a policy of deficit spending. Any economic weakness would be punished by the markets. Second, Labour had failed to be elected throughout the 1980s because they were perceived as economically incompetent. This led to the conclusion that they would not be elected unless they could convince the electorate of their sound economic credentials.

New Labour: embedding Thatcherite neo-liberalism?

Many commentators have argued that New Labour has fully embraced the Thatcherite agenda. Furthermore, in the course of its first two terms in office, it has embedded and consolidated this new settlement (Hay 1999; Heffernan 2001). What we have with New Labour, and for British politics in general is a Thatcherite polity. It is interesting that both candidates for the final round of the 2005 Conservative leadership contest were essentially Thatcherite in their policy positions. In David Cameron and David Davis, there are offered slightly divergent Conservative versions of neo-Thatcherism. Many argue that the present Labour Party, led by either Tony Blair or Gordon Brown, offers a similar version of the same ideology.

New Labour: revisionism and reform

To see New Labour as a Labour version of Thatcherism is an oversimplification. Labour has defined the nature of new millennium politics as much as they have reacted to Thatcherism. The crisis of the 1970s and the Conservative response exacerbated the contradictions within the British political system, for example, in terms of the desire to reduce the role of the state but strengthen the power of the executive, or to increase sovereignty whilst integrating Britain into Europe.

New Labour has attempted to resolve many of these contradictions and has in fact developed a number of policies which would be anathema to the Conservatives from Thatcher onwards. A number of Labour policies have had a significant impact on the nature of the British polity. They have carried on the revolution initiated by

Thatcherism but taken it in a different direction. Among the changes that they have introduced are:

- Significant constitutional change including devolution, incorporation of the European Convention on Human Rights, freedom of information (see Chapter 10).

- The establishment of a diverse and fragmented delivery system for public services (see Chapters 13, 14 and 16).

- New forms of relationship within the core executive particularly between ministers and civil servants (see Chapters 11 and 12).

- Resolution of Britain's relationship with Europe—whilst under New Labour conflict with the EU has continued, there is no debate about whether Britain does belong within the EU. Despite political rhetoric, the EU has become a normalised part of the British polity (see Chapter 9).

- The development of a new form of sovereignty. The Blair Government is not committed to the notion of indivisible sovereignty that has characterised British government and in particular Thatcherism. It has accepted that sovereignty is based on interdependence and is often shared (see Chapters 6 and 17).

- A new model for public service such as welfare and education which is based on a commitment to public provision with high and increasing levels of expenditure but recognises the need for multiple delivery systems (see Chapters 27 and 28).

- The development of new forms of participation (see Chapter 23).

What we can see with New Labour is the development of real changes to the British political system and whilst these changes could not be understood without placing them within the context of Thatcherism, Labour has not simply adopted a Thatcherite position. What they have done is adapt to the circumstances presented to them following the crisis of Keynesianism, a changing international environment and the reforms of the last Conservative Administration (see Kenny and Smith 2000; Driver and Martell 2002; Ludlam and Smith 2004). Again it is a question of structure and agency. New Labour leaders have had to make choices within a changed structural context. Labour in turn have changed the structural context. Therefore, the new Conservative leader, David Cameron, is now engaged in a process of attempting to reform the policies of Conservative Party in order to adapt to this change in the political terrain. The question that we finally then return to is whether with all these changes, the Westminster model can still offer an informed understanding of the British political system.

Is the Westminster model still relevant?

In the light of all these changes to what extent is it plausible to say that the Westminster model still has any resonance? For many commentators the Westminster model went long ago. We have argued that despite many of the key features of the Westminster model being undermined, the myth of the Westminster model continues to shape understandings of politics in Britain (see Chapters 2 and 3). Nevertheless it is clear that there have been significant changes to assumptions of the Westminster model. First, the core principle of the Westminster model was the notion of parliamentary sovereignty; that sovereignty had an internal and an external dimension. Internally it meant that Westminster was the final source of authority that could not be overruled. Externally, it meant that the boundaries of Britain were impermeable to other states.

It is clear that internal sovereignty has been significantly circumscribed. Devolution, membership of the European Union, the increased use of referenda, the incorporation of the European Convention on Human Rights, all limit the domestic sovereignty of Westminster. It is true that in principle Westminster could revoke all of these measures but the reality is that this will not happen; at least for the foreseeable future. Consequently, there are sources of authority that challenge the sovereignty of Westminster. Britain has always been characterised as a highly centralised state, and whilst it is true that many powers still reside with the executive, the creation of devolved bodies has created distinct spheres of authority which can operate outside of the formal Westminster system (although, of course, it is completely dependent on, and part of Westminster).

Externally, it is also true that there is an increasing place for international authority in domestic politics. One clear example is the development of the peace process in Northern Ireland. The process has only progressed as far as it has because of the crucial role of the United States. Without the intervention of Bill Clinton in particular, progress would have been much slower. The Good Friday Agreement means that the process of decommissioning weapons is overseen by a Canadian, General John de Chastelain, and it institutionalises a role for the Republic of Ireland in the affairs of Northern Ireland (see Chapter 17). A number of different nations have permeated the political system in relation to the peace process.

Other aspects of the Westminster model have also been severely curtailed. Now that policy implementation is fragmented into hundreds of public, private and voluntary bodies, notions of ministerial responsibility are now extremely weak. With the increasing institutionalisation of prime ministerial power, collective Cabinet decision-making seems to be declining. Moreover, the idea of a neutral and unified Civil Service is increasingly being questioned as a consequence of the increased number of outsider, more political appointments and different conditions of services across the regions of the United Kingdom. In addition, more and more of politics is taking place beyond Westminster through people taking direct action or organising collective goods independently of the state.

Understanding change

Britain has not changed in a Whiggish, and incremental manner. Over the past 30 years the changes have been rapid and radical. In terms of governmental reform, there has been something of a permanent revolution which is reflected in change in the economy and society. Patterns of work and lifestyle have also changed dramatically. More women work than ever before, family life has changed, and Britain has become increasingly multicultural. The 'sense' of shared values that existed in the post-war years seems to have disappeared (see Chapter 5). Britain has become less a collectivist and more individualist society, rediscovering, as Greenleaf pointed out, the libertarian values that dominated in the 19th century. If we compare Britain to Germany or France, as Tony Blair said in his 2005 Labour Party Conference speech, Britain has adapted much more rapidly to a changing world than its European counterparts. In Germany, the need for consensus and the cost of unification have made adaptation difficult and in France the willingness of the public to protest again welfare and employment reform has prevented radical change. Ironically, in Britain the fact that the Westminster model allows a concentration of power in the centre, and the fact that the Thatcher Government neutralised the sites of opposition by reducing the power of the trade unions and the role of local government meant, that government has been able to push through reforms drawing on the already established individualist/libertarian tradition.

The Britain of the 21st century is a polity where the trade unions are politically much weaker, wealth and inequality have increased, the market is accepted as the most effective mechanism of distribution, and managerialism suffuses the public sector. The framework for the economy is now fiscal conservatism not Keynesianism. There is recognition of the limits as to what the state can do and the questioning of whether it is the best mechanism for supplying public goods. The existence of this framework does not mean that there is a consensus between the parties. Whilst both Labour and Conservatives have accepted an increased role for markets and a reduced role for the states, their position on both the state and markets is different. For Labour, public provision is a good thing that can achieve goals that are desired by everyone—a reduction in poverty, higher levels of education and better health care. However, what is important is outcomes, and if the market can provide the best outcome it should be used, but where the state is more effective at delivering services then public provision is more appropriate. The Conservative position is that markets are generally preferable to the state and that there should be a clear limit on state activity and state expenditure. For the Conservatives, the state is more likely to produce bad outcomes and its uses should be clearly limited. Although under David Cameron, this appears to be changing as the Conservatives shift their ideological position.

'Endism' and British politics

How does what we have discussed relate to the perspectives related to 'endism' raised in the Introduction? Notions of endism have arisen within the context of the issues that this chapter has discussed. The apparent consensus over the role of the market has led to the discussion of the end of politics, the decline in participation has led to a discussion concerning the end of public space and globalisation has led to discussions about the end of the nation-state. However, it is clear as events across the world demonstrate, politics has not gone away. With the war in Iraq, new political fissures are developing and if anything, the development of greater global pressures has led to a reinvigoration of the nation-states as political leaders attempt to develop mechanisms for dealing with, and controlling, international forces.

Conclusion

To return to the ways of understanding politics outlined in Chapter 2, it is easy to characterise the British political system as one of democratic elitism. Britain was governed by an elite, but it was an elite that was constrained and circulated through the process of elections, and the existence of free associations, and a relatively free media. Power though could be located largely within the Westminster/Whitehall nexus but with some powerful groups such as the unions and business also having high levels of influence.

One argument could be that the system has become more pluralistic. Power does seem to have moved out of the Westminster arena to other areas such as Europe, supranational organisations, devolved assemblies, international organisations, social movements and even judges. There are now many more sources of information with more television channels and the growth of the internet. Even if the news media are controlled by a few small organisations, the internet can provide an alternative and critical voice. Moreover, people appear to have less faith in the traditional parties and are more willing to act through social movements rather than political parties.

On the other hand, there are many people who argue that the world has become less pluralistic and less democratic. What has occurred as a consequence of forces such as Europeanisation and globalisation is that power has been lost upwards from the nation-state. Increasingly, states are faced with issues such as avian flu or global warming that cannot be tackled at the national level and as a consequence, are subject to regulations that come from the international arena. Decisions about key social and economic policies are now being made in international organisations such as the G8. As a consequence, citizens are further away from decisions than ever before, and this has led to an increasing democratic deficit, which cannot be overcome with new forms of representation.

There is also a growing sense that whilst in the post-war period the external frame for politics was the Cold War, in the new millennium it is the war on terrorism. Increasingly, a whole set of international relations, foreign policy decisions and domestic security policy are being changed as a consequence of 9/11. We have seen a shift from politics as the art of the possible to politics at the extreme (see Chapter 1). For example, in October 2005, the High Court in London considered the issue of whether information gained under torture could be legitimately used as evidence. This demonstrates the extent to which acts of terrorism and the framework of the war on terror shapes what is deemed acceptable within domestic British politics. Indeed, the war on terror reaches deep into domestic policy affecting policies in areas like race relations and immigration.

It is difficult to make any generalisations about where power lies in Britain. What we need to understand is how the political system has changed. Whilst on the one hand the state has hollowed out to the local and the international levels, it is also the case that central government had developed new mechanisms for control (see Chapter 14). Whilst the Westminster model no longer provides an accurate organising perspective of how the British political system works, the characteristics which underpin the model and which in turn shapes the actions of the political elites, does still mean that the executive continues to control considerable resources and does have a mechanism though its control of

Parliament to claim or reclaim powers. So for example, in response to the bombings in London on 7 July 2005, we can see that the central state is able to develop new powers and attempt to control its territory (see Chapter 30). The state has responded to the threats to its borders and authorities by trying to introduce new powers such as ID cards whilst at the same time curtailing existing individual rights such as the principle of *habeas corpus* in cases of suspected terrorist activity. What is important as students of politics is that we understand the framework within which politics occurs so that we can analyse the actors, interests and institutions involved in a particular decision. What is clear is that while the nature of political development has been shaped by the Westminster model, the way the political system operates has changed considerably over the past 25 years.

 Visit the Online Resource Centre that accompanies this book
for links to more information on this chapter topic

BIBLIOGRAPHY

Acheson, D (1998) *Independent Inquiry into Inequalities in Health Report*, London: Stationary Office.

Adam, B, Beck, U and Van Loon, J (2003) *The Risk Society and Beyond*, London: Sage.

Adam, S and Shaw, J (2003) *A Survey of the UK Tax System*, Institute of Fiscal Studies, Briefing Note 9.

Addison, P (1994) *The Road to 1945* (2nd edn), London: Pimlico.

Allen, G (2001) *The Last Prime Minister: Being Honest about the UK Presidency*, London: House of Commons.

Anderson, B (1974) *Capital Accumulation in the Industrial Revolution*, London: Dent.

Archer, C (2001) *International Organisations* (3rd edn), London: Routledge.

Aron, R (1968) *Democracy and Totalitarianism*, London: Weidenfeld and Nicolson.

Bache, I and Flinders, M (2004) *Multi-Level Governance*, Oxford: Oxford University Press.

Bache, I and Jordan, A (2006) *The Europeanisation of British Politics*, London: Palgrave Macmillan.

Bachrach, P and Baratz, M (1962) 'Two Faces of Power', *American Political Science Review*, 56: 947–52.

Baker, D, Gamble, A and Ludlam, S (1993) 'Whips or Scorpions: The Maastricht Vote and the Conservative Party', *Parliamentary Affairs*, 46(2): 151–66.

Baker, K (1993) *The Turbulent Years: My Life in Politics*, London: Faber and Faber.

Bale, T (1999) 'The Logic of No Alternative' *British Journal of Politics and International Relations*, 1(2): 192–204.

Balfour, Lord (1927) *Introduction to Bagehot: The English Constitution*, London: World Edition.

Ball, S and Seldon, A (eds) (2005) *Recovering Power: The Conservatives in Opposition Since 1867*, Basingstoke: Palgrave.

Ball, S and Seldon, A (eds) (2005) *The Tory Party in Recovery*, Basingstoke: Palgrave.

Barberis, P (2000) 'Prime Minister and Cabinet' in R Pyper and L Robins (eds) *United Kingdom Governance*, Basingstoke: Macmillan.

Barnett, C (1986) *The Audit of War: The Illusion and Reality of Britain as a Great Nation*, London: Macmillan.

Barnett, C (1995) *The Lost Victory. British Dreams, British Realities 1945–1950*, London: Macmillan.

Barry, B and Goodin, R (1992) *Free Movement: Ethical Issues in the Transnational Movement of People and Money*, Hemel Hempstead: Harvester Wheatsheaf.

Bartholomew, J (2004) *The Welfare State We're In: The Failure of the Welfare State*, London: Politicos.

Baston, L (2001) 'The Party System' in Seldon, A (ed) *The Blair Effect*, London: Little Brown, pp 159–84.

Baston, L and Henig, S (2005) 'The Labour Party' in A Seldon and D Kavanagh (eds) *The Blair Effect 2001–5*, Cambridge: Cambridge University Press.

Bastow, S, Dunleavy, P and Margetts, H (2003) 'Progress in Implementing E-Government at Central and Local Levels in England, 1998–2003', paper to the UK Political Studies Association Conference, University of Leicester, 15–17 April.

Baylis, J and Smith, S (2001) *The Globalisation of World Politics: An Introduction to International Relations* (2nd edn), Oxford: Oxford University Press.

Beer, S (1964) *Modern British Politics*, London: Faber.

Benn, M (2000) 'New Labour and Social Exclusion', *Political Quarterly*, 71(3): 309–18.

Benn, T (1985) 'The Case for a Constitutional Premiership' in A King (ed), *The British Prime Minister* (2nd edn), London: Macmillan.

Berger, P and Luckman, T (1967) *The Social Construction of Reality*, Penguin: Harmondsworth.

Bevir, M and O'Brien, D (2001) 'New Labour and the Public Sector in Britain', *Public Administration Review*, 61(5): 535–47.

Bevir, M and Rhodes, R A W (2003) *Interpreting British Governance*, London: Routledge.

Billig, M, Condor, S, Edwards, D, Gane, M, Middleton, D and Radley, A (1990) *Ideological Dilemmas*, London: Sage.

Birch, A (1964) *Representative and Responsible Government*, London: Allen and Unwin.

Blackburn R and Kennon A (2003) *Parliament: Functions, Practices and Procedures*, London: Sweet and Maxwell.

Blackburn, R and Plant R (eds) (1999) *Constitutional Reform: The Labour Government's Constitutional Reform Agenda*, London: Longmans.

Blair, T (2004) *PM Hails Crime Clampdown Plan* http://www.number-10.gov.uk/output/Page6131.asp.

Blom-Cooper, L (2005) 'Government and the Judiciary' in A Seldon and D Kavanagh (eds) *The Blair Effect 2001–5*, Cambridge: Cambridge University Press.

Blumler, J and McQuail, D (1968) *Television in Politics*, London: Faber.

Blumler, J, Gurevitch, M and Nossiter, T (1989) 'The Earnest versus the Determined: Election News-making at the BBC' in I Crewe and M Harrop (eds) *Political Communications: The British General Election Campaign of 1987*, Cambridge: Cambridge University Press.

Bogdanor, V (1981) *The People and the Party System*, Cambridge: Cambridge University Press.

Bogdanor, V (1989) 'The Constitution' in D Kavanagh and A Seldon (eds) *The Thatcher Effect*, Oxford: Oxford University Press.

Bogdanor, V (1997) *Power and the People*, London: Victor Gollancz.

Bogdanor, V (1999) *Devolution in the United Kingdom*, Oxford: Oxford University Press.

Boyce, D G (1999) *Decolonisation and the British Empire 1775–1997*, Basingstoke: Macmillan.

Brittan, S (1973) *Capitalism and the Permissive Society*, London: Macmillan.

Brittan, S (1978) *The Economic Consequences of Democracy*, London: Temple Smith.

Brittan, S (2000) 'Reflections on British Decline' in R English and M Kenny (eds) *Rethinking British Decline*, London: Palgrave.

Brown, A H (1968) 'Prime Ministerial Power (Part I), *Public Law*, Spring: 28–51.

Brown, G (1972) *In My Way*, Harmondsworth: Penguin.

Bruce-Gardyne, J and Lawson, N (1976) *The Power Game*, London: Macmillan.

Buchanan, J and Tullock, G (1962) *The Calculus of Consent: Logical Foundations of Constitutional Democracy*, Ann Arbor, Mich: Michigan University Press.

Bulmer, S (1983) 'Domestic Politics and European Community Decision-Making', *Journal of Common Market Studies*, 21(4): 349–63.

Bulmer, S and Burch, M (1998) 'Organizing for Europe: Whitehall, the British State and the European Union', *Public Administration*, 76: 601–28.

Bulpitt, J (1983) *Territory and Power in the United Kingdom*, Manchester: Manchester University Press.

Bulpitt, J (1986) 'The Discipline of the New Democracy: Mrs Thatcher's Domestic Statecraft', *Political Studies*, 34: 19–39.

Burch, M (1988) 'British Cabinet: a Residual Executive', *Parliamentary Affairs*, 41: 34–47.

Burch, M and Holliday, I (1996) *The British Cabinet System*, Hemel Hempstead: Prentice Hall.

Burke, E (1834) 'To the Electors of Bristol', *Selected Writings of Edmund Burke*, New York: Henry Holt and Co.

Burke, K and Cairncross, A (1992) *Goodbye Great Britain: The 1976 IMF Crisis*, New Haven, Conn: Yale University Press.

Burley, A-M and Mattli, W (1993) 'Europe Before the Court: A Political Theory of Legal Integration', *International Organization*, 47(1): 41–76.

Butler, D and Kitzinger, U (1976) *The 1975 Referendum*, London: Macmillan.

Butler, D and Stokes, D (1974) *Political Change in Britain*, London: Macmillan.

Butler, D, Adonis, A and Travers, T (1994) *Failure in British Government: The Politics of the Poll Tax*, Oxford: Oxford University Press.

Butler, Lord (1971) *The Art of the Possible: The Memoirs of the Late Lord Butler*, London: Hamish Hamilton.

Cabinet Office (2000) *What's in IT for citizens?*, London: Cabinet Office.

Callaghan, J (1982) 'Cumber and Variables', *The Home Office: Perspectives on Policy and Administration Bicentenary Lectures*, London: RIPA.

Callaghan, J (1997) *Great Power Complex: British Imperialism, International Crises and National Decline, 1914–51*, London: Pluto Press.

Campbell, C and Wilson, G (1995) *The End of Whitehall: Death of a Paradigm*, Oxford: Basil Blackwell.

Campbell, J (1993) *Edward Heath: A Biography*, London: Jonathon Cape.

Camps, M (1964) *Britain and the European Community 1955–1963*, Oxford: Oxford University Press.

Carrington, P (1988) *Reflect on Things Past; The Memoirs of Lord Carrington*, London: Collins.

Castells, M (1998) *The Information Age, Volume III: The End of the Millennium*, Oxford: Blackwell.

Castle, B (1980) *The Castle Diaries 1974–76*, London: Weidenfeld and Nicolson.

Catney P (2004) 'Partnership Governance: Theoretical Perspectives and Interpretation of New Labour's Approach', Sheffield Working Paper, Department of Politics, University of Sheffield.

Cawson, A (1986) *Corporatism and Political Theory*, Oxford: Basil Blackwell.

Childs, S and Withey, J (2004) 'Women Representatives Acting for Women', *Political Studies*, 52: 552–64.

Chitty, C (2002) 'Education and Social Class', *Political Quarterly*, 73(2): 208–10.

Cini, M (1996) *The European Commission: Leadership, Organisation and Culture in the EU Administration*, Manchester: Manchester University Press.

Clark, J (2000) 'Reflections on British Decline' in R English and M Kenny (eds) *Rethinking British Decline*, London: Palgrave.

Clarke, H et al (2004) *Political Choice in Britain*, Oxford: Oxford University Press.

Cm 3638 (1968) *The Civil Service Report by the Fulton Committee*, London: HMSO.

Cm 4262-I (1999) *The Stephen Lawrence Inquiry: Report Of An Inquiry By Sir William Macpherson Of Cluny*, London: Stationery Office.

Cm 5571 (2002) *2002 Spending Review: Public Service Agreements*, London: Stationery Office.

Cmnd 2764 (1966) *The National Plan*, London: HMSO.

Coates, D (2005) *Prolonged Labour*, Basingstoke: Palgrave.

Cockett, R (1995) *Thinking the Unthinkable: Think-tanks and the Economic Counter-Revolution 1931–83*, London: Fontana Press.

Cohen, N (1999) *Cruel Britannia*, London: Verago.

Cohen, N (2003) *Pretty Straight Guys*, London: Faber and Faber.

Cohen S (1972) *Folk Devils and Moral Panics: The Creation of the Mods and Rockers*, Oxford: Martin Robinson.

Committee on Standards in Public Life, House of Commons (2003) *Defining the Boundaries within the Executive: Ministers, Special Advisers and the Permanent Civil Service*, Norwich: HMSO.

Conservative Party (2005) *The Conservative Election Manifesto 2005: Are You Thinking What We're Thinking? It's Time for Action*, London: Conservative Party.

Cook, R (2003) *Point of Departure*, London: Simon and Schuster.

Cooper, R (1998) 'Irony and Foreign Policy', *Prospect*, no 36, December.

Cowley, P (2002) *Revolts and Rebellions: Parliamentary Revolting under Blair*, London: Politicos.

Cowley, P and Stuart, M (2005) 'Parliament' in A Seldon and D Kavanagh (eds) *The Blair Effect 2001–5*, Cambridge: Cambridge University Press.

CRE (1999) Ethnic Minorities in Britain, Fact Sheet, CRE.

Crick, B (1964) *In Defence of Politics*, Harmondsworth: Penguin.

Crosland, A (1956) *The Future of Socialism*, London: Jonathan Cape.

Crossman, R (1963) 'Introduction' to W Bagehot, *The English Constitution*, London: Fontana.

Crossman, R (1972) *Inside View*, London: Jonathan Cape.

Crouch, C (2003) 'Commercialisation or Citizenship: Education Policy and the Future of Public Services', *Pamphlet 606*, London: Fabian Society.

Curtice, J and Seyd, B (2003) 'Is There a Crisis of Political Participation?' in *British Social Attitudes, The 20th Report*, London: Sage.

Curtice, J and Seyd, B (2004) 'Is There a Crisis of Political Participation' in A Park, J Curtice, K Thomson, L Jarvis and C Bromley (eds) *British Social Attitudes: Continuity and Change over Two Decades—the 20th Report*, London: Sage.

Curtice, J and Steed, M (1997) 'Statistical Appendix' in D Butler and D Kavanagh (eds) *The British General Election of 1997*, Basingstoke, Macmillan.

Cutler, T and Waine, B (2000) 'Managerialism Reformed? New Labour and Public Sector Management', *Social Policy and Administration*, 34(3): 3–18.

Dahl, R (1957) 'The Concept of Power', *Behavioural Science*, 2(3): 201–15.

Daintith, T and Page, A (1999), *The Executive in the Constitution*, Oxford: Oxford University Press.

Darwin, J (1988) *The Retreat from Empire in the Post-War World*, Basingstoke: Macmillan.

Davis, G and Keating, M (eds) (2000) *The Future of Governance*, St Leonards, NSW: Allen and Unwin.

Deakin, N and Parry, R (2000) *The Treasury and Social Policy*, Basingstoke: Macmillan.

Deedes, W (1968) *Race Without Rancour*, London: Conservative Political Centre.

Dehousse, R (1998) *The European Court of Justice: The Politics of Judicial Integration*, Basingstoke: Macmillan.

Delap, C (2001) 'Citizens Juries: Reflections on the UK Experience', PLA Notes, 40: 39–42.

Denham, A and Garnett, M (2001) *Keith Joseph*, London: Acumen.

Denver, D (2002) *Elections and Voting Behaviour in Britain*, Hemel Hempstead: Harvester Wheatsheaf.

DiMaggio, P J and Powell, W W (1991) 'Introduction' in P J DiMaggio and W W Powell (eds) *The New Institutionalism in Organizational Analysis*, Chicago: University of Chicago Press.

Doherty, B, Plows, A and Wall, D (2003) 'The British Direct Action Movement', *Parliamentary Affairs*, 56(4): 669–86.

Doherty, B, Paterson, M, Plows, A and Wall, D (2003) 'Explaining the fuel protest', *British Journal of Politics and International Relations*, 5: 1–23.

Dorey, P (1995) *British Politics Since 1945*, Oxford: Blackwell.

Downes, D and Morgan, R (1997) 'Dumping the "Hostages to Fortune": The Politics of Law and Order in Post-War Britain' in M Maguire, R Morgan and R Reiner (eds) *The Oxford Handbook of Criminology* (2nd edn), Oxford: Oxford University Press.

Driver, S and Martell, L (2002) *Blair's Britain*, Oxford: Polity Press.

Dudley, G and Richardson, J J (1996) 'Why Does Policy Change over Time? Adversarial Policy Communities, Alternative Policy Arenas and British Trunk Road Policy 1945–1995', *Journal of European Public Policy*, 3: 318–38.

Dumbrell, J (2001) *A Special Relationship: Anglo-American Relations in the Cold War and After*, Basingstoke: Palgrave Macmillan.

Dunleavy, P (1991) *Democracy, Bureaucracy and Public Choice. Economic Explanations in Political Science*, London: Harvester.

Dunleavy, P (1999) 'Electoral Representation and Accountability: The Legacy of Empire' in I Holiday, A Gamble, and G Parry (eds) *Fundamentals in British Politics*, London: Macmillan.

Dunleavy, P (2003) 'Analysing Political Power' in P Dunleavy, A Gamble, R Heffernan, and

G Peele (eds) *Developments in British Politics 7*, London: Palgrave.

Dunleavy, P and Rhodes, R A W (1990) 'Core Executive Studies in Britain', *Public Administration*, 68: 3–28.

Dyson, K (2000) 'Europeanisation, Whitehall Culture and the Treasury as Institutional Veto Player', *Public Administration*, 78(4): 897–914.

Elbaum, B and Lazonick, W (1986) *The Decline of the British Economy*, Oxford: Clarendon Press.

Ellison, J (1970) *Threatening Europe. Britain and the Creation of the European Community 1955–1958*, Basingstoke: Macmillan.

Emerson, C, Frayne, C and Love, S (2003) *A Survey of Public Spending in the UK*, Institute of Fiscal Studies, Briefing Note 43.

English, R and Kenny, M (2000) *Rethinking British Decline*, London: Palgrave.

Farrell, D (2001) *Electoral Systems. A Comparative Introduction*, Basingstoke: Palgrave.

Favell, A (2001) *Philosophies of Integration: Immigration and the Idea of Citizenship in France and Britain*, Basingstoke: Palgrave.

Fay, M T and Meehan, E (2000) 'British Decline and European Integration' in R English and M Kenny (eds) *Rethinking British Decline*, London: Palgrave.

Feigenbaum, H, Henig, J and Hamnett, C (1998) *Shrinking the State*, Cambridge: Cambridge University Press.

Ferguson, R and Howell, M (2004) *Political Blogs—Craze or Convention?*, London: Hansard Society.

Fielding, S (2003) *The Labour Party*, Basingstoke: Palgrave.

Finer, S E (1956) 'The Individual Responsibility of Ministers', *Public Administration*, 34: 377–96.

Finer, S E (1958) *Anonymous Empire*, London: Pall Mall.

Finer, S E (1970) *Comparative Government*, London: Allen Lane.

Fitzpatrick, T (2004) *After the New Social Democracy*, Manchester: Manchester University Press.

Flinders, M (1999) 'Setting the Scene: Quangos in Context' in M Flinders and M J Smith (eds) *Quangos, Accountability and Reform*, London: Macmillan.

Flinders, M (2002) 'Shifting the Balance: Parliament, the Executive and the British Constitution', *Political Studies*, 50(2): 23–42.

Flinders, M (2004) 'Distributed Governance in the European Union', *Journal of European Public Policy*, 11: 520–44.

Flinders, M (2004a) 'Distributed Public Governance in Britain', *Public Administration*, 82: 883–910.

Foley, M (1992) *The Rise of the British Presidency*, Manchester: Manchester University Press.

Foley, M (1999) *The Politics of the British Constitution*, Manchester: Manchester University Press.

Foley, M (2000) *The Blair Presidency*, Manchester: Manchester University Press.

Foster, C D (1997) *A Stronger Centre of Government*, London: Constitutional Unit.

Foster, C (2001) 'The Civil Service Under Stress: The Fall in Civil Service Power and Authority', *Public Administration*, 79: 725–49.

Foster, C (2005) *British Government in Crisis or the Third English Revolution*, Oxford: Hart.

Foster, C and Plowden, F (1996) *The State under Stress*, Buckingham: Open University Press.

Foster, L (1999) 'The Encroachment of the Law on Politics', *Parliamentary Affairs*, 53: 2.

Fowler, R (1991) *Language in the News: Discourse and Ideology in the Press*, London: Routledge.

Franklin, B (1994) *Packaging Politics*, London: Arnold.

Franklin, M, Marsh, M and McLaren, L (1994) 'Uncorking the Bottle: Popular Opposition to European Unification in the Wake of Maastricht', *Journal of Common Market Studies*, 32(4): 455–72.

Freeden, M (1999) 'The Ideology of New Labour', *Political Quarterly*, 70(1): 42–52.

Freedman, L (1999) *The Politics of British Defence 1979–1998*, London: Macmillan.

Freedman, L (2001) 'Defence' in A Seldon (ed) *The Blair Effect*, London: Little Brown.

Fukyama, F (1992) *The End of History and the Last Man*, London: Hamish Hamilton.

Gains, F (2004) 'Hardware, Software or Network Connection? Theorizing Crisis in the UK Next Steps Agencies', *Public Administration*, 82: 547–67.

Gamble, A (1988) *The Free Economy and the Strong State*, Basingstoke: Macmillan.

Gamble, A (1990) 'Theories of British Politics', *Political Studies*, 38(3): 404–20.

Gamble, A (1994) *The Free Economy and the Strong State* (2nd edn), London: Macmillan.

Gamble, A (1995) *Britain in Decline*, London: Macmillan.

Gamble, A (2000) 'Theories and Explanations of British Decline' in R English and M Kenny (eds) *Rethinking British Decline*, London: Palgrave.

Gamble, A (2000a) *Politics and Fate*, London: Polity.

Gamble, A (2000b) 'Economic Governance' in J Pierre (ed) *Debating Governance*, Oxford: Oxford University Press.

Gamble, A (2003) *Between Europe and America: The Future of British Politics*, London: Palgrave Macmillan.

Game, C and Leach, S (1994) *The Role of Political Parties in Local Democracy*, London Commission for Local Democracy.

Garner, R and Kelly, R (1998) *British Political Parties Today*, Manchester: Manchester University Press.

Garnett, M and Lynch, P (eds) (2003) *The Conservatives in Crisis*, Manchester: Manchester University Press.

Geddes, A (1997) 'Europe: Major's Nemesis' in A Geddes and J Tonge (eds) *Labour's Landslide: The 1997 British General Election*, Manchester: Manchester University Press.

Geddes, A (2002) 'In Europe, not interested in Europe' in A Geddes and J Tonge (eds) *Labour's Second Landslide: The 2001 British General Election*, Manchester: Manchester University Press.

Geddes, A (2004) *The European Union and British Politics*, London: Palgrave Macmillan.

Geddes, A (2005) 'Immigration and European Integration as Election Issues' in A Geddes and J Tonge (eds) *Britain Decides: The 2005 UK General Election*, London: Palgrave Macmillan.

Geddes, A and Tonge, J (eds) (2005) *Britain Decides: The 2005 UK General Election*, London: Palgrave Macmillan.

George, S (ed) (1992) *Britain and the European Community: The Politics of Semi-Detachment*, Oxford: Clarendon Press.

George, S (1998) *An Awkward Partner: Britain in the European Community*, Oxford: Oxford University Press.

George, S and Bache, I (2002) *Politics in the European Union*, Oxford: Oxford University Press.

Gibbins, J R and Reimer, B (1999) *The Politics of Post-Modernity*, London: Sage.

Gibson, R, Ludoli, W and Ward, S (2005) 'Online Participation in the UK: Testing a "Contextualised" Model of Internet Effects', *British Journal of Politics and International Relations*, 7: 561–83.

Giddens, A (1986) *The Constitution of Society*, Cambridge: Polity.

Giddens, A (1998) *The Third Way*, Oxford: Polity.

Giddens, A (2000) *The Third Way and its Critics*, Oxford: Polity.

Gilmour, I (1992) *Dancing with Dogma*, London: Simon and Schuster.

Goodhart, D (2004) 'Too Diverse?', *Prospect*, February.

Gould, P (1997) *The Unfinished Revolution*, London: Little Brown.

Gowland, D and Turner, A (2000) *Reluctant Europeans: Britain and European Integration 1945–1998*, Harlow: Longman.

Grant, W (2000) *Pressure Groups and British Politics*, Basingstoke: Macmillan.

Gray, J (1995), *Liberalism*, Milton Keynes: Open University Press.

Green Cowles, M, Caporaso, J and Risse, T (2000) *Transforming Europe: Europeanization and*

Domestic Change, Ithaca, NY: Cornell University Press.

Greenleaf, W H (1983) *The British Political Tradition Vols 1 & 2*, London: Methuen.

Greenleaf, W H (1987) *The British Political Tradition Vol 3*, London: Methuen.

Griffith, J (1997) *The Politics of the Judiciary* (5th edn), Oxford: Clarendon Press.

Guardian (2001) *President Blair*, leader article, 6 October.

Gyford, J (1985) *The Politics of Local Socialism*, London: Allen and Unwin.

Hailsham, Lord (1976) *Elective Dictatorship*, BBC.

Hall, P (ed) (1989) *The Political Power of Economic Ideas: Keynesianism Across Nations*, Princeton, NJ: Princeton University Press.

Hall, S (1988) *The Hard Road to Renewal: Thatcherism and the Crisis of the Left*, London: Verso.

Hansard Society (2001) *The Challenge for Parliament. Making Government Accountable*, London: Vacher Dod.

Hansen, R (2000) *Citizenship and Immigration in Post-War Britain*, Oxford: Oxford University Press.

Harling, P (2001) *The Modern British State: an Historical Introduction*, Cambridge: Polity.

Harris, J (1996) 'Political ideas on the welfare state' in D Marquand and A Seldon (eds) *The Ideas that Shaped Post-War Britain*, London: Fontana.

Harrison, K and Boyd, T (2003), *Political Ideas and Movements*, Manchester: Manchester University Press.

Harrison, N (1985) *TV News: Who's Bias?*, Hermitage, Berks: Policy Journals.

Harrop, M (1986) 'Press Coverage in Post-War British Elections' in I Crewe and M Harrop (eds) *Political Communications: The British General Election Campaign of 1983*, Cambridge: Cambridge University Press.

Hay, C (1996) *Restating Social and Political Change*, Buckingham: Open University Press.

Hay, C (1999) *The Political Economy of New Labour*, Manchester: Manchester University Press.

Hay, C (2002) *Political Analysis*, London: Palgrave.

Hay, C and Richards, D (2000) 'The Tangled Webs of Westminster and Whitehall', *Public Administration*, 78(1): 1–28.

Hay, C and Rosamond, B (2002) 'Globalisation, European Integration and the Discursive Construction of Economic Imperatives', *Journal of European Public Policy*, 9(2): 147–67.

Hazell, R (ed) (1999) *Constitutional Futures*, Oxford: Oxford University Press.

Hazell, R et al (2002) 'The Constitution: Coming in from the Cold', *Parliamentary Affairs*, 55: 2.

HC 247 (2004) *Report of the Inquiry into the Circumstances Surrounding the Death of David Kelly C M G*, London: Stationery Office.

Headey, B (1974) *British Cabinet Ministers*, London: George, Allen and Unwin.

Healey, D (1990) *Time of My Life*, London: Norton and Co.

Heath, A et al (1991) *Understanding Political Change*, Oxford: Pergamon Press.

Heath, A, Jowell, R and Curtice, J (1994) *Labour's Last Chance: The 1992 Election and Beyond*, Aldershot: Dartmouth.

Heath, E (1998) *The Course of My Life: My Autobiography*, London: Hodder and Stoughton.

Heclo, H and Wildavsky, A (1974) *The Private Government of Public Money* (2nd edn, 1981), London: Macmillan.

Heffer, S (2000) *Nor Shall my Sword: Reinvention of England*, London: Phoenix.

Heffernan, R (2001) *New Labour and Thatcherism: Political Change in Britain*, London and New York: Palgrave Macmillan.

Heffernan, R (2005) 'Exploring (and Explaining) the Prime Minister', *British Journal of Politics and International Relations*, 7(4): 605–20.

Heinlein, F (2002) *British Government Policy and Decolonisation 1945–1963: Scrutinising the Official Mind*, London: Frank Cass.

Henn, M, Weinstein, M and Wring, D (1999) *Young People and Citizenship: A Study of Opinion in Nottinghamshire*, Nottingham: Nottinghamshire County Council.

Hennessy, P (1986) *Cabinet*, Oxford: Blackwell.

Hennessy, P (1989) *Whitehall*, London: Fontana.

Hennessy, P (1992) *Never Again: Britain 1945–51*, London: Pantheon Books.

Hennessy, P (2000) *The Blair Revolution in Government*, University of Leeds: Institute for Politics and International Studies.

Hennessy, P (2001) *The Prime Minister: The Office and its Holders Since 1945*, London: Penguin.

Hennessy, P (2004) '*An End to the Poverty of Aspirations? Parliament since 1979*', published lecture.

Heywood, A (2000) *Key Concepts in Politics*, Basingstoke: Palgrave.

Hill, A and Whichelow, A (1964) *What's Wrong with Parliament?* Harmondsworth: Penguin.

Hills, J (1998) 'Thatcherism, New Labour and the Welfare State', *CASE Paper 13*, London School of Economics: Centre for the Analysis of Social Exclusion.

Hirschman, A (1970) *Exit, Voice and Loyalty: Responses to Decline in Forms, Organizations and States*, Oxford: Oxford University Press.

Hitchens, P (1999) *The Abolition of Britain*, London: Quartet Books.

Hix, S (2000) *The Political System of the European Union*, Basingstoke: Palgrave Macmillan.

HM Government (1984) 'Europe: The Future', *Journal of Common Market Studies*, 23(1): 74–81.

HM Treasury (2000) *Good Practice in Performance Reporting in Executive Agencies and Non-Departmental Bodies: A Report by the Comptroller and Auditor General*, HC 272, London: Stationery Office.

HM Treasury (2002) *European Community Finances: Statement on the 2002 Budget and Measures to Counter Fraud and Mismanagement*, London: HM Treasury.

HM Treasury (2003) *UK membership of the single currency: An assessment of the five economic tests*, London: HM Treasury.

HM Treasury (2004) *2004 Spending Review* www.hm-treasury.gov.uk/spending_review/ spend_sr04/spend_sr04_index. cfm.

HM Treasury (2005a) *Public Service Performance Index* www.hm-treasury.gov.uk/performance/ index.cfm.

HM Treasury (2005b) *Performance: Department of Health* www.hm-treasury.gov.uk/performance/ Health.cfm.

Hobsbawn, E (1968) *Industry and Empire: An Economic History of Britain Since 1750*, London: Weidenfeld and Nicolson.

Hoffmann, S (1966) 'Obstinate or Obsolete: The Fate of the Nation State and the Case of Western Europe', *Daedalus*, 95: 892–908.

Hogg, S and Hill, J (1995) *Too Close to Call*, London: Little Brown.

Holliday, I (2000) 'Is the British State Hollowing Out?', *Political Quarterly*, 71(2): 167–76.

Holliday, I (2002) 'Executives and Administrations' in P Dunleavy, A Gamble, R Heffernan and G Peele (eds) *Developments in British Politics 6* (revised edn), London: Palgrave.

Holmes, C (1988) *John Bull's Island: Immigration and British Society 1871–1971*, Basingstoke: Macmillan.

Holmes, M (1996) *The Eurosceptical Reader*, Basingstoke: Macmillan.

Hood, C, James, O and Scott, C (2000) 'Regulation or Government: Has it Increased, is it Increasing, Should it be Diminished?', *Public Administration*, 78(2): 283–304.

Hood, C, James, O, Scott, C and Travers, T (1999) *Regulation Inside Government*, Oxford: Oxford University Press.

Hooghe, L and Marks, G (2001) *Multi-Level Governance and European Integration*, Maryland: Rowman and Littlefield.

Hutton, W (1995) *The State We're In*, London: Jonathan Cape.

Hutton, W (2003) *The World We're In*, London: Abacus.

Hyman, P (2005) *1 out of 10: From Downing Street Vision to Classroom Reality*, London: Vintage.

Hyndman, N and Eden, R (2002) 'Executive Agencies, Performance Targets and External Reporting', *Public Money & Management*, 22(3): 14–24.

Ingham, B (2003) *The Wages of Spin*, London: Aurum.

Inglehart, R (1997) *Culture Shift in the Advanced Industrial Societies*, Princeton, NJ: Princeton University Press.

James, O (2003) *The Executive Agency Revolution in Whitehall*, London: Palgrave.

Jayasuriya, K (2004) 'The New Regulatory State and Relational Capacity', *Policy and Politics*, 32(4): 487–501.

Jefferys, K (1999) *Anthony Crosland: A New Biography*, London: Richard Cohen.

Jenkins, R (1991) *A Life at the Centre*, London: Macmillan.

Jenkins, S (2004) *Big Bang Localism. A Rescue Plan for British Democracy*, London: Policy Exchange.

Jennings, I (1954) *Queen's Government*, Harmondsworth: Penguin.

Jessop, B (1990) *State Theory: Putting Capitalist States in Their Place*, Cambridge: Polity.

Jessop, B (1994) 'The Transition to post-Fordist and the Schumpeterian Workfare State' in R Burrows and B Loader (eds) *Towards a Post-Fordist Welfare State?*, London: Routledge.

Jessop, B (2004) 'Multi-level Governance and Multi-level Meta Governance' in I Bache and M Flinders (eds) *Multi-level Governance: Interdisciplinary Perspectives*, Oxford: Oxford University Press.

Jessop, B, Bonnett, K, Bromley, S and Ling, T (1988) *Thatcherism*, Cambridge: Polity Press.

Johnson, N (1999) 'The Constitution' in I Holliday et al (eds) *Fundamentals in British Politics*, London: Macmillan.

Jones, G (1975) 'Development of the Cabinet' in W Thornhill (ed) *The Modernisation of British Government*, London: Pitman.

Jones, N (1999) *Sultans of Spin*, London: Gollancz.

Jones, N (2001) *Campaign 2001*, London: Politicos.

Jones, N (2002) *Control Freaks*, London: Politicos.

Joppke, C (1999) *Immigration and the Nation State; The United States, Germany and Great Britain*, Oxford: Oxford University Press.

Jordan, A (2002) *The Europeanisation of British Environmental Policy: A Departmental Perspective*, Basingstoke: Palgrave.

Jordan, G and Richardson, J (1987) *Government and Pressure Groups in Britain*, Oxford: Clarendon Press.

Jordan, G, Maloney, W and McLaughlin, A (1994) 'Characterizing Agricultural Policy-making, *Public Administration*, 72: 505–27.

Jordana, J and Levi-Faur, D (eds) (2004) *The Politics of Regulation: Institutions and Regulatory Reforms for the Age of Governance*, London: Edward Elgar.

Joseph, K (1966) *Changing Housing*, London: Conservative Political Centre.

Judge, D (1993) *The Parliamentary State*, London: Sage.

Judge, D (1999) *Representation*, London: Routledge.

Kaiser, W (1996) *Using Europe, Abusing the Europeans: Britain and European Integration 1945–1963*, Basingstoke: Macmillan.

Kandiah, D and Seldon, A (eds) (1996a) *Ideas and Think-Tanks in Contemporary Britain, Volume 1*, London: Frank Cass.

Kandiah, D and Seldon, A (eds) (1996b) *Ideas and Think-Tanks in Contemporary Britain, Volume 2*, London: Frank Cass.

Kaufmann, G (1997) *How To Be a Minister*, London: Faber.

Kavanagh, D (1990) *Thatcherism and British Politics: The End of Consensus?*, Oxford: Oxford University Press.

Kavanagh, D (1994) 'Changes in Electoral Behaviour and the Party System', *Parliamentary Affairs*, 47: 598–612.

Kavanagh, D (1995) *Election Campaigning: The New Marketing of Politics*, Oxford: Blackwell.

Kavanagh, D and Butler, D (2005) *The British General Election of 2005*, London: Palgrave.

Kavanagh, D and Richards, D (2002) 'Prime Ministers, Ministers And Civil Servants in Britain', *Comparative Sociology*, April: 1–28.

Kavanagh, D and Seldon, A (1999) *The Powers Behind the Prime Minister*, London: Harper Collins.

Kellas, J (1989) *The Scottish Political System* (4th edn), Cambridge: Cambridge University Press.

Kellner, P (2004) 'Britain's Culture of Detachment', *Parliamentary Affairs*, 57(4): 830–43.

Kemp, P (1993) *Beyond Next Steps: A Civil Service for 21st Century*, London: Social Market Foundation.

Kennedy, P (1988) *The Rise and Fall of the Great Powers: Economic Change and Military Conflict from 1500–2000*, London: Unwin Hyman.

Kenny, M and Smith, M J (2000) 'Interpreting New Labour: Constraints, Dilemmas and Political Agency' in S Ludlam and M J Smith (eds) *New Labour in Government*, Basingstoke: Macmillan.

Keohane, D (2000) *Security in British Politics*, London: Macmillan.

King, A (1975) 'Overload: Problems of Governing in the 1970s', *Political Studies*, 23(2/3): 284–96.

King, A (1976) 'Modes of Executive Relations: Great Britain, France and West Germany', *Legislative Studies Quarterly*, 1: 11–36.

King, A (1977) *Britain Says Yes. The 1975 Referendum on the Common Market*, Washington, DC: American Enterprise Institute for Public Policy Research.

King, A (1985) 'Margaret Thatcher: the Style of a Prime Minister' in A King (ed) *The British Prime Minister*, Basingstoke: Macmillan.

King, A (1985) *The British Prime Minister*, London: Macmillan.

King, A (2001) *Does the United Kingdom Still Have a Constitution?*, London: Sweet and Maxwell.

Klein, R (1995) *The New Politics of the National Health Service* (3rd edn), London: Longman.

Kooiman, J (2000) 'Levels of Governing: Interactions as a Central Concept' in J Pierre (ed) *Debating Governance*, Oxford: Oxford University Press.

Krasner, S (1999) *Sovereignty: Organized Hypocrisy*, Princeton, NJ: Princeton University Press.

Kurlansky, M (2004) *1968: The Year That Rocked the World*, London: Jonathan Cape.

Labour Party (1964) *Crime—A Challenge to Us All*, London: The Labour Party.

Labour Party (1997) *New Labour: Because Britain Deserves Better*, London: The Labour Party.

Landers, B (1999) 'Of Ministers, Managers and Mandarins' in M Flinders and M J Smith (eds) *Quangos, Accountability and Reform*, London: Macmillan.

Lawson, N (1994) 'Cabinet Government in the Thatcher Years', *Contemporary Record*, 8: 440–7.

Lawson, N and Bruce Gardyne, J (1976) *The Power Game*, Basingstoke: Macmillan.

Layton-Henry, Z (1992) *The Politics of Immigration: Immigration, 'Race' and 'Race Relations' in Britain*, Oxford: Blackwell.

Le Grand, J (2003) *Motivation, Agency and Public Policy: Of Knight and Knaves, Pawns and Queens*, Oxford: Oxford University Press.

Le Grand, J and Bartlett, W (1993) *Quasi-Markets and Social Policy*, London: Macmillan.

Leach, R (2002), *British Political Ideologies*, Oxford: Philip Allan.

Leadbetter, C (1999) *Living on Thin Air: The New Economy*, London: Viking.

Lee, J, Jones, G and Burnham, J (1998) *At the Centre of Whitehall*, London: Macmillan.

Lee, S (1994) 'Law and the Constitution', in D Kavanagh and A Seldon (eds) *The Major Effect*, London: Macmillan, pp 122–44.

Lees-Marchment, J (2001) *Political Marketing and British Political Parties*, Manchester: Manchester University Press.

Leonard, M and Leonard, T (2001) *The Pro-European Reader*, Basingstoke: Palgrave.

Levin, B (1998) 'An Epidemic of Education Policy: (What) Can we Learn from Each Other?', *Comparative Education*, 34(2): 131–41.

Levitas, R (1999) *The Idea of Social Exclusion*, Ottawa: Social Inclusion Research Conference www.ccsd.ca/events/inclusion/index.htm.

Liaison Committee (2002) 'Minutes of Evidence' www.publications.parliament.uk/pa/cm200102/cmselect/cmliaisn/1095/2071601.htm, 16 July.

Liberal Democrats (2005) *The Real Alternative*, London: Liberal Democrats.

Ling, T (2002) 'Delivering Joined–up Government in the UK: Dimensions, Issues and Problems', *Public Administration*, 80(4): 615–42.

Littlechild, S (1983) *Regulation of British Tele-communications' Profitability: A Report by Stephen C Littlechild*, London: Department of Industry.

Lloyd, J (2003) *What the Media are doing to our Politics*, London: Constable and Robinson.

Lowe, R (2004) *The Welfare State in Britain* (3rd edn), Basingstoke: Palgrave Macmillan.

Ludlam, S (2001) 'New Labour and the Unions: the End of the Contentious Alliance?' in S Ludlam and M J Smith (eds) *New Labour in Government*, London: Palgrave.

Ludlam, S and Smith, M J (eds) (2004) *Governing as New Labour: Politics and Policy under Blair*, Basingstoke: Palgrave.

Lukes, S (2004) *Power: A Radical View* (2nd edn), London: Palgrave.

MacDonagh, O (1958) 'The Nineteenth-Century Revolution in Government: A Reappraisal', *Historical Journal*, 1: 52–67.

Mackintosh, J P (1963) *The British Cabinet* (3rd edn), London: Stevens and Sons Limited.

Mackintosh, J P (1977) *The Politics and Government of Britain*, London: Hutchinson.

Macpherson, W (1999) *The Stephen Lawrence Inquiry*, London: Stationery Office (Cm 4262-I).

Majone, G (1994) 'The Rise of the Regulatory State', *West European Politics*, 14: 77–101.

Majone, G (1996) *Regulating Europe*, London: Routledge.

Majone, G (2002) 'The New European Agencies: Regulation by Information', *Journal of European Public Policy*, 4(2): 262–75.

Marks, G Hooge, L and Blank, K (1996) 'European Integration from the 1980s: State Centric versus Multi-Level Governance', *Journal of Common Market Studies*, 34: 341–78.

Marquand, D (1988) *The Unprincipled Society: New Demands and Old Politics*, London: Fontana.

Marquand, D (2004) *Decline of the Public*, Oxford: Polity.

Marsh, D (1992) *The New Politics of British Trade Unionism*, Basingstoke: Palgrave Macmillan.

Marsh, D (2002) 'Pluralism and the Study of British Politics: it is always the happy hour for men with money, knowledge and power' in C Hay (ed) *British Politics Today*, Cambridge: Polity.

Marsh, D and Rhodes, R A W (1992) *Policy Networks in British Government*, Oxford: Clarendon Press.

Marsh, D, Richards, D and Smith, M J (2000) 'Bureaucrats, Politicians and Reform in Whitehall: Analysing the Bureau-Shaping Model', *British Journal of Political Science*, 30(3): 461–82.

Marsh, D, Richards, D and Smith, M J (2001) *Changing Patterns of Governance*, Basingstoke: Palgrave.

Marsh, D, Richards, D and Smith, M J (2003) 'Unequal Power: Towards An Asymmetric Power Model of the British Polity', *Government and Opposition*, 38(3) (Summer): 306–22.

Marsh, D et al (1999) *Post-War British Politics in Perspective*, Basingstoke: Palgrave.

Marsh, P (1994) *Joseph Chamberlain: Entrepreneur in Politics*, London: Yale University Press.

Marshall, G (1971) *Constitutional Theory*, Oxford: Oxford University Press.

Marshall, G, Swift, A and Roberts, S (1997) *Against the Odds? Social Class and Social Justice in Industrial Societies*, Oxford: Oxford University Press.

Marsland, D (1996) *Welfare or Welfare State?*, Basingstoke: Macmillan.

McConnell, A (2000) 'Issues of Governance in Scotland, Wales and Northern Ireland' in R Pyper and L Robins (eds) *United Kingdom Governance*, Basingstoke: Macmillan.

McEachern, D (1990) *The Expanding State: Class and Economy since 1945*, Hemel Hempstead: Harvester Wheatsheaf.

McKenzie, R (1963) *British Political Parties*, London: Heinemann.

McKenzie, R T (1974) 'Politics, Pressure Groups and the British Political Process' in R Kimber and J Richardson (eds) *Pressure Groups in Great Britain*, London: Dent.

McLean, I (2001) *British Politics and Rational Choice*, Oxford: Oxford University Press.

McNaughton, N and McNaughton, R (1999) 'Best Value: A Fresh Start for Local Government', *Politics Review*, vol 83.

McRobbie, A (1994) *Postmodernism and Popular Culture*, London: Routledge.

Middlemas, K (1979) *Politics in Industrial Society*, London: Andre Deutsch.

Miliband, R (1969) *The State in Capitalist Society*, London: Quartet.

Miliband, R (1972) *Parliamentary Socialism*, London: Merlin.

Miliband, R (1984) *Capitalist Democracy in Britain*, Oxford: Oxford University Press.

Mitchell, J (1999) 'From Unitary State to Union State: Labour's Changing View of the United Kingdom and its Implications', *Regional Policy and Politics*, 9: 9–13.

Mitchell, J (2002) 'Towards the New Constitutional Settlement' in C Hay (ed) *British Politics Today*, Oxford: Polity.

Moore, B (1966) *Social Origins of Dictatorship and Democracy: Lord and Peasant in the Making of the Modern World*, Boston, Mass: Beacon Press.

Moran, M (2001) 'The Rise of the Regulatory State in Britain', *Parliamentary Affairs*, 54(1): 19–34.

Moran, M (2003) *The British Regulatory State: High Modernism and Hyper Innovation*, Oxford: Oxford University Press.

Moravcsik, A (1991) 'Negotiating the Single European Act: National interests and conventional statecraft in the European Community' in R Keohane and S Hoffmann (eds) *The New European Community: Decision-Making and Institutional Change*, Boulder, Colo: Westview.

Moravcsik, A (1994) *Why the European Community Strengthens the State: Domestic Politics*, Center for European Studies Working Paper Series, Harvard University, No 52.

Mount, F (1992) *The British Constitution Now: Recovery or Decline?*, London: Heinemann.

Mueller, H (1984) *Bureaucracy, Education and Monopoly: Civil Service Reforms in Pressure and England*, Berkeley, Cal: University of California Press.

Mulgan, G (1994) *Politics in an Anti-Political Age*, Oxford: Polity Press.

Mulgan, G (ed) (1999) *Life after Politics: New Thinking for the Twenty-First Century*, London: Fontana.

Muncie, J (2002) 'A New Deal for Youth? Early Intervention and Corrrectionalism' in G Hughes, E McLaughlin and J Muncie (eds) *Crime, Prevention and Community Safety: New Directions*, London: Sage.

Munro, E (2004) 'State Regulation of Parents' *Political Quarterly*, 75(2): 180–4.

Myers, A R (1952) *England in the Late Middle Ages*, London: Penguin.

Nairn, T (1977a) 'The Twilight of the British State', *New Left Review*, 101–102.

Nairn, T (1977b) *The Break-Up of Britain*, London: NLB.

Nairn, T (1979) 'The Future of the British Crisis', *New Left Review*, 113.

Nairn, T (1981) *The Break-up of Britain: Crisis and Neo-Nationalism* (2nd edn, 2000), London: Verso.

Naughtie, J (2001) *The Rivals: The Intimate Story of a Political Marriage*, London: Fourth Estate.

Negrine, R (1998) *Television and the Press since 1945*, Manchester: Manchester University Press.

Newman, O (1981) *The Challenge of Corporatism*, London: Macmillan.

Newton, K (1992) 'Is Small Really so Beautiful?', *Political Studies*, 30: 190–206.

Norris, P (1997) *Electoral Change Since 1945*, Oxford: Oxford University Press.

Norris, P (2002) 'Gender and Contemporary British Politics' in C Hay (ed) *British Politics Today*, Cambridge: Polity.

Norton, P (1980) *Dissention in the House of Commons 1974–1979*, Oxford: Oxford University Press.

Norton, P (1993) *Does Parliament Matter?*, Hemel Hempstead: Harvester Wheatsheaf.

Norton, P (2001) 'Parliament' in A Seldon (ed) *The Blair Effect*, London: Little Brown.

Norris, P (ed) (2006) *Britain Votes 2005*, Oxford: Oxford University Press.

Norton, P and Aughey, A (1981), *Conservatives and Conservatism*, London: Temple Smith.

Norris, P et al (1999) *On Message*, London: Sage.

Nugent, N (2001) *The European Commission*, Basingstoke: Palgrave.

Nugent, N (2003) *The Government and Politics of the European Union* (5th edn), London: Palgrave.

O'Sullivan, N (1975), *Modern Ideologies: Conservatism*, London: Dent.

O'Toole, T (2003) 'Engaging with Young People's Conceptions of the Political' *Children's Geographies*, vol 1/1, February.

O'Toole, T, Marsh, D and Jones, S (2003) 'Political Literacy Cuts Both Ways', *Political Quarterly*, 74(3): 349–59.

Oakeshott, M (1951) *Political Education*, Cambridge: Bowes.

Oborne, P and Walters, S (2004) *Alastair Campbell: New Labour and the Rise of the New Media Class*, London: Aurum.

Olson, M (1982) *The Rise and Decline of Nations: Economic Growth, Stagflation and Social Rigidities*, New Haven, Conn: Yale University Press.

Olson, M (1982) *The Rise and Fall of Nations*, New Haven: Yale University Press.

Orwell, G (1970) *The Collected Essays, Journalism and Letters of George Orwell, Volume 2, My Country Right or Left*, Harmondsworth: Penguin.

Osborne, D and Gaebler, T (1992) *Reinventing Government*, Reading, Mass: Addison-Wesley.

Painter, C (1999) 'Public Service Reform from Thatcher to Blair: a Third Way', *Parliamentary Affairs*, 52: 94–112.

Parekh, B (2000) *The Future of Multi-ethnic Britain: Report of the Commission on the Future of Multi-Ethnic Britain*, London: Profile Books.

Park, A (1998) *Young People's Social Attitudes 1998: Full Report of Research Activities and Results*, Keele: ESRC.

Park, A and Surridge, P (2003) 'Charting Change in British Values' in Park et al (eds) *British Social Attitudes: The 20th Report*, London: Sage.

Parkinson, J (2004) 'Hearing Voices: Negotiating Representation Claims in Public Deliberation', *British Journal of Politics and International Relations*, 6: 370–88.

Parliamentary Office of Science and Technology (2001) Postnote, 'Online Voting', May, No 155.

Pattie, C, Seyd, P and Whiteley, P (2004) *Citizenship in Britain: Values, Participation and Democracy*, Cambridge: Cambridge University Press.

Paul, K (1997) *Whitewashing Britain: Race and Citizenship in the Post-War Era*, Ithaca, NY: Cornell University Press.

Peacock, A T and Wiseman, J (1967) *The Growth of Public Expenditure in the United Kingdom*, London: George Allen and Unwin.

Peden, G C (1991) *British Economic and Social Policy: Lloyd George to Margaret Thatcher*, London: Phillip and Allen.

Peele, G (1999) 'The Growth of the State' in I Holliday, A Gamble and G Parry, (eds) *Fundamentals in British Politic*, Basingstoke: Macmillan.

Perri, 6 and Peck, E (2004) 'New Labour's Modernization in the Public Sector: A Neo-Durkheimian Approach and the Case of Mental Health Services', *Public Administration*, 82(1): 83–108.

Peters, B G (2000) 'Governance and Comparative Politics' in J Pierre (ed) *Debating Governance*, Oxford: Oxford University Press.

Phillis, B (2004) *An Independent Review of Government Communications*, London: Stationery Office.

Pierre, J (2000) 'Introduction: Understanding Governance' in J Pierre (ed) *Debating Governance*, Oxford: Oxford University Press.

Pierre, J and Peters, B G (2000) *Governance, Politics and the State*, Basingstoke: Macmillan.

Pierre, J and Stoker, G (2000) 'Towards Multi-Level Governance' in P Dunleavy, A Gamble, I Holliday and G Peele (eds) *Developments in British Politics 6*, Basingstoke: Macmillan.

Pierson, C (1996) 'Social Policy' in D Marquand and A Seldon (eds) *The Ideas that Shaped Post-War Britain*, London: Fontana.

Pimlott, B (1988) 'The Myth of Consensus' in L Smith (ed) *The Making of Britain: Echoes of Greatness*, London: Macmillan.

Pirie, M and Worcester, R M (1998) *The Millennial Generation*, London: Adam Smith Institute.

Plant, R (2001) 'Blair and Ideology' in A Seldon, (ed) *Blair Effect*, London: Little Brown.

Political Quarterly (1999) Special Issue, 70: 368–416.

Pollard, S (1983) *The Development of the British Economy 1918–1980*, London: Edward Arnold.

Pollard, S (1992) *The Development of the British Economy, 1914–1990* (4th edn), London: Edward Arnold.

Pollitt, C (1990) *Managerialism in the Public Services*, Oxford: Blackwell.

Pollock, A (2004) *NHS plc: The Privatisation of our Healthcare*, London: Verso.

Ponting, C (1986) *Whitehall: Tragedy and Farce*, London: Hamish Hamilton.

Prabhakar, R (2004) 'Whatever Happened to Stakeholding?', *Public Administration*, 82(3): 567–84.

Pryce, S (1997) *Presidentialising the Premiership*, London: Macmillan.

Public Administration Select Committee (2001) 'Public Administration—Minutes of Evidence', www.publications.parliament.uk/pa/cm20010/cmselect/cmpupadmin, 18 March.

Putnam, R (1995) 'Bowling Alone: America's Social Capital', *Journal of Democracy*, 6: 65–78.

Pym, F (1984) *The Politics of Consent*, London: Hamish Hamilton.

Radaelli, C (2000) 'Whither Europeanisation: Concept Stretching and Substantive Change', *European Integration On-Line Papers*, 4(8), http://eiop.or.at/eiop/texte/2000–008a.htm.

Randall, N (2004) 'New Labour's Home Office' in S Ludlam and M J Smith (eds) *Governing as New Labour*, Basingstoke: Palgrave.

Rawnsley, A (2001) *Servants of the People: The Inside Story of New Labour*, London: Penguin.

Reif, K and Schmitt, H (1980) 'Nine National Second Order Elections: A Systematic Framework for the Analysis of European Elections Results', *European Journal of Political Research*, 8(1): 3–44.

Rhodes, R (1988) *Beyond Westminster and Whitehall*, London: Unwin-Hyman.

Rhodes, R A W (1981) *Control and Power in Central-Local Relations*, Aldershot: Gower.

Rhodes, R A W (1986) *The National World of Local Government*, London: Allen and Unwin.

Rhodes, R A W (1995) 'From Prime Ministerial Power to Core Executive' in R A W Rhodes and P Dunleavy, *Prime Minister, Cabinet and Core Executive*, London: Macmillan, pp 11–37.

Rhodes, R A W (1996) 'The New Governance: Governing without Government', *Political Studies*, 44: 652–67.

Rhodes, R A W (1997) *Understanding Governance: Policy Networks, Governance, Reflexivity and Accountability*, Buckingham: Open University Press.

Rhodes, R A W (1999) *Control and Power in Central—Local Government Relations* (2nd edn), Aldershot: Ashgate.

Rhodes, R A W (2000) 'Governance and Public Administration' in J Pierre, (ed) *Debating Governance*, Oxford: Oxford University Press.

Rhodes, R A W (2005) 'Presidents, Barons, Court Politics and Tony Blair', paper presented at the Political Science Association Annual Conference, University of Leeds, Leeds, 4–6 April.

Rhodes, R A W and Dunleavy, P (1995) *Prime Minister, Cabinet and Core Executive*, London: Macmillan.

Rhodes, R A W, Carmichael, P, Macmillan, J and Massey, A (2003) *Decentralizing the Civil Service: From Unitary State to Differentiated Polity in the United Kingdom*, Buckingham: Open University Press.

Rhodes James, R (1986) *Anthony Eden*, London: Weidenfeld and Nicolson.

Richard, I and Welfare, D (1999) *Unfinished Business: Reforming the House of Lords*, London: Vintage.

Richards, D (1997) *The Civil Service under the Conservatives 1979–1997: Whitehall's Political Poodles?* Brighton: Sussex Academic Press.

Richards, D (2005) 'Delivery of Public Services' in A Geddes and J Tonge (eds) *Britain Decides: the 2005 General Election*, Basingstoke: Palgrave.

Richards, D and Smith, M J (2000) 'Power, Knowledge and the British Civil Service: the Living Chimera of the Public Service Ethos', *West European Politics*, 23(3): 45–66.

Richards, D and Smith, M J (2001) 'New Labour, the State and the Constitution' in S Ludlam and M J Smith (eds) *New Labour in Government*, Basingstoke: Macmillan.

Richards, D and Smith, M J (2002) *Governance and Public Policy in the United Kingdom*, Oxford: Oxford University Press.

Richards, D and Smith, M J (2004a) 'Interpreting the world of Political Elites: Some Methodological Issues', *Public Administration*, 82(4): 777–800.

Richards, D and Smith, M J (2004b) 'New Labour and the Reform of the State' in S Ludlam and M J Smith (eds) *Governing as New Labour: Policy and Politics under Blair*, Basingstoke: Palgrave, pp 106–25.

Richardson, J J (2000) 'Government, Interest Groups and Policy Change', *Political Studies*, 48: 1006–25.

Richardson, J J and Jordan, G (1979) *Governing under Pressure*, Oxford: Martin Robertson.

Riddell, P (2000) *Parliament under Blair*, London: Politicos.

Riddell, P (2004) *Blair: The Unfulfilled Prime Minister*, London: Politico.

Ridley, F (1988) 'There is no British Constitution: A Dangerous Case of the Emperor's Clothes', *Parliamentary Affairs*, 41: 339–60.

Ridley, F (1992) 'What Happened to the Constitution under Mrs Thatcher?' in B Jones and L Robins (eds) *Two Decades in British Politics*, Manchester: Manchester University Press.

Roberts, J and Devine, F (2004) 'Some Everyday Experiences of Voluntarism: Social Capital, Pleasure and the Contingency of Participation', *Social Politics*, 11(2): 280–96.

Rose, R (1982) 'Is the United Kingdom a State? Northern Ireland as a Test Case' in P Madgwick, and R Rose (eds) *The Territorial Dimension in the United Kingdom Politics*, London: Longman, pp 100–36.

Rose, R (1984) *Do Parties Make a Difference?* (2nd edn), London: Macmillan.

Rose, R (2001) *The Prime Minister in a Shrinking World*, Oxford: Polity.

Rose, R and Davies, P (1995) *Inheritance and Public Policy: Change without Choice in Britain*, New Haven, Conn: Yale University Press.

Rosenau, J (2000) 'Change, Complexity and Governance in a Globalizing Space', in J Pierre (ed), *Debating Governance*, Oxford: Oxford University Press.

Rosenberg, J (1997) *Trial of Strength. The Battle Between Ministers and Judges over Who Makes Law*, London: Richard Cohen.

Rothon, C and Heath, A (2003) 'Trends in racial prejudice' in Park et al (eds) *British Social Attitudes The 20th Report*, London: Sage.

Rubinstein, W (1993) *Capitalism, Culture and Decline in Britain 1750–1993*, London: Routledge.

Ruggie, J G (1998) *Constructing the World Polity*, London: Routledge.

Russell, M (2000) *Reforming the Lords: Lessons From Abroad*, London: Macmillan.

Saggar, S (1992) *Race and Politics in Britain*, Hemel Hempstead: Harvester Wheatsheaf.

Saggar, S (2000) *Race and Representation: Ethnic Pluralism and Electoral Politics*, Manchester: Manchester University Press.

Sampson, A (1982) *The Changing Anatomy of Britain*, London: Hodder and Stoughton.

Sanders, D (1990) *Losing an Empire, Finding a Role*, London: Macmillan.

Sanders, D, Clarke, H, Stewart, M and Whiteley, P (2003) 'The Dynamics of Protest in Britain', *Parliamentary Affairs*, 56: 687–99.

Saunders, P (1985) 'Corporatism and Urban Service Provision' in W Grant (ed) *The Political Economy of Corporatism*, London: Macmillan.

Saunders, P (1996) *Unequal but Fair? A Study of Class Barriers in Britain*, London: IEA.

Saward, M (1997) 'In Search of the Hollow Crown' in P Weller, H Bakvis, and R Rhodes, (eds) *The Hollow Crown: Countervailing Trends in Core Executives*, Basingstoke: Macmillan.

Scammell, M (1995) *Designer Politics: How Elections are Won*, London: Macmillan.

Scammell, M and Harrop, M (2006) 'The Press for Blair in Spite of Blair' in D Kavanagh and D Butler (eds) *The British General Election of 2005*, Buckingham: Palgrave.

Scott, D (2004) *Off Whitehall: A View from Downing Street by Tony Blair's Adviser*, London: I.B. Tauris.

Scott, R (1996) *Report of the Inquiry into the Export of Defence Equipment and Dual Use Goods to Iraq and Related Prosecutions*, London: HMSO.

Searing, D (1994) *Westminster World: Understanding Political Roles*, Cambridge, Mass: Harvard University Press.

Seldon, A (1997) *Major: A Political Life*, London: Weidenfeld and Nicolson.

Seldon, A (2004) *Blair*, London: Fontana.

Seldon, A and Ball, S (eds) (1995) *The Conservative Century*, Oxford: Oxford University Press.

Seldon, A and Hickson, K (2004) *New Labour, Old Labour*, London: Routledge.

Seldon, A and Kavanagh, D (eds) (2005) *The Blair Effect 2001–5*, Cambridge: Cambridge University Press.

Senvirante, M (2002) *Ombudsmen: Public Services and Administrative Justice*, London: Butterworths.

Seyd, P (2002) 'Labour Government—Party Relationships: Maturity or Marginalisation?' in A King (ed) *Britain at the Polls 2001*, London: Chatham House.

Seymour-Ure, C (1996) *The British Press and Broadcasting Since 1945*, Oxford: Blackwell.

Seymour-Ure, C (2001) 'New Labour and the Media' in A King (ed) (2001) *Britain at the Polls*, London: Chatham House.

Sharpe, J (1982) 'The Labour Party and the Geography of Inequality' in D Kavanagh (ed) *The Politics of the Labour Party*, London: Allen and Unwin.

Shaw, E (1966) *The Labour Party Since 1945*, Oxford: Oxford University Press.

Shell, D (1992) *The House of Lords* (2nd edn), London: Harvester Wheatsheaf.

Shonfield, A (1958) *British Economic Policy Since the War*, Harmondsworth: Penguin.

Short, C (2004) *An Honourable Deception?: New Labour, Iraq, and the Misuse of Power*, London: Free Press.

Smith, G and Wales, C (2000) 'Citizens' Juries and Deliberative Democracy', *Political Studies*, 48: 51–65.

Smith, M J (1993) *Pressure, Power and Policy: State Autonomy and Policy Networks in Britain and the United States*, London: Harvester Wheatsheaf.

Smith, M J (1998) *The Core Executive in Britain*, London: Macmillan.

Smith, M J (2000) 'Institutional approaches to Britain's relative economic decline' in R English and M Kenny (eds) *Rethinking British Decline*, London: Palgrave.

Smith, M J (2004) 'Mad Cows and Mad Money: Problems of Risk in the Making and Understanding of Policy', *British Journal of Politics and International Relations*, 6(2): 1–21.

Smith, M J (2005) 'The Economy' in A Geddes and S Tonge (eds) *Britain Decides*, Basingstoke: Palgrave.

Solomos, J (2003) *Race and Racism in Britain* (3rd edn), London: Palgrave.

Spencer, I (1997) *British Immigration Policy since 1939: The Making of Multi-Racial Britain*, London: Routledge.

Stephens, P (1996) *Politics and the Pound: The Conservatives Struggle with Sterling*, London: Macmillan.

Stephens, P (2004) *Tony Blair: The Price of Leadership*, London: Politicos.

Stevens, A and Stevens, H (2001) *Brussels Bureaucrats: The Administration of the European Union*, Basingstoke: Palgrave.

Stewart, J D (1958) *British Pressure Groups*, Oxford: Oxford University Press.

Stoker, G (ed) (1999) *The New Politics of British Local Governance*, London: Macmillan.

Stoker, G (2000) *The New Politics of British Local Governance*, London: Macmillan.

Stoker, G (2001) 'Life is a Lottery: New Labour's Strategy for the Reform of Devolved Governance', *Public Administration*, 80(3) (Autumn 2002): 417–34(18).

Stone Sweet, A and Sandholtz, W (1998) *European Integration and Supranational Governance*, Oxford: Oxford University Press.

Stones, R (1996) *Sociological Reasoning: Towards a Post-Modern Sociology*, London: Macmillan.

Thatcher, M (1993) *The Downing Street Years*, London: Harper Collins.

Thompson, H (1996) *The British Government and the European Exchange Rate Mechanism, 1979–1994*, London: Pinter.

Thomas, G (1998) *Prime Minister and Cabinet Today*, Manchester: Manchester University Press.

Tivey, L (1988) *Interpretations of British Politics*, Hemel Hempstead: Harvester Wheatsheaf.

Toke, D (2002) 'UK GM Crop Policy: Relative Calm before the Storm?', *Political Quarterly*, 73(1): 67–75.

Toynbee, P (2003) *Hard Work*, London: Bloomsbury.

Toynbee, P and Walker, D (2001) *Did Things Get Better? An Audit of Labour's Success and Failures*, London: Penguin.

Toynbee, P and Walker, D (2005) *Better or Worse? Has Labour Delivered?*, London: Bloomsbury.

Travers, T (2001) 'Local Government' in A Seldon (ed) *The Blair Effect*, London: Little Brown.

Usher, K (2003) 'Is Rising Inequality a Problem? The UK Experience' in M Browne, and P Diamond, (eds) *Rethinking Social Democracy*, London: Policy Network.

Vickers, R (2003) *Labour and the World, Vol 1, Labour's Foreign Policy 1900–51*, Manchester: Manchester University Press.

Vincent, D (1998) *The Culture of Secrecy: Britain 1832–1998*, Oxford: Oxford University Press.

Wakeham Commission (1999) *Unfinished Business: Reforming the House of Lords*, London: Stationery Office (Cmnd 4534).

Wakeham, J (1994) 'Cabinet Government', *Contemporary Record*, 8: 473–83.

Walden, G (2001) *The New Elites*, London: Penguin.

Wall, S (2002) *Insider Interview, Global Thinking*, Spring 2002, London: Foreign Policy Centre.

Wallace, H and Hayes-Renshaw, F (1997) *The Council of Ministers*, Basingstoke: Macmillan.

Wallace, W (1986) 'What Price Interdependence? Sovereignty and Interdependence in British Politics', *International Affairs*, 62(3): 357–69.

Waltz, K (1979) *Theory of International Politics*, London: Addison Wesley.

Ward, H (1995) 'Rational Choice Theory' in D Marsh, and G Stoker, (eds) *Theory and Methods in Political Science*, London: Macmillan.

Warleigh, A (2003) *Democracy and the European Union: Theory, Practice and Reform*, London: Sage.

Watkins, A (1991) *A Conservative Coup*, London: Duckworth.

Webb, P (2000) *The Modern British Party System*, London: Sage.

Weir, D and Beetham, D (1994) *Political Power and Democratic Control in Britain*, London: Routledge.

Weller, P (2000) 'In Search of Governance' in G Davis and M Keating (eds) *The Future of Governance*, St Leonards, NSW: Allen and Unwin.

White, N (1999) *Decolonisation: The British Experience Since 1945*, London: Longman.

White, S (ed) (2001) *New Labour. The Progressive Future?*, Basingstoke: Palgrave.

Whitely, P et al (eds) (1994) *True Blues: The Politics of Conservative Party Membership*, Oxford: Oxford University Press.

Whyte, J (1990) *Interpreting Northern Ireland*, Oxford: Oxford University Press.

Wiener, M (1981) *English Culture and the Decline of the Industrial Spirit*, Cambridge: Cambridge University Press.

Wight, C (2003) 'The Agent Structure Problem and Institutional Racism', *Political Studies*, 51: 706–21.

Wilson, D (1999) 'Threats and Promises: New Labour and Local Government', *Politics Review*, vol 84.

Wilson, D and Game, C (2002) *Local Government in the United Kingdom* (3rd edn), Basingstoke: Palgrave.

Winder, R (2004) *Bloody Foreigners: The Story of Immigration to Britain*, London: Time Warner.

Wodehouse, D (2002) 'The Law and Politics: In the Shadow of the Human Rights Act', *Parliamentary Affairs*, 55: 2.

Woodhouse, D (2004) 'UK Ministerial Responsibility in 2002: The Tale of Two Resignations', *Public Administration* 82(1): 1–19.

World Bank (1992) *Governance and Development*, Washington, DC: World Bank.

Wright, A (1987) *Socialism: Theories and Practices*, Oxford: Oxford University Press.

Wright, A (1994) *Citizens and Subjects*, London: Routledge.

Wring, D (2005) *The Politics of Marketing the Labour Party*, London: Palgrave.

Young, H (1999) *This Blessed Plot: Britain and Europe from Churchill to Blair*, London: Papermac.

Young, J (1993) *Britain and European Unity 1945–1963*, Basingstoke: Macmillan.

INDEX

L

N